SAXON®
GEOMETRY

Practice Workbook

SAXON®

HOUGHTON MIFFLIN HARCOURT
Supplemental Publishers

www.SaxonPublishers.com
800-531-5015

ISBN 13: 978-1-6027-7565-7
ISBN 10: 1-6027-7565-6

Printed in the United States of America

10 11 12 13 14 15 16 2266 20 19 18
4500747610

Table of Contents

Table of Contents

Name ______________________ Date __________ Class __________

Points, Lines, and Planes

LESSON 1

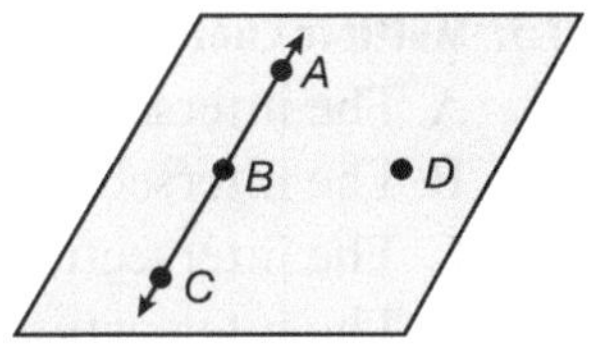

1. In the diagram, which set of three points are collinear? Which point cannot be included in a collinear set of three points?
(1)

2. Can two points be noncollinear?
(1)

3. Can two noncoplanar lines intersect?
(1)

4. Name three undefined basic figures of geometry.
(1)

5. What term describes two lines that have a point in common?
(1)

6. **Generalize** Can three points be noncoplanar? Explain.
(1)

7. Name the coplanar points shown on plane $\mathcal{M}$.
(1)

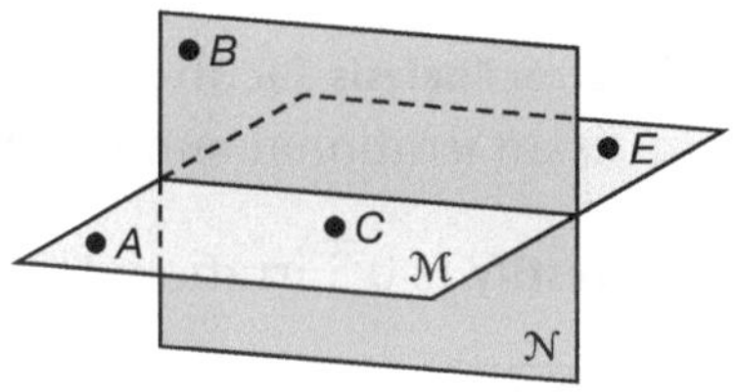

8. **Write** The floor, ceiling, and walls of a room are all parts of planes. How many planes intersect the plane of the floor in your classroom? What geometric figures are formed where the planes intersect? Explain.
(1)

Use the diagram to answer problems 9–11.

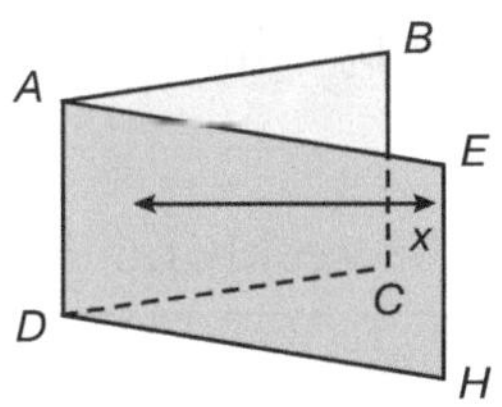

9. What is the intersection between the planes?
(1)

10. **Justify** Are $\overleftrightarrow{AD}$, $\overleftrightarrow{CD}$, and $\overleftrightarrow{CH}$ coplanar? Explain.
(1)

11. State the intersection point of $\overleftrightarrow{BC}$ and line x.
(1)

12. **Multiple Choice** Which statement is true?
(1)
   A Any two lines are coplanar.
   B Any three lines are coplanar.
   C Any two intersecting lines are coplanar.
   D Any two perpendicular lines are noncoplanar.

13. How many different points can a line contain?
(1)

14. How many different lines can a plane contain?
(1)

15. (1) **Multiple Choice** Which statement is true?
A The intersection of two lines forms a one-dimensional figure.
B The intersection of two planes forms a two-dimensional figure.
C The intersection of two planes forms a one-dimensional figure.
D The intersection of two lines forms a two-dimensional figure.

16. (1) **Error Analysis** Miri used two points to name a plane. What mistake did Miri make in naming the plane?

17. (SB 1) Evaluate: $5 - (7 + 8) \div 5 + (-2)^3$

18. (SB 2) Name the property of addition shown by this equation:
$(+3) + (-4) = (-4) + (+3)$

19. (SB 3) **Error Analysis** Jacob said that -3 is a rational number. Aaron said that -3 is an irrational number. Who is correct? Explain.

20. (SB 3) **Justify** Is $0.\overline{3}$ irrational? Why or why not?

21. (SB 41) **Baseball** A ball player is at bat 55 times and hits the ball 33 times. What ratio of his times at bat does he not hit the ball?

22. (SB 1) Evaluate: $(-3)^3 - \left(\frac{1}{3}\right)^{-3}$

23. (SB 6) Simplify: $2\sqrt{12} + 6\sqrt{27}$

24. (SB 9) **Construction** A concrete pad has dimensions 9 feet by 9 feet by 4 inches. How many cubic yards of concrete does it contain?

25. (SB 11) **Meteorology** Determine the mean and median values for the weekly rainfall data.

Day	Monday	Tuesday	Wednesday	Thursday	Friday	Saturday	Sunday
Rainfall (mm)	0.5	2	0	4	2.5	5	7

26. (SB 10) **Physics** On average, the acceleration due to gravity is 9.807 m/s^2. A science student measured it as 9.760 m/s^2. To the nearest hundredth of a percent, what was the student's percent error?

27. (SB 13) **Coordinate Geometry** Plot these points on the coordinate plane: (2, 1), (−1, −1), (0, 0), and (3, −1).

28. (SB 14) **Algebra** Evaluate the expression $xy^{-2} + \frac{x}{y}$, where $x = -2$, $y = \frac{1}{2}$.

29. (SB 16) **Algebra** Transform the formula $I = Prt$ to solve for r.

30. (SB 19) **Algebra** State the slope of the line $3x + 4y - 15 = 0$.

Name ______________________ Date __________ Class __________

Segments

LESSON 2

1. (2) Measure the line segments at right to determine which segments are congruent.

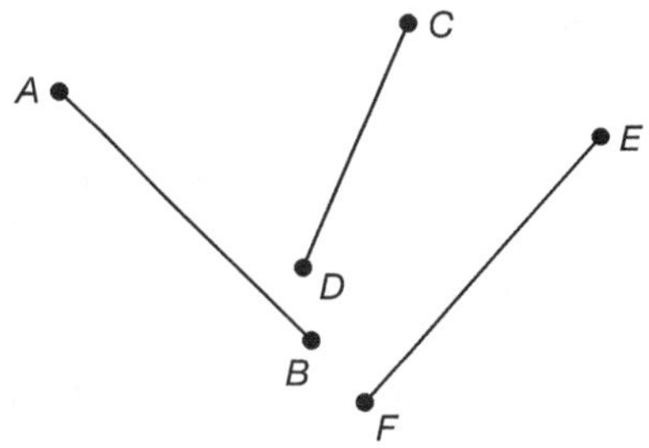

2. (SB 6) Estimate $\sqrt{32}$ to the nearest tenth.

3. (SB 2) What property is illustrated by this statement?

If a and b are real numbers, then $a + b = b + a$.

4. (1) **Multiple Choice** What is the least number of points that can determine a plane?

A 1 **B** 2

C 3 **D** 4

Calculate the length of each segment using the diagram below.

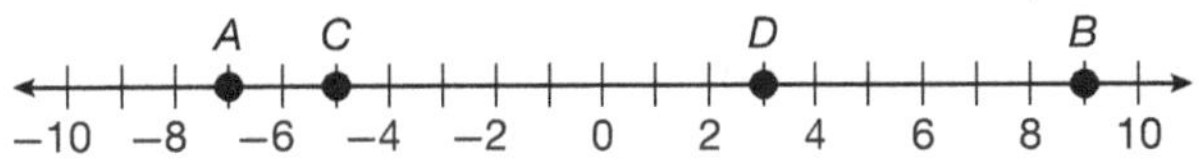

5. (2) $\overline{AD}$

6. (2) $\overline{BC}$

7. (2) $\overline{DA}$

8. (2) $\overline{AC}$

9. (SB 11) **Data Analysis** The numbers in this set are the math test scores for a class. Find the mode.

$\{62, 53, 74, 55, 66, 72, 80, 83, 83, 86, 92, 93, 40, 51, 61, 71\}$

10. (SB 14) Evaluate $3m^2 - 5m + 17$ for $m = -3$.

11. (SB 13) In what quadrant is point S if its coordinates are $(2, -4)$?

12. (SB 11) Find the median of the set $\{2, 2, 3, 5, 6, 7, 7, 8, 9\}$.

13. (2) **Algebra** A, B, and C are collinear, $AB = 5x - 19$, and $BC = 3x + 4$. Find an expression for AC if B is between A and C.

14. (2) **City Planning** The city is planning to install streetlights and wants five lights along a walkway of 60 yards. If there is a light at the beginning and at the end of the walkway and the lights are evenly spaced, what is the distance between each light?

15. (1) **Error Analysis** Sunil stated that three points determine a unique plane. Explain Sunil's error and and give a corrected statement.

16. (2) **Algebra** Suppose $AB = 3x$, $BC = 2y + 16$, $AC = 60$, and B is the midpoint of AC. Find the values of x and y.

17. (2) **Analyze** Points D, E, and F are collinear with E between D and F. $DE = 15$, $EF = x + 17$, and $DF = 3x - 10$. Find EF and DF.

18. (1, 2) **Write** Describe how equality and congruence are used to describe two line segments and their lengths.

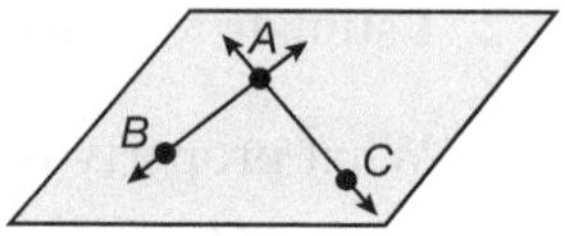

19. (1) Are points A, B, and C collinear, coplanar, both, or neither?

20. (1) How many points are required to determine a line?

21. (1) **Multiple Choice** Which of these statements is false?
A Two distinct points determine a line.
B Three noncollinear points determine a plane.
C Two noncoplanar lines determine a space.
D Four noncoplanar points determine a space.

22. (1) Lines MN and PQ intersect at point E. Name two sets of three collinear points.

23. (SB 18) Factor: $2x^2 - 16x - 66$

24. (SB 18) Expand: $(x - 4)(x + 7)$

25. (SB 9) **Carpentry** A piece of wood that is 8 feet long needs to be 7 feet 4 inches long. How much has to be cut off? Express your answer in feet.

26. (SB 6) Simplify: $\frac{-36x^{-4}y^5}{12x^2y^{-3}}$. Express your answer with positive exponents.

27. (SB 4) **Sales Tax** If sales tax is 6%, estimate the sales tax on an item that retails for \$48.99.

28. (SB 5) Estimate the sum to the nearest whole number.
$1.8 + 2.345 + 0.65 + 13.56$

29. (SB 9) **Multi-Step** There are 1000 liters in a cubic meter and approximately 3.85 liters in one gallon. A swimming pool measures 8 meters wide by 4 meters long by 1.5 meters deep. Approximately how many gallons of water can the pool hold?

30. (SB 9) **Physics** In a free fall, acceleration due to gravity is approximately 9.8 m/s^2. Convert this rate into ft/s^2.

Name ______________________ Date __________ Class __________

Angles

LESSON 3

Use the diagram to classify and find the measure of each angle.

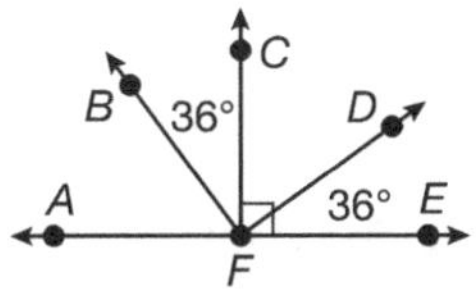

1. (3) $\angle AFC$

2. (3) $\angle CFD$

3. (3) $\angle BFD$

4. (3) $\angle AFD$

5. (3) **Multiple Choice** $\overrightarrow{LJ}$ bisects $\angle ILK$. What is the measure of $\angle GLJ$?

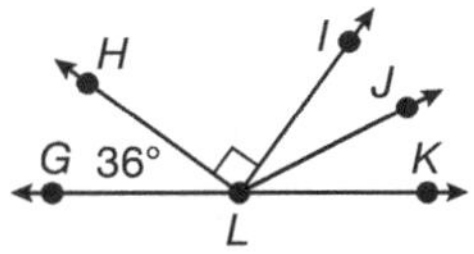

A 27° **B** 117°

C 54° **D** 153°

6. (3) What is the measure of a straight angle?

7. (2) Find AB.

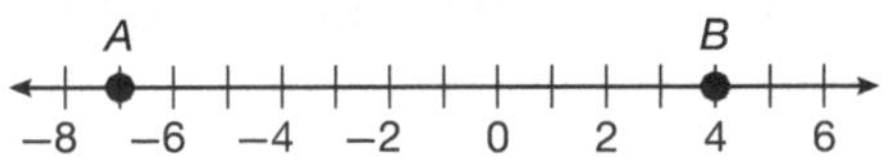

8. (SB 4) Which of the following triplets are equivalent?

A $\frac{1}{2}$, 50%, 5:10 **B** $\frac{20}{20}$, 100%, 7:7

C $\frac{30}{36}$, $83.\overline{3}$%, 5:6 **D** All of the above

9. (1) What is the fewest number of points that can determine a line?

10. (SB 7) How many significant digits are there in 10,001?

11. (2) **Error Analysis** Jackson said, "Congruent segments are the same as equal segments." Explain how he has misunderstood congruence and equality.

12. (3) **Algebra** Ray BD bisects $\angle ABC$. If $m\angle ABD = (x^2 + x + 12)°$ and $m\angle DBC = (x^2 + 3x + 4)°$, find x and $m\angle ABC$.

13. (2) **Landscaping** A homeowner wants to put up a fence around her square yard. She has 8 posts, which must be equally spaced. If the perimeter of her yard is 16 meters, how far apart must the posts be?

14. (2) **Verify** If $\overline{MN} \cong \overline{NH}$ and $\overline{NH} \cong \overline{ES}$, then $\overline{MN} \cong \overline{ES}$. What property justifies this?

15. (2) Points A, B, and C are collinear. Point B is between points A and C. $AB = 12$, $AC = 7x + 5$ and $BC = 4x - 1$. Find x.

16. (2) Find the midpoint of the segment connecting points with coordinates −142 and 53 on a number line.

17. (1) **Write** If four points are collinear, are they also coplanar? Explain.

18. The ratio of boys to girls at the camp is 14:17. If there are 186 children at the camp altogether, how many are boys?
(SB 4)

19. **Algebra** Factor: $10x^2 + x - 21$
(SB 18)

20. The mean of these six numbers is 20.38. What is the missing number?
(SB 11)
25.14, 17.22, ______, 23.04, 20.21, 21.27

21. **Surveying** A surveyor measured a building lot. She recorded the corner points of the lot as $M(-80, 210)$, $N(-80, -120)$, $P(130, 210)$, and $Q(130, -120)$. The coordinates represent the distances, in feet, from the axes of a coordinate grid. Calculate the area of the lot.
(SB 13)

22. **Farming** A farmer wishes to plant a field with flax. According to his budget, the total cost of planting and harvesting cannot exceed $12,000. The planting and harvesting costs are $0.015/square yard for flax. What is the maximum area the farmer could plant with flax while keeping within the budget?
(SB 22)

23. How does the graph of $f(x)$ compare to the graph of $f(x) + 3$?
(SB 17)

24. Solve the equation $\sqrt{6g} = (j + y)$ for g.
(SB 16)

25. A stone is dropped from a cliff into a river. The function $h(t) = 82 - 4.9t^2$ gives the height h of the stone in meters t seconds after it is dropped. What is the height of the stone, to the nearest tenth of a meter, after 1.7 seconds?
(SB 22)

26. **Solar System** Sirius, the brightest visible star in the sky, is about 8.6 light years away from Earth. One light year is 9.46×10^{15} kilometers. Find the distance between Earth and Sirius in kilometers. Express your answer in scientific notation with 3 significant figures.
(SB 7)

27. The instructions on a juice concentrate container read "Five parts water, 1 part concentrate." How much juice can you make if you have 500 mL of concentrate?
(SB 4)

28. To what sets of numbers does the number -8 belong?
(SB 3)

29. Is the square root of any prime number a real number?
(SB 3)

30. **Chemistry** Liquid nitrogen is extremely cold. The freezing point for nitrogen is approximately −346°F and the boiling point for nitrogen is approximately −320°F. Use this data to find the range.
(SB 1)

Name ______________________ Date __________ Class __________

Postulates and Theorems About Points, Lines, and Planes

LESSON 4

* **1.** (4) **Multiple Choice** Which of the following is a set of noncollinear points?

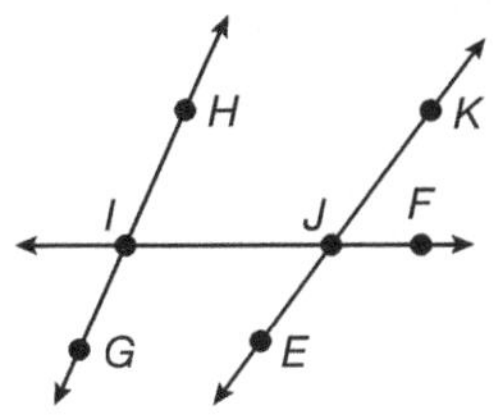

A H, I, G **B** I, J, F
C H, I, K **D** K, J, E

* **2.** (4) **Write** Describe the difference between collinear points and coplanar lines.

* **3.** (4) Find the theorem or postulate that justifies the following statement.
If two lines are on the same plane, they will only intersect at one point.

Draw each of the following.

* **4.** (4) Two planes that intersect at a line.

* **5.** (4) Two lines that intersect on a plane at point O.

* **6.** (4) Is this statement always true, never true, or sometimes true?
If two lines intersect then they are both contained in a single plane.

Use the figure to answer problems 7–9.

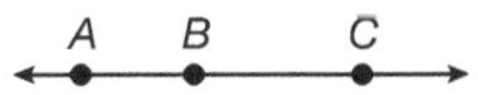

* **7.** (3) Name two rays.

* **8.** (3) What is the measure of $\angle ABC$?

* **9.** (3) What name is given to this type of angle?

***10.** (3) The base of a crane at a construction site makes an angle of 30° with the ground. As it lifts its load to clear an obstruction, the base makes an additional angle of 13°. What is the base's angle with the ground after lifting the load?

***11.** (3) If $m\angle ABC = 62°$ and $\overline{DB}$ bisects $\angle ABC$, what is the measure of $\angle ABD$?

***12.** (2) **Write** Describe how to locate the quarter points of a line segment, $\overline{AB}$.

***13.** (2) **Algebra** Find the expression to represent AC if $AB = 2x + 5$, $BC = 5x - 16$ and A, B and C are collinear. B is between A and C.

14. (SB 12) **Probability** Handel flips a fair coin seven times and it comes up heads seven times. What is the probability his next flip will be heads? Why?

*15. (2) **Traffic** There are three traffic lights on a street. If the second traffic light is 75 yards from the first, and all three traffic lights span 120 yards, how far is the second traffic light from the third one?

*16. (1) **Multiple Choice** Which statement is true? Make a drawing to show why each other statement is not always true.

A Any two lines are coplanar.

B Any two intersecting lines are coplanar.

C Any three intersecting lines are coplanar.

D Any two perpendicular lines are noncoplanar.

*17. (1) How many points are between any two points on a line?

*18. (1) What word describes two coplanar lines that never meet?

19. (SB 17) What is the parent function of $\frac{15 - 6x^2}{2}$?

20. (SB 17) **Analyze** Graph $y = |x - 3|$. Is it a function?

21. (SB 16) **Algebra** Solve for j. $\frac{4j - 12x^2}{3} = j$

22. (SB 15) **Algebra** Solve for m. $-4m + 2 < 26$

*23. (2) Determine AC.

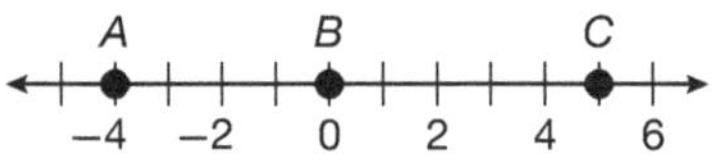

24. (SB 10) Jaime measures the volume of a container to be 1.15 liters. If its actual volume is 1.25 liters, what was Jaime's percent error?

25. (SB 9) Convert 18 centimeters to inches. Round to the nearest tenth.

26. (SB 9) How many inches equal one-half of a mile?

27. (SB 7) Express 23,000,000 in scientific notation.

28. (SB 6) Evaluate 3^5.

29. (SB 5) Round 34,016.45 to the nearest ten.

30. (SB 2) What property of arithmetic is shown by $(a)(0) = 0$?

Name ______________________ Date __________ Class __________

More Theorems About Lines and Planes

LESSON 5

1. *(1)* Draw a diagram showing three planes that intersect at a common line.

* 2. *(4)* **Error Analysis** Damon states that at least four collinear points are needed to determine a plane. Is Damon correct? Explain.

3. *(4)* **Write** Why is a plane not defined by the three given points?

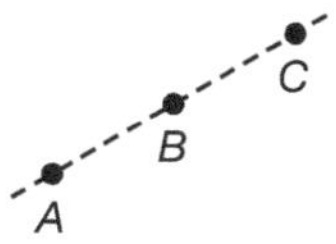

4. *(SB 3)* **Predict** The Pythagorean Theorem, $a^2 + b^2 = c^2$, relates the lengths of the legs of right triangle, a and b, to the length of the hypotenuse, c. There are cases where all three numbers are positive integers. One example is $3^2 + 4^2 = 5^2$. Find one other example. Are there an infinite number of positive integers that satisfy the Pythagorean Theorem?

5. *(3)* What is the measure of the angle between two opposite rays?

* 6. *(5)* **Justify** Can two lines be drawn from a point not on a line that will meet the line at a right angle? at a 45° angle? Explain each answer.

7. *(SB 9)* There are 100 centimeters in 1 meter. How many square centimeters are there in 1 square meter? Explain how you found your answer.

8. *(SB 1)* **Algebra** Simplify $\frac{2(2+4)}{6} - |-2|$.

* 9. *(5)* Consider $\overline{AB}$ in this figure. Name a segment that is skew, one that is parallel, and one that is perpendicular to $\overline{AB}$.

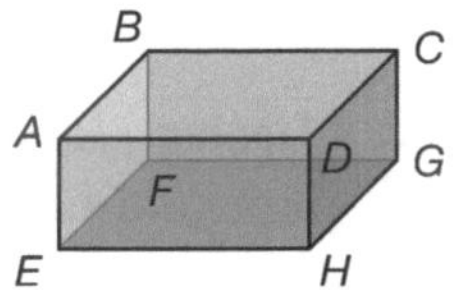

10. *(2)* Which property is used to state, "If $5 = x$, then $x = 5$"?

11. *(SB 13)* Plot the points $A(0, 0)$, $B(4, 0)$, $C(4, 4)$ and $D(0, 4)$ on a coordinate grid. Describe the shape that results when the points are connected in alphabetical order.

*12. *(4)* **Air Traffic Controller** An air traffic controller requested that a pilot taxi on the runway from point A to point B by traveling in a straight line. How many different options does the pilot have to get from point A to point B? How do you know?

13. *(SB 17)* For the function $f(x) = 3x^2 - 2x + 5$, find $f(1)$, $f(-2)$ and $f(a)$.

14. *(SB 13)* **Multiple Choice** Which point has the coordinates $(3, -3)$ on the graph shown?

A W **B** Y
C X **D** Z

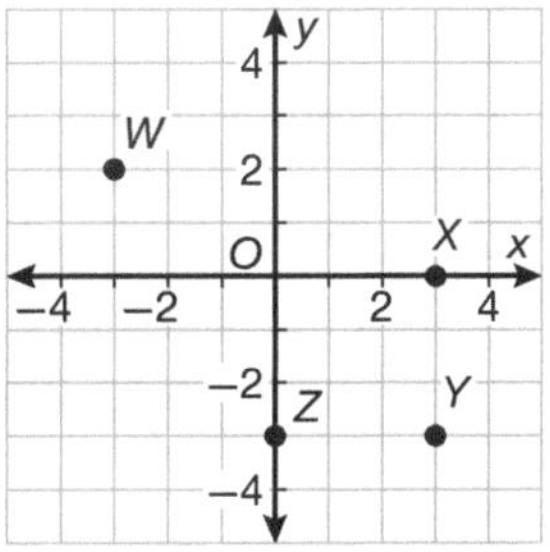

More Theorems About Lines and Planes

LESSON 5

15. (4) **Photography** It is very important that a camera be held as still as possible when using certain photographic techniques. Explain why professional photographers use tripods to hold their cameras steady instead of a stand with four or more legs. Name a postulate or theorem in your explanation.

*16. (5) If $\overleftrightarrow{XY}$ is parallel to $\overleftrightarrow{LM}$, what is the relationship between $\overleftrightarrow{XY}$ and $\overleftrightarrow{UT}$?

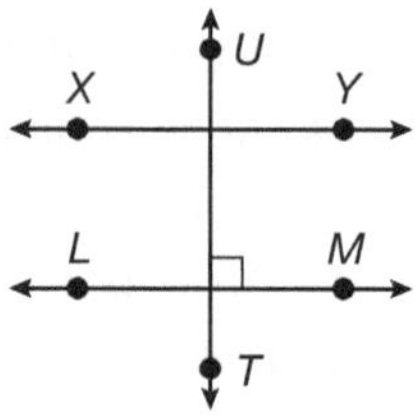

17. (SB 4) **Food Preparation** The instructions on a container of juice concentrate read, "Seven parts water per 1 part juice concentrate." How much juice can this container make if it holds 250 milliliters of juice concentrate?

18. (1) Are the points (1, 1), (5, 5), and (7, −4) collinear or coplanar? Explain.

19. (SB 16) Transform this formula to solve for b: $a^3 + b^3 + c^3 = d^3$.

20. (SB 12) What is the probability, as a fraction, of rolling an even number on a six-sided number cube?

21. (2) **Justify** How can you use a ruler to determine if a point M is the midpoint of a segment AB?

22. (SB 4) **Tipping** In some places, it is customary to give a tip of 15% at restaurants. Does it make a difference whether the 15% is paid on the bill before taxes are added or after taxes are added? Explain.

23. (4) **Write** How many lines connect points A and B? Explain.

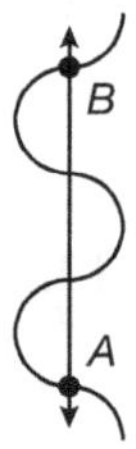

24. (SB 13) **Generalize** What are the properties of all ordered pairs in Quadrant II of the coordinate plane?

25. (3) Are angles A and B in the triangles shown congruent? Explain.

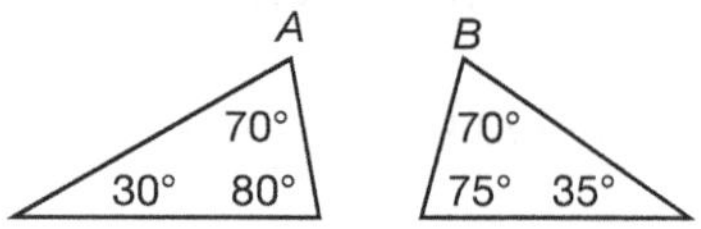

26. (SB 16) **Algebra** Transform the formula for the area of a triangle to solve for the height, h.

*27. (5) In most rooms, the floor is perpendicular to the wall and the wall is perpendicular to the ceiling. What can you say about the relationship between the floor and ceiling of most rooms if those two statements are true?

28. (3) **Generalize** Give an example of two acute angles whose measures could be added together to form another acute angle. Give an example of two acute angles whose measures could be added together to form an obtuse angle.

29. (SB 22) **Music** Musical notes can be identified by their frequencies. The frequency doubles when going up an octave. Middle C is denoted as C_4 and has a frequency of 261.63 hertz. What is the frequency of the note C_5, which is one octave above C_4?

*30. (5) Does the diagram at right show $\overleftrightarrow{AB}$ perpendicular to $\overleftrightarrow{DE}$? Explain.

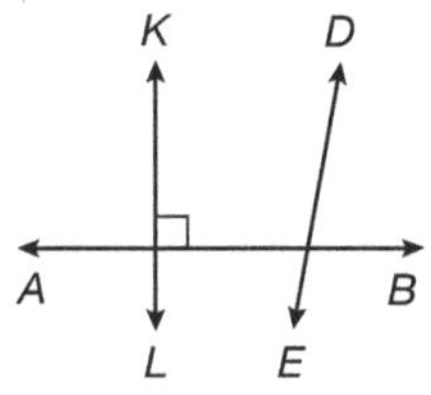

Name ______________________ Date __________ Class __________

Identifying Pairs of Angles

LESSON 6

* **1.** (6) An angle measuring 32° has a complement that measures $(2x - 16)°$. What is the value of x?

* **2.** (6) An angle measures 51°. What is the measure of its supplementary angle?

3. (SB 1) **Algebra** Compute $|3 \times 2 - 8| \times 2$.

4. (4) Four noncoplanar points define space, but could they be used to form two intersecting planes? Explain why or why not.

* **5.** (6) Find the value of x in the diagram at right.

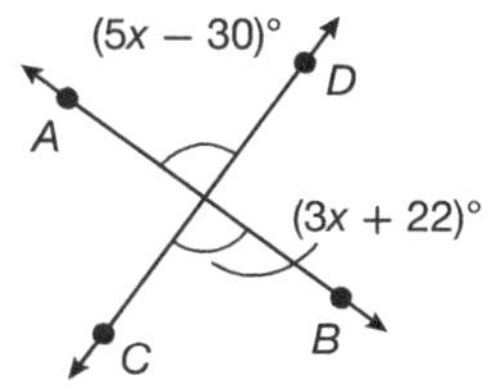

6. (4) **Write** Stanley says, "If a point is not on a line, then the line and the point exist on exactly one plane." If the point *is* on the line, how would his statement need to be changed?

7. (2) **Mapping** On a grid of their community, Silvio lives at the point (7, 3) and his friend Andy lives at the point (−11, 3). If they decide to meet halfway between their houses, at what point on the grid will they meet?

8. (SB 14) Evaluate the expression $3xy + 5x + 2y$ for $x = 2$ and $y = -1$.

* **9.** (6) What angle is equal to its complementary angle?

10. (SB 12) What is the probability, expressed as a percentage, of choosing a red marble if a bag of marbles contains 20 red, 15 green, 25 orange, and 40 blue marbles?

11. (1) **Error Analysis** A student says that two points define a line, three points define a plane, and four points define space. Are the student's definitions correct? Explain.

12. (2) Find the midpoint of the values 4 and 8 on the x-axis and the midpoint of the values 1 and 7 on the y-axis.

13. (3) If D is in the interior of $\angle ABC$, which measures 74°, and $m\angle ABD = 32°$, what is $m\angle DBC$?

14. (SB 12) **Competition** In 2007, the World Rock-Paper-Scissors Championship was held in Toronto, Ontario, Canada. What is the probability that any two competitors will both have the same combination in a game of rock-paper-scissors, expressed as a fraction?

***15.** (5) Simone has been given the challenge of drawing two coplanar lines that are perpendicular to the same line, but the lines must not be parallel to each other. Will she succeed? Explain why or why not.

***16.** (5) **Write** Two planes are parallel to each other and are both intersected by a third plane. Describe the property of each intersection and how these intersections are related.

13. (1) **Write** Explain what is meant when a term in mathematics is said to be *undefined.*

14. (SB 15) **Algebra** Find the value of x in the equation $\frac{2x-5}{3} = \frac{x+10}{4}$.

15. (SB 22) **Landscaping** A rectangular field that is 119 square yards in area is to be covered with sod. It is known that the field is 3 yards longer than twice the width. Find the dimensions of the field.

16. (SB 13) **Travel** Marcella lives at (4, 22) on a city grid, and Arnault lives at (−3, −4) on the same grid. One grid line represents one mile. If Arnault's mom drives him to Marcella's house by driving on a road that is parallel to the x-axis, then turns and drives along a road that is parallel to the y-axis, how many miles does Arnault's mom drive?

*17. (7) **Write** Can a conjecture be proved or disproved by studying examples or cases of the conjecture? Explain.

18. (3) **Algebra** Ray BD is the angle bisector of $\angle ABC$. What is the value of x?

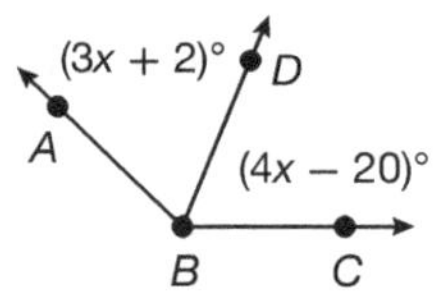

*19. (4) Sketch an example of two lines that are coplanar.

20. (SB 7) How many significant figures does the number 0.0100 have?

*21. (5) Draw a line parallel to and a line perpendicular to $\overleftrightarrow{AB}$ from each of the points K and L. Discuss the relationship between these drawn lines.

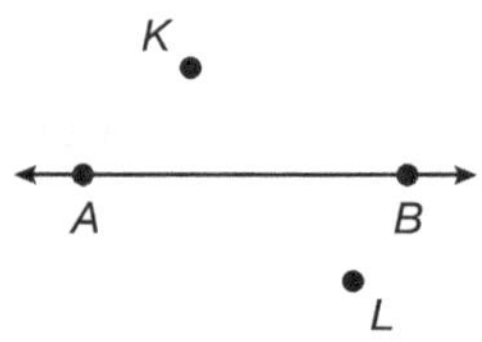

*22. (7) What type of reasoning is used in the statement below? Provide a counterexample to the conjecture if possible.

Every car I have ever owned ran on gas, therefore all cars run on gas.

23. (SB 16) **Multi-Step** The formula for converting kilometers to miles is $m = 1.609k$, where m is miles and k is kilometers. Transform this formula to find a formula for converting miles to kilometers. Use this formula to determine the number of kilometers in 539 miles and in 7380 miles, rounded to the nearest kilometer.

24. (6) **Justify** Can two acute adjacent angles form a linear pair? Explain why or why not.

25. (SB 16) **Temperature** The conversion for temperature from degrees Celsius to degrees Fahrenheit is given by the formula $F = \frac{9}{5}C + 32$. Transform this formula to find a formula to convert degrees Fahrenheit to degrees Celsius.

26. (4) **Multiple Choice** Which statement is true?

A Two distinct coplanar lines can intersect at two points.
B Two distinct coplanar lines can intersect at one point or never intersect if they are parallel.
C Two distinct coplanar lines can intersect at one point or intersect everywhere.
D Two distinct coplanar lines intersect at every point if they are parallel.

27. (6) The sum of the measures of three congruent angles is 180°. What would be the complementary angle to each of the angles?

***28.** (1) **Justify** Is it possible for three planes to intersect at a point? Explain why or why not, and if it is possible, sketch an example showing how.

29. (2) If B is the midpoint of $\overline{AC}$, find the value of x.

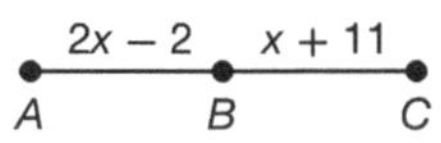

30. (3) The measure of $\angle XYZ$ is 110°. What would the resulting angles' measures be if the angle bisector to $\angle XYZ$ were drawn?

Name ______________________ Date __________ Class __________

Using Formulas in Geometry

LESSON 8

1. Complete the following conjecture.
(7) *The product of an even and an odd number is* _______.

2. (Plants) A bean sprout grows 3 inches in its first week, 2 inches in its second week,
(7) and 1.333… inches in its third week. If the sprout's growth follows this pattern, how much will the bean sprout have grown in its fourth week?

3. What are three undefined terms of geometry?
(1)

4. **Coordinate Geometry** State the quadrant in which each point is located.
(SB 13) **a.** $(-2, -2)$ **b.** $(-2, 2)$ **c.** $(2, -2)$

5. If there are twelve turtles in the pet store, what is the probability that a turtle chosen
(SB 12) at random will weigh more than the median turtle weight?

6. **Algebra** The area of a rectangle is 54 cm^2. The side lengths are $2x + 1$ and $x + 2$.
(8) What is the measure of each side?

7. **Analyze** Can a line be intersected at the same point with two different perpendicular
(5) lines? Explain why or why not.

8. How far does a jogger travel to reach the midpoint between a jogging track and
(2) a parking lot that are 0.25 miles apart?

9. Find the next item in the pattern. 2, 4, 8, 16, 32, …
(7)

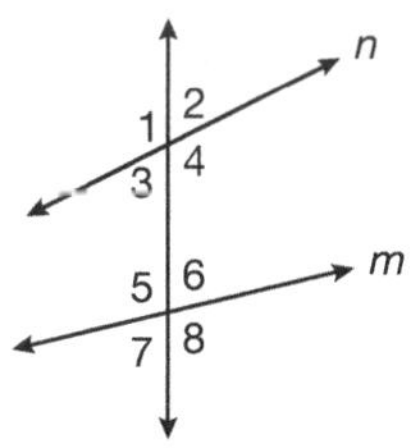

10. **Multiple Choice** Which pair of angles are congruent?
(6)
A $\angle 1$ and $\angle 8$ **B** $\angle 2$ and $\angle 3$
C $\angle 1$ and $\angle 2$ **D** $\angle 5$ and $\angle 6$

11. **Multiple Choice** Which pair of angles are a linear pair?
(6)
A $\angle 5$ and $\angle 6$ **B** $\angle 6$ and $\angle 7$
C $\angle 1$ and $\angle 4$ **D** $\angle 4$ and $\angle 6$

12. Name all the pairs of supplementary angles formed by line m.
(6)

13. **Write** Karl wrote that any three points define a plane. Is his statement true? If not,
(4) rewrite his statement so that it is true.

14. **Verify** A rectangle has side lengths of 30 meters and 36 meters. If the side lengths of
(8) the rectangle are doubled, verify that the perimeter also doubles.

15. **Error Analysis** A student has solved the equation for Pythagorean Theorem in the
(8) following way. It is given that $a = 5$ and $b = 12$.

$$a^2 + b^2 = c^2$$
$$(a + b)^2 = c^2$$
$$(5 + 12)^2 = c^2$$
$$17^2 = c^2$$
$$\sqrt{289} = \sqrt{c^2}$$
$$17 = c$$

Where did the student make an error? What is the actual answer?

16. Identify the intersection between planes $\mathcal{P}$ and $\mathcal{Q}$.
(4)

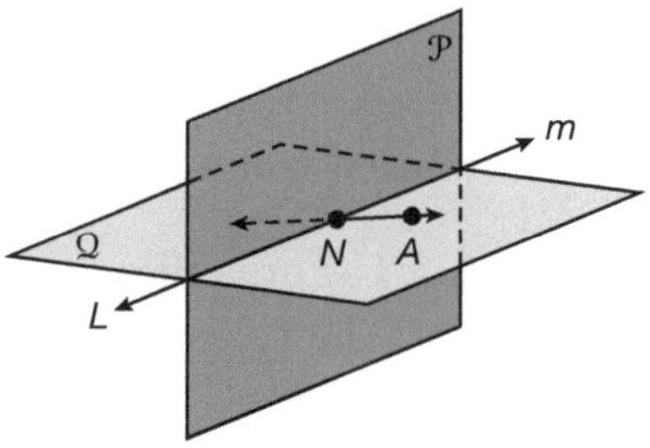

17. Name the two rays that make $\angle LNA$.
(3)

18. What figure is formed at the intersection of two lines?
(1)

19. **Multiple Choice** Which of the following terms cannot describe lines?
(5)

A perpendicular **B** congruent
C skew **D** parallel

20. Evaluate the expression $\frac{x + (3x)^2 + x}{2}$ for $x = \sqrt{2}$. Express the answer in simplified radical form.
(SB 14)

21. **Music** Musical notes are identified by their frequencies, which are recorded in hertz (Hz). Middle C is denoted as C_4 and has a frequency of 261.63 Hz. What is the frequency of the C_3 note, which is one octave below C_4? (Frequency doubles when going up an octave.)
(SB 22)

22. Find the perimeter of a triangle if each side length is 136 millimeters.
(8)

23. If $f(x) = 3x + x^2$, what does $f(2)$ equal?
(SB 17)

24. **Statistics** What is the mode of the following set? {A, B, M, M, H, H, J, P}
(SB 11)

25. What is the angle between two opposite rays?
(3)

26. **Biology** In a lab experiment, there is a culture that contains 25 bacteria at 2:00. At 2:15, there are 50 bacteria. At 3:15, there are 800 bacteria. Make a conjecture about the rate at which the bacteria increases.
(7)

27. By what property is the statement $AB = AB$ justified?
(2)

28. **Banking** King is baking a recipe that serves 6 and calls for 1.5 cups of flour. He expects 8 guests and decides to increase the recipe so that it can serve 8. How much flour will he need to make the larger recipe?
(SB 22)

29. *(8)* **Building** A housing developer wants to build a fence around the backyard of a house. If the backyard forms a square and one side is bounded by the house, what formula could the developer use to calculate the amount of fence required?

30. *(SB 2)* **Verify** Show that the Commutative and Associative Properties of Addition are true when adding the linear functions $f(x) = 3x + 2$, $g(x) = -2x + 3$, and $h(x) = 0$. The first line of each is given below.

Associative Property of Addition	Commutative Property of Addition
$[f(x) + g(x)] + h(x) = f(x) + [g(x) + h(x)]$	$f(x) + g(x) = g(x) + f(x)$

16. (9) **Fencing** If Sven has a rectangular yard with the corners given in the diagram, to the nearest hundredth meter, how much fencing will he need to divide the yard into two triangles? Each unit on the grid represents one meter.

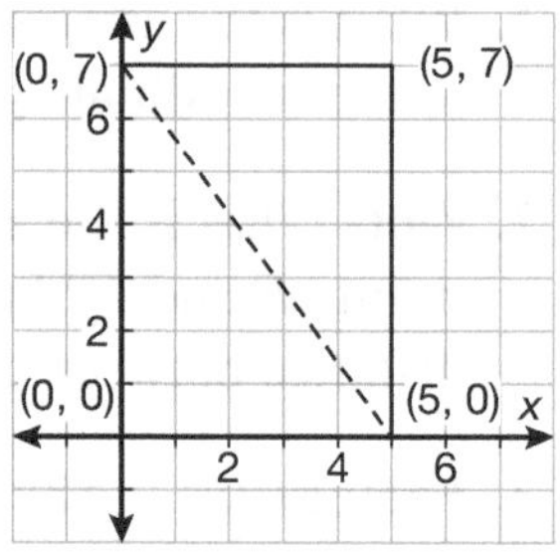

17. (SB 12) There are six bananas, two oranges, and seven apples in a bag. At random, pieces of fruit are chosen from the bag. What is the probability that an apple is chosen first and an orange is chosen second?

18. (3) What is the measure of $\angle BXC$?

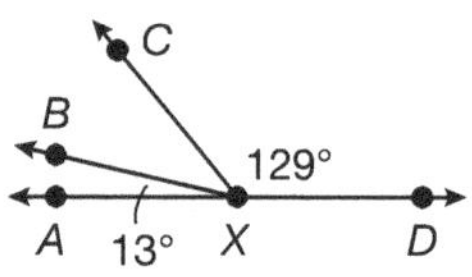

19. (8) **Multiple Choice** Which of the following is not a formula?
A distance formula
B perimeter formula
C Pythagorean Theorem
D protractor formula

20. (SB 18) Find the product of $(2x - 2)$ and $(x + 1)$.

21. (2) What property justifies this statement?
If $\overline{AB} \cong \overline{XY}$ *and* $\overline{CD} \cong \overline{XY}$, *then* $\overline{AB} \cong \overline{CD}$.

22. (1) **Explain** Can two noncoplanar lines intersect? Explain.

23. (SB 22) **Shopping** If a carton of eggs costs \$2.05 with tax included, how many cartons can you buy with \$10? Explain how you estimated the answer.

24. (6) **Multiple Choice** Which of the following is not a pair of angles?
A supplementary
B adjacent
C right
D vertical

25. (2) **Algebra** If B is the midpoint of $\overline{AC}$, and $AB = \frac{5}{2}x + 12$ and $AC = 12x - 4$, what is the length of $\overline{BC}$?

26. (SB 17) What is the domain of the function $f(x) = \sqrt{x}$?

27. (9) How does the distance formula simplify when finding the distance between two points which are directly above each other on a coordinate grid?

Name ______________________________ Date ____________ Class ____________

Using Conditional Statements

LESSON 10

1. (2) **Driving** Three cities lie on a straight highway. Dawson City is between Orangebourgh and Danteville. If the distance from Dawson City to Danteville is 19 miles and the distance from Orangebourgh to Danteville is 32 miles, what is the distance from Orangebourgh to Dawson City? Name a theorem or postulate that justifies your answer.

* 2. (8) **Signs** What is the perimeter of a regular, triangular yield sign with a side length of 15 inches?

3. (4) **Justify** If two lines are parallel, are they contained in a plane? Why or why not?

* 4. (10) Use the Venn diagram to write a conditional statement.

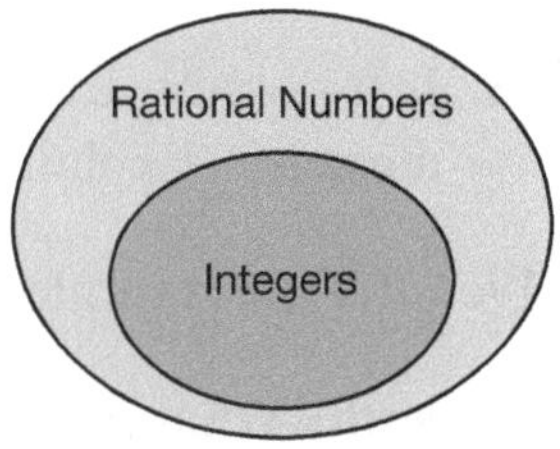

5. (SB 18) Factor: $x^2 - 4x - 21$.

6. (SB 1) Can the expression $\frac{|x^2 - 4x + 3|}{2}$ ever be a negative number? Explain.

*7. (9) **Multiple Choice** The point (4, 7) is an endpoint of a line segment. The segment is 5 units long. Which point is a possible second endpoint of the line?

A (1, 4) **B** (1, 11)
C (−1, 6) **D** (0, 3)

8. (3) **Write** What is the difference between the Ruler Postulate and the Protractor Postulate?

* 9. (10) **Write** A certain conditional statement's conclusion is always true when its hypothesis is true, so the conditional statement is always true. Can you determine for certain that the statement's converse will always be true? Explain and give an example to support your answer.

*10. (10) **Life Span** If an animal is a loggerhead sea turtle, then its expected life span is approximately 70 years. Is this a conditional statement? If it is not, rewrite it as a conditional statement. If so, write its converse.

11. (SB 10) An experiment designed to find the speed of sound shows that it is 768 miles per hour. If the speed of sound is actually 770 miles per hour, what is the experiment's percent error, to the nearest hundredth?

12. (SB 16) Transform the formula $E = mc^2$ to solve for m.

13. (5) **Model** Copy the figure at right and draw a line through the point that is parallel to $\overleftrightarrow{AB}$. Try to draw a different line through the point that is also parallel to $\overleftrightarrow{AB}$. Is it possible to draw a second line? Why or why not?

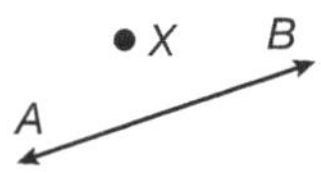

*14. Find the distance between the two points (2, 3) and (−4, 1) to the nearest hundredth.
(9)

*15. The length of a line segment is 7. Its endpoints are (1, 3) and (k, 3). Solve for k. Is there more than one solution? Explain.
(9)

16. **Model** Is it possible to draw two intersecting lines where the vertical angles are not equal? Why or why not?
(6)

17. Two streets intersect and are not perpendicular. Two different corners of the streets are at angles that have equal measures. What is another term to describe the angle pair?
(6)

18. Is it possible to compare two quantities that are recorded in different units of measure? Explain how.
(SB 9)

19. Give an example of a situation in which scientific notation is commonly used.
(SB 7)

20. **Justify** What property justifies the statement $x = x$?
(2)

*21. **Gardening** A gardener wants to split a rectangular bed of flowers diagonally to make two separate triangular beds. What is the area of one of the right triangles the gardener will form if the diagonal is 13 feet and one side is 12 feet?
(8)

22. Find the next number in this pattern: 3, 9, 27, 81, …
(7)

23. Evaluate the expression mc^2 for $m = 1$ and $c = 3 \times 10^8$. Express your answer in scientific notation.
(SB 7)

*24. **Algebra** Complete the conditional statement.
(10)

If $2x + 7 = 13$, then $x =$ ____.

*25. **Error Analysis** Kareem wrote the following statement.
(10)

If the measures of three angles combined equal 180°, then the angles are all acute.

Use an example to disprove Kareem's conditional statement, then write a true conditional statement.

26. **Error Analysis** A student multiplied the binomial below. Explain where the student made an error. Multiply the binomial correctly.
(SB 18)

$(x + 2)(x - 3) = x^2 + x - 6$

27. List all the sets of numbers to which −2.8 belongs.
(SB 3)

28. **Analyze** Find the value of the expression $|3 + (-4) + 6|$. Now find the value of the expression $|3| + |-4| + |6|$. Why are the answers different?
(SB 1)

29. **Multiple Choice** Which pair of terms is equivalent?
(6)
A supplementary angles and vertical angles
B vertical angles and complementary angles
C linear pair and adjacent, supplementary angles
D linear pair and adjacent angles

*30. Draw a Venn diagram to show the relationship in the conditional statement.
(10)
If a number is a natural number, then it is a whole number.

Name ______________________ Date __________ Class __________

Finding Midpoints

LESSON 11

1. (11) What is the midpoint of the segment connecting 2 and 9 on a number line?

2. (11) Determine the midpoint M of $\overline{AB}$ connecting $A(3, 2)$ and $B(7, 4)$.

3. (11) Determine the midpoint M of $\overline{PQ}$ connecting $P(-3, 2)$ and $Q(2, -2)$.

4. (11) **Algebra** Use the number line to determine the value of a, where the midpoint of a and 5 is 2.

5. (11) **Error Analysis** Fred claims that the midpoint of $\overline{AB}$ connecting $A(-2, 5)$ and $B(2, 0)$ is $(0, 5)$. What mistake did he make?

Refer to the figure to answer each question.

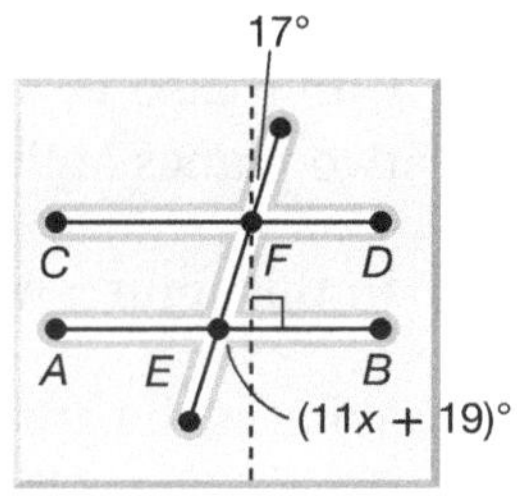

6. (Inv 1) **Drafting** Hoyt used engineering software to draft a sketch of a metal plate etched with grooves that is needed to complete a highly secure lock. Segments CD and AB are parallel, and $\overline{EF}$ intersects each at 17° from vertical. What is the measure of $\angle AEF$?

7. (Inv 1) **Drafting** What is the value of x?

8. (Inv 1) **Verify** What theorem or postulate can be used to justify the statement $\angle 1 \cong \angle 7$?

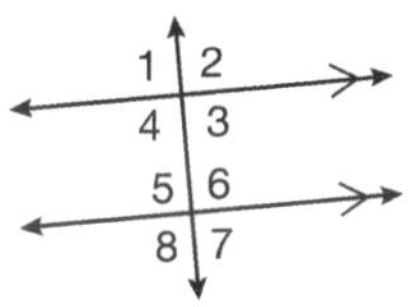

Determine whether each conditional statement is true. If the statement is false, give a counterexample.

9. (10) If it is winter, then the month is January.

10. (10) If $2x + 2y = 6$, then $x = 2$ and $y = 1$.

11. (9) Find the distance between points $(3, 4)$ and $(-9, 7)$ to the nearest hundredth.

12. (9) Find the distance between points $(-1, 4)$ and $(5, -6)$ to the nearest hundredth.

13. (8) **Skiing** A 180-yard ski slope is 120 yards high. What is the horizontal distance of the hill to the nearest yard?

14. (8) Find the perimeter of a right triangle with two legs which each measure 6 units. Round to the nearest hundredth.

15. (8) Find the side length of a square with a perimeter of 458 centimeters.

16. **Generalize** Fill in the next three rows of the following pattern:
(7)

1
1 1
1 2 1
1 3 3 1
1 4 6 4 1

17. Use inductive reasoning to determine the next term:
(7)
1, 3, 9, 27, 81, 243, _____

18. **Write** Morgan has been following college football for many years and makes the statement that her team will win if she wears her lucky sweater. Comment on the validity of her conjecture.
(7)

19. Find the complement of a 14° angle.
(6)

20. Find the supplement of an 85° angle.
(6)

21. Two coplanar lines are parallel when a third line intersects these two lines at 90°. Can it also be said that two planes are parallel if a third plane intersects these two planes at 90°?
(5)

22. In this figure, what is the value of k?
(5)

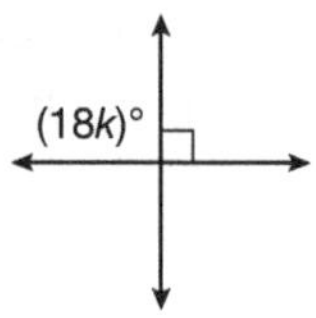

23. What is the greatest number of planes determined by three points? What is the least?
(4)

24. Is this statement always, sometimes, or never true? *Two lines intersect at one point.*
(4)

25. **Multi-Step** If $\overleftrightarrow{SU}$ lies in the right angle $\angle RST$ and $\angle RSU$ is one-fourth the measure of $\angle UST$, what is $m\angle UST$?
(3)

26. **Clocks** What is the angle of a clock's hands when it is 2:30?
(3)

27. **Write** Explain the difference between congruence and equality. Use an example.
(2)

28. Given that P, Q, and R are collinear and Q is between P and R, what postulate can be used to justify this addition? $PQ + QR = PR$
(2)

29. **Error Analysis** Joy made the statement, "Any three points are noncollinear." Explain where Joy made an error and suggest a new, true statement.
(1)

30. **Multiple Choice** Which statement is true?
(1)
A Any two planes are coplanar.
B Any two points are noncollinear.
C Any two points are coplanar.
D Any two lines are coplanar.

Name ______________________ Date ____________ Class ____________

Proving Lines Parallel

LESSON 12

* **1.** Prove that lines m and n are parallel.
(12)

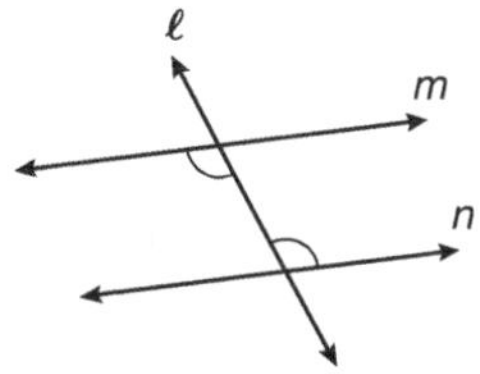

2. **Justify** What type of reasoning is being used in forming the following statement?
(7)

The numbers 5, 10, 15, 20, and 25 all end in either a 5 or a 0, and can all be divided by 5. Therefore, all numbers ending in 5 or 0 can be divided by 5.

* **3.** **a.** Use the Converse of the Corresponding Angles Postulate to prove that lines x and y are parallel.
(12)

b. Identify the same-side interior angles in the figure.

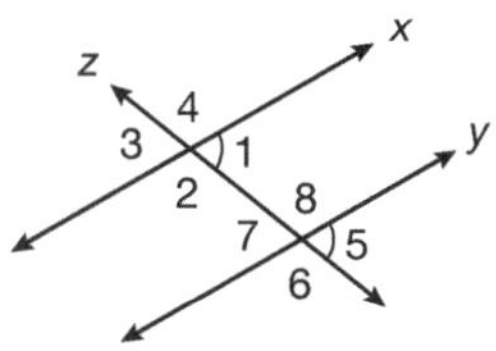

* **4.** **Write** A pair of same-side interior angles formed by a transversal across two lines measure $(3x + 10)°$ and $(2x)°$. Explain how to find a value of x that would indicate that two lines are parallel.
(12)

5. What is the midpoint of the segment connecting 4 and 8 on the number line?
(11)

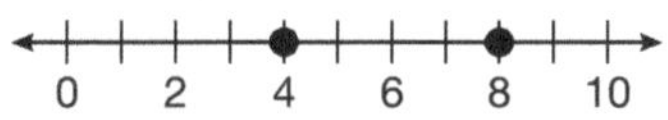

6. **Carpentry** Karen drilled holes in a 12-inch wooden ruler at 1 inch, 6 inches, and 11 inches along its length. She wants to drill two more holes at the midpoints between the holes she already has. Where should the new holes go?
(11)

7. **Write** One endpoint of a segment lies on the origin. If the second endpoint is known to lie on the line $x = 4$, and the segment is a units long, explain how you could find the coordinates of the other endpoint.
(9)

Refer to the figure to find the requested points.

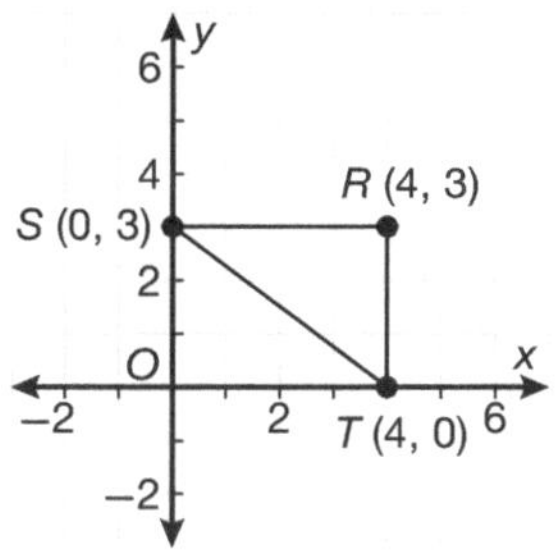

8. What is the midpoint of $\overline{SR}$? of $\overline{RT}$?
(11)

9. What is the midpoint of $\overline{ST}$?
(11)

Determine whether each conditional statement is true. If the statement is false, give an example why it is false.

10. If you have two points, then they can be connected by exactly one line.
(10)

11. **Track and Field** If a runner wins the gold medal, then that runner was the fastest in the race.
(10)

12. (6) **Algebra** Two angles are supplementary. One measures $(4x + 2)°$ and the other $(6x + 8)°$. What is the value of x?

13. (8) **Building** A builder wants to build a diagonal beam across a decorative window. If the window is 3 feet by 5 feet, then to the nearest hundredth, how long is the diagonal?

14. (11) What is the midpoint of the segment connecting the points $(-3, -4)$ and $(4, 3)$?

15. (4) Is this statement always, sometimes, or never true?

Two planes intersect in exactly one line.

16. (8) Find the side length of a square with an area of 182.25 m^2.

17. (8) **Tiling** A square ceramic tile is 18 inches in length. If a room is 12 feet by 18 feet, how many tiles are needed?

18. (5) The parallel planes PQT and SRU are cut by the plane PQR. Name one pair of parallel lines in the figure.

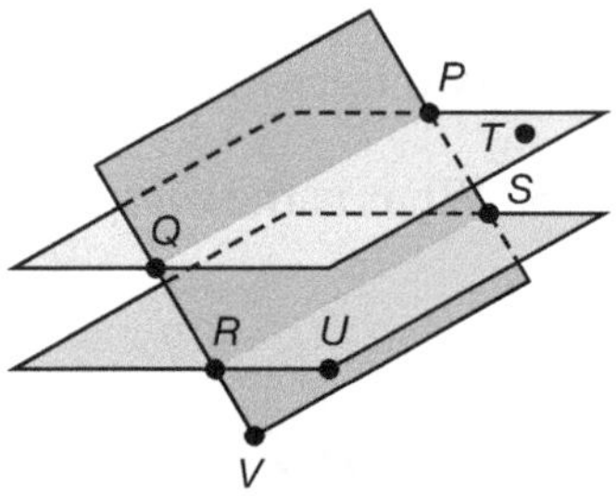

***19.** (12) Prove that lines a and b are parallel.

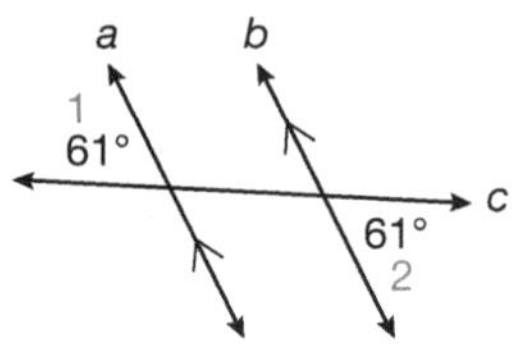

20. (6) **Landscaping** A support wire to a newly planted tree makes a 32° angle with the ground. Determine the angle made by the wire at the point of contact to the tree by finding the complement of 32°.

21. (10) **Multiple Choice** Which statement disproves the following conditional statement?

If $y = 2x^2 - 5$, then y is positive.

A $x = 1$ **B** $x = 2$

C $x = 3$ **D** $x = 100$

22. (5) Is $\overline{AB}$ parallel to $\overline{DF}$? Explain.

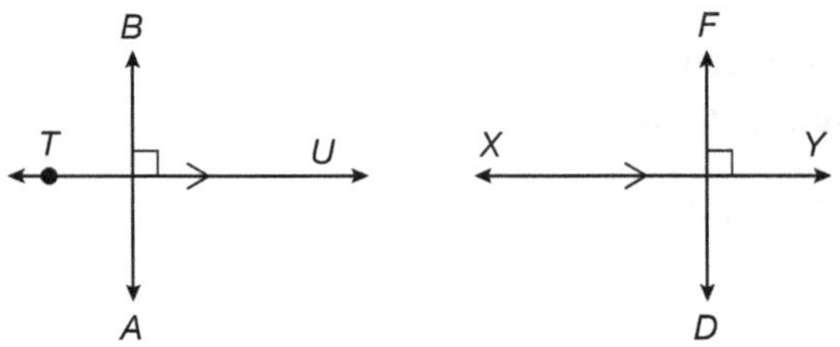

23. *(7)* **Multiple Choice** Use inductive reasoning to determine the next item in the sequence.

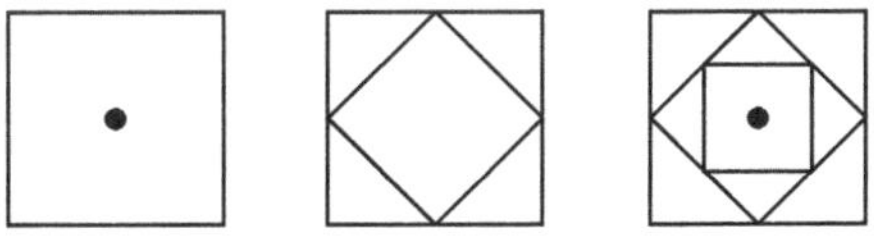

A 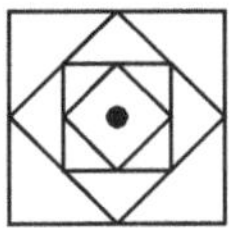

B 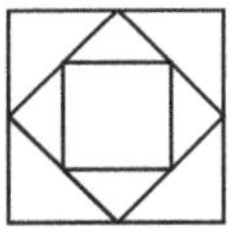

C 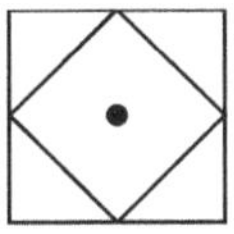

D 

24. *(5)* **Write** How many different ways can coplanar lines intersect? Explain each situation.

25. *(8)* **Multi-Step** Find the approximate area of the rectangle if the perimeter is 84 inches.

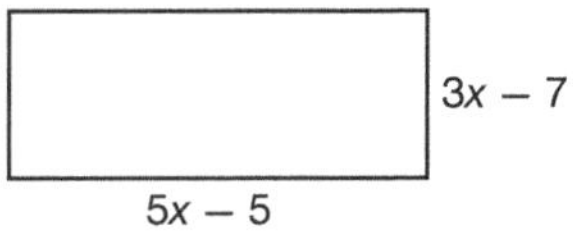

26. *(4)* **Error Analysis** Sarita said that if there are two lines, they are both contained in the same plane. Explain a situation where she could be wrong.

27. *(3)* **Clocks** What is the angle made by the hands of a clock when it is 8 o'clock?

28. *(2)* **Multiple Choice** Which of the following is not a property of congruence?

A Mirror Property | **B** Transitive Property
C Symmetric Property | **D** Reflexive Property

29. *(2)* Point C lies between A and B on $\overline{AB}$. If $CB = 18$ and $AB = 42$, what is AC?

30. *(1)* How many possible points of intersection can three different coplanar lines have?

Name ______________________ Date ____________ Class ____________

Introduction to Triangles

1. Identify a pair of angles in the diagram that can be used to prove lines parallel using the Converse of the Same-Side Interior Angles Theorem.
(12)

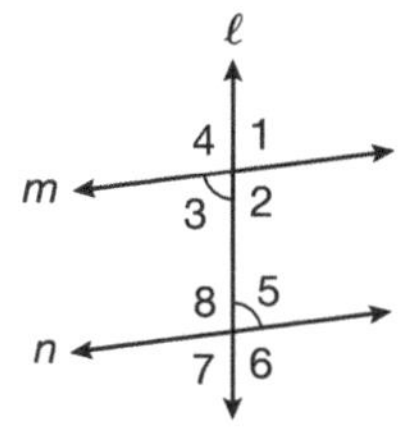

2. **Write** Write a conditional statement that has a false converse.
(10)

3. Classify $\triangle ABC$ as acute, right, or obtuse.
(13)

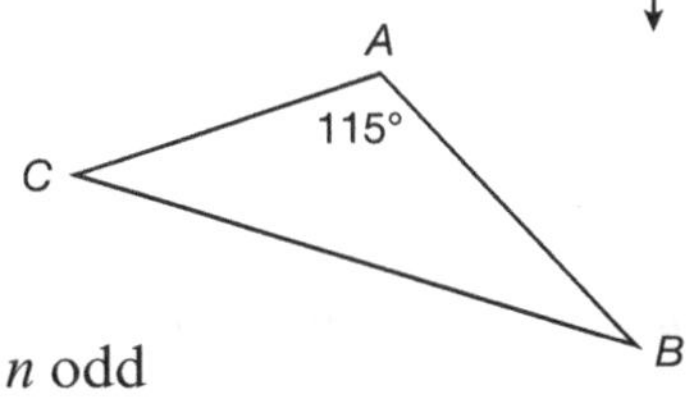

4. **Analyze** Is it possible to draw three points that are noncoplanar? What about drawing four points?
(4)

5. **Algebra** Test the conjecture that the sum of the first n odd whole numbers is given by n^2 using $n = 3$, $n = 5$, and $n = 7$.
(7)

Use the diagram for the next two questions. Round to the nearest hundredth.

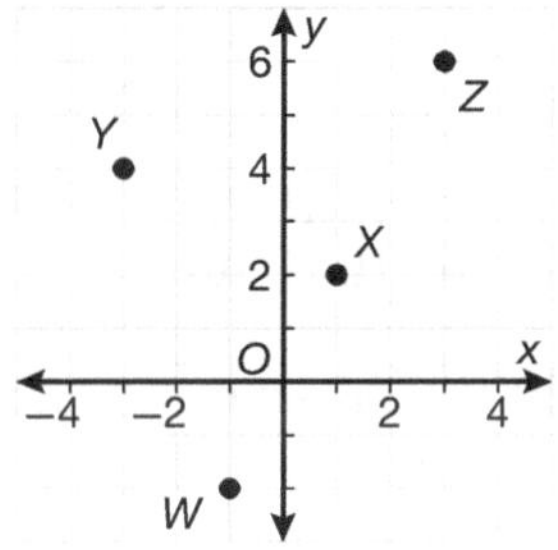

6. What is the length of $\overline{YZ}$?
(9)

7. What is the length of $\overline{WX}$?
(9)

8. **Surveying** A hedge surrounds the field shown on the grid. There are openings at the midpoints of the northern and southern sides of the hedge for a hiking trail. Determine the coordinates of the openings in the hedge.
(11)

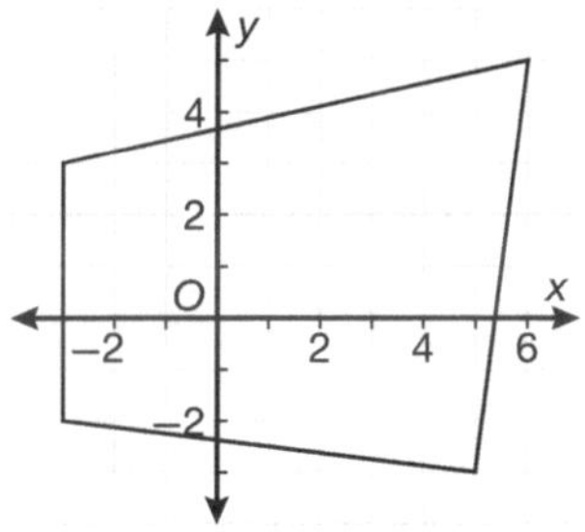

9. **Write** Shanice hears that the weather forecast predicts rain tomorrow. She thinks, "Since they have been wrong every day this week, it will not rain." Is Shanice's conjecture valid? Explain.
(7)

10. Is $\overleftrightarrow{AB}$ perpendicular to $\overleftrightarrow{DE}$? Explain.
(5)

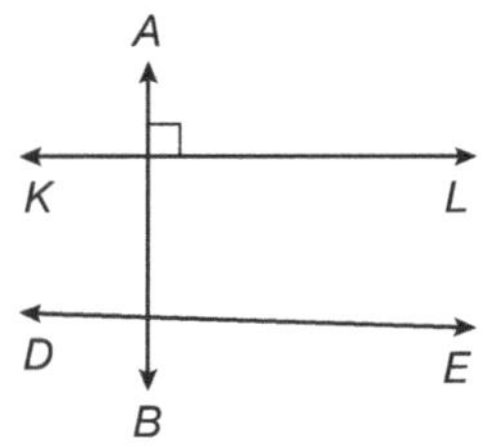

11. Suppose $\angle 3$ and $\angle 8$ are supplementary. Which postulate or theorem should be used to prove that lines a and b are parallel?
(12)

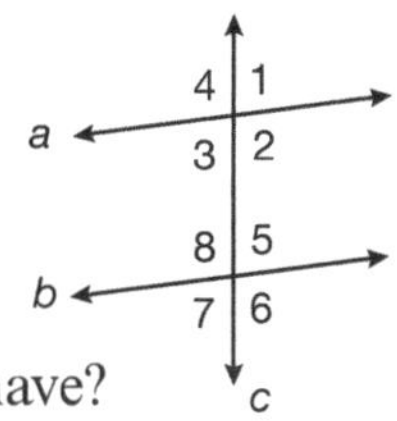

12. **Multiple Choice** What is the greatest number of intersection points that four coplanar lines can have?
(1)

A 0 **B** 2
C 4 **D** 6

13. Classify $\triangle DEF$ by its sides. Is $\triangle DEF$ also equilateral?
(13)

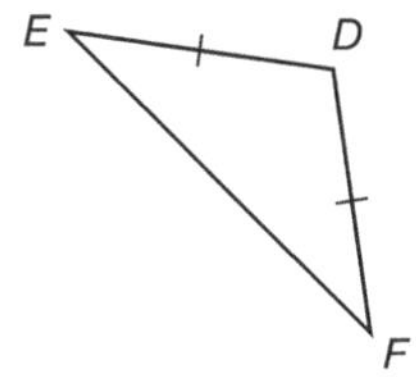

14. **Error Analysis** Alejandro and Jessica were asked to find the next number in the sequence 2, 4, ____. Alejandro makes the conjecture that the next number will be 6, while Jessica makes the conjecture that the number will be 8. Who is correct?
(7)

15. (11) **Multiple Choice** Which point is the midpoint of the segment connecting −4 and 11?

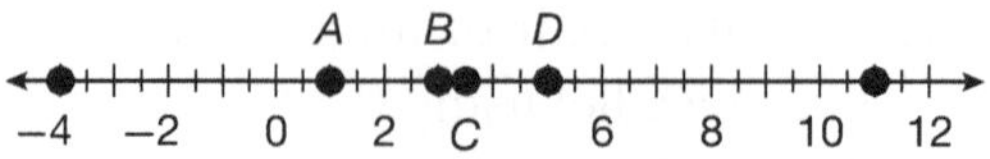

A 1 B 3
C 3.5 D 5

16. (3) **Write** Explain why an obtuse angle cannot be congruent to an acute angle.

17. (10) **Passports** Write a conditional statement from the following statement.
People born in the United States can have an American passport.

18. (8) **Agriculture** A farmer is building a rectangular pen for his chickens with an area of 40 square feet. If one side measures 8 feet, what is the length of the other side?

19. (Inv 1) Draw a pair of parallel lines and label them n and m. Then draw a transversal that is not perpendicular to either line and label it k. Mark all congruent acute angles on the figure.

20. (13) **Architecture** A certain tower has eight triangular faces. Four of these faces have approximate base lengths of 200 feet and heights of 1280 feet. Estimate the number of panes of glass needed for one of these faces, if each pane of glass has an area of approximately 45 ft^2.

21. (10) Write the converse of the following conditional statement.
If a bird is a flamingo, then it is pink.

22. (6) **Justify** Is $\angle ABD$ congruent to $\angle CBE$? Justify your answer.

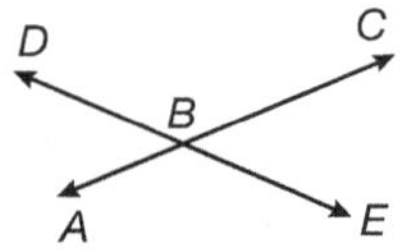

23. (4) Is the following statement always, sometimes, or never true?
Three noncoplanar points are contained in a single space.

24. (13) **a.** Of the three triangles shown, which triangle is a right triangle?
b. Which triangle is obtuse?
c. Which triangle is equiangular?

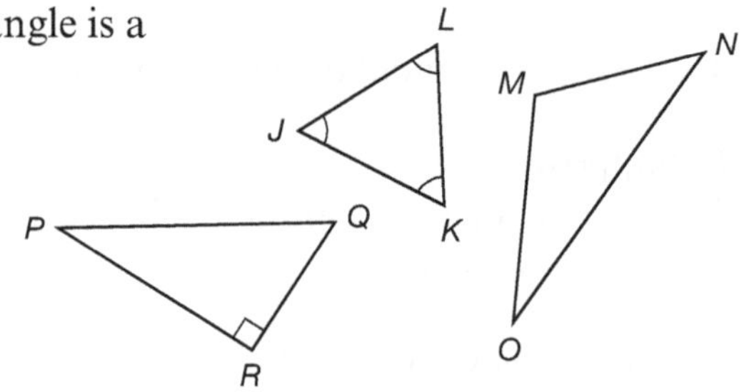

25. (11) **a.** Find the midpoint of the segment connecting −5 and 0.
b. Draw a number line containing −5 and 0. Label the midpoint.

26. (8) What is the perimeter of the pentagon shown?

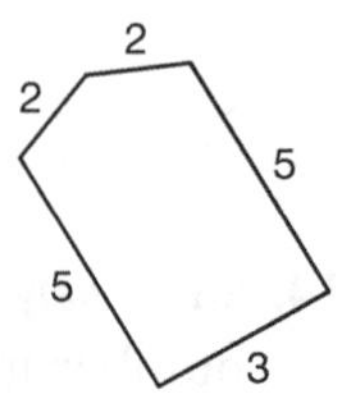

27. (2) **Algebra** Suppose E is the midpoint of $\overline{CD}$, $CD = 2x + 7$, and $DE = 4x - 13$. What is CE?

28. **Justify** Three planes, *BCD*, *ABE*, and *ACD* are arranged so that they intersect in pairs, forming the plane arrangement shown at right. Is the information given sufficient to determine that $\overline{AE} \parallel \overline{CD}$? Explain.
(5)

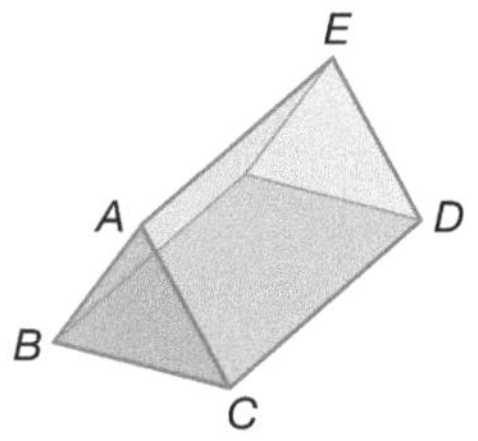

29. **Civil Engineering** Each diagonal girder on this bridge forms a transversal with the upper and lower horizontal girders.
(12)

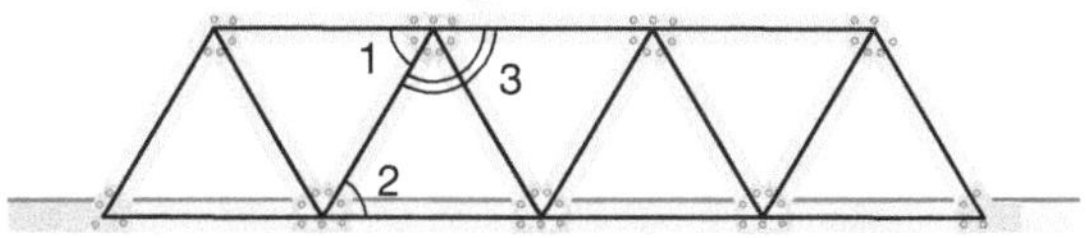

a. Suppose the angles 1 and 2 are congruent. Prove that the upper and lower girders are parallel.

b. Describe another way you could prove that the upper and lower girders are parallel.

30. If the measure of an acute angle is $(12x + 30)°$, what is the range of values for x?
(3)

Name ______________________ Date __________ Class __________

Disproving Conjectures with Counterexamples

LESSON 14

1. (14) This table shows the base lengths and areas of some triangles.

Base Length (cm)	Area (cm^2)
5.2	15.3
2.9	9.7
1.8	5.6
10.3	20.6
0.5	2.4

a. (12) Does the table give a counterexample to this conjecture? Explain. *If the base length of a triangle is less than 3 centimeters, then its area is less than 10 cm^2.*

b. Draw a triangle, not listed in the table, that is a counterexample to the conjecture.

2. (1) Classify the following statement as sometimes true, always true, or never true. *Three points can be noncoplanar.*

3. (8) **Analyze** How could you find the perimeter of an isosceles right triangle if you already know the area? Is it possible to find the leg lengths?

4. (6) List two adjacent angles and a linear pair from the diagram.

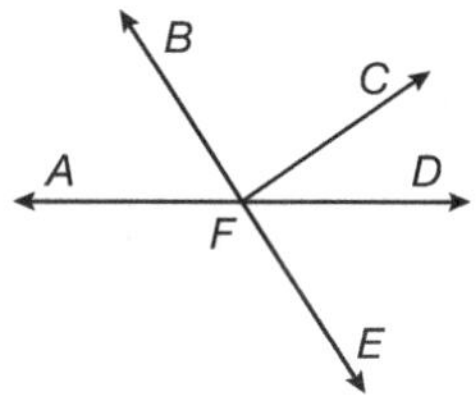

5. (8) **Algebra** If a regular triangle has a perimeter of $12x + 3$, what is an expression for the length of one of its sides?

6. (Inv 1) Line p is a transversal that intersects parallel lines m and n. If two of the alternate exterior angles measure $(2x - 10)°$ and $(-3x + 20)°$, what is the measure of each exterior angle?

7. (14) Consider this conjecture. *If a shape is a pentagon, then all its interior angles are obtuse.*

a. What is the hypothesis of the conjecture? What is its conclusion?

b. Find a counterexample to the conjecture.

8. (11) **Multiple Choice** Which point is the midpoint of -13 and 5?

A -3 **B** -4

C -6 **D** -8

9. (5) An angle in a triangle is labeled as $\angle ABC$. Explain why $\overleftrightarrow{AB}$ and $\overleftrightarrow{BC}$ can be used to define a plane.

10. (13) **a.** In this figure, which triangle is acute?

b. Which triangle is obtuse?

c. Which triangle is equiangular?

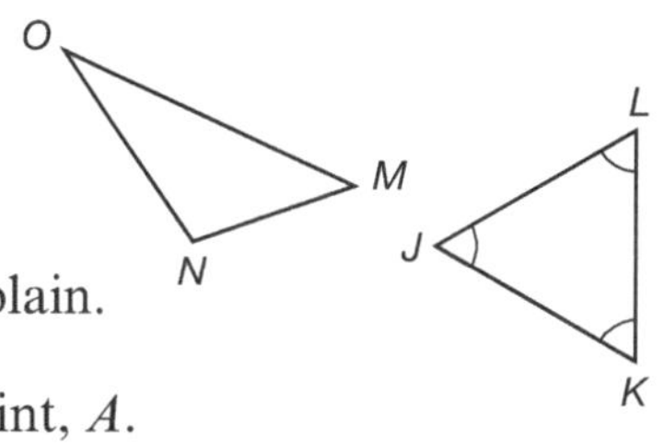

11. (6) **Write** Do complementary angles need to be adjacent? Explain.

12. (4) Draw and label two opposite rays with a common endpoint, A.

13. (10) Identify the hypothesis and conclusion of this statement. *If one dozen eggs cost \$2.49, then two dozen eggs cost \$4.98.*

14. (9) **Error Analysis** A student calculated the distance between G (12, 4) and H (12, 2) as approximately 12.81. Where did the student make the error and what should the answer be?

Disproving Conjectures with Counterexamples

LESSON 14

15. (13) **Multi-Step** A star-shaped logo for a shop consists of three isosceles triangles, each with a base length of 12.5 millimeters and a height of 24.5 millimeters, fitted around an equilateral triangle with a base length of 12.5 millimeters and a height of 10.8 millimeters. Find the approximate sum of the four triangles' areas.

16. (Inv 1) State the converse of the statement below.
If two lines are cut by a transversal and the alternate interior angles are congruent, then the lines are parallel.

Write a conditional statement from each sentence.

17. (10) **Football** The team scores three points if the kicker makes a field goal.

18. (10) A number squared is a positive number.

19. (14) Find a counterexample to this conjecture. *If* $(1 - a)(1 - b) = 0$, *then* $a = b = 1$.

20. (13) **Packaging** This figure shows the triangular shaped label for a brand of cheese wedges. Classify the triangle by its sides and angles.

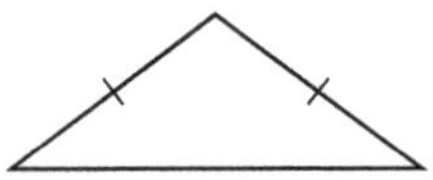

21. (Inv 1) If a pair of parallel lines are cut by a transversal, which pairs of angles will be supplementary?

22. (9) **Analyze** If you are given the first endpoint of a segment and the length of the segment, how many possible locations are there for the second endpoint of the segment? Explain.

23. (12) **Visual Arts** Seth is creating an abstract design with parallel lines, shown here. He adds angle markings as a reminder that the angles are congruent. How do you know that $a \parallel b$?

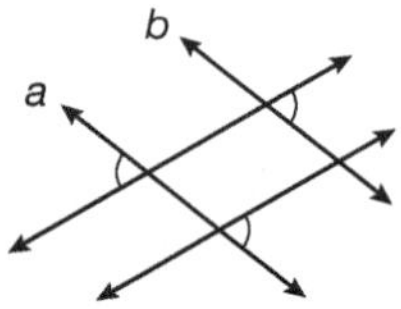

24. (7) **Write** When can a conjecture be considered a theorem?

25. (11) Determine the midpoint of each side of $\triangle KLM$ with coordinates $K(-2, -5)$, $L(-7, 4)$, and $M(0, -1)$.

26. (5) Describe all of the possible types of intersections of three planes.

27. (7) Use inductive reasoning to find the next term: $-4, -1, 2,$ ______

28. (14) Find a counterexample to this conjecture. *If a triangle is isosceles, then it is equilateral.*

29. (8) **Painting** A man wants to paint the walls of a room. If the floor is a rectangle that is 10 feet by 12 feet and the ceiling is 10 feet high, what is the area he will have to paint?

Disproving Conjectures with Counterexamples

30. (11) **Geography** Jacob lives in Philadelphia and his friend Antonio lives in Baltimore. The two plan to meet in the town that is closest to the midpoint of these two cities.

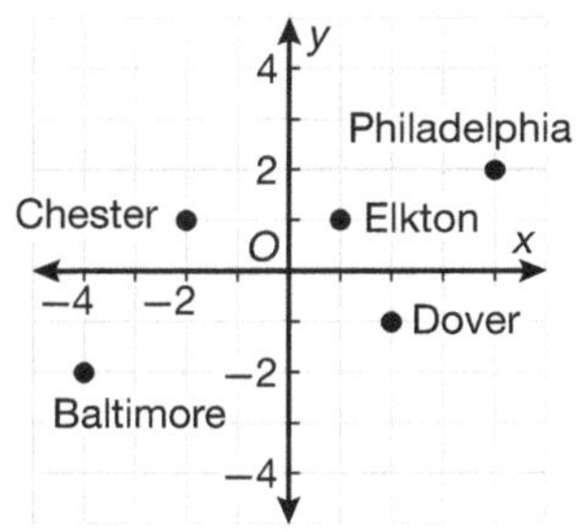

a. What are the coordinates of the midpoint of Philadelphia and Baltimore on the grid?

b. What is the name and the coordinates of the town where Jacob and Antonio will meet?

Name ______________________ Date __________ Class __________

Introduction to Polygons

LESSON 15

1. (14) **Write** Explain why the pair of numbers 3 and 3 is a counterexample to this statement.
If the sum of two numbers is even, then both numbers are even.

2. (5) **Agriculture** A farm is being divided so that each section of land has equal access to the canal running through the property for watering crops. If the road on the opposite side of the property runs parallel to the canal, explain how this can be done.

3. (8) **Wallpaper** A family wants to install wallpaper around the bottom half of a room. If the room has 12-foot tall ceilings and each wall is 14 feet long, calculate the area the wallpaper will cover.

4. (15) In polygon *JKLMN*, name each angle and identify it as an interior or exterior angle.

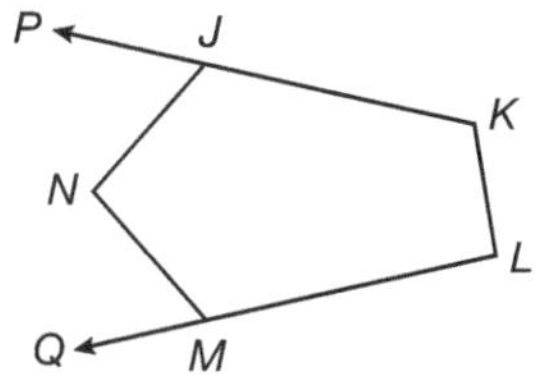

Write a conditional statement from each sentence.

5. (10) The absolute value of a number is a nonnegative number.

6. (10) A bilingual person speaks two languages.

7. (11) Determine the midpoint M of $\overline{XY}$ connecting $X(0, 2)$ and $Y(6, 1)$.

8. (14) **Model** Find a counterexample to this conjecture.
If two lines intersect, then any third coplanar line intersects both of them.

9. (7) Use inductive reasoning to determine the pattern in the following sequence:

$$2, 3, 5, 9, 17, 33, 65$$

10. (2) Identify the property that justifies this statement:
$a = b$ *and* $b = c$, *so* $a = c$.

11. (Inv 1) Name all the pairs of angles that are congruent when a transversal cuts a pair of parallel lines.

12. (9) Find the length of the segment connecting (1.3, 4.1) and (2.8, 6.1).

13. (13) **Verify** Rectangle *PQRS* is divided into two triangles by diagonal $\overline{QS}$.

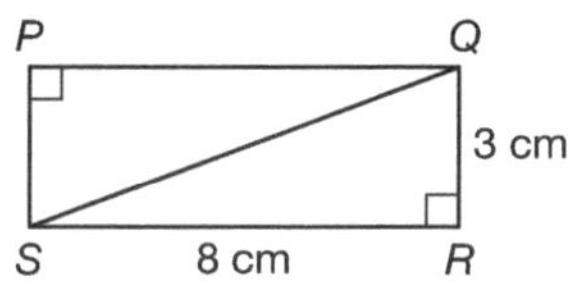

a. Determine the area of rectangle *PQRS*.
b. Given that $\triangle PQS$ and $\triangle QRS$ have equal areas, use your answer to part **a** to determine the area of $\triangle PQS$.
c. Verify that the formula for the area of a triangle gives the same answer as part **b** for the area of $\triangle PQS$.

14. (15) Classify this polygon. Is it equiangular? Is it equilateral? Is it regular?

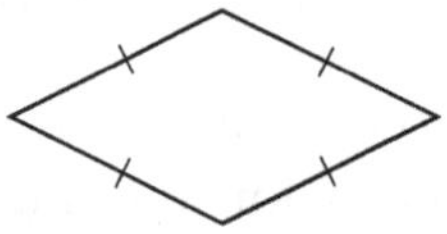

15. (12) **Home Renovation** Tasha is using two wooden rails to construct a pair of stair rails along the walls of a staircase. To make sure that the rails are parallel, she measures the acute angle each rail makes with the vertical edge of the wall at the base of the stairs.

a. What type of angles are these?

b. Tasha measures each angle to be 42°. Explain how she can make sure that the rails are parallel.

16. (14) **Verify** Confirm that this quadrilateral is a counterexample to the conjecture.

If a quadrilateral has two pairs of congruent sides, then both pairs of opposite sides are parallel.

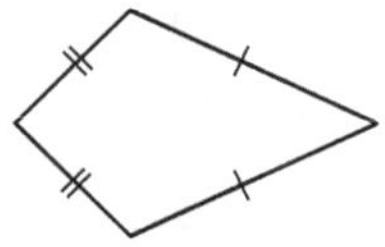

17. (Inv 1) If two parallel lines are cut by a transversal and one pair of same-side interior angles has angles that measure $(10x + 90)°$ and $(4x + 6)°$, what is the measure of each angle?

18. (12) **Write** In this figure, the transversal line ℓ intersects lines m and n. Write a paragraph explaining how you know that m and n are parallel.

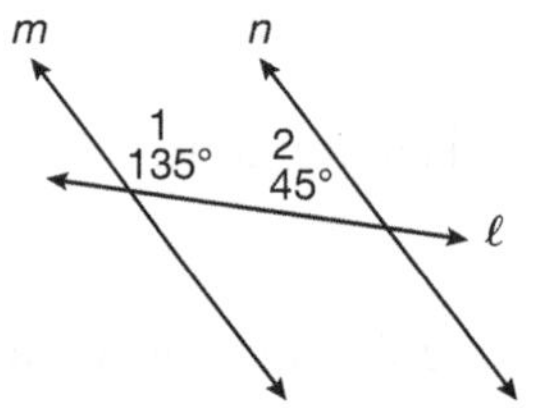

19. (15) This figure shows a polygon with one vertex and two sides missing.

a. Copy the figure and add a point G that makes $ABCDEFG$ concave.

b. Make a second copy of the figure and add a point H that makes $ABCDEFH$ convex.

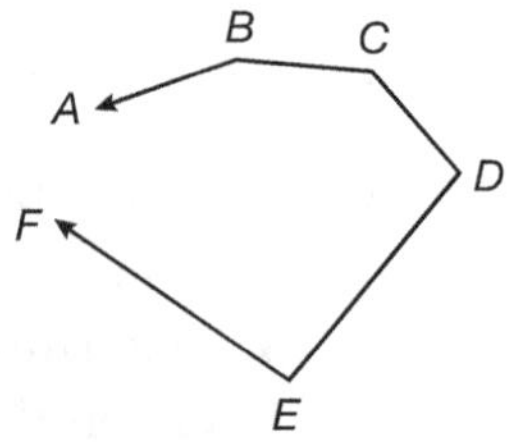

20. (Inv 1) Name every pair of corresponding angles in the diagram.

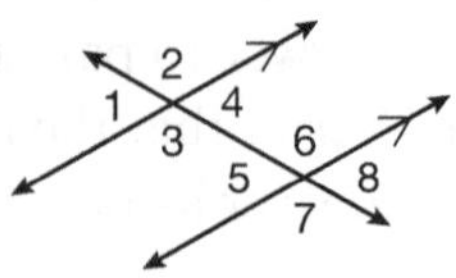

21. (8) **Building** A builder wants to add a diagonal beam to add support to a structure. The beam needs to extend across a height of 15 feet and a distance of 28 feet. What will the length of the beam be to the nearest hundredth of a foot?

22. (11) Determine the midpoint of each side of $\triangle ABC$.

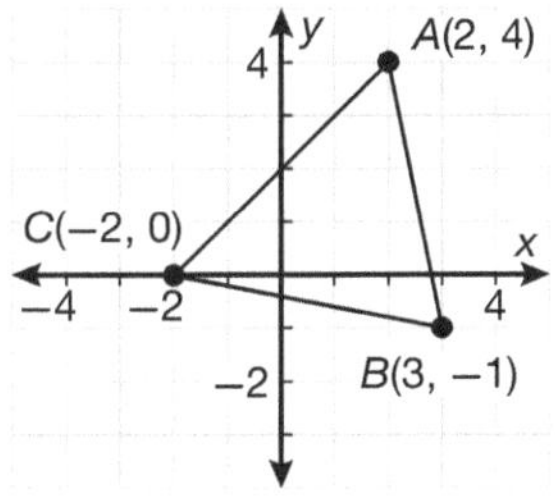

23. (13) **Algebra** The height of a triangle is 12.7 centimeters and its area is 31.75 square centimeters. Use the Triangle Area Formula to determine its base length.

24. (4) **Multiple Choice** Which statement is always true?
A Two planes intersect in a straight line.
B Two lines are contained in exactly one plane.
C Two lines can intersect at two points.
D Any four points can be contained in exactly one plane.

25. (12) **Multiple Choice** If $\angle 1$ and $\angle 2$ are congruent, which of these should be used to prove that lines p and q are parallel?
A Converse of the Alternate Exterior Angles Theorem
B Converse of the Alternate Interior Angles Theorem
C Converse of the Corresponding Angles Postulate
D Converse of the Same-Side Interior Angles Theorem

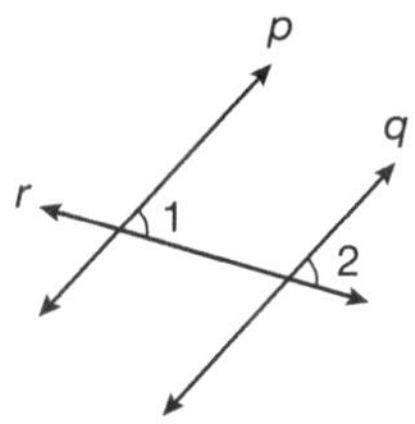

26. (7) **Predict** Use inductive reasoning to find the next term in this sequence. Explain the rule for the pattern.

2, 3, 5, 9, 17, ...

27. (8) **Multi-Step** Find the perimeter of a square if its area is 289 square centimeters.

28. (Inv. 1) If two parallel lines are intersected by a transversal, what is the sum of the measures of all four interior angles that are formed?

29. (8) Find the perimeter of a regular hexagon with side lengths of 6.8 inches

30. (15) If the points A, B, C, D, and E are connected, is polygon $ABCDE$ convex or concave?

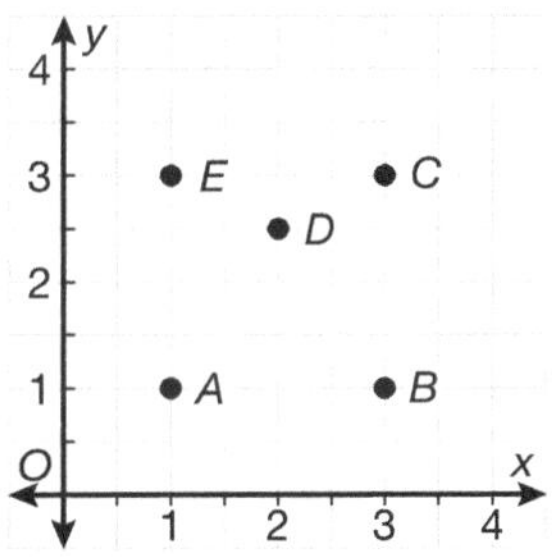

Name ______________________ Date __________ Class __________

Finding Slopes and Equations of Lines

LESSON 16

1. (15) **Packaging** This figure shows the cardboard which will be folded into a package.

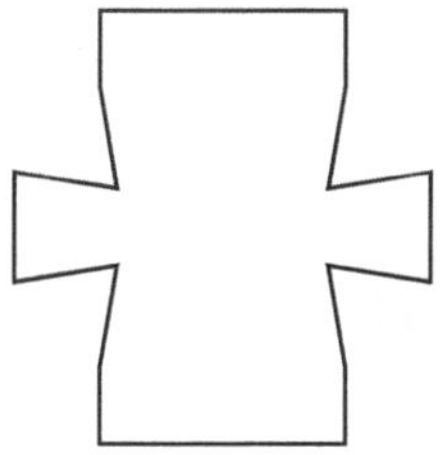

a. Determine whether the shape is equiangular and whether it is equilateral.

b. Determine whether the shape is regular or irregular.

c. Determine whether the shape is concave or convex, and explain how you know.

2. (16) Determine the slope of the line passing through (3, 1) and (5, 5).

3. (12) **Verify** Which postulate or theorem can you use to determine that x and y in this figure are parallel? Explain.

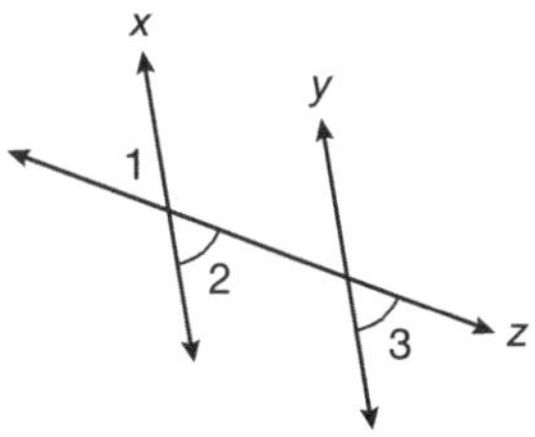

4. (16) **a.** Determine the slope of this line.

b. Write an equation for the line.

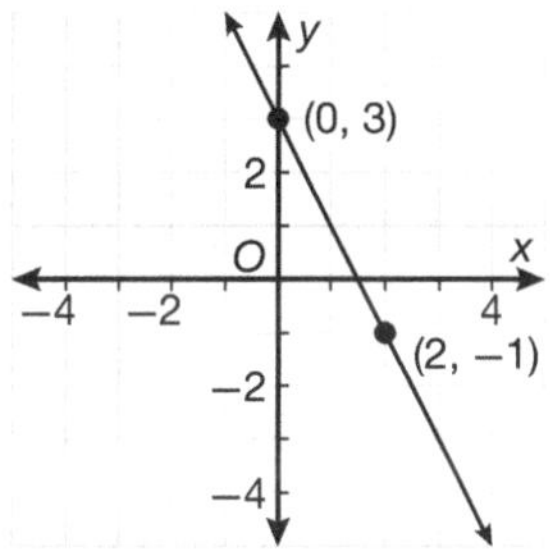

5. (10) **Write** Write a conditional statement that has a false converse.

6. (8) **Tiling** The area of a single tile is exactly 1 square foot. If a developer wants to put tile in a room that measures 17 feet by 14 feet and each tile costs \$1.29, how much will it cost to tile the room?

7. (16) Graph the line with equation $y + 2x = 0$.

8. (Inv 1) Two parallel lines cut by a transversal form corresponding angles that measure $(2x)°$ and $(4x - 60)°$. What is the measure of each angle?

9. (11) **Multi-Step** If the midpoint of the segment connecting $(-8, x)$ and $(x, 4x)$ is (y, y), what is the value of y?

10. (11) **Space Exploration** NASA plans to launch Terrestrial Planet Finder 1, a telescope array that uses five spacecraft flying in formation to search for Earth-like planets in other solar systems. Suppose the locations of the top-left and bottom-right telescopes in the picture are $(-100, 40)$ and $(40, -60)$. Given that the central combiner telescope lies exactly halfway between these two, what are the coordinates of the central combiner telescope?

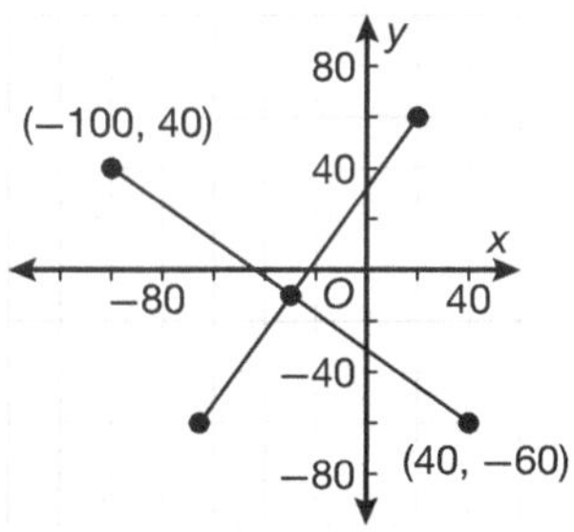

11. (8) **Farming** A plow has a length of 6 feet. If the plow has dimensions as shown, how far off the ground are the plow handles, to the nearest hundredth of a foot?

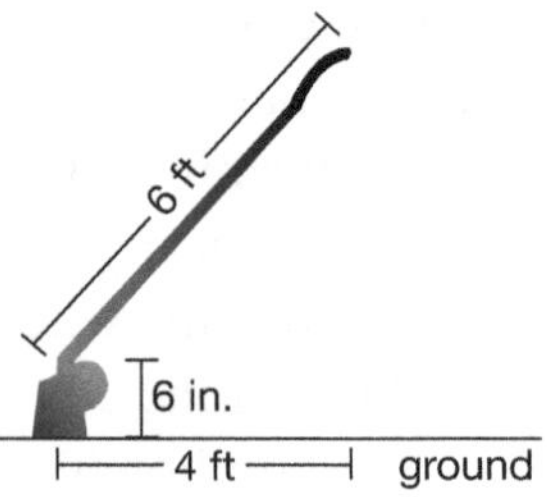

12. (3) **Multi-Step** If $\overrightarrow{BD}$ intersects straight angle $\angle ABC$ and $\angle ABD$ is one-eighth the size of $\angle DBC$, what is $m\angle DBC$?

13. (13) **Algebra** The base of a triangle measures 4.5 inches and its area is 24.75 in^2. Use the Triangle Area Formula to determine its height.

14. (5) **Error Analysis** Mohammed reads a theorem that says there is exactly one line through a point not on a given line that is perpendicular to that line, and extends this statement to read that a point on the line would also have one perpendicular line through it. Comment on the validity of his conclusion in two dimensions and in three dimensions.

15. (15) Copy polygon *UVWXYZ* and draw in all diagonals. Classify polygon *UVWXYZ* as convex or concave.

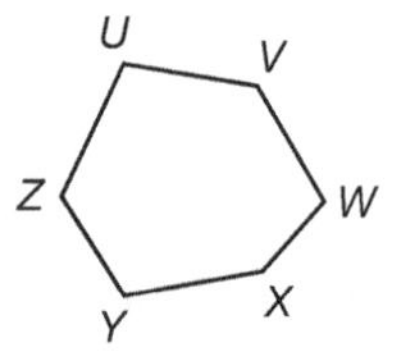

16. (8) Find the area of a right triangle with a hypotenuse of 36 inches and a leg of 15 inches. Round to the nearest hundredth.

17. (5) In the right triangular prism shown, list pairs of lines that appear to be parallel, perpendicular, and skew.

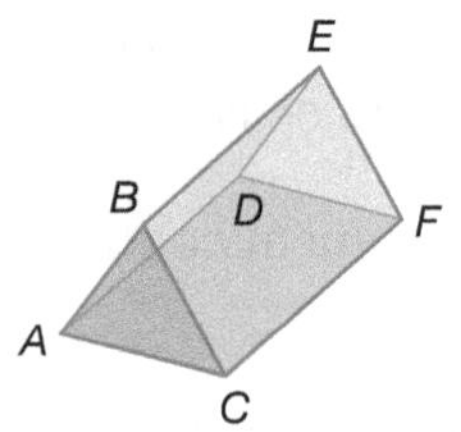

18. (4) **Verify** Points *A*, *B*, *C*, and *D* all lie on the same line. Are the points also coplanar? Which postulate or theorem can be used to justify your response?

19. (7) **Formulate** Show that the conjecture "$2n - 1$ is a prime number" is true for $n = 3$ and $n = 4$.

20. (6) **Multiple Choice** Which angle measure is supplementary to 80°?

A 100° **B** 10°

C 80° **D** 110°

21. $\angle ABD$ and $\angle CBE$ are right angles. Are $\angle ABC$ and $\angle DBE$ congruent? Explain.
(6)

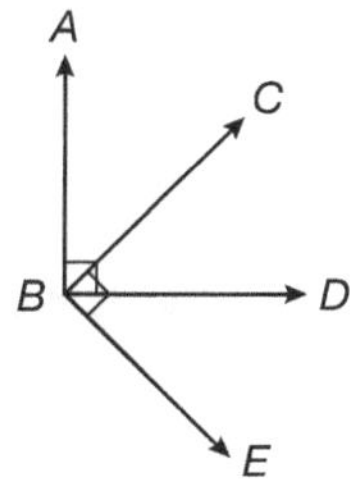

22. Does the line $y = -1.2x + 3$ slope up or down when you move left to right? How do you know?
(16)

23. **Analyze** Is it possible to draw two planes that intersect at a point? Explain.
(4)

24. **Write** In this figure, the transversal line r intersects lines q and p. Write a paragraph explaining why q and p are parallel.
(12)

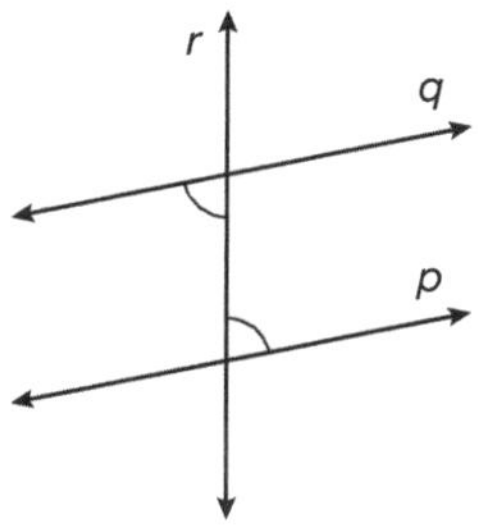

25. Use inductive reasoning to determine the next term in the series: 11, 16, 15, 20, 19, 24, 23, ______
(7)

26. What are the values of x and y in the diagram, given that $m \parallel n$?
(Inv 1)

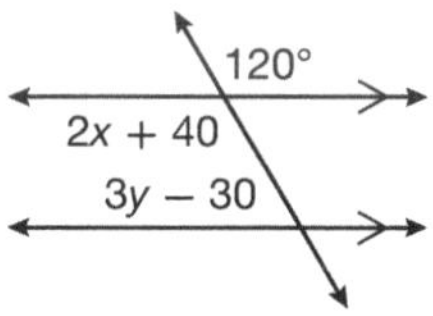

27. **Write** State the hypothesis and the conclusion of this conjecture. *If the product of two numbers is at least 4, then both numbers are at least 2.* Is the conjecture true? Explain how you know.
(14)

28. Determine the slope of this line.
(16)

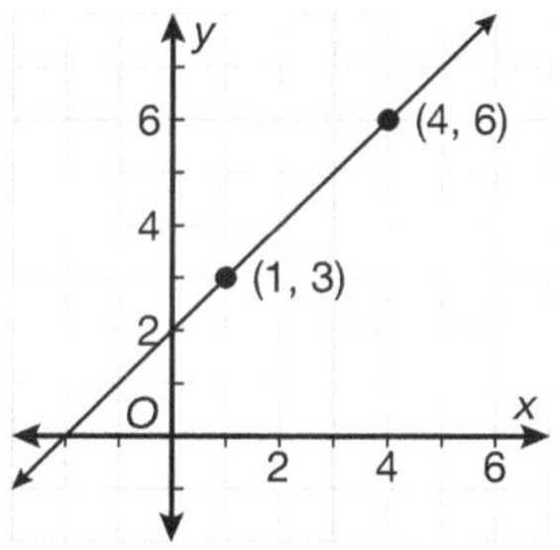

29. (13) **Model** Use a straightedge and a protractor to draw a scalene, an isosceles, and an equilateral triangle. Mark each congruent angle with arc marks and each congruent side with tick marks.

30. (14) **Multiple Choice** Which is a counterexample to the following conjecture? *If two numbers are not positive, then their product is positive.*

A 2 and −3 **B** −1 and 0
C −4 and −1 **D** 2 and 7

More Conditional Statements

LESSON 17

1. (13) **Music** Chris is planning to make an electric guitar in this shape.
   a. What area of material will he need for the face of the triangular body, to the nearest square inch?
   b. Chris wants to edge the body in luminescent material. If the body is $\frac{3}{4}$ inch. thick, what area of material will he need for the edging? (Round to the nearest square inch.)

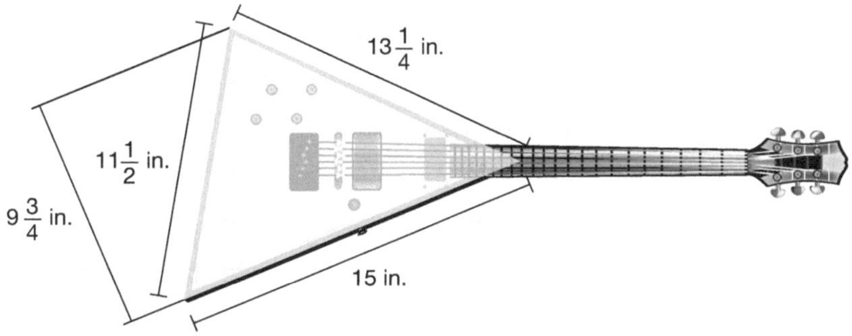

2. (14) **Economics** A cost function relates the total cost (C) of production to the number of items (x) produced per day. Acme Industries has a cost function $C_1 = 300x + 500$, while Amalgamated Widgets' cost function is $C_2 = 420x + 250$. Using these facts, find a counterexample to this conjecture.

   For any value of x, Acme Industries has lower costs than Amalgamated Widgets.

3. (8) If a right triangle has a base of 6 inches and a height of 12 inches, what is the length of the hypotenuse to the nearest inch?

4. (11) **Formulate** Points $G(7, 1)$ and $H(-1, 4)$ lie on the coordinate plane.
   a. Think of the x-coordinates 7 and -1 as points on a number line. What is the midpoint of the segment connecting them? What is the midpoint of the segment connecting y-coordinates 1 and 4? What is the midpoint of $\overline{GH}$?
   b. Use part **a** to write a statement of the form:
   $\left(\frac{\_+\_}{2}\right), \left(\frac{\_+\_}{2}\right) = (\_, \_)$

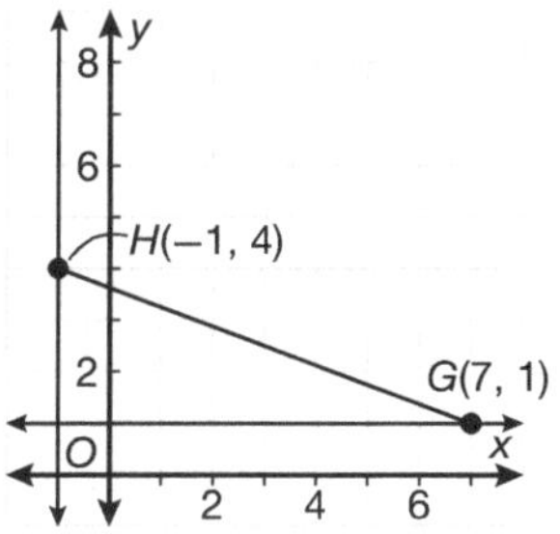

5. (17) Write the inverse of this statement. *If Noah has pasta for lunch, then it is Tuesday.*

6. (1) Classify the statement as sometimes true, always true, or never true. Explain why.

   If two lines are noncoplanar, then they are skew.

7. (10) This conditional statement is not in if-then form. Rewrite it in if-then form, then identify the hypothesis and the conclusion.

   All PE students wear blue shorts to class.

8. (12) **Multiple Choice** In this figure, ∠5 and which other angle can prove the lines parallel using the Alternate Exterior Angles Converse?

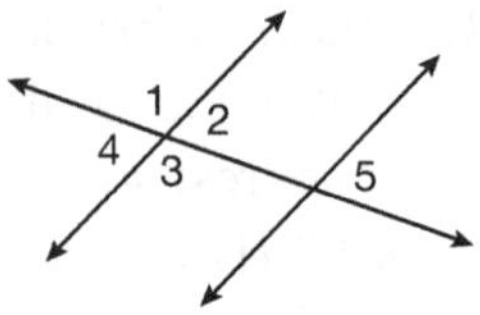

A 1
B 2
C 3
D 4

9. (12) **Write** In this figure, the transversal line z intersects lines x and y. Write a paragraph explaining how to show that x and y are parallel.

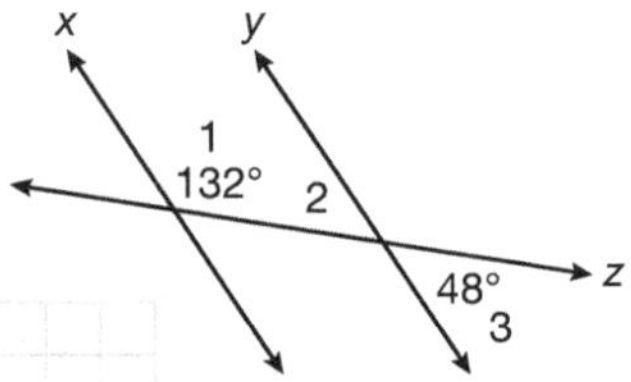

10. (16) **Multiple Choice** The slope of this graph is:

A 0.5
B 2
C −0.5
D −2

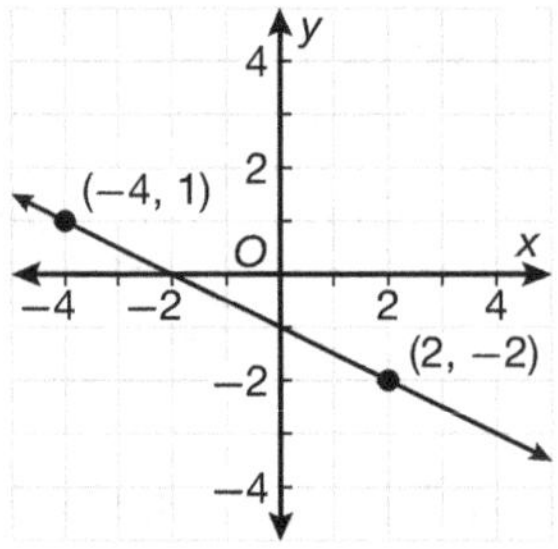

11. (17) **Algebra** Examine the statement, "If $x^2 > 4$, then $x > 2$." Is the statement true or false? Write its converse. Is the converse true or false?

12. (11) **Write** Explain why the midpoint of a and $-a$ on a number line is 0, for any value of a.

13. (16) **Physics** This graph shows the distance a train must travel in miles against the length of time of its journey in minutes. Determine the slope of the line. What does it represent?

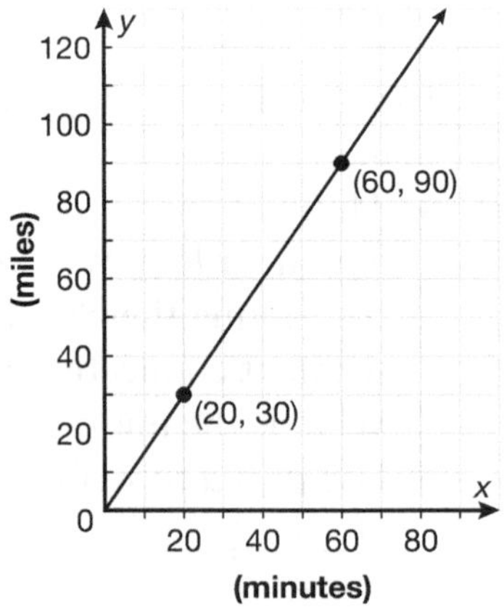

14. (2) Identify the property that justifies the statement: $WX = YZ$, so $YZ = WX$.

15. (7) Draw an acute, a right, and an obtuse triangle to test the conjecture made by Marc that the side which is opposite the largest angle in a triangle is the largest side in the triangle.

16. (12) Prove that lines r and q in this figure are parallel.

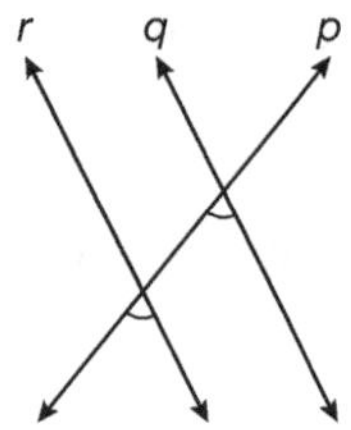

17. Copy and complete this table showing the side lengths of several triangles.
(13)

Side Lengths	Isosceles or Scalene?	Equilateral?
3, 4, 5		
7, 13, 7		
39, 39, 39		

18. State the contrapositive of this statement.
(17)

If a bird is black, then it is not a swan.

Does an individual white swan prove the contrapositive statement? If all the swans you have ever seen are white, does that prove the statement? Does it provide evidence to support the statement? Explain your reasoning.

19. **Verify** Confirm that a triangle with side lengths of 5, 4, and 3 units is a counterexample to this statement.
(14)

If a triangle has no congruent sides, then it is obtuse or acute.

20. **Multiple Choice** Many rooms have a baseboard that lines the room where the walls and floor intersect. Which of the following best describes this situation?
(4)

A Two unique points make a line.
B Two noncollinear points define a plane.
C Two noncoplanar lines make a plane.
D Two distinct planes intersect in a line.

21. Identify the hypothesis and conclusion of this statement.
(10)

A drink is a soda if it has bubbles.

22. **Civics** An opinion poll shows support for Sally Smith at 60% in her congressional race. Assuming the poll is accurate, plot a line to represent how many votes Smith would get against different voter turnouts. Use scales from 0 to 300,000 in steps of 50,000.
(16)

23. Find a counterexample to this conjecture. *If three lines in a plane are all non-parallel, then they divide the plane into seven regions.*
(14)

24. Write the converse of this statement. *If a polygon is a triangle, then the sum of its angle measures is 180°.*
(17)

25. **Algebra** Find a counterexample to this conjecture.
(14)

If $xy < 1$, *then* $x < 1$ *and* $y < 1$.

26. **Multi-Step** Find the length of the given segments shown and determine if they are congruent.
(9)

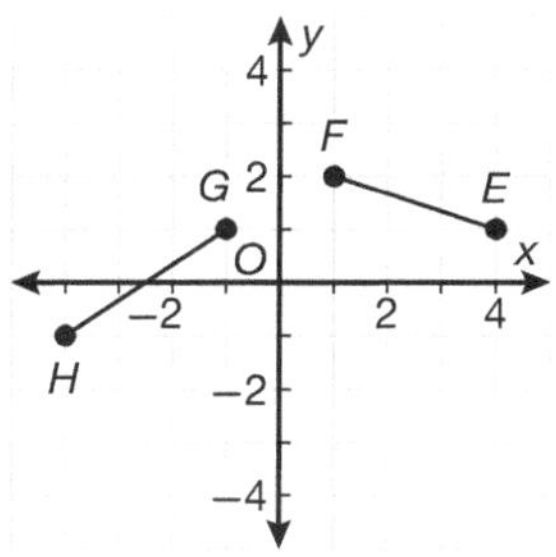

27. (15) **Analyze** A heptagon has sides with positive integer lengths. If the heptagon is regular, what can you conclude about its perimeter? Explain.

28. (8) Find the area of a right triangle with the hypotenuse of 17 centimeters and a leg of 10 centimeters. Round to the nearest hundredth.

29. (8) **Multi-Step** Find the perimeter of a right triangle with both legs equal, if the area is 32 square meters. Round to the nearest hundredth.

30. (15) Draw an irregular convex hexagon. Draw and label an exterior angle and the associated interior angle. What is the relationship between these two angles?

Name ________________ Date ________ Class ________

Triangle Theorems

LESSON 18

1. Use $\triangle XYZ$ to answer problems **a** and **b**.
(8)
   a. In $\triangle XYZ$, what is the length of side $\overline{YZ}$? Round to the nearest eighth of an inch.
   b. Determine the perimeter of $\triangle XYZ$.

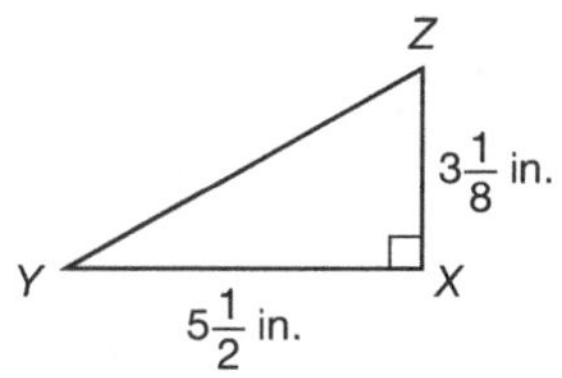

2. **Algebra** Two congruent angles are complementary to a 22° angle. These angles are defined by the expressions $3x + 5$ and $7y - 2$, respectively. What are the values of x and y?
(6)

3. **Geology** Consider this statement. *If a rock is metamorphic, then it is crystalline.*
(17)
   a. Write the inverse of this statement.
   b. Assuming that the original statement is true, can you conclude that its inverse is true?

4. **Verify** Two of the labeled points on this coordinate grid have a third labeled point as their midpoint. Identify the two points and their midpoint, and verify your answer.
(11)

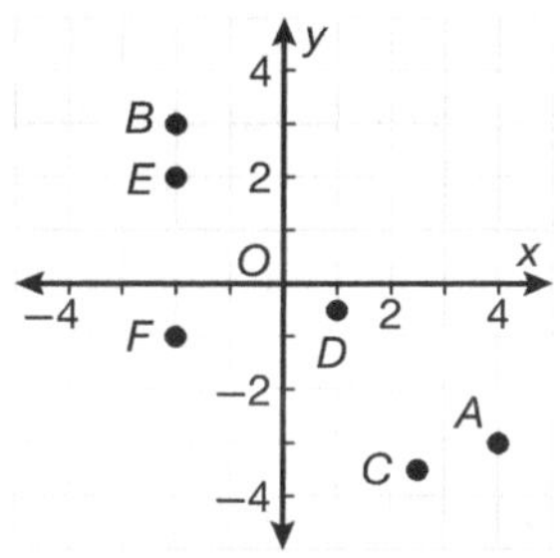

5. Find an example to disprove the converse of the following statement.
(10)

   If $x = -4$, *then* $x^2 = 16$.

6. **Multiple Choice** If a line has the length of 5 units and it has one endpoint of $(3, -2)$, what is a possible second endpoint?
(9)
   A $(0, 1)$ **B** $(-1, 2)$
   C $(-1, 1)$ **D** $(6, -6)$

7. Is $\overleftrightarrow{EF}$ parallel to $\overleftrightarrow{AB}$? Explain.
(5)

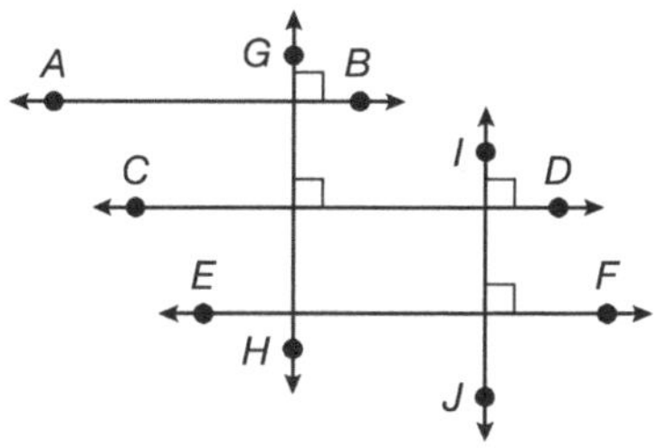

8. **Algebra** A rectangle has a perimeter of 40 inches. If the longer side is $(4x + 8)$ inches and the shorter side is $(3x - 2)$ inches, what are the dimensions of the rectangle?
(8)

9. What is the measure of angle 1 in the diagram?
(Inv 1)

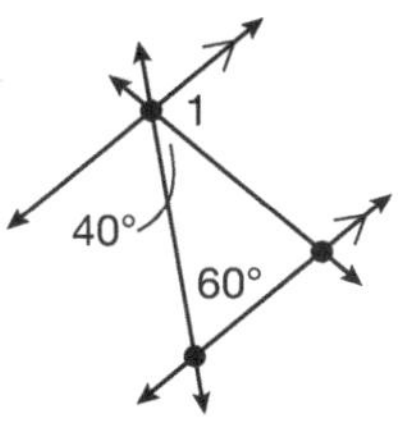

10. (15) **Geography** Mia, a traveling sales representative, has to stop at five customers' locations in one day: A, B, C, D, and E. She begins and ends at her hotel, H. Mia figures that she will drive the shortest total distance if she makes the stops in the sequence A, C, D, E, B. Classify the polygon that her route, $HACDEB$ forms, including any features which are congruent, and whether it is convex or concave.

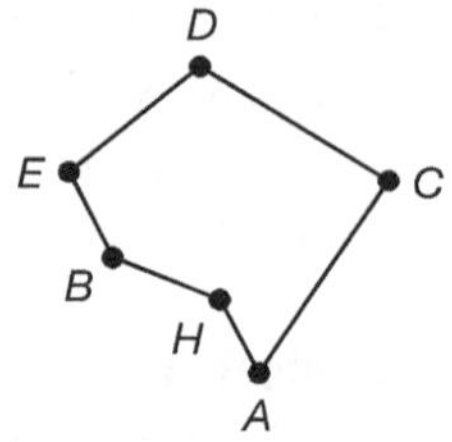

11. (Inv 1) If two parallel lines are cut by a transversal that is perpendicular to both lines, which pairs of angles will be supplementary?

12. (Inv 1) **Analyze** Use the Alternate Interior Angles Theorem to explain why corresponding angles are congruent.

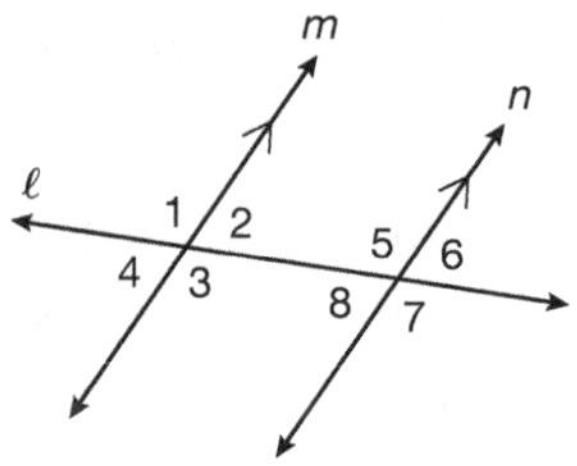

13. (7) **Justify** Use inductive reasoning to create the next item in the sequence, and explain your reasoning.

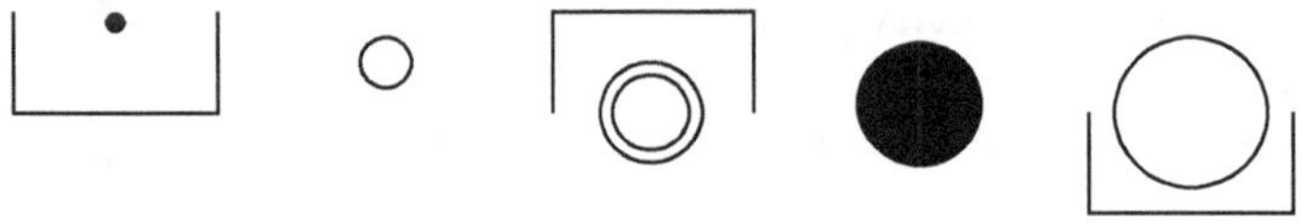

14. (18) Two angles of a triangle measure 30° and 45°. What is the measure of the third angle?

15. (16) **Algebra** Transform the equation $x - 3y = 6$ to put it in slope-intercept form.

16. (18) Determine the measure of the exterior angle at C in $\triangle ABC$.

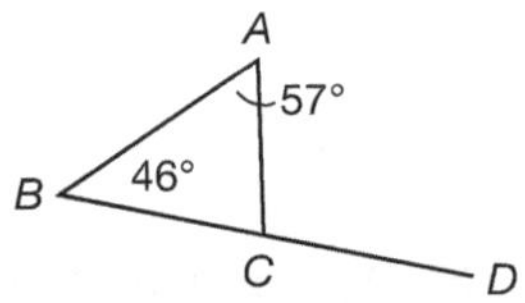

17. (17) **Verify** Consider this statement. "If a polygon is irregular, then it is concave."

a. Write the converse of the statement.

b. Write the inverse of the original statement.

c. Verify that the inverse statement and converse statement have the same truth value.

18. (18) All exterior angles of a certain triangle are obtuse. Classify the triangle by its angles and explain how you know.

19. (14) **Computer Science** An "OR" logic gate has two inputs and one output, related by the table shown.

a. Find a counterexample to this conjecture.
If the output of an OR logic gate is 1, input B is 1.

b. Violet made the conjecture: *If neither input of an OR gate is 1, the output is 0.* Does the table contain a counterexample to her conjecture?

In		Out
A	*B*	
0	0	0
0	1	1
1	0	1
1	1	1

20. (17) Write the inverse of this statement, "If a triangle has all three sides congruent, then it is obtuse." Which is true: the statement, its inverse, both, or neither?

21. (10) **Write** Write a conditional statement that has a true converse.

22. (8) Find an expression for the perimeter of a regular hexagon if the sides are $2x - 6$.

23. (12) **Optics** This optical diagram shows the paths of light rays in a reflecting telescope. Identify the two angles you need to prove congruent in order to prove that rays a and b are parallel. Which postulate or theorem would you use, and why?

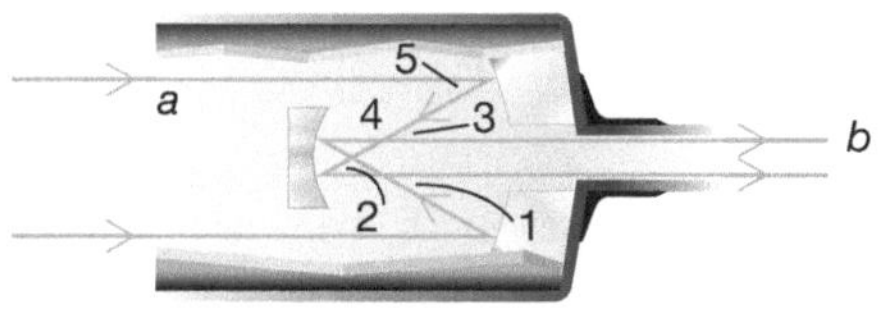

24. (15) **Multiple Choice** Polygon $JKLMN$ is a(n):

A irregular pentagon **B** equiangular nonagon

C irregular hexagon **D** regular pentagon

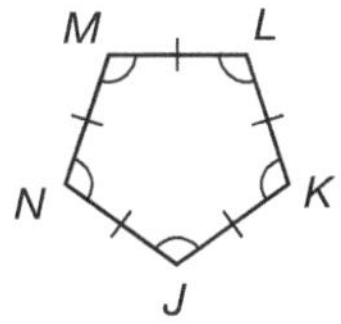

25. (10) **Multi-Step** How many true conditional statements can you write using the following three statements?

p: $\angle 1$ and $\angle 2$ are complementary

q: $m\angle 1 + m\angle 2 = 90°$

r: $\angle 1$ and $\angle 2$ are acute

26. (16) **Error Analysis** Ricardo has drawn this graph for the line with equation $x - 2y = -4$. Identify two errors Ricardo has made.

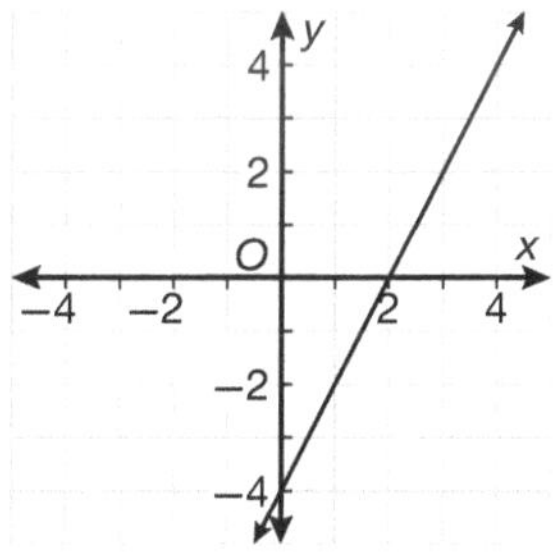

27. (9) **Write** Explain why the distance formula is not needed to determine if three points lie on the same line.

28. (18) In $\triangle DEF$, the exterior angle at D measures 58° and $m\angle E = 36°$. Determine $m\angle F$.

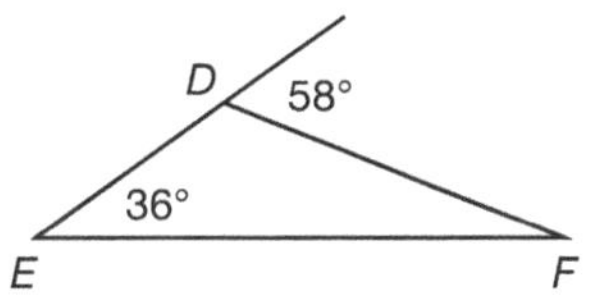

29. (13) Classify $\triangle DEF$ by its angles.

30. (4) Two distinct lines which are not contained in plane H intersect plane H. At how many points could the lines intersect the plane?

Name ______________________ Date __________ Class __________

Introduction to Quadrilaterals

LESSON 19

* **1.** (19) In quadrilateral *STUV*, $\overline{ST}$ and $\overline{TU}$ both measure 2.5 centimeters, and $SV = UV = 5.0$ centimeters. Sketch *STUV*.

2. (13) **Multiple Choice** Choose the best classification of $\triangle PQR$ by its angles.

A right | **B** acute and equiangular
C acute | **D** obtuse

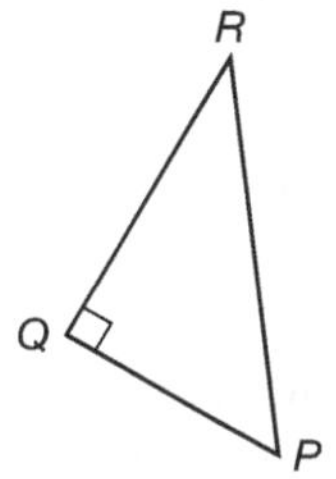

* **3.** (17) **Write** Write the negation of the Converse of Alternate Exterior Angles Theorem.

4. (13) **Algebra** A triangle has a perimeter measuring 133.1 centimeters, and two of its sides measure 23.8 centimeters and 49.3 centimeters, respectively. The height from the third side to the opposite vertex is 19.0 centimeters. Determine the triangle's area.

5. (16) Determine the slope of this line.

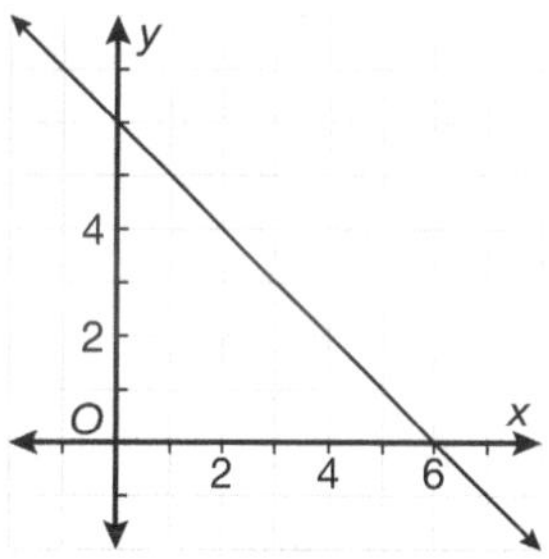

6. (7) **Generalize** Use inductive reasoning to determine the missing value: 11, 13, 17, 19, 23, ____, 31, 37

7. (Inv 1) A pair of lines is cut by a transversal, forming a pair of alternate interior angles that measure 85° and $(3x - 17)°$. For what value of x are the lines parallel?

8. (4) What is the intersection of a line, a plane containing the line, and a point on the line?

9. (15) Find a diagonal in polygon *PQRSTUVW* that lies partly in the exterior of the polygon. Classify polygon *PQRSTUVW* as convex or concave.

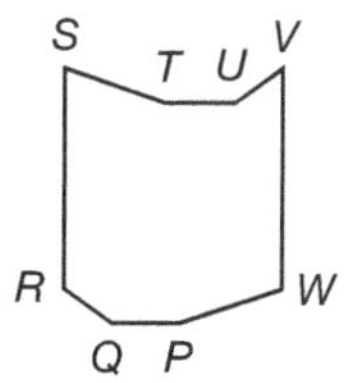

***10.** (18) Two angles of a triangle measure 68° and 43°, respectively. What is the measure of the third angle?

***11.** (19) Classify this quadrilateral.

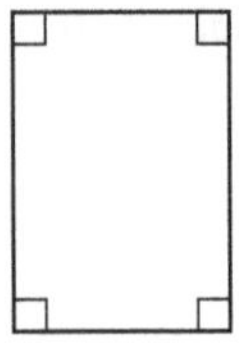

12. (14) **Verify** Confirm that a triangle with side lengths 5, 5, and 3 units is a counterexample to the statement, "If a triangle has two congruent sides, then it is obtuse."

13. (10) Identify the hypothesis and conclusion of this conditional statement. *If you have the blood type O, then you are the universal donor.*

14. (5) **Air Traffic Control** On her screen, Rita notices that two planes are flying paths that are parallel to each other. She knows that if they continue flying straight, their paths will never cross What theorem or postulate can be used to justify Rita's conclusion?

15. (11) Determine the midpoint of the points $P(-3, 0)$ and $Q(-7, -3)$.

***16.** (17) **Write** Write the inverse of the statement.

If an animal is warm-blooded, then it is a mammal.

17. (11) **Verify** Let M be the midpoint of $A(3, 7)$ and $B(5, 1)$ on the coordinate plane. Verify that M lies on $\overline{AB}$ and that $AM = BM$.

18. (8) Find an expression for the area of a rectangle if one side is twice as long as the other side.

***19.** (19) Larissa is redecorating her room. The ceiling will be white and she plans to paint the walls blue. The diagram shows the room's dimensions.

a. What is the area to be painted white?

b. To the nearest square foot, what is the area to be painted blue?

c. The actual area to be painted blue does not include the 6-by-2 foot door and does not include one 3-by-4 foot window. Find the actual area to be painted.

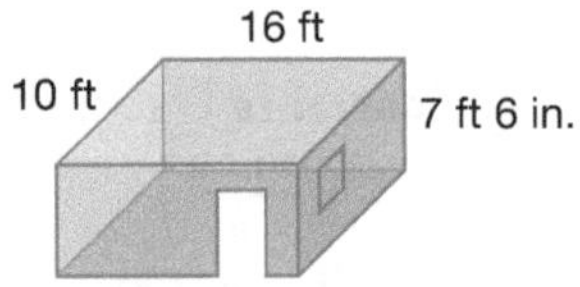

***20.** (14) **Engineering** This table shows the gas mileage of a car at various cruising speeds. Do the data give a counterexample to the conjecture, "The product of cruising speed and gas mileage is constant"? Explain.

Cruising Speed (mi/h)	Gas Mileage (mi/gal)
37	35
56	30
75	22

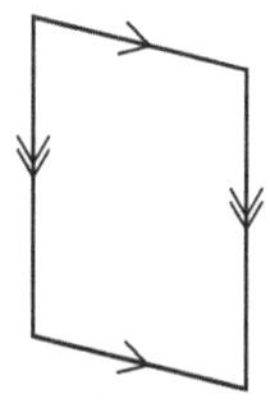

***21.** (18) In triangles JKL and MNO, $\angle J$ is congruent to $\angle M$, and $\angle K$ is congruent to $\angle N$. What can you say about $\angle L$ and $\angle O$?

***22.** (19) Classify this quadrilateral.

23. (11) What is the midpoint of $(-4, 1)$ and $(4, -1)$?

24. (7) **Write** In a biological experiment looking at the migratory patterns of geese, all of the geese that were observed actually flew to a warmer climate during the cold winter months. Is the conjecture, "All geese fly to warmer climates for the winter," valid? Why or why not?

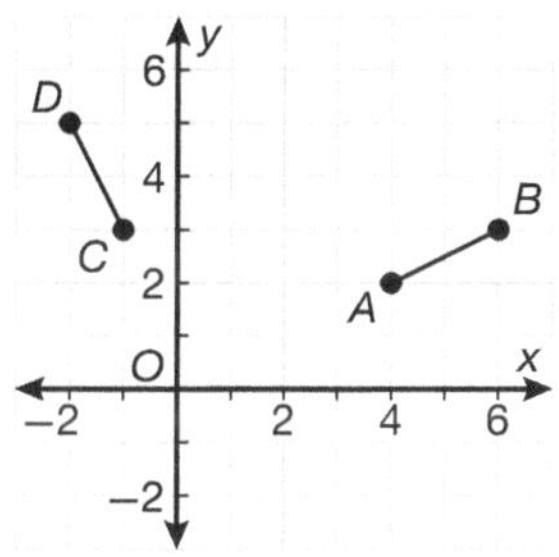

25. (9) **Multi-Step** Find the length of the given segments and determine if they are congruent.

26. (2) Identify the property that justifies the statement. *If* $\overline{AB} \cong \overline{CD}$, *then* $\overline{CD} \cong \overline{AB}$.

27. (Inv 1) **Analyze** Use the Same-Side Interior Angles Theorem to explain why corresponding angles are congruent. Assume that m is parallel to n.

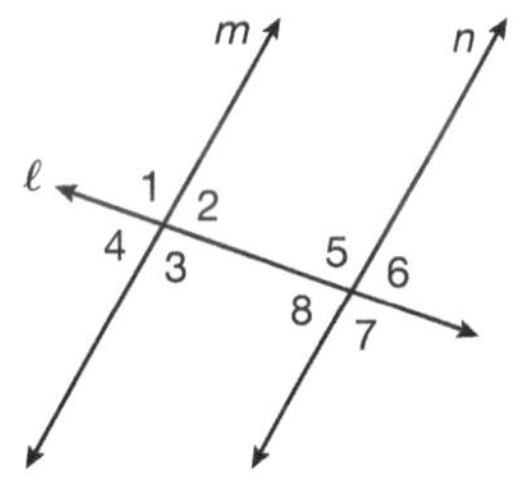

28. (16) **Write** an equation for the line passing through $(3, 0)$ and $(5, -1)$.

***29.** (18) **Geography** Three streets in Chicago, Illinois—N. Wabash St., N. Rush St., and E. Chestnut St.—make a city block in the shape of a right triangle. The acute angle at the north end of the block measures 28°. What is the exterior angle measure at N. Rush St. and E. Chestnut St.?

30. (6) **Error Analysis** Victoria states that angles that measure 50° and 130°, respectively, are complementary, but her friend Shen disagrees, stating that they are not complementary, but instead are supplementary. Who is correct?

Name ______________________________ Date __________ Class __________

Interpreting Truth Tables

LESSON 20

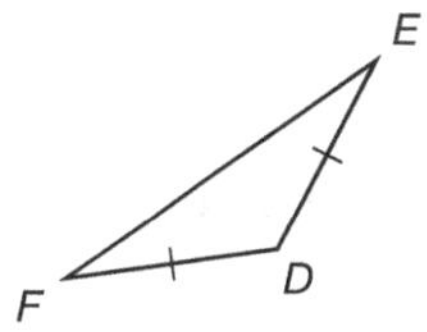

1. (16) Graph the line with equation $y = 0.5x - 1.5$.

2. (13) Classify $\triangle DEF$ by its sides.

* **3.** (20) Find the converse of the statement, "If two angles are congruent, then their measures are equal," and write a biconditional statement equivalent to them.

* **4.** (19) **Architecture** Each floor of an office building has 30 rectangular windows measuring 57 inches by 38 inches. The building has 23 floors.

a. Determine the total area of glass in all the windows, in square inches.

b. Express this area in square feet.

5. (10) Draw a Venn diagram to represent the following conditional statement.
A number is an integer if it is a whole number.

6. (4) **Aim** Julio is playing a game where he rolls a ball from one corner of the room to the opposite corner, without touching the walls. In how many different directions could Julio roll the ball to reach its target? How do you know?

7. (10) Find the converse of the following statement.
If you are an only child, then you do not have a brother.

8. (14, 19) **Multiple Choice** Which is a counterexample to the conjecture, "If a quadrilateral is equiangular, then it is equilateral"?

A A rectangle that is not a rhombus **B** A rhombus that is not rectangular
C Any square **D** Any parallelogram

9. (17) **Geography** Write the converse of the following statement.
If a state lies to the east of longitude 125° W, then it is one of the lower 48 states.

10. (3) **Write** Can an obtuse and an acute angle make a straight angle? Can an obtuse and acute angle make a right angle? Explain.

11. (7) **Write** Explain why testing a conjecture is not a generally accepted method of proof.

12. (12) **Analyze** Given two lines m and n with a transversal ℓ, consider these statements:
p: *Alternate interior angles formed by ℓ are congruent.*
q: *Alternate exterior angles formed by ℓ are congruent.*
r: *Lines m and n are parallel.*

a. Prove that if statement p is true, then statement q is true.

b. Use part **a** and the Converse of the Alternate Exterior Angles Theorem to prove the Converse of the Alternate Interior Angles Theorem.

13. Determine the midpoint of each side of square *ABCD*.
(11)

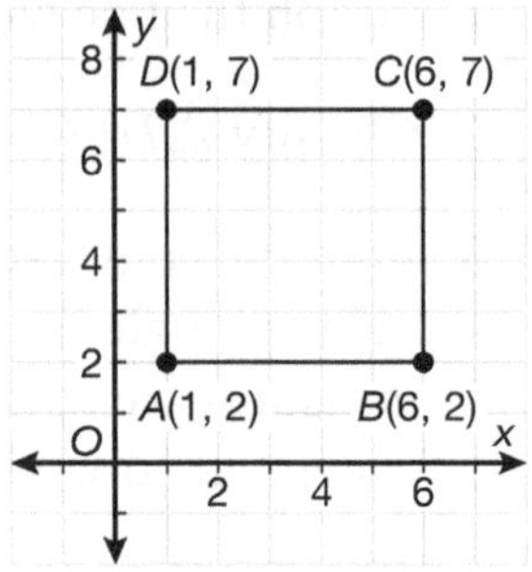

14. **Write** What can be done to disprove a conjecture? Explain.
(14)

*15. **Error Analysis** A student calculates the area and perimeter of a rectangle with length 7.5 cm and width 3 cm as follows:
(19)

$A = 3(7.5)$ and $P = 3 + 7.5$

$= 22.5\text{ cm}^2$ $= 10.5\text{ cm}$

Explain the student's error.

*16. a. State the converse of the statement, "If a quadrilateral is a square, then it has four congruent sides." Write the statement and its converse as a biconditional statement.
(20)

b. Determine whether the biconditional is true. Use a truth table to explain why or why not.

*17. **Games and Puzzles** This tangram set includes two quadrilaterals. Classify them.
(19)

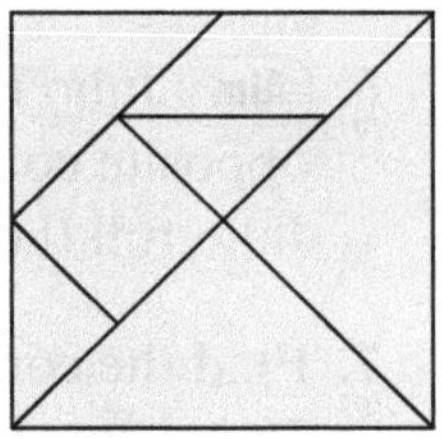

*18. An exterior angle of a triangle is a right angle. What can you say about the two remote interior angles? Explain.
(18)

19. **Algebra** What value of x allows you to apply the Converse of the Corresponding Angles Theorem to this figure? If x has this value, how are lines m and n related?
(12)

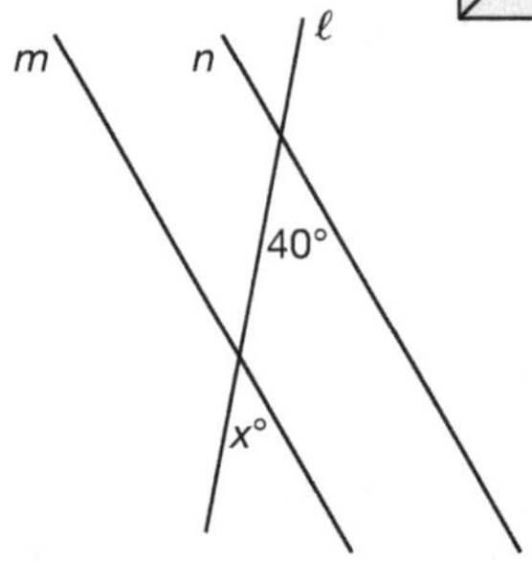

20. Determine the slope of the line passing through (3, 6) and (6, 0).
(16)

21. **Write** Can the sum of the angles in a triangle be considered a group of supplementary angles? Explain.
(6)

Use the diagram at right for the next two questions. Round to the nearest hundredth.

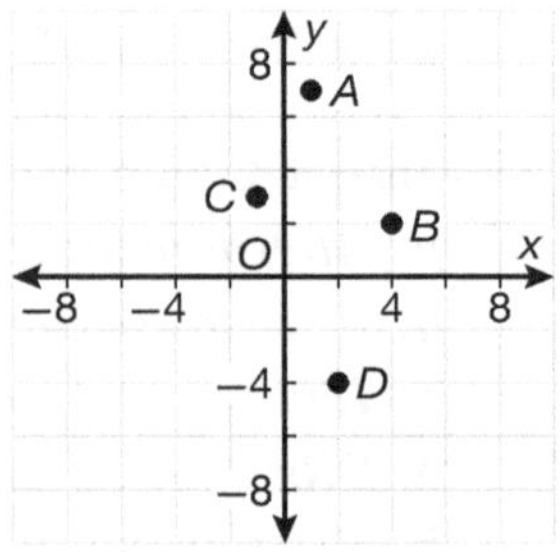

22. What is the length of $\overline{AB}$?
(9)

23. What is the length of $\overline{CD}$?
(9)

*24. Either Soo-Lin takes cheese sandwiches to school or she takes a salad, but not both or neither. On days when she takes cheese sandwiches, she takes milk. Sometimes she takes milk even if she does not take cheese sandwiches. Consider the statements "Soo-Lin takes cheese sandwiches," "Soo-Lin takes a salad," and "Soo-Lin takes milk." Write two disjunctions that are true, each using two of these statements.
(20)

25. Is this conditional statement true? If so, explain why. If not, give a counterexample.
(15) *If a polygon is regular, then it is equiangular.*

26. **Astronomy** This star chart shows the constellation Triangulum. Given that there is an almost perfect right angle at β ("beta"), what can you say about the angles at the other two vertices?
(18)

***27.** **a.** State the converse of the statement, "If the month is December, then it has 31 days."
(10)
b. Determine whether the statement is true, and whether its converse is true.

28. **Woodworking** Scarlet measures two sides of a board of wood as 14 inches and 7 inches. If she wants to find out the perimeter of the board, what formula should she use? What is the perimeter of the board?
(8)

29. Determine the midpoint of each side of triangle KLM with coordinates $K(-3, 8)$, $L(1, 4)$, and $M(5, 2)$.
(11)

30. If a pair of parallel lines is cut by a transversal, and the alternate exterior angles measure $(160 - 2x)°$ and $(5x + 55)°$, what is the measure of each angle?
(Inv 1)

Name ________________________ Date ____________ Class ____________

Laws of Detachment and Syllogism

LESSON 21

* **1.** (21) **Analyze** What conclusion can be drawn from these statements?

If the quality of the granite is high, then our company will purchase it.
The quality of the granite is high.

2. (8) What is the length of a rectangle with a perimeter of 300 feet and a width of 32 feet?

3. (16) **Error Analysis** Tim states that the slope between the points (1, 1) and (5, 5) is (4, 4). Yasmini states that the slope is $\frac{4}{4} = 1$. Who is correct? Explain.

4. (20) **Probability** Write the converse of this statement and state whether the converse is always true. If both the statement and its converse are always true, write it as a biconditional statement.

If it is certain that a sock I pull out of the drawer will be red, then all the socks in the drawer are red.

5. (Inv 1) **Verify** Genji says that angle A measures 108°. Is she correct? What theorem can be used to justify her answer?

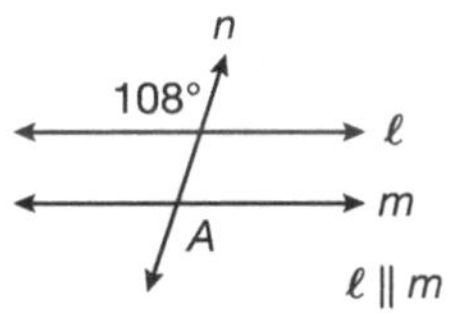

* **6.** (19) **Landscaping** A landscape designer needs to fence in the area indicated in the diagram. How much fencing will be needed for the whole area?

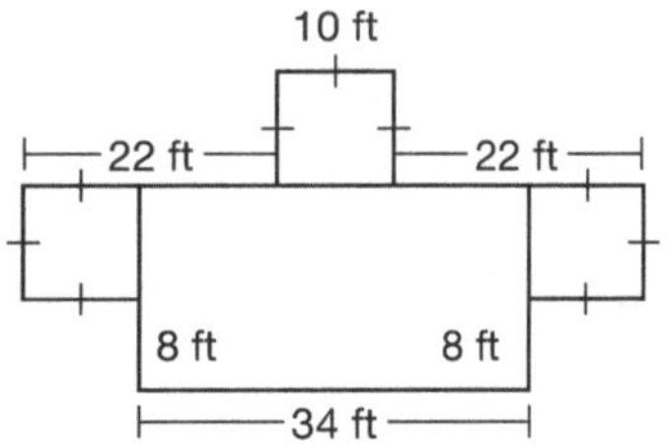

7. (9) Find the distance between the points $A(4, 5)$ and $B(7, 1)$.

* **8.** (20) **Multiple Choice** A defense lawyer in court states in her cross examination of a witness, "You were either at the scene of the accident or you were not. Which is it?" What type of statement is she using?

A a compound statement
B a disjunction
C both **A** and **B** are correct
D neither **A** nor **B** is correct

Laws of Detachment and Syllogism

LESSON 21

9. (Inv 2) **Safety** It is recommended that the ratio of $a{:}b$ in the figure at right be 4:1 to prevent the ladder from shifting. According to this ratio, how far from the base of the wall should you place the foot of a 16-foot ladder? Round to the nearest inch.

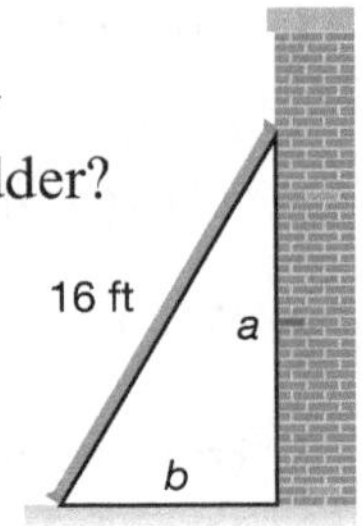

10. (14) **Write** Disprove the statement by writing a counterexample.

All numbers that are either one more or one less than a multiple of 6 are prime.

***11.** (18) Use the Triangle Angle Sum Theorem to find the missing angles in the triangle.

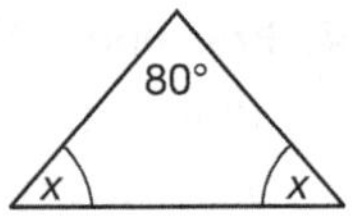

Write the converse of each given statement, then determine whether the converse is true.

12. (17) **Analyze** *If* $3x + 4 = 10$, *then* $x = 2$.

13. (17) **Analyze** *If a number is prime, then it is odd.*

14. (19) Classify the following quadrilaterals.

a. 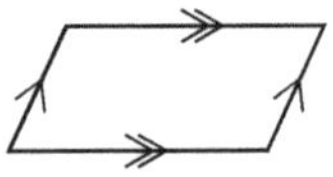

b. 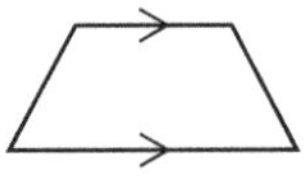

15. (11) Find the midpoint of the points $(-2, 5)$ and $(6, 9)$.

***16.** (21) Use the Law of Detachment to draw a valid concluding statement from the following:

If the bread has just come out of the oven, then it is fresh. The bread has just come out of the oven.

17. (14) Disprove the statement, "All irregular polygons are concave polygons," by drawing a counterexample.

18. (12) **Justify** Are the lines *m* and *n* parallel? Explain.

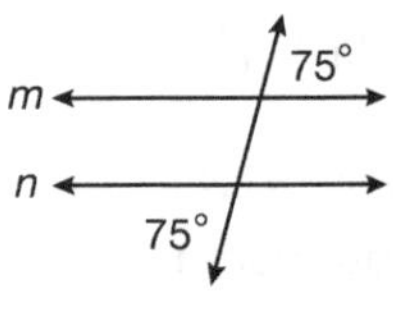

19. (Inv 1) Find the missing angles in the figure on the right.

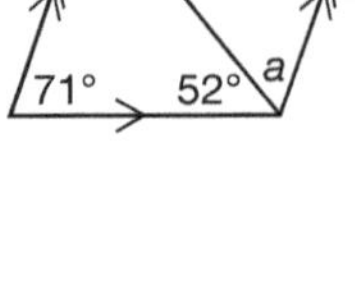

20. (16) **Algebra** Find the slope of the line segment that joins points E and F.

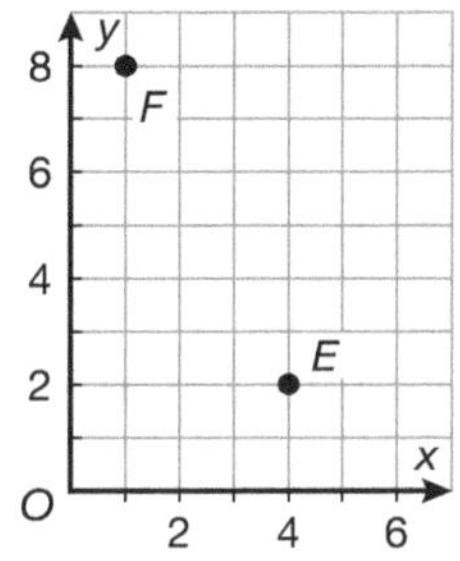

***21.** (20) Convert the following statements into a compound statement with a disjunction.

a. *Some numbers between 20 and 30 are prime numbers. The other numbers between 20 and 30 are composite numbers.*

b. *The lunch special can come with a soup. The lunch special can come with a salad.*

22. (15) Is this polygon concave or convex? Explain.

***23.** (21) Write a third conditional statement using the Law of Syllogism:

If the season is rainy, then the crops will flourish.
If the crops flourish, then there will be plenty of corn for the livestock.

***24.** (21) Write a statement that can be deduced from the following statements.

All the children in the Dument family are the tallest in their classes at school.
Lucy is a child in the Dument family.

25. (16) **Formulate** Find the equation of the line that passes through points A and B on the graph.

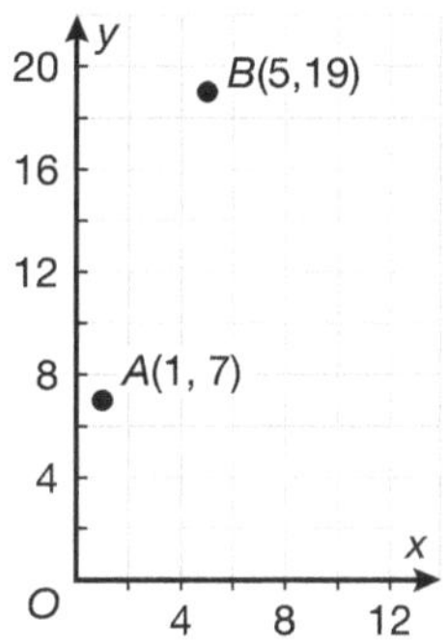

26. (13) **Sewing** Thomas is sewing a tent with a triangular flap for a door. If the height of the door is 4 feet and the door is $4\frac{1}{2}$ feet wide, how many square feet of fabric will he need to make the door?

27. (12) **Justify** Are the lines *m* and *n* parallel? Explain.

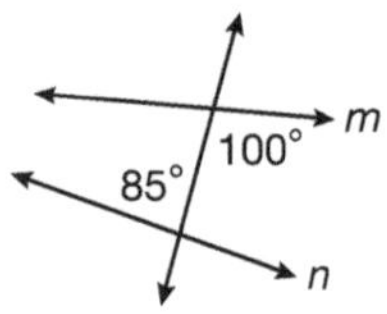

***28.** (20) Convert the following statements into compound statements with a conjunction.

a. *Today it is cold. Today it is snowing.*

b. *Later this week is the big game at our school. Anita is playing in the big game.*

29. (Inv 1) **Parking** A construction firm is designing a large parking lot. The lines that mark the widths of the spaces will be parallel. For optimum parking safety and visibility when backing out, the measure of $\angle 1$ should be half the measure of $\angle 2$. What are the measures of both angles?

30. (Inv 1) Find the measure of each angle in this figure. Lines *AB* and *CD* are parallel.

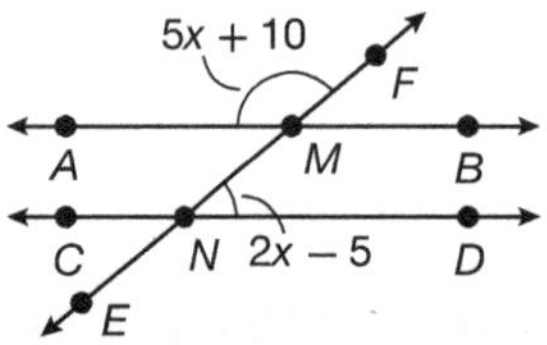

Name ______________________ Date __________ Class __________

Finding Areas of Quadrilaterals

LESSON 22

* **1.** (22) Find the area of a rectangle with a diagonal measuring 25 inches and one side that measures 20 inches.

2. (15) **Analyze** Are the following pairs of polygons congruent? Explain.

a.

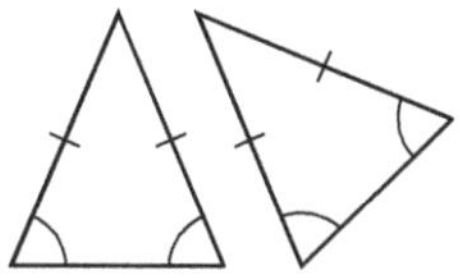

b.

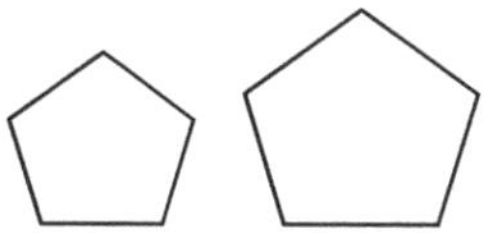

3. (8) **Multiple Choice** The exact conversion from Celsius to Fahrenheit is $°F = \frac{9}{5}(°C) + 32$. The actual temperature at which the two temperature scales have the same numerical value is

A −30 degrees **B** 30 degrees
C −40 degrees **D** 40 degrees

4. (21) Use deductive reasoning to write a valid conclusion to this statement.

All games played at the baseball tournament were decided by one run. Allentown played Holdenville at the baseball tournament.

* **5.** (22) Find the area of the following quadrilaterals.

a.

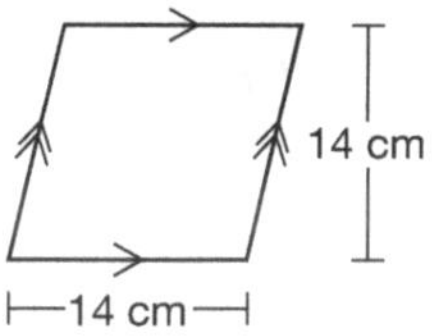

b.

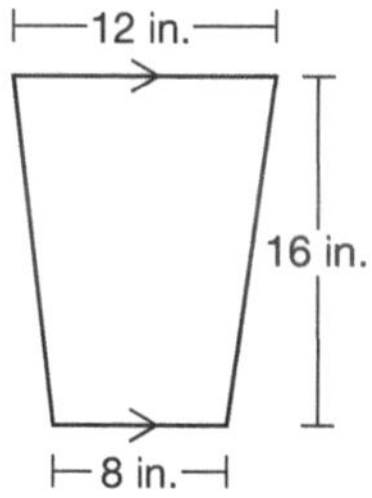

6. (10) **Justify** Write the converse to each conditional statement. State if each converse is true.

a. *If $x + 11 = 5$, then $x = -6$.*

b. *If it rains, then I bring my umbrella to work.*

7. (18) **Justify** What is the value of x? Explain how you found it.

8. (6) State whether the following statements are true or false.

a. Linear pairs of angles are supplementary.

b. Complementary angle pairs can be linear.

c. The adjacent angles formed by two intersecting lines are called vertical angles.

d. If two angles are in the same plane and share a vertex and a side, but no interior points, then the two angles are adjacent angles.

xy² * **9.** **Algebra** Determine the measure of each angle.
(18)

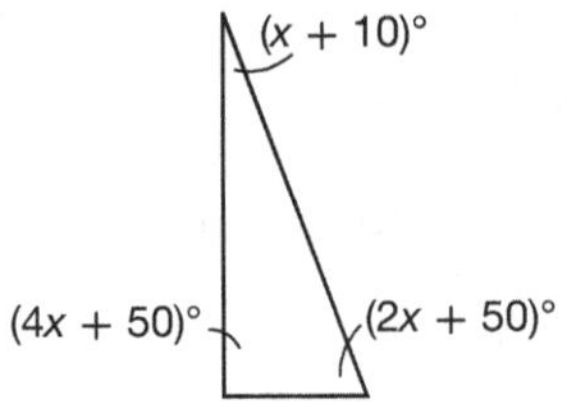

***10.** Use the Law of Detachment to write a concluding statement.
(21)

If today is Thursday, then it is Mrs. Wu's turn to drive the children to their piano lesson. Today is Thursday.

11. **Urban Planning** On a scale map of a state, each square represents 5 square miles. The water works company needs to connect two purification stations that are located at the points (3, 11) and (14, 26) on the grid. About how many miles apart are these two stations?
(9)

***12.** Write each set of statements as a biconditional statement.
(20)

a. Two angles are congruent if they have the same measure. Two angles that have the same measure are congruent.

b. A triangle is equilateral if it has three lines of symmetry. A triangle that has three lines of symmetry is equilateral.

13. The following statement is an example of a ____________.
(20)
(*conjunction, disjunction*)

A set of two statements can often be joined as a conjunction or a disjunction.

***14.** Find the areas of the following shapes.
(22)

a.

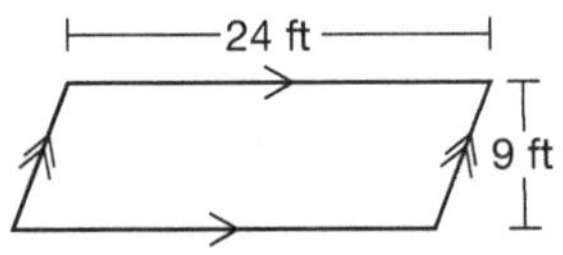

b.

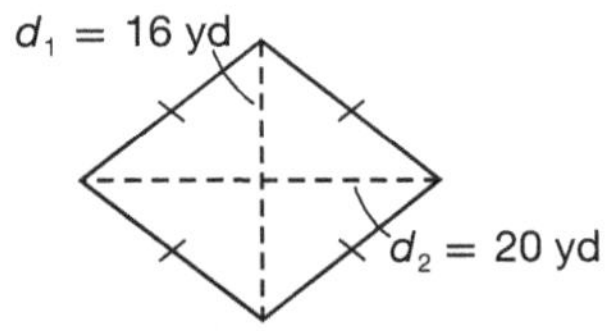

15. Find the equation of the line that:
(16)

a. passes through the point (0, 5) with a slope of -2.

b. passes through the point (4, 11) with a slope of $\frac{1}{2}$.

16. Classify each triangle according to its sides.
(13)

a.

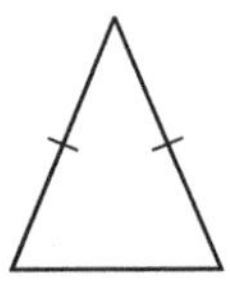

b.

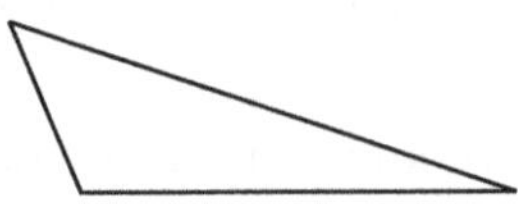

17. **Yachting** A race course for a yachting regatta is in the form of a right triangle. If the two legs of the triangle are 6 miles and 8 miles long, how much distance does the race cover?
(13)

*18. (16) **Error Analysis** Veronica thought the equation of the line that passes through the points (1, 5) and (5, 17) is $y = 2x + 3$, but then she found out that her answer was incorrect. What has she done wrong and what is the correct equation?

19. (12) **Analyze** Are the following pairs of lines parallel? Explain.

a.

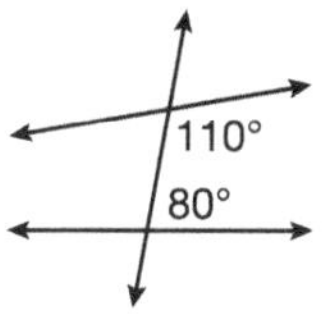

b.

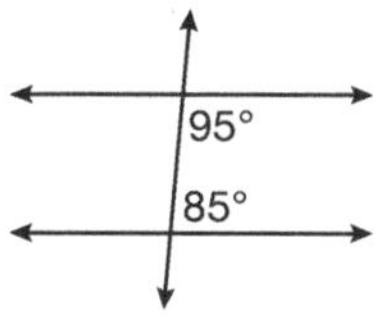

20. (15) **Write** Draw an equiangular octagon with sides that are each 2 centimeters long. Is it regular? Explain.

*21. (19) **Landscaping** The following diagram represents a patio that is to be covered instones. Determine the total area of the patio.

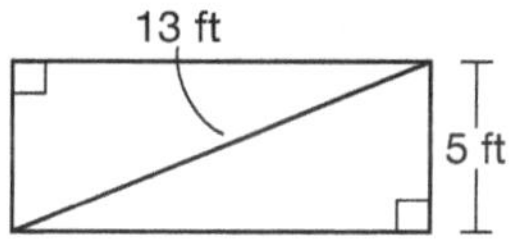

22. (11) **Urban Planning** Three transformer stations exist on a grid at positions *A*, *B*, and *C*. The power company needs to locate the three points that are exactly halfway between each of the three stations to determine where new stations must be built. If the existing stations are located at grid points *A*(5, 9), *B*(4, −4), and *C*(8, 17), find the locations of the new stations.

23. (16) Graph the line $y = 3x + 1$ using a table of values.

24. (10) Identify the hypothesis and the conclusion in each conditional statement.

a. *If today is Wednesday, then Jasmine needs to take out the trash.*

b. *If* x − *3 = 5, then* x = *8.*

25. (9) **Emergency Response** Two fire stations are located at grid points *A*(4, 8) and *B*(17, 29). The closest fire station should respond to any emergency call. Which station should respond to a fire located at the grid point (9, 21)?

*26. (21) Use the Law of Syllogism to write a third conditional statement.

If Mark's pen runs out of ink, then he must get a new pen to finish his assignment.
If Mark must get a new pen to finish his assignment, then he must go to the store.

27. (8) An approximate method for converting from Celsius to Fahreneit is to double the Celsius temperature and add 30. Use this method to convert 25° C and −30° C to Fahrenheit.

*28. (22) **Landscaping** A landscape architect needs to place sod on the area within the shape shown below. How many square feet of sod are needed to cover the area?

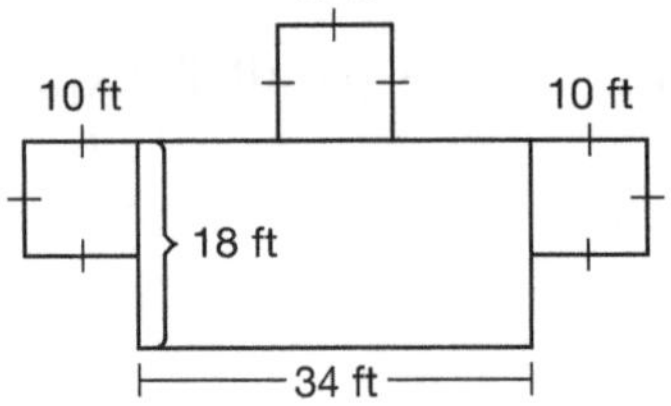

29. (Inv 1) Find the measure of each acute angle and each obtuse angle in the diagram. Line *a* is parallel to line *b*.

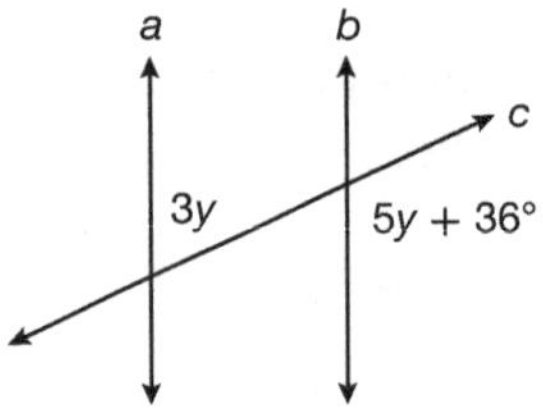

30. (5) **Predict** Draw a line *l*, and a point *P* not on *l*. Then, construct a line parallel to *l* through point *P*. Can you construct a different line that is parallel to *l* through the same point *P*? Write a conjecture about the number of lines parallel to *l* through point *P*.

Name ______________________ Date __________ Class __________

Introduction to Circles

LESSON 23

* **1.** To the nearest kilometer, how far would you go if you traveled along the circumference of the equator, assuming the equator is a circle with a radius of 6378 kilometers? Use 3.14 for π.
(23)

2. **Write** Explain what it means for a mathematical statement to be a conjecture and give an example.
(7)

3. **Algebra** Find the hypotenuse of a right triangle with legs measuring $3x$ and $4x$.
(Inv 2)

* **4.** **Handball** A semicircular area of the gym floor has been marked off with tape to make room for a handball game. If the radius of the semicircle is 16 feet, about how much tape is needed? Use 3.14 for π and round to the nearest tenth of a foot.
(23)

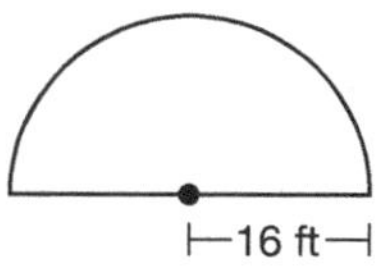

5. **Multi Step** Find the distance between the point (5, 7) and the midpoint of the points (1, 4) and (11, 6).
(9)

6. Find the area of a trapezoid that is 12 centimeters tall, and whose bases are 12 centimeters and 10 centimeters long.
(22)

7. Give three possible sets of dimensions for a right triangle with an area of 36 square inches.
(13)

8. Can the number of sides of a polygon be different than its number of vertices?
(15)

9. **Coordinate Geometry** Find the midpoint of each side of triangle *DEF*.
(11)

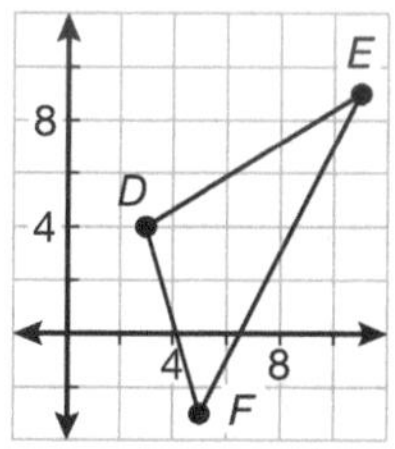

10. Draw a regular convex octagon.
(15)

***11.** **Write** Use the Law of Detachment to draw a conclusion to the following statements.
(21)

If I have the correct combination, then I can open the safe. I have the correct combination.

12. **Algebra** Find the hypotenuse of a right triangle with congruent leg lengths that are both b.
(Inv 2)

***13.** Name the conditional statement and the converse that are true if the following biconditional statement is true.
(20)

The rooms in the arena will get a new coat of paint if and only if new funding from the local council is approved.

14. (15) **Multiple Choice** Which of these choices *cannot* describe a polygon?
A more than 12 sides **B** a curved side
C closed **D** concave

15. (6) State the measure of the angle that is supplementary to each angle.
a. 75° **b.** 126°

***16.** (19) Draw two different rectangles, each with a perimeter of 100 centimeters, and calculate the area of each.

***17.** (12) **Carpentry** A carpenter is going to use a protractor to determine if the sides of the door she just installed are parallel to the corresponding sides of the door frame. To do this, she attaches a brace to the door, as shown, and measures the indicated angles. How can she use the values of these two angles to determine if the sides of the door are aligned correctly?

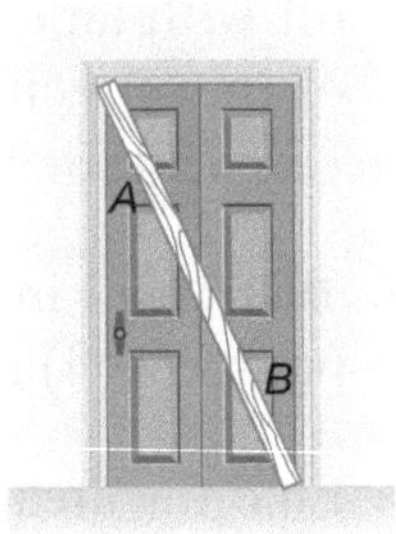

18. (21) **Multiple Choice** In this set of statements using syllogism, one of the statements is missing. Which one of the given statements below would correctly complete this syllogism?

If I plant a seedling in my yard, then a tree will grow.
AND

____

THEN
If I plant a seedling in my yard, then my house will be worth more.

A *If I don't plant a seedling in my yard, then my house will be worth less.*
B *If a tree grows in my yard, then my house will be worth more.*
C *If my house is worth more, then a tree will grow in my yard.*
D *If my house is worth more, then I will plant a seedling in my yard.*

19. (18) **Error Analysis** Dustin reasons that the missing angle in this triangle is 53°. Is he correct? If not, what is the measure of the missing angle?

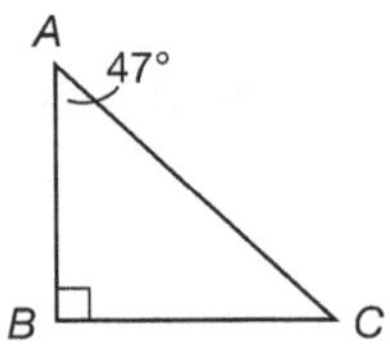

***20.** (23) **Sewing** Rhonda is making a circular pillow with a diameter of 18 inches, and she needs to sew trim around the edge. To the nearest tenth of an inch, how much trim would Rhonda need to sew around the edge of the pillow? Use 3.14 for π.

***21.** (17) **Write** Write a true conditional statement whose inverse is also true.

22. (13) **Painting** If one can of spray paint can cover 32 square feet, how many cans of spray paint are needed to paint a wall in the shape of an isosceles triangle with a base of 18 feet and a height of 12 feet?

23. (16) **Surveying** Civil engineers are drafting plans for a road with a slope that cannot exceed a value of 0.08. If the total rise of the road from the bottom to the top point needs to be 24 meters, how long must the horizontal distance of the road be to maintain the 0.08 slope?

24. (14) Disprove the conditional statement by giving a counterexample.

If a figure is formed by connecting five points with line segments, then the figure is a polygon.

*25. (23) Two circles on the ground at the baseball field are to be painted red for the upcoming playoffs. If the diameter of each circle is 6 feet, what is the total area to be painted? Use 3.14 for π and round to the nearest tenth of a square foot.

26. (13) The coordinates of the vertices of a right triangle are $R(3, 4)$, $S(9, 4)$, and $T(3, 11)$. If each unit on the grid represents one foot, determine the approximate perimeter and exact area of the resulting triangle.

27. (Inv 1) Ana knows that $\angle B$ measures 72°. She says that if lines l and m are parallel, then $\angle G$ also measures 72°. What theorem supports Ana's claim?

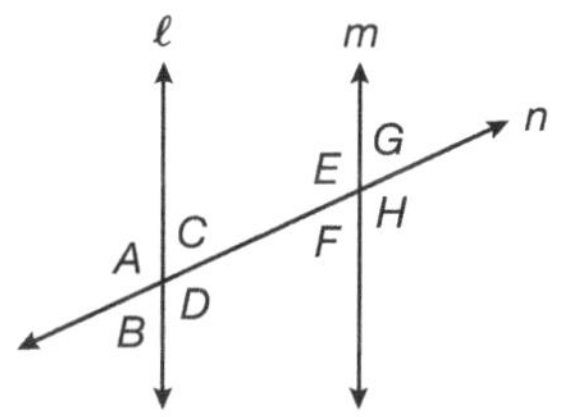

*28. (13) A right triangle has side lengths of 15, 36, and 39 centimeters. What is the area of the triangle?

29. (22) **Algebra** Find the area of a trapezoid with a height of $\frac{1}{4}x$ and base lengths of $3x$ and $5x$.

30. (19) **Justify** Compare the areas of these two trapezoids. Do the figures have the same area? Explain your reasoning.

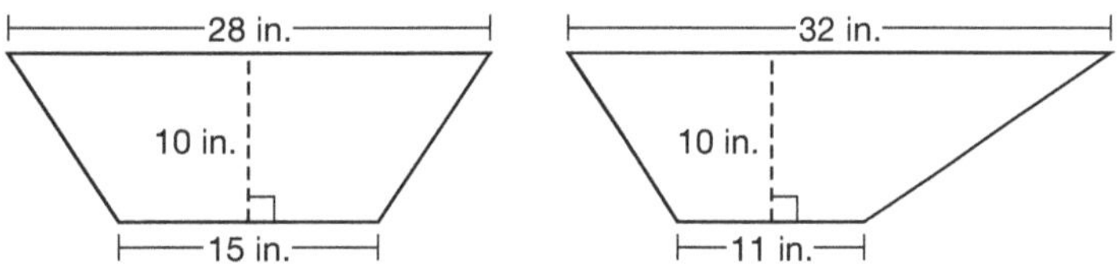

Name ______________________ Date __________ Class __________

Algebraic Proofs

LESSON 24

1. (Inv 2) **Monitors** Computer monitors are usually measured in terms of the lengths of their diagonals. If a 20-inch monitor has a horizontal/vertical aspect ratio of 4:3, what are the horizontal and vertical dimensions of the monitor?

2. (12) **Write** Explain how to check if two shelves are parallel by dropping a string and measuring the angles between the string and the shelves.

3. (Inv 1) Write the converse of the theorem, "If two parallel lines are cut by a transversal, then the same-side interior angles are supplementary." Is the converse true?

* **4.** (24) **Error Analysis** Minh and Soon Yu are asked to solve the expression $2(x + 1) = 12$. Here are their two solutions. Is Minh's solution correct? Is Soon Yu's solution correct? Explain.

Minh's solution:

$2(x + 1) = 12$	Given
$2x + 2 = 12$	Distributive Property
$2x = 10$	Subtraction Property of Equality
$x = 5$	Division Property of Equality

Soon Yu's solution:

$2(x + 1) = 12$	Given
$x + 1 = 6$	Division Property of Equality
$x = 5$	Subtraction Property of Equality

5. (17) Write the converse of the following statement. *If the window is open, then it is not closed.* Is the converse true?

* **6.** (24) **Multiple Choice** If $x = 3$ and $3 = y$, then $x = y$. This is an example of which property of equality?

A Symmetric **B** Reflexive **C** Transitive **D** Comparative

7. (8) **Multi Step** What is the width of a rectangular driveway with an area of 2592 square feet and a length of 27 yards?

8. (18) **Generalize** What is the relationship between the interior angle and its adjacent exterior angle at any vertex of any polygon?

9. (13) **Art** Tony wants to paint a triangular pattern on a rectangle which is 10 feet long and 4 feet wide. He divides the rectangle into four triangles by stretching wire across the diagonals. Determine the area of triangles A and B.

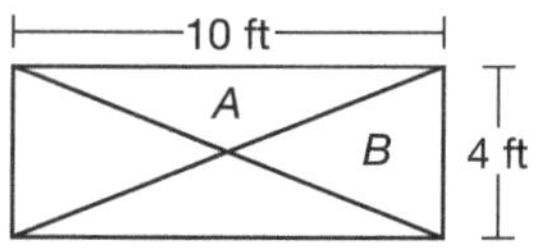

10. (15) Draw a convex hexagon with all sides congruent and a concave hexagon with all sides congruent.

*11. **Write** Write the converse of the following statement and state whether it is true. If the
(20) converse is true, write the two statements as a biconditional.

If all of the students in the school achieve over 70% on the state exams, then the school will receive a new computer lab from the district.

12. **Justify** If the diagonals of a rectangle form two equilateral triangles,
(13) classify the other two triangles by their angles. How do you know?

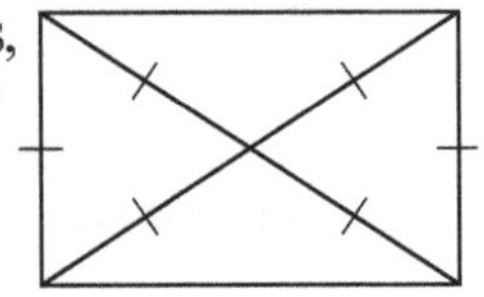

*13. Outline the solution and justification for each step in solving the
(24) equation $2x - 1 = 5$.

14. **Multiple Choice** Suzanne suggests that multiples of 3 never end in a 4, but her friend
(14) Maxine disproves her by stating that 24 is a multiple of 3. What has Maxine just used to disprove Suzanne's suggestion?

A a conjecture | **B** inductive reasoning
C a theorem | **D** a counterexample

*15. **Algebra** Miguel painted an equal number of squares with sides measuring
(22) 6 centimeters and 12 centimeters, respectively. How many of each type of square did he paint if the squares cover 4500 cm^2?

16. Graph the equation $2x + 3y - 15 = 0$ using the slope and y-intercept.
(16)

17. **Landscaping** A patio in the shape of a trapezoid is to be covered in flagstone. The
(22) parallel sides of the trapezoid measure 20 feet and 32 feet respectively, and are separated by a perpendicular distance of 14 feet. How many square feet need to be covered?

*18. A figure skater is practicing her figure-eights by repeatedly skating around two circles
(23) that join to form a figure "8." If the diameter of the circles is 30 feet each, how much total distance, to the nearest foot, will she cover in 5 full trips around the figure?

19. A right triangle has a side length of 6 inches and a hypotenuse of 10 inches. What is
(8) the length of the third side?

20. Write the inverse of the following statement. Then state whether the inverse is true.
(17)

If it is raining, then I will use my umbrella.

*21. A right triangle has side lengths of 48 meters, 20 meters, and
(13) 52 meters. What is the area of this triangle?

22. Name an interior and an exterior angle of the figure at right.
(15)

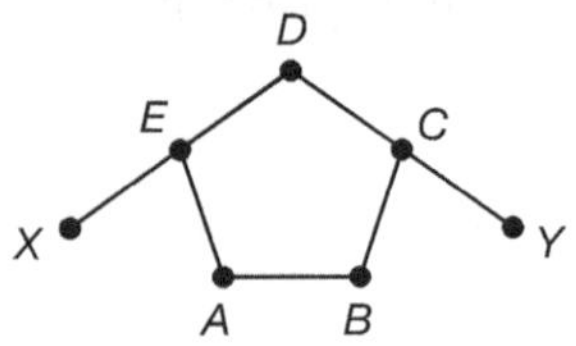

23. The midpoint of (4, 5) and a second point is (7, 1). What is
(11) the second point?

24. (6) **Balancing** A rectangular box sitting on a ramp must not be inclined more than 30° from vertical or it will slide down the ramp. What is the relationship between $\angle ABD$ and $\angle CBE$? How do you know? What is the greatest value $\angle EBC$ can have before the box slides?

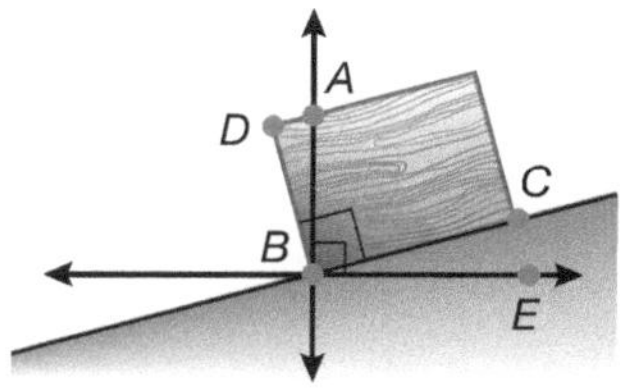

***25.** (23) Jack is drawing circles on a playground for a game. If he draws a circle with a radius 3 feet, what is the area of the circle, to the nearest square foot?

26. (16) **Fitness Membership** At a fitness club, the equation for the cost of a membership is given by $C = 30m + 200$, where C is dollars and m is months. In this application of a linear equation, what is the slope and what does it represent? How much does it cost to be a member of this gym for 5 months?

27. (7) **Error Analysis** Explain why the following inductive reasoning is not a valid proof.

All the birds I have seen in this park have brown feathers. All the birds in this park must have brown feathers.

***28.** (21) For any given angle, if the angle is obtuse, then it cannot be acute. A given angle is found to be obtuse. What conclusion can be made from this and which law was used to reach this conclusion?

29. (16) Write the equation of a line with slope $\frac{1}{2}$ that passes through (3, 4).

***30.** (24) **Verify** To solve the linear equation $3(x + 5) = 9$, Cynthia begins her solution like this:

$$3(x + 5) = 9$$
$$3(x + 5) - 5 = 9 - 5$$
$$3x = 4$$

Is Cynthia proceeding correctly? If not, what mistake has she made?

Name ____ Date ____________ Class ______________

Triangle Congruence: SSS

LESSON 25

1. (8) **Art** A painting covers a wall as shown. What is the perimeter of the painting, to the nearest tenth of a meter?

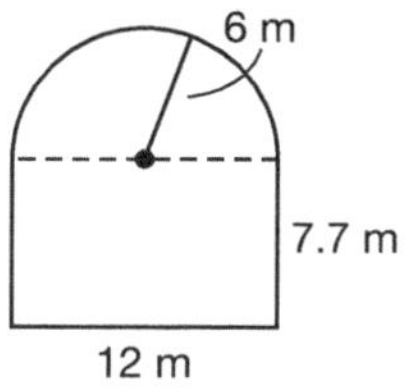

*2. (23) An area of 400 square meters is to be roped off for a farmers' market that is to be in the shape of a circle. What will be the diameter of this circle, to the nearest tenth of a meter?

*3. (25) Give the congruence statement for the triangles shown.

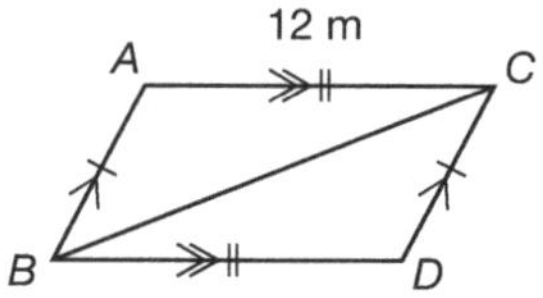

4. (19) Classify the quadrilateral shown here.

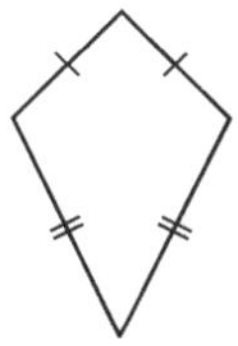

*5. (22) **Baseball** The bases on a baseball diamond form a square that is 90 feet on each side. What is the minimum distance that would be covered when running around all four bases?

6. (Inv 1) **Railroads** Railway tracks consist of two parallel steel rails. If an inspector places a meterstick across the rails and determines that the measures of the alternate interior angles differ by several degrees, is there anything wrong? Explain.

*7. (25) **Model** Draw two congruent triangles that correspond to the following statements: $\angle E \cong \angle N$, $\angle F \cong \angle L$, $\angle G \cong \angle M$, $\overline{EF} \cong \overline{NL}$, $\overline{EG} \cong \overline{NM}$, and $\overline{FG} \cong \overline{LM}$.

8. (14) Find a counterexample to prove that the following conjecture is false.

For every natural number n, $4n > n^2$.

Use the grid to determine how far each friend lives from the other. Each grid unit is 0.1 mile. Round to the nearest hundredth of a mile.

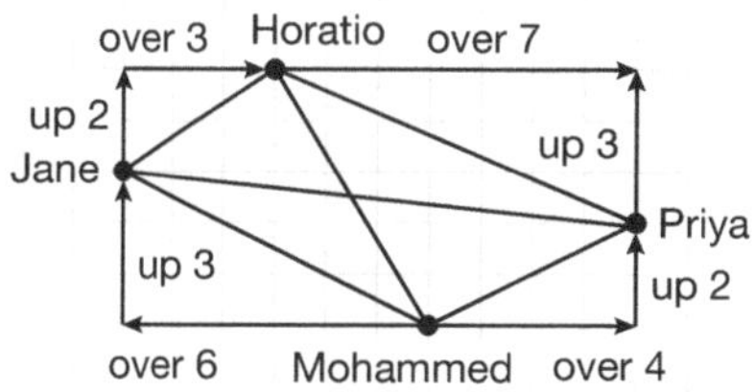

9. (9) How far apart do Jane and Horatio live?

10. (9) How far apart do Horatio and Priya live?

*11. (25) **Error Analysis** Polly determines that for $\triangle ABC$ and $\triangle XYZ$, $\angle A \cong \angle X$, $\angle B \cong \angle Y$, and $\angle C \cong \angle Z$. She also concludes that $\overline{AB} \cong \overline{XY}$, $\overline{BC} \cong \overline{XZ}$, and $\overline{AC} \cong \overline{YZ}$. Are her conclusions correct? Explain.

*12. (24) **Algebra** Triangles ABC and DEF are congruent. If $AB = 2x + 10$ and $DE = 4x - 20$, find the value of x and include justifications for each step in the solution.

*13. **Multiple Choice** Use the Law of Detachment to identify a valid concluding statement.
(21)

If we get more than 12 inches of snow in the next hour, then the roads will be closed. The weather network predicts that there will be 15 inches of snow in the next hour.

A *Based on the weather network, the roads will be open in the next hour.*
B *The snow should stop after 15 inches of snow has fallen.*
C *Based on the weather network, the roads will be closed in the next hour.*
D *It will continue to snow, even after 12 inches of snow has fallen.*

14. Classify the quadrilateral.
(19)

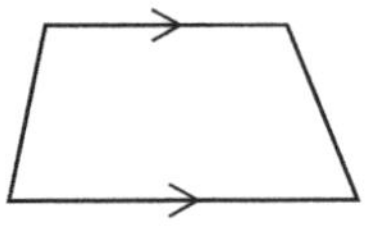

15. **Write** What can be deduced from the following statements?
(21)

The oldest person in each class in the school is wearing a blue shirt. Kelly is the oldest person in one of the classes in the school.

16. Is the statement below a biconditional statement? If so, are both conditional statements true?
(20)

An angle is a right angle if and only if it measures 90°.

17. Solve for x in the equation $\frac{x + 5}{3} = 3$. Justify each step.
(24)

Determine whether each figure is a polygon. If it is, name it.

18.
(15)

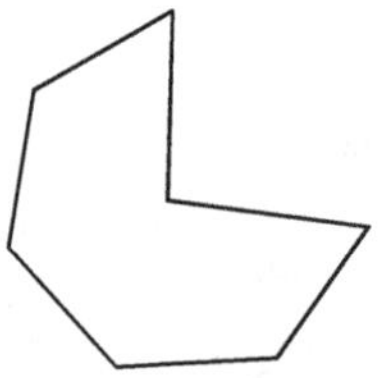

19.
(15)

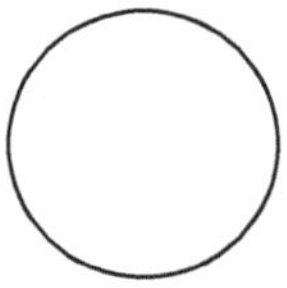

20. **Justify** Is the following statement true or false? If true, provide a theorem to support it. If false, provide a counterexample.
(19)

If the sides of a quadrilateral have equal length, then it is a square.

*21. In the triangles shown, $\angle C \cong \angle N$ and $\overline{AC} \cong \overline{LN}$. If $\triangle ABC \cong \triangle LMN$, provide four more congruence statements using CPCTC.
(25)

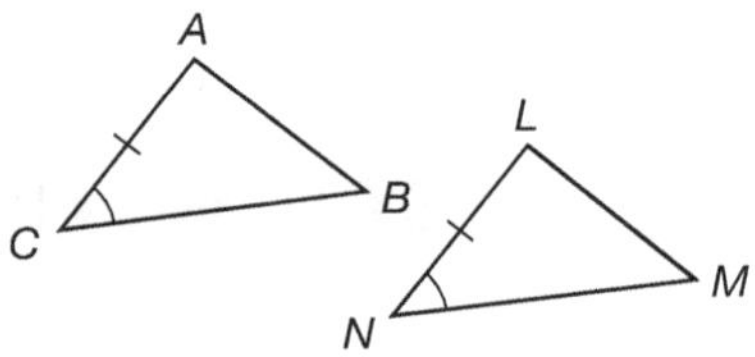

*22. **Algebra** Find the value of x for two supplementary angles if the larger angle is 20° more than three times the smaller angle. Justify each step.
(24)

23. **Urban Planning** Find the slope between two grid points marked on a road: $A(-3, 4)$ and $B(6, -4)$. Is the road going uphill or downhill from A to B? Explain.
(16)

24. (20) Identify whether the statement is conditional or biconditional.

A phone rings if and only if someone is calling.

25. (14) Find a counterexample to prove that the conjecture is false.

$\frac{1}{n}$ *is a rational number for every whole number.*

26. (23) **Construction** Workers are stringing caution tape around a circular parking lot that has just been repaired. To the nearest foot, how much tape is needed if the parking lot has a diameter of 40 feet?

***27.** (21) **Formulate** What conclusion can be drawn from these statements? How do you know?

If the team wins the remainder of the games, then they will make the playoffs.
The team won the remainder of their games.

28. (17) **Write** What is the contrapositive of the following statement?

If a bee is the queen bee, then it does not leave the hive.

29. (Inv 1) **Model** Line ℓ_1 and ℓ_2 are parallel lines. Point P lies on ℓ_1, and point M lies on ℓ_2. Draw a line through P and M. Label one pair of alternate interior angles, and label one pair of corresponding angles.

30. (18) Find m∠1 and m∠2 if m∠1 $= 2x^2 + 2x + 3$ and m∠2 $= 3x^2 - 5x + 3$.

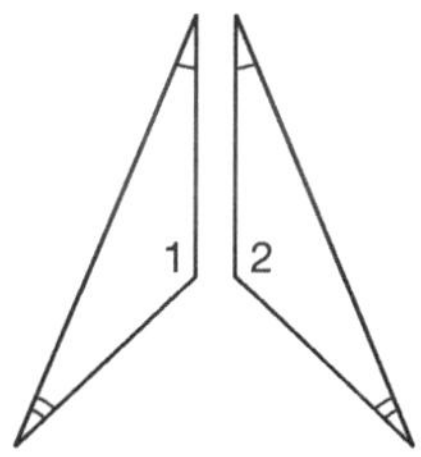

Name ______________________ Date __________ Class __________

Central Angles and Arc Measure

LESSON 26

1. *(16)* Find the slope of the line containing points $C(7, 3)$ and $D(12, -2)$.

* **2.** *(21)* **Analyze** What conclusion can be drawn from the following statements?

All plants require water to develop. A cactus is a plant.

3. *(13)* **Algebra** Triangle ABC has side lengths of $AB = x^2 - x + 5$, $BC = 5x - 4$, and $AC = 3x^2 - 2x - 1$. If $\triangle ABC$ is isosceles where $AB = BC$, find the lengths of all sides.

* **4.** *(23)* **Geography** The Kentland Impact Crater in Indiana is in the shape of a circle whose diameter is approximately 13 kilometers. To the nearest kilometer, how far would Farah walk if she were to travel the full distance around the outside of the crater?

5. *(20)* Construct a truth table for not P and not Q.

* **6.** *(26)* What is the measure of a central angle of a circle if the associated minor arc has an angle measure of 65°?

7. *(13)* **Multiple Choice** Which of the following classifications allows you to know the measures of the triangle's angles with no additional information? What are the angle measures of such a triangle?

A equilateral **B** equiangular

C isosceles **D** both **A** and **B**

8. *(20)* **Geography** Use A and B to determine the truth value of the statement, "A and not B".

A: New York City is the most populous city in the United States.
B: New York City is near the Pacific Ocean.

9. *(6)* **Algebra** The supplement of an angle is four times more than its complement. Find the measure of the angle.

10. *(14)* Find a counterexample to the conjecture $n^3 < 3n$.

11. *(16)* **Algebra** If the slope of $\overline{XY}$ is 0, and $X(2, 3)$ and $Y(-1, k)$, find k.

12. *(Inv 1)* Angles A and B are a pair of alternate interior angles on a pair of parallel lines intersected by a transversal, and $\angle A$ and $\angle C$ are a pair of same-side interior angles on the same figure. If $m\angle B = 30°$, what is $m\angle C$?

***13.** *(25)* Which side of $\triangle PRG$ corresponds to $\overline{XT}$, if $\triangle XTW \cong \triangle PRG$?

14. *(14)* **Error Analysis** A student wrote the following conjecture. Find a counterexample and explain the error.

If x is a positive even number and y is any integer, then the product xy will be positive.

***15.** (25) Write the congruence statement for the given triangles.

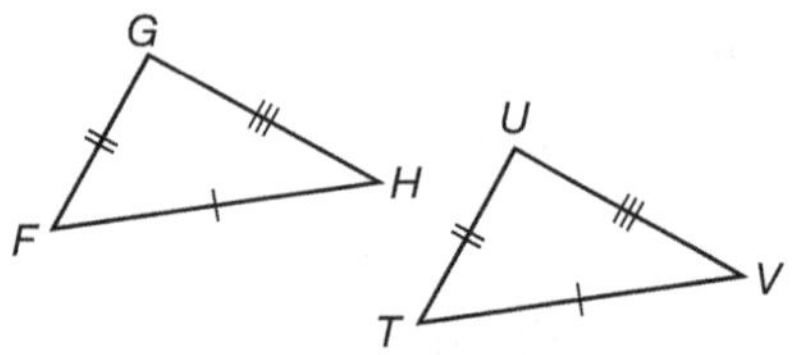

16. (17) **Write** What is the inverse of the following statement?

If a building has more than four floors, then it has an elevator.

17. (Inv 1) If lines f and g are parallel, find x.

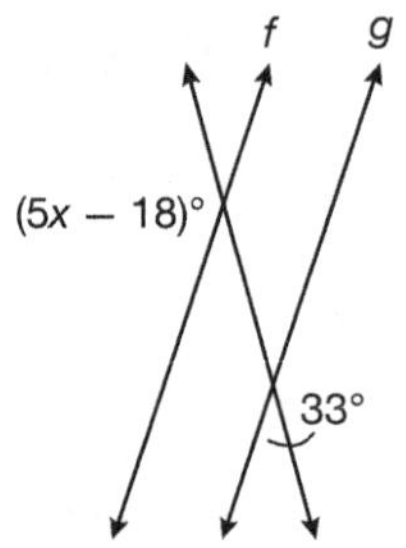

***18.** (26) **Multiple Choice** If there are a total of 6 non-overlapping adjacent minor arcs in a circle, the Arc Addition Postulate gives

A a total arc measure of 90°.
B a total arc measure of 180°.
C a total arc measure of 360°.
D a total that is the sum of the measures of the adjacent arcs.

19. (15) Is this figure a polygon? If so, name it. If not, explain why not.

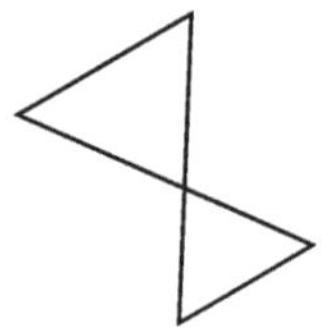

20. (13) What is the area of this triangle?

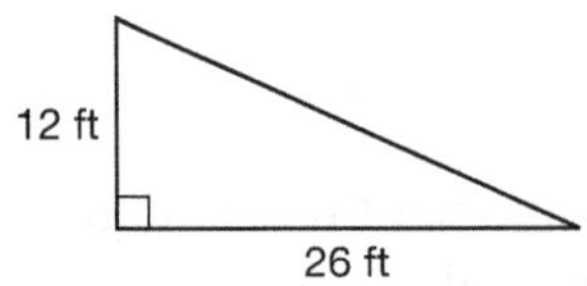

21. (24) Janie has just solved an equation for x and found $4 = x$. She writes her answer as $x = 4$.
What property of equality is she using to do this?

22. (16) **Phone Plans** To calculate monthly charges, a cell phone provider uses the equation $C = 0.25m + 60$, with C being dollars and m representing minutes used beyond the ones provided with the plan. In this linear equation, what is the value of the vertical intercept and what does it represent?

***23.** (26) **Algebra** Two congruent arcs have central angle measures that are $3x + 10$ and $50 - 2x$.
Find x and the measure of the arcs.

***24.** (25) Write six congruence statements for $\triangle ABC \cong \triangle WXY$.

25. (17) **Write** Write the contrapositive of the following statement.

If a polygon is a triangle, then it has three sides.

*26. (24) What property of equality is used as a justification in solving for x in the problem below?

$$x + 5 = 11$$
$$x + 5 - 5 = 11 - 5$$
$$x = 6$$

27. (Inv 2) **Geography** Roderick calculated the distance from New York City to Montreal using indirect measurement. On his map, New York City is 188 miles from Boston. Boston is 253 miles from Montreal, Canada. Assuming the angle from New York City to Boston to Montreal is 90°, what is the distance between New York City and Montreal, to the nearest mile?

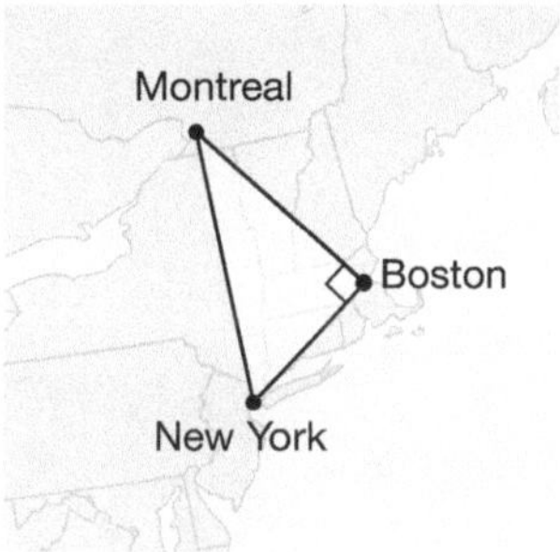

*28. (26) A major arc has a measure of 227°. What is the corresponding minor arc measure?

29. (7) **Write** The Fibonacci Sequence is a famous pattern which begins: 1, 1, 2, 3, 5, 8, 13, 21, ... Describe the pattern and give the next four terms.

30. (19) What are four different names for this quadrilateral?

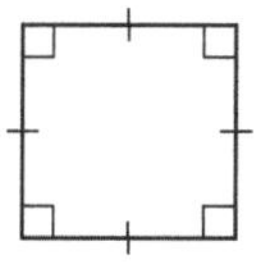

Name ______________________ Date __________ Class __________

Two-Column Proofs

LESSON 27

***1.** (26) **Write** Explain the difference between a minor arc and a major arc.

2. (19) Is the statement, "A square is a rhombus," sometimes, always, or never true?

3. (13) **Error Analysis** Parveer calculated the area of the given triangle as follows. Is he correct? Explain.

$A = \frac{1}{2}bh$

$= \frac{1}{2}(5)(6)$

$= 15$

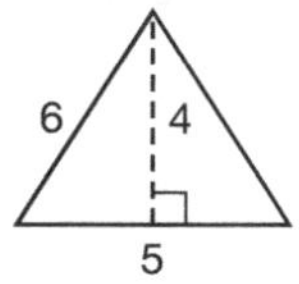

4. (27) Prove Theorem 10-2: If two parallel lines are cut by a transversal, then the alternate exterior angles are congruent.

Given: $m \parallel n$, transversal

Prove: $\angle 1 \cong \angle 2$

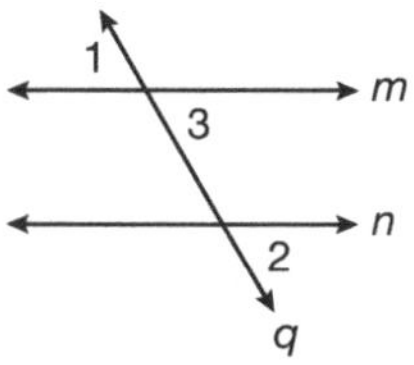

***5.** (23) **Landscaping** A sprinkler system used for watering a field sprays water in a circular pattern with a radius of 20 feet. To the nearest square foot, what area is covered by this sprinkler?

***6.** (27) **Verify** If M is the midpoint of $\overline{AB}$, write a two-column proof to show that $AM = \frac{1}{2}AB$.

7. (11) **Coordinate Geometry** Find the coordinates of the midpoints of $\overline{AB}$ and $\overline{CD}$ given the following coordinates: $A(8, 1)$, $B(14, 7)$, $C(7, 11)$, and $D(5, 5)$.

8. (21) **Write** Use the Law of Syllogism to write a valid conclusion.

If all the math classes are full, then Raymond must enroll in an elective.
If Raymond must enroll in an elective, then he will enroll in theater.

9. (23) **Furniture Design** The seating surface of a stool is a woolen circle with a diameter of 14 inches. To the nearest tenth of a square inch, how much material is used for the top surface of the stool?

10. (8) **Woodworking** If a rectangular table with an area of 35 square feet has a width that is 2 feet less than the length, what are the dimensions of the table?

11. (20) Write the disjunction of the statements "Priyanka takes the bus," and "Priyanka goes to work early."

12. (27) Prove Theorem 5-6: All right angles are congruent.

Given: Angle 1 and angle 2 are right angles.

Prove: $\angle 1 \cong \angle 2$

13. (Inv 1) Adrienne claims that for transversals of two lines, all the acute angles generated by the transversal are congruent and all the obtuse angles are congruent. Is she correct? Explain.

14. (22) **Road Repair** In the diagram, a parallelogram-shaped area of a parking lot is to be repaved. How many square meters are to be repaved?

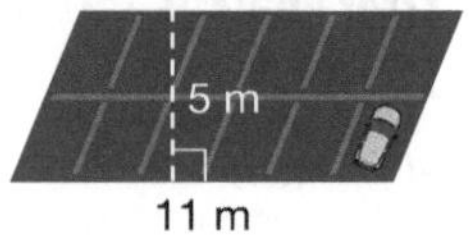

***15.** (27) Prove Theorem 5-7: If two lines are parallel to the same line, then they are parallel to each other.

Given: $\overleftrightarrow{AB} \parallel \overleftrightarrow{CD}$ and $\overleftrightarrow{EF} \parallel \overleftrightarrow{CD}$
Prove: $\overleftrightarrow{AB} \parallel \overleftrightarrow{EF}$

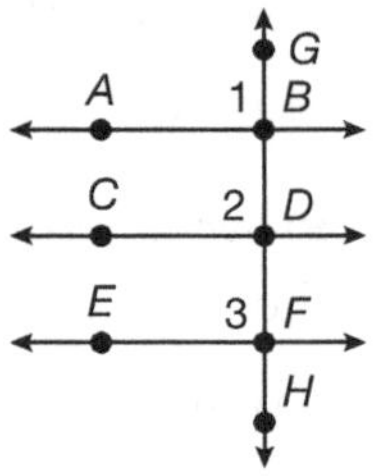

16. (19) Draw a quadrilateral with no two sides parallel. Classify this shape.

17. (12) Prove Theorem 12-1: If two lines are cut by a transversal and the alternate interior angles are congruent, then the lines are parallel.

Given: $\angle 1 \cong \angle 2$
Prove: $m \parallel n$

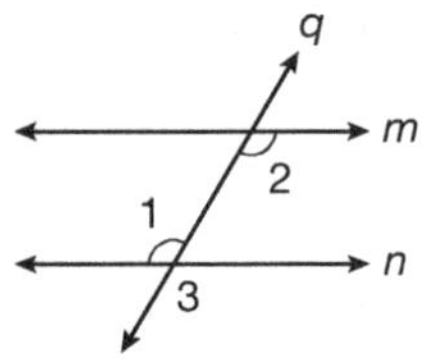

18. (23) What is one-fourth of the circumference of a circle with a diameter of 10 meters?

19. (25) **Construction** A construction worker is framing a new roof and needs to make a triangular structure congruent to one already on the roof. If she only has tools for linear measurement, what measurements should she take to ensure that the triangles are congruent?

***20.** (24) **Justify** Write an algebraic proof to solve $4x = 8 - 2x$ for x.

21. (16) **Algebra** Solve for y, if the slope between points U and V is $-\frac{2}{3}$, with points $U(-2, -3)$ and $V(-5, y)$.

***22.** (25) Which angle corresponds to $\angle R$, if $\triangle XTW \cong \triangle PRG$?

23. (13) **Multiple Choice** Which triangle classification pertains to the lengths of the sides of a triangle?

A scalene | **B** equiangular
C acute | **D** right

24. (19) **Algebra** Quadrilateral $PQRS$ is a rhombus. If $PQ = 4x + 7$ and $QR = 8x - 5$, what is the length of $\overline{QR}$?

***25.** (26) Two congruent arcs have measures $3(x + 4)°$ and $4(x - 5)°$. What is the value of x?

26. Construct and label a diagram based on the following information:
(Inv 1)

Transversal k intersects lines m and n to produce corresponding angles $\angle 1$ and $\angle 2$ that are both acute, alternate interior angles $\angle 3$ and $\angle 4$ that are both obtuse, and alternate exterior angles $\angle 1$ and $\angle 5$ that are both acute.

27. Jameer states that the difference between any two even integers is positive. Give a counterexample to disprove this conjecture.
(14)

*28. Which property of equality supports the statement if $x = k$ and $k = y$, then $x = y$?
(24)

*29. **Track and Field** The area used for shot-put events is a sector of a circle with a central angle of 45°. What would be the arc measure (x) 50 meters away from the center of the area?
(26)

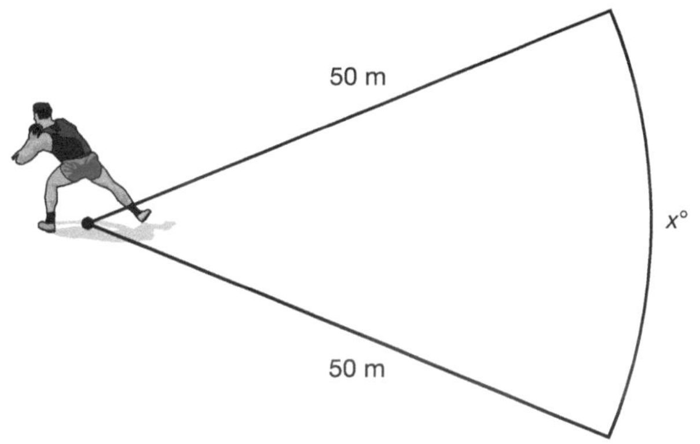

30. Classify $\triangle DEF$ by its angles and sides.
(13)

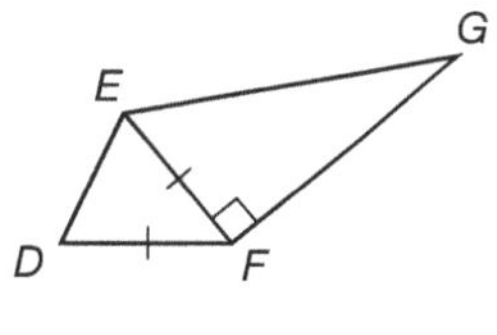

Name ______________________ Date __________ Class __________

Triangle Congruence: SAS

LESSON 28

1. Henry wants to hang a picture frame on to the wall but does not have a leveling tool. However, the striped wallpaper on the wall has parallel lines that form 45-degree angles to the floor and the ceiling. How can Henry use a protractor to hang the picture frame so that it is not tilted?
(Inv 1)

2. **Justify** Is the following conclusion valid? Why or why not?
(21)
Some skates that fit well are expensive. For my feet to be comfortable, I need skates that fit well. As a result, it is expensive to keep my feet comfortable.

xy² * 3. **Algebra** Two congruent arcs have measures $(x^2 - 4x - 1)°$ and $(x^2 - 3x + 10)°$. What is the value of x?
(26)

* 4. If two angles form a linear pair, then they are supplementary.
(27)
Given: ∠1 and ∠2 are a linear pair.
Prove: m∠1 + m∠2 = 180°

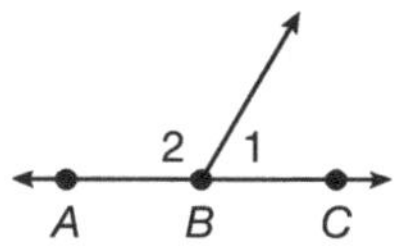

5. **City Planning** A rectangular city block measures 105 meters by 88 meters. The city council wants to divide the block into two triangles of equal area. What is the length of the hypotenuse of each triangular area?
(8)

6. A minor arc has a measure of 122°. What is the measure of the corresponding major arc?
(26)

7. Find the measure of ∠P in the figure shown.
(18)

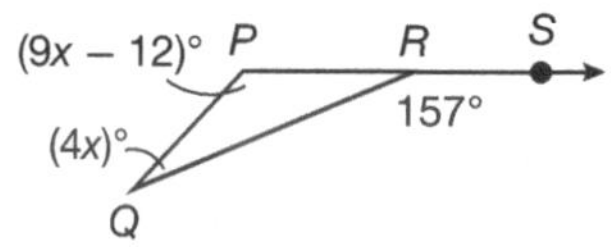

8. **Generalize** The numbers in the geometric sequence $1, \frac{1}{4}, \frac{1}{9}, \frac{1}{16}, \ldots$ continue to get smaller in value. Make a general formula for the sequence. State whether a term of the sequence will ever have a value of 0.
(7)

* 9. **Error Analysis** Is the following proof for congruent triangles correct? Explain.
(28)

1. $\overline{AC} \cong \overline{DE}$ $\angle ABC \cong \angle EDF$ $\overline{BC} \cong \overline{DF}$	1. Given
2. $\triangle ABC \cong \triangle EFD$	2. SAS Postulate

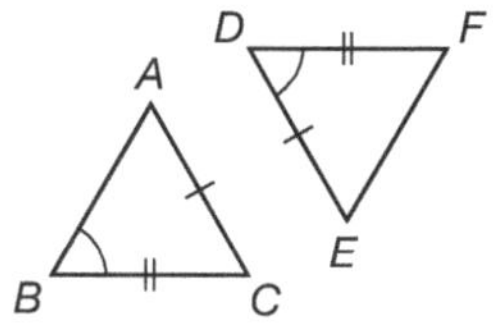

10. **Multiple Choice** What are the coordinates of the midpoint of a segment that connects the points (1, 1) and (−3, 5)?
(11)
A (2, 3) **B** (−1, −3)
C (−1, 3) **D** (4, 6)

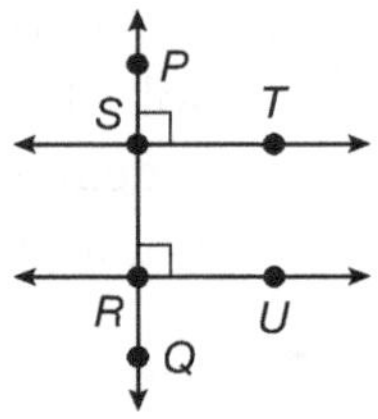

***11.** *(27)* Prove Theorem 5-2: If two lines in a plane are perpendicular to the same line, then they are parallel to each other.
Given: $\overleftrightarrow{ST} \perp \overleftrightarrow{PQ}, \overleftrightarrow{RU} \perp \overleftrightarrow{PQ}$
Prove: $\overleftrightarrow{ST} \parallel \overleftrightarrow{RU}$

12. *(17)* **Write** What is the inverse of this statement?
If John is at least 5'10" tall, then he is taller than Herschel.

***13.** *(28)* **Write** When can the SAS Postulate be used?

14. *(23)* **Art** Paolo was hired to do an abstract mural on the side of a building. His mural includes three circles. The first circle has a diameter of 34 feet, the second has a diameter of 30 feet, and the third has a diameter of 26 feet. What is the total circumference of the three circles, to the nearest foot?

***15.** *(23)* Explain this statement: In $\odot P$, with two points anywhere on the circle, K and L, $\overline{KP} \cong \overline{LP}$.

***16.** *(19)* **Algebra** Figure $DEFG$ is a parallelogram. If $m\angle D = 8x + 17$ and $m\angle E = 5x^2 - 2$, what are the measures of the other two angles?

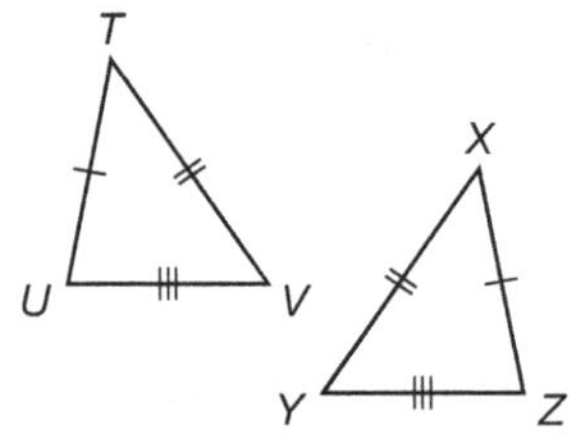

17. *(25)* Write a congruence statement for the triangles and give a justification.

18. *(16)* Write the equation of line AB in slope-intercept form if A is at $(-2, -3)$ and B is at $(2, -1)$.

19. *(21)* Given these statements, is the conclusion valid?
Wilhelm will be in Paris on Friday if he leaves New York by Wednesday.
Wilhelm was not in Paris on Friday.
Wilhelm did not leave New York by Wednesday.

20. *(25)* **Write** If $\triangle KLM \cong \triangle TUV$ by the SSS Postulate, is $m\angle K \cong m\angle U$? Explain.

21. *(22)* A rhombus has diagonals that measure 22 inches and 14 inches. What is the area of the rhombus?

22. *(21)* **U.S. History** Use the Law of Detachment to make a valid conclusion based on these statements.
If you live in Arkansas, then you live in the 25th state to enter the Union.
Clark lives in Arkansas.

23. *(23)* **Farming** A crop disease has started at a central point in a field. The disease is spreading in a circular pattern whose radius increases at a rate of 2 meters per day. At this rate, how large an area will be affected in 3 days, to the nearest square meter?

*24. **Write** If two triangles are proven congruent by the SAS Postulate, what can be said about the third sides of the two triangles?
(28)

*25. **Model** Graph the line $y = 2x + 4$.
(16)

*26. A properly-tied bow tie can be modeled as two congruent triangles. If $\overline{BA} \cong \overline{BD}$ and $\overline{BE} \cong \overline{BC}$, prove $\triangle ABE \cong \triangle DBC$.
(28)

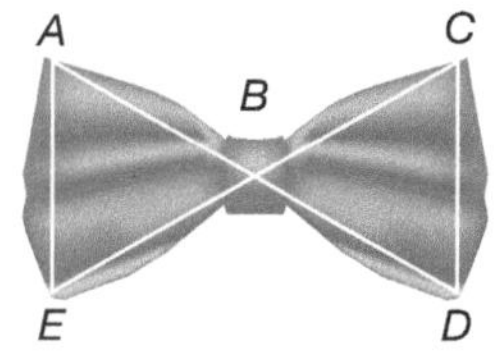

27. **Road Signs** A triangular yield sign is to be rust-proofed with a layer of plastic. Its base is 18 inches and its height is 24 inches. How many square feet of plastic are needed to cover both the front and the back of the sign?
(13)

28. **Algebra** What is the hypotenuse of a triangle whose legs are a and $\sqrt{3}a$?
(Inv 2)

29. Find m$\angle W$ and m$\angle J$.
(18)

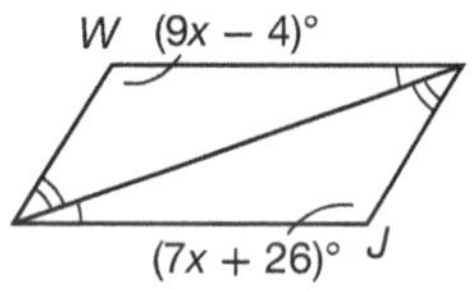

30. Find the area of the trapezoid.
(22)

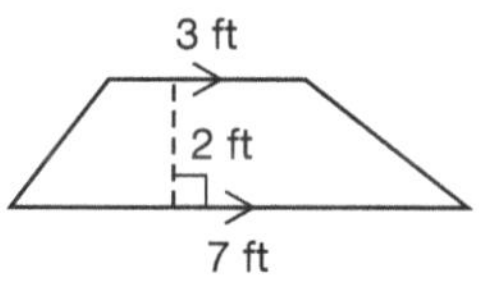

Name ______________________________ Date ____________ Class ____________

Using the Pythagorean Theorem

LESSON 29

* **1.** (12) **a. Algebra** In the figure shown, if $x = 5$, find $m\angle 1$ and $m\angle 2$ where $m\angle 1 = (x^2 + 3x - 5)°$ and $m\angle 2 = (x^3 - 2x^2 - 2x - 10)°$.

b. Is $\overleftrightarrow{DE}$ parallel to $\overleftrightarrow{FG}$?

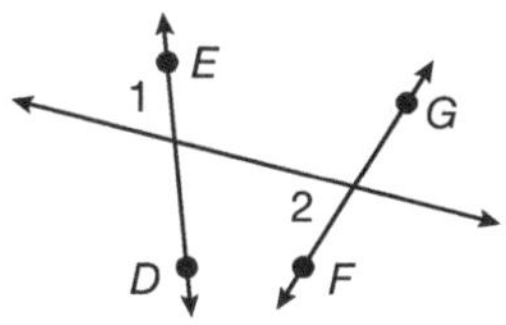

2. (23) **Air Traffic Controller** An air traffic controller uses radar to scan the airspace above an area near the airport. A controller's radar covers a circular area of 250,000 square kilometers. What is the radius of the circle, to the nearest kilometer?

3. (20) Construct a truth table for "*s* and not *t*," where *s* and *t* are logical statements.

* **4.** (25) **Write** Are the two triangles congruent? Explain.

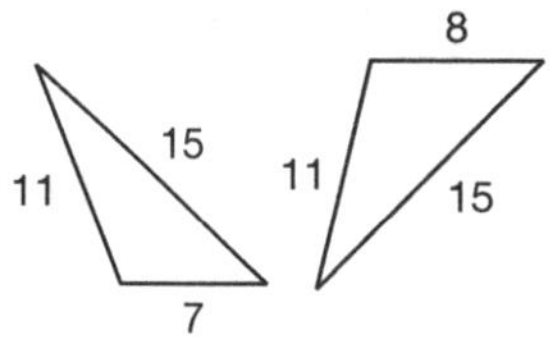

* **5.** (28) **Write** When can SAS congruency be used to conclude two triangles are congruent?

6. (18) In $\triangle DEF$, $m\angle D = 71°$ and the measure of exterior angle F is 107°. Find $m\angle E$.

7. (15) **Road Signs** While driving, Anil saw the following signs. Which of these is not a regular polygon?

A 

B 

C 

D 

8. (21) What conclusion can be drawn from the following statements using the Law of Syllogism?

My family room is a place where I like to study.
The places where I like to study are quiet.

* **9.** (28) Write the congruency statement for the triangles shown below.

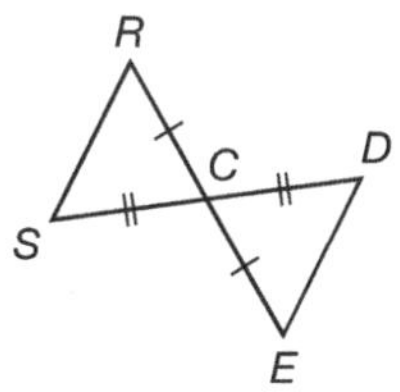

10. (25) **Justify** The congruence statement for the two triangles is written as $\triangle DEF \cong \triangle PQR$. Find the values of x and y.

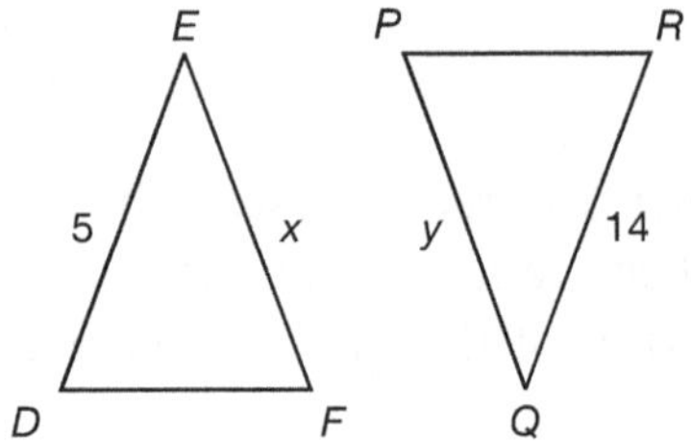

11. (14) **Multiple Choice** Which of the following conjectures is false?

A If x is odd, then $2x$ is even.

B If x is prime, then $x + 1$ is not prime.

C The product of two odd numbers is odd.

D Division of an integer by a prime number gives a rational number.

12. (11) **Geography** On a grid map, Albuquerque is located at $(-10, 4)$ and Oklahoma City is at $(4, 2)$. If Amarillo is the midpoint between the two cities, where is it located?

***13.** (27) If a point lies on the perpendicular bisector of a segment, then the point is equidistant from the endpoints of the segment.

Given: A lies on the perpendicular bisector of $\overline{BC}$.
Prove: $AB = AC$

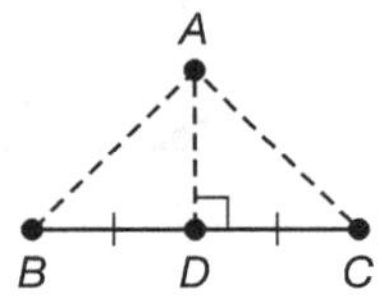

14. (23) A small car has a turning radius of 22 feet. If the car makes a complete 360° turn at this radius, what is the area of the circle made to the nearest square foot?

15. (18) Find $m\angle Q$.

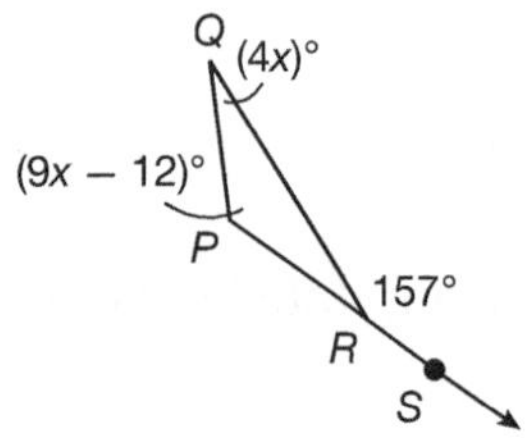

***16.** (29) Find the unknown length of the side in the triangle.

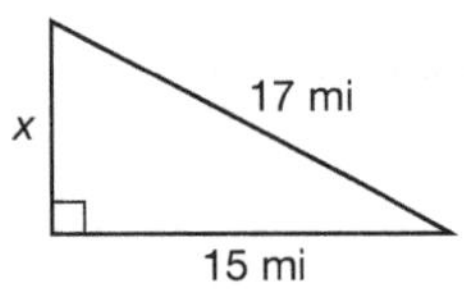

***17.** (26) If an arc of 120° were to be divided into three equal arcs, what would be the measure of each arc?

18. (INV6) Prove Theorem 10-3: If two parallel lines are cut by a transversal, then the same-side interior angles are supplementary.
Given: $m \parallel n$, transversal q
Prove: $\angle 1$ is supplementary to $\angle 2$.

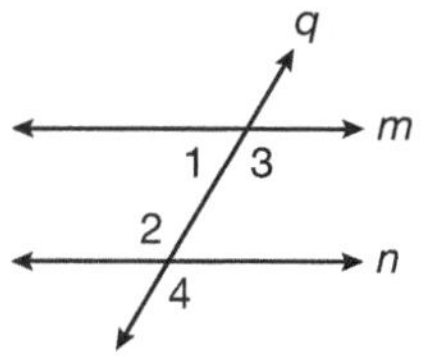

19. (23) **Astronomy** The moon orbits the Earth with an average radius of 380,000 kilometers. Assuming the orbit is circular, what is the distance the moon travels in one orbit, to the nearest kilometer?

20. (16) Graph the line $y = -3x - 6$.

21. (13) Classify $\triangle EFG$ by its angles and sides.

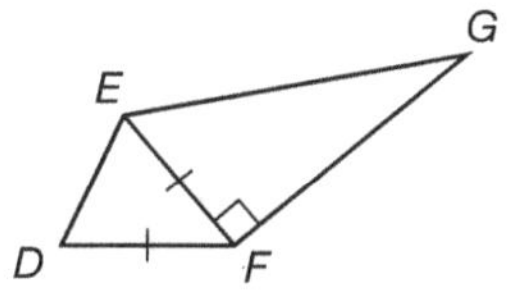

22. (5) Prove Theorem 5-1: If two parallel planes are cut by a third plane, then the lines of intersection are parallel.
Given: Planes CDE and ABF are parallel. Plane ABC is a transversal intersecting both planes.
Prove: $\overleftrightarrow{AB} \parallel \overleftrightarrow{CD}$

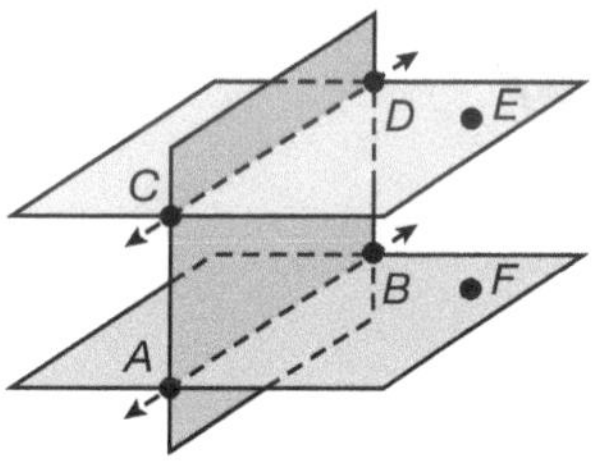

23. (22) **Landscaping** A school's soccer field is rectangular with dimensions 110 yards by 60 yards. If the field is temporarily fenced and covered with a protective tarp during the off-season, how many yards of fence are needed? How many square yards of tarp are needed?

24. (20) **Analyze** Use the statements to determine the truth value for "*A* and not *B*."
A: Thanksgiving is a holiday.
B: Thanksgiving is celebrated in January.

***25.** (29) **Error Analysis** Oshwinder found the solution 13.9 feet when solving for the length of one leg of a right triangle with a hypotenuse of 13 feet and a side length of 5 feet. Is he correct? Explain.

***26.** (28) These two triangles are congruent, $\triangle KLM \cong \triangle TVU$. Find the values of x and y.

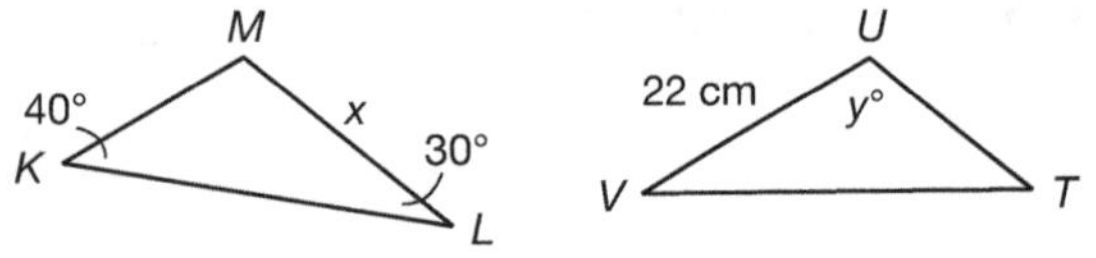

27. (14) **Error Analysis** A student wrote the following as a conjecture. Is he correct? If not, provide a counterexample.

Any sequence starting with $\frac{1}{2}$ which keeps increasing will eventually include a term greater than 1.

***28.** (29) Give two Pythagorean triples that are related to the triple (7, 24, 25).

29. (19) Is the statement, "A parallelogram is a rectangle," always, sometimes, or never true?

***30.** (29) **Carpentry** A shelf bracket is needed to secure the shelf in the diagram. Use the Pythagorean Theorem to find the length of the support.

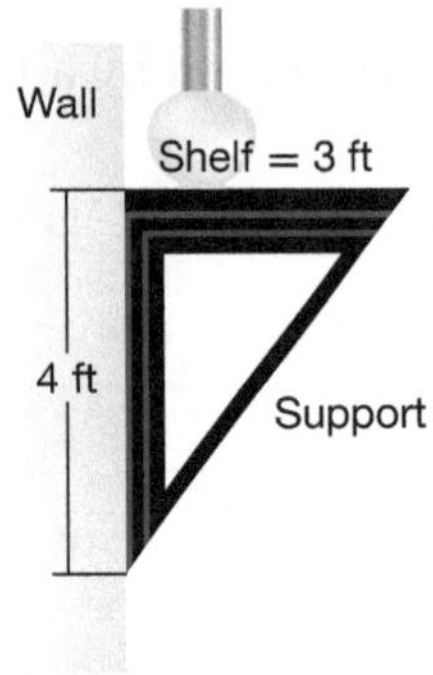

Name ______________________ Date __________ Class __________

Triangle Congruence: ASA and AAS

LESSON 30

1. (20) Construct a truth table for the biconditional statement, "(if x, then y) and (if y, then x)."

2. (9) **Mapping** After walking 0.5 kilometers north and 0.4 kilometers east of her house, Juanita is one-third the distance to her grandfather's house. If the coordinates of Juanita's house are (1, 2), what are the coordinates of her grandfather's house?

3. (29) **Landscaping** A newly planted tree will be secured by wires, each attached to the ground 1.5 meters from the base of the tree. If each wire is 4 meters long, how high up the tree should each wire be attached, to the nearest tenth of a meter?

4. (28) **Justify** Can the SAS Postulate be used to prove these triangles congruent? Explain.

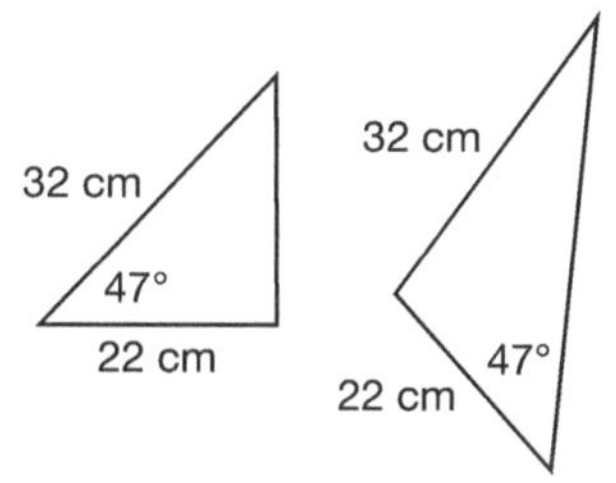

*** 5.** (30) Prove that the two triangles are congruent.

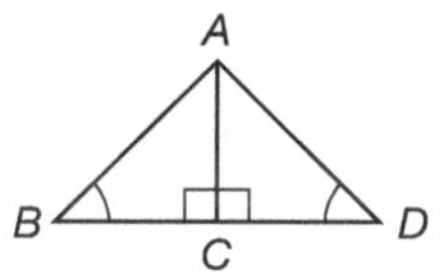

6. (24) **Algebra** Solve the equation $\frac{2x-5}{5} = 3$, and justify each step.

7. (27) **Justify Given:** $PQRS$ is a parallelogram.
Prove: $\angle 1 \cong \angle 5$, $\angle 2 \cong \angle 4$ and $\angle 6 \cong \angle 3$.

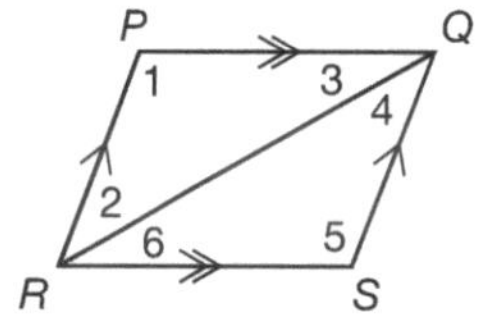

8. (23) **Safety** A lid is needed to cover a well that has a 14-foot circumference. What is the area of the lid that is needed to cover the well, to the nearest tenth of a square foot?

*** 9.** (30) If the triangles are congruent, what is the perimeter of $\triangle PRQ$?

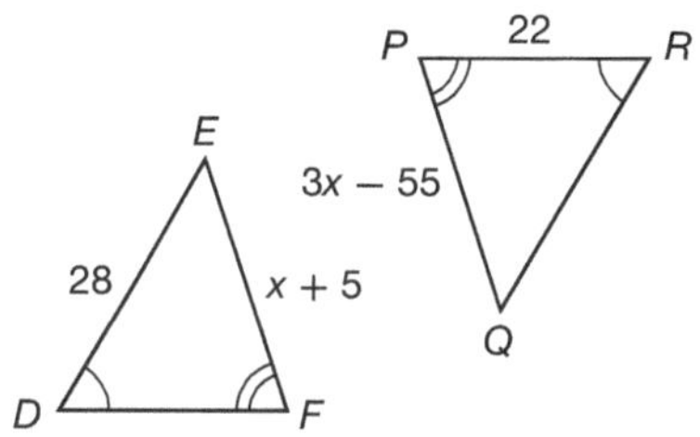

10. (26) **Algebra** The expressions $12x - 62$ and $8x + 86$ represent a pair of congruent arcs. What is the value of x in the expressions?

***11.** (28) Determine the value of x.

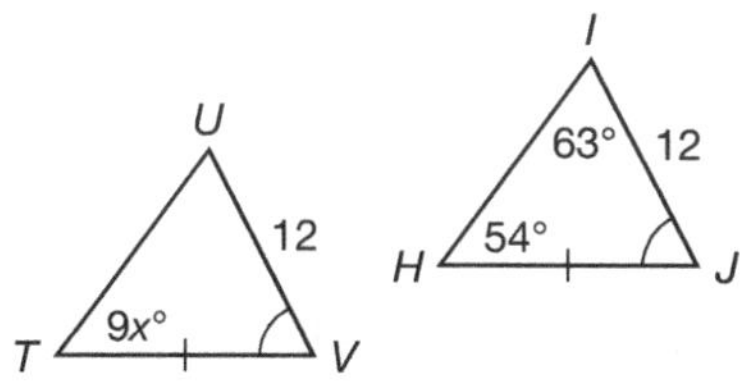

Triangle Congruence: ASA and AAS

LESSON 30

*12. Given that $\triangle ABC \cong \triangle DEF$, write the six congruence statements for the triangles.
(25)

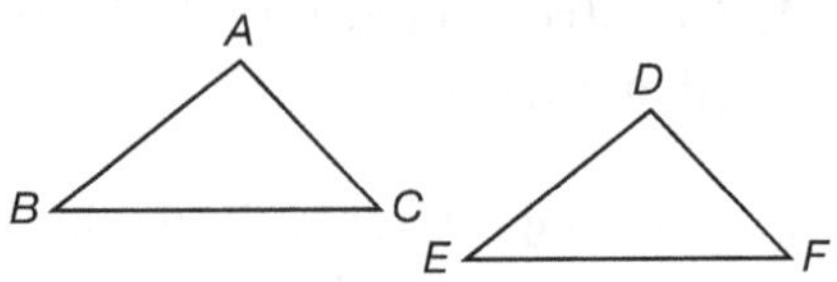

13. **Muiltiple Choice** What is the relationship between these two statements?
(17)

If Ming rides the bus to school, then she will not ride with Debra.
If Ming rides with Debra, then she will not ride the bus to school.

A They are converses. **B** They are contrapositives.
C They are inverses. **D** none of the above

*14. **Write** What theorem or postulate can be used to prove that the two triangles are congruent? Explain.
(30)

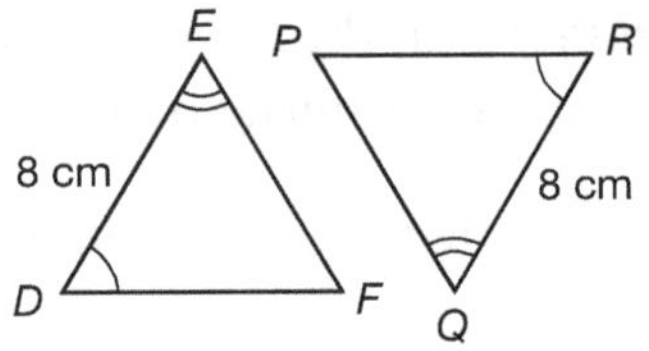

15. **Justify** Use *a, b,* and *c* to determine the truth value of "*a* or (*b* and *c*)".
(20)

a: New York City is the most populous city in the United States.
b: Florida is the most northwestern of all states.
c: The first president of the United States was George Washington.

16. Find a counterexample for the following conjecture.
(14)

The difference between x and y is a positive, even integer.

17. **Algebra** Find the length of each leg of an isosceles right triangle with a hypotenuse of 24 inches, to the nearest inch.
(29)

18. **Analyze** Draw a valid conclusion from the following statements.
(21)

Whoever dropped the bowl made a mess.
The clerk dropped the bowl.

*19. A minor arc has a measure of 135°. If the corresponding major arc is divided into 5 equal parts, what is the measure of each part?
(26)

*20. **Surveying** A road is to be built on an incline to reach a new bridge. The surveyor measures a horizontal distance of 660 yards and a vertical distance of 60 yards for the incline. How long is the actual road surface, to the nearest yard?
(29)

21. **Multi-Step** In $\triangle GHI$, $m\angle G = 33°$ and the measure of an exterior angle at I is 141°. Find $m\angle H$.
(18)

22. The diagonals of a rhombus are 14 centimeters and 22 centimeters long, respectively. If the rhombus is cut apart and reassembled into a rectangle with a width of 5 centimeters, what would be the length of the rectangle?
(22)

*23. (30) **Error Analysis** Jamal says that $\overline{AB} \cong \overline{DE}$ is needed to prove that $\triangle ABC \cong \triangle DEC$ by the AAS Theorem. Identify and correct Jamal's mistake.

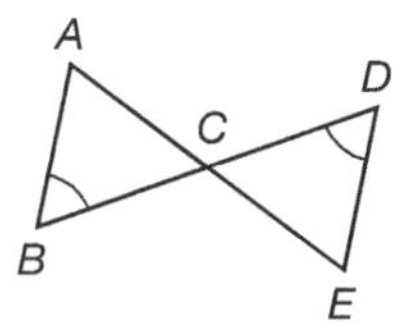

*24. (27) Prove Theorem 6-7: If a point lies on the bisector of an angle, then the point is equidistant from the sides of the angle.
Given: K lies on the angle bisector of $\angle HIJ$.
Prove: $HK = JK$

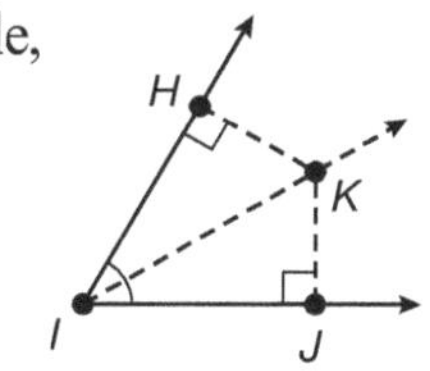

25. (16) **Multi-Step** Find the slope and the y-intercept of the line $C(1, 1)$ and $D(-2, 3)$.

26. (23) A circular lid has an area of 42 square inches. If the lid rolls 8 times, what distance will it cover, to the nearest inch?

*27. (25) **Model** How many triangles could you construct if you were given three different line segments? Explain.

28. (18) The measure of one acute angle in a right triangle is y. What is the measure of the other acute angle?

29. (22) **Stereo Equipment** The front of a speaker box is shaped like a trapezoid with a height of 2 feet, a lower base of 4 feet, and an upper base of 3 feet. How many square feet of mesh is needed to cover the front of the speaker?

30. (17) What is the relationship between the following two statements?

If a rectangle is regular, then it is a square.
If a rectangle is not regular, then it is not a square.

Name ______________________________ Date ____________ Class ____________

Flowchart and Paragraph Proofs

LESSON 31

* **1.** (Inv 3) **Baseball** Vernon is standing on the pitcher's mound of a baseball field. He turns from looking toward home plate to first base. If the pitcher's mound is at the center of the regular polygon made by the bases, how many degrees did Vernon rotate?

2. (28) **Analyze** In the diagram given, prove that $\overline{AD} \cong \overline{BC}$, using a two-column proof.

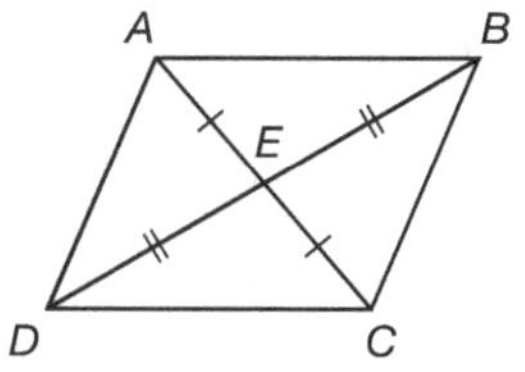

3. (18) Determine $m\angle Y$ in $\triangle XYZ$.

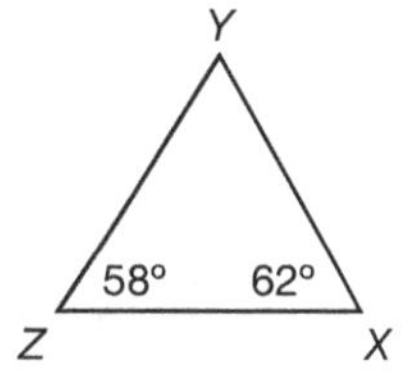

4. (22) **Algebra** Erin drew a parallelogram with an area of 18 square centimeters and a base of 6 centimeters. What was the height?

5. (26) If $m\widehat{AB} = 70°$, what is the measure of the associated major arc?

* **6.** (31) Write a paragraph proof.
Given: $a \parallel b$, $n \parallel m$
Prove: $\angle 1 \cong \angle 5$.

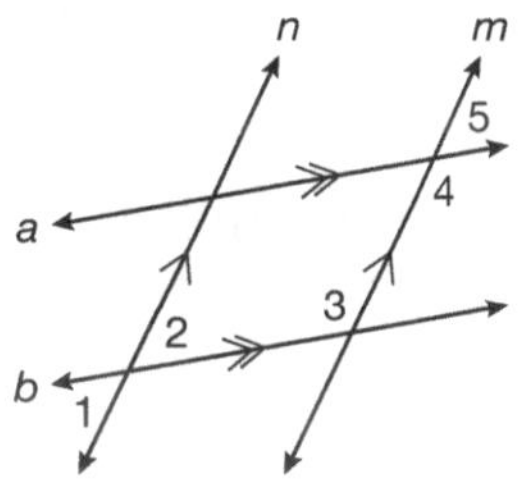

7. (25) **Algebra** $\triangle ABC$ and $\triangle DEF$ are congruent triangles with $m\angle A = 90°$, $AB = 7$, and $DF = 24$. Based on the given information, what is the length of BC?

* **8.** (29) **Home Repair** A contractor arrives at a house with a ladder that is 4 meters long. If the closest he can safely place the ladder to the house is 1.5 meters, will the top of the ladder reach the edge of the roof, which is 3.8 meters above the ground?

* **9.** (Inv 3) **Design** Whitney is making a stop sign, a regular octagon. What should be the measure of each angle of her sign?

10. (22) **Kites** Mohinder wants to make a rhombus-shaped kite with an area of 224 square inches and a frame using one diagonal crosspiece that is 14 inches long. What is the length of the other diagonal crosspiece?

* **11.** (31) Write a flowchart proof.
Given: $\overrightarrow{BD}$ bisects $\angle ABC$ and $\angle 1$ is congruent to $\angle 3$.
Prove: Angle 2 is congruent to $\angle 3$.

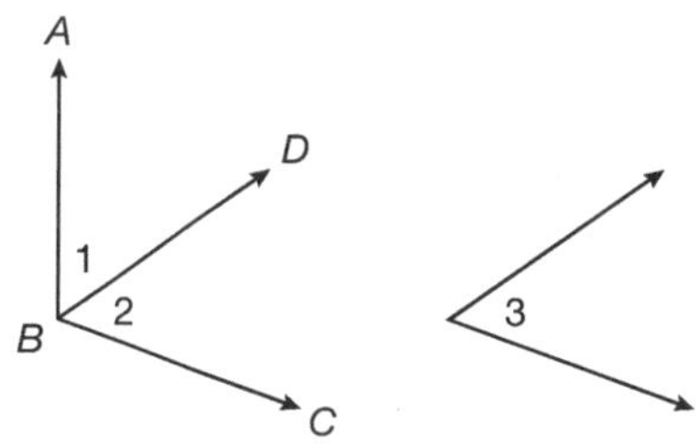

12. (25) **Justify** If $\triangle ABC \cong \triangle LMN$ and $\triangle LMN \cong \triangle XYZ$, write the congruence statements between $\triangle ABC$ and $\triangle XYZ$. What property justifies these conclusions?

13. (27) **Landscaping** Prove that if the area of a rectangular patio *ABCD* is 25 square units and one of the lengths is 5 units, then *ABCD* is a square.

14. (17) Write the converse of the following statement.

If two numbers have midpoint 0 on a number line, then they are opposites.

Is the original statement true? Is the converse?

***15.** (29) **Multiple Choice** The length of a leg of a right triangle with a hypotenuse of 20 centimeters and another leg of 12 centimeters is _________.

A 6 centimeters **B** 4 centimeters
C 16 centimeters **D** 10 centimeters

16. (16) Determine the equation of each line graphed on this grid.

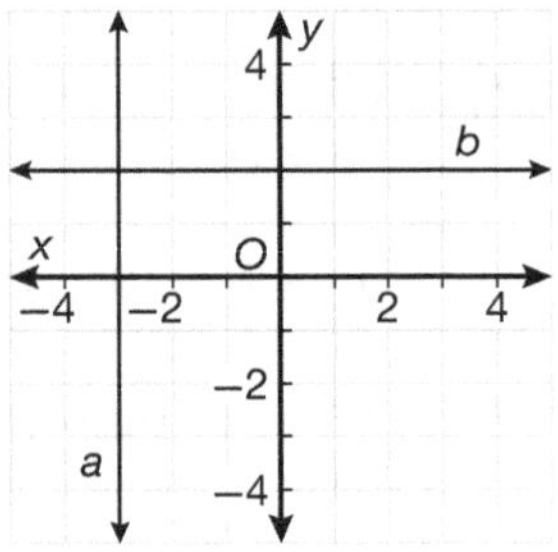

17. (21) **Meteorology** When cumulus clouds appear, there is a good chance of rain later in the day. When it rains, the air cools and descends, creating wind. What can students conclude from these statements if they see cumulus clouds forming?

***18.** (30) **Error Analysis** Suresh and Gayle are having a debate. Suresh believes that since each angle in an equilateral triangle measures 60°, all equilateral triangles are congruent. Gayle disagrees since she can draw two equilateral triangles that are different sizes. Who is correct? Explain.

19. (14) **Algebra** Find a counterexample to the conjecture.

A linear equation in one unknown has exactly one solution.

***20.** (30) Using the diagram given, prove that $\overline{AE} \cong \overline{CE}$.

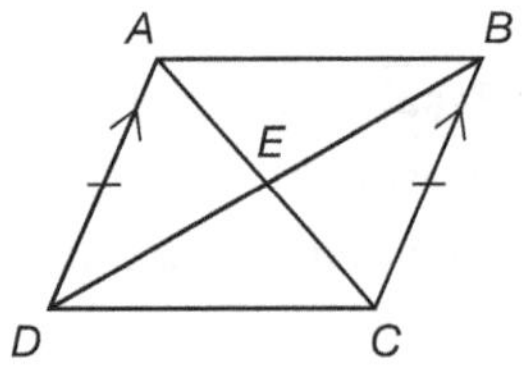

***21.** (31) Write a paragraph proof.
Given: $\overline{AD}$ bisects $\overline{CB}$ and $\overline{AD} \perp \overline{CB}$.
Prove: $\triangle ACD \cong \triangle ABD$.

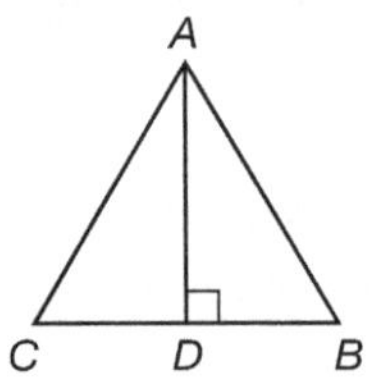

22. (24) City Hall is located at (1, 1) on a coordinate grid of a city. The police station is located at point $(x - 3, 4x + 1)$. If the police station is 5 units away from City Hall and x is positive, what are the numeric coordinates of the police station? Provide a justification for each step.

23. (16) Write an equation for the line passing through (−3, 2) that has slope 4.

***24.** (31) Write a flowchart proof.
Given: $\overline{LP}$ is congruent to $\overline{MN}$ and $\overline{LO}$ is congruent to $\overline{MO}$.
Prove: $\overline{OP}$ is congruent to $\overline{ON}$.

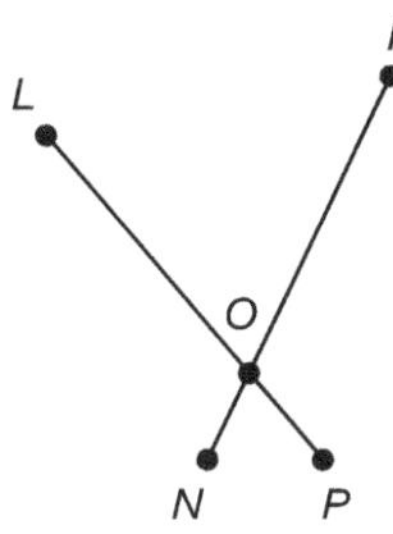

***25.** (28) **Generalize** If $\triangle ABC$ and $\triangle DEF$ are right triangles, $\angle B$ and $\angle E$ are right angles, $AC = DF$, and $AB = DE$, is it possible to conclude that $\triangle ABC \cong \triangle DEF$? If yes, use the SAS Theorem to prove it. If no, explain why.

26. (13) **a.** A right triangle has a base length of 1.5 meters and a height of 1.2 meters. Determine its area.
b. The other side of the same triangle has a length of 0.81 meters. Determine the triangle's perimeter.

***27.** (20) **a. Generalize** Rewrite the statement, "If p, then q" as a compound statement involving p, q, and/or their negations.
b. Write the negation of the statement, "p or q" as a compound statement involving p, q, and/or their negations.
c. Write the negation of your answer to part **a** as a compound statement involving p, q, and/or their negations.

28. (15) In the figure below, name each angle marked with a dot and identify it as an interior or exterior angle.

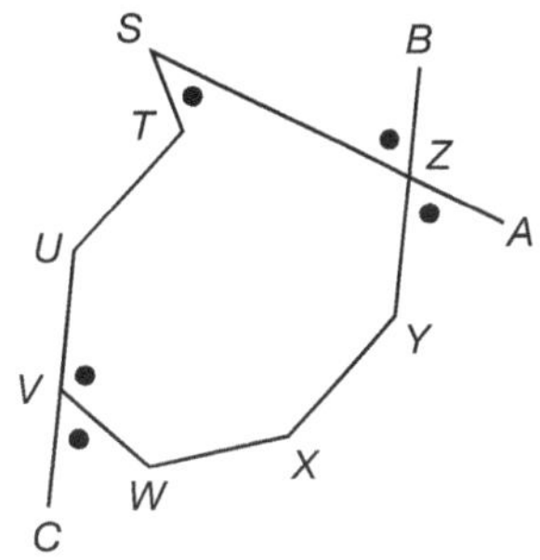

29. (23) **Verify** For a circle with a diameter of 13 centimeters, Sal calculated the circumference to be 81.64 centimeters. Is Sal's calculation correct?

***30.** (30) **Algebra** If in $\triangle ABC$, $AB = (3x + 11)$, $m\angle ABC = 45°$, $m\angle BCA = 75°$, and $BC = 15$, and in $\triangle DEF$, $DE = (7x - 9)$, $m\angle DEF = 45°$, $m\angle EFD = 75°$, and $EF = 15$, what is the value of x?

Name ____ Date ____________ Class ______________

Altitudes and Medians of Triangles

LESSON **32**

1. (26) **Formulate** An arc measure of 180° creates a semicircle. Use this fact to derive a formula for the area of a semicircle.

2. (19) Three sides of convex quadrilateral *ABCD* are congruent, but the fourth is not. What possible shape(s) could *ABCD* be?

3. (22) **Algebra** A trapezoid has an area of 22, a height of 4, and bases of $x + 2$ and $3x - 3$. Solve for x.

4. (7) Make a conjecture about the next item in the list and explain the basis of your conjecture.

Triangle, square, pentagon, hexagon, heptagon…

*** 5.** (32) A median of a triangle connects a vertex and the ________ of the opposite side.

6. (15) **Marketing** In the diagram, a corporate logo is designed in the shape shown at right.

a. Name the polygon.
b. Determine whether the polygon is equiangular, equilateral, regular, irregular, or more than one of these.
c. Determine whether the polygon is concave or convex. Explain.

7. (14) Consider the conjecture.

If $\triangle$MNO *is an acute triangle,* D *lies on* $\overline{MN}$*, and* E *lies on* $\overline{MO}$*, then* $\triangle$MDE *is an acute triangle.*

a. What is the hypothesis of the conjecture? What is its conclusion?
b. Find a counterexample to the conjecture.

8. (27) In the diagram given, $\overline{RU}$ and $\overline{ST}$ are diameters of the circle and O is the center of the circle. Prove that $m\angle SRO = m\angle UTO$.

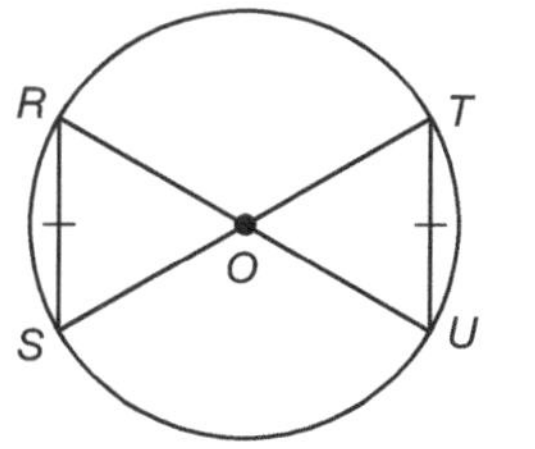

Use the diagram to answer the next two questions.

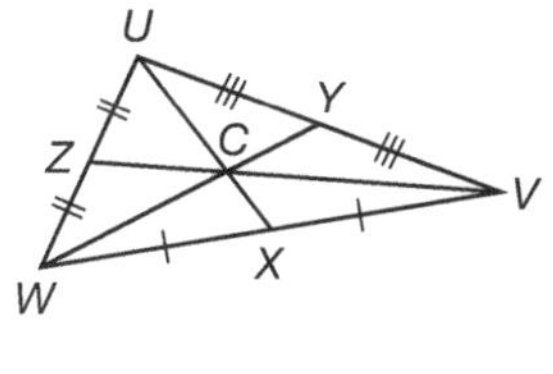

*** 9.** (32) If the length of $\overline{ZV}$ is 72, determine the length of $\overline{VC}$.

***10.** (32) If the length of $\overline{CX}$ is 18, determine the length of $\overline{UC}$.

11. (28) **Designing** Spencer is making two triangular flags, $\triangle ABC$ and $\triangle DEF$, for the upcoming football game. Given that if $\triangle ABC$ is a right triangle at $\angle B$ and $\triangle DEF$ is a right triangle at $\angle E$ with $\overline{AB} \cong \overline{DE}$ and $\overline{BC} \cong \overline{EF}$, which congruence postulate would prove $\triangle ABC \cong \triangle DEF$?

*12. Using the diagram shown, prove $KM = LM$.
(30)

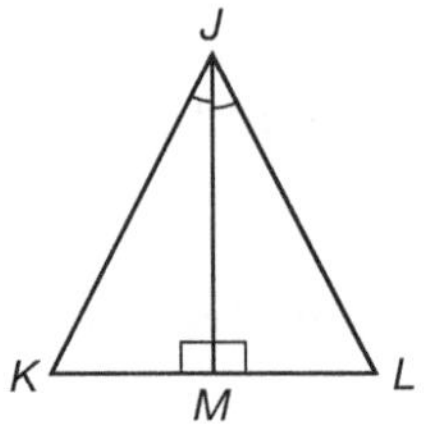

13. Art Using a technique known as vanishing point to give a three-dimensional perspective to the painting, an artist drew a rectangular table as a trapezoid with a height of 3 inches and with upper and lower bases of 3 and 4 inches, respectively. What is the area of the painting of the table?
(22)

*14. Write a paragraph proof.
(31)
Given: $\overline{AB} \cong \overline{BC}$ and $\overline{BC} \cong \overline{DE}$
Prove: $\overline{AB} \cong \overline{DE}$

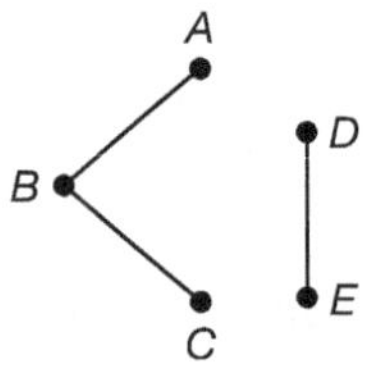

15. Prove that if all angles in $\triangle PQR$ are equal, then each angle is 60°.
(27)

16. **Error Analysis** In calculating the length of a hypotenuse, Beatrice and Amelie both got an answer of $\sqrt{360}$. However, when asked to provide their answer in simplified radical form, Beatrice's answer was $36\sqrt{10}$ and Amelie's was $6\sqrt{10}$. Who is incorrect and why?
(29)

*17. Write a paragraph proof.
(31)
Given: Angle 1 and ∠2 are complementary.
Angle 3 and ∠4 are complementary.
∠2 ≅ ∠3
Prove: ∠1 ≅ ∠4

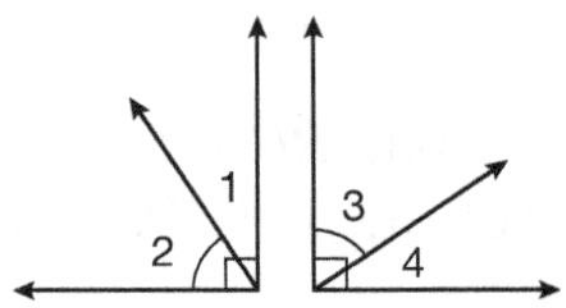

18. **Algebra** Two vertical angles measure $(4x - 4)°$ and $(3x + 7)°$. What is the measure of each angle? Provide a justification for each step.
(24)

19. Consider the following conjecture.
(14)

If the product of three numbers is positive, then all three numbers are positive.

a. What is the hypothesis of the conjecture? What is its conclusion?
b. Find a counterexample to the conjecture.

20. Use the Law of Detachment to fill in the missing statement in this conjecture.
(21)

____

M is the midpoint of $\overline{WX}$.
Therefore, $WM = MX$.

21. **Verify** A triangle has an exterior angle measuring 98°. One remote interior angle
(18) measures 49° and the other remote angle is congruent to it. Verify the Exterior Angle Theorem for this exterior angle.

22. **Machinery** Two gears are interlocked. One has a radius of 10 centimeters and for
(23) each complete rotation, it rotates the second gear 0.77 of a full turn.
a. What is the relationship between the circumferences of the two gears?
b. What is the second gear's radius, to the nearest centimeter?

23. Prove that if the heights of two parallelograms, h_1 and h_2, lie on the same
(27) parallel lines and have the same base, b, then the parallelograms are equal in area.

*24. **Multiple Choice** If the length of a median of a triangle equals 4.5, what is the distance
(32) from the centroid to the opposite side?

A 4.5 **B** 3
C 2.25 **D** 1.5

25. **Analyze** In the diagram given, prove that $\triangle ABC \cong \triangle BDC$ using the SAS
(28) Triangle Congruence Theorem. *Hint: Show* $m\angle BAC = m\angle DBC$.

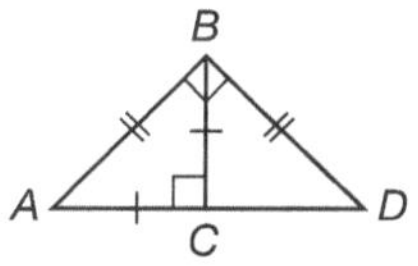

26. **Generalize** Complete the table by writing the contrapositive of each statement.
(17)

Statement	Contrapositive
If p, then q	If $\sim q$, then $\sim p$
If $\sim p$, then q	
If p, then $\sim q$	
If $\sim p$, then $\sim q$	

*27. **Design** Ian is making a kite he has labeled $VWXY$. He has already made
(30) $m\angle VWY = m\angle XWY$. What pair of angles can he make equal to ensure $\triangle VWY \cong \triangle XWY$?

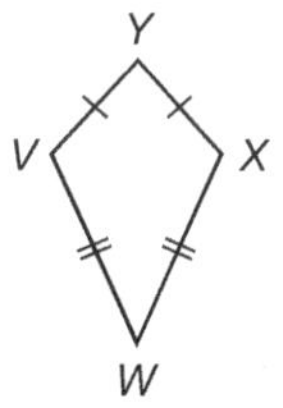

28. $\triangle HIJ \cong \triangle LKN$ and $m\angle H = 50°$, $m\angle K = 100°$, and $HI = 5$ centimeters.
(25) What is $m\angle J$?

***29.** (31) Write a flowchart proof. Refer to the figure shown.
Given: m∠*BAC* = m∠*EAF*, m∠*CAD* = m∠*DAE*
Prove: m∠*BAD* = m∠*DAF*

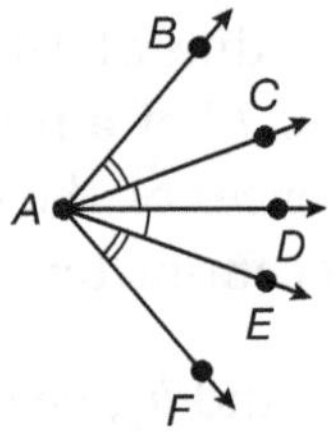

30. (20) **Generalize** What is the negation of the statement, "If *p*, then *q*?" Write a truth table to help you.

Name ______________________ Date __________ Class __________

Converse of the Pythagorean Theorem

LESSON 33

1. *(25)* The two triangles at right are congruent. Write the six congruency statements for them.

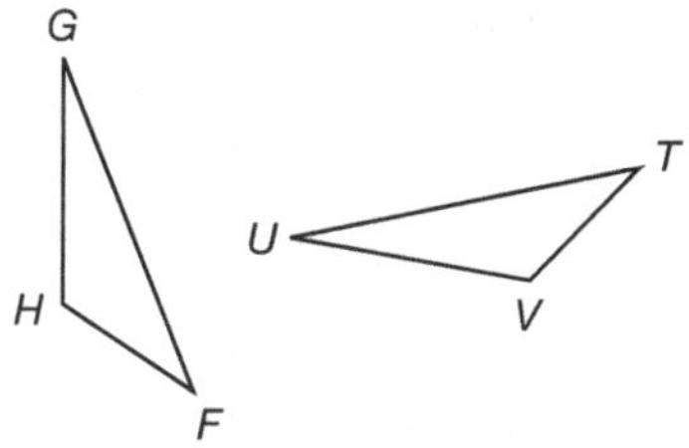

2. *(30)* In $\triangle ABC$, $m\angle BAC = 57°$, $AB = 10$, and $m\angle ABC = 52°$. In $\triangle DEF$, $m\angle EDF = 57°$, $DE = 10$, and $m\angle DFE = 71°$. Is $\triangle ABC \cong \triangle DEF$? Explain.

*** 3.** *(33)* **Multi-Step** What is the value for x if the triangle is a right triangle? Write an inequality to show the smallest value for x that makes the triangle an obtuse triangle. Write your answer in simplified radical form.

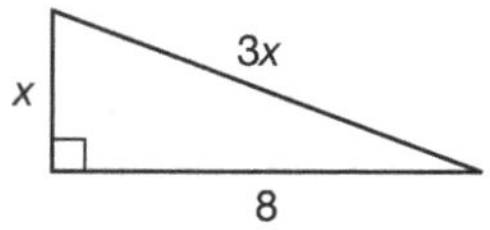

4. *(17)* Write the converse of the following false statement.
If a triangle is isosceles, then it is obtuse.

*** 5.** *(31)* Write a paragraph proof.
Given: $\angle STV \cong \angle TVU$, $\angle STU \cong \angle UVS$
Prove: $\angle SVT \cong \angle UTV$

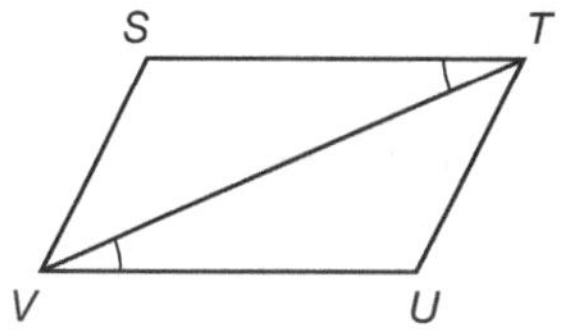

6. *(28)* The angles of $\triangle ABC$ are $m\angle BAC = 9x - 77°$, $m\angle ABC = 5x + 17°$, and $m\angle ACB = 6x - 33°$. If $m\angle DEF = 90°$, $\overline{AB} \cong \overline{DE}$, and $\overline{BC} \cong \overline{EF}$, is $\triangle ABC \cong \triangle DEF$?

7. *(22)* Find an expression for the area of a parallelogram with a height of $2y$ and a base of $3x$.

*** 8.** *(33)* **Architecture** The Leaning Tower of Pisa in Italy would be 185 feet tall if it were standing vertically.

a. If you are standing 80 feet from the base of the tower, and the tower is leaning away from you, what type of triangle would be formed? What is the minimum length of y?

b. If you are standing 125 feet from the base of the tower, and the tower is leaning toward you, what type of triangle would be formed? What is the maximum length of x?

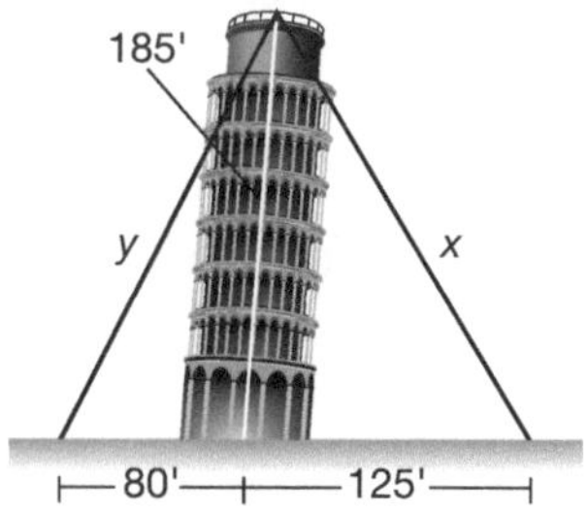

9. *(17)* **Verify** Write the inverse of the statement, "If a triangle does not have an obtuse angle, then it is acute." Which is true: the statement, its inverse, both, or neither? Explain.

***10.** *(31)* Write a flowchart proof.
Given: $\overline{EF} \cong \overline{HI}$, H is the midpoint of $\overline{GI}$
Prove: $\overline{EF} \cong \overline{GH}$

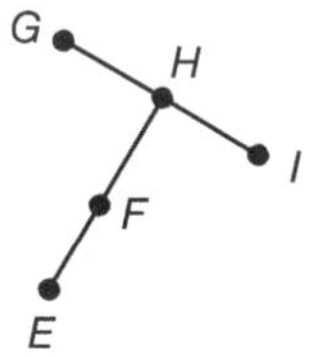

11. *(23)* **a. Generalize** How many different radii does a circle have?
b. How many different measures do the radii of a circle have?

*12. **Algebra** Write an inequality to show the largest value for x that makes the triangle obtuse if the longest side length is 11.
(33)

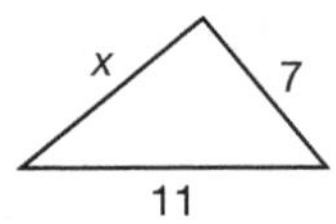

13. **Write** Explain how the slope-intercept form of a line can be used to sketch its graph, without creating a table of values.
(16)

14. **Geology** A volcano is active if it has erupted recently and is expected to do so again soon. It is dormant if it is not active, but is expected to erupt again at some future time. It is extinct if it is not ever expected to erupt again.
(20)
   a. Write the conjunction of the statements, "A volcano is active," and "A volcano is not ever expected to erupt again." Is this conjunction true? Explain.
   b. Write the disjunction of the same two statements. Is the disjunction true? Why or why not?

15. **Gardening** Ashanti has a 40-square foot garden in the shape of a trapezoid. If the diagram shows the garden's dimensions, what are the lengths of the two bases? Provide a justification for each step.
(24)

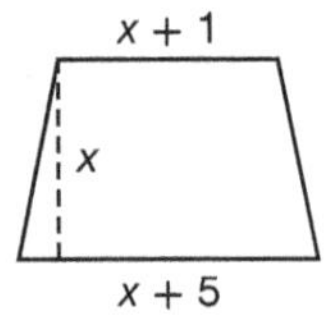

*16. **Multiple Choice** The altitudes are used to find which of the following?
(32)
A orthocenter **B** median
C area **D** centroid

17. In the figure, name each angle marked with a dot and identify it as an interior or exterior angle.
(15)

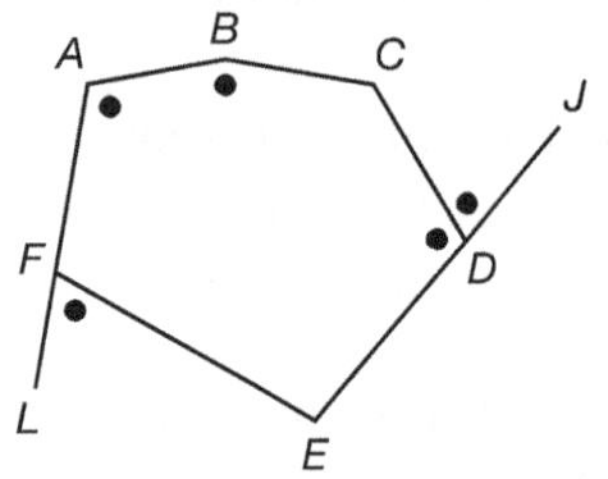

18. **Algebra** A convex polygon has interior angles $(x + 4)°$, $(2x + 5)°$, $(3x + 6)°$, $(4x + 7)°$, and $(5x + 8)°$. What is the value of x?
(Inv 3)

*19. **Furniture** The height of a triangular cabinet is 8 feet. There are four shelves which are evenly spaced. What is the distance from the top of the cabinet to each of the shelves along the hypotenuse, to the nearest inch?
(29, 33)

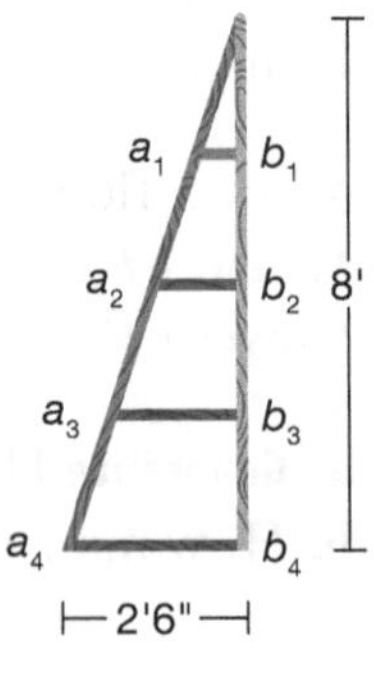

20. (21) **Error Analysis** From the statements, "If a, then b. If c, then b. a is a true statement," a student incorrectly concluded, "c is a true statement." What mistake did the student make? What conclusion should have been made?

21. (Inv 3) What is the measure of each exterior angle in a regular dodecahedron?

22. (18) **Justify** An exterior angle of a triangle measures 136°. One remote interior angle measures 56°. Determine the other two interior angle measures, justifying each step in your reasoning.

23. (26) **Algebra** In the diagram, $m\widehat{TU} = (5x + 10)°$, $m\widehat{UV} = (3x + 12)°$ and $m\widehat{TV} = (6x + 50)°$. What is the value of x?

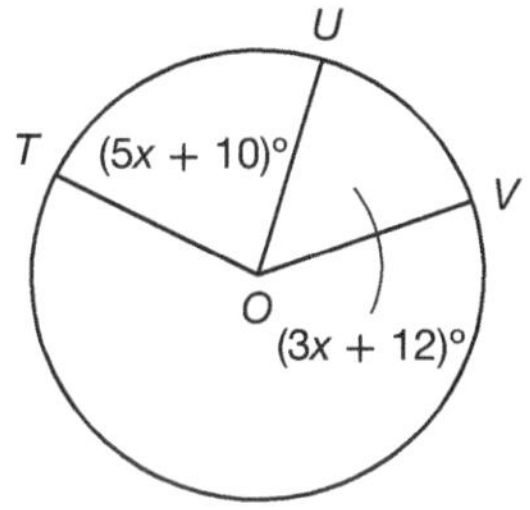

24. (16) **Write** Describe how to write the equation of a line, given that its slope is −1 and that the point (4, 5) lies on it.

Use the diagram to answer the following questions.

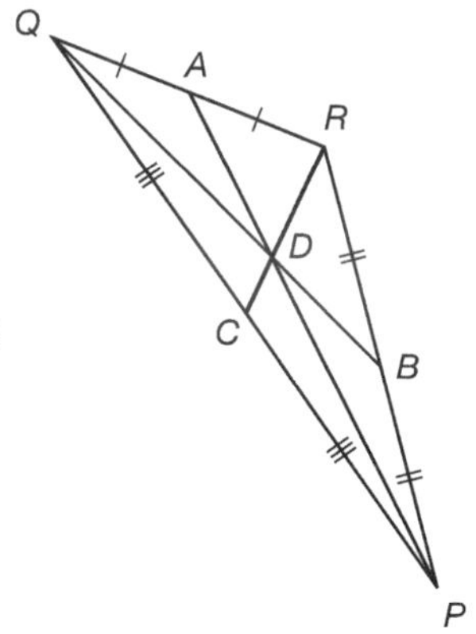

*25. (32) Given that $AP = 123$, determine the length of $\overline{AD}$.

*26. (32) Given that $BD = 63$, determine the length of $\overline{DQ}$.

27. (29) **Gardening** Julian installed a total of 10 yards of fence which runs along the perimeter of his square garden. He decides to run a watering hose between two opposite corners. What length of hose will he need, to the nearest tenth of a yard?

28. (26) If $m\widehat{AB} = 23°$ and $m\widehat{BC} = 33°$, what is the measure of $\widehat{AC}$ if $\widehat{AB}$ and $\widehat{BC}$ are non-overlapping, adjacent arcs?

29. (11) Determine the midpoint M of the line segment $\overline{CD}$ with endpoints $C(0, 6)$ and $D(5, 2)$.

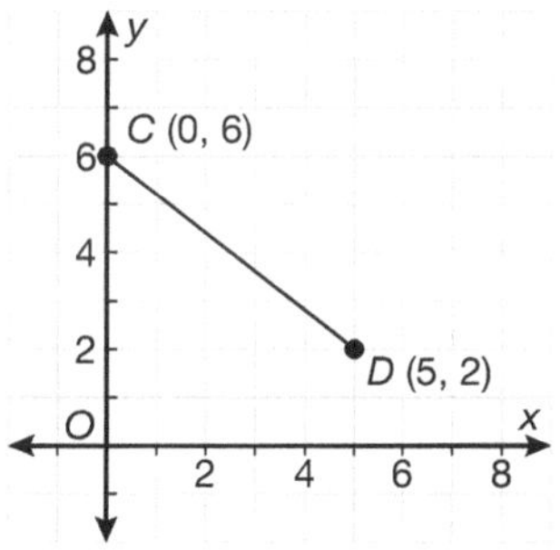

30. (23) What is the circumference of a circle with a radius measure of $7x$? Express your answer in terms of π.

Name ______________________ Date __________ Class __________

Properties of Parallelograms

LESSON 34

* **1.** *(34)* **Multi-Step** Figure $KLMN$ is a parallelogram. Find the length of the diagonals.

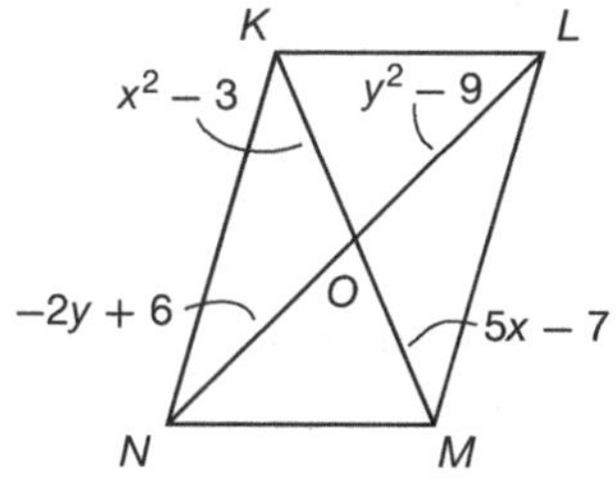

2. *(28)* If $\triangle ABC \cong \triangle DEF$, $m\angle ACB = 9x - 77°$, and $m\angle DFE = 4x + 33°$, what is the value of x?

3. *(19)* **Analyze** Classify this quadrilateral, and explain how you know.

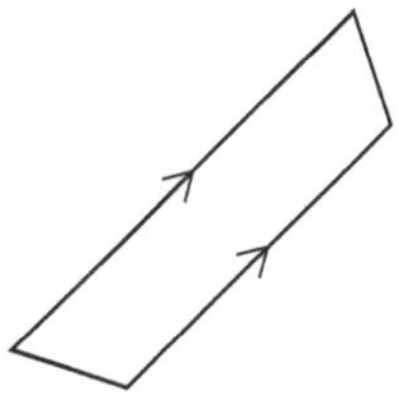

4. *(21)* Draw a valid conclusion from these conditional statements:
If Molly does her homework, then she learns the material.
If she learns the material, then she will do well on the test.
If she does well on the test, then she will get a good grade in the course.

5. *(27)* **Justify** In the diagram, $AC = BC$, and $DC = BC$. Prove that $m\angle BCD = 2x + 2y$.

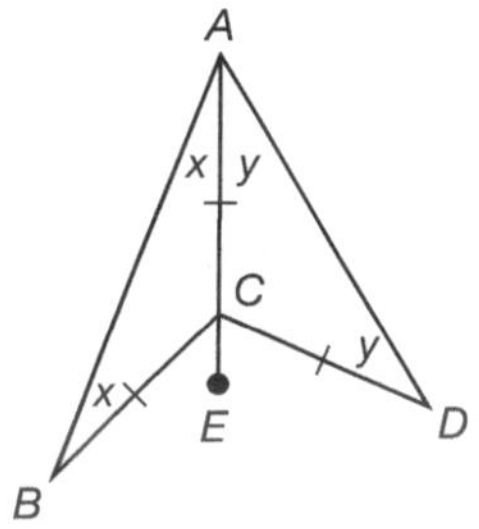

* **6.** *(22)* **Construction** In order to place a square toolshed in his backyard, Landon measures an area with a diagonal length of 12 feet. What area of the yard will the shed occupy? *Hint: Use the Pythagorean Theorem to find the length of one side of the shed.*

7. *(17)* **Multiple Choice** Consider the following statements.
If Martha wears jeans, then it is the weekend.
If it is the weekend, then Martha wears jeans.

The second statement is the __________ of the first.

A inverse **B** negation
C contrapositive **D** converse

8. *(31)* Write a flowchart proof.
Given: $\angle 2$ and $\angle 3$ are supplementary.
Prove: $\angle 1$ and $\angle 3$ are supplementary.

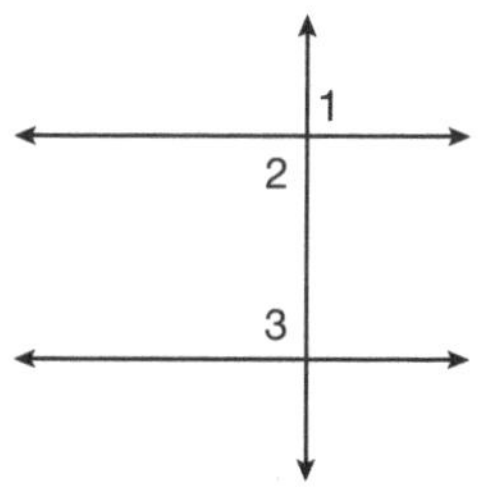

9. *(Inv 3)* What is the sum of all the interior, exterior, and central angles in a convex hexagon?

10. *(18)* **Write** Explain why the measure of an exterior angle of a triangle is equal to the sum of its two remote interior angles.

*11. (34) Briefly state the four properties of parallelograms.

12. (22) What is the area of a rectangle with a length of 4 and a diagonal length of 5?

13. (17) **Error Analysis** For the contrapositive of the statement, "If a bus is green, then it is a downtown bus," Keisha has written, "If a bus is not green, then it is not a downtown bus." Identify any errors Keisha has made.

14. (30) **Multiple Choice** Which of these statements describes these triangles?

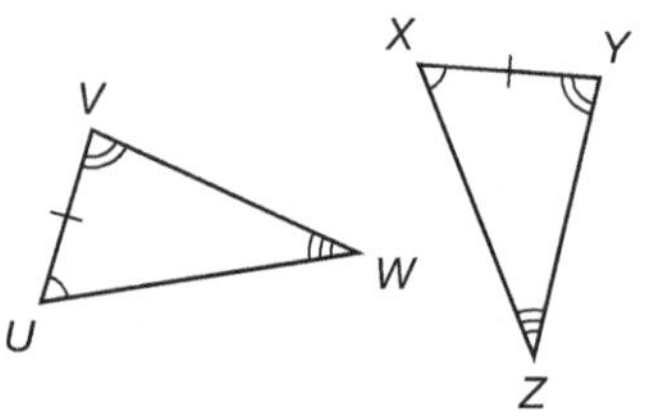

A $\triangle VWU \cong \triangle ZYX$ **B** $\triangle XYZ \cong \triangle WVU$
C $\triangle WUV \cong \triangle ZXY$ **D** $\triangle YZX \cong \triangle UWV$

15. (23) **Irrigation** In order to water plants efficiently, many farmers use a long metal pole which sweeps over a circular area, spraying water on the crops below. If the radius of one such device is 150 feet, what is the area of the circle that gets watered, to the nearest ten square feet?

*16. (33) **Multiple Choice** Which of the following sets of numbers represents the leg lengths of an acute triangle?
A 7, 4, 8 **B** 4, $2\sqrt{2}$, 5
C 9, 7, $2\sqrt{3}$ **D** 14, 15, 4

17. (16) **Chemistry** Linear alkanes are a class of organic molecules with only hydrogen (H) and carbon (C) atoms. This graph plots the number of carbon atoms of some linear alkanes on the x-axis and the number of hydrogen atoms on the y-axis. What is the equation of the line connecting them?

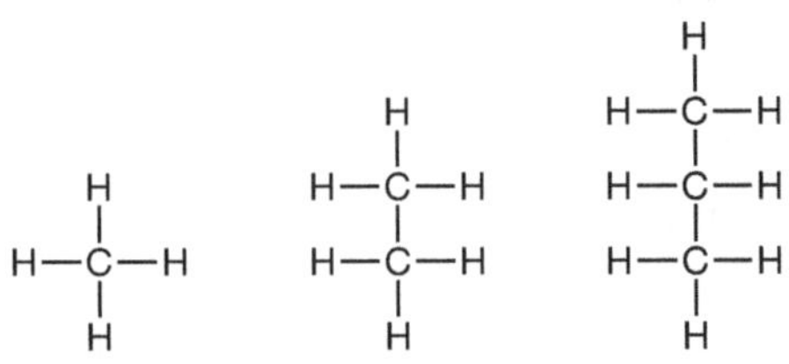

methane **ethane** **propane**

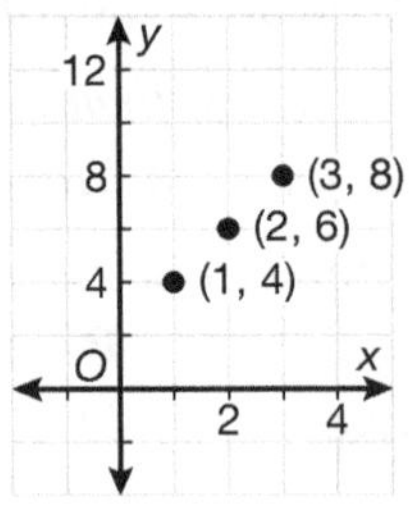

18. (19) **Write** Quadrilateral $WXYZ$ has two pairs of parallel sides. Describe the steps needed to sketch $WXYZ$, and then sketch it.

*19. (34) $HIJK$ is a parallelogram. Find the measure of each angle.

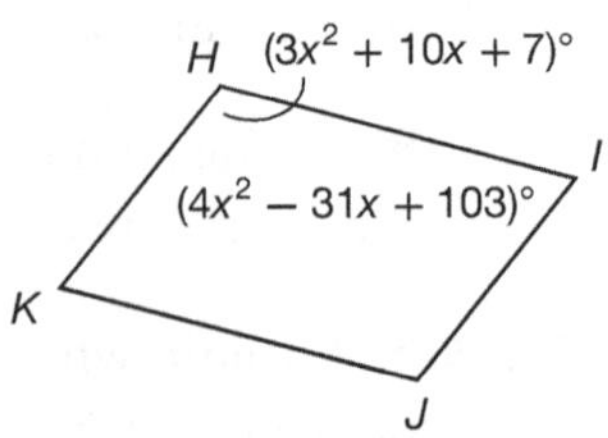

20. (28) Name the included angle between the sides $\overline{RS}$ and $\overline{TR}$ of $\triangle RST$.

*21. (29, 33) **Architecture** The Seattle Space Needle is 184 meters tall. If a person is standing 160 meters away from the base, how far is the person from the top, to the nearest meter?

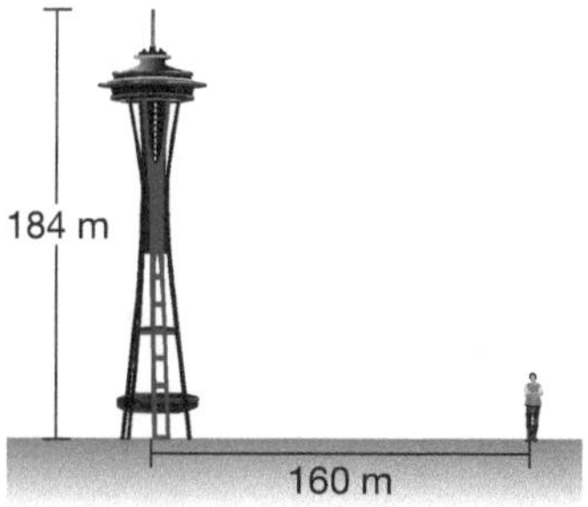

*22. (31) **Generalize** Are there any proofs that can be done as a flowchart proof but cannot be proved with a paragraph proof? If so, give an example. If not, explain why.

23. (30) **Algebra** In $\triangle ABC$, $m\angle BAC = 67°$, $AB = (5x - 7)$, and $m\angle ABC = 23°$. In $\triangle DEF$, $m\angle EDF = 67°$, $EF = (2x + 4)$, $DE = (3x + 1)$, and $m\angle DEF = 23°$. What is the length of $\overline{EF}$?

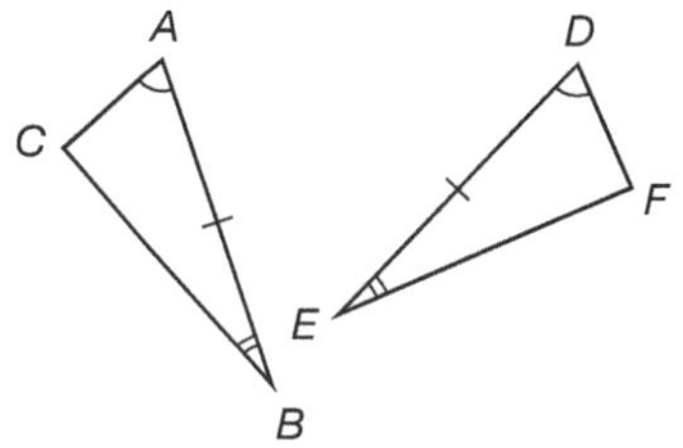

24. (29) **Algebra** A right triangle has a hypotenuse of 15 inches, with one leg twice the length of the other leg. What is length of each leg, to the nearest tenth of an inch?

25. (24) **Justify** Solve the equation $3(x - 2) = 4(x + 1)$ with a justification for each step.

*26. (34) Three vertices of parallelogram $ABCD$ are $A(-1, 5)$, $B(4, 5)$ and $C(3, 2)$. Find the coordinates of D.

Use the diagram to find the following measures.

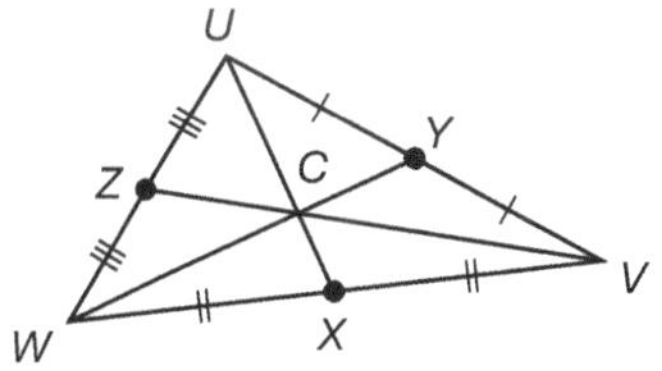

27. (32) Given that $CX = 18$, determine the length of $\overline{UX}$.

28. (32) Given that $ZV = 72$, determine the length of $\overline{ZC}$.

29. (20) **Algebra** Consider the following statement.

If two positive numbers are less than 1, then their product is positive and less than 1.

a. Rewrite the statement using inequalities.

b. State the converse and biconditional of your statement from part **a**. Is the biconditional true? Explain why or why not.

*30. (33) **Algebra** Determine the value of x. Write your answer in simplified radical form.

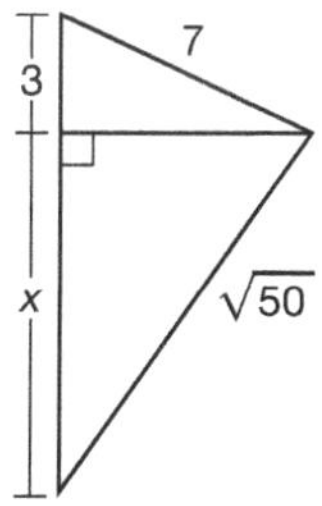

Name ______________________ Date __________ Class __________

Finding Arc Lengths and Areas of Sectors

LESSON 35

* **1.** (35) **Write** Explain how the formula for arc length is similar to the formula for the area of a circle.

* **2.** (32) **Model** Find the centroid of $\triangle HIJ$ with vertices at $H(-6, 10)$, $I(-4, 2)$, and $J(-14, 6)$.

3. (25) Given that $\triangle BCD \cong \triangle EFG$, write the six congruence statements for the triangles.

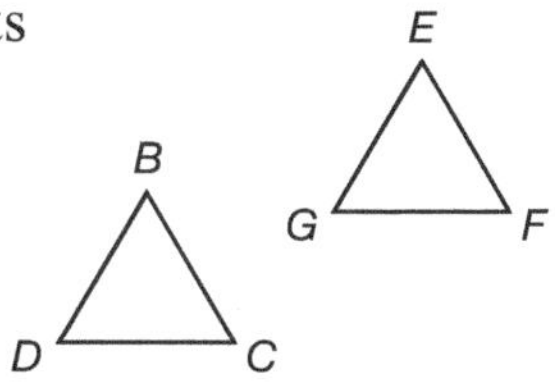

4. (21) **Analyze** What conclusion can be drawn from these statements?

If my computer is not working properly, then I will restart it.
My computer is not working properly.

* **5.** (34) Three vertices of parallelogram $HIJK$ are $H(0, 10)$, $I(2, 10)$, and $K(-2, 0)$. Find the coordinates of J.

6. (18) **Visual Arts** An artist is making a motif design using the two triangles shown. The measurements must be exact in order to make the repeating pattern of the motif. What are the measurements of x, y, and z?

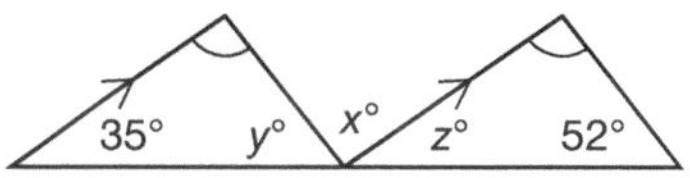

7. (26) **Multiple Choice** A minor arc has a measure of $(5x + 20)°$. Its corresponding major arc has a measure of $(8x - 50)°$. What is the correct value of x?

A 23.3 **B** 30
C 170 **D** 190

8. (20) **a.** State the converse of the following statement,
If a triangle is obtuse, then it has exactly two acute angles.

b. Determine whether the statement is true, and whether its converse is true.

* **9.** (34) $QRST$ is a parallelogram. Find the length of the diagonals $\overline{TR}$ and $\overline{QS}$.

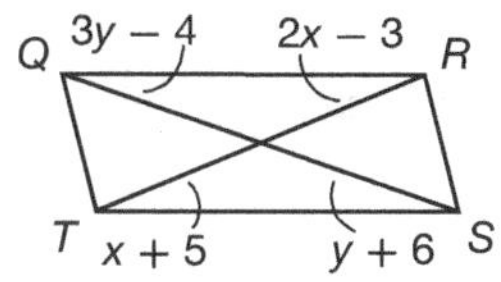

10. (Inv 3) **Carpentry** Margot is making a coffee table with a top in the shape of a regular hexagon. What measure should she make each angle of the table top?

11. (24) **Algebra** Solve the equation $x + 3 = \frac{4x + 5}{2}$, and justify each step.

12. (29) Find the unknown length in the triangle. Are these side lengths a Pythagorean triple?

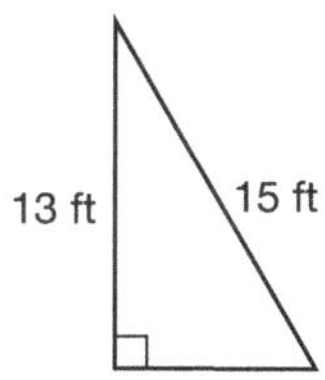

13. (26) Prove Theorem 26-1: In the same or congruent circles, congruent arcs have congruent central angles.
Given: $\overset{\frown}{JK} \cong \overset{\frown}{HI}$
Prove: $\angle 1 \cong \angle 2$

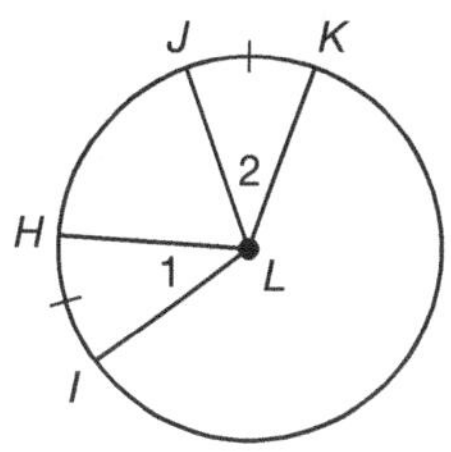

14. (33) The side lengths of a triangle are $4\sqrt{2}$, $4\sqrt{3}$, and 9. Is it a right triangle?

15. (22) **Calendars** A page of a calendar is 10 inches by $12\frac{1}{4}$ inches. The page is divided into 5 rows of 7 congruent boxes. What is the area of each of these boxes?

16. (27) Write a two-column proof.
Given: $\angle KLM$ and $\angle NML$ are right angles and $\angle 2 \cong \angle 3$.
Prove: $\angle 1 \cong \angle 4$

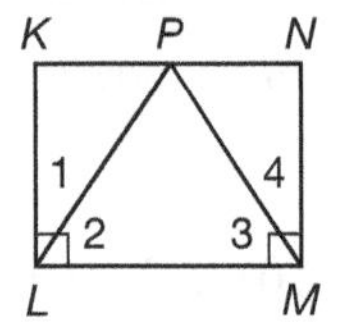

***17.** (35) **Error Analysis** Two students tried to find the area of the shaded region in the circle shown. Which solution is incorrect? Explain where the error was made.

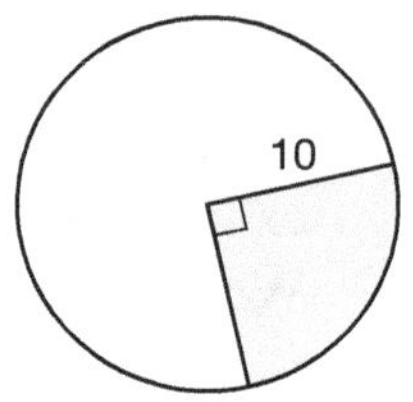

Marc	**Stephanie**
$A = 2\pi r\left(\frac{m^\circ}{360^\circ}\right)$	$A = \pi r^2\left(\frac{m^\circ}{360^\circ}\right)$
$A = 2\pi(10)\left(\frac{90^\circ}{360^\circ}\right)$	$A = \pi(10)^2\left(\frac{90^\circ}{360^\circ}\right)$
$A = 5\pi$	$A = 25\pi$
$A \approx 15.71$	$A \approx 78.54$

18. (21) What conclusion can be drawn from these statements?
If I lose my driver's license, then I need to go get a new one.
If I need to go get a new driver's license, then I will have to go to the DMV.

***19.** (35) **Games** D.J. is designing a spinner for a game. He wants the spinner to have a $\frac{3}{8}$ probability of landing on a particular sector. What size arc should he assign to this sector?

***20.** (30) These triangles are congruent. What is the perimeter of $\triangle LMN$?

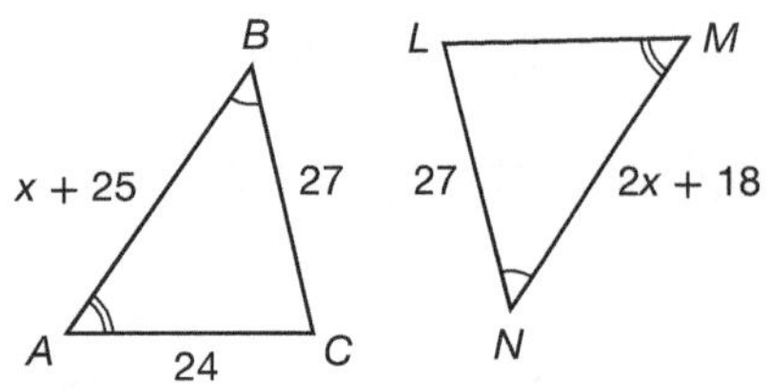

21. (20) State the disjunction of the statements, "A triangle is acute," and "A triangle has exactly two acute angles." Is the disjunction true or false?

*22. **Multi-Step** The major arc of a circle measures 240° and has a length of 18 centimeters. What is the length of the minor arc?
(35)

23. **Justify** Alejandro made the conjecture, "For every integer x, $x^2 + 2x - 1$ is divisible by 2." Is the conjecture true of false? If it is false, provide a counterexample.
(14)

24. Given that $\triangle QSR \cong \triangle TUV$, find the area of each triangle.
(30)

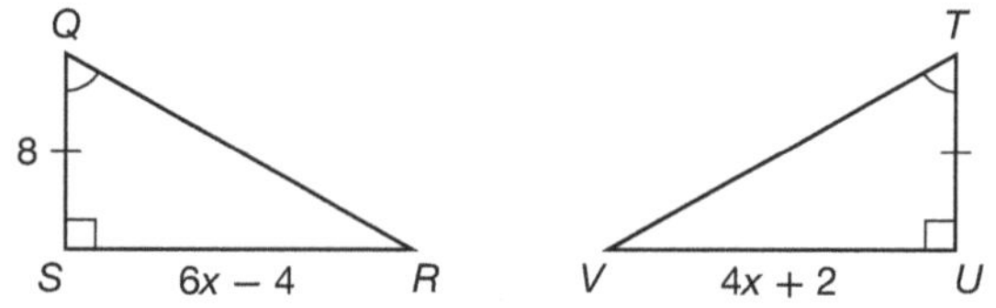

25. Write the converse of the following statement.
(17)

If a triangle is a right triangle, then it has two acute angles.

*26. **Algebra** Find the radius of a circle with an arc length of 40 centimeters and an arc measure of 60°.
(35)

*27. Is $\triangle EFG$ an obtuse, acute, or a right triangle?
(33)

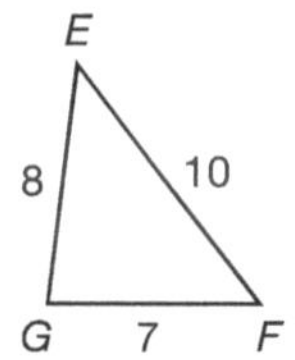

28. **Verify** For a circle with a radius of 7 inches, Vanessa calculated the area to be about 43.98 square inches. Is Vanessa's calculation accurate? If not, what is the actual area of the circle to the nearest hundredth?
(23)

29. Give two Pythagorean triples that are related to the triple (5, 12, 13).
(29)

30. *ABCD* is a parallelogram. Find the measure of each angle.
(34)

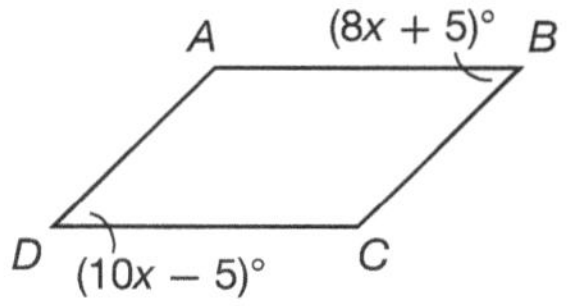

Name ______________________ Date __________ Class __________

Right Triangle Congruence Theorems

LESSON **36**

* **1.** Using the diagram, prove that $\triangle OPQ \cong \triangle TRS$. Name any theorems used.
(36)

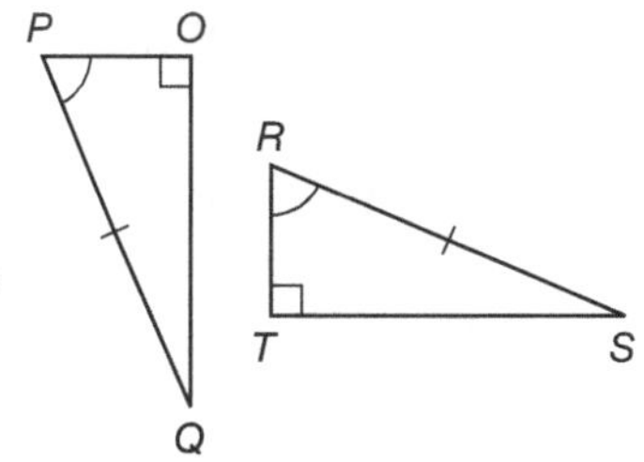

2. **Generalize** If $\widehat{AB}$, $\widehat{BC}$, and $\widehat{CD}$ are non-overlapping adjacent arcs, what is an expression for the measure of $\widehat{AD}$?
(26)

3. **Arts and Crafts** The diagram shows a square piece of paper that is folded to make a kite. The kite is composed of four triangles. Prove that the triangles labeled 1 and 2 are congruent.
(19, 36)

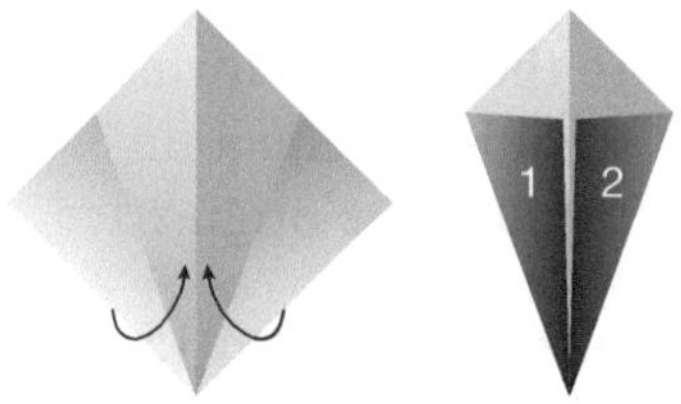

* **4.** **Error Analysis** Greta is calculating the area of a sector of a circle with a diameter of 5. The sector covers 24°. What error has she made?
(35)

$$\left(\frac{24°}{360°}\right)\pi(5)^2 = \left(\frac{1}{15}\right)(\pi)(25)$$

$$\frac{5}{3}\pi \approx 5.24$$

5. In a right triangle, the length of one leg is 1.2 yards and the length of the hypotenuse is 1.3 yards. What is the length of the third side?
(29)

* **6.** Use the Leg-Leg Congruence Theorem to prove that $\triangle JKL \cong \triangle MNO$.
(36)

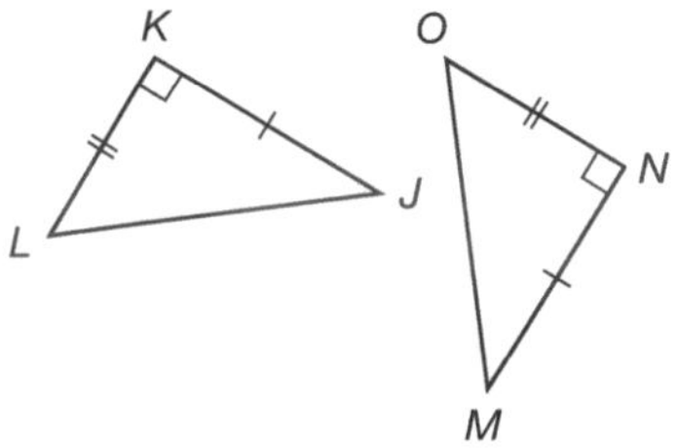

7. Calculate the circumference of the circle to the nearest centimeter.
(26)

* **8.** **a.** Write the formula for the area of a trapezoid.
(22)
b. Transform the formula to solve for height.

9. Write a paragraph proof showing that if point X is equidistant from points A and B in the triangle shown, then it lies along the perpendicular bisector of $\overline{AB}$.
(31)
Hint: Draw a line through X *that is perpendicular to* $\overline{\text{AB}}$ *at* Y.

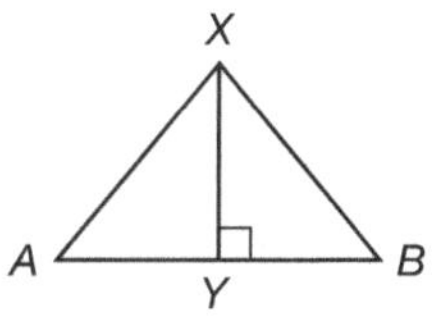

10. Calculate the area of the circle shown to the nearest hundredth.
(23)

* **11.** **Catering** The catering service is dividing a small pizza, with a diameter of 8 inches, into four slices. What is the area of each slice, to the nearest tenth?
(35)

12. **Algebra** If $m\widehat{AB} = (5x + 11)°$ and $m\widehat{CD} = (7x - 9)°$, what is the value of x if $\widehat{AB}$ and $\widehat{CD}$ are congruent?
(26)

13. Using information given in the diagram, determine the area of each triangle.
(30)

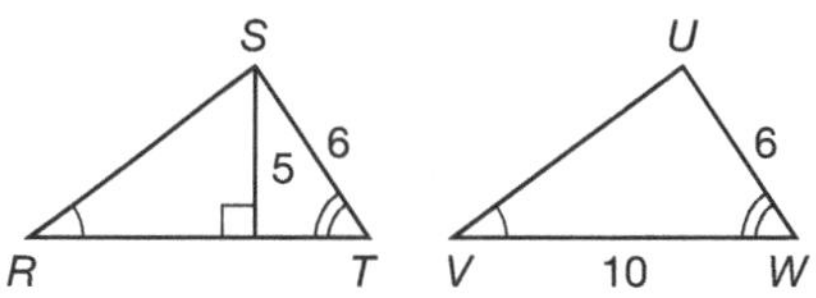

Right Triangle Congruence Theorems

LESSON 36

14. (18) **Multiple Choice** Which statement about an equiangular triangle is not true?

A Each pair of interior angles is complementary.

B The sum of the interior angle measures is 180°.

C Each exterior angle measures 120°.

D Each interior angle measures 60°.

15. (34) Find the value of h in parallelogram $STUV$.

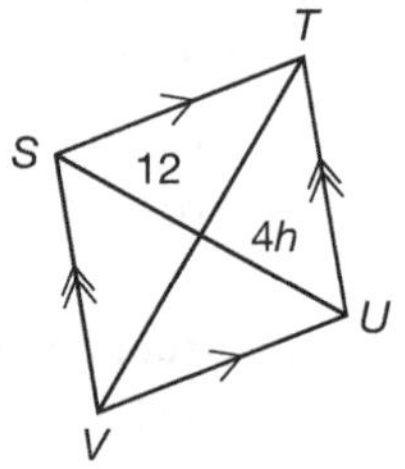

***16.** (32) In the triangle formed by the points (2, 2), (4, 0), and the origin, what is the equation of the line containing the median passing through the origin?

17. (25) In $\triangle ABC$, $AB = 15$, $BC = 20$, and $AC = 25$. In $\triangle DEF$, $DE = 25$, $EF = 15$, and $DF = 20$. Write the congruency statement for the triangles.

***18.** (35) What is the arc measure of one-sixth of a circle? What is the area of one-sixth of a circle that has a radius of 12, in terms of π?

19. (30) In the diagram given, prove that $\triangle ABE \cong \triangle CDE$.

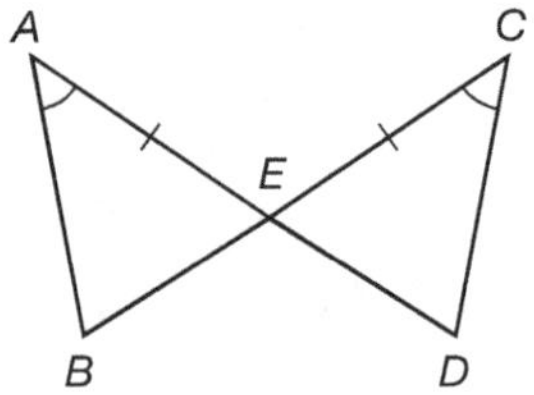

20. (25) **Write** If in $\triangle JKL$, $JK = 9$, $KL = 11$, and $JL = 12$, and in $\triangle PQR$, $PQ = 9$, $QR = 11$, and $PR = 11$, explain why $\triangle JKL$ and $\triangle PQR$ are not congruent.

***21.** (27) Complete the following proof showing that if a point in the interior of an angle is equidistant from the sides of the angle, then it is on the bisector of the angle.

Given: $\overline{VX} \perp \overline{YX}$, $\overline{VZ} \perp \overline{YZ}$, $VX = VZ$

Prove: V is on the bisector of $\angle XYZ$.

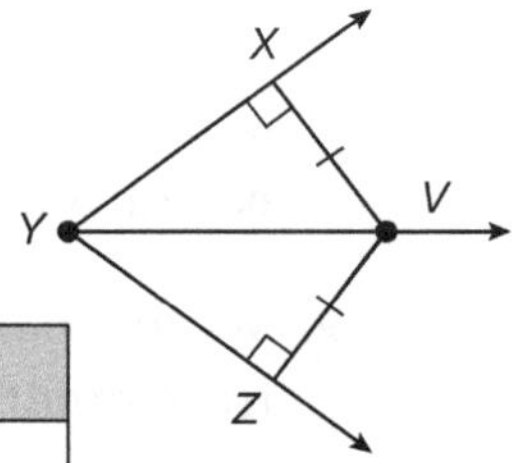

Statements	Reasons
1. $\overline{VX} \perp \overline{YX}$, $\overline{VZ} \perp \overline{YZ}$, $VX = VZ$	1. Given
2.	2. Definition of perpendicular
3.	3. Reflexive Property
4. $\triangle YXV \cong \triangle YZV$	4.
5. $\angle XYV \cong \angle ZYV$	5.
6. $\overrightarrow{YV}$ bisects $\angle XYZ$	6. Definition of angle bisector

22. (34) Find the value of x in the parallelogram.

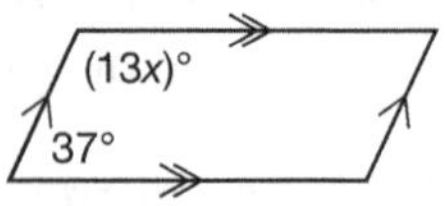

23. (33) **Gardening** A gardener tried to plant a garden in the shape of a right triangle. The longest side was 14 feet long and the two shorter sides were 5 feet and 13 feet long, respectively. Did the gardener succeed in making the garden a right triangle? If not, what kind of triangle describes the shape of the garden?

24. (28) **Write** Use the SAS Congruence Theorem to show that a diagonal of a square divides the square into two congruent triangles.

25. (28) For what values of x are these two triangles congruent?

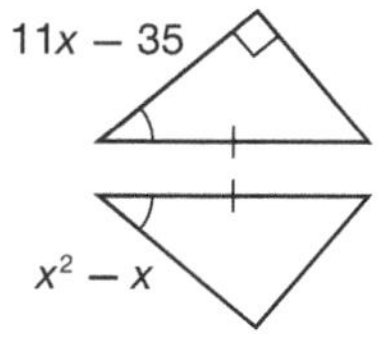

26. (20) **Biology** Consider the following statements.

An organism is an animal.
An organism has leaves.

a. Make a truth table for the disjunction of these statements.
b. Explain why the disjunction is false.

***27.** (36) Use the Leg-Angle Congruence Theorem to prove that $\triangle JKL \cong \triangle MNO$.

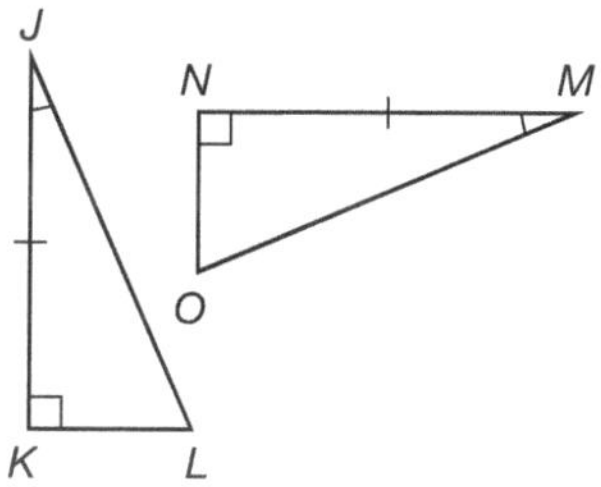

28. (33) **Verify** Naomi measures the sides of a triangle as 5, 8, and 9 units, respectively, and declares the triangle to be acute. Is she correct? How do you know?

***29.** (27, 36) **Analyze** Copy and complete this two-column proof of the LA Congruence Theorem.

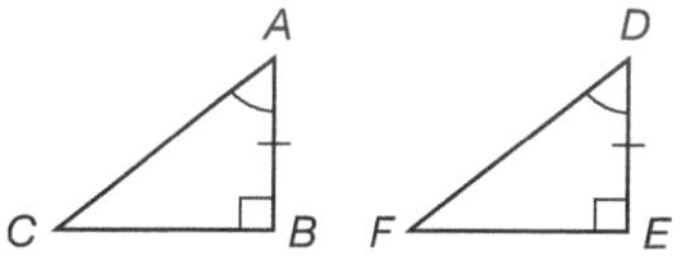

Statements	Reasons
1. $\triangle ABC$ and $\triangle DEF$ are right triangles	1. Given
2.	2. Given
3. $\angle A \cong \angle D$	3.
4. $\angle B$ and $\angle E$ are right angles	4.
5.	5.
6. $\triangle ABC \cong \triangle DEF$	6.

30. (32) **Write** Explain why only two altitudes of a triangle need to be drawn to find the orthocenter of the triangle.

Writing Equations of Parallel and Perpendicular Lines

LESSON 37

1. (29) **Analyze** Find the unknown length in the triangle shown. Do the side lengths form a Pythagorean triple?

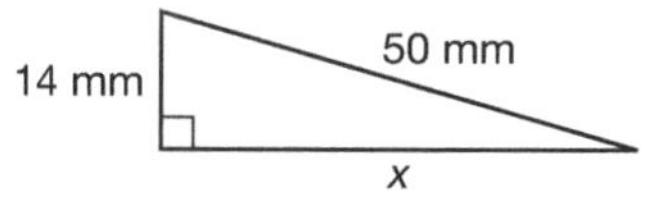

2. (35) What is the area of a 30° sector of a circle with a radius of 9 miles? Express your answer in terms of π.

3. (21) Kyle says that if Marcy goes to the party, then he will go to the party. Marcy said she goes to every party. Assuming both statements are true, will Kyle go to the party?

4. (34) Find the value of a and b in the rhombus $WXYZ$ at right.

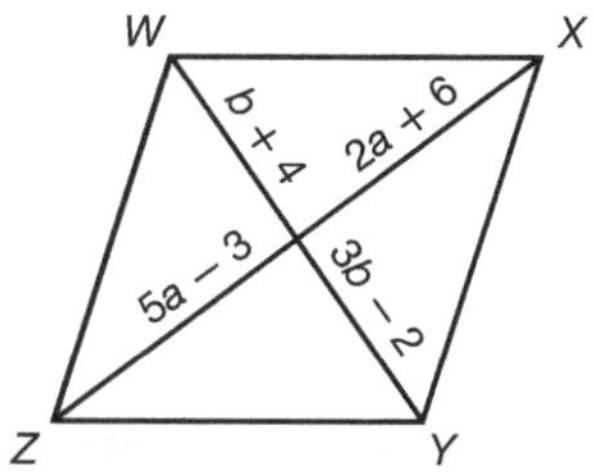

***5.** (37) Write the equation of the line through (3, 7) that is perpendicular to $y = 3x - 4$.

6. (Inv 3) **Generalize** Can the sum of the central angles for any convex polygon be determined? Explain.

7. (23) **Basketball** The rim of the basket in a basketball court encloses a circle with an area of about 0.16 square meters. What is the diameter of the basket, to the nearest hundredth of a meter?

8. (22) Find the area of the parallelogram at right.

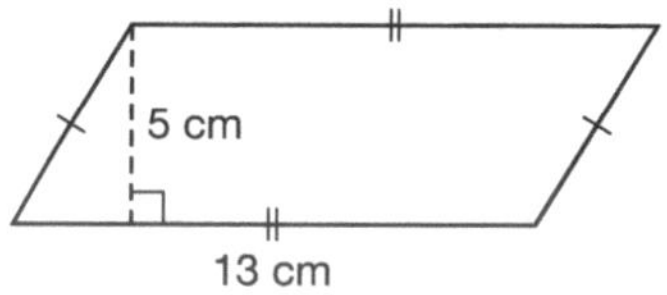

9. (32) Find the orthocenter of a triangle with vertices at (−3, 0), (3, 0), and (−1, 4).

***10.** (37) **Algebra** The equations of two parallel lines are $y = \frac{3}{k}x + 14$ and $y = \frac{h}{2}x + 3$. Find the values of k and h.

11. (14) Consider the following conjecture.

If a, b, *and* c *are lines in a plane, then they divide the plane into seven regions.*

a. What is the hypothesis of the conjecture? What is its conclusion?

b. Find a counterexample to the conjecture.

***12.** (36) Which congruence theorem applies to these triangles?

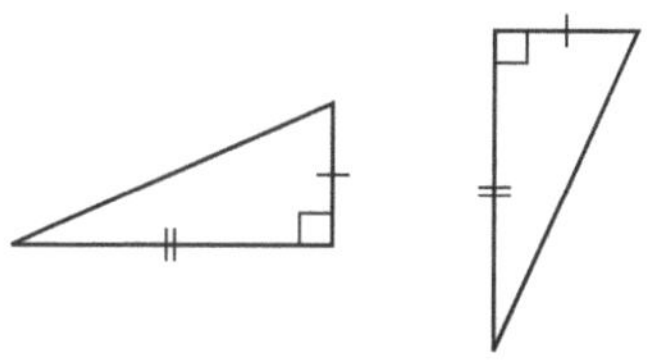

Writing Equations of Parallel and Perpendicular Lines

LESSON 37

***13.** (27, 36) Complete this two-column proof of the LL Right Triangle Congruence Theorem: If two legs of a right triangle are congruent to the two legs of another right triangle, then the triangles are congruent.
Given: $\overline{AB} \cong \overline{DE}$, $\overline{BC} \cong \overline{EF}$, $\triangle ABC$ and $\triangle DEF$ are right triangles.**Prove:** $\triangle ABC \cong \triangle DEF$

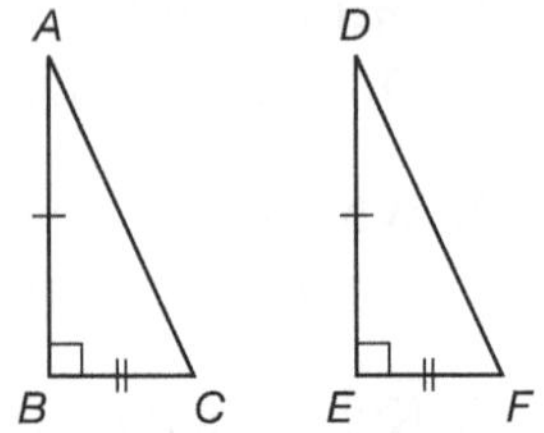

Statements	Reasons
1. $\overline{AB} \cong \overline{DE}$, $\overline{BC} \cong \overline{EF}$	1. Given
2.	2. Definition of right triangle
3. $\angle B \cong \angle E$	3.
4. $\triangle ABC \cong \triangle DEF$	4.

Complete the following statements:

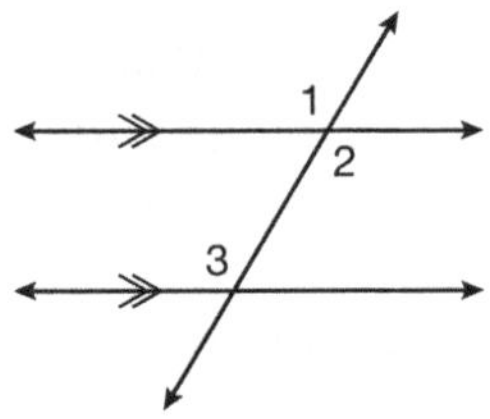

14. (Inv 1) Angle 1 is congruent to $\angle 2$ by the ____________________.

15. (Inv 1) Since $\angle 1$ is congruent to $\angle 2$, and $\angle 2$ is congruent to $\angle 3$ by the Alternate Interior Angles Theorem, by the ____________________________, $\angle 1$ is congruent to $\angle 3$.

***16.** (37) **Error Analysis** A student says the equation of a line perpendicular to $y = \frac{12}{13}x + \frac{47}{13}$ is $y = \frac{13}{12}x + \frac{47}{13}$. Explain the student's error.

***17.** (36) **Optics** In this optical diagram, $\triangle ABC$ and $\triangle DBC$ are congruent. Explain why.

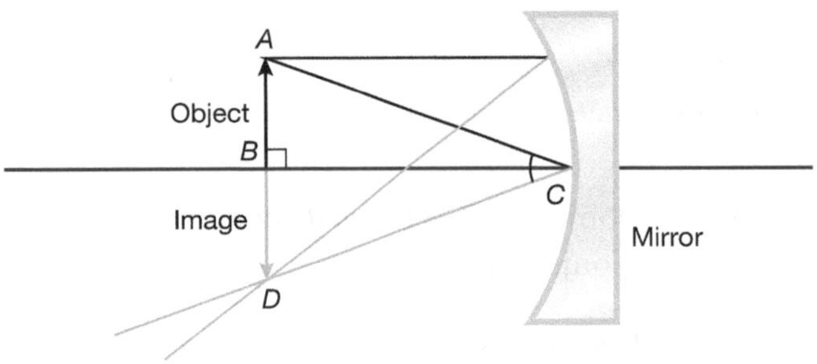

18. (32) In $\triangle HIJ$, $HE = 12$ and $GI = 4.6$. Find GF and GE.

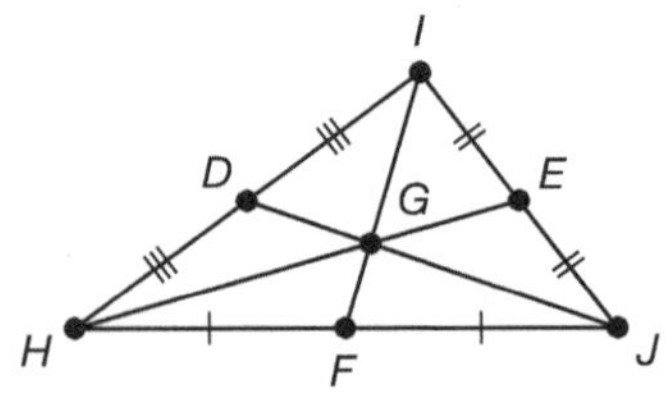

19. (29) **Multiple Choice** Which of the following is a Pythagorean triple?
A (6, 9, 10) **B** (7, 24, 25)
C (3, 6, 9) **D** (1, 2, 3)

20. (35) The radius of $\odot J$ measures 8 inches. Points K and L lie on $\odot J$. If the length of $\widehat{KL}$ is 1.2 inches, what is the measure of $\widehat{KL}$ to the nearest tenth?

21. (19) **Design** A wind power energy company's logo is made up of three parallelograms as shown. Copy the logo and indicate with tick marks all pairs or sets of parallel sides.

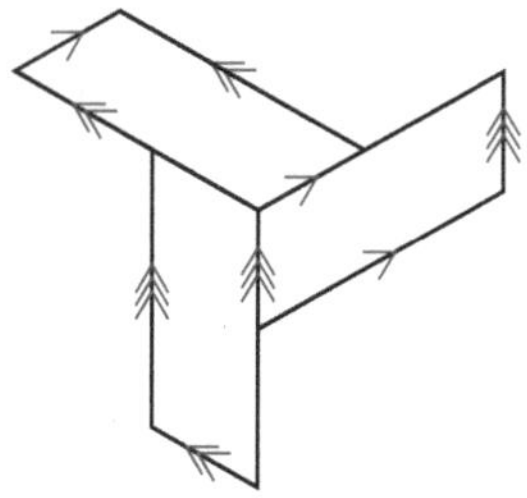

22. (33) Parallelogram $EFGH$ has adjacent side lengths of 13 and 17 units. One of its diagonals is 20 units long. Could the parallelogram be a rectangle?

23. (26) **Generalize** If $\widehat{AC}$ is a minor arc, and $\widehat{AB}$ and $\widehat{BC}$ are non-overlapping adjacent arcs, what is an expression for the measure of the major arc associated with $\widehat{AC}$ in terms of $\widehat{AB}$ and $\widehat{BC}$?

24. (34) In the diagram, $PQRS$ is a parallelogram. Find the value of x and y.

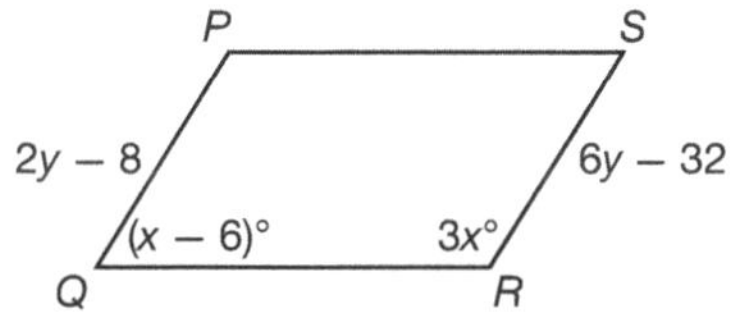

25. (Inv 3) **Design** Shen is drawing a Canadian one-dollar coin, which is a regular 11-sided polygon. Approximately what size should he make each angle?

***26.** (37) **Highways** The interstate system consists of divided highways with parallel lanes of traffic. Suppose the path of the eastbound lanes is modeled by $y = \frac{4}{3}x$, and the highway is intersected by a bridge that is perpendicular to the highway. Write equations to model both the path of the westbound lanes and the path of the bridge.

27. (34) **Coordinate Geometry** Parallelogram $JKLM$ on the coordinate plane has vertices at $J(-1, 2)$, $K(5, 2)$ and $L(2, 6)$. Where is the fourth vertex of $JKLM$ located?

***28.** (36) Which congruence theorem applies to these triangles?

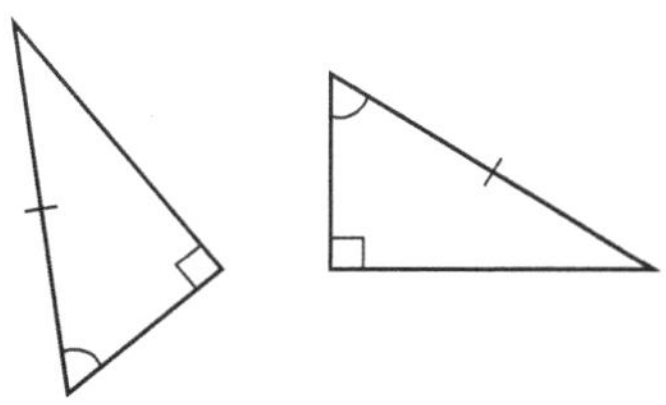

29. (33) **Formulate** In any isosceles right triangle, what is the ratio of the length of the hypotenuse to the length of a leg? Would a higher ratio indicate that the triangle is acute or obtuse?

30. (22) Find the area of the figure at right.

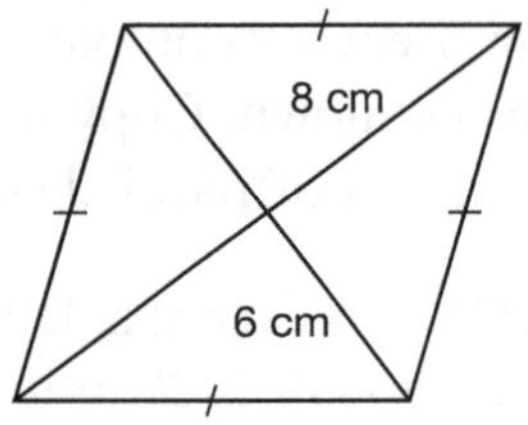

Name ______________________ Date __________ Class __________

Perpendicular and Angle Bisectors of Triangles

LESSON 38

1. (33) Classify the following triangles as acute, obtuse, or right, based on the three side lengths given.

a. 5, 9, 12

b. 6, 17, 17.5

c. 9, 12, 15

*** 2.** (38) **Fire Stations** Three towns want to build a fire station that can serve them all. Explain how the towns might go about finding the optimal location for the fire station.

3. (29) **Analyze** Find the unknown length in the triangle. Do the side lengths form a Pythagorean triple?

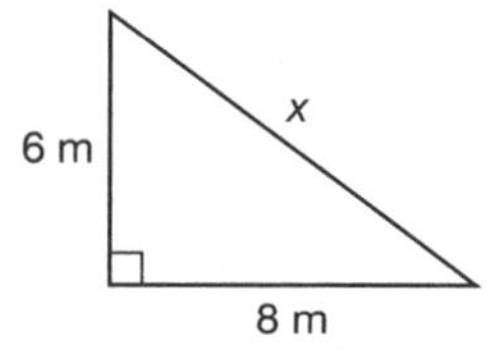

4. (7) **Algebra** Test the conjecture that the sum of the first n squares is given by the expression $\frac{1}{6}n(n + 1)(2n + 1)$.

5. (24) Letty is solving the equation $3x - 4 = 21$. Which property of equality should she use first?

6. (28) What is the included side of $\angle QRS$ and $\angle QRT$?

*** 7.** (37) **Predict** If line x is parallel to line y and line y is perpendicular to line z, describe the relationship between lines x and z.

8. (23) **Driving** A traffic circle is a round intersection. The first one built in the United States is the Columbus Circle in New York City, and has a circular monument in the center covering approximately 148,000 square feet. What is the radius of the monument, to the nearest hundredth?

*** 9.** (Inv 3) Determine the sum of the measures of the angles in the polygon shown at right.

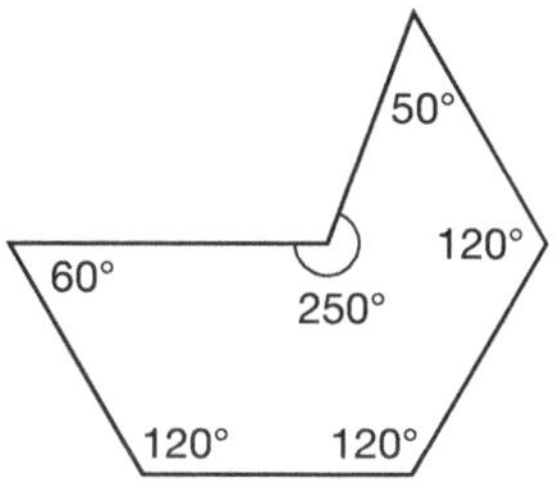

10. (25) **Generalize** If $\triangle LMN \cong \triangle DEF$, what can you determine about the heights of the triangles as measured from side $\overline{LM}$ and from side $\overline{DE}$, respectively?

11. (21) **Verify** Hamid reasoned, "All safety glasses protect your eyes. Sunglasses protect your eyes. Therefore, all sunglasses are safety glasses." What is wrong with Hamid's conclusion?

***12.** (37) Find the line parallel to $y = -\frac{1}{2}x - 2$ that passes through the origin.

***13.** (38) In the diagram at right, P is the incenter of $\triangle QRS$. Find PT.

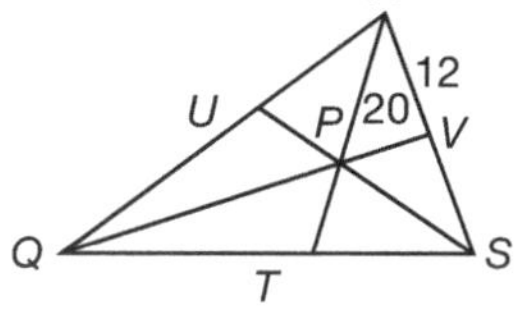

Perpendicular and Angle Bisectors of Triangles

LESSON 38

14. **Baking** Louis is baking a cake for a party that celebrates the birthdays of three different people. He wants to use three different kinds of frosting, making three equal sections on the top of the round cake, each with a person's name on it. If the cake has a radius of 5 inches, what is the surface area of each wedge of the cake that Louis needs to cover with frosting, to the nearest hundredth?
(35)

*15. **Error Analysis** Mira states that she can use the Leg-Angle Congruence Theorem to prove these triangles congruent. Is she correct about the triangles being congruent? Is her justification correct? Explain.
(36)

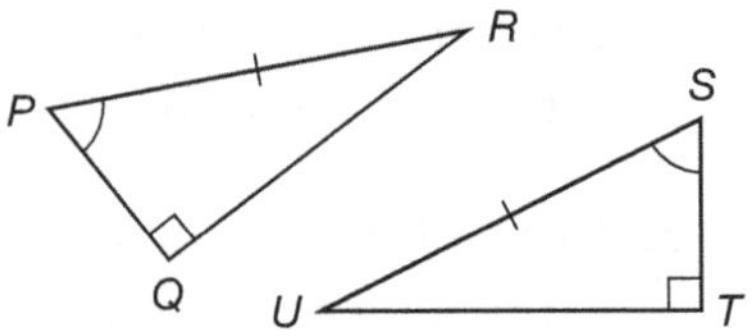

*16. **Construction** A contractor wants to cut a circular piece of stone out of a scrap piece that is shaped like a right triangle. She wants the circle to be as large as possible. How should she determine how to cut the piece of stone in order to get the largest possible circle out of it? Explain your reasoning and support your answer with a drawing.
(38)

17. **Coordinate Geometry** Find the centroid of a triangle with vertices at (1, 4), (5, 6), and (5, 0).
(32)

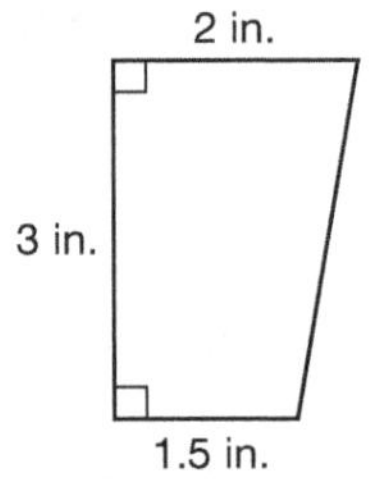

18. What is the area of the trapezoid in the diagram?
(22)

19. **Analyze** Helen wrote the following proof:
(24)

Statements	Reasons
1. $x = y$	1. Given
2. $x^2 = xy$	2. Multiplication Property of Equality
3. $x^2 - y^2 = xy - y^2$	3. Subtraction Property of Equality
4. $(x - y)(x + y) = y(x - y)$	4. Factor.
5. $\frac{(x - y)(x + y)}{(x - y)} = \frac{y(x - y)}{(x - y)}$	5. Division Property of Equality
6. $x + y = y$	6. Simplify.
7. $x + y - y = y - y$	7. Subtraction Property of Equality
8. $x = 0$	8. Simplify.

Is there something wrong with Helen's proof? If so, which step is wrong and why?

20. **Multiple Choice** Which statement is *not* true of a rhombus?
(34)
A Consecutive angles are supplementary.
B The diagonals bisect each other.
C Opposite angles are complementary.
D All sides are congruent.

Perpendicular and Angle Bisectors of Triangles

LESSON 38

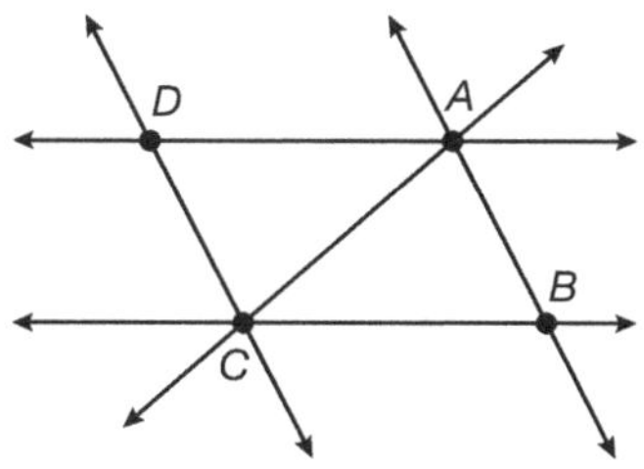

21. *(31)* In the diagram, $\overline{AD} \parallel \overline{BC}$ and $\overline{DC} \parallel \overline{AB}$. Prove that $\triangle ACB \cong \triangle CAD$ using a flowchart or paragraph proof.

22. *(29)* **Home Maintenance** A window washer needs the top of his ladder to rest against the bottom of a window that is 25 feet above the ground. However, the shrubs against the house require him to place the ladder 10 feet away from the house. Assuming that the ground and house meet at right angles, what length of ladder will he need, to the nearest foot?

***23.** *(38)* Using the diagram find FG if G is the incenter of $\triangle HIJ$.

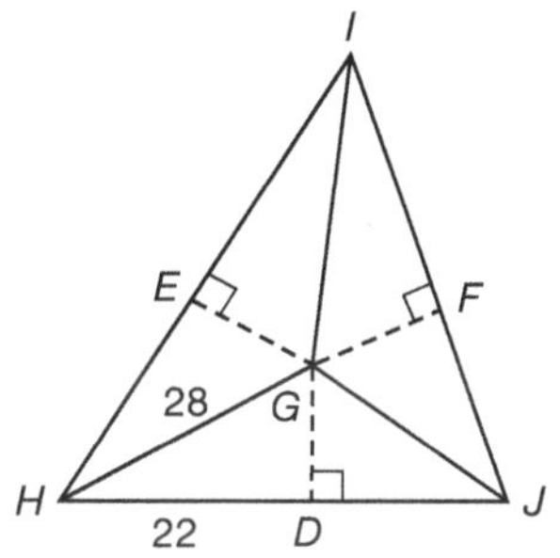

24. *(20)* In the city of Logica, downtown buses are blue and suburban buses are green. State the conjunction of the two statements, "A bus is a downtown bus," and "A bus is green." Is the conjunction true or false?

25. *(29)* Find the unknown length of the side in the triangle.

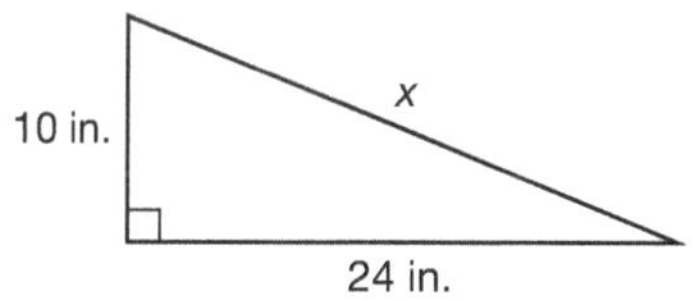

26. *(35)* In $\odot C$, $\overset{\frown}{AB}$ measures 44° and the radius AC is 5 centimeters. What is the area of sector ACB, to the nearest hundredth?

***27.** *(37)* Find the line parallel to $y = \frac{3}{2}x + \frac{1}{2}$ that passes through the point (3, 4).

***28.** *(36)* In $\triangle JKL$ and $\triangle PQR$, $\angle J$ and $\angle P$ are right angles, $\overline{KL} \cong \overline{QR}$, and $\angle Q \cong \angle K$. Use the Hypotenuse-Angle Congruence Theorem to prove that $\triangle JKL \cong \triangle PQR$.

29. *(30)* Prove that if $m\angle ABC = m\angle ACB$, then $AB = AC$. *Hint: Prove* $\triangle ABC \cong \triangle ACB$.

30. *(34)* Find the value of x and y in parallelogram $KLMN$.

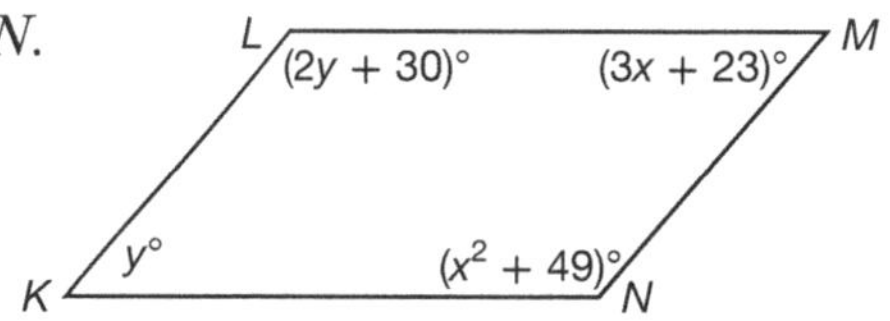

Name ________________________ Date __________ Class __________

Inequalities in a Triangle

LESSON 39

1. In $\triangle GHJ$ and $\triangle KLM$, it is given that $\angle G$ and $\angle K$ are right angles, $\overline{GH} \cong \overline{KL}$, and $\angle H \cong \angle L$. Prove that $\triangle GHJ \cong \triangle KLM$.
(36)

*2. Write the side lengths of $\triangle ABC$ in order from least to greatest.
(39)

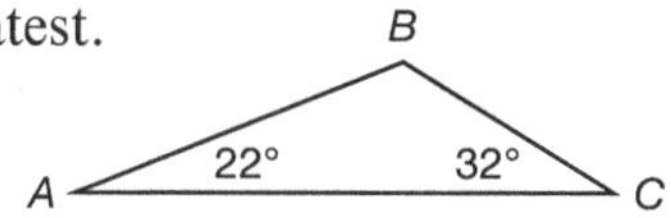

3. **Algebra** An isosceles right triangle has a hypotenuse of 10 inches. What is the length of each leg, to the nearest tenth of an inch?
(29)

4. **Security** To protect a circular area of a park, cameras are placed on a lamppost in the center of the area. If each camera can observe an arc measure of 75°, how many cameras are needed to observe the entire area around the lamppost?
(26)

5. **Model** Draw a right triangle and sketch the altitude of each vertex. Where is the orthocenter of the triangle located? Will the orthocenter be located in the same place on every right triangle?
(32)

*6. **Multiple Choice** Which group of line segment lengths can be used to form a triangle?
(39)
A 4, 4, 9 **B** 3, 7, 12
C 1, 5, 7 **D** 3, 4, 6

*7. **Analyze** Explain whether or not it is possible to construct a triangle with side lengths of 34 inches, 14 inches, and 51 inches.
(39)

8. If rectangle *STUV* has an area of 27 square units, and $ST = 3(TU)$, find the length of each side of *STUV*.
(34)

9. **Error Analysis** On $\overline{AD}$, B is the midpoint of $\overline{AC}$ and C is the midpoint of $\overline{BD}$. The paragraph proof below was written to prove that $AB = CD$. Identify the mistake in the proof.
(31)

Since B *is the midpoint of* $\overline{\text{AC}}$, AB = BC *by the definition of midpoints. Since* C *is the midpoint of* $\overline{\text{BD}}$, BC = CD *by the definition of midpoints. By the Reflexive Property,* AB = CD.

*10. **Nautical Maps** Three lighthouses surround a harbor, as shown in the drawing. The lighthouses are equidistant from a buoy in the harbor. Copy the diagram and draw the location of the buoy based on the locations of the lighthouses.
(38)

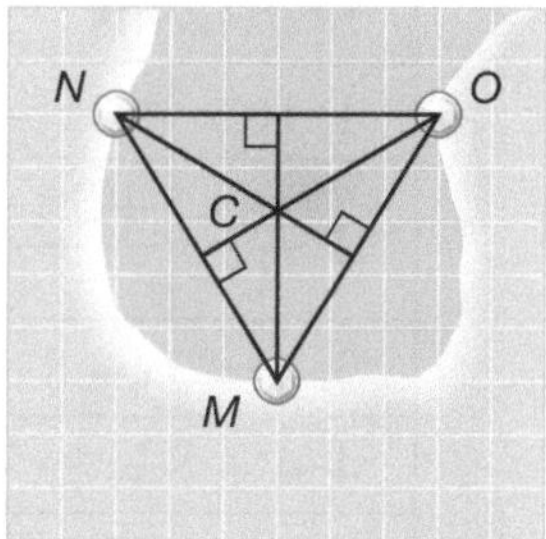

11. **Engineering** A bridge uses several girder sections that are right triangles. Each section is made so that its legs are 10 feet and 12.5 feet long, respectively. Explain why the sections are congruent to each other.
(36)

12. **Decorating** Kirsten is buying carpet for a rectangular room that is 11 feet by 13 feet. How many square feet of carpet does she need?
(22)

13. Find the centroid of a triangle with vertices at (0, −2), (0, −6), and (2, −4).
(32)

14. What is the included angle of $\overrightarrow{TS}$ and $\overrightarrow{TR}$?
(28)

***15.** **Algebra** Using the diagram at right, find MN in terms of x if $NO = 2$, $OP = 4x$, and $MP = x + 7$.
(38)

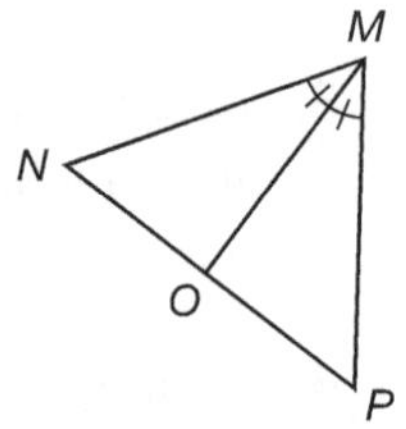

***16.** **Multiple Choice** Which expression represents two parallel lines?
(37)

A $y = 2x + 3, y = -2x + 3$ **B** $y = -2x + 4, y = -6 - 2x$

C $y = \frac{1}{2}x + 3, y = -2x - 3$ **D** $y = 3x + 7, \frac{1}{3}y = -x - 7$

17. **Urban Development** A development company plans to build three square single-story buildings that completely surround a triangular park. Buildings A and B will be situated at right angles to each other and have an area of 1296 square feet and 2500 square feet, respectively. What will be the area of building C? Explain.
(Inv 2)

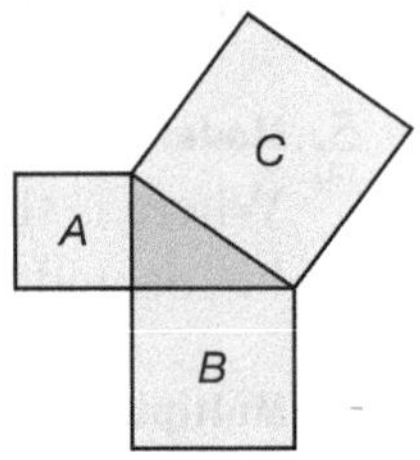

***18.** Using the diagram, P is the incenter of $\triangle QRS$. Find PU.
(38)

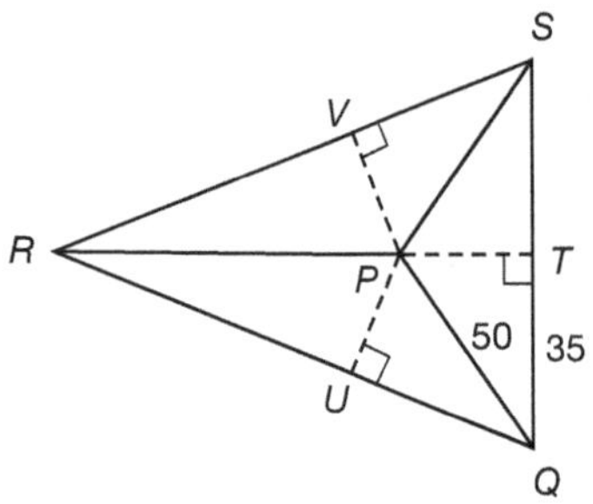

19. **Write** Explain why the size of each central angle in a regular polygon decreases as the number of sides increases.
(Inv 3)

20. **Justify** Provide a justification for each step of the proof. The first one is done for you.
(24)

Statements	Reasons
1. $16 = 4(3x - 8)$	1. Given
2. $\frac{16}{4} = \frac{4(3x - 8)}{4}$	2.
3. $4 = 3x - 8$	3.
4. $4 + 8 = 3x - 8 + 8$	4.
5. $12 = 3x$	5.
6. $\frac{12}{3} = \frac{3x}{3}$	6.
7. $4 = x$	7.
8. $x = 4$	8.

*21. Find the line parallel to $y = 2x + 3$ that passes through the point $(-1, -1)$.
(37)

22. Use an inequality to indicate the minimum length of the longest side, x, of $\triangle ABC$ if the two shorter sides of the triangle measure 8 and 7 and $\triangle ABC$ is obtuse.
(33)

23. Calculate the area of sector QRS in the diagram to the nearest hundredth of a centimeter.
(35)

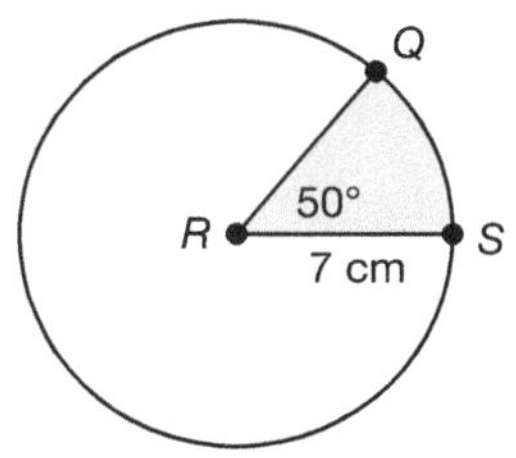

24. Davindra, who is 15 years old, is one year older than twice the age of her younger sister, Preetha. Find the age of Preetha and justify each step.
(24)

25. In the diagram, $\overline{AB} \parallel \overline{DE}$. Write a paragraph to prove that $m\angle CAB + m\angle ACB = m\angle DEF$.
(31)

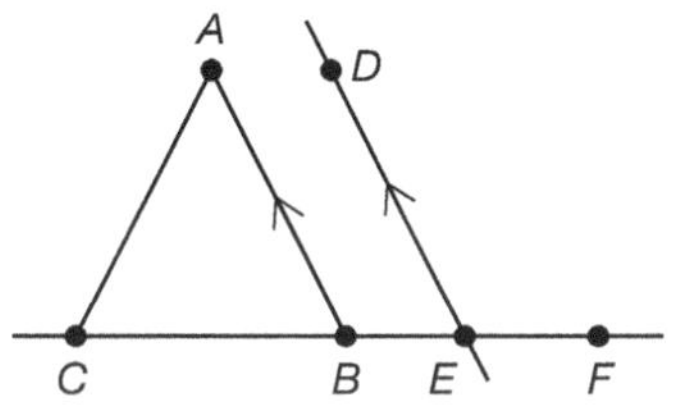

26. A circle with a radius of 6 meters has an arc that measures 35°. If this arc and its associated sector are completely removed from the circle, what is the length of the major arc that remains, to the nearest tenth of a meter?
(35)

27. Classify the following triangles as acute, obtuse, or right, based on the three side lengths given.
(33)

a. 4, 4, $\sqrt{34}$

b. 6, 5, 8

c. 10, 24, 26

*28. **Construction** An important part of many structures is the structural support truss, a series of interlocking metal rods that form triangles, which gives the structure its rigidity. The diagram below shows a section of a support truss for a geodesic dome. What is the shortest length of metal used in this section of a geodesic dome structural support truss?
(39)

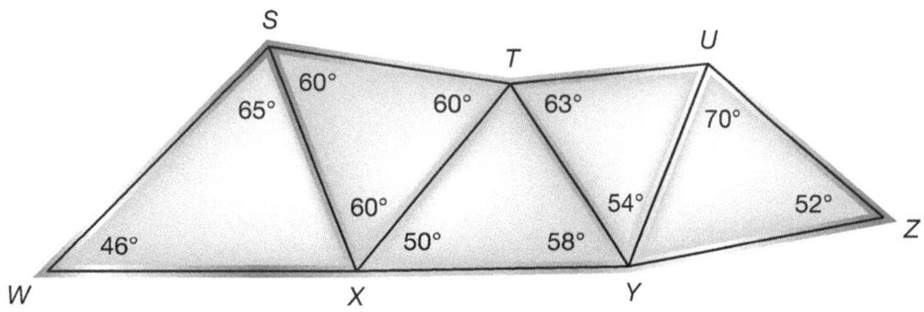

*29. (37) **Predict** If line a is perpendicular to line b and line c is perpendicular to line b, describe the relationship between lines a and c.

30. (29) Find the value of x in the figure shown. Give your answer in simplified radical form.

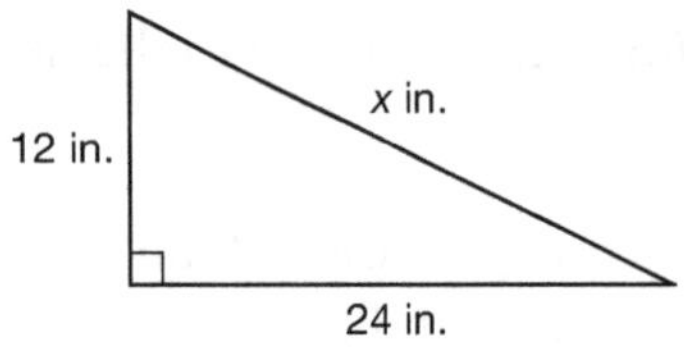

Name ________________________________ Date ___________ Class ___________

Finding Perimeters and Areas of Composite Figures

LESSON 40

1. (37) **Multi-Step** Find the slope of the line that passes through the points $X(2, -3)$ and $Y(4, 1)$. Then, find a perpendicular line that passes through point $Z(-2, 2)$.

2. (29) **Error Analysis** Isabelle has determined that the legs in a right triangle are 21 centimeters and 75 centimeters long, and the hypotenuse is 72 centimeters long. What error has she made?

3. (33) If a triangle has side lengths of $2x$, $3x$, and $4x$, is it an acute, obtuse, or a right triangle?

4. (37) Find the line perpendicular to $y = \frac{1}{4}x + 7$ that passes through the origin.

*** 5.** (40) These figures are the first two stages of an abstract design. Determine the perimeter and area of each figure.

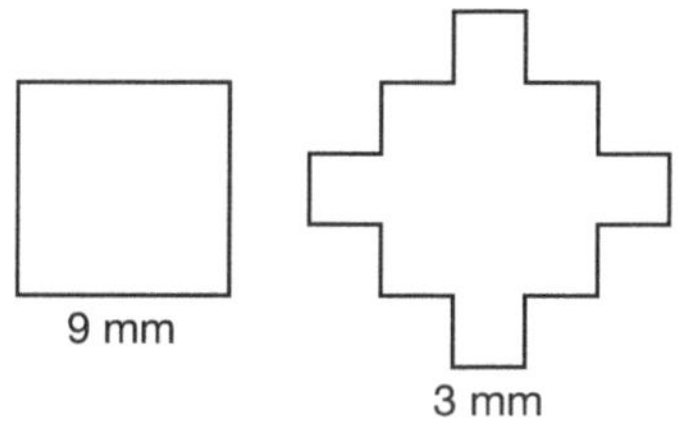

6. (21) **Write** For two statements p and q, what can be determined about the truth value of p when "if p, then q" is a true statement and q is false? Why?

7. (36) What congruence theorem is used to prove that $\triangle HJK \cong \triangle LNM$? Explain.

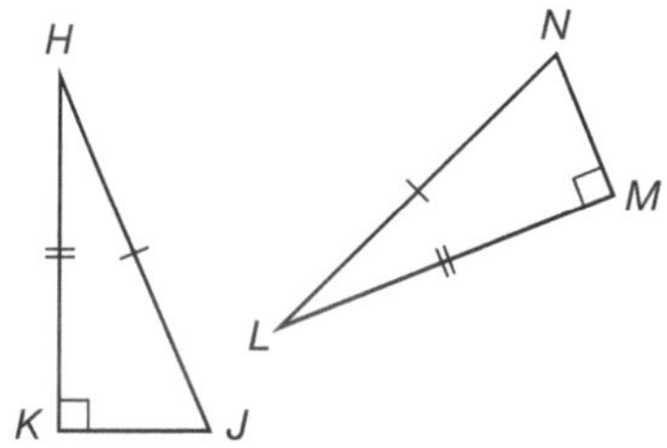

8. (23) The U.S. dime has a radius of 8.96 millimeters. Estimate the area of one side of a dime to the nearest whole square millimeter.

*** 9.** (38) Use a compass and a straightedge to find the incenter of a triangle whose vertices are at (0, 0), (5, −3), and (−1, −4) in a coordinate plane.

10. (29) Antoine solved for the length of a hypotenuse in a right triangle and found that $c^2 = 490$. What is the value of c, in simplified radical form?

11. (32) In the diagram, $QW = 14$ and $TR = 9$. Find QV and TW.

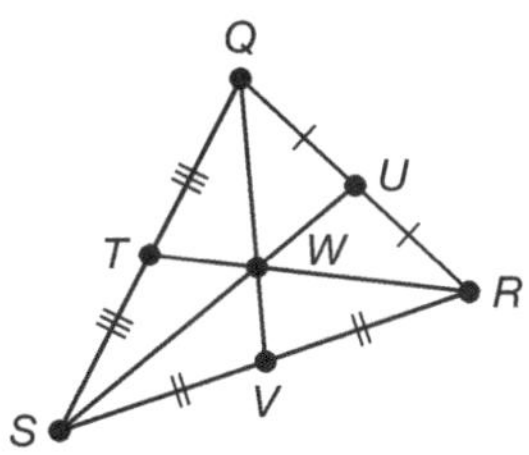

12. (26) **Track and Field** Tara is running along a circular track and Petra is standing at the center of the circle. Petra observes Tara running an arc measure of 56° clockwise, then a measure of 34° counterclockwise, and then a measure of 67° clockwise. What is the measure of the arc from her starting point to where Tara stands now?

*13. If a triangle were constructed with the smallest third side possible, which angle
(39) would measure the greatest, if the two given sides measure 14 yards and 31 yards?

14. In ⊙C, $\widehat{AB}$ measures 65°, and the area of sector ABC is 9 square units. What is the
(35) radius of ⊙C, to the nearest hundredth unit?

15. **Error Analysis** Using the diagram, Lily decided that $\triangle ABE \cong \triangle CDE$. She wrote a
(31) paragraph proof, which is given below. What mistake did Lily make?

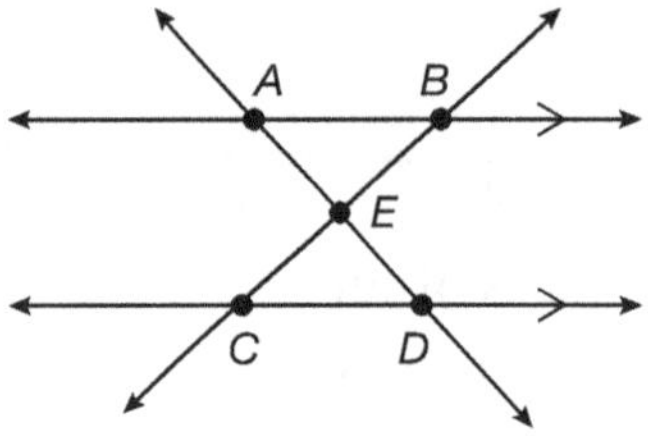

The diagram shows that $\overline{AB} \parallel \overline{CD}$. *Therefore, because alternate interior angles are congruent,* $\angle BAE \cong \angle EDC$ *and* $\angle ABE \cong \angle ECD$. *Since* $\angle AEB$ *and* $\angle CED$ *are vertical angles,* $\angle AEB \cong \angle CED$. *Since the corresponding angles of the triangles are all congruent,* $\triangle ABE \cong \triangle DCE$.

*16. A composite figure is made up of a rectangle that is 4 inches wide by 10 inches
(40) long and two semicircles that fit exactly on two adjacent sides of the rectangle. Determine the figure's perimeter and area. Express your answers in terms of π.

*17. Write the angles of $\triangle SEP$ in order from least to greatest
(39) measure.

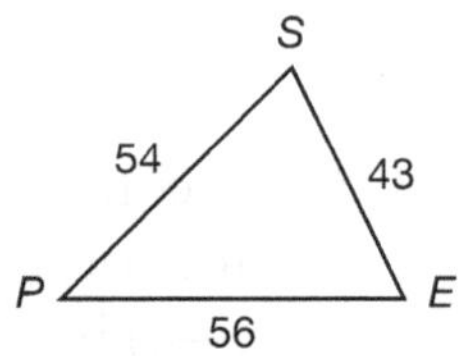

18. In triangles UVW and XYZ, $\angle V$ and $\angle Y$ are right angles,
(36) $\overline{UW} \cong \overline{XZ}$, and $\angle U \cong \angle X$. Use the Hypotenuse-Angle Congruence Theorem to prove that $\triangle UVW \cong \triangle XYZ$.

19. **Security** A camera covers an arc measure of 45°. What fraction of
(26) a full rotation does the camera cover? How many cameras would be needed to be able to look in all directions?

20. In the rectangle $ABCD$, $BD = 2x - 3$. What is the
(34) value of x? What is the length of $\overline{AC}$?

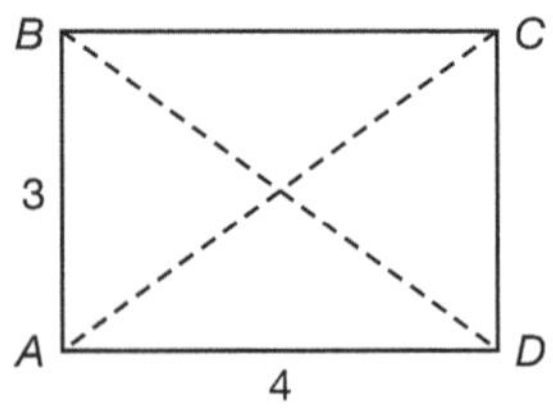

21. **Forestry** A tree's circular trunk has a circumference of
(23) 4 feet 9 inches. To the nearest inch, how wide is its trunk?

22. **Multiple Choice** Find the pair of perpendicular lines.
(37)

A $2x - 3y = 4$, $y = -\frac{2}{3}x - 3$

B $y = \frac{1}{2}x + 7$, $y = 2x - 5$

C $-3y + 2x + 7 = 0$, $-3x + 2y - 4 = 0$

D $2x + y = 8$, $x - 2y = 1$

23. (Inv 3) **Write** Explain why the size of each exterior angle in a regular polygon decreases as the number of sides increases.

***24.** (39) **Justify** Can a triangle have sides with the lengths of 8 feet, 8 feet, and 16 feet?

Use the diagram to complete the problems.

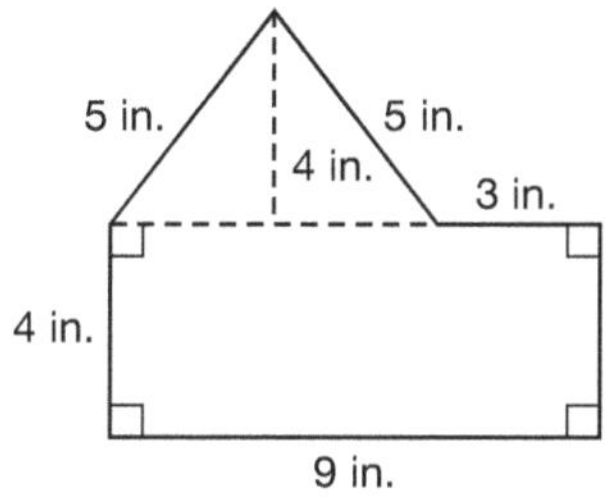

***25.** (40) Determine the perimeter of the figure.

***26.** (40) Determine the area of the figure.

***27.** (38) **Algebra** Find the value of x that makes P the incenter of the triangle shown.

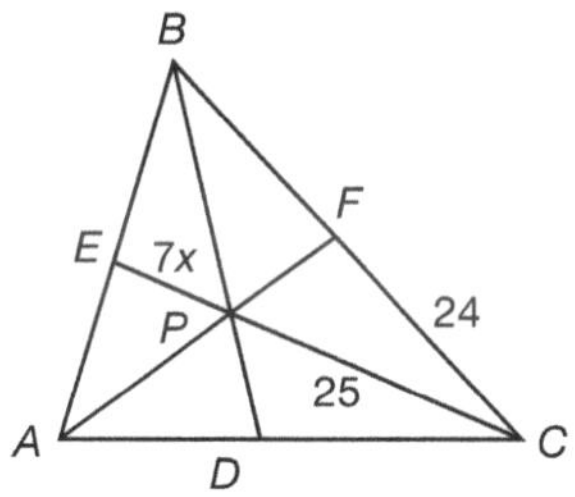

28. (29) **Driving** A car drives 20 miles east and then 45 miles south. To the nearest hundredth of a mile, how far is the car from its starting point?

Use the given diagram. Round to the nearest hundredth.

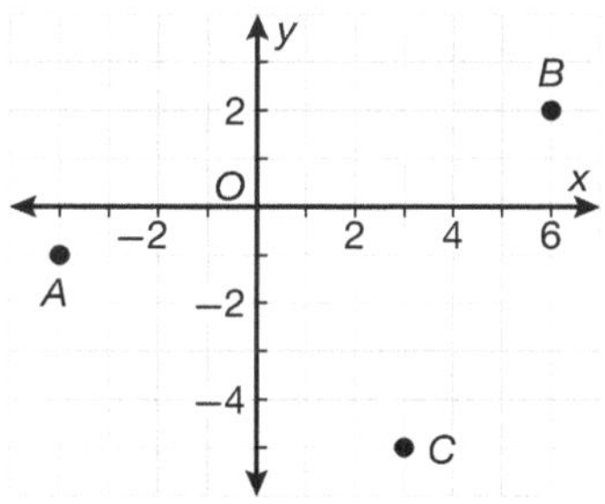

29. (9) Find the length of $\overline{AB}$.

30. (9) Find the length of $\overline{BC}$.

Name ______________________ Date ____________ Class ____________

Ratios, Proportions, and Similarity

LESSON 41

1. **Error Analysis** Alexander made a convex pentagon and a convex quadrilateral. He measured and then added the measures of all the exterior angles, finding a sum of 900°. Is this possible? Explain.
(Inv 3)

* 2. If the quadrilaterals at right are similar, what is the measure of $\angle E$? What is the length of $\overline{XY}$?
(41)

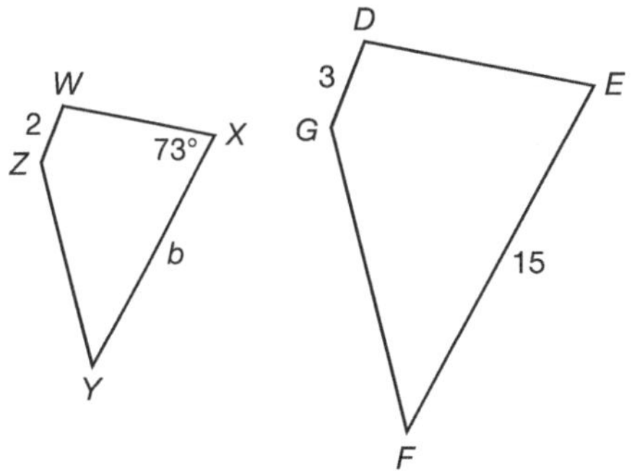

3. **Reunions** Three friends who live far away from each other want to meet for a reunion. Explain how the friends might go about finding a location for the reunion that is equidistant from each friend.
(38)

4. Compare the lengths of $\overline{AB}$ and $\overline{DE}$.
(Inv 4)

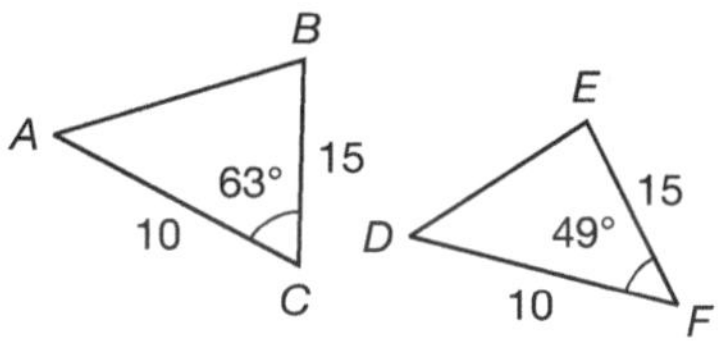

5. **Predict** If line l is perpendicular to line m and line n is parallel to line m, describe the relationship between lines l and n.
(37)

* 6. What is the value of x in the proportion $\frac{9}{x+2} = \frac{27}{9}$?
(41)

7. If $x = 5$ and $y = x$, which property of equality can be used to conclude that $y = 5$?
(24)

8. Name this polygon. Is it equiangular? Is it equilateral? Is it regular or irregular?
(15)

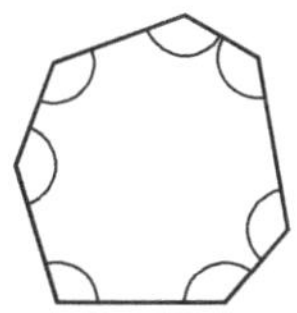

9. **Generalize** Given that the sum of all the angle measures in a triangle is 180°, prove that the interior angles in convex quadrilateral *ABCD* sum to 360°.
(27)

10. **Verify** Use the formula for the sum of the interior angles of a convex polygon to verify the Triangle Sum Theorem.
(Inv 3)

*11. **Multi-Step** Determine the area of this figure. Express your answer in terms of π.
(40)

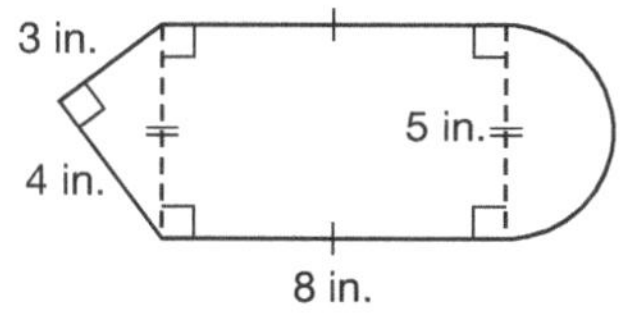

12. **Wheels** A car's wheels are 18 inches across. To the nearest hundredth of an inch, how far will the car move with four complete rotations of its wheels?
(23)

13. Give a Pythagorean triple that is proportional to the triple (7, 24, 25).
(29)

14. **Engineering** Determine the area of this metal plate.
(40)

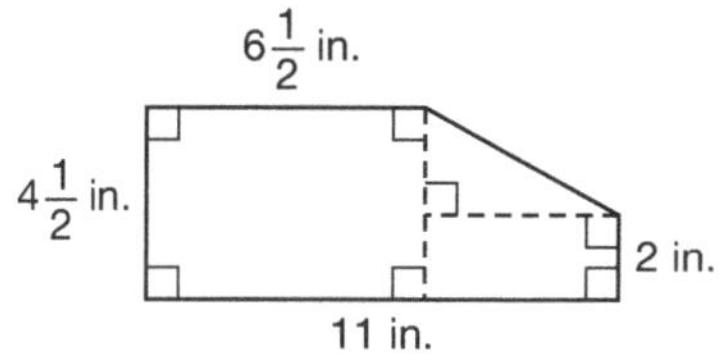

15. (25) Triangle JKL is congruent to $\triangle MNO$. What triangle is $\triangle OMN$ congruent to?

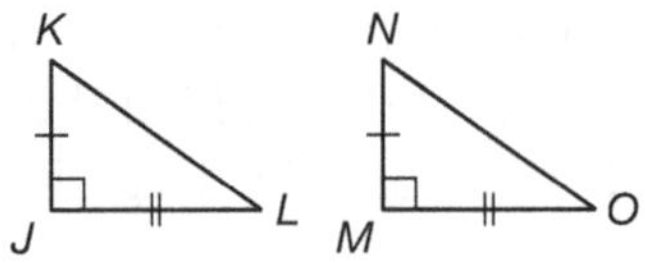

***16.** (31) Complete the flowchart to prove the Pythagorean Inequality Theorem.
Given: $(BC)^2 > (AB)^2 + (AC)^2$, $\triangle DEF$ is a right triangle, $\overline{AB} \cong \overline{DE}$, $\overline{AC} \cong \overline{DF}$
Prove: $\triangle ABC$ is an obtuse triangle.

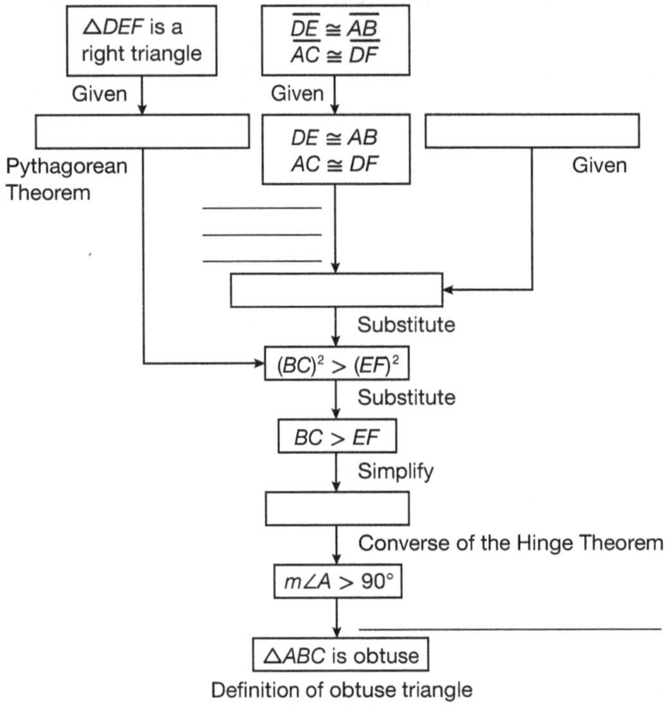

17. (32) In a triangle with vertex D, $\overline{DM}$ is a median, and C is the centroid of the triangle. What is the length of $\overline{DC}$ if $\overline{DM}$ measures 70.2 centimeters? What theorem or postulate justifies your answer?

18. (22) What is an expression for the area of the trapezoid?

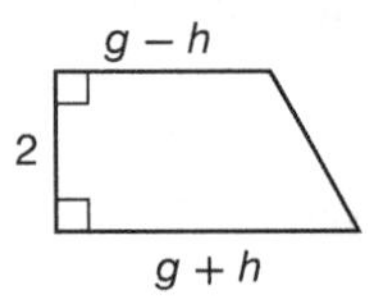

19. (30) In $\triangle MNO$, $m\angle MNO = 37°$, $m\angle NOM = 53°$, $NO = 50$ feet, $MO = 40$ feet, and $MN = 30$ feet. In $\triangle RST$, $m\angle RST = 53°$, $m\angle TRS = 37°$, and $RS = 50$ feet. Determine all other lengths.

20. (36) **Geography** Two right triangles have been marked on a map of Seattle, WA. The distance from Pike Street to Broadway along E. Madison Street is equal to the distance from Marion Street to Boren Avenue along Broadway. Also, Marion Street and E. Madison Street run parallel. Prove that the triangles are congruent.

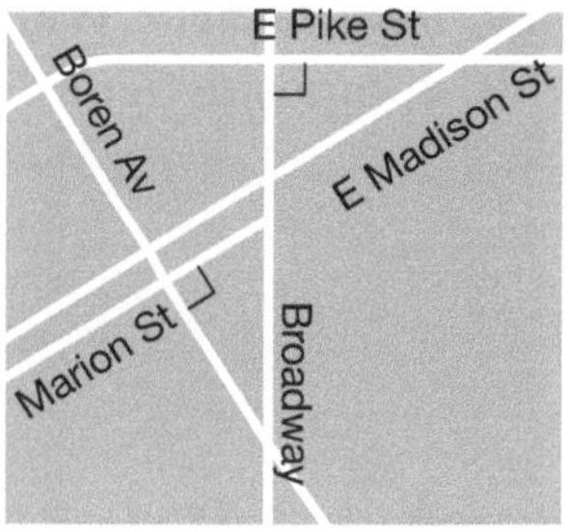

*21. (41) **Photography** A rectangular 8-by-10-inch photograph has to be reduced to $\frac{1}{4}$ its original dimensions to be placed in a magazine. What will be the dimensions of the reduced photograph?

Use the figure to find the unknown measures. Quadrilateral *PQRS* is a parallelogram.

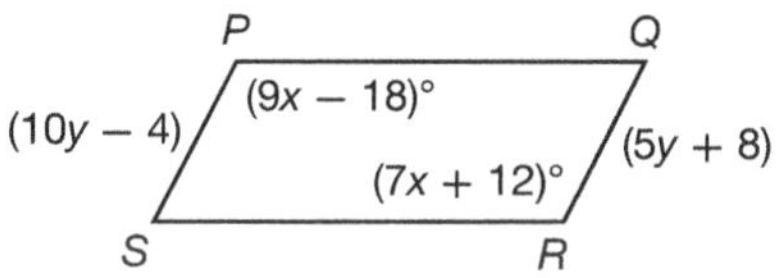

22. (34) Solve for x, then find the measure of each interior angle of the parallelogram.

23. (34) Solve for y, then find the perimeter if $PQ = 2PS$.

24. (Inv 4) Fill in the blanks with the correct words.

If two sides of one ________ are congruent to two sides of another triangle and the included _______ of the first triangle is greater than the included angle of the second triangle, then the third side of the first triangle is longer than the third _____ of the second triangle.

25. (39) **Write** Can a triangle have a side length that is the sum of the other two side lengths? Explain.

26. (30) If in $\triangle ABC$, $AB = 10$, $m\angle ABC = 5°$, and $m\angle CAB = 60°$, and in $\triangle DEF$, $m\angle EFD = 5°$, $m\angle DEF = 60°$, and $FE = 10$, write a congruency statement for these triangles.

27. (39) **Algebra** If $x = 1$, which angle would have the least measure in the triangle?

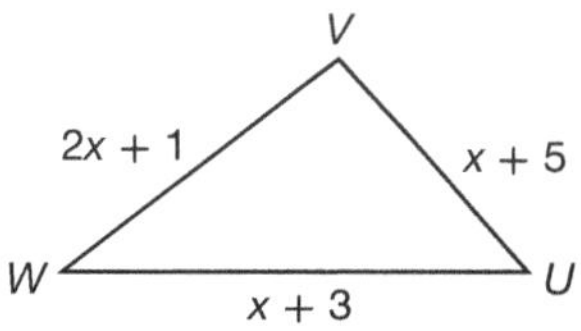

28. (23) For two circles, the first circle has a radius of 0.5 units, and the second radius is the circumference of the first. Using 3.14 for π, what is the area of the second circle?

29. (40) **Multiple Choice** Which two formulas are used to calculate the area of this composite figure?

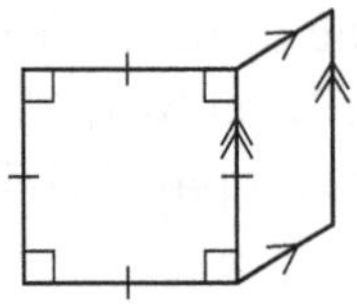

A $A_1 = 4s, A_2 = \frac{1}{2}bh$
B $A_1 = \frac{1}{2}\ell w, A_2 = bh$
C $A_1 = s^2, A_2 = bh$
D $A_1 = \ell w, A_2 = \frac{1}{2}bh$

30. (22) **Write** Explain why you can use the formula, $A = \frac{1}{2}d_1d_2$, for both the area of rhombuses and the area of squares.

Name ______________________ Date __________ Class __________

Finding Distance from a Point to a Line

LESSON 42

1. (36) **Carpentry** Denzel needs to cut a replacement support for the roof of his house. The existing supports are 18 inches long and fit against the wall 10 inches below the roof. Explain how Denzel can make sure the triangles in this diagram are congruent.

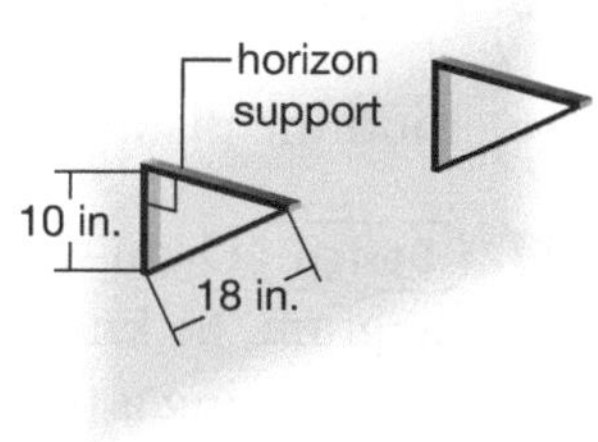

2. (23) The outer circumference of Stonehenge, a ring of standing stones in England, is about 328 feet. To the nearest tenth of a foot, what is the length of the radius?

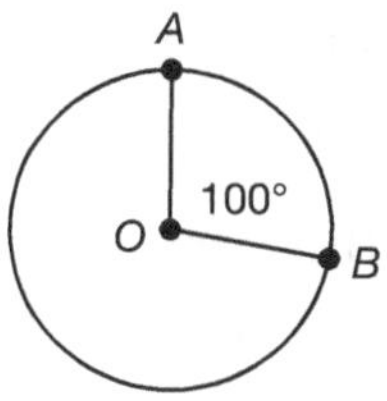

3. (26) What is the measure of $\widehat{AB}$ in this circle?

4. (33) The side lengths of a triangle are 5, 12, and c, respectively. If $c = 14$, is the triangle obtuse, acute, or right? …if $c = 13$? …if $c = 12$?

***5.** (Inv 4) **Multi-Step** Which side is longer, $\overline{AB}$ or $\overline{DE}$? Explain.

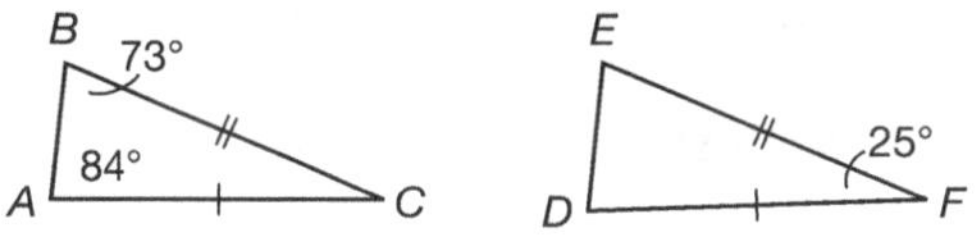

***6.** (27) Complete this two-column proof.
Given: $\angle 1$ and $\angle 2$ are straight angles
Prove: $\angle 1 \cong \angle 2$

***7.** (41) **Multiple Choice** The sides of a triangle are 6, 9, and 12 inches long. If the shortest side of a similar triangle is 19.2 inches, what is the longest side of the triangle?
A 25.2 in. **B** 25.6 in.
C 28.8 in. **D** 38.4 in.

***8.** (36) In $\triangle ABC$ and $\triangle DEF$, $\angle B$ and $\angle E$ are right angles, $\overline{BC} \cong \overline{EF}$, and $\angle C \cong \angle F$. Use the Leg-Angle Congruence Theorem to prove that $\triangle ABC \cong \triangle DEF$.

***9.** (42) Find the distance between (4, 5) and the line $y = -\frac{3}{2}x - 2$.

10. (37) **Algebra** Line j passes through points (4, 6) and (3, 2). Line k passes through points $(x, -1)$ and $(-3, 3)$. What value of x makes these lines parallel?

11. (40) Determine the area of this figure.

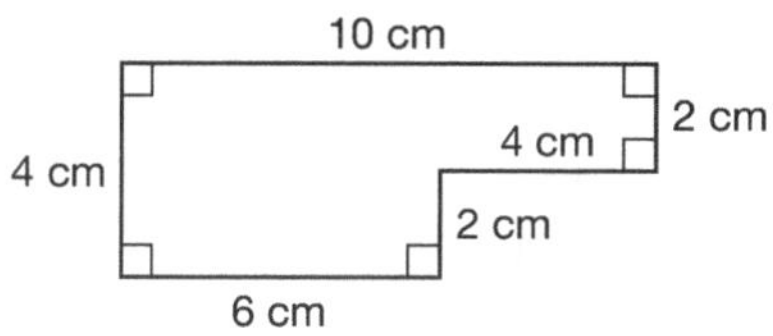

12. (29) **Framing** Justine has built a frame for her painting that measures 27 by 36 inches. In order for the corners of the frame to be at right angles, what length must the diagonal be?

13. (29) Give two Pythagorean triples that are proportional to the triple 5, 12, 13.

***14.** (27) **Analyze** In the diagram shown, prove that $m\angle BAC = m\angle ABC$.

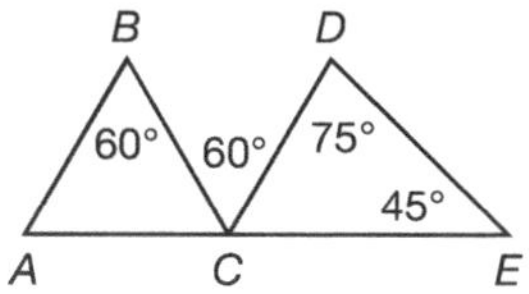

*15. **Analyze** Find the distance between the line $y = 4x - 1$ and the point (4, 15).
(42)

*16. Find the distance from (−2.15, 3.28) to the line $x = 11.3$.
(42)

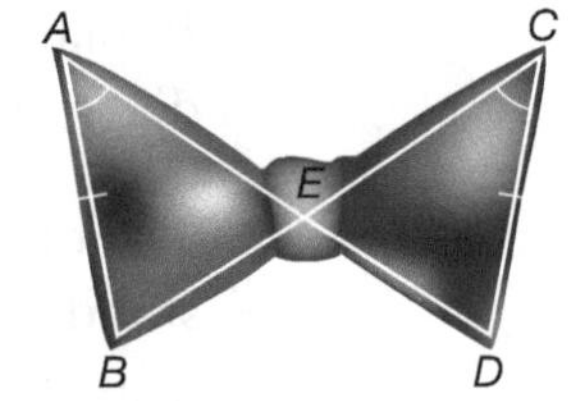

17. **Design** Dean wants to make a symmetric bowtie. As in the diagram, he knows that $AB = CD$, and $m\angle BAE = m\angle DCE$. Prove, using a two-column proof, that $\triangle ABE \cong \triangle CDE$.
(30)

18. What is the included side of $\triangle RST$ that is between $\angle TRS$ and $\angle RST$?
(28)

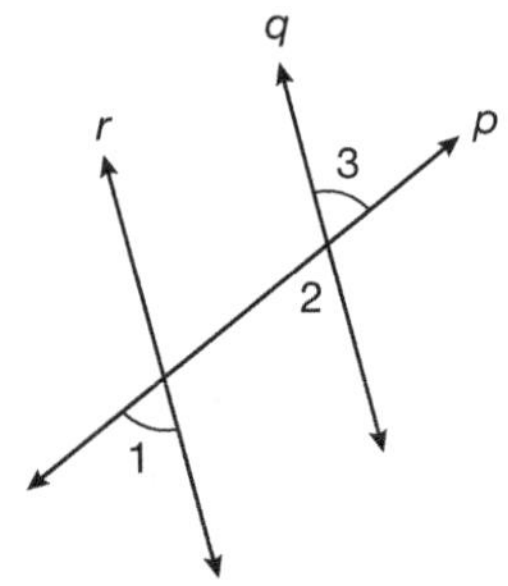

19. Use the Converse of the Corresponding Angles Postulate to prove that lines q and r in this figure are parallel.
(12)

20. **Write** Three side lengths in a triangle are given by the expressions $2x$, $4x$, and $3x$. Which would be opposite to the angle with the greatest measure? Explain.
(39)

21. **Multi-Step** Find the slope of the line that passes through the points (3, 4) and (−1, 3). Then find a parallel line that passes through point (4, 2).
(37)

22. The steps of the algebraic proof below are correct. However, the justifications for each step are out of order. Determine the correct order for the justifications.
(24)

Statements	Reasons
1. $9x = 3(2x + 3)$	1. Simplify
2. $9x = 6x + 9$	2. Division Property of Equality
3. $9x - 6x = 6x + 9 - 6x$	3. Given
4. $3x = 9$	4. Simplify
5. $\frac{3x}{3} = \frac{9}{3}$	5. Subtraction Property of Equality
6. $x = 3$	6. Distributive Property

*23. Find the distance from (−1.2, 1.7) to the line $x = 3$.
(42)

24. State the converse of the following statement, and write the two statements as a biconditional.
(20)

If two numbers are positive, then their product is positive.

25. A triangle has an area of 4, a base of $2x + 4$, and a height of $x - 1$. Solve for x and provide a justification of each step.
(24)

*26. **Algebra** If rectangles $KLMN$ and $QRST$ are similar, and $LM = 4$, $RS = 9$, and QR is 5 greater than KL, write and solve a proportion to find the measures of $\overline{KL}$ and $\overline{QR}$.
(41)

27. In this diagram, find the value of x and the lengths of $\overline{PC}$, $\overline{CM}$, and $\overline{PM}$ if C is the centroid of the triangle.
(32)

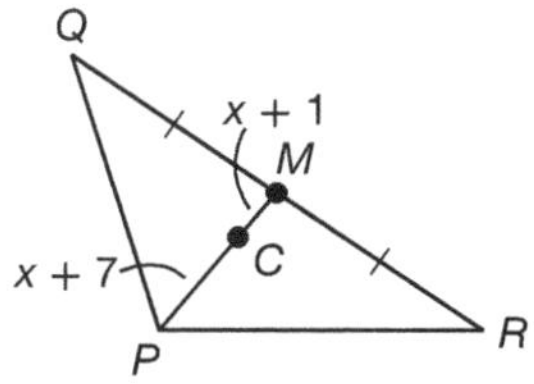

*28. **Generalize** Explain why each statement is true or false.
(41)

a. *Two squares are always similar.*

b. *A rectangle and a square are always similar.*

29. **Justify** A triangle has side lengths that are 5, 8, and 11. Classify the triangle by its angles. Cite a theorem or postulate to justify your answer.
(33)

30. **Games and Puzzles** Determine the area of each tangram piece.
(40)

a. 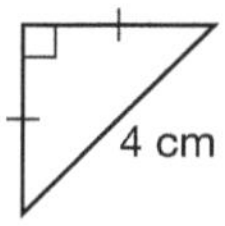

b. 

c. 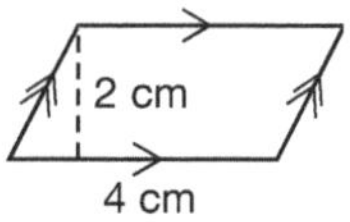

d. 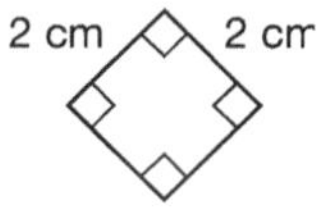

e. 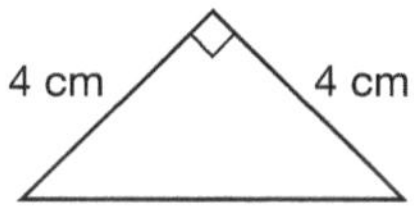

Name ______________________________ Date ___________ Class ___________

Chords, Secants, and Tangents

LESSON 43

1. Which of the following is not a parallelogram?
(34)
A rhombus B rectangle
C square D trapezoid

* 2. **Farming** A farmer has 264 feet of fencing to enclose a triangular field. If the farmer wants the sides of the triangle to be in the ratio 3:4:5, what is the length of each side of the field?
(41)

3. **Algebra** A convex polygon has exterior angles $(4x + 10)°$, $(5x + 2)°$, and $(x + 8)°$. What is the value of x?
(Inv 3)

* 4. Find the point on the line $y = -0.25x + 9$ that is closest to $(1, -4)$.
(42)

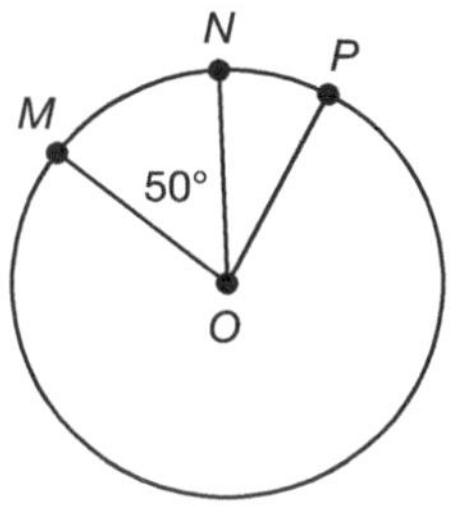

5. In the diagram, $m\widehat{MN} = 50°$ and $m\widehat{MP} = 80°$. What is the measure of $\widehat{NP}$?
(26)

* 6. **Formulate** If $\angle 1$ and $\angle 2$ are adjacent central angles of a circle, show that the sum of their associated sector areas is equal to the sector area of their angle sum.
(35)

* 7. Identify each line or segment that intersects the circle at right. What type of intersecting line is each one?
(43)

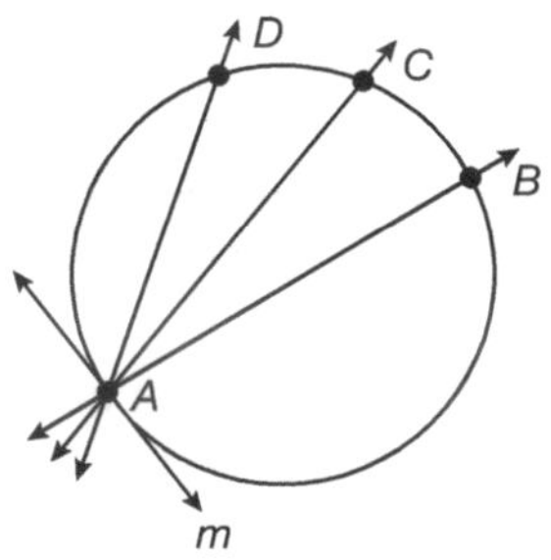

8. **Multi-Step** Graph the line and find the slope of the line that passes through the points $D(4, 2)$ and $E(-3, 6)$. Then find the equation of a perpendicular line that passes through the point $F(-1, 2)$.
(37)

9. **Error Analysis** A composite figure is made up of a semicircle and a rectangle. The width of the rectangle is 3 centimeters, and the diameter of the semicircle is 5 centimeters. Derek calculated the perimeter of the figure like this:
(40)

$P = 3 + 3 + 5 + \pi d$
$\quad = (11 + 5\pi)$ cm

Find and correct Derek's error.

10. **Carpentry** A 25-meter-long diagonal piece of wood runs across a rectangular platform that has a length-to-width ratio of 4:3. What are the dimensions of the platform?
(29)

11. When are all the medians and altitudes of a triangle congruent?
(32)

12. **Multiple Choice** Which congruence theorem applies to these triangles?
(36)
A Leg-Leg Theorem B Leg-Angle Theorem
C Hypotenuse-Leg Theorem D Hypotenuse-Angle Theorem

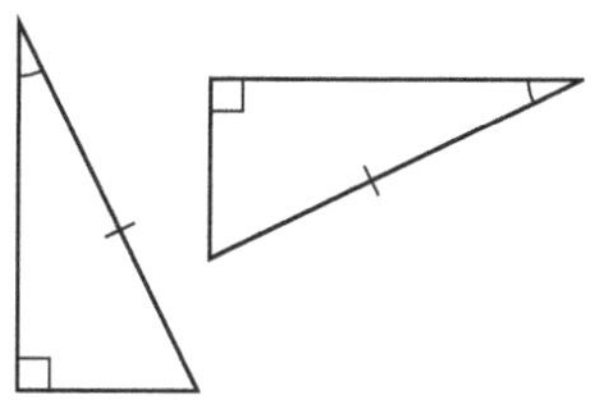

13. **Algebra** Each central angle of a regular polygon is 1°. How many sides does the polygon have?
(Inv 3)

14. Solve the equation $3(2x - 1) = 15$ with a justification for each step.
(24)

*15. A circle has a diameter of 22 centimeters. A chord in the circle is 11 centimeters long. What is the *exact* distance from the chord to the center of the circle?
(43)

16. **Given:** $\overline{BE}$ is the perpendicular bisector of $\overline{AC}$ at point D.
Prove: $\triangle ABD \cong \triangle CBD$
(38)

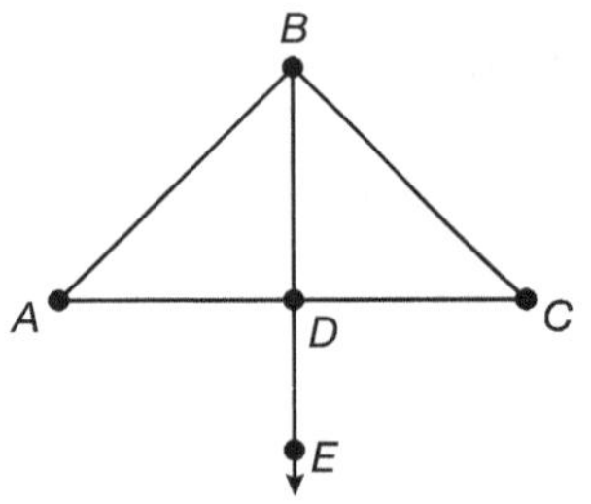

*17. **Algebra** Given the equation $y = 2x + 1$, and $R(4, 4)$, find the point on the line that is closest to R.
(42)

18. **Multi-Step** Find the orthocenter of $\triangle MNP$ with vertices $M(2, 2)$, $N(2, 8)$, and $P(-6, 4)$.
(32)

19. **Formulate** An arc measure of 180° forms a semicircle. Use this fact to derive a formula for the perimeter of a semicircle.
(26)

20. **Disc Golf** In disc golf, a player tries to throw a flying disc into a metal basket target. Four of the disc golf targets are shown in the diagram. Which of the targets are closest together?
(39)

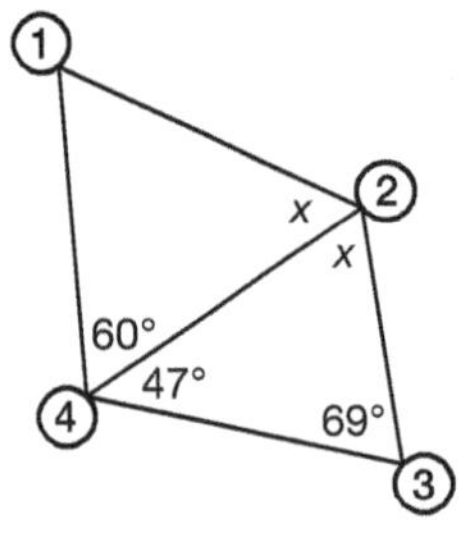

21. Identify the hypothesis and conclusion of the following statement.
(10)

If two planes intersect, then they intersect on exactly one line.

*22. **Write** Explain the relationship between two chords that are equidistant from the center of a circle.
(43)

23. The area of a circle is 40.6 square meters. If an arc's length is 2.8 meters, what is the arc's measure?
(35)

24. **Driving** Esther normally takes Exeter Avenue to work, but it is closed for repairs. For the detour, she must travel south on Central Street for 2.2 miles and then east on Court Street for 3.4 miles. How much longer is the detour than her normal route, to the nearest tenth of a mile?
(29)

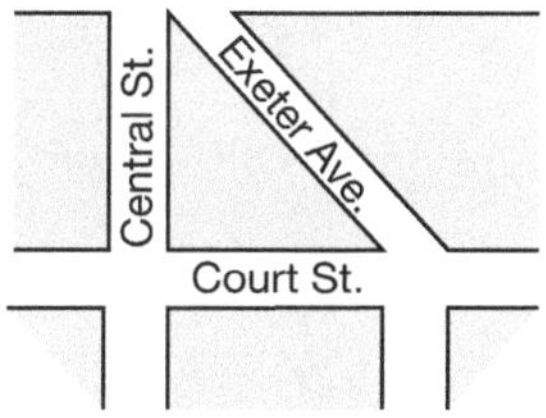

*25. Find the distance between the two parallel lines $y = 3x + 1$ and $y = 3x - 18$.
(42)

*26. **Model** Can the following be modeled with straws? If not, explain.
(41)

a. Two similar equilateral triangles.

b. Two equilateral triangles that are not similar.

27. Write a paragraph proof.
(31)

Given: Angle 1 is congruent to $\angle 2$.

Prove: Angle 2 and $\angle 3$ are supplementary.

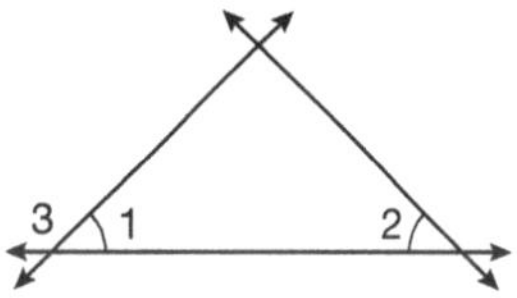

28. **Skiing** Developers are designing a new ski hill in the Rocky Mountains. They use the standard difficulty rating of ski runs as green (easy), blue (medium), and black (difficult). To determine what color each of the runs should be, developers use a slope formula. Green runs have a slope of $\frac{1}{3}$. Blue runs have a slope of $\frac{1}{2}$. Black runs have a slope of 1. If all the runs start at 150 yards high, what is the length of each run, to the nearest tenth of a yard?
(29, 33)

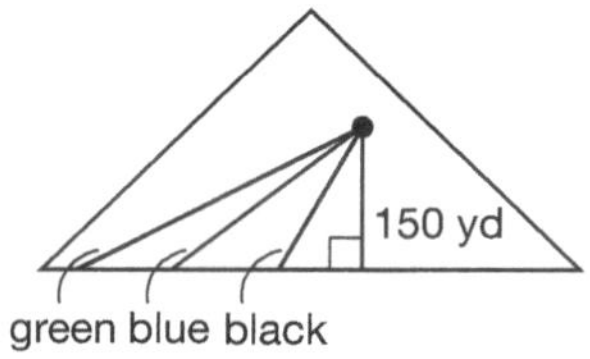

*29. Find the distance from the center of a circle with a diameter of 2.6 inches to a chord that is 1.2 inches in length, to the nearest hundredth of an inch.
(43)

30. **Justify** Which is the longer side, x or y? Explain.
(Inv 4)

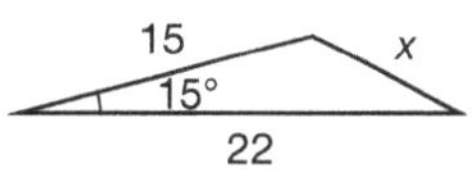

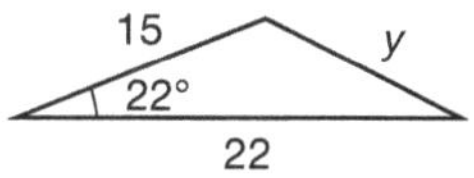

Name ______________________ Date ____________ Class ____________

Applying Similarity

LESSON 44

1. If the triangles shown are similar so that $3:4:5 = x:y:15$, what are the values of x and y? (41)

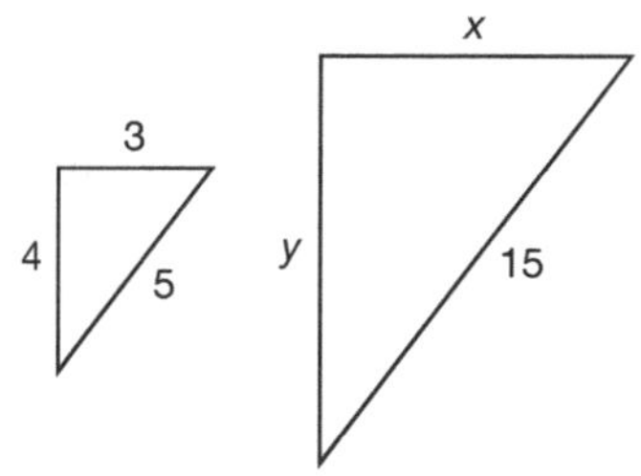

2. **Design** Billy is making a kite $STUV$. He knows that $\overline{ST}$ and $\overline{TU}$ are the same length. Which angles does he need to know are equal to ensure that the two halves of the kite, $\triangle STV$ and $\triangle UTV$, are congruent? (28)

3. **Restaurants** A restaurant owner plans to add a triangular patio to her restaurant, as shown. She wants to position a fountain on the patio that is the same distance from each edge. Where should she position the fountain? Explain your reasoning. Support your answer with a diagram. (38)

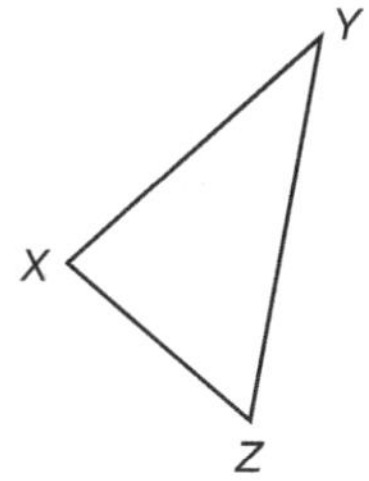

4. **Write** Explain how the Pythagorean Theorem can be used to ensure that two pieces of metal in a frame are at right angles to each other. (29)

5. **Verify** Name two properties of parallelograms that can be used to justify the congruency marks on this diagram. (34)

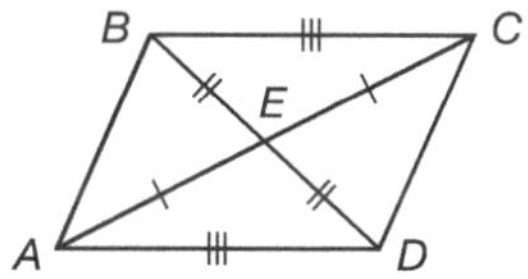

*6. Given $\triangle FGH \sim \triangle MNP$, with $FG = 8$ and $MN = 16$, what is the reduced ratio of their corresponding sides? (44)

7. (16)
   a. Determine the slope and y-intercept of this graph of a line.
   b. Write the equation of the line.

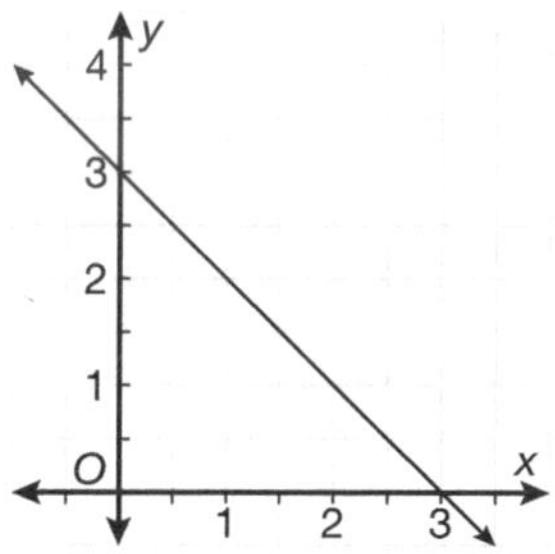

*8. Figure $RSTU$ is similar to figure $KLMN$. The ratio of their corresponding sides is 1:2. If the perimeter of $RSTU$ is 10 inches, what is the perimeter of $KLMN$? (44)

9. **Verify** Wesley has two triangles, $\triangle ABC$ and $\triangle XYZ$. He knows that $m\angle ABC = 67°$, $m\angle BAC = 23°$, $AB = 5$ units, $BC = 13$ units, $m\angle XYZ = 67°$, $m\angle YXZ = 23°$, and $ZY = 13$ units. He concludes that $XY = 5$ units. Verify that Wesley is correct. (30)

*10. **Multi-Step** Determine the perimeter of this figure. Express your answer in terms of π. (40)

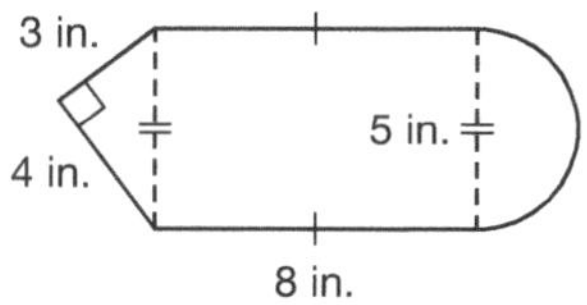

*11. The radius of a circle is 15 centimeters. If a chord measuring 24 centimeters is perpendicular to the radius and cuts it into two parts, find the length of each part of the radius. (43)

12. **Write** When finding a perpendicular or parallel line to a given line, why is the y-intercept not used? (37)

*13. (44) Elijah wants to change the size of the tires on his bike. The old tires have a radius of 12 inches. The new tires have a radius of 15 inches. What is the ratio of the radius of the old tires to that of the new tires?

14. (39) **Justify** Explain how you know a triangle can have side lengths measuring 11, 15 and 21.

*15. (42) Given the equation $y = \frac{2}{3}x - 2$ and $G(1, 3)$, find the point on the line that is closest to G.

Refer to this diagram to answer the next two questions.

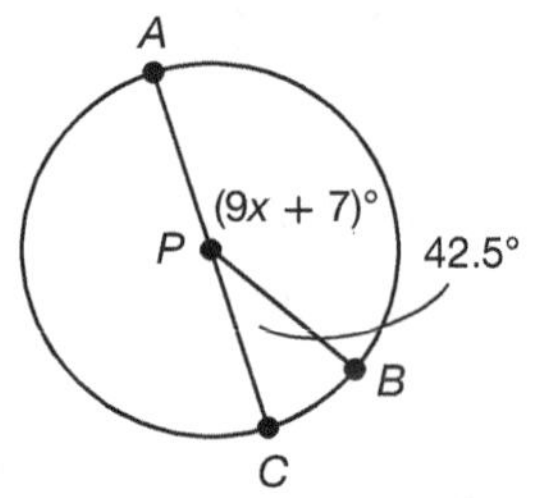

16. (35) **a.** If $\overline{AC}$ is a diameter, what is the value of x?
b. If $PA = 10$ centimeters, what is the length of $\widehat{AB}$ to the nearest tenth of a centimeter? Of major arc $\widehat{ACB}$?

17. (35) If the radius of the circle is 25 inches, what is the area of sector BPC to the nearest tenth square inch?

*18. (42) Find the distance from $(-1, 2)$ to the line $y = \frac{3}{2}x - 3$.

19. (Inv 3) **Error Analysis** Lionel calculated the sum of the interior angles of a convex polygon to be 1710°. Explain how you know he made an error.

20. (33) Is a triangle with side lengths that measure 3.6, 4.8, and 6.2 a right, obtuse, or acute triangle?

*21. (43) Using the diagram below, determine the value of x.

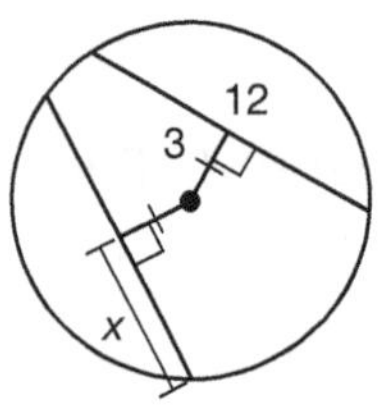

22. (38) **Emergency Alert** A town wants to place a weather emergency siren where the three schools can all hear the siren to alert them in case of an emergency. Explain how the town might go about finding the optimal location for the siren.

23. (41) **Multiple Choice** If the triangles are similar, which of these is the length of $\overline{BC}$?

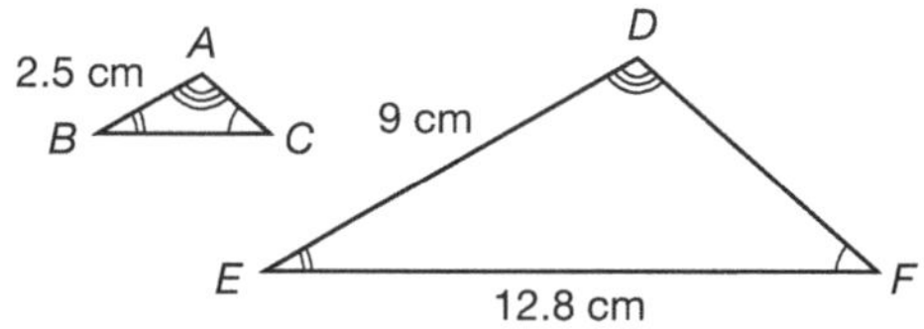

A 1.3 centimeters
B 1.8 centimeters
C 3.2 centimeters
D 3.6 centimeters

24. (Inv 3) If the sum of the measures of the interior angles in a regular polygon is 1260°, how many sides does the polygon have?

25. (29) **Analyze** Jason is walking around an empty field, from the southwest corner to the northeast corner. The field is 140 yards long and 90 yards wide. How much farther will Jason have to walk if he walks around the edge of the field than if he cuts through the middle of the field, to the nearest yard?

***26.** (44) $\triangle CDE$ is an equilateral triangle. Its perimeter is 45 inches. If $\triangle CDE \sim \triangle VWX$, and the ratio of their corresponding sides is 3:1, what are the lengths of the sides of $\triangle VWX$?

27. (40) A composite figure is made up of a right triangle and three squares. The triangle has a base length of 8 centimeters and a height of 15 centimeters. Each square fits exactly along one side of the triangle.
a. Determine the side length of the largest square.
b. Determine the perimeter of the figure.
c. Determine the area of the figure.

28. (37) **Algebra** Line p passes through points (4, 7) and (4, 3). Line q passes through points (–2, 1) and (5, 1). Are the lines parallel, perpendicular, or neither?

29. (25) **Carpentry** Deklynn and Bonita are making two congruent triangles out of wood. Deklynn's triangle, $\triangle FGH$ has $m\angle G = 70°$ and $m\angle H = 80°$. If Bonita's triangle is $\triangle PQR$ and $\triangle FGH \cong \triangle PQR$, how large should she make $m\angle P$?

***30.** (43) Identify each line or segment that intersects the circle. What type of intersecting line is each one?

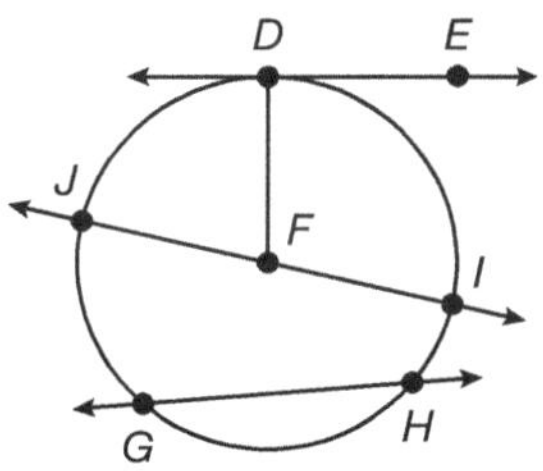

Name ____________________ Date __________ Class __________

Introduction to Coordinate Proofs

LESSON 45

1. (45) **Coordinate Geometry** An isosceles triangle has vertices $K(0, 0)$, $L(-2, 2)$, and $M(x, y)$. Find the coordinates of one possible position of M.

2. (44) Similar pentagons $EFGHI$ and $QRSTU$ are regular and have a similarity ratio of 5:3. Find the value of x if $FG = 30$ and $TU = x - 11$.

3. (43) If $\overline{CD}$ is a diameter of circle P in the diagram, and it is perpendicular to $\overline{AB}$, what is the value of x?

4. (43) In the circle at right if $YZ = 30.2$, what is the value of y?

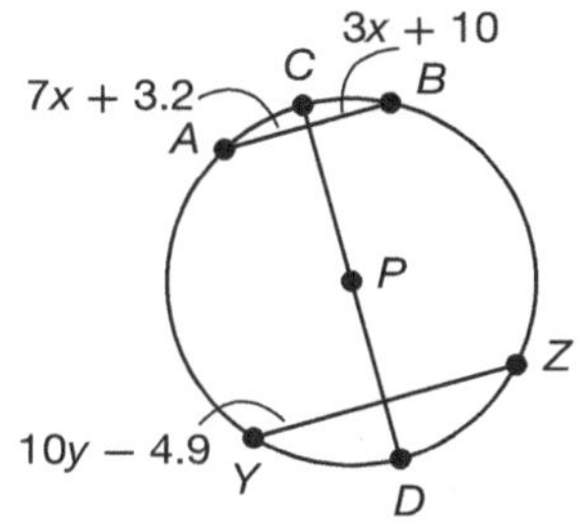

5. (42) Find the distance from the line $y = \frac{5}{4}x - 4$ to $(-1, 5)$.

6. (45) $KLMN$ is a parallelogram. Find the coordinates of $L(x, y)$.

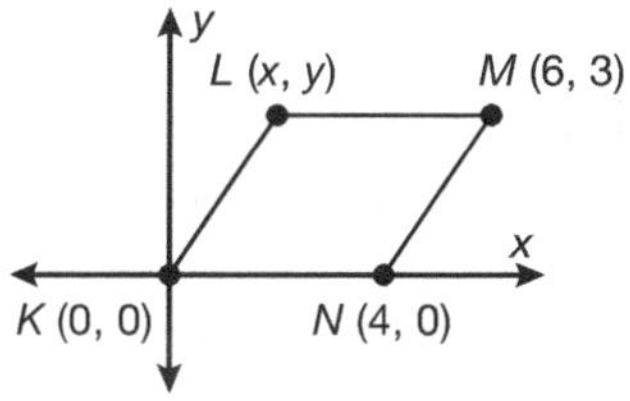

7. (35) What is the arc length of the minor arc bounded by a 60° central angle in a circle with a radius of 30 centimeters? Use 3.14 for π.

8. (34) Angela draws diagonals on a quadrilateral and notices that they bisect each other. Without knowing any other information about the shape, can you classify it as a parallelogram? As a rectangle? Explain.

9. (45) **Coordinate Geometry** Parallelogram $JKLM$ has vertices $J(0, 0)$, $K(2, 2)$, $L(x, y)$, and $M(5, 0)$. Find (x, y).

10. (41) If $\triangle ABC \sim \triangle XYZ$, what are the measures of $\angle A$ and $\angle Y$?

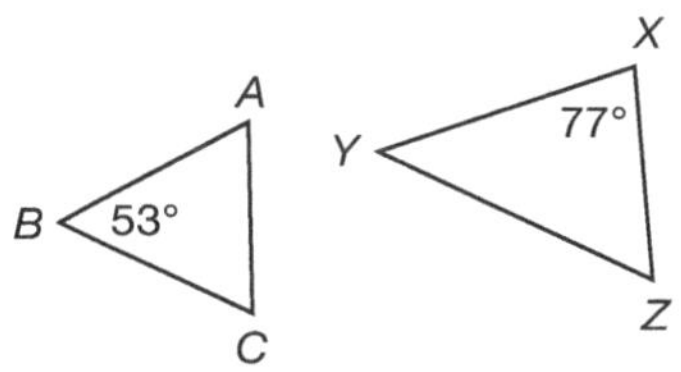

11. (41) **Analyze** The side lengths of rectangle A are 16.4 inches and 10.8 inches. The side lengths of rectangle B are 10.25 inches and 6.75 inches. Determine whether the two rectangles are similar. If so, find the similarity ratio. If not, explain why.

12. (40) **Architecture** How much veneer siding is required to cover the front of this house? Do not include the 3-by-7-foot door or the three 6-by-3-foot windows.

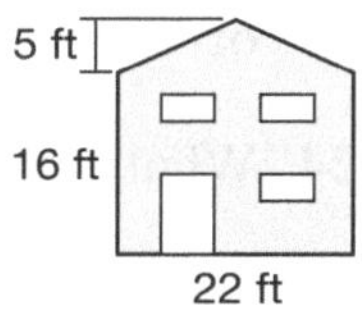

13. (40) **Packaging** The cardboard pattern for a gift box is shown at right. The two trapezoids are congruent. The two end rectangles are also congruent.

a. Calculate the area of card stock used for the box.

b. If the box is cut from a square sheet with side lengths of 21 centimeters each, how much card stock is wasted?

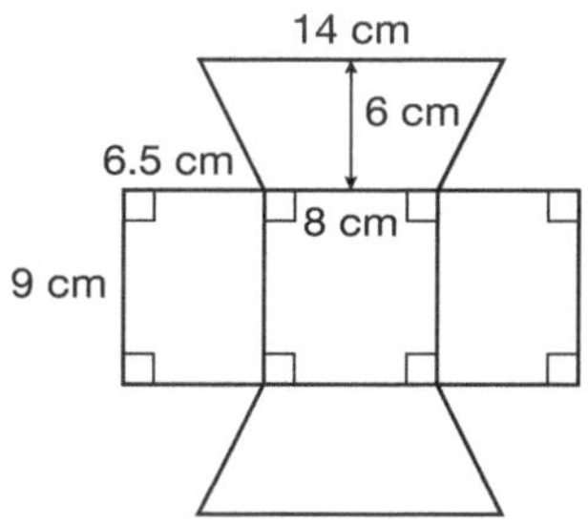

14. (44) Lauren and her grandmother have tables that are similar rectangles. The ratio of their corresponding sides is 2:3. Lauren's table is 5 feet wide and 6 feet long, and her grandmother's is the larger table. What is the perimeter of her grandmother's table?

15. (39) **Construction** The measurements in the diagram were taken from the attic space in a new home. What is the range of possible lengths of the unknown side? Explain.

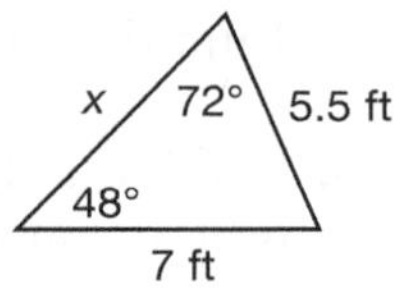

16. (44) Given $\triangle LMN \sim \triangle UVW$, with $LM = 10$, and $UV = 4$, what is the ratio of their corresponding sides?

17. (38) **Algebra** Using the diagram at the right, find the length of $\overline{AD}$ in terms of x if $BC = 3x$, $DC = 2x$, and $AB = 9$.

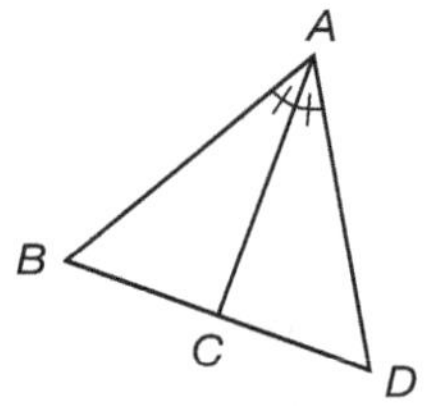

18. (37) Find the line parallel to $2y + 4 = 6x - 5$ that passes through the origin. Write it in slope-intercept form.

19. (37) **Justify** If $y = 2x + 3$ and $y = 2x + k$ is parallel to it, what are all the possible values of k? Why does changing the value of k not make the lines intersect?

20. (36) **Design** The math faculty of Pythagoras College uses this logo. All four triangles are right triangles, the whole logo is a square, and the inner quadrilateral is also a square. Prove that the right triangles are all congruent.

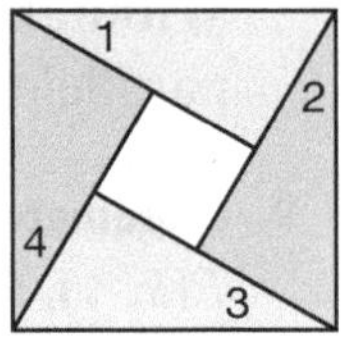

21. (28) **Analyze** In $\triangle ABC$, $AB = (x + 3)$, $m\angle ABC = (16x + 8)°$, and $BC = (4x - 8)$. In $\triangle DEF$, $DE = (2x - 1)$, $m\angle DEF = (18x)°$, and $EF = (3x - 6)$. Is it possible for $\triangle ABC \cong \triangle DEF$? Explain.

22. (33) A triangle has side lengths that are 100, 240, and 265 units long. Classify the triangle by side lengths and by angles.

23. (32) Draw an equilateral triangle using a protractor and straightedge. Locate and label its orthocenter and centroid. What do you notice about the two points?

24. (Inv 3) What is the sum of the interior angle measures of a convex, irregular octagon?

25. (30) **Error Analysis** Mick has two triangles, $\triangle MNO$ and $\triangle DEF$. He knows that $m\angle MNO = m\angle DEF$, $m\angle NOM = m\angle EFD$, and $NO = DF$. Mick concludes that $\triangle MNO \cong \triangle DEF$. Is he correct? Explain.

26. (28) For a circle with center O and diameters $\overline{AB}$ and $\overline{CD}$, prove $\triangle AOC \cong \triangle BOD$.

27. (34) In the parallelogram shown, what is the measure of $\angle IFG$? $m\angle FGH$? $m\angle HGE$?

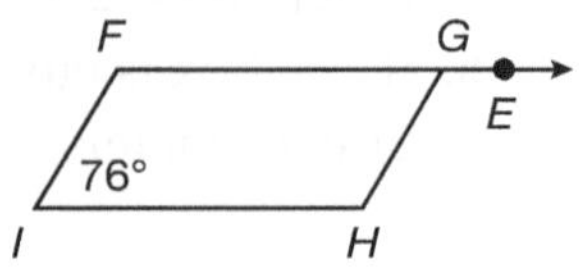

Introduction to Coordinate Proofs

LESSON 45

28. (45) Write a coordinate proof showing that the midpoint of a hypotenuse of a right triangle is equidistant from the three vertices.

29. (26) **Algebra** If $m\overset{\frown}{AB} = (2x + 10)°$ and $m\overset{\frown}{BC} = (4x + 5)°$ are non-overlapping adjacent arcs, $m\overset{\frown}{XY} = (x + 19)°$ and $m\overset{\frown}{YZ} = (2x + 11)°$ are non-overlapping adjacent arcs and $\overset{\frown}{AC}$ and $\overset{\frown}{XZ}$ are congruent, what is the measure of each arc?

30. (10) **Multiple Choice** What is the conclusion of this conjecture?

If a polygon is regular, then it is equilateral and equiangular.

A A polygon is equilateral.
B A polygon is regular.
C A polygon is equilateral and equiangular.
D A polygon is equiangular.

Name ______________________________ Date ____________ Class ____________

Triangle Similarity: AA, SSS, SAS

LESSON 46

1. (42) Find the distance from $(-1, 7)$ to the line $x = 3$.

* **2.** (9) **Flying** Two aircraft depart from an airport at (10, 12). The first aircraft travels to an airport at $M(-220, 80)$, and the second aircraft travels to an airport at $N(100, -400)$. If each unit on the grid represents one mile, what is the distance to the nearest mile between the two aircraft after they both land?

3. (41) **Analyze** The side lengths of rectangle A are 18.3 inches and 24.6 inches. The side lengths of rectangle B are 24.4 inches and 32.8 inches. Determine whether the two rectangles are similar. If so, write the similarity ratio.

4. (37) **Multiple Choice** Which of the following lines is parallel to $y = 7$?

A $y = 2x$ **B** $y = -\frac{1}{7}x$

C $y + 7 = 0$ **D** $y = \frac{7}{x}$

5. (Inv 3) What is the central angle measure of a regular octagon?

* **6.** (27) Write a two-column proof to prove the SAS Similarity Theorem: If two sides of one triangle are proportional to two sides of another triangle and the included angles are congruent, then the triangles are similar.

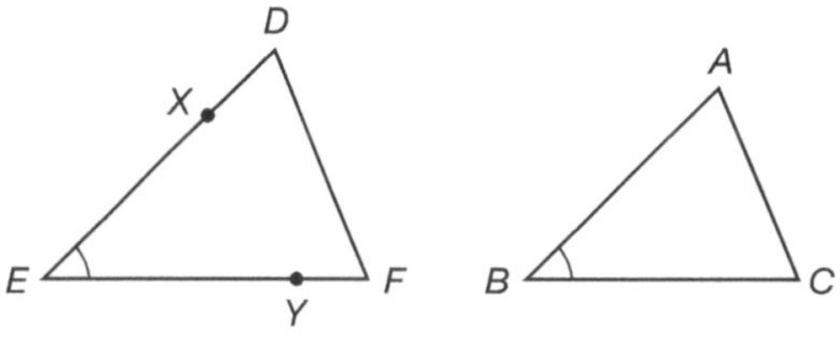

Given: $\angle B \cong \angle E, \frac{AB}{DE} = \frac{BC}{EF}$

Prove: $\triangle ABC \sim \triangle DEF$

Hint: Assume that $AB < DE$ and choose point X on $\overline{DE}$ so that $\overline{EX} \cong \overline{BA}$. Then choose point Y on $\overline{EF}$ so that $\angle EXY \cong \angle EDF$. Show that $\triangle XEY \sim \triangle DEF$ and that $\triangle ABC \cong \triangle XEY$.

7. (34) **Error Analysis** A student drew the figure at right and called it a parallelogram. Explain where the student erred.

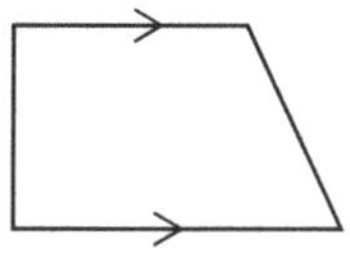

* **8.** (46) **Landscaping** A gardener wants all of the triangular gardens in a yard to be similar shapes. The first garden has sides that are 3, 4, and 6 feet long. If the second garden has to have sides of 12 and 16 feet corresponding to the 3- and 4-foot sides of the other garden, what is the length of the third side?

9. (44) Given $\triangle JKL \sim \triangle EFG$, with $JL = 25$ and $EG = 15$, what is the ratio of their corresponding sides?

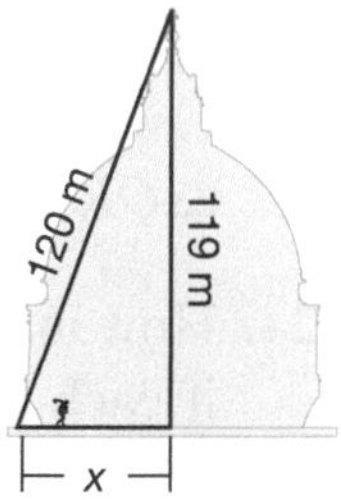

10. (29, 33) **Architecture** The Dome of St. Peters in Vatican City is 119 meters tall. If you are standing 120 meters away from the zenith of the dome, how far are you from standing directly underneath it?

11. (20) **Algebra** Suppose the conjunction, "$x^2 < 9$ and $x^2 > 4$" is true. Write a disjunction of two statements, involving x but not x^2, which must be true.

12. (38) **Algebra** Find the value of x that makes N the incenter of this triangle.

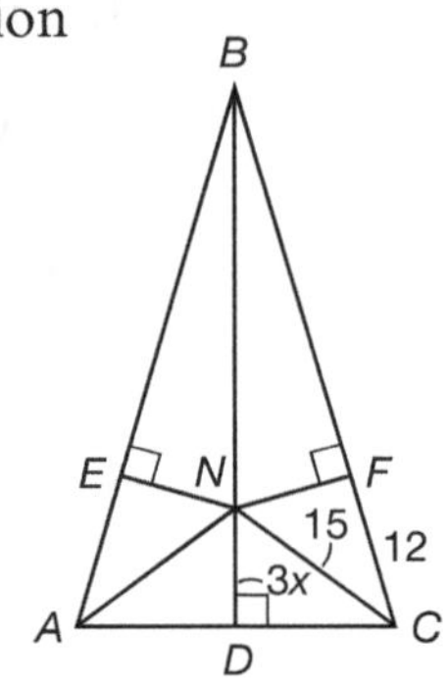

***13.** (45) A square on the coordinate plane has side lengths that are each 6 units long. A vertex is at the origin. Find the coordinates of each vertex.

14. (43) **Write** Explain the difference between a tangent line and a secant line with respect to circles.

15. (29) The legs in a right triangle are 9 inches and 12 inches long. What is the length of the hypotenuse?

16. (36) Use the LL Congruence Theorem to prove that $\triangle HJK \cong \triangle LMN$.

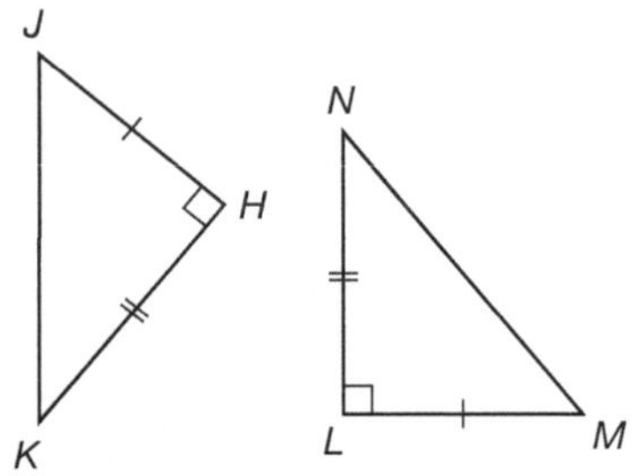

***17.** (46) **Algebra** Given that $\triangle ABC \sim \triangle DEF$, $AB = 12$, $DE = 16$, and $EF = 20$, what is the length of BC?

***18.** (45) An isosceles triangle on the coordinate plane has side lengths of 8, 5, and 5 units, respectively. The long side is along the x-axis. Find the coordinates of each vertex.

19. (Inv 4) **Justify** In the two triangles shown, which is greater, x or y? Explain.

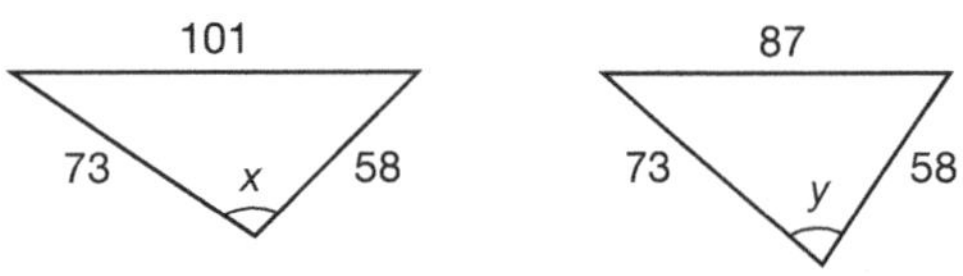

***20.** (46) **Construction** A house has triangular roof structures, or gables, which are similar to the gables of the attached garage. If the base of the house gable is 25 feet and the base of the garage gable is 40 feet, what is the similarity ratio between the two lengths?

***21.** (46) Explain why the triangles are similar, then find the value of x.

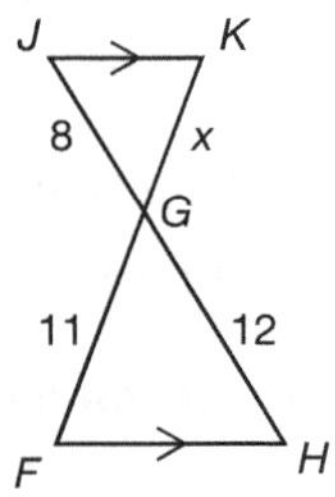

22. (7) **Wordplay** Formulate a conjecture that describes the following pattern. *pop, noon, level, redder, racecar.*

23. (38) Using the diagram at right, P is the incenter of $\triangle QRS$. Find RV.

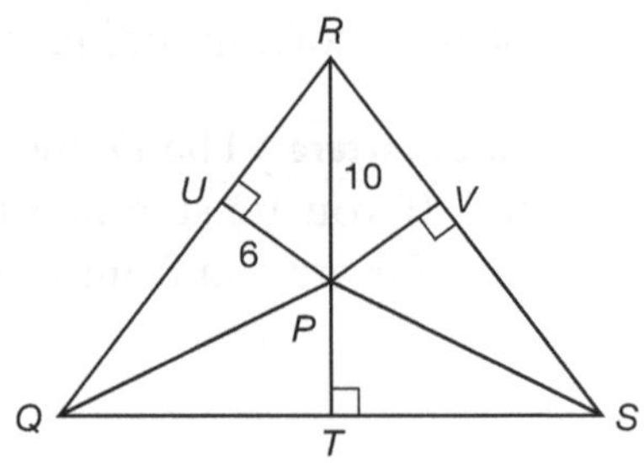

24. (Inv 3) How many sides does a convex polygon have, if each interior angle is equal to 179°?

***25.** (37) **Generalize** Line m is given by $ax + by = j$. Line n is given by $-bx + ay = k$. Is n perpendicular to m?

Find the lengths of the minor arcs given. Round to the nearest hundredth of a centimeter.

26. $\widehat{EF}$
(35)

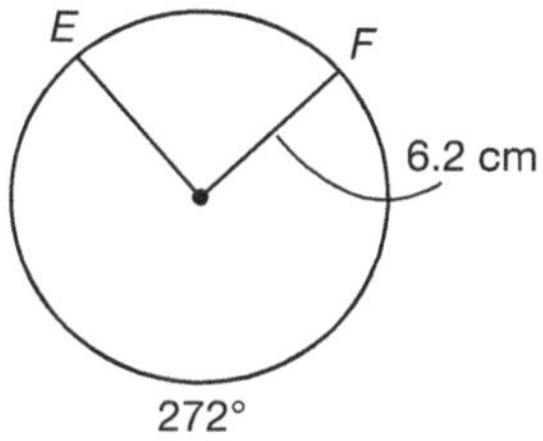

27. $\widehat{GH}$
(35)

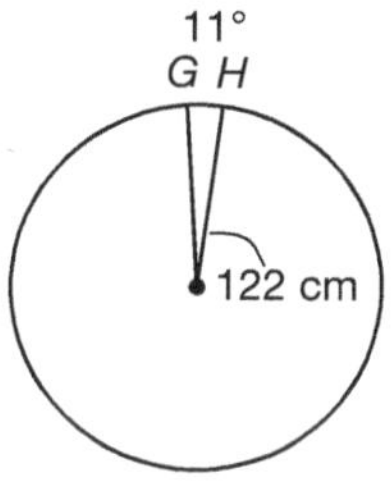

28. **Algebra** Find the length of $\overline{CY}$.
(32)

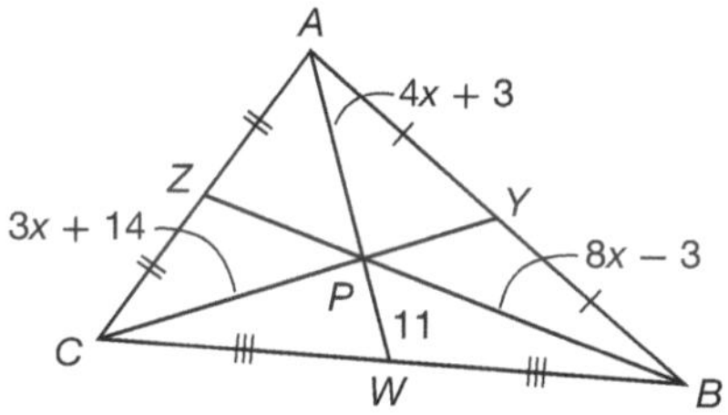

***29.** In triangles RST and UVW, $\angle T$ and $\angle W$ are right angles, $\overline{RT} \cong \overline{UW}$, and $\overline{ST} \cong \overline{VW}$. Prove that $\triangle RST \cong \triangle UVW$.
(36)

***30.** **Write** Suppose you know $\triangle ABC \sim \triangle DEF$, and you are given the lengths of all three sides of one triangle and the length of one side of the other. Explain how you would find the lengths of all six sides and the ratio of the corresponding sides.
(44)

Name ______________________ Date __________ Class __________

Circles and Inscribed Angles

LESSON 47

* **1.** (27) Write a two-column proof, proving that if a quadrilateral is inscribed in a circle, then it has supplementary opposite angles.
Given: *ABCD* is inscribed in a circle.
Prove: $\angle A$ is supplementary to $\angle C$.

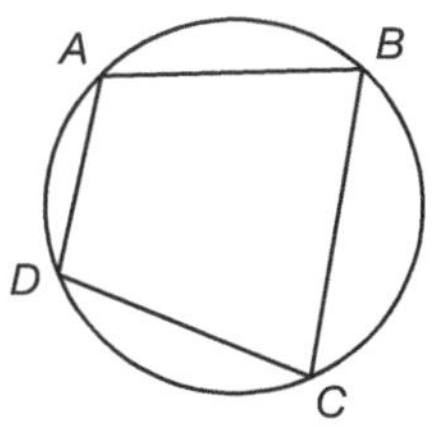

2. (41) **Electrical Wire** An electrician cuts a 45-inch cable cord into three pieces, with a ratio of 2:3:4. What are the lengths of the three pieces of cable?

* **3.** (47) **Formulate** Quadrilateral *ABCD* is inscribed in a circle. Write two equations that show the relationships of the angles of the quadrilateral.

4. (39) **Justify** Ariel is fencing off a triangular area with some caution tape. One side of the triangle must be 14 feet and a second side must be 22 feet. If the roll of tape is 40 feet long, can he use it to fence off the whole triangular area? Explain.

5. (45) **Bicycling** Norma started her cycling trip at (0, 7). Eduardo started his trip at (0, 0). They crossed paths at (4, 2). Draw their routes on a coordinate plane.

6. (40) **Analyze** A composite figure is made up of a square and an equilateral triangle. If the figure has five sides, what is the relationship between the perimeter P and the square side length s? Explain.

* **7.** (46) **Algebra** Find the value(s) of x that make $\angle FGH \sim \angle JKL$.

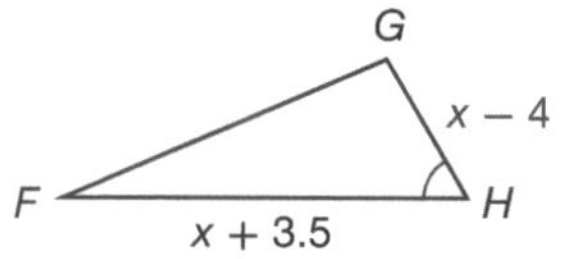

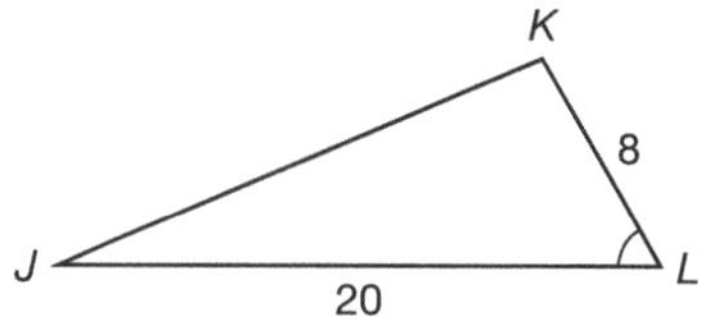

8. (44) **Hardware** If one socket wrench has a $\frac{5}{8}$-inch diameter and the other has a $\frac{3}{4}$-inch diameter, what is the ratio of the diameter of the bigger wrench to that of the smaller wrench?

9. (30) If in $\triangle ABC$, $AB = 7$, $m\angle ABC = 55°$, and $m\angle BCA = 60°$, and in $\triangle DEF$, $m\angle DEF = 60°$, $m\angle DFE = 55°$, and $FD = 10$, is $\triangle ABC \cong \triangle DEF$?

10. (40) **a. Multi-Step** Determine the figure's perimeter. Express your answer in terms of π.
b. Multi-Step Determine the figure's area. Express your answer in terms of π.

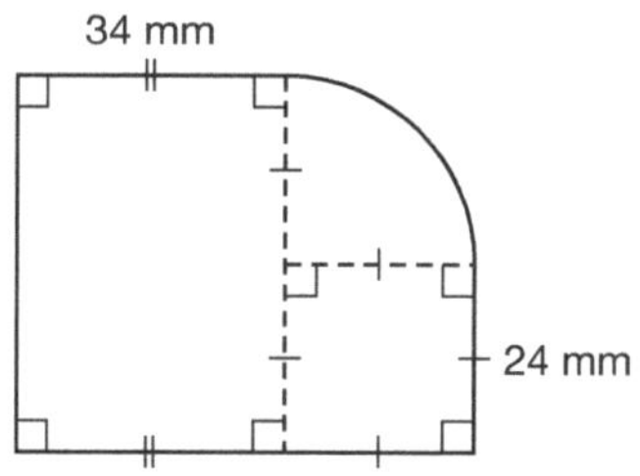

* **11.** (47) **Analyze** If a triangle is inscribed in a circle such that one edge of the triangle goes through the center of the circle, what statement can be made about the measure of one of the angles in the triangle?

12. (29) Give an example of a Pythagorean triple that is not a multiple of 3, 4, 5.

13. (12) There are two theorems or postulates you could use to prove that lines m and n in this figure are parallel. Which are they? What other facts are you using?

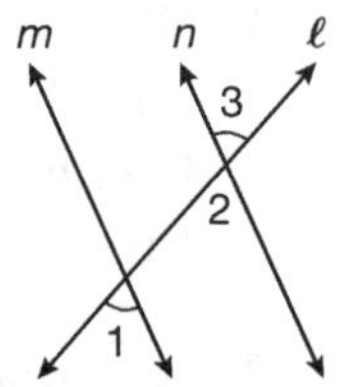

14. (43) A pipe with a diameter of 2.2 centimeters is being used for a drainage system. If a cross section of the pipe reveals the water level creates a chord 2 centimeters long, how close to the center of the pipe is the water level to the nearest hundredth of a centimeter?

15. (Inv 3) What is the measure of each interior angle in a regular heptagon? Round your answer to the nearest degree.

16. (43) Find the length of the chord CE.

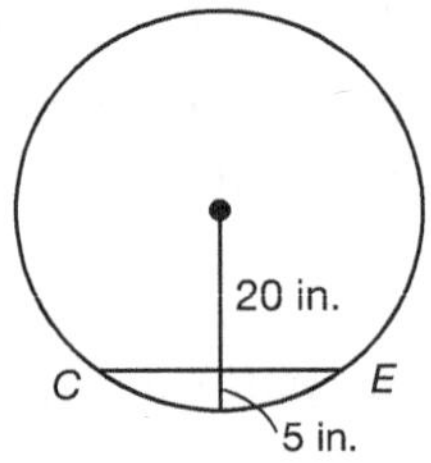

17. (17) Consider the following statement.

If the month is April, then it is spring in the Northern Hemisphere.

a. Write the negation of this statement's hypothesis.

b. Write the negation of the statement's conclusion.

c. Write the contrapositive of the statement.

18. (Inv 4) **Error Analysis** Rosalba was studying the given triangles and determined that $\overline{DF}$ must be longer than $\overline{AC}$. Is she correct? Explain.

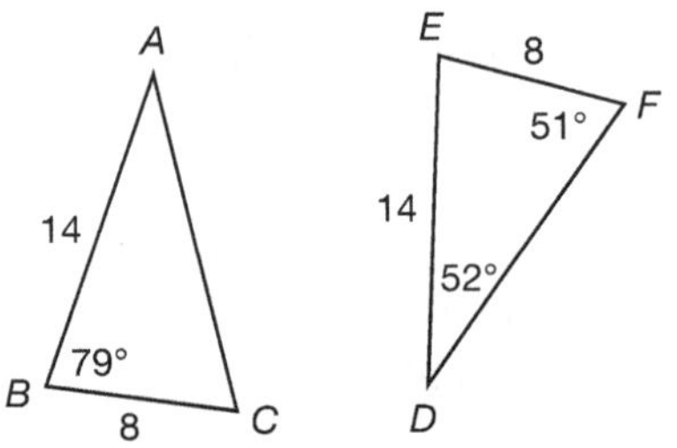

19. (37) What is the relationship between the lines $y = \frac{-1}{2}x + b$ and $2x - y = -\sqrt{b}$?

xy² ***20.** (47) **Algebra** Find the measure of $\angle ZWY$.

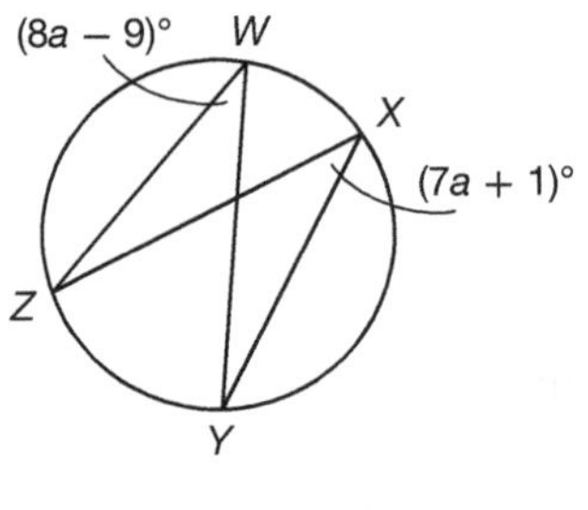

21. (41) What is the value of y in the proportion $\frac{2}{y-3} = \frac{4}{y}$?

22. (45) **Generalize** A square centered at the origin of the coordinate plane has a side length, k. Find expressions for the coordinates of each vertex.

23. Find the unknown length of the side in the triangle shown.
(29)

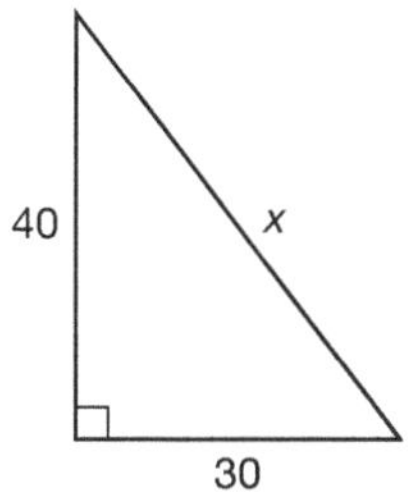

***24.** Use a ruler and a protractor to find the approximate circumcenter of a triangle with vertices at (−5, −2), (2, 3), and (−2, 4).
(38)

25. If in $\triangle ABC$ and $\triangle XYZ$, $m\angle ACB = m\angle XYZ$, $AC = XY$, and $CB = XZ$, is it true that $\triangle ACB \cong \triangle XYZ$? How do you know?
(28)

***26.** **(Baking)** Tomas is making a layered cake out of 2 individual triangular cakes. The cakes need to be similar triangles so Tomas can stack the smaller one on top of the larger cake. Prove that the two pieces of cake shown are similar. What is the measure of EF?
(46)

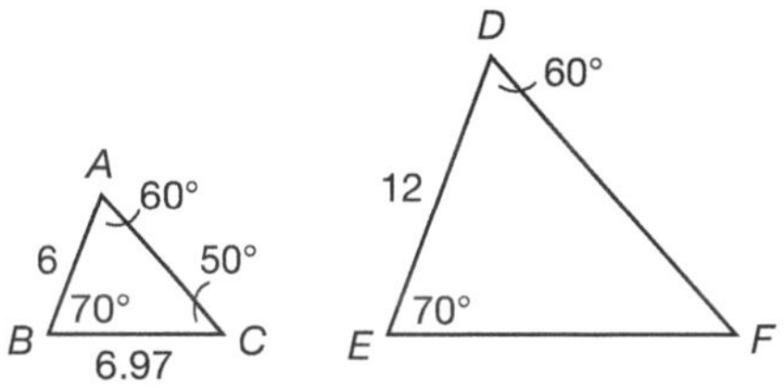

27. The ratio of the angle measures in a triangle is 3:5:10. What are the measures of the angles?
(41)

28. Which congruence theorem applies to these triangles?
(36)

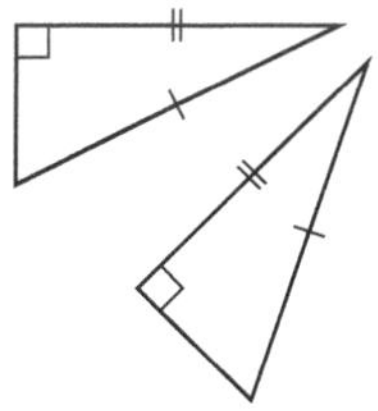

***29.** **Multiple Choice** The measure of an inscribed angle is _____________ the measure of the intercepted arc.
(47)

A half **B** one third

C one fourth **D** twice

***30.** **(Carpentry)** Gwen is building a truss for her roof. She needs to find the length of segment DE. Use similar triangles to help Gwen find the measurement she needs.
(46)

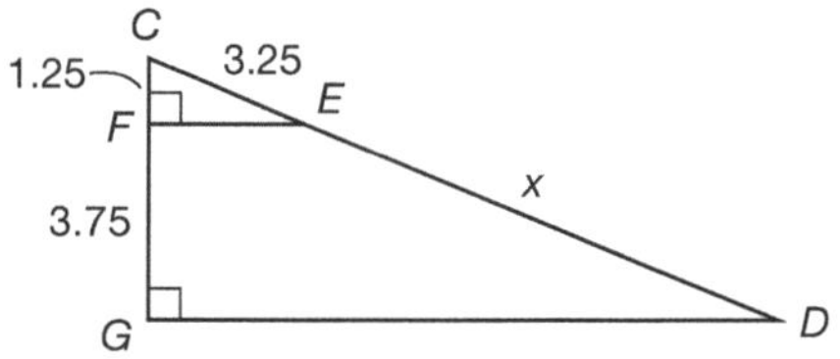

Name ______________________________ Date __________ Class __________

Indirect Proofs

LESSON 48

1. (16) **Verify** Choose two points on the line $y = 3x - 4$ and use them to verify that the value $m = 3$ from the equation is actually the slope of the line.

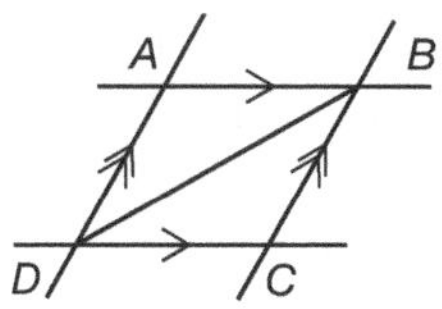

2. (30) In the diagram shown, prove that $AD = BC$.

3. (42) Find the distance from $(-6, 4)$ to the line $y = x$.

4. (39) **Floor Plans** In Thuy's room, the distance from the door D to the closet C is 4 feet, and the distance from the door D to the window W is 5 feet. The distance from the closet C to the window W is 6 feet. On a floor plan, she draws $\triangle CDW$. Order the angles from the least to the greatest measure.

***5.** (47) **Justify** If the measures of the angles in a quadrilateral are 132°, 90°, 48°, and 90°, can the quadrilateral be inscribed in a circle? Explain.

6. (32) **Error Analysis** Arturo wanted to find the orthocenter of the triangle shown. Explain the error Arturo made.

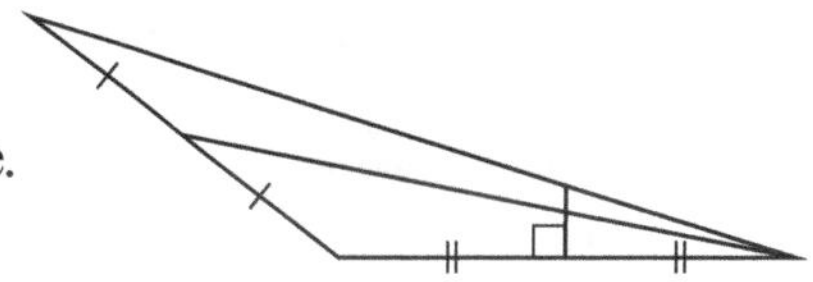

7. (41) Given $\triangle MNP \sim \triangle HJK$, with $MN = 3$ and $HJ = 66$, what is the ratio of the corresponding sides?

8. (40) **Landscaping** A lawn for an ornamental garden is designed as shown. Determine the area of grass needed for the lawn, to the nearest square meter. The semicircular regions have radius lengths of 2.5 meters each.

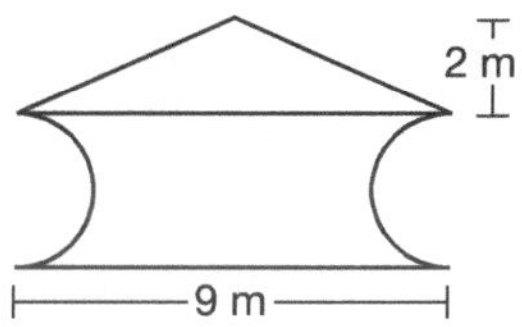

9. (41) Solve the proportion for g. $\frac{6}{16} = \frac{g}{12}$

***10.** (45) Triangle STU has vertices $S(0, 0)$ and $T(h, k)$. Find the coordinates of vertex U such that the triangle is isosceles.

11. (35) **Gardening** Oksana needs to fertilize her gardens for the winter, so she needs to find out how many square feet both gardens occupy. If the two gardens are sectors of a circular area, what is the area to be fertilized, to the nearest tenth?

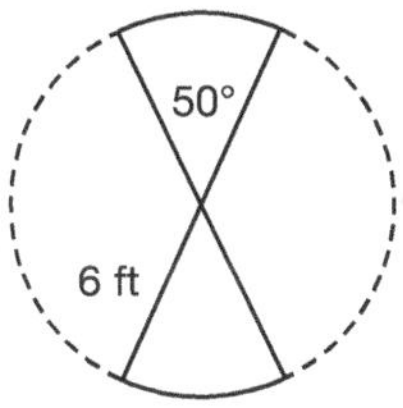

12. (28) If in $\triangle ABC$ and $\triangle DEF$, $AB = DE$ and $m\angle ABC = m\angle EDF$, what other piece of information is needed to show that $\triangle ABC \cong \triangle EDF$ by the SAS postulate?

***13.** (48) Use an indirect proof to prove the Converse of the Hinge Theorem. Refer to $\triangle PQR$ and $\triangle XYZ$ in the diagram.
Given: $\overline{PQ} \cong \overline{XY}$, $\overline{PR} \cong \overline{XZ}$, $QR > YZ$
Prove: $m\angle P > m\angle X$

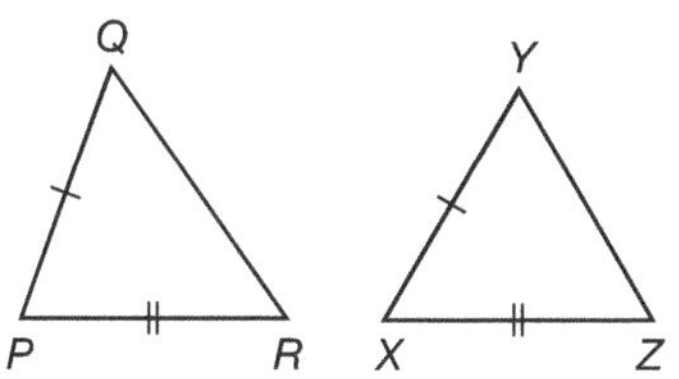

14. Find the length of a circle's radius given a 12-centimeter chord that is 5 centimeters away from the center of the circle.
(43)

15. Verify that $\angle ABC \sim \angle MNP$.
(46)

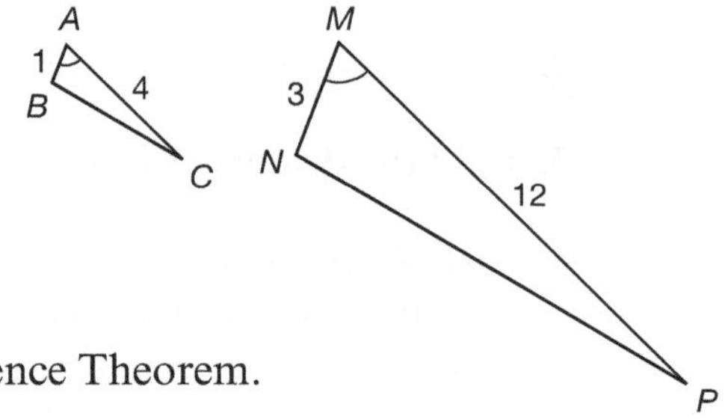

16. **Multiple Choice** The diagonals of parallelogram *RSTU* intersect at *P*. Which of the following is true?
(34)

A $m\angle RSP = m\angle UTP$ **B** $RP + SP = RT$
C $m\angle UPT = m\angle RPU$ **D** $2TP = RT$

17. Write a flowchart proof of the Right Angle Congruence Theorem.
(31)
Given: $\angle 1$ and $\angle 2$ are right angles.
Prove: $\angle 1 \cong \angle 2$

*18. Write an indirect proof showing that if two lines intersect, then there exists exactly one plane that contains them.
(48)

19. **Outdoor Cooking** Two pairs of tongs are being designed for a barbecue kit, each being of the same length. One is to be used to pick up larger items while the other is to be used to pick up smaller items. Which should be set with a smaller maximum spread angle? Explain.
(Inv 4)

*20. **Skating** Brianna skates in straight lines across a circular rink until she reaches a wall. She starts at *P*, turns 75° at *Q*, and turns 100° at *R*. How many degrees must Brianna turn at *S* to return to her starting point?
(47)

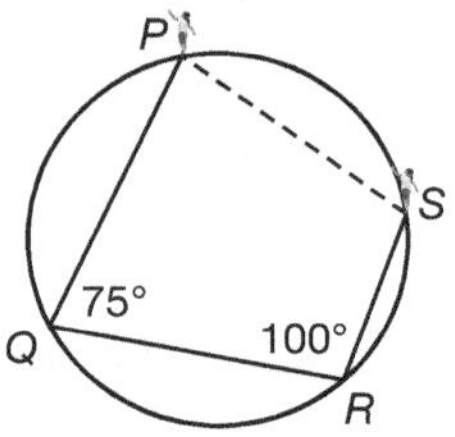

21. A diameter intersects an 8-unit long chord at right angles. What is the length of each of the two chord segments cut by the diameter?
(43)

22. **Multi-Step** Determine the perimeter and area of this figure.
(40)

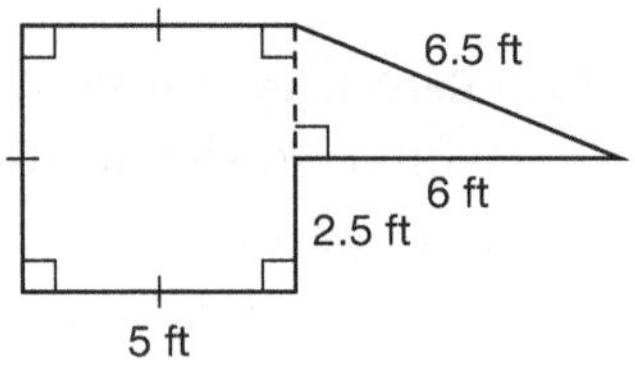

*23. **Algebra** In an *n*-sided convex polygon, the sum of the interior angles is $2x + 80$. In a $2n$-sided convex polygon, the sum of the interior angles is $5x + 20$. Determine the value of *n* and *x*.
(Inv 3)

*24. Use an indirect proof to prove the following.
(48)
Given: $\triangle HIJ \cong \triangle KJL$
Prove: $\angle KJL \cong \angle MIN$

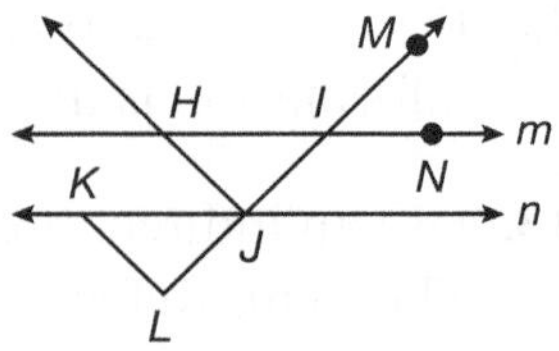

25. Triangles *ABC* and *DEF* are right triangles with right angles *B* and *E*, respectively. If $m\angle C \cong m\angle F$, $AC = DF = 25$, and $EF = 7$, what is *AB*?
(36)

26. (47) **Algebra** Find the measure of $\overset{\frown}{AB}$.

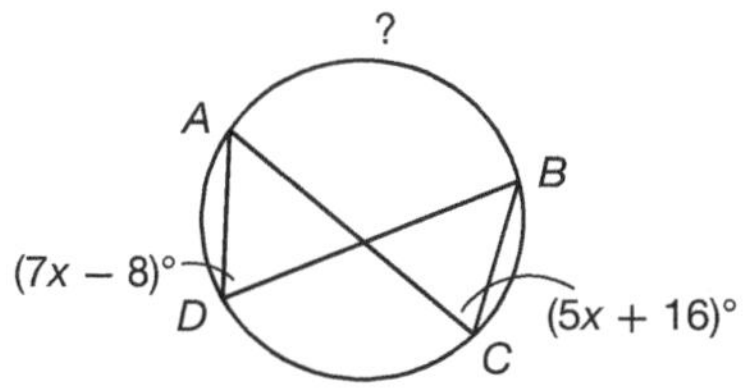

27. (35) **Write** Explain how the method for finding arc length is similar to the formula for the circumference of a circle.

28. (46) Explain why the triangles *STU* and *VWU* are similar, then find the missing length.

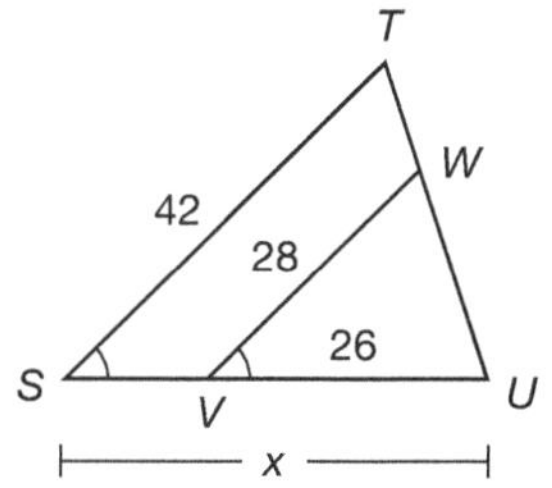

29. (36) **Model** Fold a standard 8-by-11-inch sheet of paper along one diagonal. Carefully cut or tear along the diagonal to make two triangles. Explain why the hypothesis of the Leg-Leg Congruence Theorem is true for these two resulting right triangles.

***30.** (48) Write an indirect proof showing that through a line and a point not on the line, there exists exactly one perpendicular line to the given line.
Given: P not on $\overleftrightarrow{AB}$
Prove: There exists exactly one perpendicular line through P to $\overleftrightarrow{AB}$.

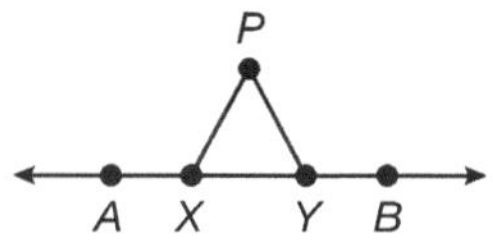

Name ______________________ Date ____________ Class ____________

Introduction to Solids

LESSON 49

1. (46) **Verify** Using the information shown, verify that $\triangle DEF \sim \triangle MNP$.

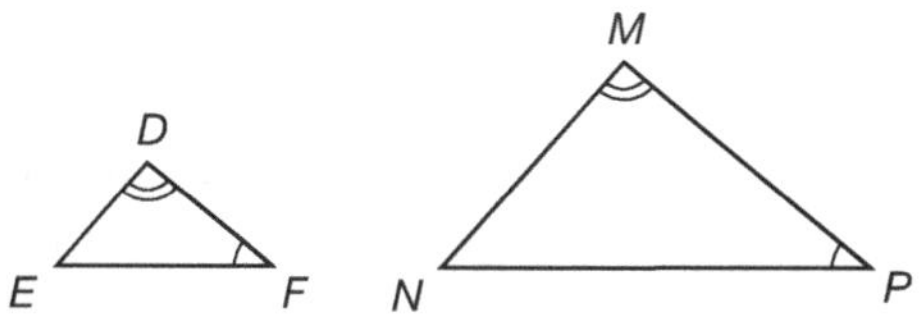

*** 2.** (48) State the assumption you would make to start an indirect proof if asked to prove the following statement.

If a polygon is a hexagon, then the sum of the interior angles is 720°.

*** 3.** (48) **Multiple Choice** Which statement contradicts the fact that $\triangle ABC$ is an equilateral triangle?

A All angle measures of $\triangle ABC$ are equal.
B The altitude of $\triangle ABC$ is not a median.
C All sides lengths of $\triangle ABC$ are equal.
D All angles of $\triangle ABC$ are acute angles.

4. (38) **Algebra** Using the diagram at the right, find the length of $\overline{NO}$ in terms of x if $MP = x + 3$, $OP = x$, and $MN = 28$.

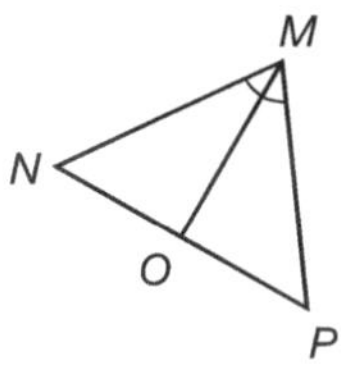

*** 5.** (49) **Generalize** Describe the resulting figures when any prism is cut parallel to its base.

6. (30) Using information from the diagram, determine the area of both triangles.

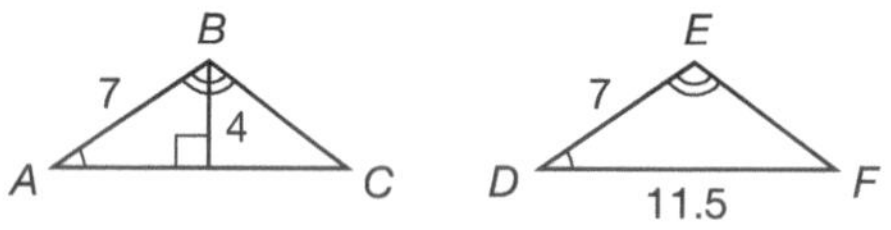

*** 7.** (45) **Multi-Step** A corner garden has vertices $Q(0, 0)$, $R(0, 2d)$, and $S(2c, 0)$. A brick walkway runs from point Q to the midpoint of RS. What is the length of the walkway?

8. (11) Determine the midpoint M of the line segment $\overline{JK}$ with endpoints $J(7, 5)$ and $K(1, 2)$.

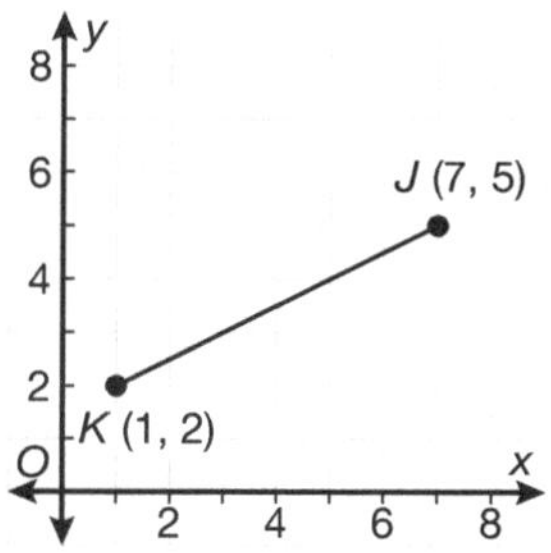

9. (28) What is the included side of $\angle LMO$ and $\angle OMN$?

***10.** (49) **Construction** A construction company wants to pre-cut all the pieces for the barn in the diagram. Each face, including the floor, is cut from a special fiberboard. Metal strips will be used along each edge, and a connector pipe placed at each vertex. How many fiberboards, metal strips, and connector pipes are needed to construct the barn?

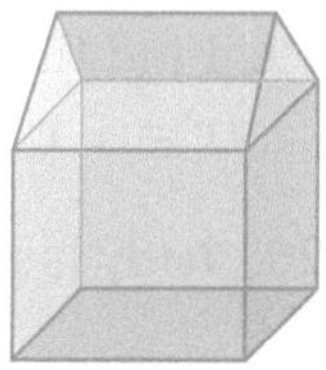

11. (43) In $\odot P$, determine the value of x.

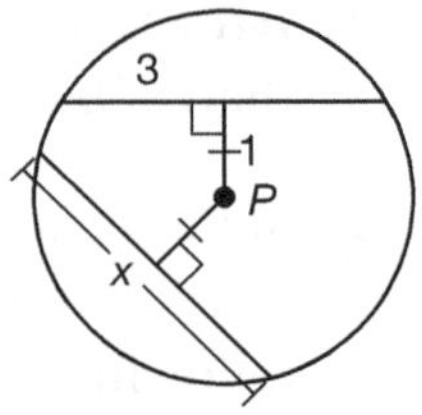

***12.** (48) If you are trying to prove indirectly that the altitude of an equilateral triangle is also a median, what assumption should you make to start the proof?

13. (44) **Carpentry** Susanna wants to increase the perimeter of her garden shed by a factor of 1.5. If the shed is 10 feet wide by 12 feet long already, what will be the perimeter of the new garden shed?

14. (41) **Zoos** The habitats of the animals at a local zoo is shown in the diagram. The zookeeper wants to keep the mammals grouped nearby each other. How far are the bears from the giraffes, to the nearest meter?

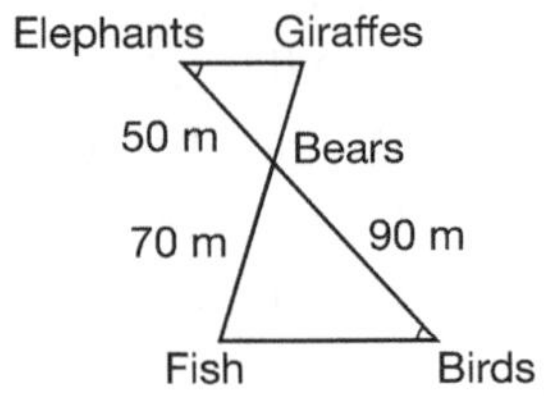

15. (41) The noncongruent angle in an isosceles triangle measures 76°. What are the measures of the three angles in a triangle that is similar to this triangle?

16. (Inv 4) **Security Cameras** A surveillance camera company needs to set up cameras that pan across three areas as indicated in the given diagram. Which camera pivots through the largest angle? … the smallest angle? Explain.

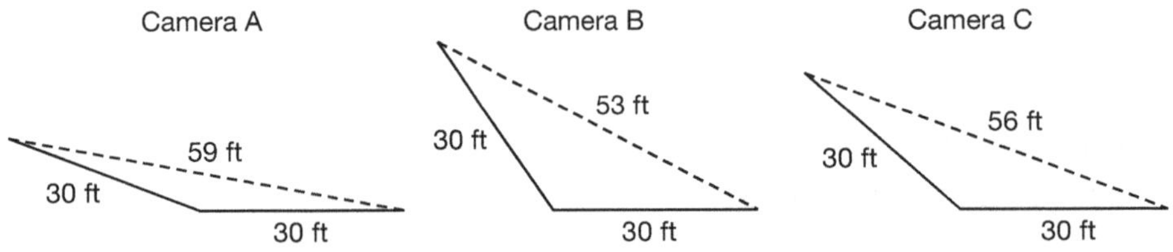

***17.** (44) **Analyze** $\triangle FGH$ and $\triangle KLM$ are similar scalene triangles. How many of their six sides do you need numerical values for in order to find all the other side lengths and the perimeters of both triangles? Explain.

18. (40) **a.** Determine this figure's perimeter.
b. Determine its area.

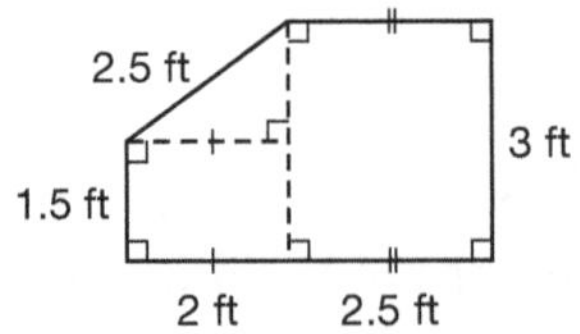

19. (42) Find the closest point on the line $y = -x - 4$ to (4, 4).

***20.** (49) **Verify** Is it possible to have a solid with 7 faces, 12 edges, and 10 vertices? Explain.

21. (29, 33) **Error Analysis** Below are two students' solutions for finding the length of the hypotenuse. Determine which is incorrect and explain where the error was made.

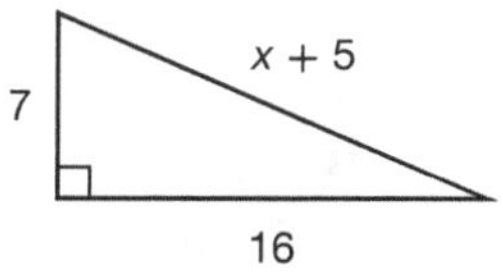

Leonardo's Solution

$$16^2 + 7^2 = (x + 5)^2$$
$$16^2 + 7^2 = x^2 + 5^2$$
$$256 + 49 = x^2 + 25$$
$$280 = x^2$$
$$x \approx 16.7$$
$$x + 5 \approx 16.7$$
$$x \approx 11.7$$

Florence's Solution

Let $x + 5 = c$
$$16^2 + 7^2 = c^2$$
$$256 + 49 = c^2$$
$$305 = c^2$$
$$c \approx 17.5$$
$$x + 5 \approx 17.5$$
$$x \approx 12.5$$

*22. (49) **Probability** Explain why a cube is the only prism used in fair probability experiments.

23. (43) Identify each line or segment that intersects the circle at right.

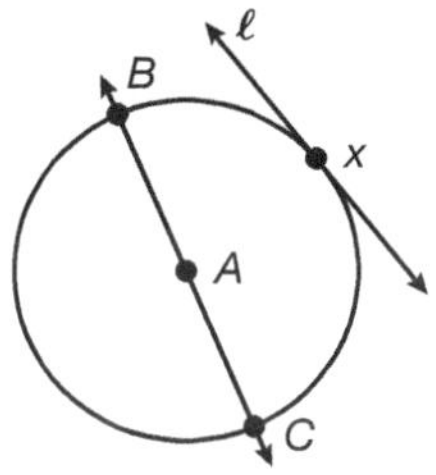

24. (47) **Write** What conclusion can you make about three inscribed angles that intercept the same arc?

25. (11) What are the coordinates of the midpoint of (2, −2) and (−7, 3)?

26. (34) **Algebra** *UVWZ* is a parallelogram. Find each length.

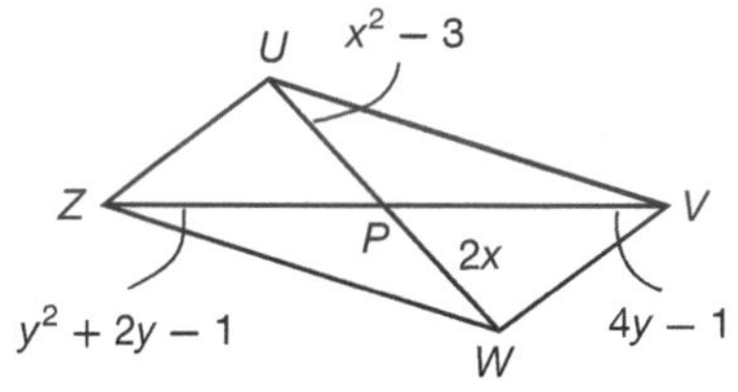

a. *UW*
b. *VP*
c. *WP*
d. *ZV*

Use the diagram to answer the next two questions.

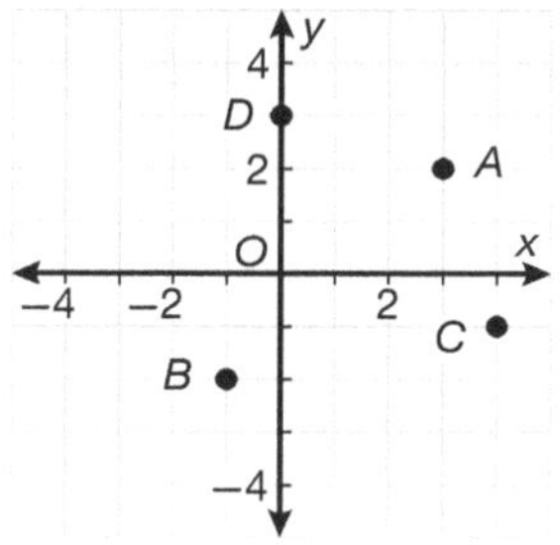

27. (9) **Multiple Choice** Which distance is closest to 5 units?
A *AB*
B *CD*
C *BC*
D *AD*

28. (9) **Multiple Choice** What is the length to the nearest hundredth of $\overline{AB}$?
A 11.49
B 8.12
C 5.66
D 5.83

29. (47) Find the measure of $\angle ABC$.

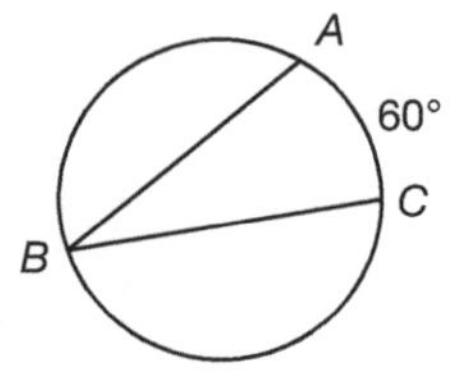

30. (39) (**Interior Design**) The kitchen sink, countertop, and refrigerator are the vertices of a triangle in a kitchen. If the distance from the refrigerator to the countertop is 9 feet and from the countertop to the sink is 8 feet, what range of values would the distance from the sink to the fridge have?

Name ______________________ Date ____________ Class ____________

Geometric Mean

LESSON 50

* **1.** What is the name of a figure that has 5 vertices and 5 faces?
(49)

2. **Interior Design** A wallpaper design is made up of repeating circles that contain inscribed angles as shown. If $m\angle ADC = 17°$, and $m\overset{\frown}{CE} = 42°$, find $m\angle ABE$.
(47)

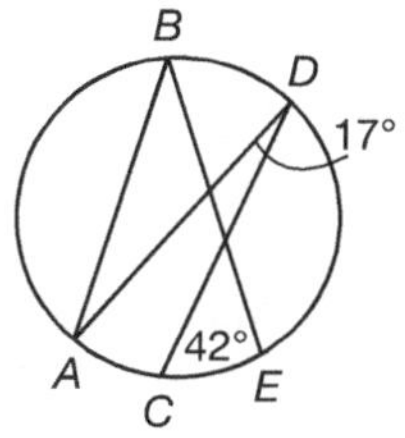

3. **Multi-Step** Parallelogram *EFGH* has three vertices at $E(-4, -2)$, $F(0, 6)$, and $G(3, 7)$. Find the coordinates of *H*.
(34)

4. **Algebra** If a chord that is perpendicular to a 6-inch long radius cuts the radius into two equal lengths, what is the length of the chord?
(43)

5. Given that $\triangle ABC$ is an isosceles triangle, find (x, y).
(45)

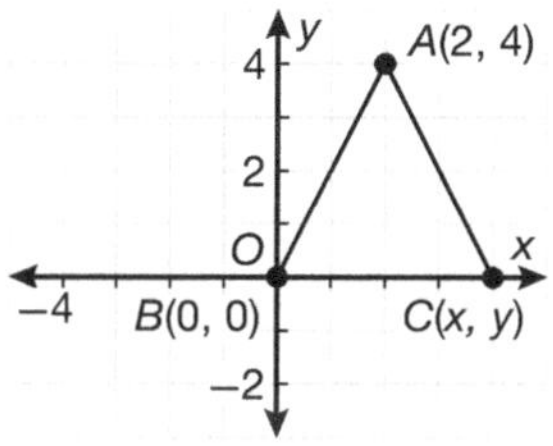

* **6.** **Write** Explain how the mean of two numbers is different from their geometric mean.
(50)

* **7.** On the diagram, $m\angle 1 \neq m\angle 2$. Prove $\overline{XA}$ is not an altitude of $\triangle XYZ$.
(48)

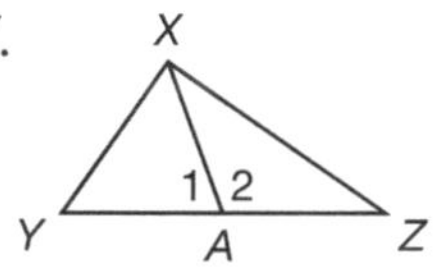

* **8.** **Algebra** Find the geometric mean of *x* and *y*.
(50)

9. Using the diagram given, complete the proof that $\triangle ABD \cong \triangle BCD$.
(30)

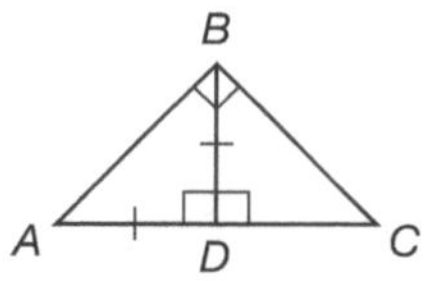

Statements	Reasons
1. $m\angle ADB = 90°$, $m\angle BDC = 90°$, $m\angle ABC = 90°$, $AD = DB$	1. Given
2.	2. Acute angles in a right triangle are complementary
3. $m\angle ABD + m\angle DBC = 90°$	3.
4. $m\angle DAB + m\angle ABD = m\angle ABD + m\angle DBC$	4. Substitution Property of Equality
5. $m\angle DAB + m\angle ABD - m\angle ABD = m\angle ABD + m\angle DBC - m\angle ABD$	5. Subtraction Property of Equality
6.	6. Simplify
7.	7. Definition of congruent angles
8.	8. All right angles are congruent
9. $\triangle ABD \cong \triangle BCD$	9.

10. (46) Name the angles that are congruent. If these triangles are similar, explain why.

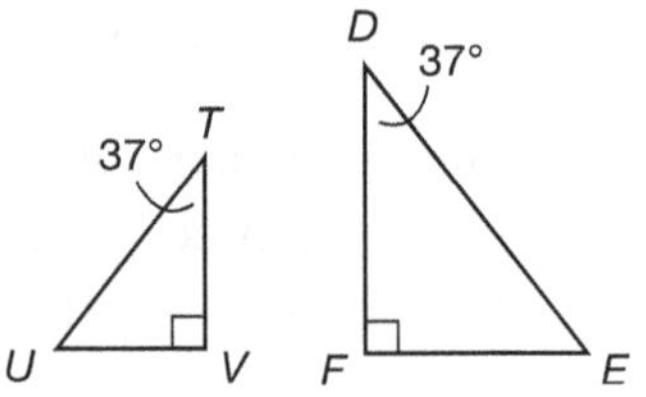

11. (Inv 3) **Algebra** The sum of the interior angles of a convex polygon is 5400°. How many sides does the polygon have?

***12.** (44) **Analyze** $\triangle XYZ$ and $\triangle MNO$ are similar equilateral triangles. How many of their six sides do you need numerical values for in order to find all the other side lengths and the perimeters of both triangles? Explain.

13. (47) **Algebra** Find the measure of $\angle G$ in the figure shown.

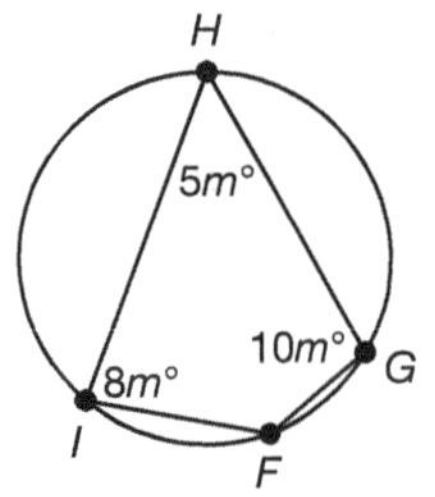

14. (42) Given the line equation $y = -\frac{2}{5}x + 4$ and $H(3, -3)$, find the point on the line that is closest to H.

15. (38) **Lifeguarding** A beach inlet has three lifeguards on duty at all times. They are spaced around the inlet so that they are all equidistant from the diving board. Copy this diagram to find the approximate location of the diving board based on the location of the lifeguards.

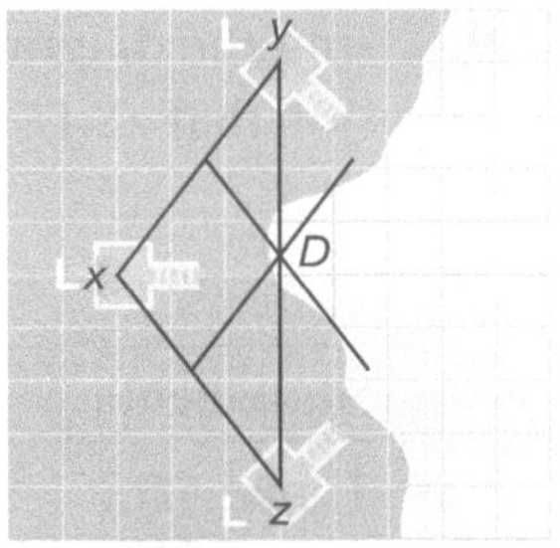

16. (39) **Justify** Explain why a triangle cannot have side lengths measuring 51, 13, and 31.

***17.** (50) **Carpentry** A builder is making a triangular eave as shown. What is the length of the brace in the center?

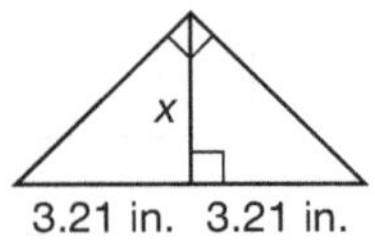

***18.** (49) **Multiple Choice** Which of the following *does not* describe a polyhedron?

A 6 vertices, 9 edges, 5 faces
B 6 vertices, 10 edges, 6 faces
C 8 vertices, 10 edges, 6 faces
D 8 vertices, 12 edges, 6 faces

***19.** (36) **Algebra** Suppose you can use the Hypotenuse-Angle Congruence Theorem to prove that these two triangles are congruent. What could the value of z be?

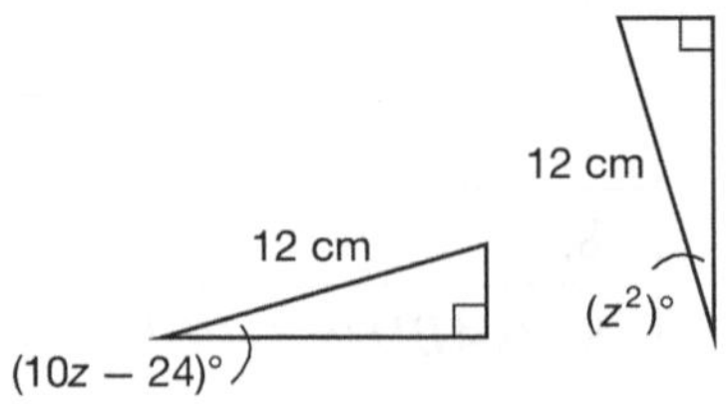

20. (29) **Landscaping** City planners have decided to build a new park that is in the shape of a triangle. Along one side of the park will be a 12-foot fence. It will meet at right angles with another fence that is 5 feet long and will run along a second side. What length will be the third side of the park?

21. (Inv 1) A transversal crossing two lines, makes a right angle with one of the lines. When does it make a right angle with the other?

22. (Inv 4) **Justify** Give a possible value for the angle at vertex C if you know that $AB < LK$. Explain your answer.

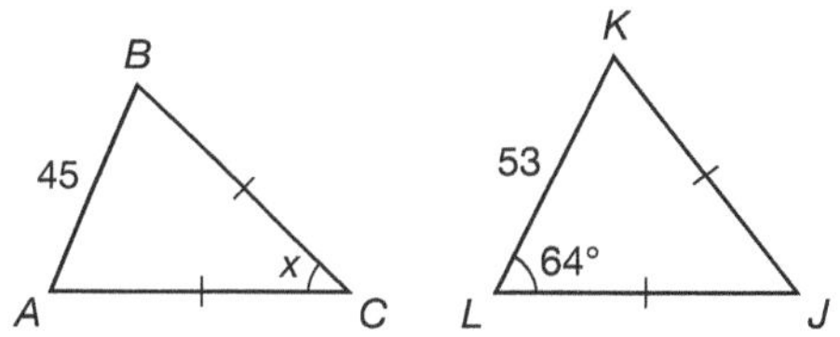

23. (45) A square on the coordinate plane has side lengths of 10 units. The midpoint of the bottom side is at the origin. Find the coordinates of the vertices.

24. (37) **Multiple Choice** Which of the following are perpendicular lines?
i) $x + y = 1$ **ii)** $-2x - y = 3$ **iii)** $2y - x = 5$
A i and ii **B** i and iii
C ii and iii **D** None is perpendicular to either of the other lines.

25. (29) **Baseball** The distance between consecutive bases in a baseball diamond is 90 feet. How far does the catcher have to throw the ball to get it from home plate to second base?

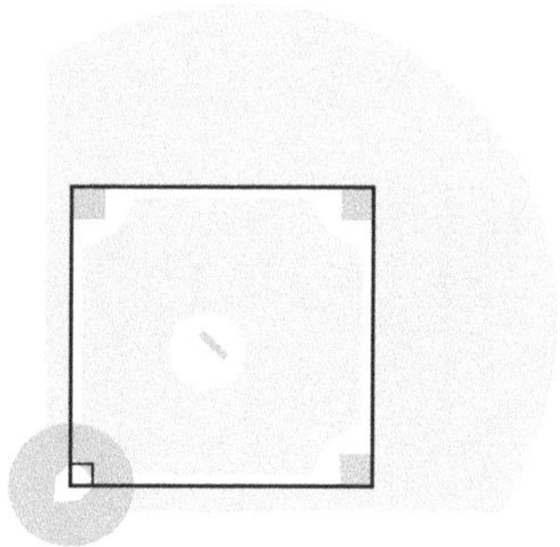

26. (35) **Analyze** Find the measure of an arc so that the associated sector has one-tenth the area of the circle.

*27. (49) **Error Analysis** Nikki counted 48 edges, 24 vertices, and 22 faces on a polyhedron. Is it possible for Nikki to be correct? Explain.

*28. (50) Find the value of x.

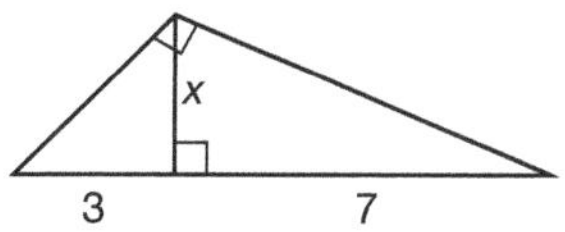

29. (28) **Algebra** If in $\triangle ABC$ and $\triangle DEF$, $AB = DE$, $m\angle ABC = m\angle EDF$, $BC = DF$, $AC = (20x - 10)$, and $EF = (15x + 15)$, what is the value of x?

30. (48) Which statement, if true, would contradict the fact that $\triangle JKL \sim \triangle PQR$?

A $JK = rPQ$ for some factor r

B $JK \neq PR$

C $\angle J \neq \angle R$

D None of the angles in $\triangle JKL$ have the same measure as any of the angles in $\triangle PQR$.

Name ______________________ Date __________ Class __________

Properties of Isosceles and Equilateral Triangles

LESSON 51

1. In $FGHJ$, $m\angle H < m\angle FJG$, $GH = 4x - 1$, and $FG = x + 8$. Find the range of values for x.
(Inv 4)

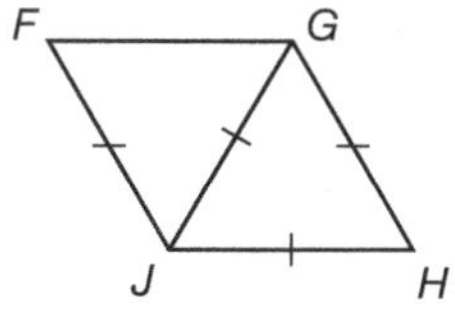

2. From the statement, "If Fabian's socks are clean, then they are in the dresser," what can you conclude about what will happen when Fabian's socks are clean?
(21)

3. **a.** Determine this figure's perimeter.
(40)
b. Determine its area.

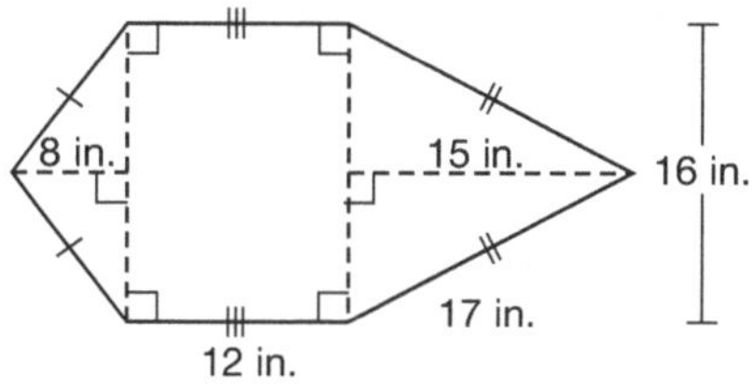

***4.** **Write** Explain how you would find the geometric mean of 4 and 7.
(50)

5. What is the measure of each exterior angle in a regular hexagon?
(Inv 3)

6. Using the diagram, find the length of $\widehat{AB}$ to the nearest hundredth of a centimeter.
(35)

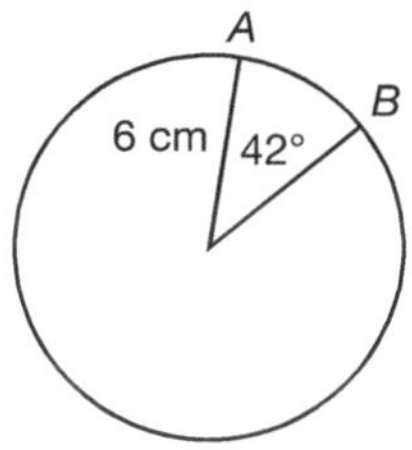

***7.** In $\triangle PQR$, $\overline{PR} \cong \overline{QR}$ and $m\angle R = 118°$.
(51)
a. Identify the vertex angle.
b. Determine $m\angle P$.

8. **Algebra** A polyhedron has 10 more edges than vertices. How many faces does the polyhedron have?
(49)

9. Find the unknown length of the side in the triangle shown.
(29)

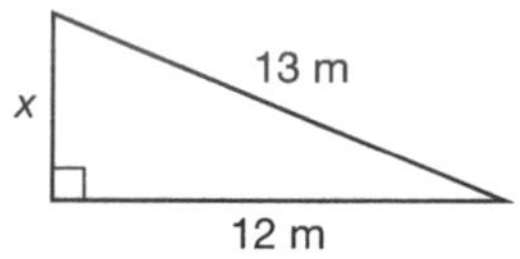

***10.** **Write** Explain why each angle of an equilateral triangle measures 60°.
(51)

11. **(Art)** In order to design part of her tile pattern correctly, Teresa needs to make the consecutive angles shown supplementary. How can she ensure the angles will be supplementary?
(34)

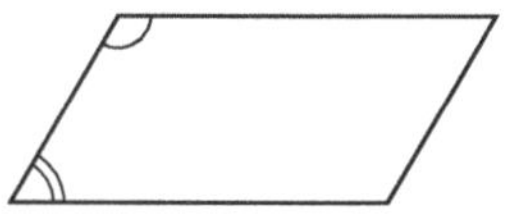

12. **Algebra** Two lines are perpendicular. One line has an equation $y = \frac{12}{m}x - 2$ and the other line has an equation of $4y = \frac{n}{9}x + 5$. Find one value for m and n.
(37)

***13.** **(Construction)** A builder needs to position a support brace as shown. What is the length of the support brace x, to the nearest tenth?
(50)

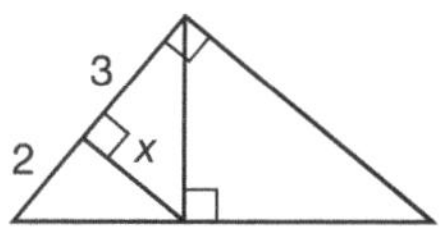

14. **Justify** Explain why $\triangle ADE \sim \triangle ABC$, then find BC.
(46)

15. Convex pentagon $PQRST$ has vertices $P(0, 0)$, $Q(-2, 2)$, $R(-1, 4)$, $S(x, y)$, and $T(2, 2)$. $QR = ST$ and $RS = 2$. Find (x, y).
(45)

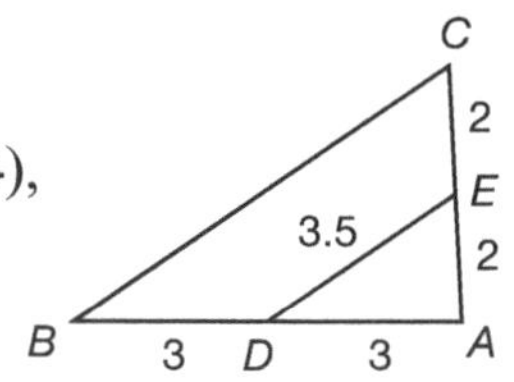

Properties of Isosceles and Equilateral Triangles

16. (18) **Surveying** Kristi, a map surveyor, is using an east-west baseline to locate various landmarks. She measures the clockwise angle from the baseline to the line passing through her surveying instrument and the landmark. Kristi takes two sightings from a clock tower, as this diagram shows.

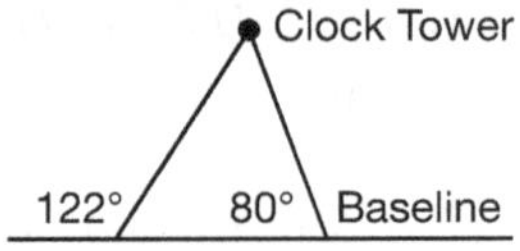

a. What measure is the angle between the two sightings?
b. What theorem did you use in part **a**?

17. (30) In the diagram shown at right, what information is needed to conclude that $\triangle TUV \cong \triangle DEF$?

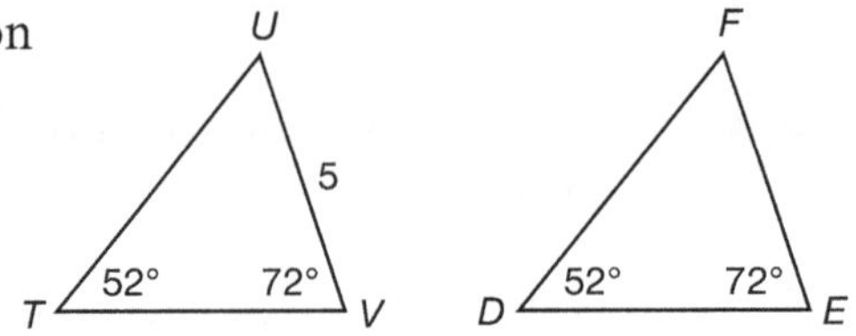

18. (45) **Generalize** Triangle GHI has vertices $G(0, 0)$ and $H(a, b)$. Find coordinates for a point I so that $\triangle GHI$ is a right triangle.

19. (36) Use the LL Congruence Theorem to show that $\triangle OPQ \cong \triangle RST$.

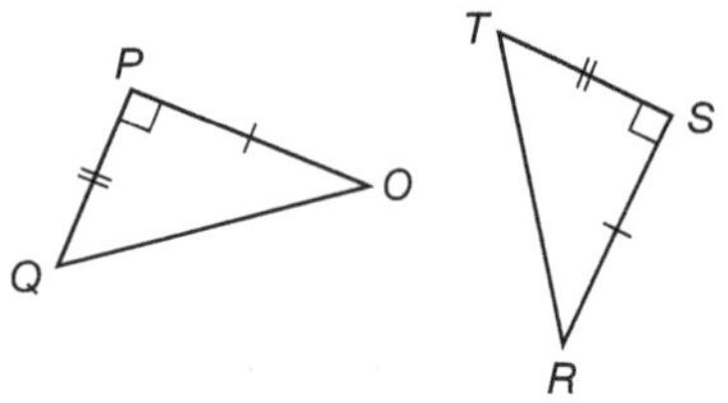

20. (37) What is the equation of a line perpendicular to $y = -4x + 12$, passing through the origin?

21. (39) **Cell Phone Towers** Three cell phone towers are the vertices of a triangle at right. The measure of $\angle M$ is 10° less than the measure of $\angle K$. The measure of $\angle L$ is one degree greater than the measure of $\angle M$. Which two towers are closest together?

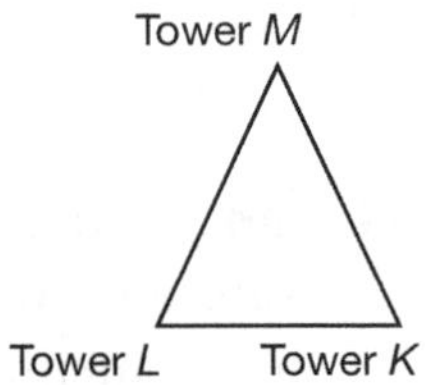

***22.** (51) **Analyze** Give a two-column proof of the Converse of the Isosceles Triangle Theorem.
Given: $\angle B \cong \angle C$
Prove: $\triangle ABC$ is isosceles.
Hint: Drop an altitude from point A to the base of $\triangle ABC$.

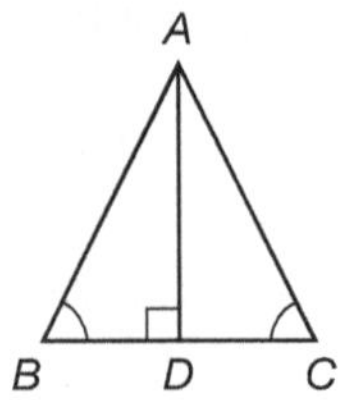

***23.** (50) Find the value of x and y on the triangle shown.

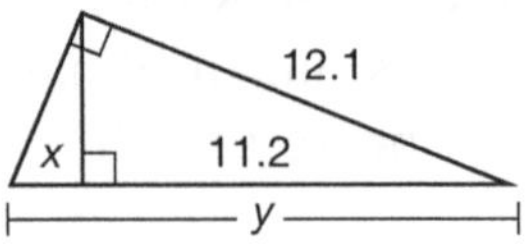

***24.** (33, 39) **Multi-Step** Determine whether each set of numbers can be the side lengths of a triangle. If they can be a triangle, determine whether it is an acute, obtuse, or right triangle.
a. $\sqrt{99}, 3\sqrt{13}, 21$
b. $\sqrt{7}, \sqrt{8}, 3$
c. 8, 7, 14

25. Determine the perimeter and area of this figure. Give exact answers.
(40)

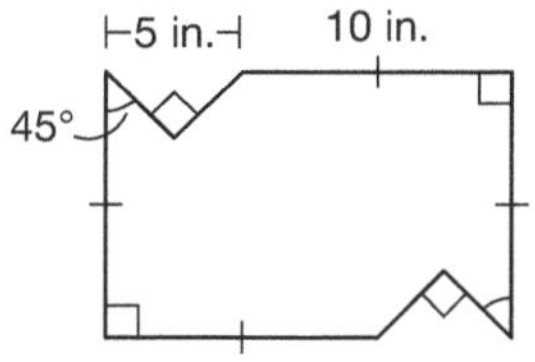

26. If $\triangle KLM \cong \triangle DEF$, what side of $\triangle DEF$ corresponds to side $\overline{KM}$?
(25)

27. Using the diagram, find PY in terms of x if $PV = 3$ and $YU = x$.
(38)
Point P is the incenter of the triangle.

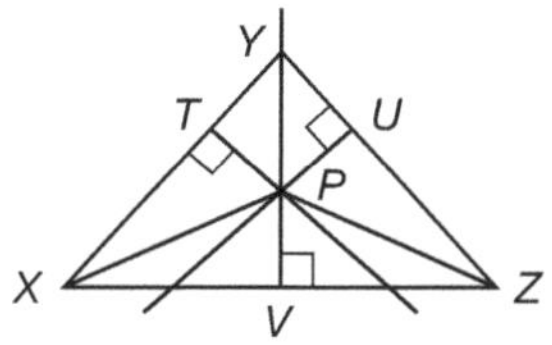

28. **Multiple Choice** The intercepted arc of an inscribed angle is a semicircle if and only if
(47)
the measure of the angle is

A 20° **B** 90°
C 100° **D** 180°

*29. Find the value of x in this figure.
(51)

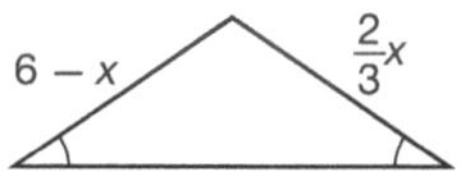

30. Prove Theorem 39-2: If one angle of a triangle is larger than another angle, then the side opposite the first angle is longer than the side opposite the second angle.
(48)

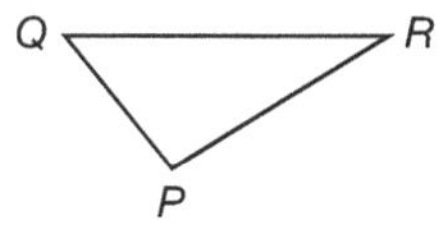

Given: $m\angle P > m\angle R$
Prove: $QR > QP$
Hint: There are two cases you must consider. One where $QR < QP$ and one where $QR = QP$.

Name ______________________ Date ___________ Class ___________

Properties of Rectangles, Rhombuses, and Squares

LESSON 52

1. *(Inv 5)* Draw a net for this polyhedron.

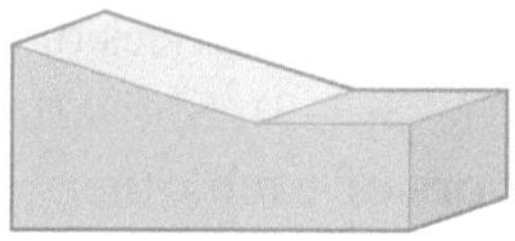

2. *(32)* **Multi-Step** Find the orthocenter of $\triangle JKL$ with vertices $J(3, 6)$, $K(3, -9)$, and $L(-5, -5)$.

3. *(49)* **Write** Compare a regular octagonal prism and a cylinder. Consider what happens as the number of sides of the base of a prism increases.

4. *(50)* **Carpentry** A cabinetmaker needs to position a support brace as shown. What is the length x of the support brace?

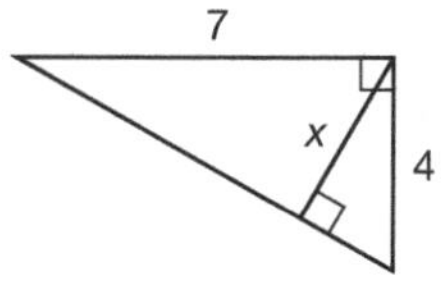

***5.** *(52)* **Art** Joni wants to use a square piece of paper for an art project. Explain how she could easily determine if a piece of paper is square.

6. *(35)* The circumference of a circle is 113 feet. If a sector has an area of 12 ft^2, what is the measure of the arc to the nearest degree?

7. *(37)* **Error Analysis** Henrietta is trying to find the slope of the line that passes through the point (8, 0) and is perpendicular to the line $y = 2x + 1$. Her answer is $y = \frac{1}{2}x + 4$. Is she correct? Why or why not?

8. *(46)* Are these two triangles similar? Give a reason to support your answer.

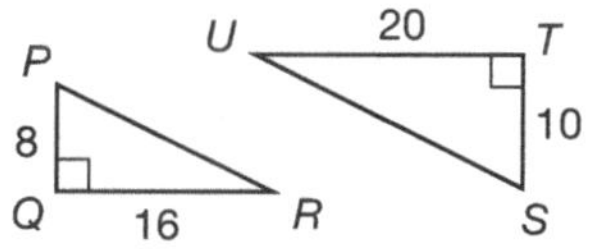

9. *(41)* **Generalize** Explain how a parallelogram could be similar to a rectangle.

***10.** *(52)* **Algebra** A rhombus has two angles that each measure $(9x + 1)°$ and two angles that each measure $(20x + 5)°$. Find the measure of each of the four angles in the rhombus.

***11.** *(50)* Find the geometric mean of $\sqrt{11}$ and $\sqrt{5}$.

***12.** *(51)* **Chemistry** This diagram shows the atoms and bonds in a water molecule. The bond angle at the oxygen (O) atom is always 104.5°. The distances from the oxygen atom to each hydrogen (H) atom are equal. What are the measures of the other two angles, to the nearest tenth?

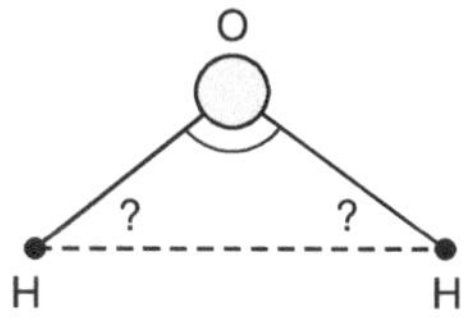

13. *(10)* **Multiple Choice** Which statement has a false converse?

A If two angles are supplementary, then they sum to 180°.
B If a triangle has two congruent angles, then it is isosceles.
C If a number is an even prime, then the number is 2.
D If two angles are complementary, then they are both acute.

14. *(45)* **Analyze** For a triangle with vertices $L(0, 0)$, $M(6, 0)$, and $N(3, y)$ to be equilateral, what must be the value of y?

*15. (52) **Multi-Step** The vertices of a square $KLMN$ are $K(0, 1)$, $L(4, -2)$, $M(1, -6)$ and $N(-3, -3)$. Show that the diagonals are congruent perpendicular bisectors of each other.

16. (35) If a circle has a circumference of $6x$, and an arc in that circle has a length of x, what is the angle measure of the associated sector?

17. (47) **Algebra** In the circle shown, find the measure of $\angle I$.

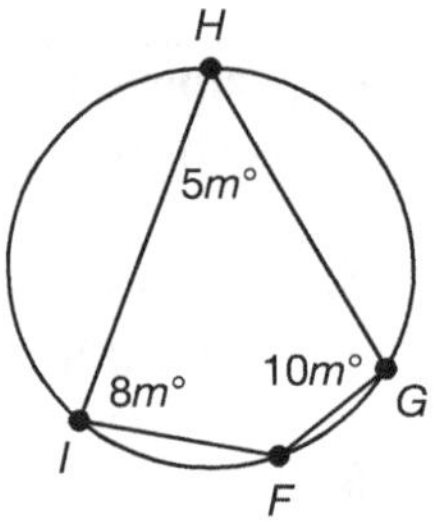

18. (51) In isosceles triangle PQR, $PQ = 28$, $QR = 28$, and $m\angle Q = 86°$.

a. Identify the vertex angle.
b. Determine $m\angle R$.

19. (47) What is the relationship between angles intercepted by the same arc?

*20. (31) Write a paragraph proof showing that if one side of a triangle is longer than another side, then the angle opposite the first side is larger than the angle opposite the second side.
Given: $RS > RQ$
Prove: $m\angle RQS > m\angle S$

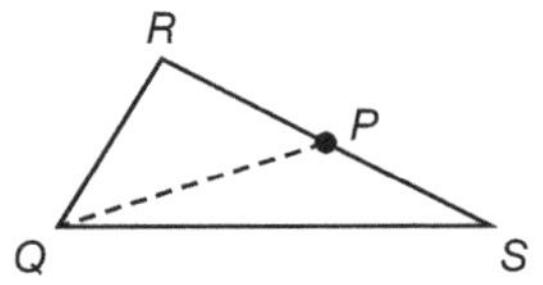

21. (51) In isosceles triangle ABC, $\overline{AB} \cong \overline{BC}$ and each base angle measures 40°. Determine $m\angle B$.

22. (33) **Algebra** Write an inequality to show the largest value for x that makes the triangle obtuse if the longest side is 9 units.

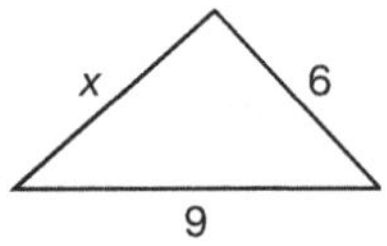

23. (29) In a right triangle, one leg is 36 feet long, and the hypotenuse is 39 feet long. What is the length of the third side?

*24. (52) **Fence Construction** A homeowner wants to build a fence gate with reinforcing diagonal braces. How can he make sure the gate is rectangular without measuring the angles?

*25. (40) **Predict** This figure is formed from three congruent rectangles.

a. Determine the perimeter of the figure.
b. Consider the figure formed by extending the pattern to four congruent rectangles. Determine the perimeter of the new figure.
c. Determine a formula for the perimeter of a figure in the same pattern formed from n congruent rectangles.

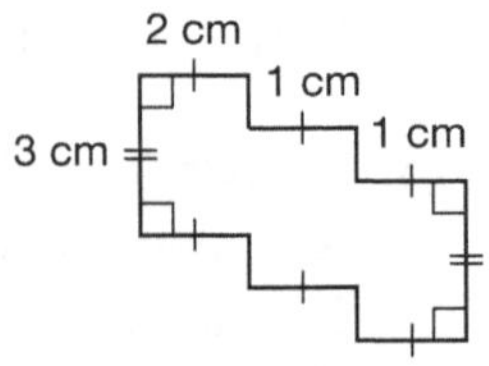

26. (46) To measure the distance *EF* across the lake, a surveyor at *S* locates points *E*, *F*, *G*, and *H* as shown. What is the length of $\overline{EF}$?

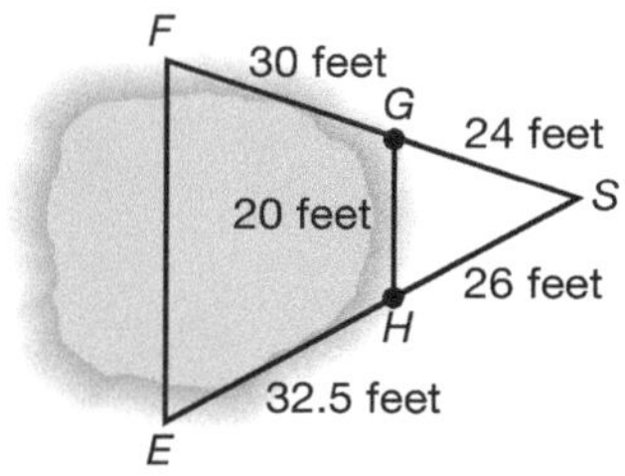

27. (38) **Write** Describe how to circumscribe a circle around an obtuse triangle.

28. (34) *ABCD* is a parallelogram. If $\overline{AB}$ is 3 times longer than $\overline{AD}$ and the perimeter of *ABCD* is 12, how long is each side?

29. (48) Suppose you are to prove $\overline{AB} \cong \overline{CD}$. State the assumption you would make to start an indirect proof.

*30. (43) **Hiking** Yvette was planning on going around a thick, circular clump of trees, but she found a shortcut through it. If the diameter of the circular area is 100 meters, how much shorter is her direct path, to the nearest meter, than traveling around the trees?

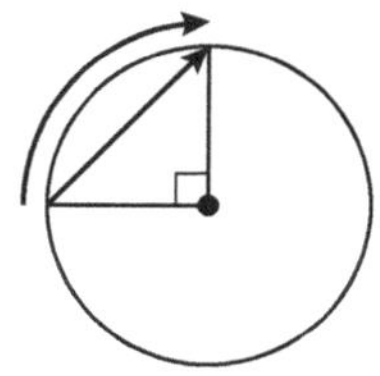

Name ______________________ Date ____________ Class ____________

45°-45°-90° Right Triangles

LESSON 53

1. (39) **Construction** The measurements in the diagram are from the attic space in a new home. If the angle measure of 72° is an inaccurate label on the diagram, what is the range of degrees that the mislabeled angle could be? It is given that the side opposite the mislabeled angle is the longest side of the triangle, and the side opposite the 48° is the shortest side.

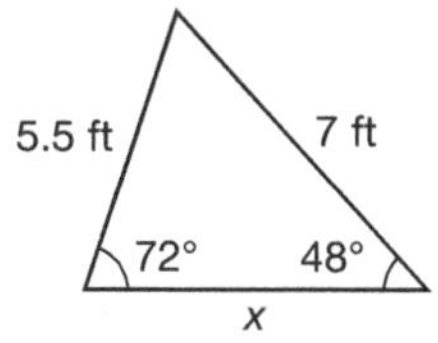

2. (49) A figure has 12 congruent edges and 8 vertices. Classify the figure.

***3.** (53) Find the exact value of the length of leg a in the triangle.

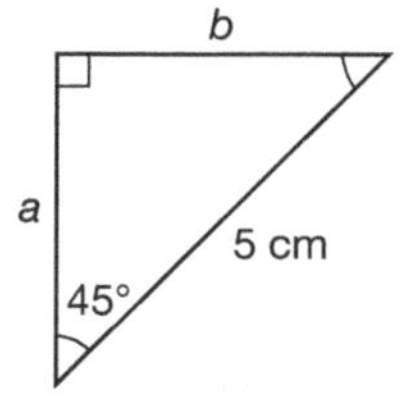

4. (32) **Center of Gravity** Are the orthocenter and the centroid both centers of gravity? If not, which one is?

***5.** (52) Is the following statement always, sometimes, or never true?
A parallelogram is a rectangle.

6. (50) Find the value of x and y in the figure at right to the nearest tenth.

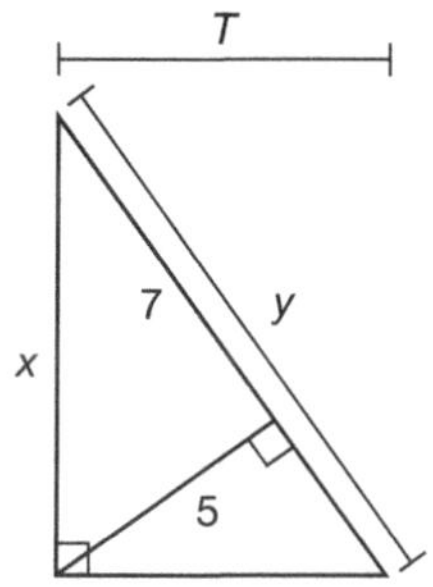

7. (40) A composite figure is formed by a rectangle with a square removed at one corner. The rectangle measures $6\frac{1}{2}$ inches by 5 inches. The removed square has side lengths of $3\frac{1}{2}$ inches.
a. Determine the perimeter of the figure.
b. Determine the area of the figure.

***8.** (53) **Write** Is every right isosceles triangle a 45°-45°-90° triangle? Explain.

9. (43) Identify each line or segment that intersects the circle shown.

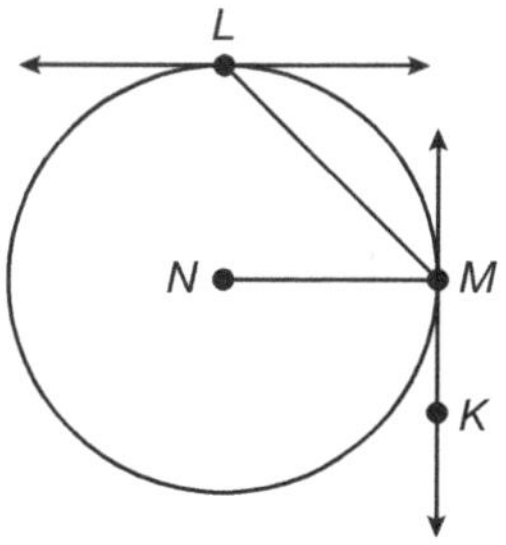

***10.** (53) **Algebra** The value of the side length in a 45°-45°-90° triangle is x inches. What would be the algebraic expression for the length of the triangle's hypotenuse?

11. (46) Write a similarity statement to explain why the two triangles shown are similar.

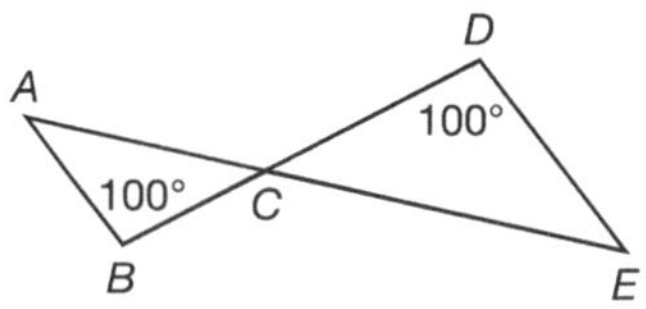

12. (44) **Analyze** What information must be known about two similar triangles in order to find the ratio of their perimeters?

***13.** (51) **Analyze** Write a flowchart proof showing that if a triangle is equilateral, then it is equiangular.

14. (35) What is the total area of the shaded sectors if the diameter of the circle is 8 meters? Write your answer in terms of π.

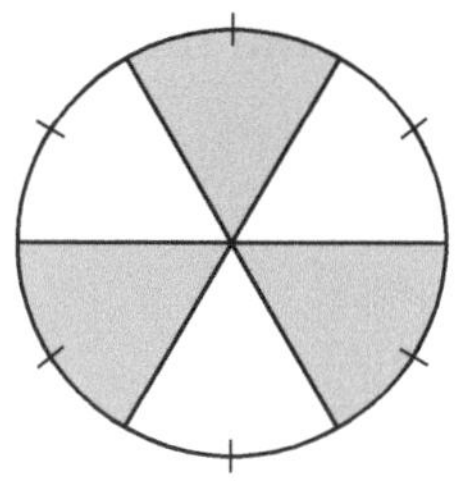

15. (42) Find the distance from $(-5, 2)$ to the line $x = 13$.

16. **Algebra** If in $\triangle ABC$, $AB = (12x + 11)$, $m\angle ABC = 12°$, $m\angle BCA = 21°$, and $AC = 7$ units, and in $\triangle DEF$, $DE = (5x + 18)$, $m\angle DEF = 12°$, $m\angle EFD = 21°$, and $DF = 7$ units, what is the value of x?
(30)

17. **Justify** Give a possible value for the length of XY. Explain your answer.
(Inv 4)

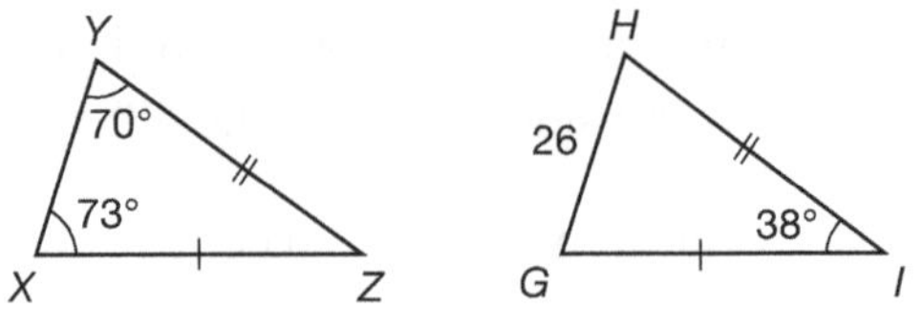

18. What is the value of b in the proportion $\frac{2}{5} = \frac{7}{b}$?
(41)

19. **Art** An artist is making a round ceramic plate with a pattern of lines on it. If $m\angle KLM = 20°$, and $m\widehat{MP} = 30°$, find $m\angle KNP$.
(47)

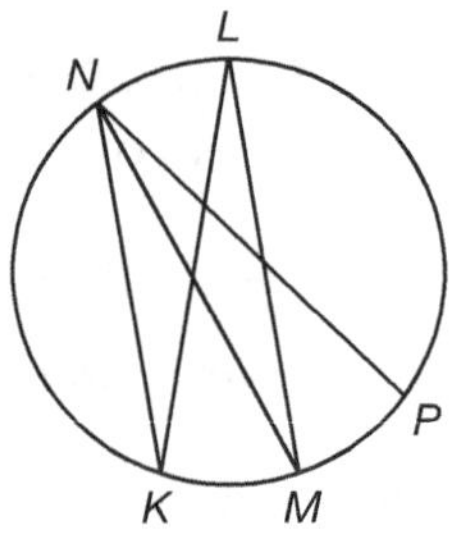

20. Suppose a chord of a circle is 10 inches long, and the radius of the circle is also 10 inches. What is the measure from the chord to the center of the circle?
(43)

*21. **Multiple Choice** What would be the perimeter of a 45°-45°-90° triangle with a hypotenuse of 73 feet, to the nearest foot?
(53)

A 52 feet **B** 176 feet
C 104 feet **D** 198 feet

22. **Design** A gift box has the net shown in this figure. Use the net to provide a counterexample to the following statement.
(14, Inv 5)

If the net of a three-dimensional figure has all lateral faces congruent, then the figure is closed.

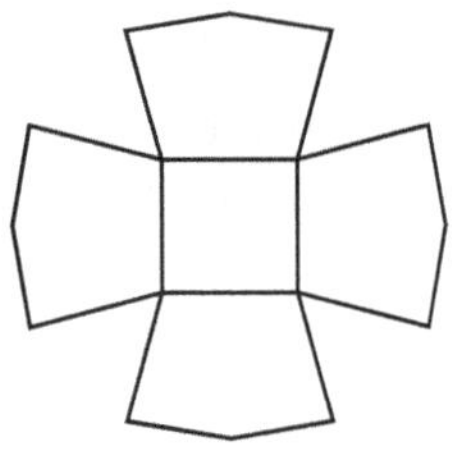

*23. $WXYZ$ is the rectangle shown. Find XY.
(52)

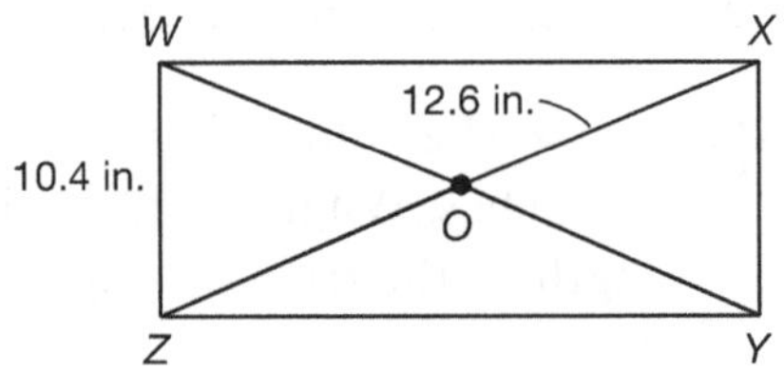

24. **Multi-Step** Find the centroid of $\triangle DEF$ with vertices $D(-3, 2)$, $E(9, 8)$, and $F(3, -4)$.
(32)

25. It is given that $\triangle ACE \sim \triangle BDF$. If AC is 3 units, CE is 12 units, and BD is 11 units, what is the length of $\overline{DF}$?
(41)

26. If two sides of one triangle are proportional to two sides of another triangle, and if their corresponding included angles are congruent to each other, then the triangles are similar by ____________________.
(46)

*27. Find the exact value of the length of the hypotenuse in the triangle.
(53)

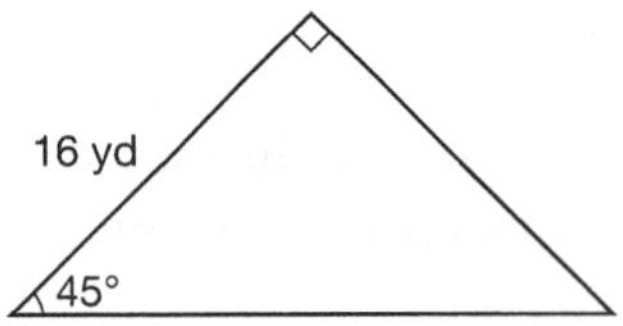

28. (36) Use the Hypotenuse-Angle Congruence Theorem to prove that $\triangle ABC \cong \triangle DEF$.

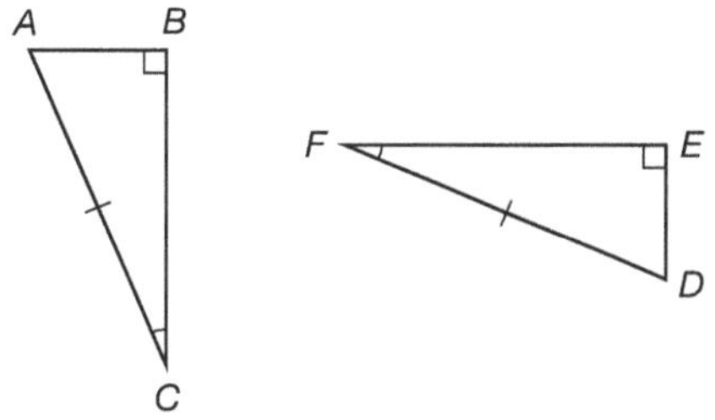

***29.** (52) **Write** Explain why the following statement is true.

If a quadrilateral is a square, then it is a rhombus.

***30.** (51) **Surveying** Renée takes the bearings of landmarks at A, B, and C from the same position, D.

Landmark	Bearing from D
A: Church Steeple	322°
B: Clock Tower	2°
C: Water Tower	42°

Suppose Renée chose point D to be equidistant from the church steeple and the water tower. What must be true about the clock tower's distance from each of the other two landmarks? Why?

Name ______________________________ Date ____________ Class ____________

Representing Solids

LESSON 54

* **1.** (54) Draw a triangular prism in one-point perspective so that the vanishing point is below the prism.

2. (52) **Write** Explain why the following statement is true.
If a quadrilateral is a square, then it is a rectangle.

3. (32) **Algebra** Find the length of $\overline{ZP}$ in the diagram.

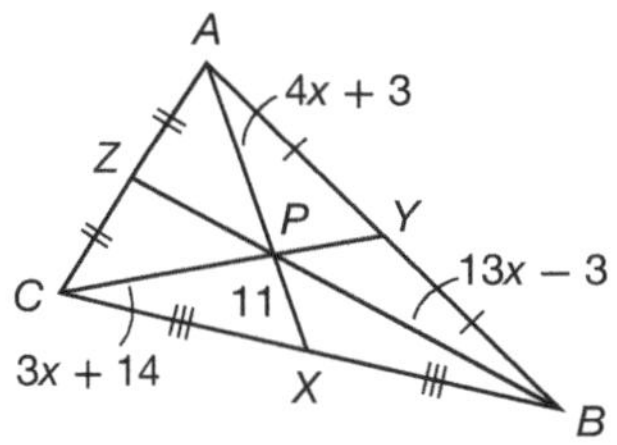

4. (42) What is the shortest distance from (5, 3) to the line $y = -2x + 8$?

* **5.** (54) **Architecture** An architect is creating different perspective drawings for a new building. The building is a rectangular prism and the client would like a drawing that focuses on the front façade of the building. Should the architect create the drawing using a one-point or two-point perspective? Sketch a sample drawing of the building.

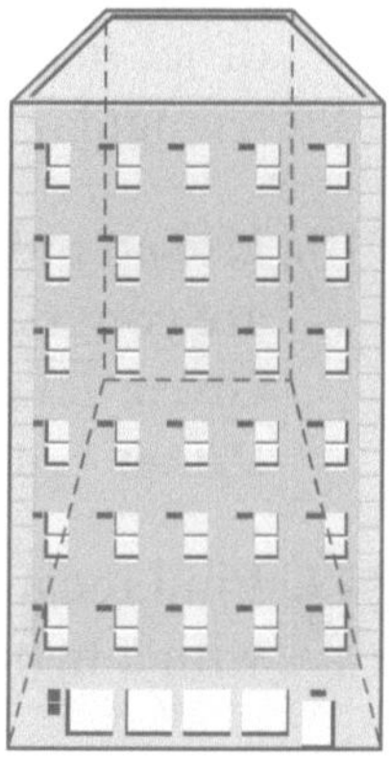

6. (49) A figure has a hexagonal base and triangular lateral faces. Classify the figure.

7. (37) **Multi-Step** Graph the line and find the slope of the line that passes through the points $L(4, 1)$ and $M(3, -1)$. Then find a perpendicular line that passes through point $N(-2, -2)$.

8. (50) Find the value of x and y in the triangle shown to the nearest tenth.

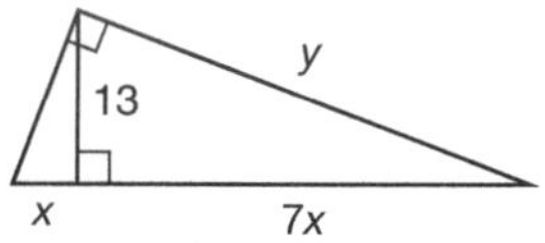

9. (Inv 3) What is the sum of the exterior angles of a convex 134-sided polygon?

10. (52) Is the following statement always, sometimes, or never true?
A parallelogram is a rectangle.

***11.** (54) Trace the figure at right on your paper. Then locate the vanishing point and the horizon line.

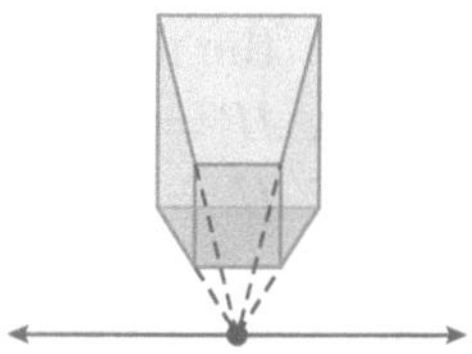

12. (30) **Algebra** In $\triangle ABC$, $m\angle ABC = 90°$, $AB = (3x - 7)$, and $m\angle BCA = 60°$, and in $\triangle DEF$, $m\angle DEF = 90°$, $DE = (5x - 17)$, and $m\angle EFD = 60°$. What value of x will make $\triangle ABC \cong \triangle DEF$?

13. (32) The point where three or more lines intersect is the ________________.

***14.** (36) Use the Hypotenuse-Angle Congruence Theorem to prove that $\triangle RST \cong \triangle UVW$.

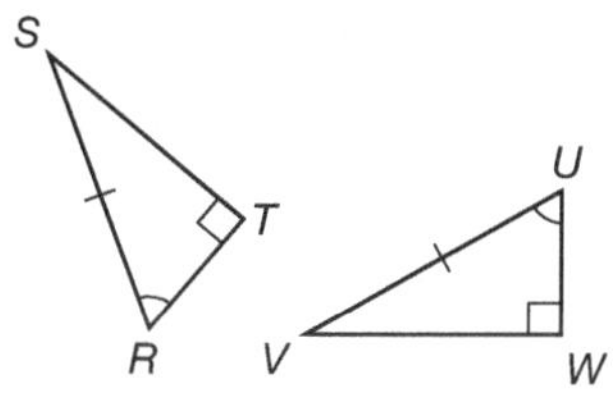

***15.** (53) Find the exact length of the hypotenuse of a 45°-45°-90° right triangle with a leg that is 57 feet long.

16. (40) **Formulate** Four congruent circles are cut out of a square as shown. Write an expression for the area of the shaded region in terms of the radius of each circle, r.

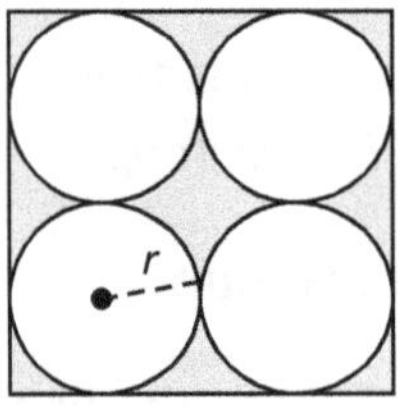

17. (51) **Aviation** Four jet aircraft are flying in a triangular formation. Jets A, B, and C form a line perpendicular to the flight heading, while jet B is midway between the other two. Jet D flies directly in front of jet B. If $m\angle ADB = 37°$, what does the vertex angle of the triangular formation measure? Which theorem did you use?

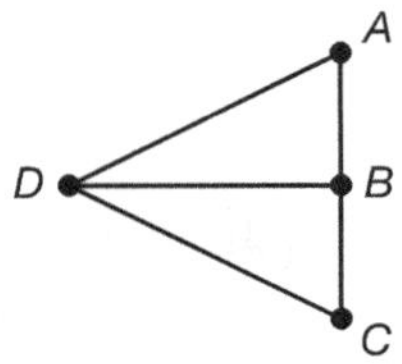

***18.** (48) Use an indirect proof to prove that if two altitudes, $\overline{BX}$ and $\overline{CY}$ of $\triangle ABC$ are congruent, then the triangle must be isosceles.
Given: $\overline{BX} \cong \overline{CY}$, $\overline{BX}$ and $\overline{CY}$ are altitudes.
Prove: $\triangle ABC$ isosceles.

***19.** (53) Find the area, to the nearest hundredth, of a 45°-45°-90° right triangle with a hypotenuse of 17 centimeters.

xy^2 **20.** (43) **Algebra** If a chord perpendicular to a radius cuts the radius in two pieces that are 7 and 2 inches long, respectively, what are the two possible lengths of the chord to the nearest tenth?

***21.** (54) **Justify** How does a two-point perspective differ when the vanishing points are located close together compared with when they are located further apart? Justify your reasoning with drawings.

22. (50) Find the geometric mean of $\sqrt{2}$ and 5.

23. (34) **Multiple Choice** If the diagonals of parallelogram $JKLM$ intersect at P, which of the following is true?

A $JP = LP$ **B** $JP = KP$
C $JL = KM$ **D** $JM = KM$

***24.** (53) **Construction** The support of a shelf forms a 45°-45°-90° right triangle, with the shelf and the wall as the legs. Exactly how long is this support?

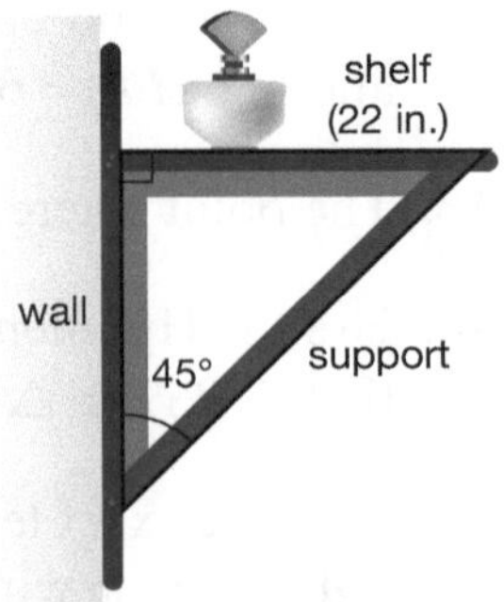

***25.** (44) **Analyze** $\triangle NPQ$ and $\triangle STV$ are similar isosceles triangles. How many of their six sides do you need numerical values for in order find all the other side lengths and the perimeters of both triangles? Explain.

26. (38) Using the diagram on the right, find the length of $\overline{MP}$ if $OP = 5$, $NO = 8$, and $MN = 18$.

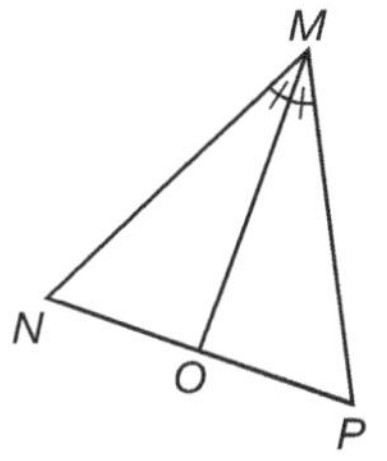

27. (Inv 4) **Cycling** Katya and Sareema start from the same location and bicycle in opposite directions for 2 miles each. Katya turns to her right 90° and continues for another mile. Sareema turns 45° to her left and continues for another mile. At this point, who is closer to the starting point?

28. (Inv 5) **Error Analysis** Darius drew this net of a number cube. Explain his error.

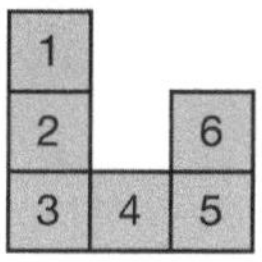

29. (45) **Analyze** Square *RSTU* has vertices at *R*(0, 4) and *S*(0, 0). What are the possible coordinates of *T* and *U*?

30. (11) **Design** A white triangle with vertices at (0, 0), (4, 0), and (0, 4) is used to create a logo. A blue triangle is added to the design so that its vertices are the midpoints of the sides of the white triangle. The blue triangle divides the white triangle into three smaller white triangles. Smaller blue triangles are placed in each small white triangle so that their vertices are the midpoints of the sides of the small white triangles.

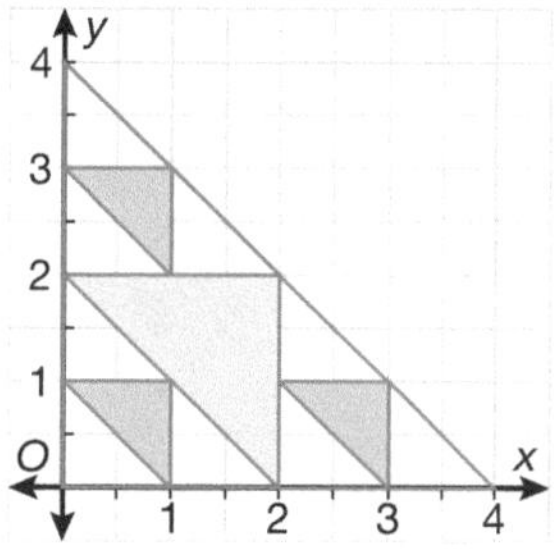

a. Find the coordinates of the vertices of the large blue triangle.

b. Find the coordinates of the vertices of each small blue triangle.

c. Which of the triangles are congruent, if any? Justify your answer.

Name ______________________ Date __________ Class __________

Triangle Midsegment Theorem

LESSON 55

* **1.** Draw a triangular prism in one-point perspective so that the vanishing point is below the prism.
(54)

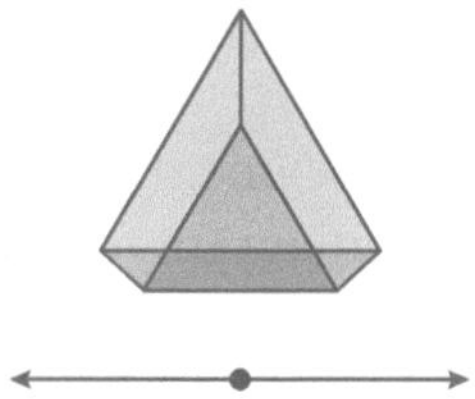

2. **Multiple Choice** Which of the following statements is *not* true of a rhombus?
(52)

A All sides are congruent.
B The diagonals are perpendicular.
C The diagonals are congruent.
D The diagonals bisect the angles.

3. **Model Trains** Gary is building a track for his model trains. He wants to ensure that the two sides of the tracks run parallel to each other, so he places crossbeams at regular intervals along them. What could Gary check to ensure the tracks are parallel?
(Inv 1)

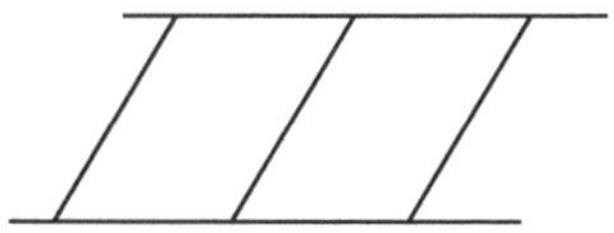

4. **Error Analysis** After reading the Triangle Inequality Theorem, which states that the sum of the lengths of any two sides of a triangle is greater than the length of the third side, Ken reasons that the theorem would mean the same if it were written, "The sum of the lengths of any two sides of a triangle cannot be less than the length of the third side." Is Ken correct? Explain.
(39)

* **5.** Trace the figure shown on your paper. Then draw the vanishing points and the horizon line of the figure.
(54)

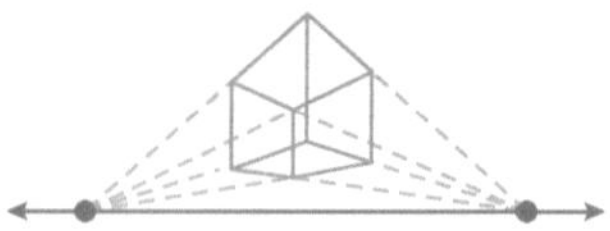

6. **Analyze** In which regular polygon is each exterior angle equal to each interior angle?
(Inv 3)

7. How many edges does a figure with 8 vertices and 6 faces have?
(49)

8. **Aviation** A pilot determines that after flying 200 kilometers on one leg of a trip and 425 kilometers on a second leg of a trip, that she has enough fuel to fly another 715 kilometers. Does she have enough fuel to get back to her starting point? Explain.
(39)

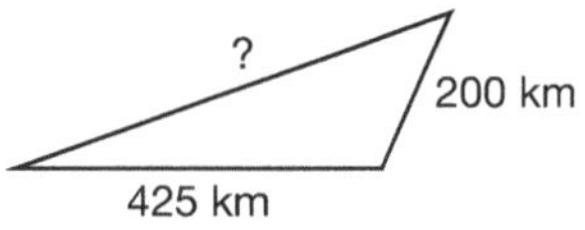

* **9.** **Analyze** Give a paragraph proof showing that if a triangle is equiangular, then it is equilateral.
(51)

10. **Golf** In his first shot of a golf tournament, illustrated here, Mitch has hit the ball too far to the left from where it should be. How far does he need to hit the ball to get it straight to the green from where it is now? Give your answer to the nearest tenth of a yard.
(53)

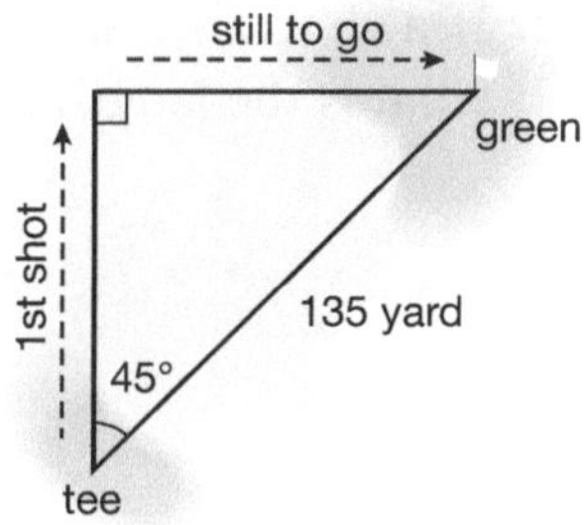

*11. (54) Draw a cube in two-point perspective.

*12. (55) Segment DE is a midsegment of $\triangle ABC$. Refer to the diagram to determine the coordinates of D and E.

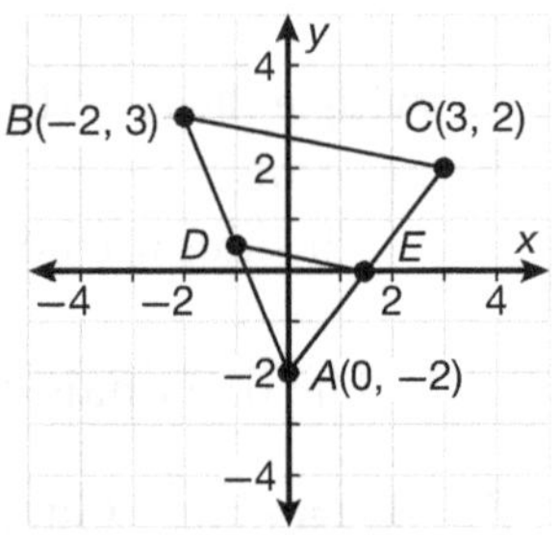

13. (46) In $\triangle QRS$, $m\angle Q = 55°$, and $m\angle R = 86°$.
In $\triangle TUV$, $m\angle T = 55°$, and $m\angle V = 39°$.
Is $\triangle QRS \sim \triangle TUV$? Explain.

14. (41) The ratio of the angle measures in a quadrilateral is 1:4:5:6. Find the measure of each angle.

*15. (55) Segment UT is a midsegment of $\triangle XYZ$. Find the values of x and y.

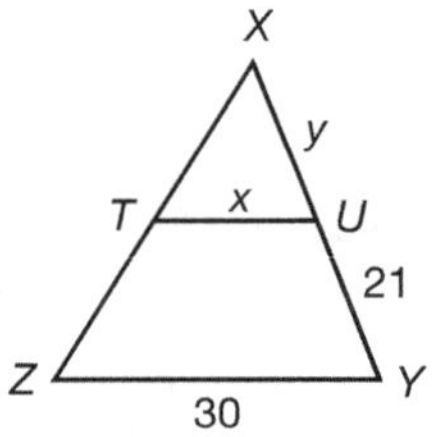

16. (32) **Multi-Step** Find the orthocenter of $\triangle GHI$ with vertices $G(-8, -9)$, $H(-2, -1)$, and $I(-2, -9)$.

17. (50) Find the geometric mean of 1 and 5.

18. (24) **Algebra** Solve the equation $2(x + 3) = \frac{5x - 1}{3}$. Provide a justification for each step.

19. (45) **Analyze** A triangle has vertices $L(0, 0)$, $M(8, 0)$, and $N(4, y)$. What value of y makes $\triangle LMN$ equilateral?

*20. (51) **Write** Explain why the median and the altitude from the vertex angle of an isosceles triangle are identical. Refer to any theorems you need to justify your explanation.

21. (31) Below is the beginning of a paragraph proof of the Triangle Inequality Theorem. Write the rest of the proof. *Hint: Use the Isosceles Triangle Theorem.*
Given: $\triangle ABC$
Prove: $AB + BC > AC$, $AB + AC > BC$, $AC + BC > AB$ One side of $\triangle ABC$ is as long or longer than each of the other sides. Let this side be $\overline{AB}$. Then $AB + BC > AC$ and $AB + AC > BC$. Therefore what remains to prove is $AC + BC > AB$. Locate D on $\overrightarrow{AC}$ such that $BC = DC$.

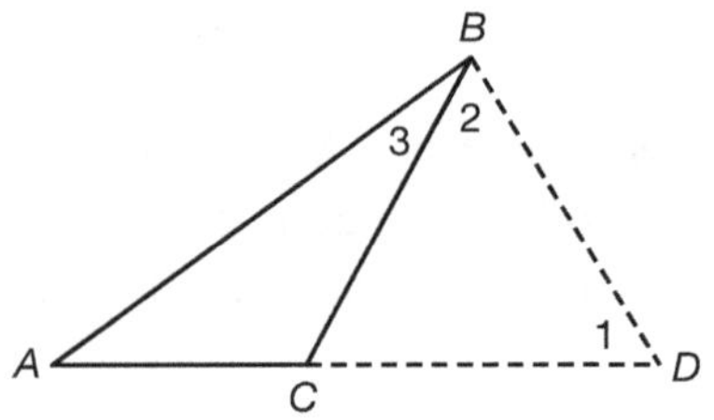

22. (43) If a chord is bisected 2 inches from the center of a circle with a diameter of 6 inches, what is the length of half of the chord to the nearest tenth of an inch?

23. (47) **Algebra** Find the measure of $\widehat{ST}$ in the circle at right.

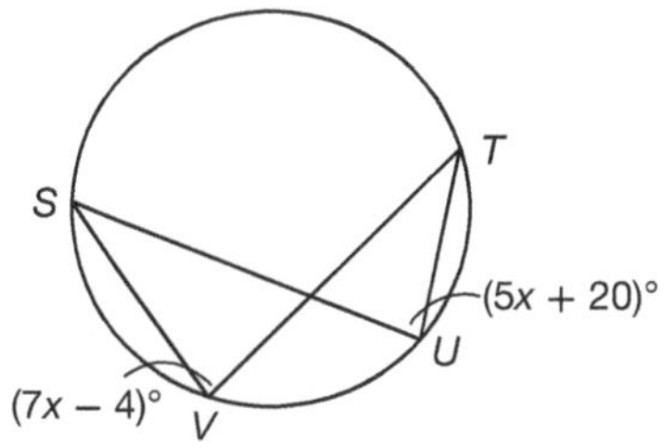

*24. (55) The midpoints of the sides of $\triangle ABC$ are as follows: midpoint of AC: $D(4, 1)$; midpoint of AB: $E(1, 3)$; and midpoint of BC: $F(1, 0)$. Draw the midsegment triangle. Find the coordinates of A, B, and C, and then draw $\triangle ABC$.

25. (53) **Travel** Marco travels from Yuma to Alamo and then from Alamo to Gadsden. Each unit on the triangle represents 30 miles. How far does he need to travel to get from Gadsden to Yuma, if he were to travel a straight path between them, rounded to the nearest mile?

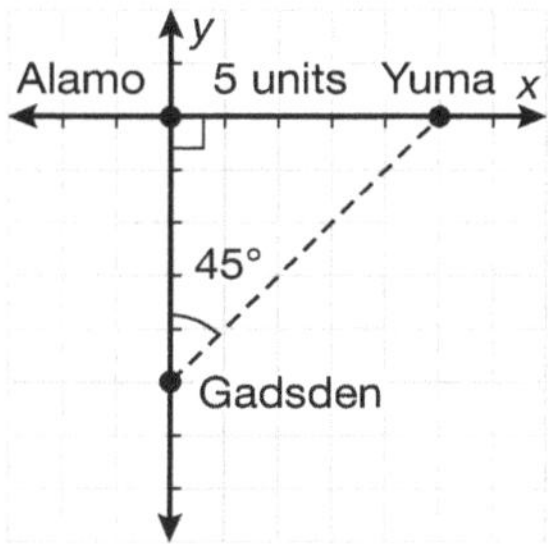

26. (53) **Landscaping** A square field is to be hydro-seeded. The field has a diagonal length of 225 yards. How many square feet need to be hydro-seeded?

27. (46) Determine if these two triangles are similar. If so, state the similarity and the reason.

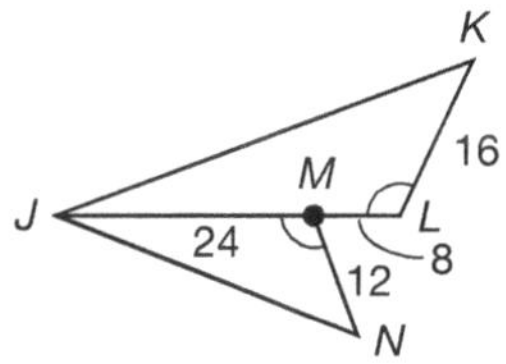

28. (50) Find the geometric mean of 11 and 1.5.

29. (Inv 1) **Write** Sketch this situation or explain why it is impossible. *Two parallel lines are intersected by a transversal so that the same-side interior angles are complementary.*

30. (55) **Algebra** Points Q, R, and S are midpoints of $\triangle FGH$. If $FH = x + 12$ and $QR = 2x - 3$, what is the length of $\overline{QR}$?

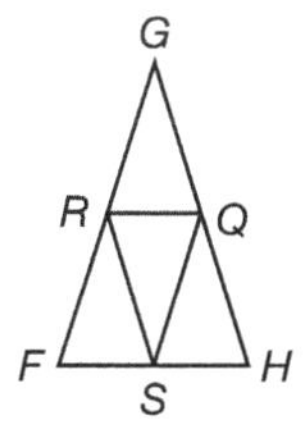

Name ______________________ Date __________ Class __________

30°-60°-90° Right Triangles

LESSON 56

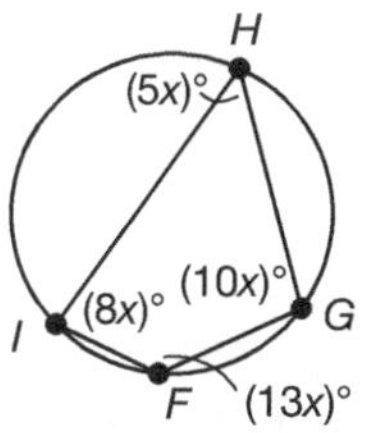

1. (47) **Algebra** Find $m\angle F$ in the figure at right.

2. (52) **Write** Explain why the following statement is true.

If a quadrilateral is a square then it is a rhombus.

*** 3.** (56) Find the hypotenuse of a 30°-60°-90° triangle if the shorter leg is 4 centimeters long.

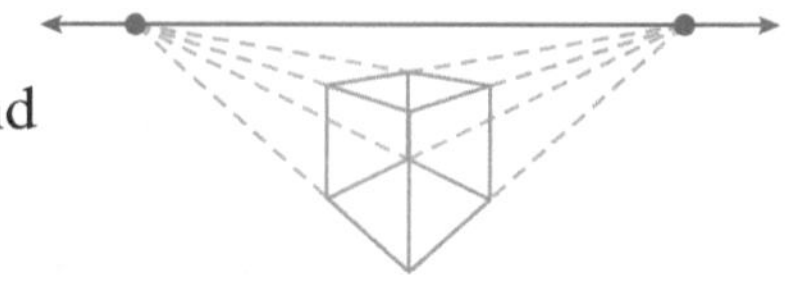

*** 4.** (54) Trace the figure at right on your paper. Then locate and draw the vanishing points and the horizon line.

5. (Inv 5) **Multiple Choice** What is the area of a net for a cube with edges that are 3 centimeters long?

A 72 cm^2 **B** 54 cm^2
C 36 cm^2 **D** 27 cm^2

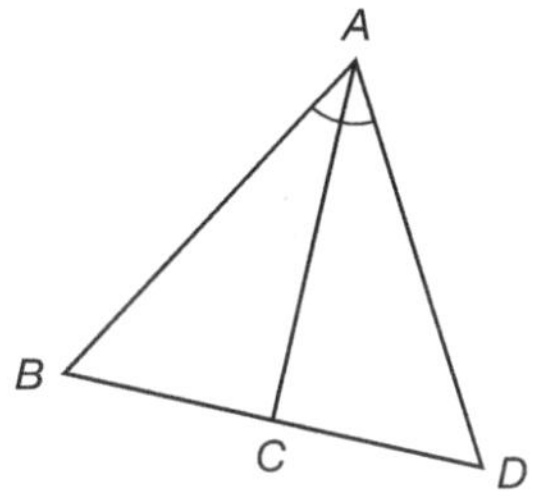

6. (38) Find the length of $\overline{BC}$ if $AD = 9$, $DC = 6$, and $AB = 12$.

*** 7.** (55) The midpoints of the sides of $\triangle PQR$ are as follows: midpoint of $\overline{PQ}$: $S(3, 1)$; midpoint of $\overline{QR}$: $T(1, -1)$; and midpoint of $\overline{RP}$: $U(-1, 1)$. Draw the midsegment triangle. Find the coordinates of P, Q, and R, then draw $\triangle PQR$.

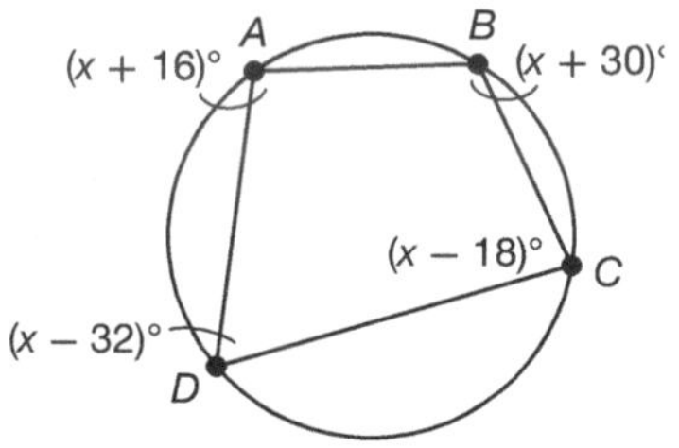

8. (47) **Algebra** Find the measure of $\angle B$ in the diagram.

*** 9.** (56) **Multiple Choice** Which set of sides does not make a 30°-60°-90° triangle?

A $4, 8, 4\sqrt{3}$ **B** $\sqrt{3}, 3, 2\sqrt{3}$
C $3, 6, 3\sqrt{3}$ **D** $2\sqrt{3}, 4\sqrt{3}, \sqrt{3}$

10. (Inv 3) What is the sum of the interior angles of a convex dodecagon?

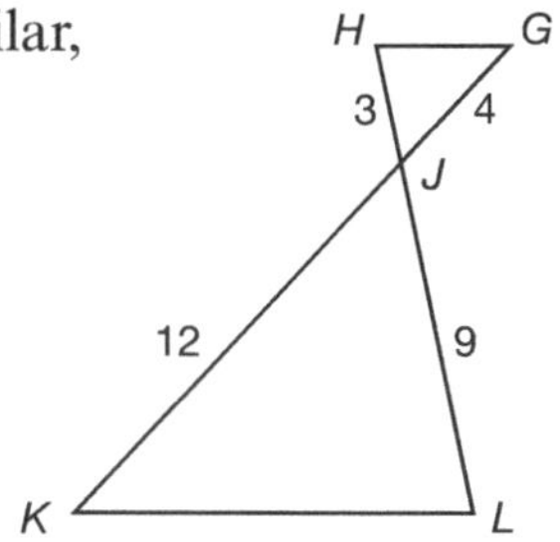

11. (46) **Justify** Explain how you know the two triangles shown are similar, and then write the similarity statement.

12. (50) Find the geometric mean of 1.55 and 5.22.

13. (53) Find the exact value of the length of the side of a 45°-45°-90° right triangle with a hypotenuse of 15 miles.

14. (51) In $\triangle DEF$, $\angle D \cong \angle F$.

a. Write a congruence statement involving the sides of $\triangle DEF$.

b. The perimeter of $\triangle DEF$ is 35 millimeters, and $DF = 14$ millimeters. Determine DE.

15. (45) **Error Analysis** Triangle PQR has vertex P at the origin. Vertices Q and R are equidistant from P, and R has coordinates $(2, -6)$. Nasim says that Q must have coordinates $(6, 2)$. Is Nasim correct? Explain.

16. (53) **Survey Science** The diagram shows a new bridge that is being built across a section of coastline. Given the surveyors' measurements of the existing road and the bridge span, by how much distance will the bridge reduce the trip, to the nearest tenth of a mile?

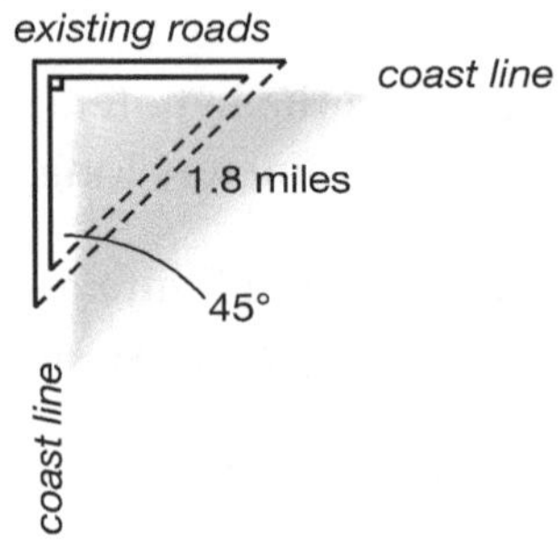

17. (51) **Algebra** Each base angle of an isosceles triangle measures $2(67 - 3y)°$.

a. Classify the base angles.

b. Write and solve an inequality for y.

***18.** (54) Draw a triangular prism in one-point perspective so that the vanishing point is above the prism.

***19.** (55) Segment VW is a midsegment of $\triangle XYZ$. Find the coordinates of V and W.

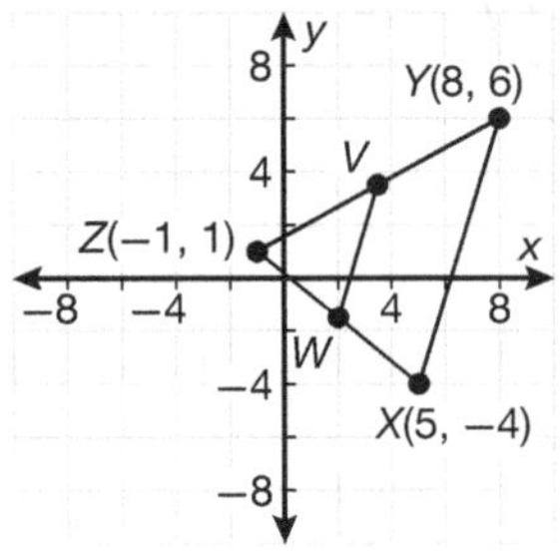

***20.** (56) **Playgrounds** A slide forms the hypotenuse of a 30°-60°-90° triangle with the ground. If the slide is 15 feet long, how long are the other two sides of the triangle?

21. (35) **Justify** Write formulas for finding arc length and area of a sector of given central angle m. Explain why the coefficient is $\frac{m}{360°}$.

***22.** (56) **Multi-Step** A triangle has coordinates of $(1, 1)$, $(4, 1)$, and $(3, 4)$. Determine whether or not this is a 30°-60°-90° triangle.

23. (38) **Analyze** If the angle bisector of one angle of a triangle is also the perpendicular bisector of the opposite side, what can you conclude about the triangle?

24. (7) **Plant Growth** A scientist conducted an experiment to see which of two plants grew faster. She recorded her results as shown.

Day	1	5	10	15	20	25
Plant *A* Height	1 cm	2 cm	4 cm	6 cm	7 cm	8 cm
Plant *B* Height	1 cm	2 cm	3 cm	4 cm	5 cm	6 cm

a. What conjecture could be reasonably drawn from the data?

b. What alternate conjecture could you draw that is consistent with the data but incompatible with the first conjecture?

*25. (55) Segment DE is a midsegment of $\triangle ABC$. Find the values of x and the lengths of $\overline{DE}$ and $\overline{BC}$.

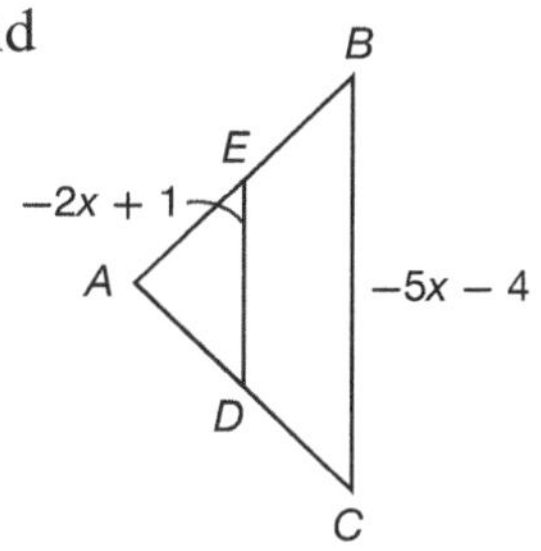

26. (37) **Generalize** The general form of a nonvertical line in slope-intercept form is $y = mx + b$. What is the general form of a line perpendicular to $y = mx + b$, in slope-intercept form?

27. (33, 39) Determine whether the set of measures (14, 15, 16) can be the side lengths of a triangle. If these measures could be a triangle, determine whether it is an acute, obtuse, or a right triangle.

28. (44) **Photography** A photographer is developing a picture of a building which is 108 feet tall.

a. What is the relationship between the building and the image of the building in the photograph?

b. If the image of the building in the photograph is 12 inches tall, what is the similarity ratio between the building and its image?

*29. (56) **Algebra** The hypotenuse of a 30°-60°-90° triangle has a length of $2r$. What are the lengths of the other two legs?

30. (18) **Design** The math faculty of Pythagoras College uses this square logo. One acute angle measure in each right triangle is 37°.

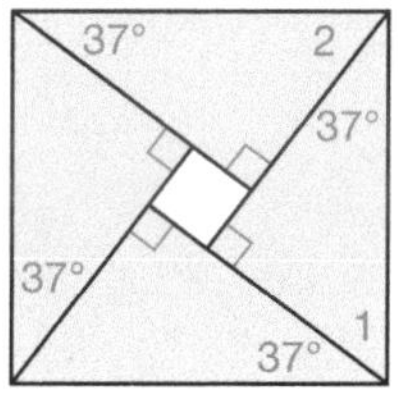

a. Determine the measure of $\angle 1$.

b. Determine the measure of $\angle 2$.

Name ______________________ Date __________ Class __________

Finding Perimeter and Area with Coordinates

LESSON 57

1. (56) **Generalize** In a 30°-60°-90° right triangle, what is the ratio of the length of the leg opposite the 30° angle to the length of the hypotenuse? What is the ratio of the length of the leg opposite the 60° angle to the length of the hypotenuse? Express your answers both exactly and to the nearest thousandth.

2. (46) What would be necessary information to add to the Side-Side-Side Similarity Theorem to transform it into the Side-Side-Side Congruence Theorem?

3. (44) **Blueprints** An architect is drawing up plans for a house. The house should have a storage closet with a triangular floor area. If the actual closet's area is to have dimensions of 10 feet, 6 feet, and 8 feet, and the architect's drawing has a longest side of $6\frac{2}{3}$ inches, what are the side lengths of the other two sides of his drawing?

4. (54) Draw a cube in one-point perspective with a vanishing point below the cube.

*5. (57) Find the area of $\triangle ABC$ with vertices $A(2, 2)$, $B(2, 5)$ and $C(-5, 1)$.

6. (43) **Algebra** Find the distance from the center of a circle with a 10-centimeter radius to a chord that is 13 centimeters long to the nearest tenth.

7. (12) Show that lines m and n in this figure are parallel.

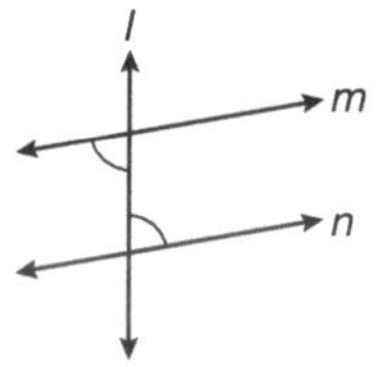

*8. (57) Find the perimeter of quadrilateral $WXYZ$ if $W(2, 4)$, $X(-2, 3)$, $Y(-1, 7)$, and $Z(4, 9)$. Give your answer in simplified radical form.

9. (35) **Multiple Choice** What is the approximate area of a sector of a circle with a radius of 6 units and an arc measure of 60°?

   A 3.14 **B** 113.10
   C 18.85 **D** 6.00

10. (34) **Justify** Find x in the parallelogram at right, and justify each step.

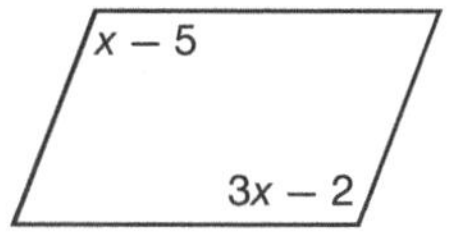

11. (53) **Framing** A photographer is building a frame for a square picture. In order to have the picture frame stand upright, a collapsible stand must be attached to the back that folds exactly across the diagonal of the back. If the frame is 8 inches on a side, how long must the stand be? Give your answer in simplified radical form and rounded to the nearest tenth.

12. (47) **Algebra** Find the measure of $\angle G$ in the circle at right.

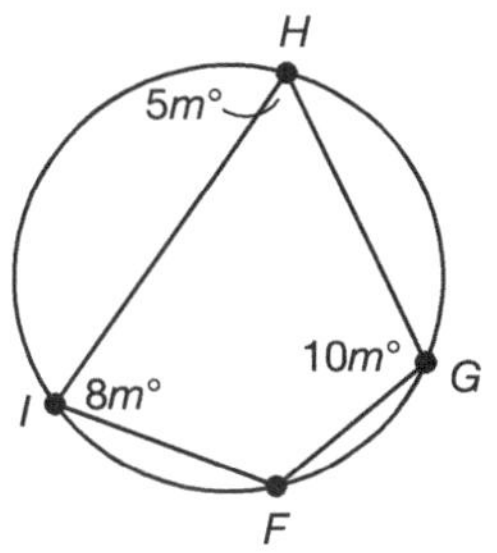

13. (36) **Analyze** Prove the Converse of the Hypotenuse-Angle Congruence Theorem.

14. (42) Find the distance from $(-1, 14)$ to the line $y = 5$.

Finding Perimeter and Area with Coordinates

LESSON 57

15. (55) **Verify** Segment JK is a midsegment of $\triangle FGH$. Find the coordinates of J and K. Use the distance formula to verify that $\overline{JK}$ is half the length of $\overline{GH}$.

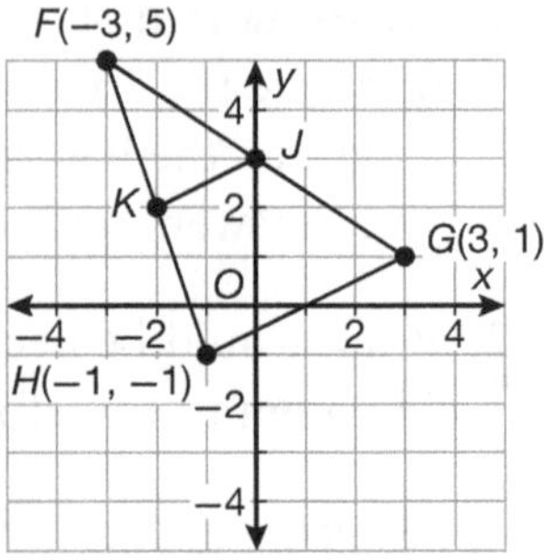

16. (44) **Automotive Engineering** An engineer needs to make a model of a car's triangular window that has side lengths of 24, 21, and 18 inches long, respectively. If the designer's model has the shortest corresponding side of the window measuring 4 inches, what are the lengths of the other two sides of the window?

***17.** (56) What is the perimeter of a 30°-60°-90° triangle with a shortest side length of 3.2 inches?

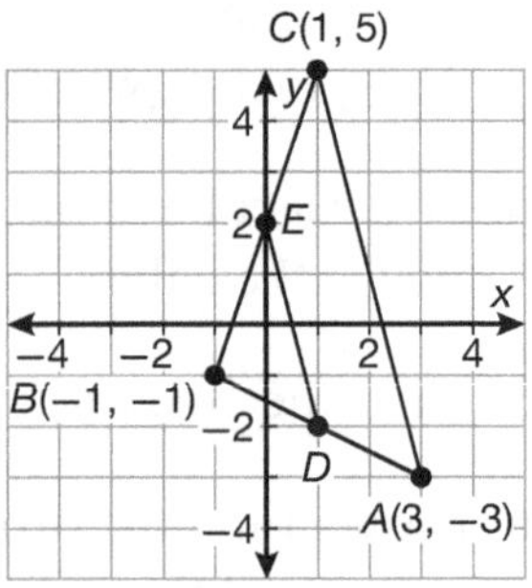

18. (17) What is the negation of, "If q, then p?"

19. (55) **Verify** In $\triangle ABC$, show that $\overline{AC} \parallel \overline{DE}$ if D and E are the midpoints of their respective sides by finding the slopes of the segments.

***20.** (57) **Multi-Step** Find the area of a polygon with vertices $J(2, 4)$, $K(-3, 2)$, $L(0, -4)$ and $M(4, 1)$.

21. (43) Determine the value of x in the circle at right.

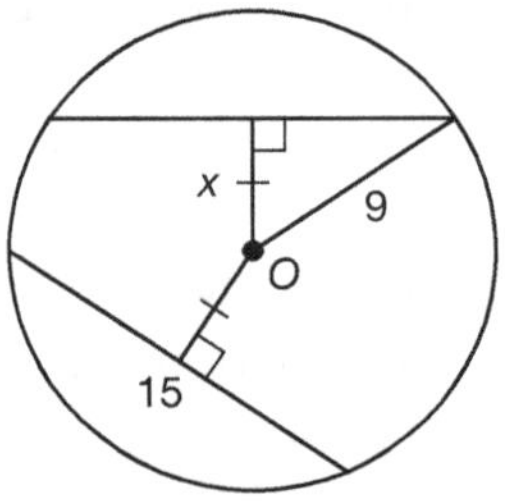

22. (48) **Multiple Choice** Which statement contradicts the fact that $\triangle HIJ \sim \triangle DEF$?

A $HI = rDE$ for some factor r

B $\angle H = \angle D$

C $\angle H \neq \angle F$

D None of the angles in $\triangle HIJ$ have the same measure as any of the angles in $\triangle DEF$.

23. (32) **Error Analysis** Carina marked the triangle at right in order to find the centroid. Explain the error she made.

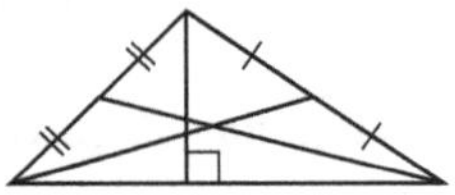

***24.** (56) **Industrial Painting** A painter needs to paint a triangular ramp. The ramp is inclined at 30° to the ground and is 30 feet high. If it takes the painter 1 minute to paint 4 square feet on average, how long will it take him to paint the side of the ramp, to the nearest minute?

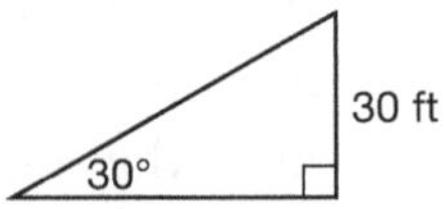

***25.** (Inv 4) **Justify** Which is the larger angle in the figure shown, $\angle DAE$ or $\angle BAC$? Explain your answer.

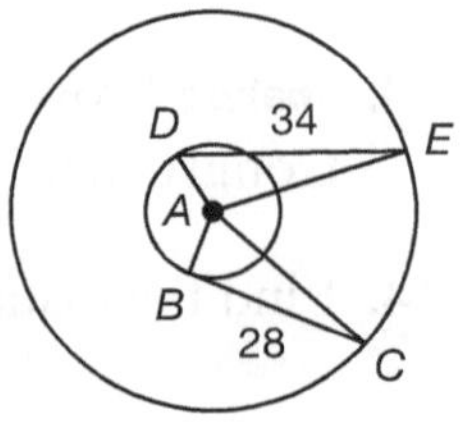

*26. (57) **Urban Planning** A city block is on a grid. If the corner of a rectangular building is at (9, 0) and another corner is 7 units to the left and 6 units up from that corner, what are the other coordinates of the building and what is its perimeter?

27. (49) **Analyze** What is the fewest number of regular triangular tiles necessary to form a polyhedron, and what is the name of the polyhedron formed?

*28. (31) Write a paragraph proof showing that in a circle or congruent circles, chords equidistant from the center are congruent.
Given: $\overline{AB}$ and $\overline{CD}$ are equidistant from P. (i.e. $PX = PY$).
Prove: $\overline{AB} \cong \overline{CD}$

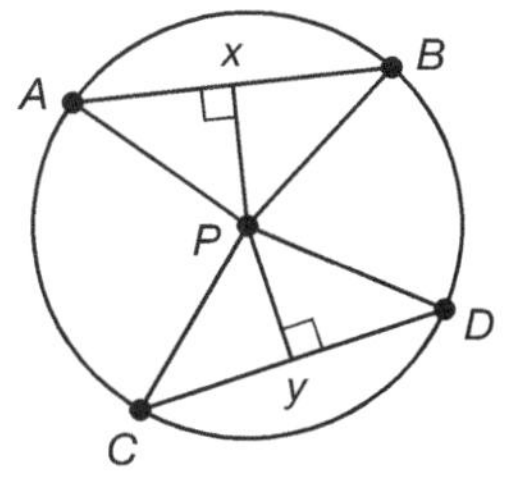

29. (12) Prove that lines d and e in this figure are parallel if $m\angle 1 = 63°$ and $m\angle 2 = 117°$.

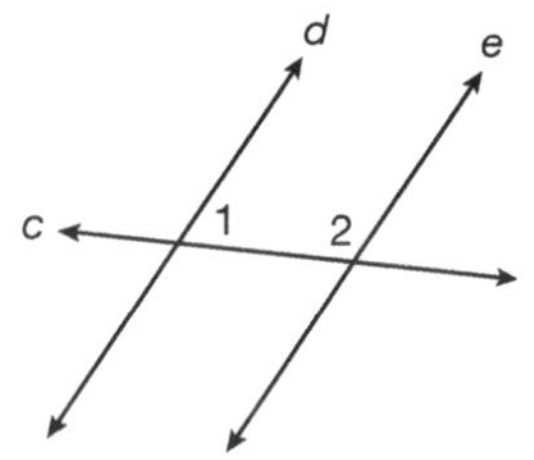

*30. (56) **Write** The hypotenuse of a right triangle is 32 meters and one leg is 16 meters. A second right triangle has a 60° angle. How can you use this information to find whether these triangles are similar? Can it be determined whether these triangles are congruent?

Name ______________________________ Date ____________ Class ____________

Tangents and Circles, Part 1

LESSON 58

* **1.** In this figure, A and Z are the centers of the circles. $\overline{AP}$ is parallel to $\overline{ZQ}$ and perpendicular to $\overleftrightarrow{PQ}$. Is $\overleftrightarrow{PQ}$ tangent to $\odot A$ and/or $\odot Z$? Explain.
(58)

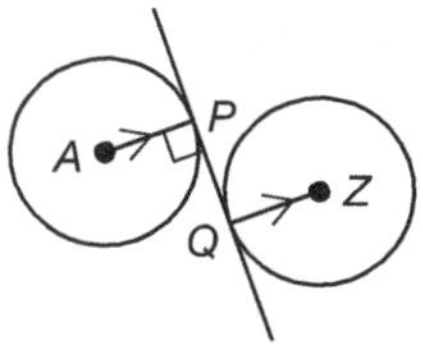

* **2.** Find ER if $FG = 36$.
(58)

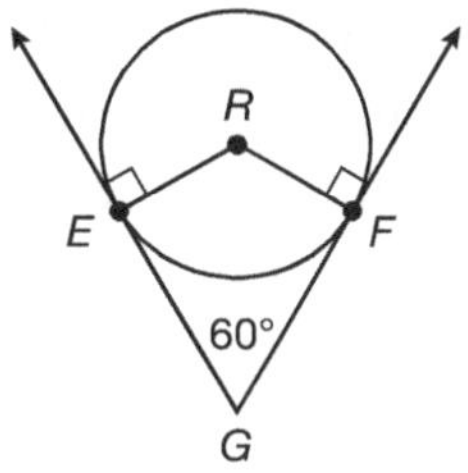

* **3.** **Estimate** Estimate the area under the curve $y = \sqrt{x}$ for $0 \le x \le 6$.
(57)

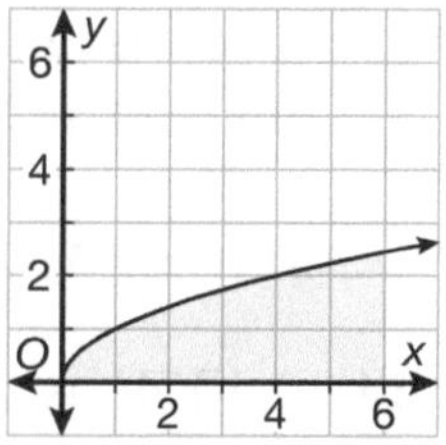

* **4.** **Multi-Step** Find the perimeter of a 30°-60°-90° triangle in which the shorter leg is 72 feet. Give your answer in simplified radical form.
(56)

5. Three fire stations are located at the vertices of a triangle as shown. Which two stations are located farthest apart?
(39)

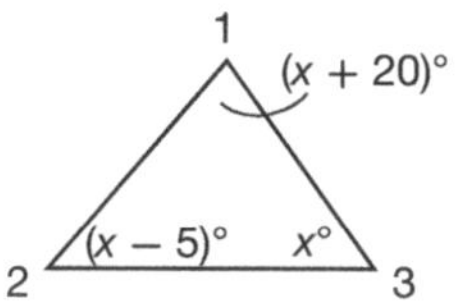

6. **Write** In $\triangle UVW$, $UW = 3.5$ inches and V is a right angle. In $\triangle XYZ$, $m\angle Z = 90°$, $m\angle X = 33°$ and $m\angle Y = 57°$. The Hypotenuse-Angle Congruence Theorem can be applied if two additional measures are known. What could they be? Explain.
(36)

7. **Dividing Cost** Hubert and three friends bought a rectangular pizza that cost \$10 for each of them to share, but the slices were not cut evenly. If the shaded region of this figure represents the portion of the pizza Hubert ate, what amount of money should he pay for his portion of the pizza?
(40)

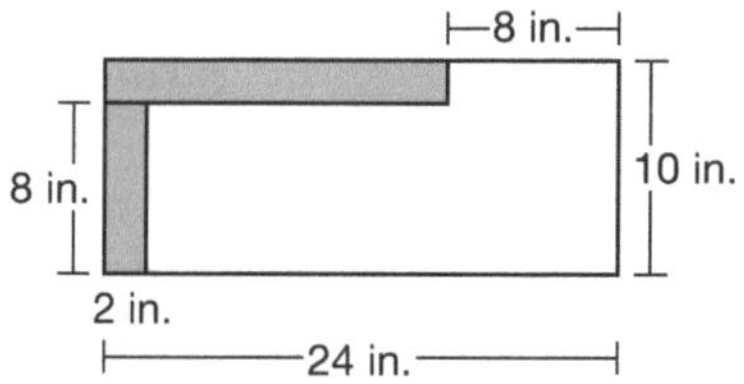

8. **Generalize** Two segments of different lengths are attached perpendicularly at the midpoint of each segment. If you draw in the segments that connect all 4 of the endpoints of the 2 segments, what kind of a quadrilateral appears? How would the shape differ if both segments were of the same length?
(52)

9. **Indirect Measure** Angelique wants to measure the diameter of a large circular pool, but she cannot reach the center. Angelique has two large pieces of rope. Explain how she can use her knowledge of chords to find the diameter.
(43)

10. **Algebra** The lengths of three line segments are given by the expressions $3x + 2$, x^2 and $2x$. Can these segments be used to create a triangle if $x = 4$? … if $x = 6$?
(39)

11. (55) **Algebra** Points J, K, and L are midpoints of $\triangle FGH$ as shown. If $GH = 5x + 2$ and $KL = 3x - 2$, what is the length of $\overline{GH}$?

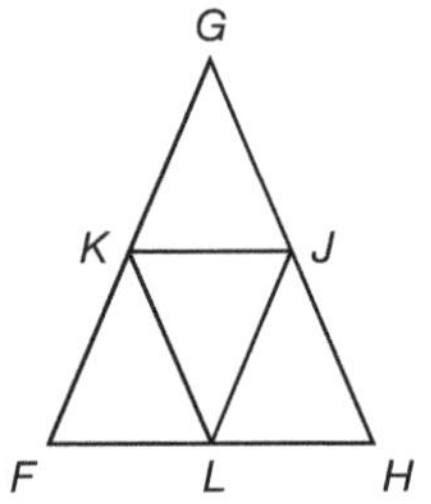

12. (9) **Framing** Derek made a frame for a picture that is 15 inches long and 8 inches wide. He wanted the frame to be a square, but now he thinks his earlier measurements were wrong. In order to determine if the frame he made is a square, Derek measured the diagonals to be 17.26 and 16.78 inches each. With these dimensions, is the frame a square? If not, by how many inches are Derek's measurements off?

***13.** (58) Line p is tangent to $\odot N$ at X, and line q passes the center of $\odot N$. Lines p and q intersect at Y.

a. Sketch $\odot N$, lines p and q, and points X and Y.

b. If $m\angle XNY = 13°$, determine $m\angle NYX$.

***14.** (56) $\triangle XYZ$ has vertices $Y(-5, 2)$ and $Z(0, 2)$. $\angle ZYX$ is a right angle, and $m\angle YZX$ is 60°. Find the coordinates of X if X is in Quadrant II.

15. (51) **Multi-Step** In equiangular $\triangle LMN$, $LN = 17$ inches. Determine the perimeter of $\triangle LMN$. Give your answer in feet and inches.

16. (54) Draw a cube in two-point perspective so that the horizon line and vanishing points are below the vertical line.

17. (37) **Multiple Choice** Which of the following is perpendicular to $2x + y = 6$?

A $2x + 4y + 7 = 0$ **B** $7x = 15y + 6$

C $2(2x + 6) - 8y = 0$ **D** $2x - y = 4$

***18.** Determine the perimeter of this quadrilateral if U is the center of the circle.

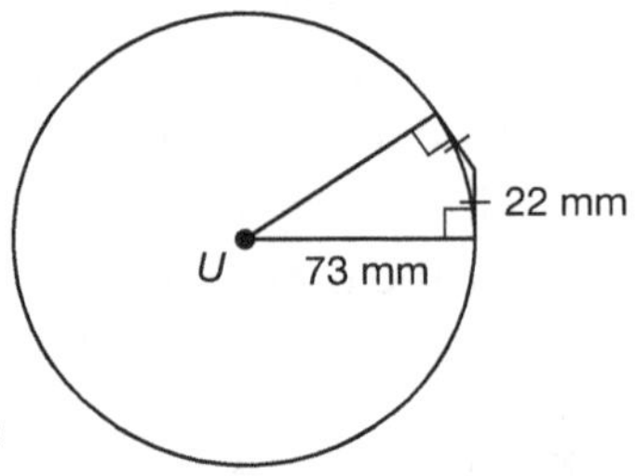

19. (57) Jose started at his home, $H(0, 0)$ and walked to a park located at $P(4, 2)$. He then went to Jacintha's house located at $F(8, 0)$. Later, he walked straight home. If each unit on the coordinate plane represents 50 feet, what is the distance that Jose walked, to the nearest foot?

20. (52) **Error Analysis** Noyemi said the following statement is sometimes true. Is she correct? Explain.

If a quadrilateral is both a rectangle and a rhombus, then it is a square.

21. (47) Find the measure of $\angle CDB$ in $\odot M$ given that $m\angle AMB = 74°$.

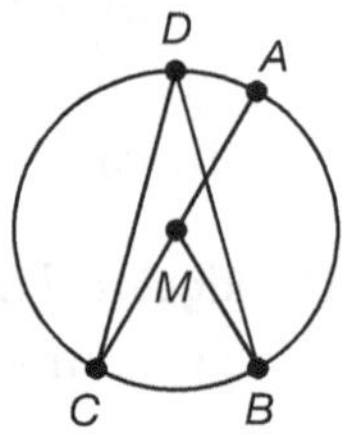

22. **Multiple Choice** An isosceles triangle has a base and height that are 2 centimeters each. The length of each leg is:
(51)
A 2 centimeters **B** $\sqrt{3}$ centimeters
C $\sqrt{5}$ centimeters **D** 3 centimeters

23. **Floor Plans** A floor plan for a square shed was left unfinished. However, Lisa can see that the diagonal of the shed is 72 feet. How many 6-foot long pieces of lumber does she need to form the perimeter of the shed?
(53)

24. A quadrilateral inscribed in a circle has interior angles of 55°, 90°, $25x$°, and $18x$°, in clockwise order. Find x.
(47)

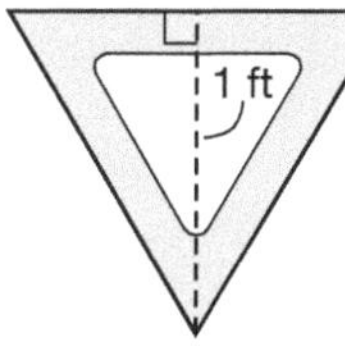

*25. **Traffic Signs** An equilateral yield sign has a height of 1 foot. What is the area of the sign in simplified radical form?
(56)

26. What is the included angle of sides $\overline{XY}$ and $\overline{ZX}$ in a triangle?
(CRN)

*27. Estimate the area of the irregular shape in the diagram.
(57)

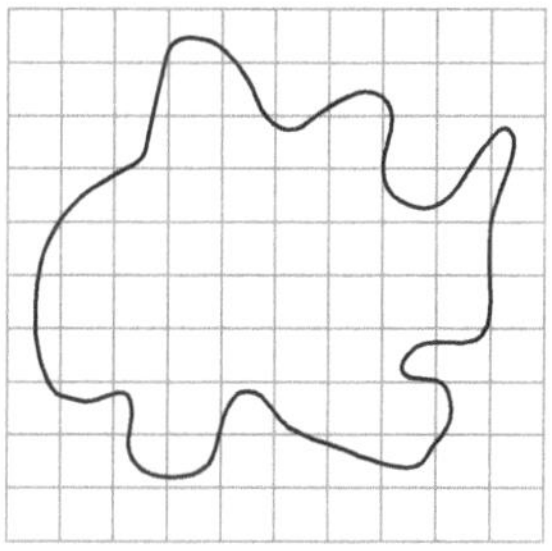

28. **Write** In parallelogram $ABCD$, $\overline{AC}$ is drawn to create $\triangle ABC$ and $\triangle CDA$. Are these triangles congruent? Explain.
(25)

29. **Predict** If two congruent septagonal prisms are joined together at their bases, with their bases aligned, what is the resulting shape?
(49)

30. **Justify** Given the information in this diagram, could RT be greater than TS? If so, find the range of values when this is true. If not, explain your answer.
(Inv 4)

Name ______________________ Date __________ Class __________

Finding Surface Areas and Volumes of Prisms

LESSON 59

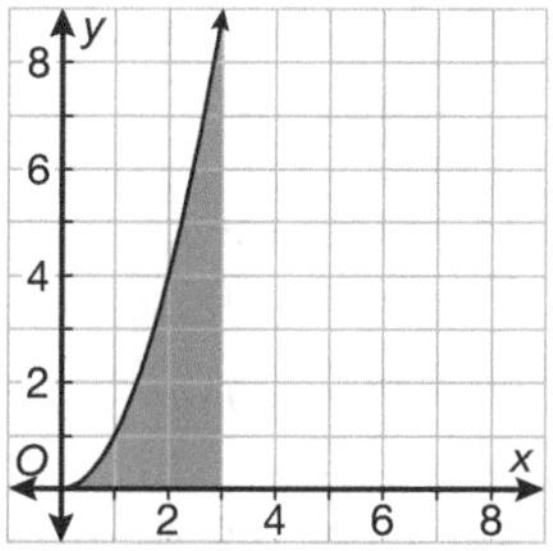

1. **Estimate** Estimate the area under the curve of $y = x^2$ for $0 \le x \le 3$.
(57)

2. Solve the proportion $\frac{9}{p} = \frac{36}{28}$.
(41)

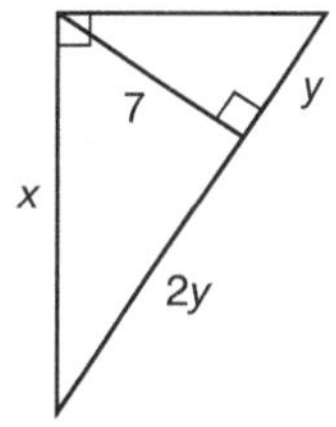

3. Find the values of x and y in the triangle shown to the nearest tenth.
(50)

4. Draw a cube in two-point perspective so that the horizon line and vanishing points are above the vertical line.
(54)

* 5. **Write** Armine needs to find the area of a square but does not have the measurements of its sides; however, he does know the diagonal length of the square. Explain how Armine can use this to find the area of the square.
(53)

6. **Design** A t-shirt designer is painting this pattern on a shirt. If each square on the grid represents 1 inch on the shirt, approximately what is the area he must cover with paint?
(57)

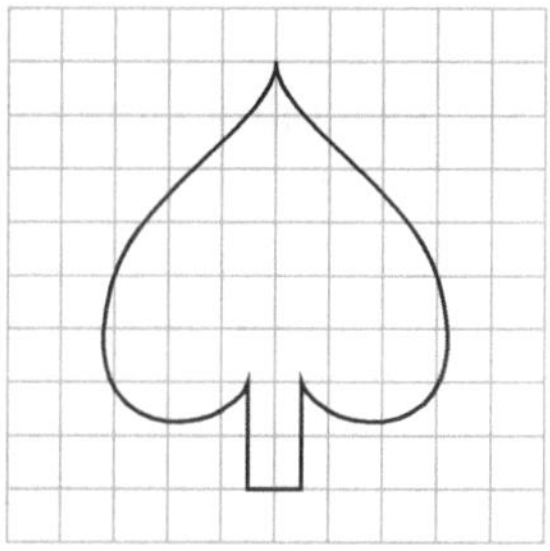

* 7. Complete this indirect proof showing that if a line is tangent to a circle, then the line is perpendicular to a radius drawn to the point of tangency.
(48)

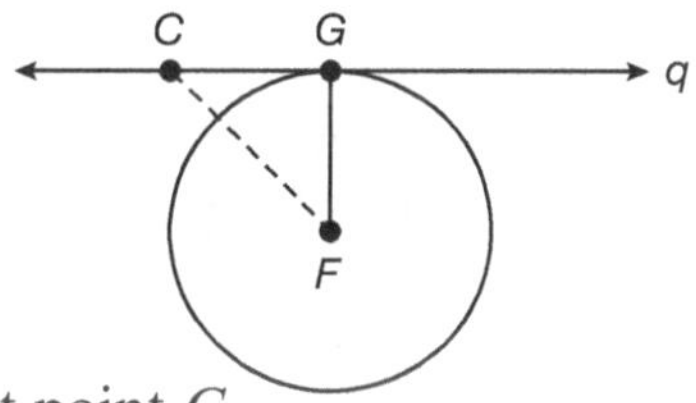

Given: Line q is tangent to $\odot F$ at point G.
Prove: $q \perp \overline{FG}$

Assume that q is not perpendicular to $\overline{FG}$. Then it is possible to draw $\overline{FC}$ such that $\overline{FC} \perp q$. If this is true, then $\triangle FCG$ is a right triangle. $FC < FG$ because ______________________________ ______________________. Since q is a tangent line, it can only intersect $\odot F$ at ___, and C must be in the exterior of $\odot F$, so $FC > FG$. Thus the assumption is false, and ______________.

8. **Error Analysis** To find the orthocenter of a triangle, Marina drew the segments shown. Explain the error she made.
(32)

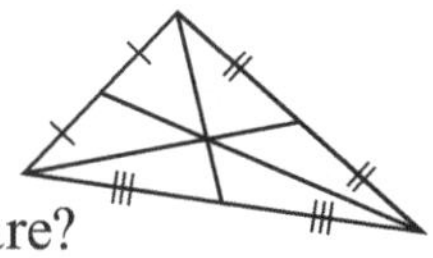

9. **Multiple Choice** Which of the following statements is *not* true of a square?
(52)
A All sides are congruent.
B The diagonals are congruent.
C The diagonals are perpendicular.
D The interior triangles created by the diagonals make two obtuse and two acute triangles.

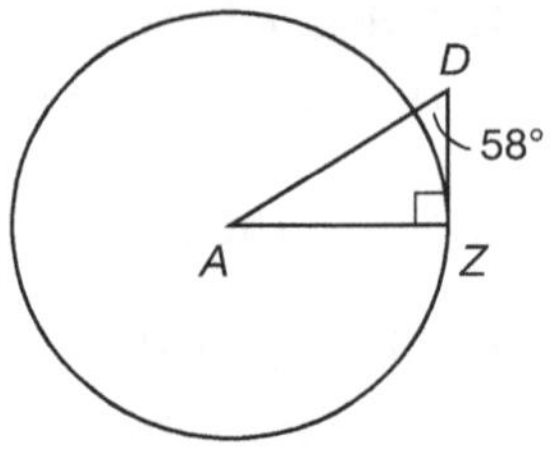

10. In this triangle, $\overline{ZD}$ is tangent to $\odot A$ at Z. Determine m$\angle DAZ$.
(58)

11. State the conjunction of these statements. Is the conjunction true or false?
(20)

The triangle is acute. The triangle has exactly two acute angles.

12. Find the value of x and of y in the triangle shown. Give your answers in simplified radical form.
(56)

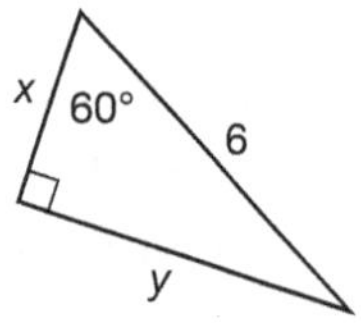

13. **Generalize** Line m is tangent to $\odot P$ at point A. Points B and C are two other distinct points on m.
(58)
   a. Classify $\angle PBC$ as acute, right, or obtuse when the order of A, B, and C along line m is B, A, C.
   b. Classify $\angle PBC$ when the order of A, B, and C along line m is A, B, C.
   c. Can $\angle PBC$ ever be a right angle? Why or why not?

14. Find the lateral area of the prism shown.
(59)

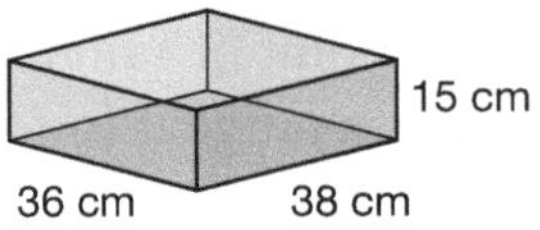

15. **Construction** Kai is trying to build a right triangle out of plastic to use as a brace for furniture. After constructing the brace, he measures its sides as 5.25 inches, 6.33 inches, and 8.25 inches. Does Kai need to cut more plastic off the hypotenuse, or does he need to find a longer piece to use for the hypotenuse? How do you know?
(33)

16. Find the volume of the right prism shown.
(59)

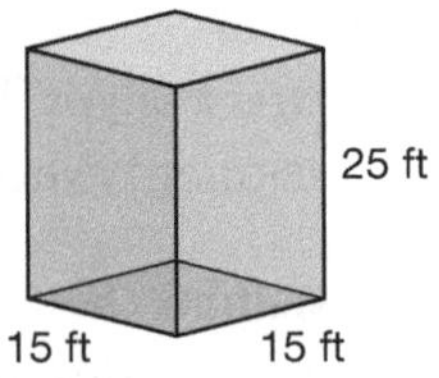

17. **Model** Draw and label two similar polygons whose corresponding sides have a ratio of 1:4.
(44)

18. Using the diagram, find PU in terms of x if $PX = 8$ and $UY = x$. Point P is the circumcenter of the triangle.
(38)

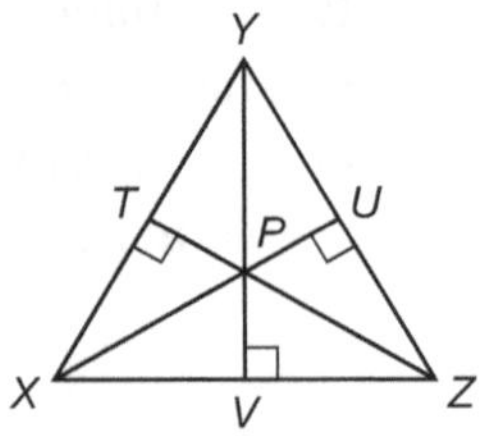

19. **Accessibility** A ramp to the library makes a 30°-60°-90° triangle with the longer leg on the ground. If the ramp is 3 feet high, how long is the ramp's surface?
(56)

20. Find the surface area of the prism shown.
(59)

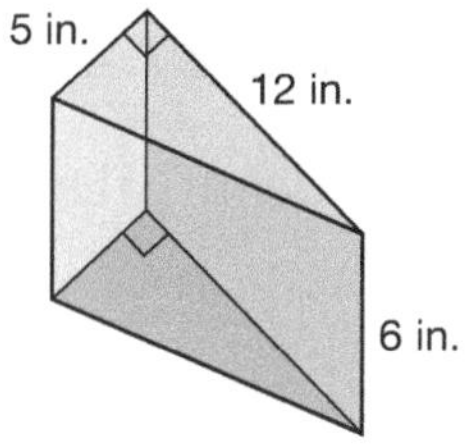

21. **Algebra** Find the area and perimeter of the triangle formed by the lines $y = -x$, $y = 2x$, and $y = 2$.
(57)

22. **Multi-Step** Isosceles $\triangle STU$ has base angles measuring 60° and a base length of 1 foot, 7 inches long. Determine the perimeter of $\triangle STU$, in feet and inches.
(51)

23. **Water Treatment** A pipe with an 8-foot radius has water flowing through it, but for safety reasons the water level must be kept at least 2.5 feet from the top of the pipe. If the water makes a chord that is 12.5 feet long, how close to the top of the pipe is the water flowing? Is the water at a safe level?
(43)

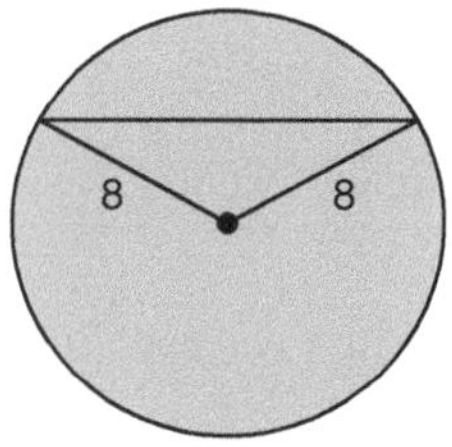

24. If a quadrilateral is inscribed in a circle, then its opposite angles are _____________.
(47)

***25.** Write a two-column proof showing the first case of this theorem: The measure of an inscribed angle is equal to half of the measure of its intercepted arc.
(27)
Hint: Draw $\overline{XA}$.
Given: $\angle ABX$ is inscribed in $\odot X$.
Prove: $m\angle ABC = \frac{1}{2}m\overset{\frown}{AC}$

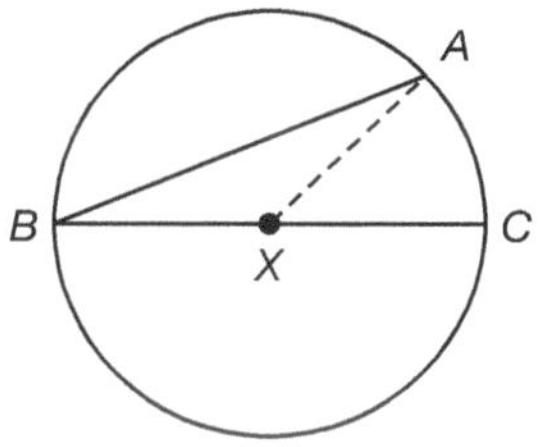

26. Explain why these two triangles are similar and give a similarity statement.
(46)

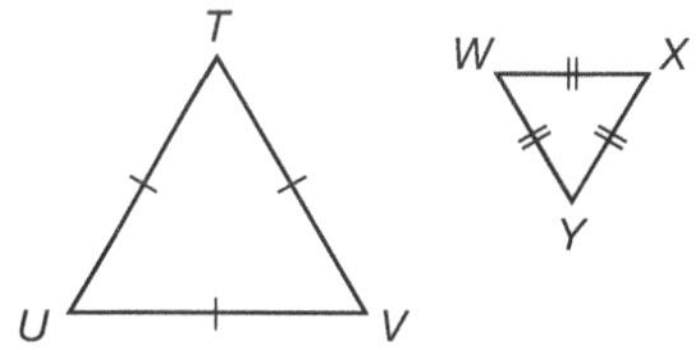

27. Find the height of a right rectangular prism whose surface area is 352 square inches. The length of the base of the prism is 8 inches and the width of the base is 4 inches.
(59)

28. **Lawnmowing** Emma is mowing her neighbors' lawns. Emma charges 1.5 cents per square foot of grass. How much should she charge to mow the lawn pictured here? *Hint: Emma does not mow the driveway.*
(40)

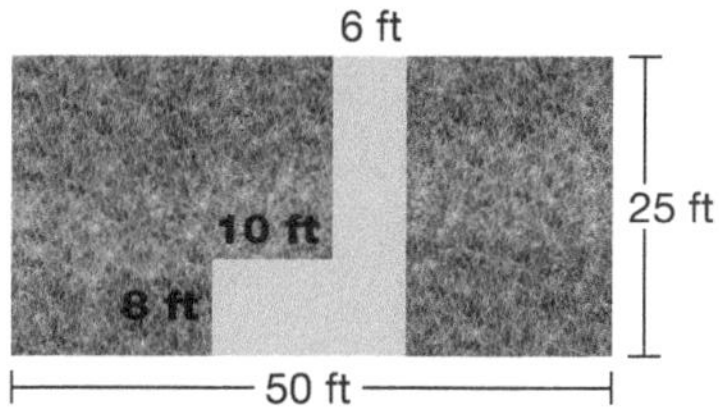

Finding Surface Areas and Volumes of Prisms

29. (18) **Justify** In two triangles, SBT and WEX, there are right angles at B and E.
a. If $\angle S \cong \angle W$, what can be said about $\angle T$ and $\angle X$? Justify your answer.
b. If $\angle T \cong \angle X$, what can be said about $\angle S$ and $\angle W$?

30. (58) Identify the tangent line(s) in this figure.

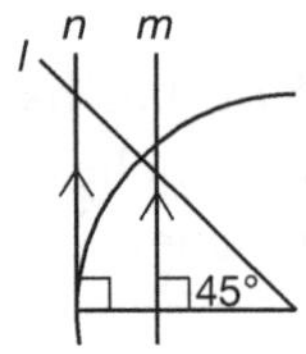

Name ______________________ Date __________ Class __________

Proportionality Theorems

LESSON 60

1. (28) For parallelogram $KLMN$, prove the triangles congruent by SAS Congruency.

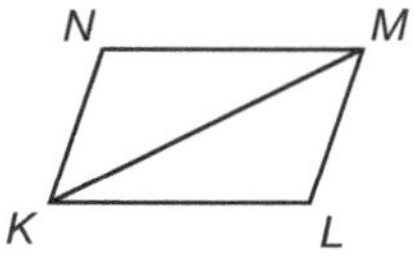

2. (38) **Algebra** Using the diagram, find WV in terms of x if $TW = 28x$, $UV = 15$, and $TU = 25x$.

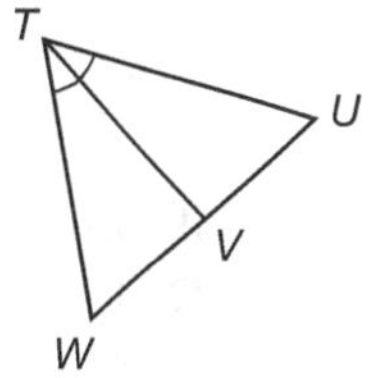

3. (42) A school is located at grid point $(-1, 2)$. If Jordan's home is on a street along the line $y = \frac{3}{2}x - 3$, what is the shortest distance Jordan could possibly live from the school?

*** 4.** (60) Fill in the blanks of the paragraph proof of the Converse of the Triangle Proportionality Theorem: If a line divides two sides of a triangle proportionally, then it is parallel to the third side.

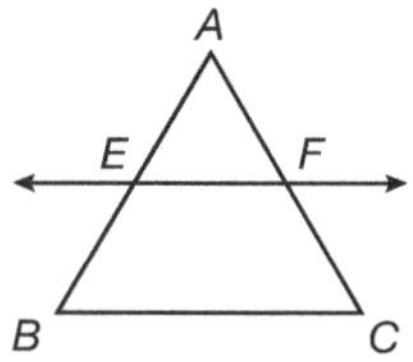

Given: $\frac{EB}{AE} = \frac{FC}{AF}$, so $\frac{AE}{AB} = \frac{AF}{AC}$.

Prove: $\overleftrightarrow{EF} \parallel \overline{BC}$

It is given that $\frac{EB}{AE} = \frac{FC}{AF}$. By the __________ Property of ____________, $\angle A \cong \angle A$, so $\triangle AEF \sim \triangle ABC$ by ____________. By definition of similar triangles, $\angle AEF \cong \angle ABC$. Finally, by the ______________________________, $\overleftrightarrow{EF} \parallel \overline{BC}$.

*** 5.** (60) **Multi-Step** In $\triangle PQR$, $\angle P$ is a right angle. Find the perimeter of $\triangle PQR$ to the nearest tenth.

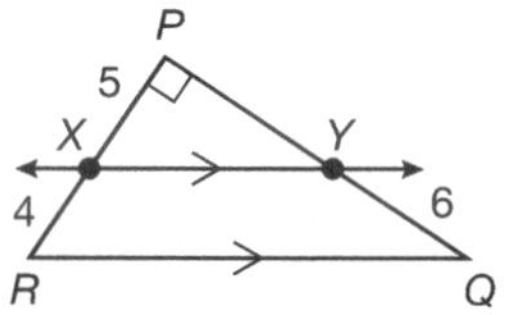

*** 6.** (59) A right rectangular prism has a length, width, and height that are all equal. The volume of the prism is 343 cubic meters. Find the surface area.

*** 7.** (31) Write a paragraph proof of the Triangle Angle Bisector Theorem: If a line bisects an angle of a triangle, then it divides the opposite side proportional to the other two sides of the triangle. *Hint: Draw* $\overline{BX}$ *parallel to* $\overline{AD}$ *and extend* $\overline{AC}$ *to X.*

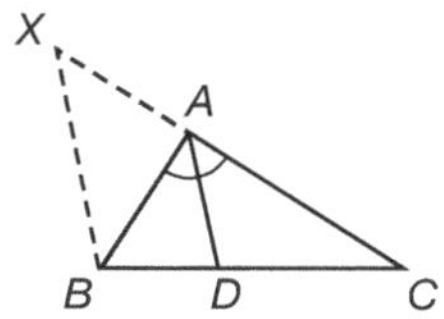

Given: In $\triangle ABC$, $\overline{AD}$ bisects $\angle BAC$.

Prove: $\frac{BD}{DC} = \frac{AB}{AC}$

8. (47) **Analyze** Find the measure of each angle in the inscribed quadrilateral.

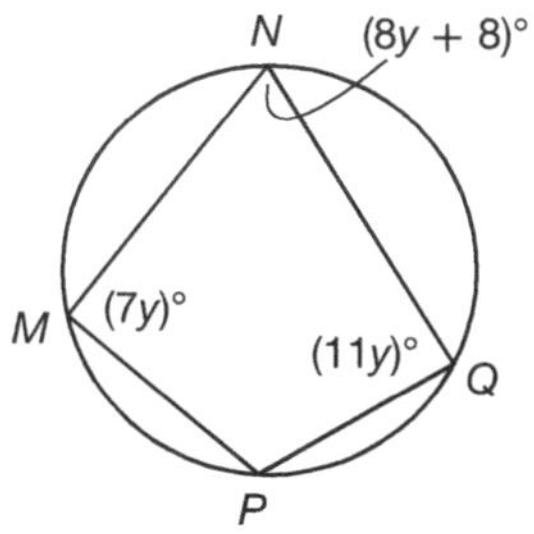

9. (21) **Sleep Patterns** Unless Cedrick has at least eight hours of sleep per night, he is tired all day. This morning he woke early and did not get eight hours of sleep. What can we conclude about Cedrick today?

10. (32) **Multi-Step** Find the orthocenter of $\triangle RTV$ with vertices $R(-2, 6)$, $T(1, 3)$, and $V(7, 3)$.

11. (58) **Error Analysis** This circle shown has center A, and $\overline{AB}$ is a radius. Mariah has calculated that $\angle A$ in $\triangle ABD$ is 65°. Why is her conclusion invalid?

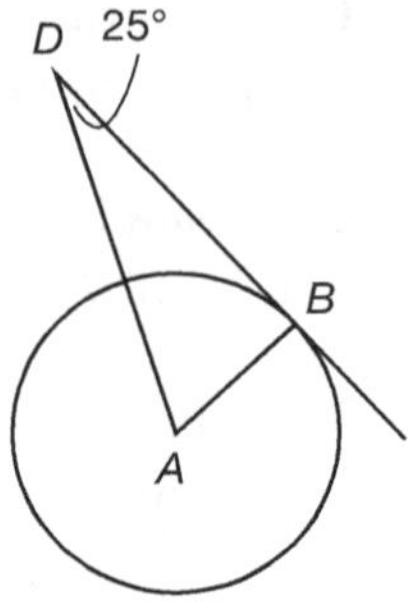

12. (50) Find the geometric mean of 33 and 27.

13. (39) **Multiple Choice** Which set of side lengths could not form a triangle?
A 4, 5, 10 **B** 1, 2, 2
C 11, 15, 20 **D** 55, 41, 37

***14.** (59) Find the surface area of the prism at right.

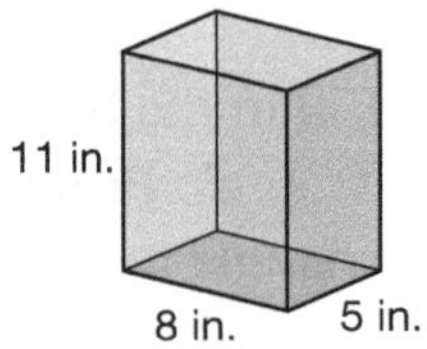

15. (53) **Floor Refinishing** Four congruent floors of a square office building need to be refinished. The diagonal of one of the floors is 175 feet. If one can of refinisher covers 8000 square feet, how many cans are needed to finish the floors?

***16.** (60) **Write** Are $\overline{JK}$ and $\overline{LM}$ parallel? Explain how you know.

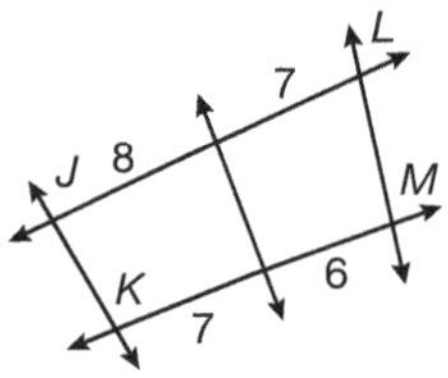

17. (55) **Verify** $\overline{DE}$ is a midsegment of $\triangle FGH$. Find the coordinates of D and E. Use the distance formula to verify that $\overline{DE}$ is a midsegment of $\triangle FGH$.

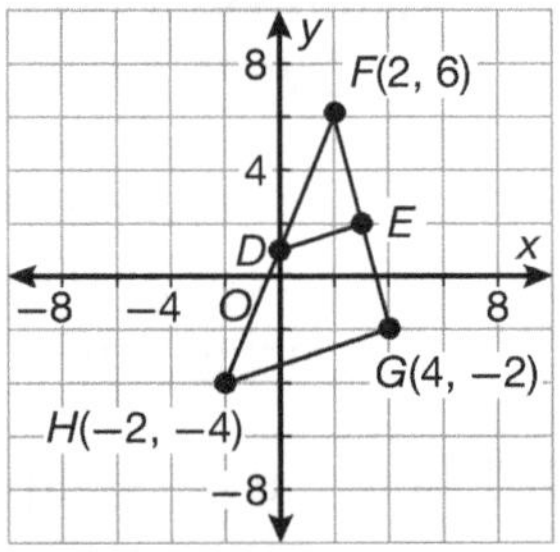

***18.** (60) **Multiple Choice** Which dimensions make $\overline{PQ} \parallel \overline{ST}$?
A $SR = 14$, $TR = 19$ **B** $SR = 10$, $TR = 13.3$
C $SR = 17.5$, $TR = 25$ **D** $SR = 13$, $TR = 20$

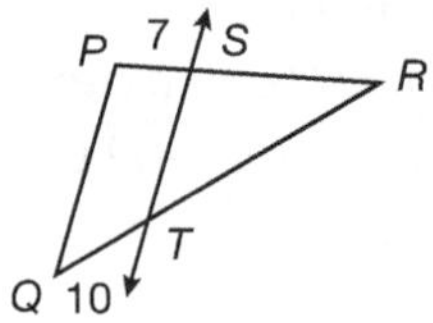

***19.** (59) Find the volume of the oblique prism shown.

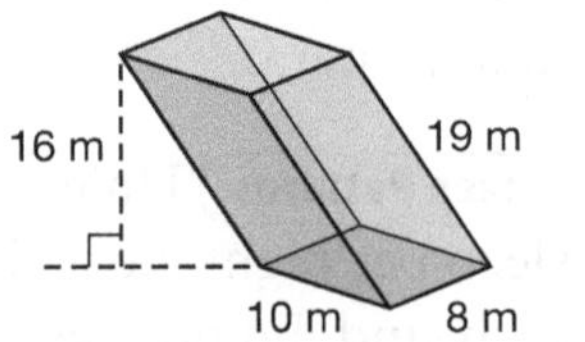

20. (58) Line ℓ is tangent to $\odot C$ at A, and line m passes through C. Lines ℓ and m intersect at B.
a. Classify $\triangle ACB$ by its angles.
b. If $m\angle ACB = 53°$, determine $m\angle CBA$.

21. (49) **Generalize** Is every solid a polyhedron? Explain.

22. (Inv 5) There are just five regular polyhedra, sometimes called the Platonic solids after the Greek philosopher Plato. Which of these polyhedra does *not* have square or triangular faces, and what shape are its faces?

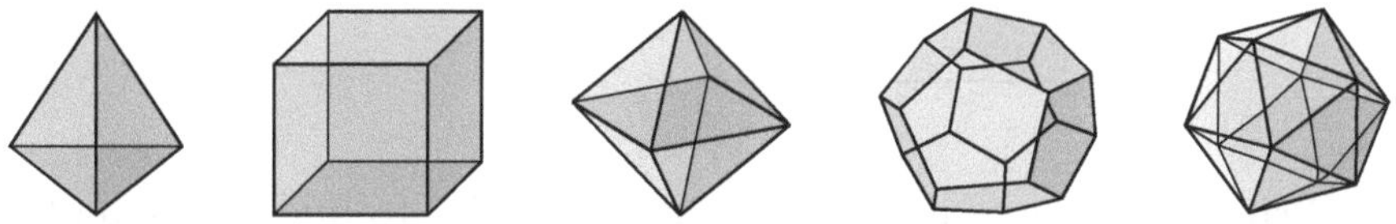

Tetrahedron 4 faces | Cube 6 faces | Octahedron 8 faces | Dodecahedron 12 faces | Icosahedron 20 faces

***23.** (48) **Justify** Use an indirect proof to prove that an altitude of an equilateral triangle is also a median.
Given: $\triangle ABC$ is equilateral with altitude $\overline{AX}$.
Prove: $\overline{AX}$ is a median of $\overline{BC}$.

24. (16) **Physics** In an experiment, wooden blocks with different masses are attached to a force meter and dragged along a rough surface. This graph shows a line that models the results. What is the equation of this line? What are the correct units for the slope?

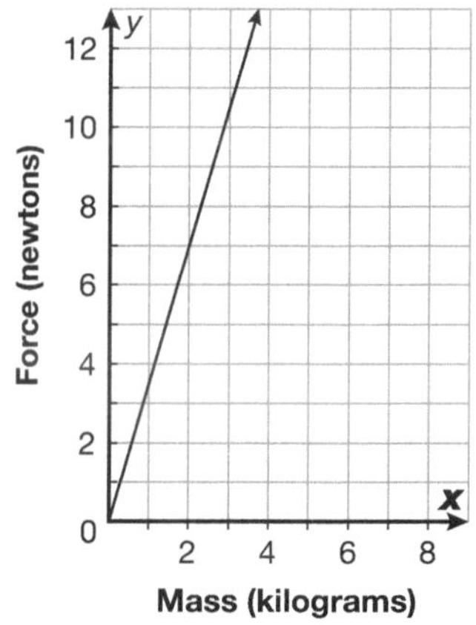

25. (49) An octahedron is a regular polyhedron. If the bases of two congruent square pyramids are glued together, the result is an octahedron. Describe the polygons that comprise the faces of an octahedron, and state the number of vertices, edges, and faces.

26. (50) Find the value of x and y in the triangle shown to the nearest tenth.

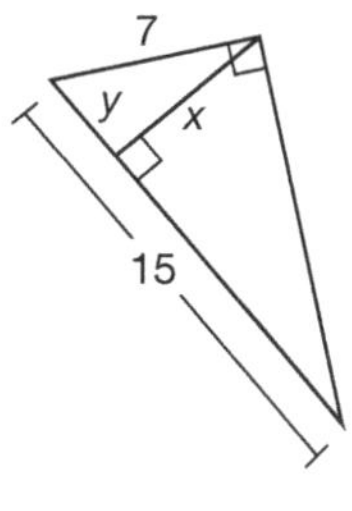

27. (35) **Geology** Large meteor craters have been found that are nearly perfectly circular. A geologist is walking around one such crater. After walking one mile, she finds that she has covered 85 degrees of arc. What is the radius of the crater, to the nearest foot?

28. (46) **Justify** Find the value of x in the figure, and justify your answer.

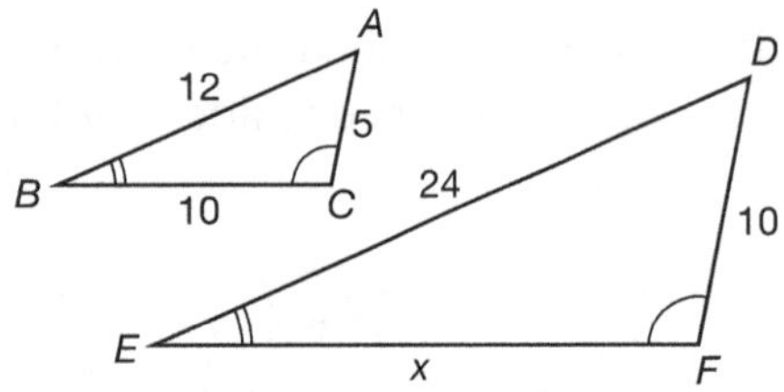

29. (56) **Formulate** Write a formula that uses only the shorter leg to find the area of a 30°-60°-90° triangle. Let the shorter leg be equal to x.

30. (57) **Traffic** A shop owner built his own stop sign according to the diagram. Find the perimeter of the stop sign to the nearest unit. Is this a regular octagon?

Name ______________________________ Date __________ Class __________

Determining if a Quadrilateral is a Parallelogram

LESSON 61

1. (50) Find the value of x and y in the triangle shown.

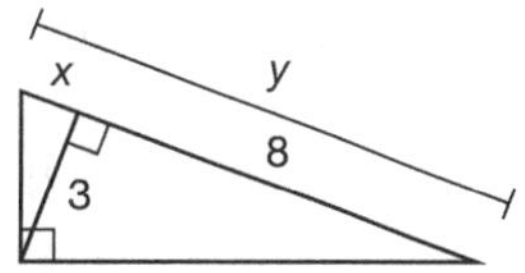

2. (53) **Crafts** Two artisans are sharing a square table measuring 1 meter on each side to display their crafts at a crafts fair. They need to divide its area equally between them before they can arrange their crafts on the table. If they mark the dividing line with tape, how much more tape will they use if they mark it diagonally than if they mark it horizontally?

3. (56) If the shorter leg of a 30°-60°-90° triangle is 17, what are the lengths of the other leg and hypotenuse?

4. (56) Find the value of x and y in the triangle shown. Give your answers in simplified radical form.

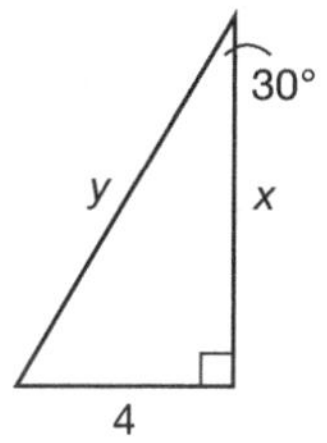

*** 5.** (Inv 6) **Model** Design a spinner with 4 sectors so that one sector is 3 times as probable as the others.

*** 6.** (60) Determine whether lines $\overline{EF}$ and $\overline{XY}$ are parallel.

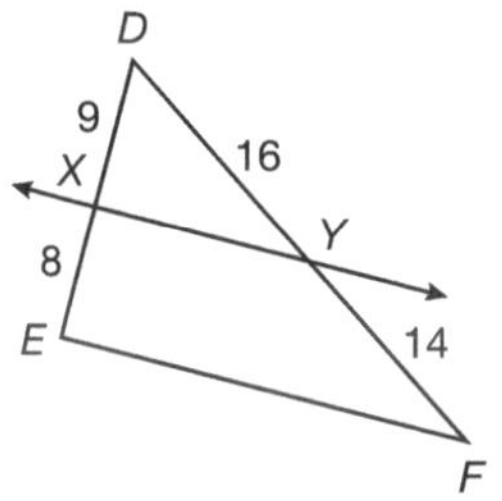

*** 7.** (61) **Urban Planning** A city block forms a parallelogram. If 3 sides are 86 meters, 86 meters, and 156 meters long, respectively, what is the only length possible for the fourth side?

8. (46) If $\triangle ABC$ and $\triangle DEF$ are similar by Angle-Angle Similarity, then the lengths of their respective sides are ___________.

9. (55) Segment QR is a midsegment of $\triangle MNP$. Find the coordinates of Q and R.

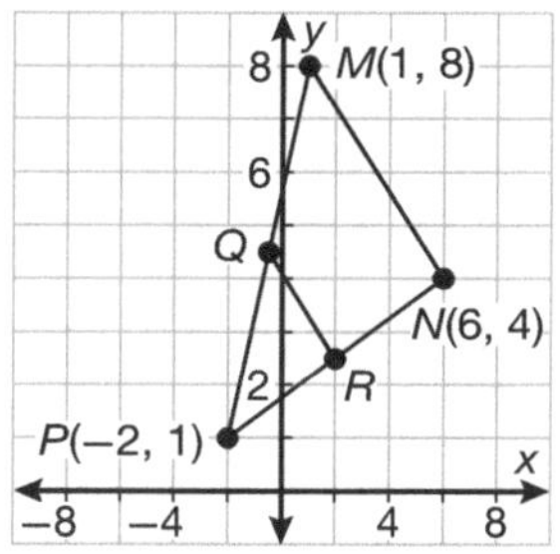

10. (53) **Radio Communications** A set of radio communicators are rated to work up to 1.35 miles apart. Smith and Claude start at the same point, and each takes a communicator. If Smith walks 1 mile east and Claude walks 1 mile north, will their communicators be able to reach each other? Explain.

11. (57) **Estimate** Estimate the area of the irregular shape at right.

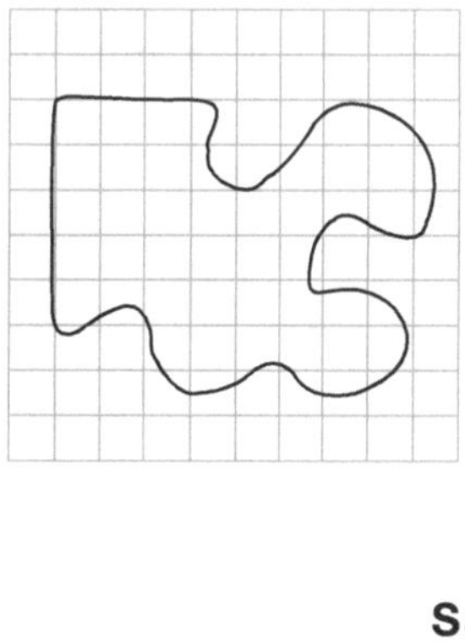

Determining if a Quadrilateral is a Parallelogram

LESSON 61

12. (11) **Multiple Choice** What is the midpoint of the line segment with endpoints $P(-7, 3)$ and $Q(0, 8)$?

A $(-3.5, 5.5)$ **B** $(-3.5, 4.5)$
C $(-2.5, 5.5)$ **D** $(-1.5, 1.5)$

13. (59) Find the surface area of the prism at right.

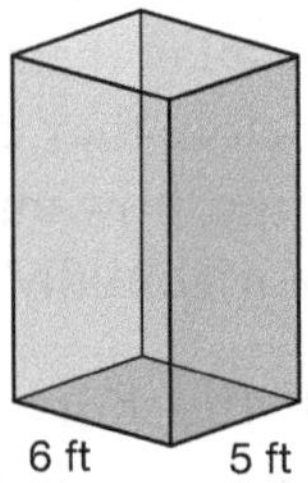

14. (59) **Painting** Aiden wants to paint the walls of his living room which measure 16 feet wide, 22 feet long, and 8 feet high. How many square feet must Aiden paint?

15. (51) $\overline{ZX}$ and $\overline{ZY}$ are tangents to $\odot C$ at X and Y, and $\triangle XYZ$ is equiangular. The radius of $\odot C$ is 5 centimeters. What is the exact perimeter of quadrilateral $CXZY$?

16. (44) Figure $ABCD$ is similar to figure $EFGH$. The ratio of their corresponding sides is 4:5. If the perimeter of $EFGH$ is 30 inches, what is the perimeter of $ABCD$?

17. (33) **Multi-Step** Write an inequality to show the values for x that make the triangle shown acute. Write an inequality to show the values for x that make the triangle obtuse. Round to the nearest tenth.

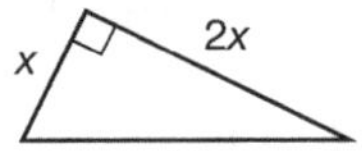

18. (35) The area of a circle is 40.6 square meters. If a sector has an arc length of 2.8 meters, what is the approximate arc measure of the central angle?

***19.** (Inv 6) **Games and Puzzles** Determine the geometric probabilities for randomly drawing each piece of this tangram.

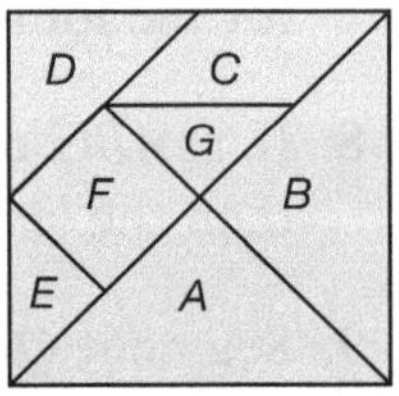

***20.** (61) **Multiple Choice** The coordinates of three vertices of a parallelogram are $(-2, 1)$, $(3, -1)$, and $(-1, -4)$. What are the coordinates of the fourth vertex?

A $(2, 5)$ **B** $(4, 5)$
C $(-4, -8)$ **D** $(-6, -2)$

***21.** (60) Find the length of $\overline{XA}$ in the triangle shown.

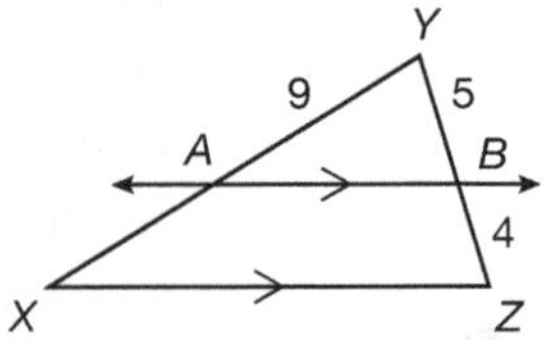

22. (58) Line ℓ is tangent to $\odot C$ at A. Line m passes through C and intersects line ℓ at B.

a. Classify $\triangle ACB$ by its angles.

b. If $m\angle ACB = 53°$, determine $m\angle CBA$.

23. **Justify** Write a paragraph proof of the following.
(31)
Given: $\angle 4 \cong \angle 3$
Prove: $m\angle 1 = m\angle 2$

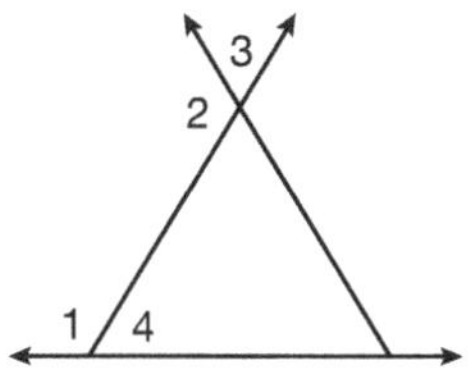

24. Is the following statement always, sometimes, or never true?
(52)
A rhombus is a rectangle.

***25.** **Algebra** If $x = 4$, then is $ABCD$ a parallelogram?
(61)
Explain why it is, or draw a diagram to prove it is not.

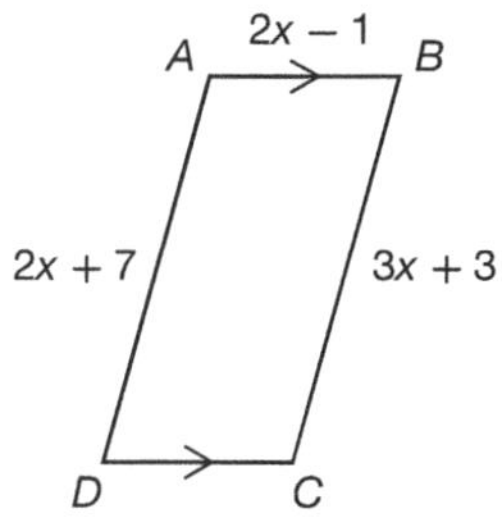

***26.** **Write** If you connect the midpoints of two sides of a triangle,
(60)
will the line you make always be parallel to the third side? Explain.

27. **Algebra** Rectangle $QRST$ has vertices $Q(0, 0)$, $R(0, 2w)$, $S(2\ell, 2w)$ and $T(2\ell, 0)$. Find the coordinates of the midpoint of $\overline{QR}$.
(45)

28. Name the shortest line segment in the diagram.
(39)

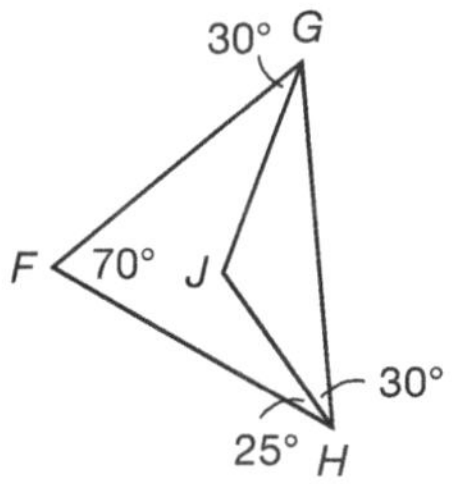

***29.** If two equilateral triangles are joined along one side,
(61)
will the result always be a parallelogram? If so, what type of parallelogram would be formed?

30. **Analyze** What can the intersection of a sphere and
(49)
a plane be?

Name ______________________ Date __________ Class __________

Finding Surface Areas and Volumes of Cylinders

LESSON 62

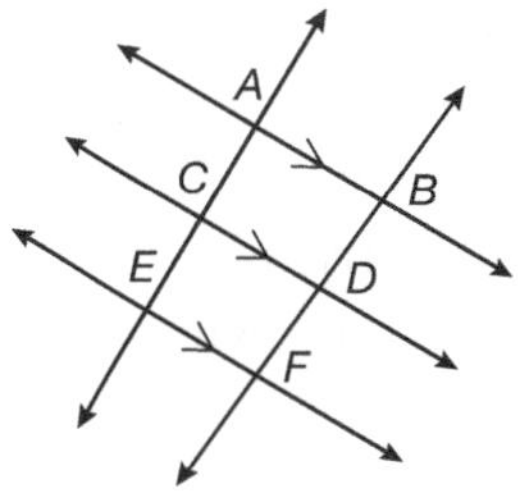

1. *(60)* Using the figure at right, complete this ratio: $\frac{AC}{CE} = \frac{\quad}{DF}$

2. *(54)* Draw a cube in one-point perspective so that the vanishing point is to the right of the cube.

3. *(25)* **Algebra** In $\triangle ABC$, $AB = 3x + 2$ and $BC = 5x - 7$. In $\triangle FED$, $DE = 4x + 13$. If $\triangle ABC$ is congruent to $\triangle FED$, then what is AB?

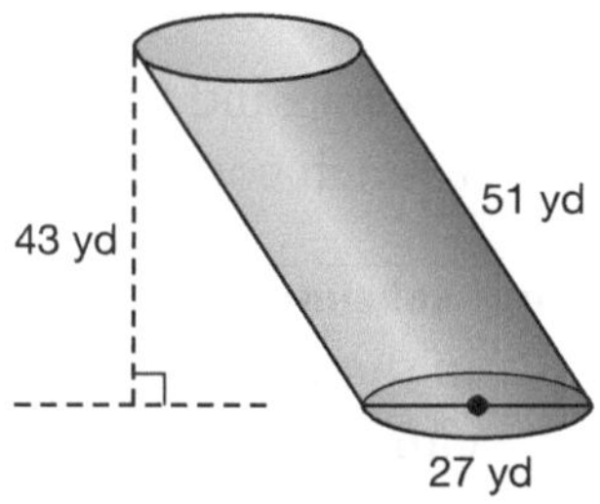

* **4.** *(62)* Find the volume of the oblique cylinder to the nearest tenth of a yard.

5. *(43)* What is the radius of a circle in which a 9.2-inch long chord is 4.3 inches from the center of a circle?

6. *(49)* Which solid does a basketball most resemble?

7. *(Inv 6)* Calculate the theoretical probabilities for each sector of this spinner.

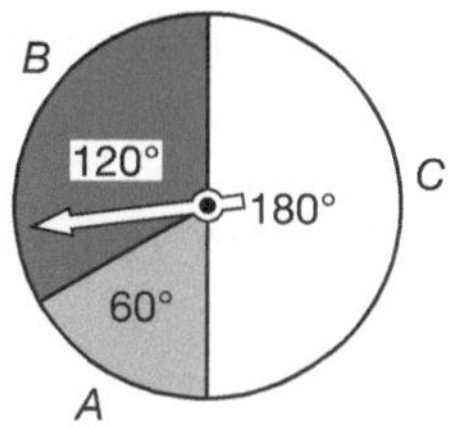

8. *(52)* What is another name for an equiangular quadrilateral?

9. *(32)* **Error Analysis** Alicia wanted to find the centroid in the diagram shown. Explain the error she made.

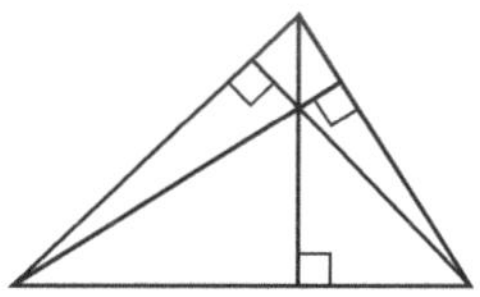

10. *(36)* **Multiple Choice** In triangles UVW and XYZ, U and Z are right angles, $\overline{UV} \cong \overline{YZ}$, and $\overline{VW} \cong \overline{XY}$. Which theorem proves these triangles are congruent?

A HA Congruence Theorem **B** LA Congruence Theorem
C LL Congruence Theorem **D** None of these

11. *(56)* **Furniture Making** The braces for a shelf are 30°-60°-90° triangles, as shown. What is the perimeter of each brace?

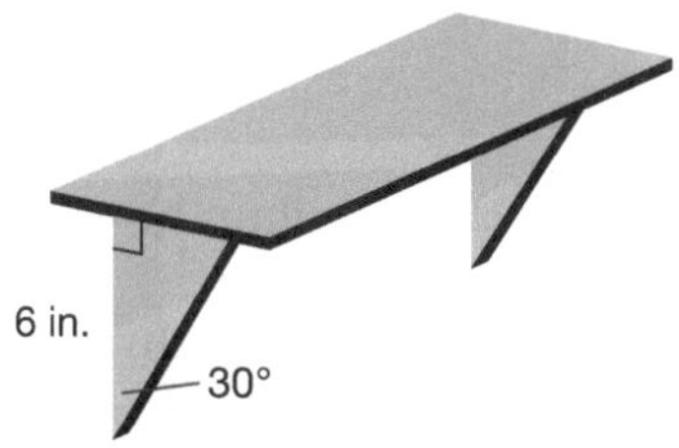

12. *(51)* In isosceles $\triangle ABC$, $\angle A$ is the vertex angle and $m\angle A = 3m\angle B$.

a. Write a congruence statement involving the angles of $\triangle ABC$. Name a postulate or theorem to justify your statement.

b. Determine the measure of each angle.

13. (52) **Formation** Lucy and her friends are walking to school as shown in the diagram. Lucy notices that she has to turn her head 90° to look from one friend to the next. Lucy decides that her friends are arranged in a square. Is this a valid conclusion? Why or why not?

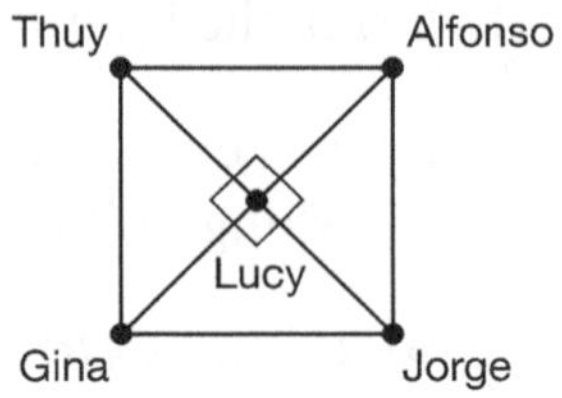

***14.** (62) Find the volume of the cylinder to the nearest hundred cubic inches.

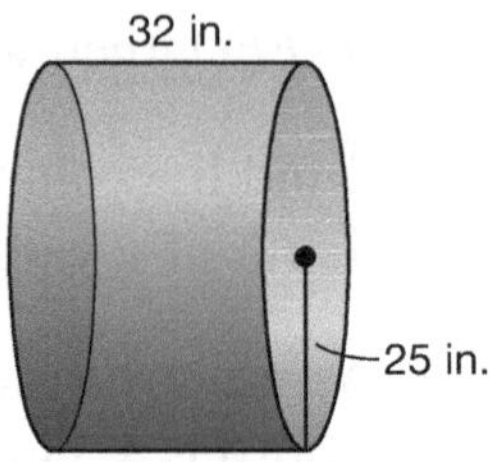

15. (43) **Algebra** Find the distance from the center of a circle to a 12-inch cord if the circle has a 20-inch diameter.

***16.** (62) **Labeling** A certain soup can measures 4 inches tall and 3 inches in diameter. If the soup company needs to fill an order for 1092 cans, what is the total area of labels the company will need to print?

17. (50) Find the value of x and y in the triangle shown.

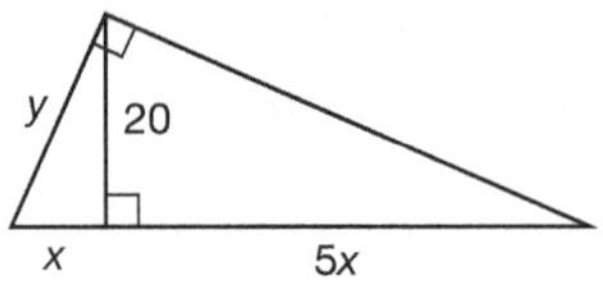

***18.** (61) **Analyze** In quadrilateral $ABCD$, $m\angle A + m\angle B = 180°$. Can it be proven that $ABCD$ is a parallelogram?

***19.** (61) **Justify** If $x = 12$, then is $ABCD$ at right a parallelogram? Explain.

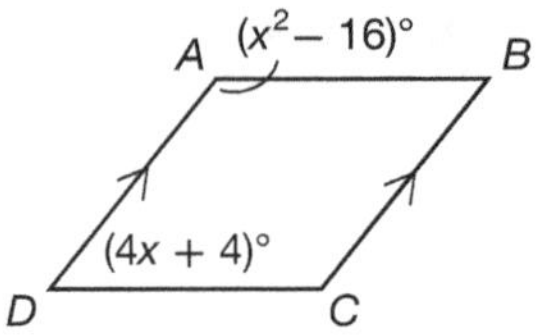

***20.** (60) **Model** Explain how the Triangle Proportionality Theorem can be thought of as a special application of Theorem 60-3 (parallel lines divide transversals proportionally). Is there a situation in which one of the theorems could *not* be used to make a triangle?

21. (58) **Engineering** A circular rod is clamped between two plates as shown. The plates have to be 20 inches wide. What is the least area of metal needed for the plates?

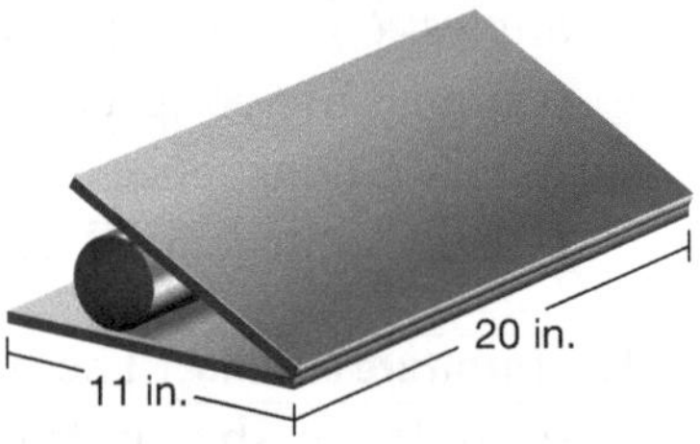

22. (50) Find the geometric mean of 17 and 13.

23. (Inv 1) **Justify** Explain how to find x in the diagram shown. What is x?

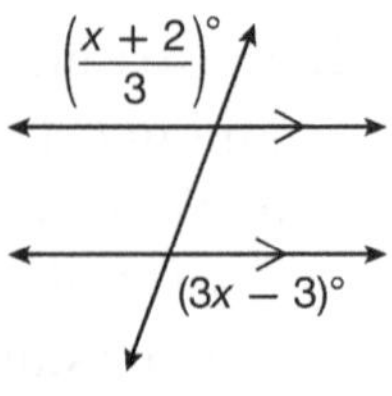

24. (Inv 6) A spinner has three colored sectors, with these central angles:

purple: 45°; yellow: 105°; orange: 210°

For each color, calculate the theoretical probability that the spinner lands on it.

25. (47) **Algebra** Find the measure of each angle in quadrilateral *QRST*.

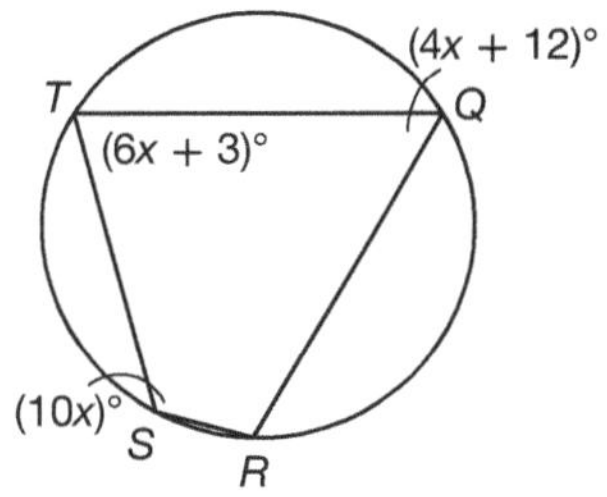

26. (59) **Packaging** Mrs. Jenkins has a jar that holds 360 cubic inches of spicy roasted almonds. She wants to transfer the almonds to gift boxes that measure 2 inches tall, 3 inches wide, and 5 inches long. How many gift boxes can she fill?

27. (42) **Multi-Step** Given the line $2y - x = 0$ and $F(-6, 2)$, find the point on the line that is closest to F.

*28. (62) Find the surface area of the cylinder shown to the nearest hundredth.

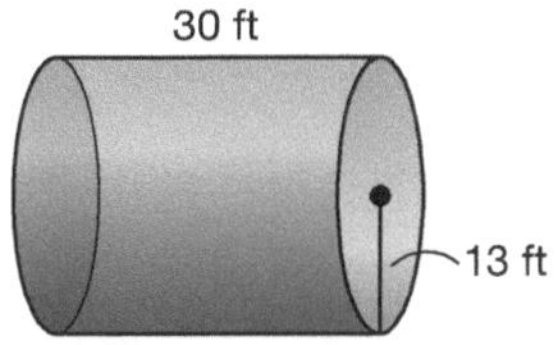

*29. (61) Is this statement sometimes, always, or never true?

A trapezoid is a parallelogram.

*30. (51) **Write** Explain how the statement, "If a triangle is equilateral, then it is equiangular," follows from the Isosceles Triangle Theorem.

Name ______________________ Date __________ Class __________

Introduction to Vectors

LESSON 63

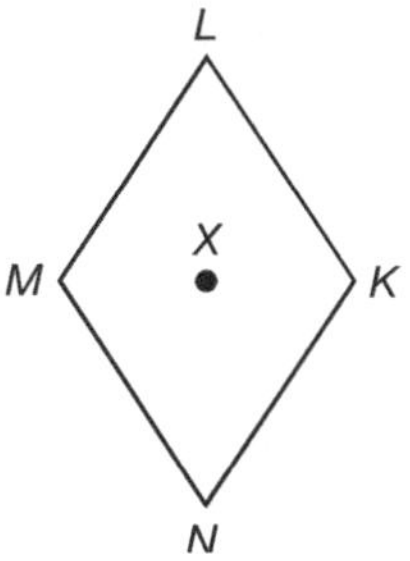

1. (52) Quadrilateral $KLMN$ is a rhombus with X at its center. If $m\angle XKL = 57°$, what is $m\angle NKL$?

* **2.** (62) Maurice has a cylindrical jar with an approximate capacity of 75.36 cubic inches. He knows the jar is 6 inches tall. What is the jar's radius?

* **3.** (63) **Algebra** The opposite vector of $\langle 4, 6\rangle$ is $\langle 2x + 2, 2x\rangle$. What is the value of x?

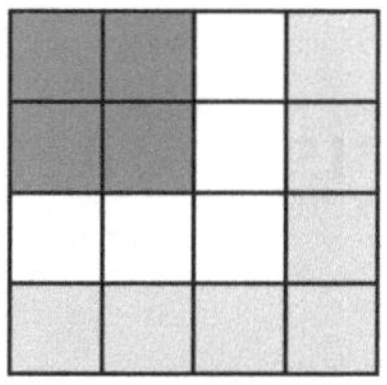

4. (Inv 6) This grid is cut up into 16 squares, which are placed in a hat. What is the probability of drawing a blue square? a white square?

* **5.** (63) **Multiple Choice** A swimmer is swimming in a river. He is swimming in the same direction as a current that is flowing 2 miles per hour. How fast must he swim if he wants to travel 4 miles per hour?

A 6 mi/hr **B** 4 mi/hr
C 2 mi/hr **D** 1 mi/hr

6. (61) Is the following statement sometimes, always, or never true?

A regular quadrilateral is a parallelogram.

7. (Inv 4) **Multi-Step** In the triangles shown, what range of values for x would cause $\angle P$ to be larger than $\angle S$? $\angle P$ to be smaller than $\angle S$?

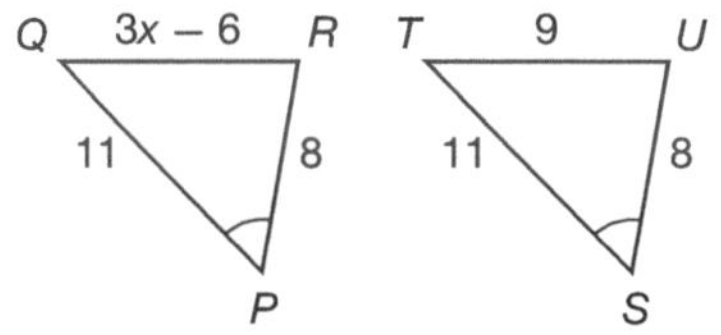

8. (48) **Analyze** Use an indirect proof to prove that if $\triangle ABC$ is isosceles where $AB = AC$ with a point D on BC such that D is not the midpoint of BC, then $\triangle ABD \neq \triangle ADC$.
Given: $\triangle ABC$ isosceles and $AD \neq DB$.
Prove: $\triangle ABD \neq \triangle ADC$.

9. (55) **Farming** A farmer wants to plant sorghum on a trapezoidal area of his field, shown by the triangle midsegment below. What is the area of the field he wishes to plant?

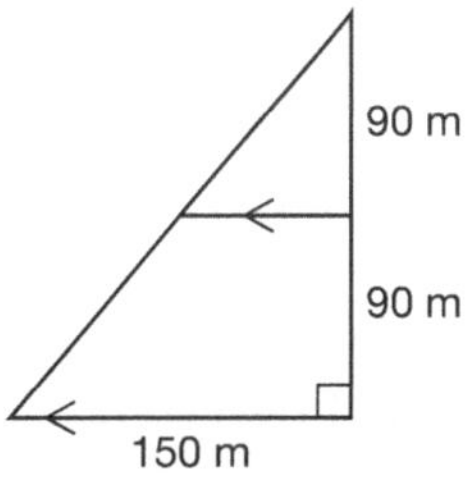

10. (34) **Multiple Choice** Which of the following is not a parallelogram?

A rhombus **B** trapezoid
C rectangle **D** square

11. (33) **Algebra** Determine the value of x in the triangle shown. Write your answer in simplified radical form.

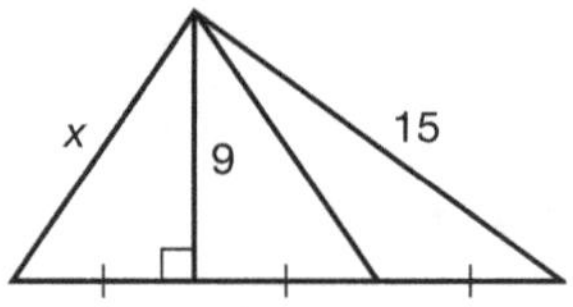

12. (58) **Analyze** When can two distinct lines which are each tangent to the same circle be parallel? Explain.

13. (60) **Error Analysis** In the figure at right, Rafael found that $BC = 6$. Where did he make an error?

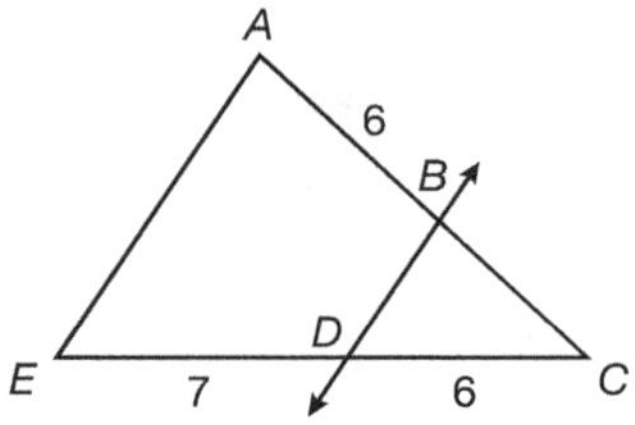

***14.** (63) What is the sum of the vectors $\langle 3, 2\rangle$, $\langle 3.7, -8.2\rangle$, $\langle 3, 2\rangle$, and $\langle -3.7, 8.2\rangle$?

***15.** (62) Find the lateral area of the cylinder below, to the nearest whole square yard.

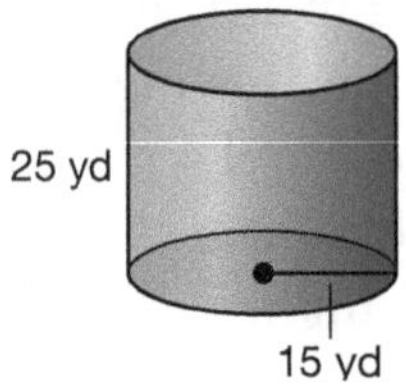

16. (44) Figure *JKLM* is similar to figure *TUWV*. The ratio of their corresponding sides is 6:1. If the perimeter of *TUWV* is 12 inches, what is the perimeter of *JKLM*?

17. (12) **Algebra** In this figure, what value of z would allow you to apply the Same-Side Interior Angles Theorem to conclude that lines j and k are parallel?

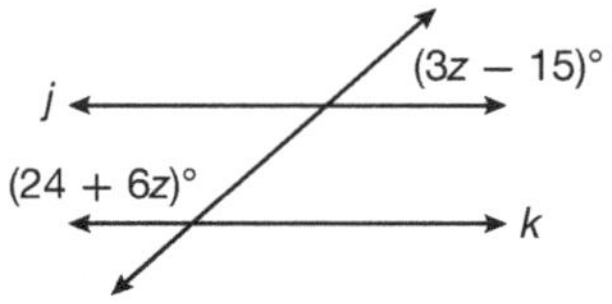

***18.** (63) **Flight** A small airplane is flying at 120 mph. If the wind is blowing at 30 mph from directly behind the airplane, at what speed is the airplane flying over the ground?

19. (58) In this figure, $\overline{AB}$ and $\overline{AD}$ are tangent to circle C. Determine the perimeter of quadrilateral *ABCD*. What type of quadrilateral is *ABCD*?

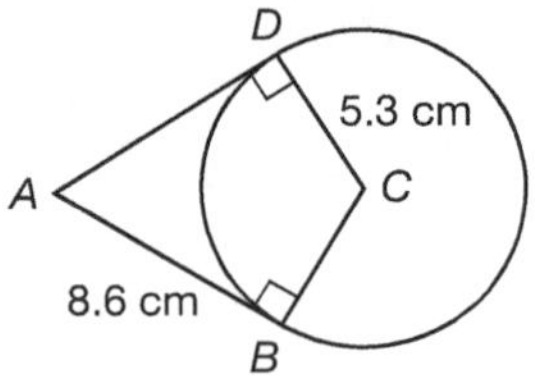

20. (56) **Formulate** Write a formula that uses only the shorter leg to find the area of a 30°-60°-90° triangle. Let the shorter leg be equal to x.

***21.** (62) Find the volume of the cylinder shown to the nearest hundredth.

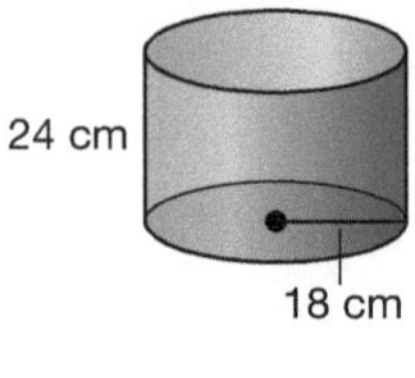

22. (54) **Generalize** How many lateral faces can a prism have? As the number of sides of the base increase, what solid does the figure look more and more like?

23. (Inv 3) **Algebra** In a certain regular polygon, each exterior angle is half the size of each interior angle. How many sides does this polygon have?

*24. (53) **Archaeology** An archaeologist is studying the ruins of a small pyramid as shown in the diagram. How can she find the original height of the pyramid? What was the original height of the pyramid?

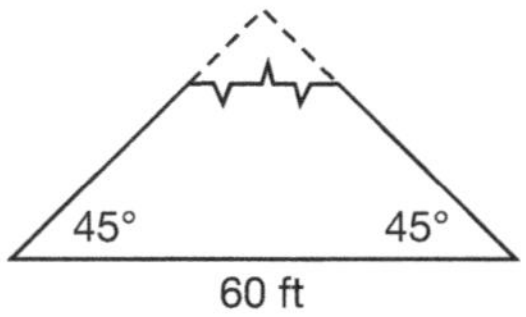

25. (51) Triangle UVW is equilateral with sides measuring 2 inches, and X is the midpoint of $\overline{VW}$.

a. Determine the exact height of $\triangle UVW$.

c. Determine the exact area of $\triangle UVW$.

26. (61) Can it be concluded that the quadrilateral at right is a parallelogram? Explain.

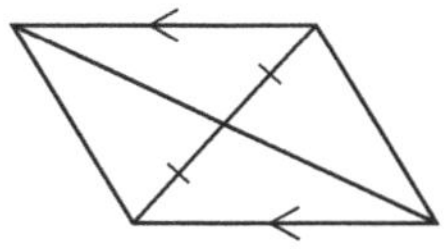

27. (59) **Driveways** Carolina is going to pave her new driveway with concrete. The space that has been dug out for the driveway is 0.5 feet deep, 20 feet long and 12 feet wide. What volume of concrete will it take to pave Carolina's driveway?

28. (57) **Estimate** Estimate the area of the heart design at right.

29. (45) For a triangle with vertices $L(0, 0)$, $M(6, 0)$, and $N(3, y)$ to be an equilateral triangle, what must be the value of y?

30. (35) **Jogging** About how many seconds does it take Henrietta to jog one-third of the way around a circular track with a 500-meter radius, if she jogs at a speed of 2 meters per second?

Name ______________________ Date __________ Class __________

Angles Interior to Circles

LESSON 64

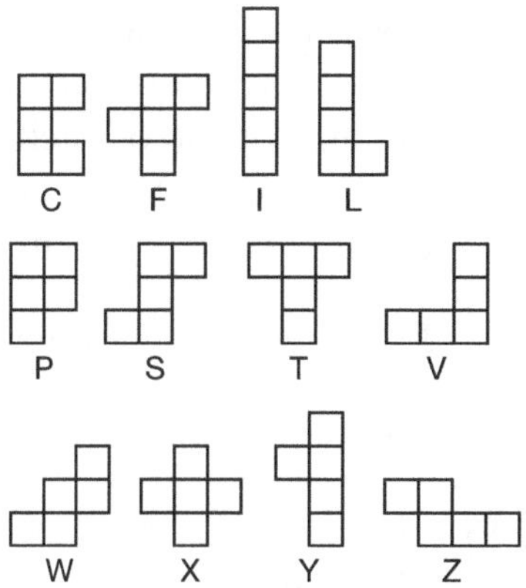

1. (Inv 6) **Predict** In this set of pentominoes, there are 12 non-congruent shapes made from 5 unit squares each.

a. A pentomino *solution* is any way of fitting the 12 pentominoes together exactly in a rectangle. What must the area of the solution rectangle be?

b. What are the geometric probabilities for each pentomino that a square chosen at random from a solution will be in that pentomino?

c. In this *partial solution*, some of the pentominoes are fit together in a smaller rectangle. What is the geometric probability in this rectangle of the V-pentomino? the T-pentomino?

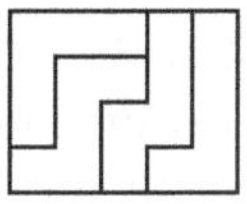

2. (49) **a. Generalize** What is the fewest number of sides a polygon can have?
b. What is the fewest number of faces a polyhedron can have?

3. (57) **Household** A child spilled a glass of grape juice on a square white pillow, as shown. Approximately what percentage of the pillow is not stained?

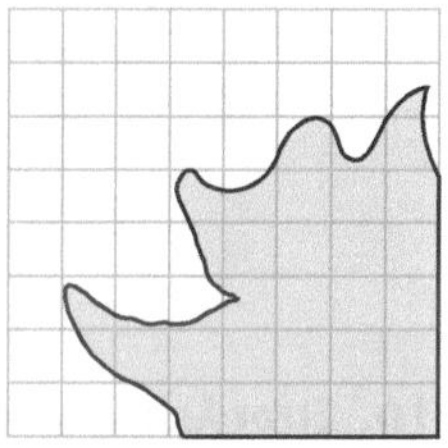

4. (34) **Multiple Choice** Which angles would be supplementary in parallelogram *KLMN*?

A $\angle K$ and $\angle M$ **B** $\angle L$ and $\angle N$
C $\angle L$ and $\angle M$ **D** Any nonconsecutive angle pair

5. (46) **Justify** Name the angles that are congruent in the triangles shown. If these triangles are similar, state why.

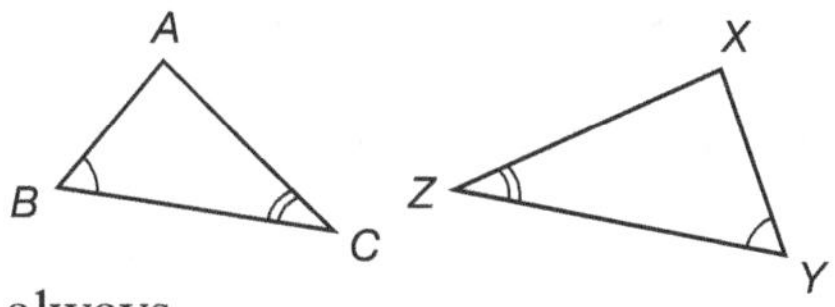

6. (61) **Write** Given any three non-collinear points, can you always find a fourth point such that the points are the vertices of a parallelogram? Explain.

7. (60) **Multi-Step** Find *EF* in the compound figure. Round to the nearest tenth.

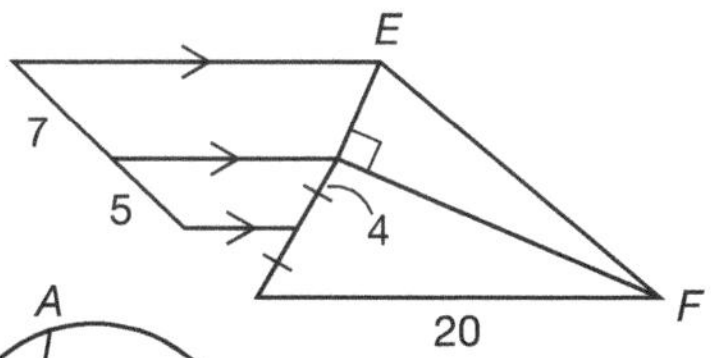

8. (50) Find the geometric mean of $4\sqrt{3}$ and $5\sqrt{2}$.

***9.** (64) Find the measure of $\widehat{ABC}$ at right. Line ℓ is tangent to the circle.

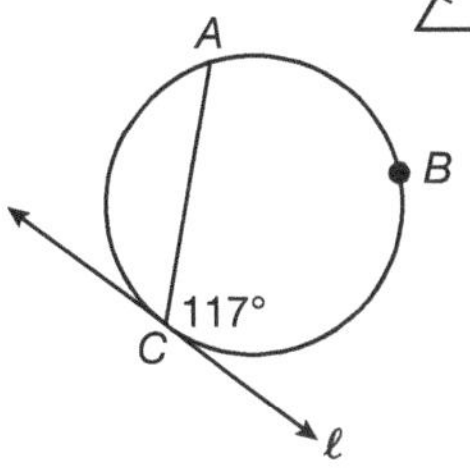

***10.** (63) Add the vectors $\langle 4, 8\rangle$ and $\langle -4, -8\rangle$. What kinds of vectors are these?

*11. (43) **Industrial Mechanics** In order to allow a series of metal cylinders with 2-inch diameters to lay flat without rolling, a machine slices off the bottom of each. If the machine cuts the cylinders so that the flat side is 1 inch across, how far down from the center of the cylinder should the cut be made?

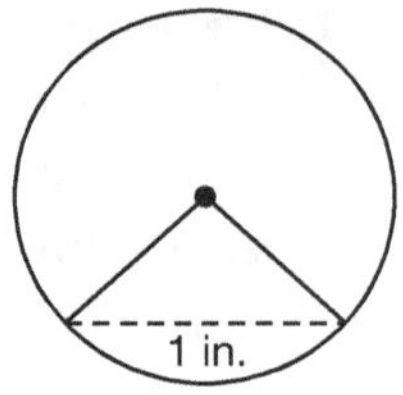

12. (46) Draw two triangles that are similar by Side-Angle-Side Theorem.

13. (47) **Algebra** Find the measure of $\angle C$ and $\angle F$ in the figure.

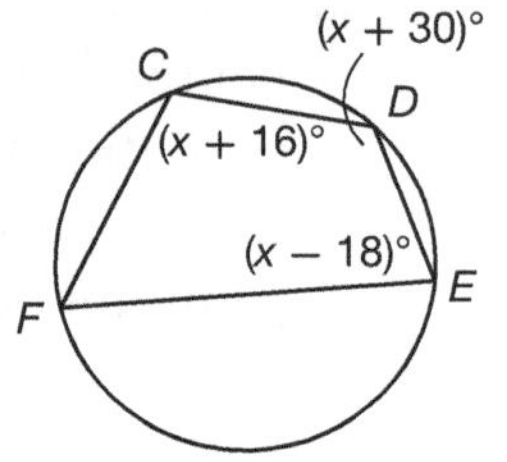

*14. (56) **Design** A carpenter wants to make a coffee table in the shape of an equilateral triangle. She doesn't have a way to measure 60°, but she can measure a right angle and the length. If she wants the table to have a perimeter of 9 feet, how should she design the table?

*15. (64) Find the measure of angle x in the circle below.

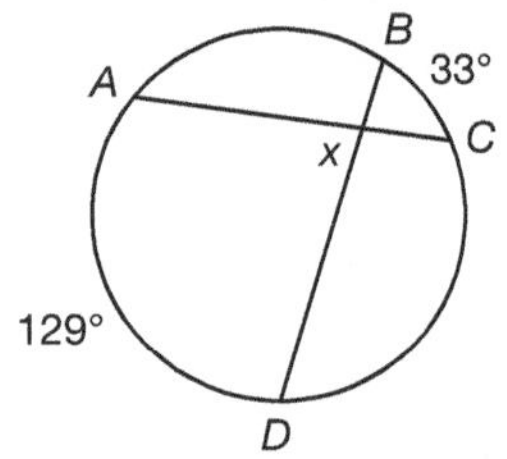

16. (53) **Error Analysis** Jessie used the properties of a 45°-45°-90° right triangle to find the length of a hypotenuse, while her friend Matthew used the Pythagorean Theorem to find the same length. Jessie found the answer to be $34\sqrt{2}$ miles, and Matthew found the answer to be about 48 miles. Who is correct?

17. (62) Find the surface area of the cylinder shown, to the nearest tenth.

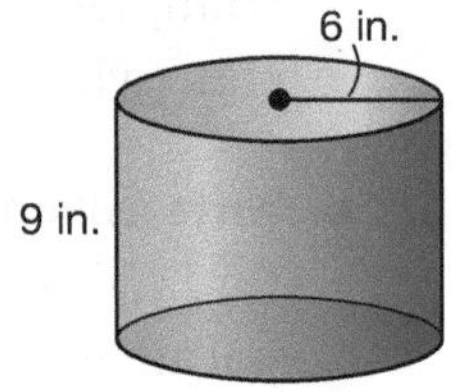

18. (37) **Algebra** Two lines are perpendicular. One line has an equation of $2y = px + 7$ and the other line has an equation of $y = \frac{q}{4}x - 4$. Find a possible set of values for p and q.

19. (Inv 5) **Multiple Choice** Which of these nets could form a regular polyhedron?

A

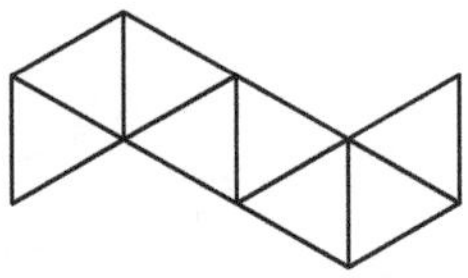

B

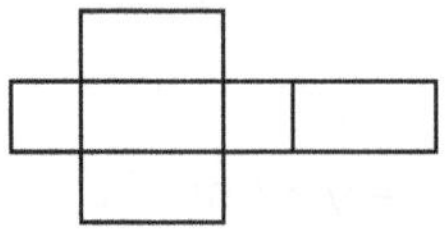

C

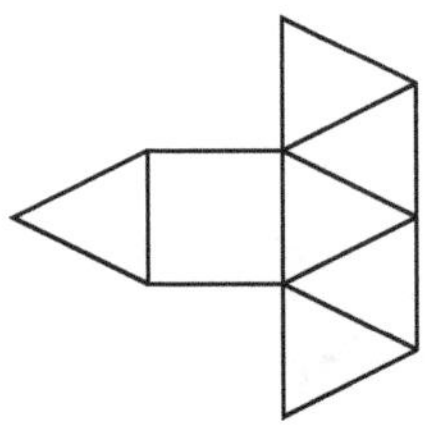

D

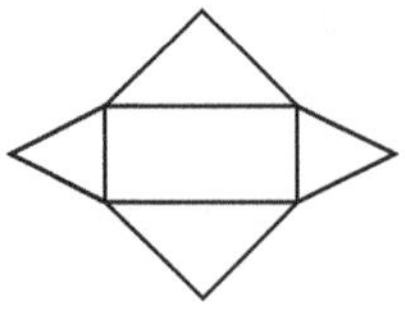

20. The ratio of the perimeters of two similar figures is 3:1. If the larger figure
(44) has a 6-unit side length, what is the length of the corresponding side on the second figure?

*21. **Stained Glass** An artist wants to use stained glass to cover the area
(40) in the rectangle and semicircle at right. If the glass he wants to use comes in 8-by-10-inch panes, what is the minimum number of panes he will need to buy to complete his project?

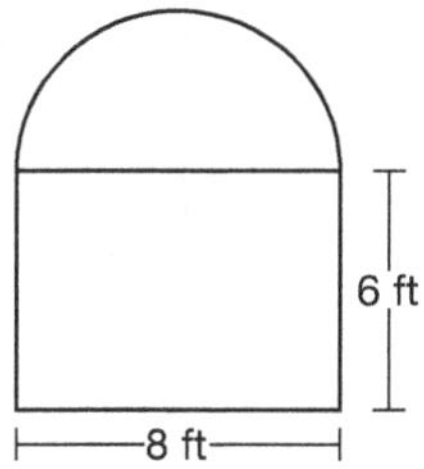

22. Find the surface area, to the nearest hundredth, of a cylinder that
(62) is 27 centimeters tall and has a 12-centimeter diameter.

23. Segment *DE* is a midsegment of $\triangle ABC$ at right. Find the values of
(55) *x* and *y*.

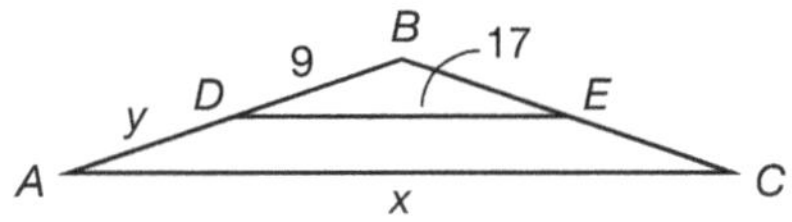

*24. Find the magnitude of vector $\langle 1, -2 \rangle$. Round your answer to the
(63) nearest tenth.

25. **Multi-Step** Find the centroid of $\triangle ABC$ with vertices $A(-2, 4)$,
(32) $B(1, -6)$, and $C(4, -4)$.

*26. Find the measure of angle *x* in the figure. Line ℓ is tangent to the circle.
(64)

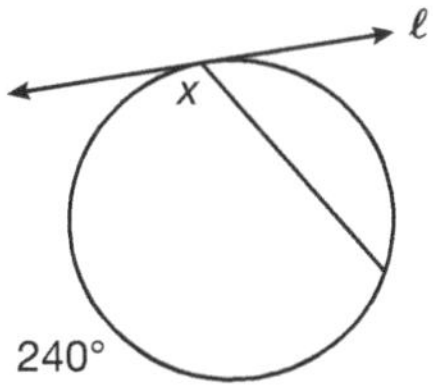

27. **Generalize** If a prism is cut parallel to its base to form two prisms, is the sum of the
(59) two prisms' volumes less than, greater than, or equal to that of the original prism? Is the sum of the two prisms' lateral areas less than, greater than, or equal to that of the original prism? Is the sum of the two prisms' total surface areas less than, greater than, or equal to that of the original prism?

*28. Find the measure of angle *x* in the circle at right.
(64)

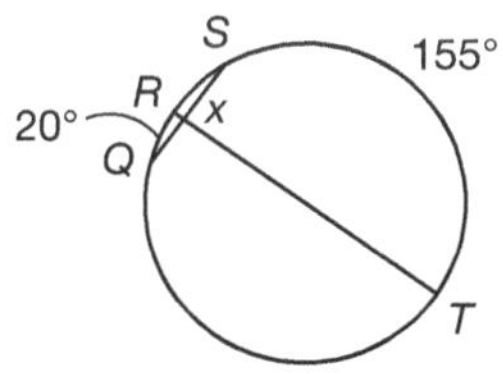

29. (16) **Biology** The estimated number of species on Earth has been declining in recent decades. One of many models for this is the equation $y = 5 - 0.025x$, where x is the number of years after 1980, and y is the number of species, in millions.

a. How many species were there in 1980?

b. Predict the number of species in the year 2100.

c. How many species are expected to become extinct in a 10-year period, according to this model?

***30.** (63) Write $\overrightarrow{f}$ in component form.

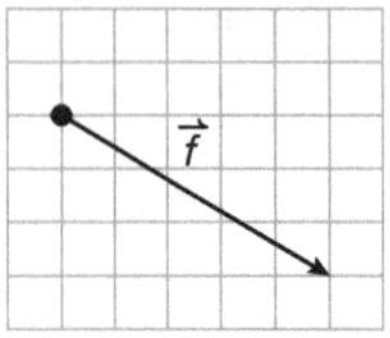

Name ______________________ Date ____________ Class ____________

Distinguishing Types of Parallelograms

LESSON 65

* **1.** (65) **Algebra** Find the value of x that would make this shape a rhombus.

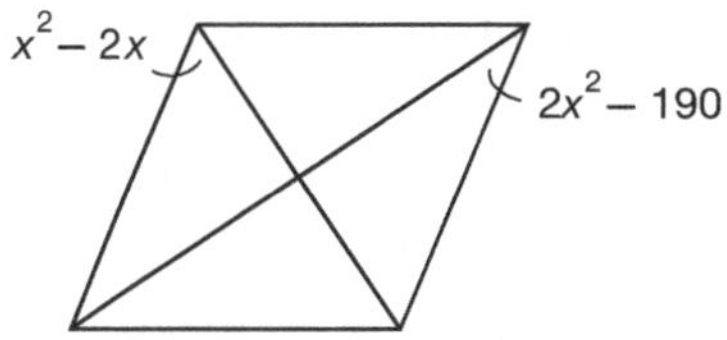

2. (35, 62) A round pie with a 10-inch diameter is 3 inches thick, and it has been cut into eight pieces. If three pieces have already been taken, what is the volume of the pie remaining to the nearest inch?

* **3.** (31) **Error Analysis** Find and correct any errors in the flowchart proof.
Given: $\angle 1$ and $\angle 2$ form a linear pair; $\angle 1 \cong \angle 3$
Prove: $\angle 2$ and $\angle 3$ are supplementary.

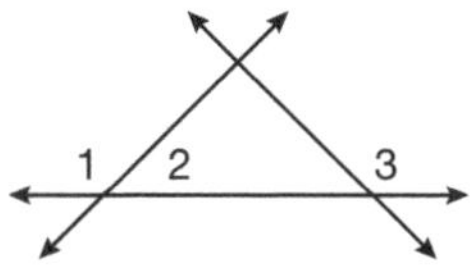

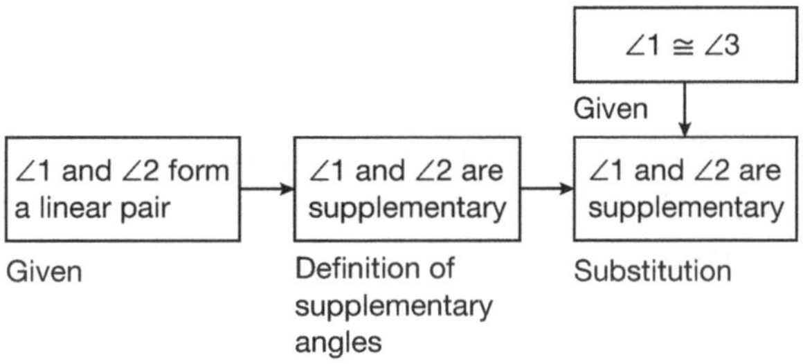

4. (57) **Algebra** This set of lines forms a triangle. Find its area and perimeter.
$y = \frac{1}{2}x + 1$, $y = x - 1$, $x = 0$

5. (59) Find the volume of the right prism shown.

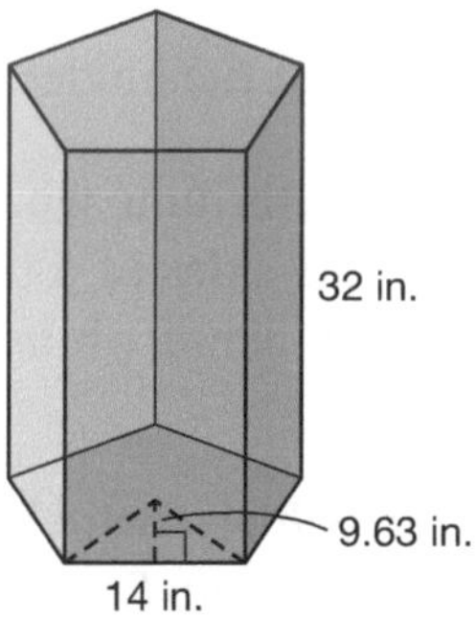

6. (63) **Sailing** The speed at which a sailboat moves over the water depends on both the current of the water and the wind. Suppose the wind is blowing at 12 miles per hour and the current is flowing at 3 miles per hour in the opposite direction. At what speed is the boat traveling relative to the shore?

* **7.** (52) Find the perimeter of the rhombus shown.

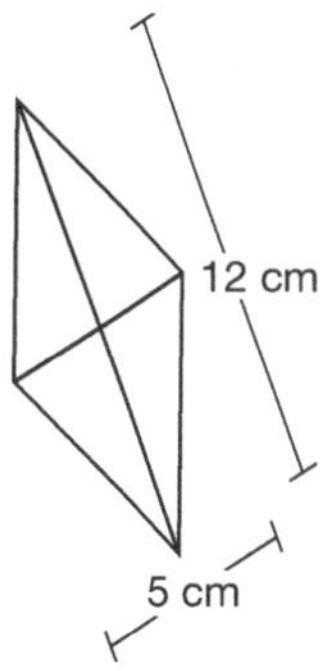

* **8.** (65) **Multi-Step** The vertices of quadrilateral $LMNP$ are $L(2, 2)$, $M(-4, 1)$, $N(-3, -5)$, and $P(3, -4)$. Classify this quadrilateral.

9. (9) **Structures** A crossbeam on a barn gate goes diagonally across a door 3 feet by 50 inches. How long is the diagonal line in feet? Round to the nearest hundredth.

***10.** *(64)* Find the measure of $\angle AXD$ in the circle at right.

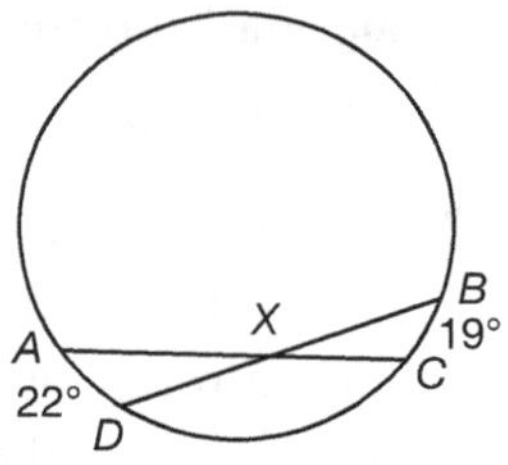

11. *(57)* **Multiple Choice** A circle with its center at (2, 4) passes through point (−1, −1). What is the area of the circle in simplified radical form?

A 34π **B** $\pi\sqrt{34}$
C $2\pi\sqrt{34}$ **D** 68π

12. *(51)* Find the missing side length and determine the perimeter of this triangle.

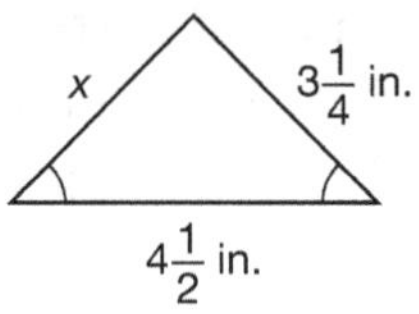

13. *(46)* **Construction** A construction worker is restoring an old staircase, and needs to find its length. She measures along the floor, from the bottom step to the wall, and finds that it is 9 feet long. She already knows that each step measures 1 foot deep and 8 inches high, and that each forms a right angle with the step above it. She conjectures that the triangular space formed by each step is similar to the triangle formed by the staircase and the wall. If she is correct, how long is the staircase, to the nearest hundredth?

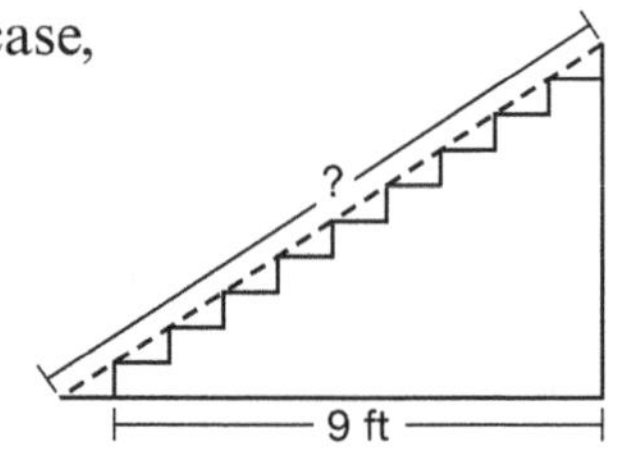

14. *(39)* List the angles of $\triangle STU$ in order from least to greatest measure.

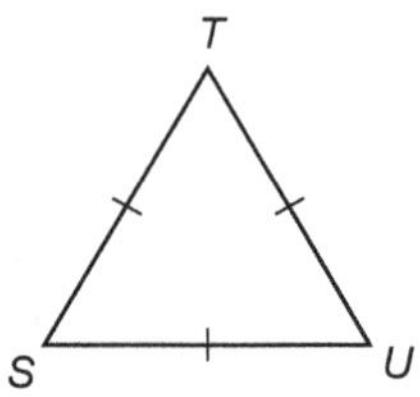

15. *(33, 39)* Determine whether {9, 40, 41} can be the set of measures of the sides of a triangle. If it is a triangle, determine whether it is an acute, obtuse, or a right triangle.

16. *(18)* **Multiple Choice** In $\triangle PQR$, $m\angle Q = 35°$ and $m\angle R = 113°$. The exterior angle at P measures:

A 32° **B** 148°
C 55° **D** 78°

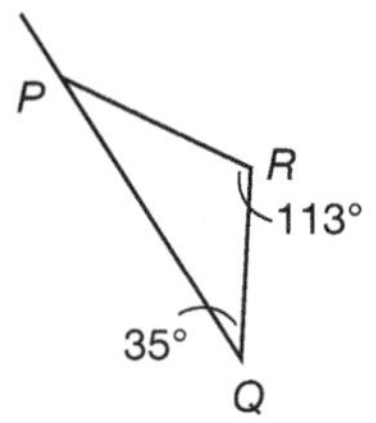

17. *(62)* **Painting** A farmer's cylindrical grain silo needs to be painted. If the silo is 75 feet tall and has a diameter of 25 feet, approximately how many square feet need to be painted?
Hint: The bottom of the silo does not need to be painted.

18. *(63)* What is the resultant vector of $\overrightarrow{e}$ and $\overrightarrow{f}$ in component form?

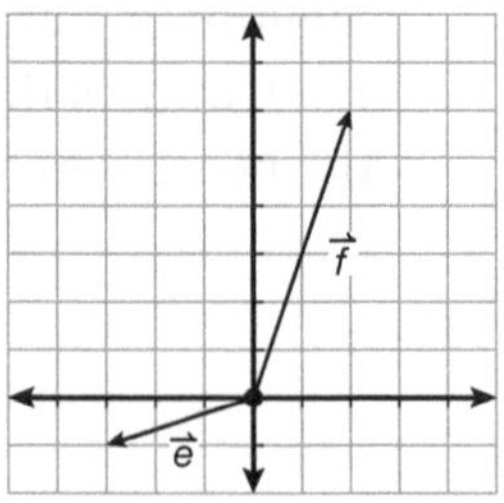

19. *(52)* **Multi-Step** The center of rhombus $DEFG$ is P. If $DP = 12$ inches, and $EP = 16$ inches, find DE.

*20. (61) **Verify** If the opposite angles of a parallelogram are supplementary, prove that the parallelogram is a rectangle. Use the diagram to help.

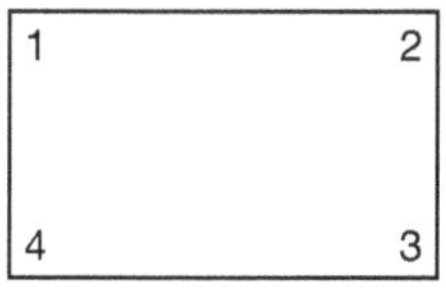

21. (41) **Shadows** The flagpole in front of a school casts a 16-foot shadow. At the same time, the student who is 5.6 feet tall casts a 3-foot shadow. How tall is the flagpole?

*22. (64) Find the value of x in the figure.

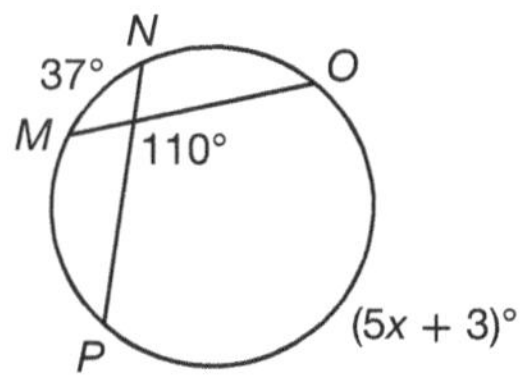

23. (59) **Analyze** What is the radius of a cylinder with a 3-millimeter height that has the same volume as a 6-millimeter cube? Round your answer to the nearest hundredth.

24. (60) **Justify** Determine whether lines $\overleftrightarrow{GH}$ and $\overleftrightarrow{KL}$ are parallel and explain how you know.

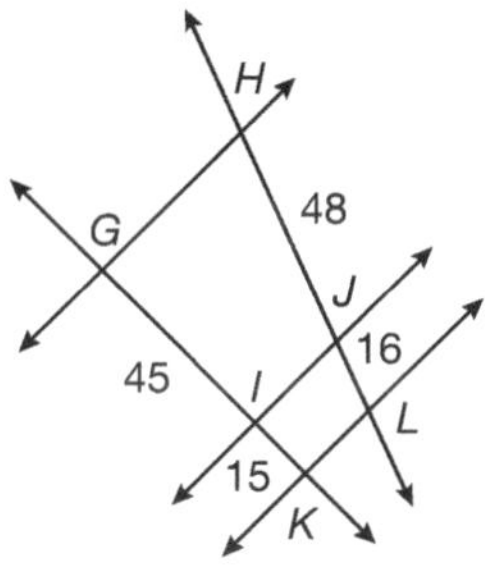

25. (45) Parallelogram *EFGH* has vertices $E(0, 0)$, $F(4, 4)$, $G(x, y)$, and $H(10, 0)$. Find a possible location of (x, y).

*26. (65) **Design** A sweater uses rhombuses to make its design, as shown. Find $\angle 1$.

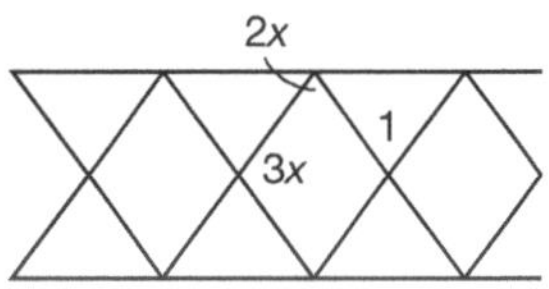

27. (53) **Write** What is unique about the circumcenter of an isosceles right triangle?

*28. (64) Find the measure of $\overset{\frown}{AC}$ in the figure. Line ℓ is tangent to the circle.

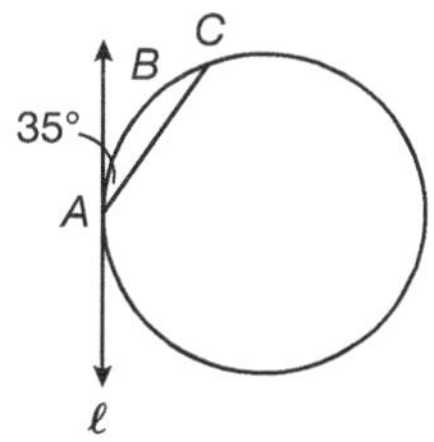

29. (43) **Algebra** If a chord cuts a radius in two pieces that measure 6 inches and 4 inches, what are the two possible lengths of the chord?

*30. (58) **Write** In the diagram, GJ is a radius of $\odot G$. Is $\overleftrightarrow{HJ}$ tangent to $\odot G$? Explain how you know.

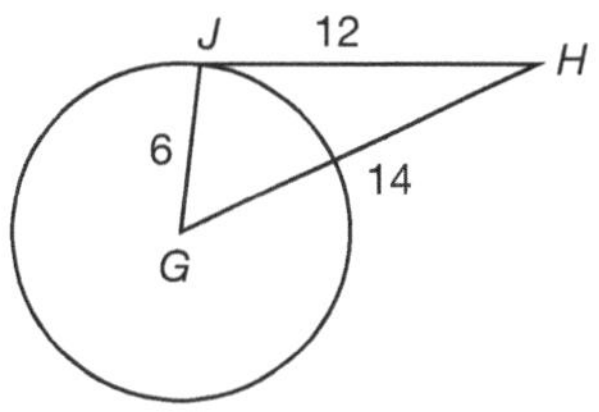

Name ______________________ Date __________ Class __________

Finding Perimeters and Areas of Regular Polygons

LESSON 66

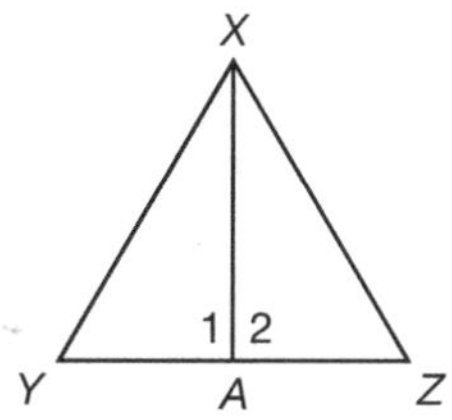

1. (48) In the diagram $m\angle 1 \neq m\angle 2$. Prove $\overline{XA}$ is not an altitude of $\triangle XYZ$ using as indirect proof.

* **2.** (66) **Rock Formations** A rock formation in Ireland is called the Giant's Causeway. It is made up of about 40,000 columns of rock that formed as lava cooled after a volcanic eruption. Most of the columns are hexagonal with average side lengths of 14 inches and an apothem that is $7\sqrt{3}$ inches long. What is the approximate area covered by the 40,000 stone columns?

* **3.** (65) Is the statement sometimes, always, or never true?

A rhombus is a rectangle.

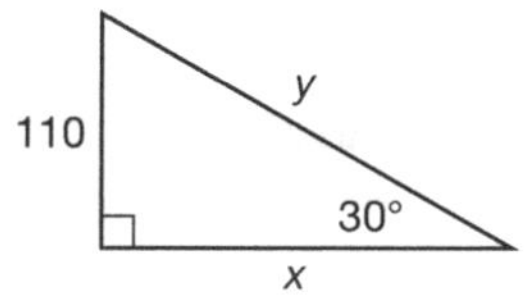

4. (56) Find the values of x and y. Give your answers in simplified radical form.

5. (61) **Analyze** What could you conclude about the bisectors of two consecutive angles of a rhombus?

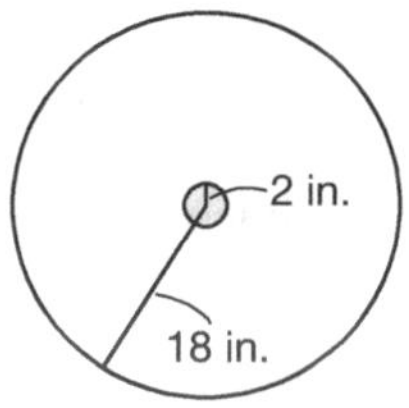

* **6.** (Inv 6) **Archery** Assuming that an amateur archer's arrow is equally likely to strike anywhere on the target *and* has a 50% chance of missing the target altogether, what is the probability of the archer hitting a bull's eye on this target?

7. (49) How many edges does a polyhedron with 10 vertices and 10 faces have?

8. (38) **Algebra** Find the value of x that makes S the incenter of the triangle shown.

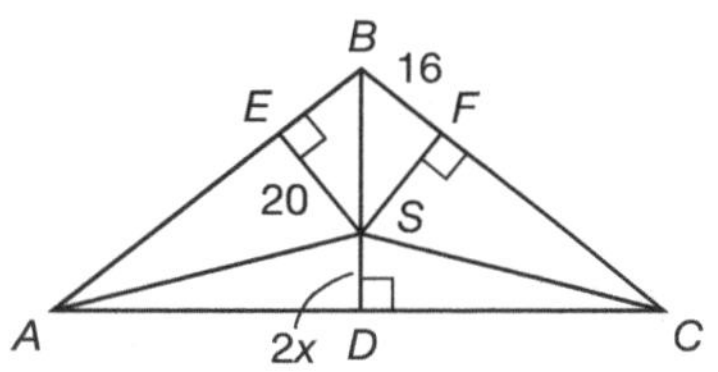

9. (58) **Space Exploration** A probe is about to use the atmosphere of Mars to aerobrake (reduce its velocity). The probe's trajectory is an almost straight line that just grazes the Martian atmosphere. The probe is currently 9600 miles from the center of Mars, and the radius of Mars is approximately 5460 miles. How far is the probe from its aerobrake maneuver? Round your answer to the nearest ten miles.

10. (63) **Write** Describe how the vector $\langle 2, 3\rangle$ is similar to the slope of the line formed by the equation $y = \frac{3}{2}x + 4$.

11. Find the value of x in the circle at right.
(64)

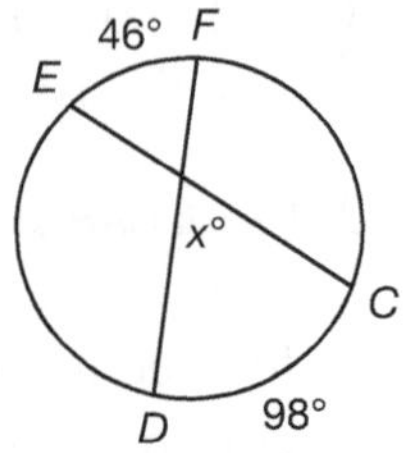

12. **Orbits** The orbit of a satellite is decaying, and it will reenter Earth's atmosphere at a random time during its next orbit. The satellite's orbit is 26,000 miles long, 17,000 miles of which is over ocean. Find the probability that fragments of the satellite will land in the ocean.
(Inv 6)

13. Segment JK is a midsegment of $\triangle FGH$. Find the values of x and the lengths of $\overline{JK}$ and $\overline{FH}$.
(55)

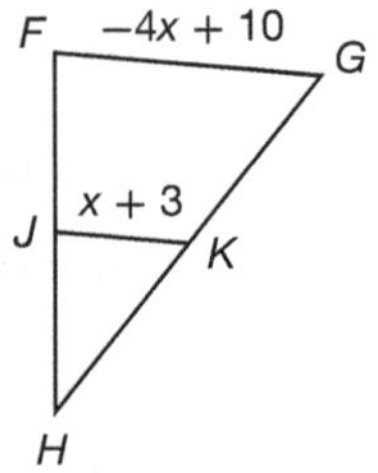

14. If an apple pie is 8 inches in diameter and a pizza is 14 inches in diameter, what is the ratio of the pie's diameter to the pizza's diameter?
(44)

15. **Justify** Which segment in the figure is greater, LM or PN? Explain how you know. Assume the circles are concentric.
(Inv 4)

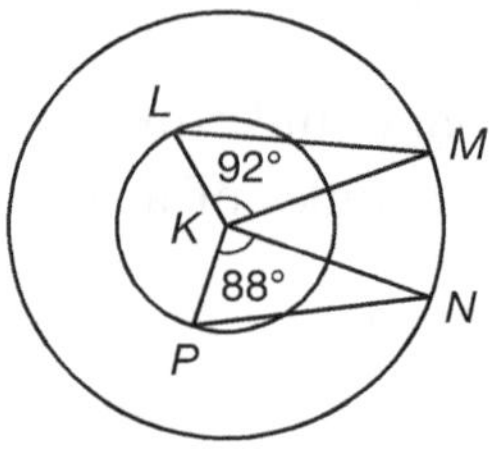

*16. Find the perimeter of a regular heptagon with sides that are each 77 feet long.
(66)

17. **Algebra** Right triangle A has leg lengths of u and v. Right triangle B has leg lengths of $2v - 1$ and $4 - u$. Given that triangles A and B are congruent, what are the possible values of u and v?
(36)

Use the diagram to answer the next two questions.

*18. If $AB = AD$ and $DB > AC$, what kind of parallelogram is the figure? List all possibilities.
(65)

*19. If $m\angle ADC = 90°$ and $\angle APB$ is an acute angle, what kind of parallelogram is the figure?
(65)

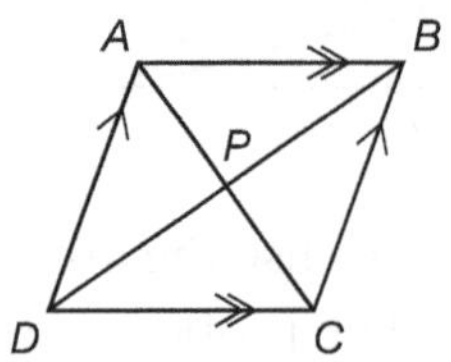

*20. **Multiple Choice** Which formula is equivalent to the formula $A = \frac{1}{2}aP$?
(66)

A $a = \dfrac{A}{2P}$ **B** $P = \dfrac{2A}{a}$

C $P = \dfrac{A}{2a}$ **D** $a = \dfrac{2A}{P}$

*21. **Error Analysis** Find and correct any errors in the flowchart proof below.
(31)

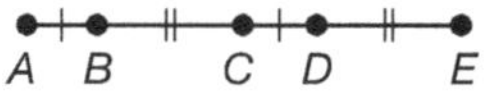

Given: $AB = CD$, $BC = DE$
Prove: C is the midpoint of $\overline{AE}$.

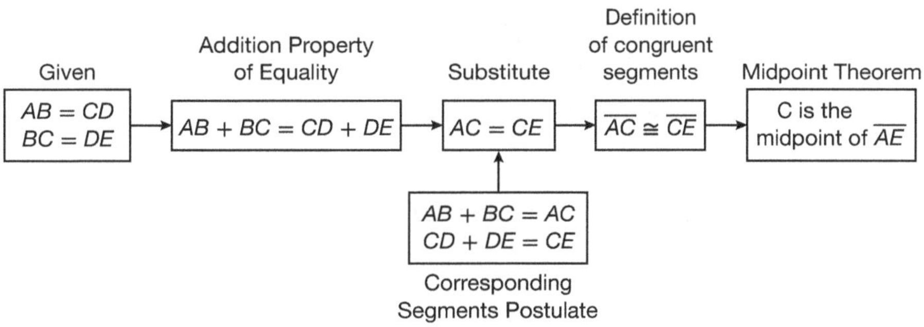

22. **Multiple Choice** Which of the following is *not* true about parallelogram $LMNP$?
(34)
A $m\angle L = m\angle N$ **B** $m\angle L = m\angle P$
C $m\angle L + m\angle P = 180°$ **D** $m\angle M = m\angle P$

23. Find x in the figure. Line ℓ is tangent to the circle.
(64)

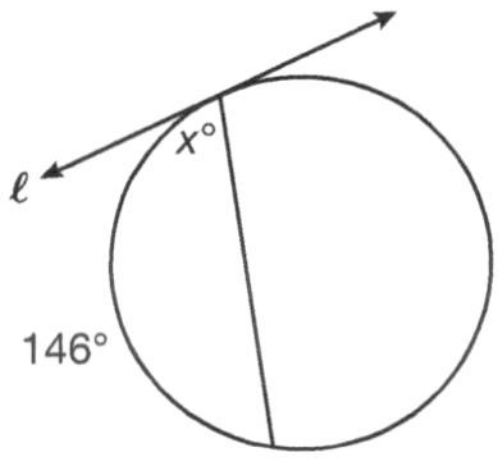

24. **Algebra** In $\triangle STU$, $m\angle TSU = 32°$, $ST = (2y - 4)$, and $m\angle STU = (5x + 12)°$.
(30)
In $\triangle DEF$, $m\angle EDF = 32°$, $DE = (x + y)$, and $m\angle DEF = (2x + 24)°$.
If $\triangle STU \cong \triangle DEF$, determine the values of x and y.

*25. **Error Analysis** The center of the circle is A. Josie says that she has determined that if FY and XH are tangent lines at Y and X, respectively, then they must be parallel, because $\angle AYF$ and $\angle AXH$ would both be right angles. Why is her conjecture false?
(58)

26. **Multi-Step** Find the area of the shaded region in the figure.
(34, 35)

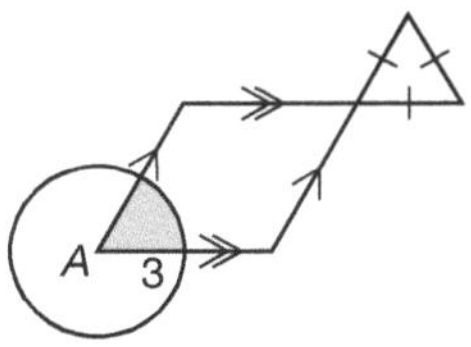

27. **Packaging** A manufacturer distributes a cylindrical tin that is 12 inches across and 6 inches tall. If the manufacturer fills each tin with mints that are assumed to be $\frac{1}{8}$ cubic inches each, to the nearest hundred, approximately how many mints are in the tin?
(62)

28. Find the distance from $(-1, 6)$ to the line $y = 2x - 7$.
(42)

29. **Justify** Determine whether $\triangle JKL$ is a right triangle, given that $\overleftrightarrow{DE}$ and $\overleftrightarrow{JK}$ are parallel. Explain how you know.
(60)

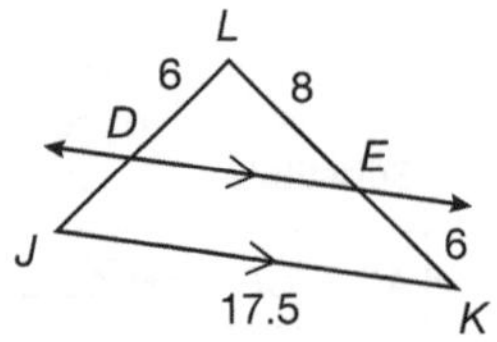

30. What are the perimeter and area of a regular hexagon with apothem 34 feet? Use exact values.
(66)

Name ______________________ Date ____________ Class ____________

Introduction to Transformations

LESSON 67

***1.** (66) Find the area of this regular pentagon, to the nearest tenth.

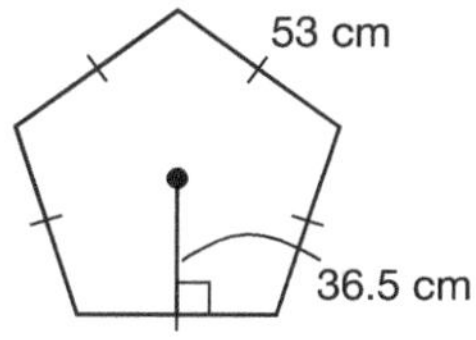

2. (53) **Meal Preparation** Mr. Jones is making sandwiches, which he wants to cut diagonally. If he uses square bread that is six inches on a side, how long a knife must he use to be able to cut each sandwich in one cut? Round your answer to the nearest half-inch.

3. (64) Find the value of x in the figure.

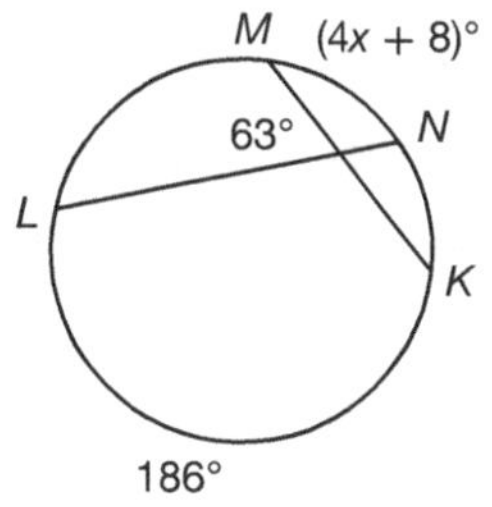

4. (42) Find the distance between the line $y = \frac{-4}{3}x + 3$ and (4, 6).

***5.** (66) Find the perimeter and area of a regular octagon with 30-foot-long sides and an apothem that is 36.2 feet long.

***6.** (67) What type of transformation takes square $STUV$ to square $S'T'U'V'$?

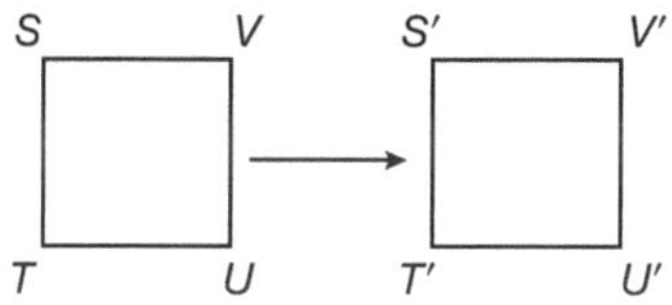

7. (63) **Flight** A dragonfly is flying at a rate of 26 feet per second. The wind is blowing at 8 feet per second in the opposite direction. How fast is the dragonfly traveling over the ground?

8. (65) Determine whether the quadrilateral at right must be a square.

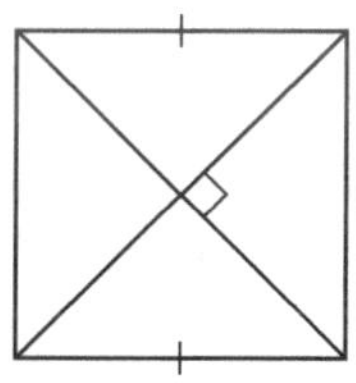

9. (14) **Algebra** Find a counterexample to the following conjecture.

If the equation $ax^2 - b = 0$ has a rational solution, then b is a perfect square.

10. (44) $\triangle ABC \sim \triangle DEF$. The ratio of their corresponding sides is 5:3. Given $AB = 3$, what is the length of $\overline{DE}$?

11. (51) Determine m$\angle X$ and m$\angle Z$ in the triangle at right.

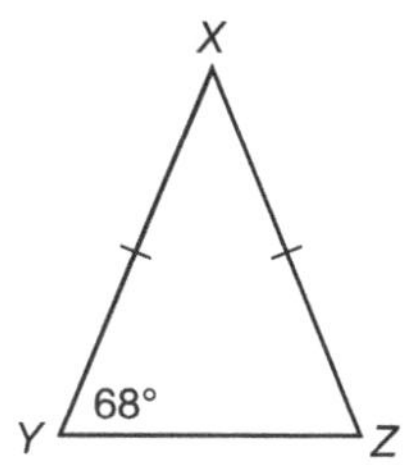

12. (59) **Painting** Cecilia is painting the walls of two rooms that are the same size. The rooms are 14 feet wide, 9 feet long, and 8 feet high. How many square feet does she need to paint?

13. (43) If two chords are congruent, and one is 5 inches from the center of the circle, then what is the distance from the center to the other chord?

Name ______________________ Date ____________ Class ____________

Introduction to Transformations

LESSON 67

***14.** (67) **Multiple Choice** Identify the type of transformation that takes $\triangle EFG$ to $\triangle E'F'G'$.

A reflection **B** translation
C rotation **D** rigid transformation

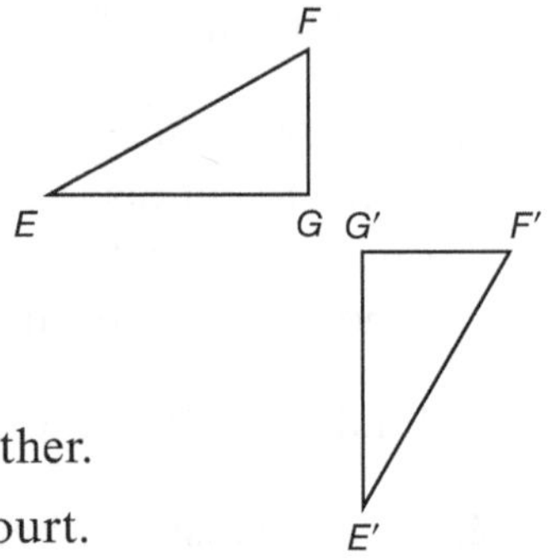

***15.** (Inv 6) **Analyze** Which of the following scenarios describes a random event?
Explain why geometric probability cannot be used for the other.

a: A tennis player hits a ball to the opponent's side of the court.
b: An astronomer scans a region of the sky looking for meteors.

16. (55) **Formulate** A trapezoid is formed by the midsegment of a triangle, as in the diagram shown. Find a formula for its area in terms of its height and its longer base, b.

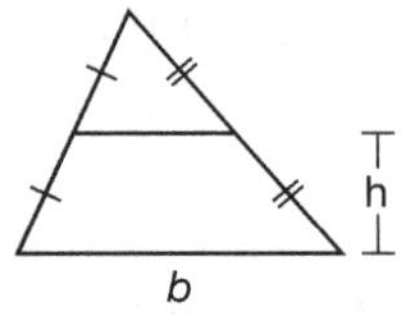

17. (62) **Painting** A cylindrical water tower needs to be painted on all sides, including the base. The tower is 115 feet tall and it has a radius of 40 feet. To the nearest square foot, how many square feet are there to be painted?

18. (58) **Multiple Choice** Which line or lines appear to be tangent to $\odot C$?

A ℓ **B** m
C m and n **D** none of these

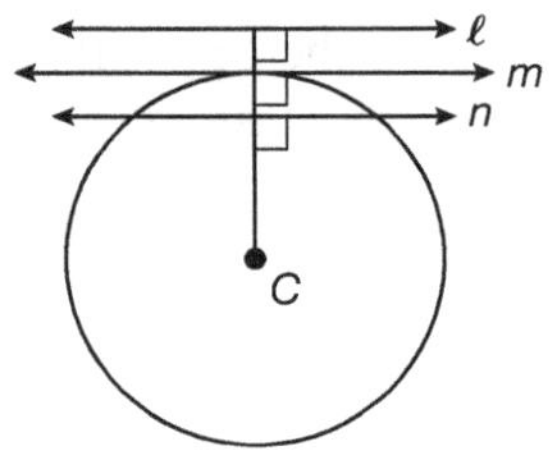

19. (37) Find the line perpendicular to $7x + 7y = 49$ that passes through the point (4, 3). Write its equation in slope-intercept form.

20. (57) **Multi-Step** Classify the polygon with vertices $C(3, -3)$, $D(-5, -3)$ and $E(3, 3)$. Find the perimeter.

21. (56) **Error Analysis** Charlie found k in rhombus $QRST$ to be roughly 3.464. What error has he made? What is the actual value of k?

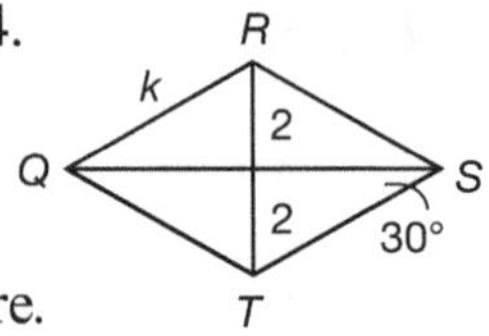

***22.** (67) **Generalize** A certain isometric transformation is performed twice and the resulting figure is in the same location as the original figure. What type or types of transformation could this be? What type or types of transformation could this *not* be?

***23.** (67) Reflect quadrilateral $PQRS$ across line n.

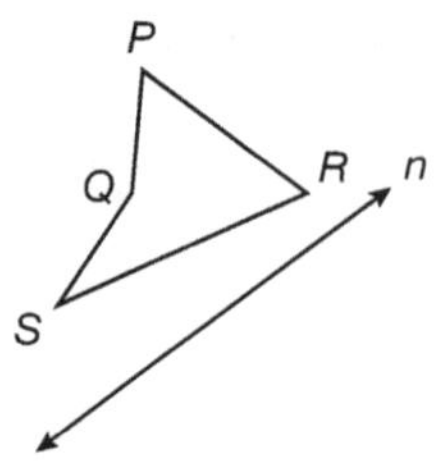

24. (48) Use an indirect proof to prove that if no two angles in a triangle are congruent, then no two sides are congruent.

Introduction to Transformations

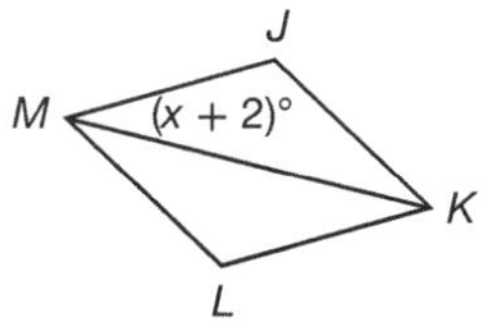

25. (65) **Formulate** What expression for m$\angle L$ makes *JKLM* a rhombus?

26. (62) **Labels** A soup can is 10 centimeters tall and has a radius of 4 centimeters. What is the area of the label that will be placed on the cans, to the nearest tenth?

27. (35) **Multiple Choice** Which choice is closest to the length of a 48°-arc of a circle that has a radius of 8.5?

A 30.26 **B** 3.56
C 7.12 **D** 60.53

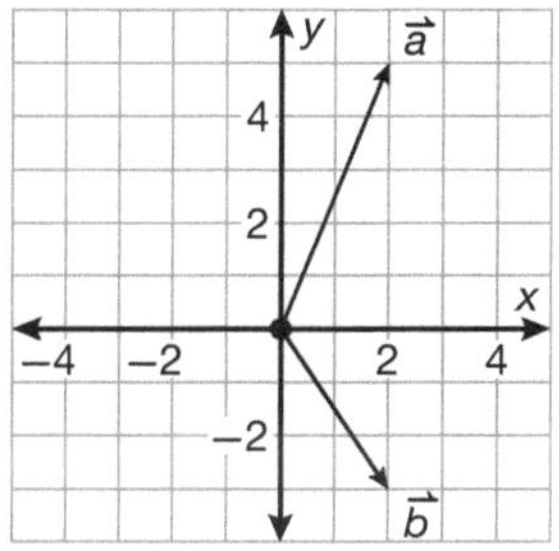

28. (63) Write the resultant vector of $\vec{a}$ and $\vec{b}$ in component form.

***29.** (66) To the nearest tenth, find the area and perimeter of an equilateral triangle with sides that are 32 feet long.

30. (32) **Generalize** Is the centroid of a triangle always in the interior of the triangle? Can the orthocenter be outside the triangle?

Name ______________________ Date __________ Class __________

Introduction to Trigonometric Ratios

LESSON 68

1. (63) **Swimming** A swimmer wants to travel at a rate of 3 miles per hour while swimming in a river. The river flows at a rate of 2 miles per hour. If she goes with the current, how fast does she need to swim? How fast does she need to swim if she goes against the current?

2. (33) **Algebra** Determine the value of x in the figure shown. Write your answer in simplified radical form.

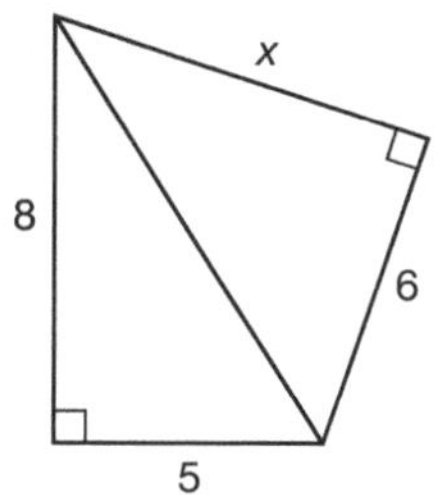

*** 3.** (68) **Building** It is unsafe to lean a ladder at less than a 70° angle with the ground. If a ladder is 8 feet tall, at least how far should the ladder be from the wall, to the nearest hundredth of a foot?

4. (58) Find h if line l is tangent to circle C.

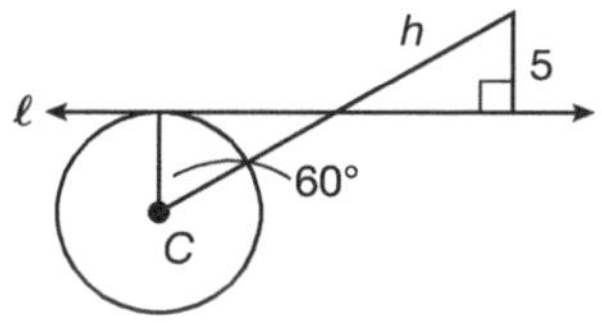

5. (45) **Multiple Choice** $\triangle DEF$ has vertices $D(0, 0)$, $E(3, 3)$, and $F(6, 0)$. What type of triangle is $\triangle DEF$?

A obtuse triangle **B** isosceles triangle
C scalene triangle **D** right triangle

6. (34) If $WXYZ$ is a parallelogram, what is the measure of $\angle Y$ if $\angle W$ is two-thirds the size of $\angle X$?

*** 7.** (68) Write expressions for the values of sin Q, cos Q, and tan Q in this figure.

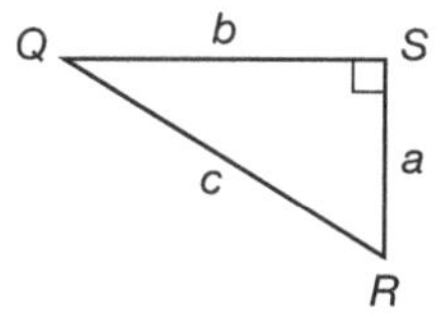

8. (65) The diagonals of parallelogram $ABCD$ meet at O. Find a measure for $\angle AOD$ that makes $ABCD$ a rhombus.

9. (Inv 6) **Predict** Predict the number of spins that would land on sector 4 in 1000 trials of the spinner at right.

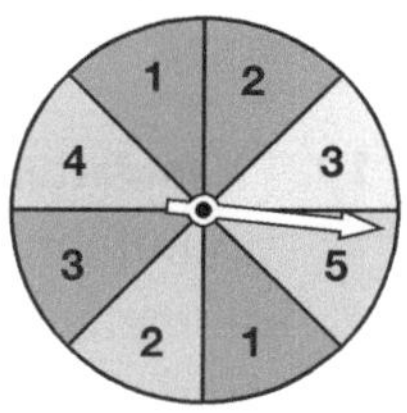

10. (52) **Multi-Step** Find the perimeter and area of a square with a diagonal length of 8 inches. Express your answer in simplified radical form.

11. (59) Find the surface area of the prism at right.

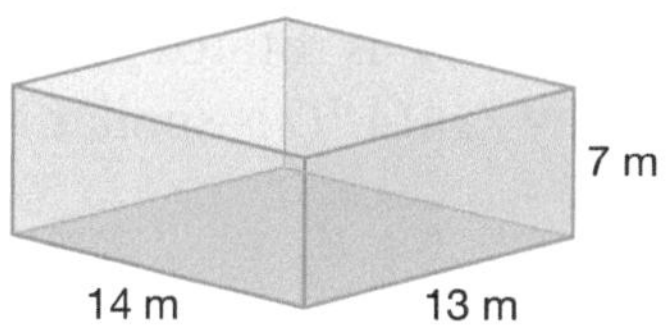

*12. **Generalize** Can a rotation of square $ABCD$ and a reflection of a square $ABCD$ ever have the same image? *Hint: Label the vertices of a square and notice their changing positions while rotating and reflecting.*
(67)

13. Elias is trying to find a coin he dropped which rolled into a dark, rectangular room. What is the probability he will find the coin within 1 foot of the wall?
(40, Inv 6)

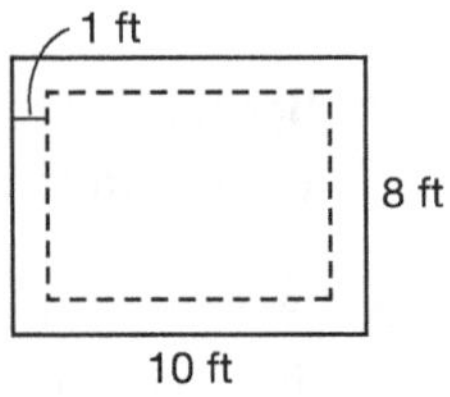

14. In the diagram at the right, G is the incenter of $\triangle HIJ$. Find EG.
(38)

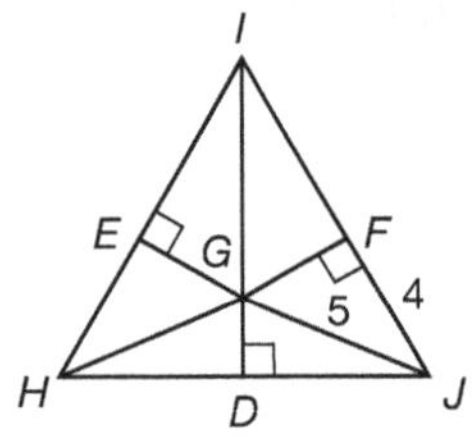

15. **Error Analysis** Marilou found the perimeter of this irregular polygon to be 19 units. What mistake has she made, and what is the actual perimeter?
(57)

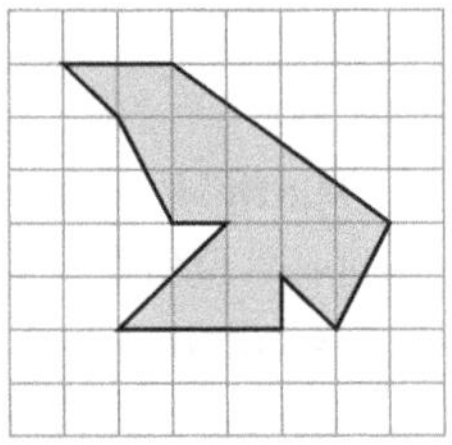

16. Determine whether $BARK$ is a parallelogram. Explain how you know.
(61)

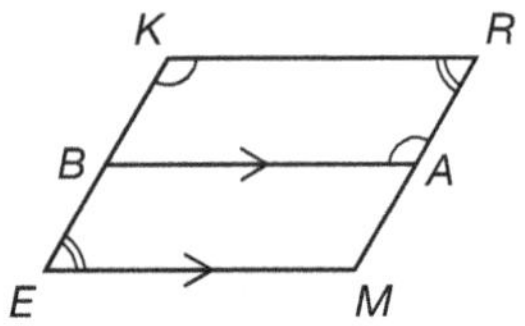

17. **Justify** Is the following a valid application of the Law of Detachment? Explain.
(21)
All birds have feathers. A whale is not a bird. Therefore, a whale does not have feathers.

18. **Tiling** A floor tile is in the shape of a regular octagon with sides that are 6 inches long. What is the perimeter of the tile?
(66)

19. **Manufacturing** To the nearest centimeter, how tall should a manufacturing company make its soup cans if the standard diameter is 7.5 centimeters and each can must hold 575 milliliters? *Hint: Recall that 1 milliliter is equivalent to 1 cubic centimeter.*
(62)

*20. Rectangle $MNOP$ is rotated clockwise about point Q. Explain why $\triangle MM'Q$ is similar to $\triangle PP'Q$.
(67)

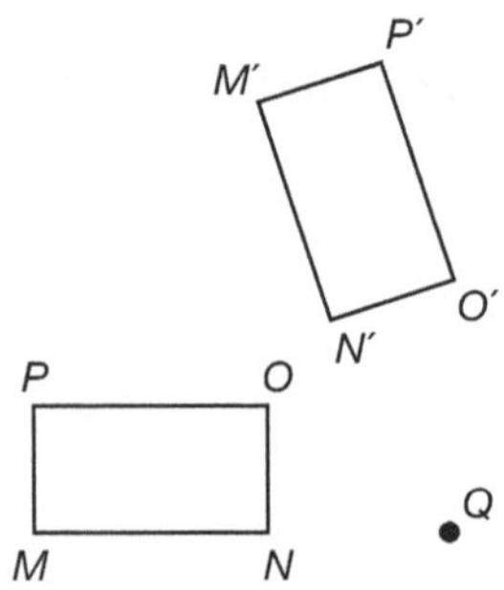

Introduction to Trigonometric Ratios

LESSON 68

21. (Inv 5) Draw a net for a rectangular prism with a length of 9, a width of 3, and a height of 12. Label each dimension.

22. (66) **Write** Can a square ever have a numerical value for its perimeter that is the same as the numerical value for its area? Explain.

23. (36) Prove that $\triangle LMN \cong \triangle QOP$.

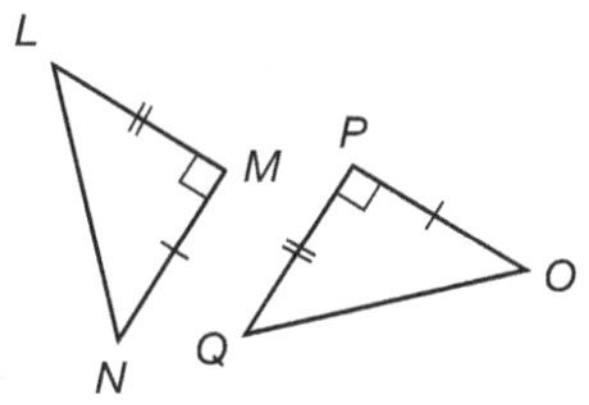

***24.** (68) **Multiple Choice** Which of the following is not a pair of equivalent functions in $\triangle ABC$ if $\angle C$ is a right angle?

A sin A and tan B **B** sin A and cos B

C tan A and $\frac{1}{\tan B}$ **D** sin B and cos A

25. (64) **Architecture** This drawing depicts the cross section of the air ducts and the support beams for a very large building. If $m\widehat{XY} = 100°$, what is the measure of the angle for the support beam, $\angle YXZ$?

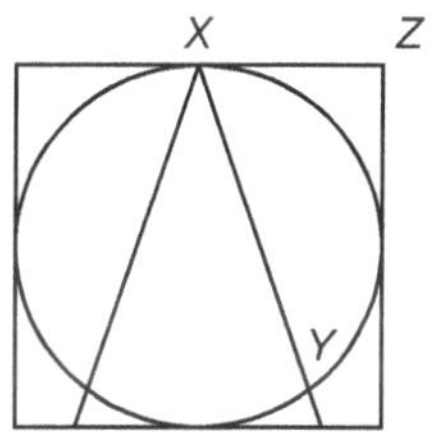

26. (50) Find the values of x and y in the triangle shown.

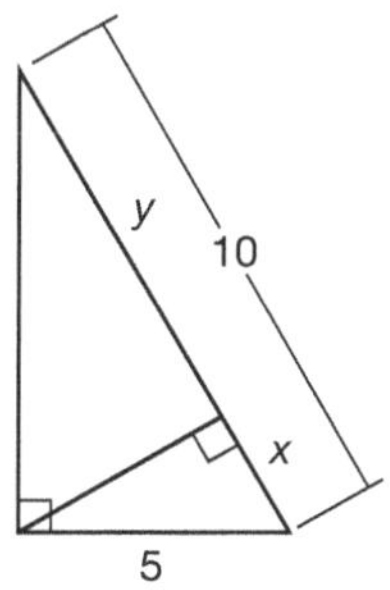

27. (31) Write a paragraph proof of the following.
Given: Ray TR bisects $\angle QTS$, $m\angle QTR = 45°$
Prove: $\angle QTS$ is a right angle.

***28.** (68) Write sin M as a fraction and then as a decimal rounded to the nearest hundredth.

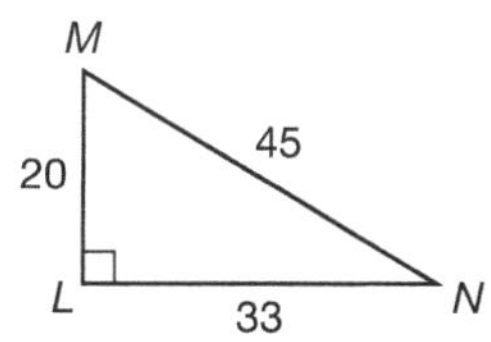

29. (60) **Justify** Determine whether lines $\overline{WX}$ and $\overline{YZ}$ are parallel. How do you know?

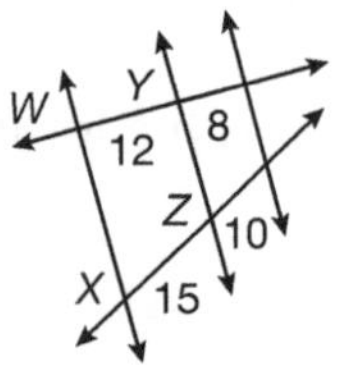

***30.** (67) **Multiple Choice** Which word *best* describes the transformation of *ABCD* into *A′B′C′D′*?

A translation **B** rotation
C reflection **D** None of the above

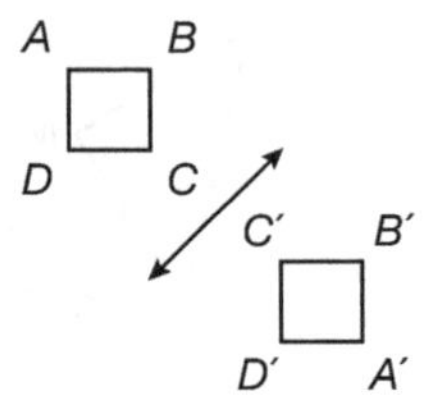

Name ______________________________ Date ____________ Class ____________

Properties of Trapezoids and Kites

LESSON 69

***1.** (69) Trapezoid *FHJL* has midsegment $\overline{GK}$. Find *FL*.

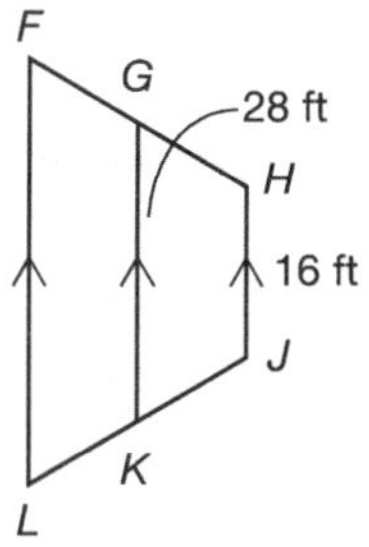

2. (61) **Verify** Show that quadrilateral *WXYZ*, with vertices *W*(4, −9), *X*(5, −1), *Y*(0, 2), and *Z*(−1, −6) is a parallelogram.

3. (39) Use the fact that m∠*DEF* < 140° to write an inequality for *x* in the triangle.

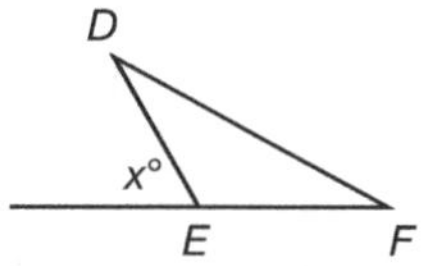

4. (63) **Swimming** A salmon is swimming against the flow of the current. Suppose the salmon is swimming at 21 miles per hour (mph) and the current is flowing at 7 mph. How fast is the salmon traveling over the riverbed below?

5. (Inv 4) **Write** In the circle, the chord $\overline{AB}$ is longer than chord $\overline{EF}$. Which angle is larger, ∠*APB* or ∠*EPF*? Explain.

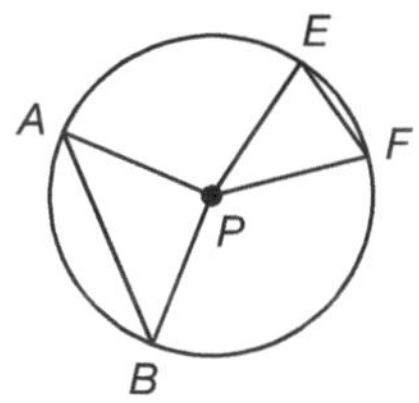

6. (10) Identify the hypothesis and conclusion of the following statement.
If $x^2 + 16 = 25$, *then* $x = 3$.

*** 7.** (68) What is the sine of a 30° angle if the hypotenuse is 10? What is the cosine of a 60° angle if the hypotenuse is 100?

8. (59, 62) **Comparison Shopping** Elissa is buying brake fluid for her car. There are two containers that are both priced the same, shown below. Is there more fluid in the rectangular container or in the cylindrical can?

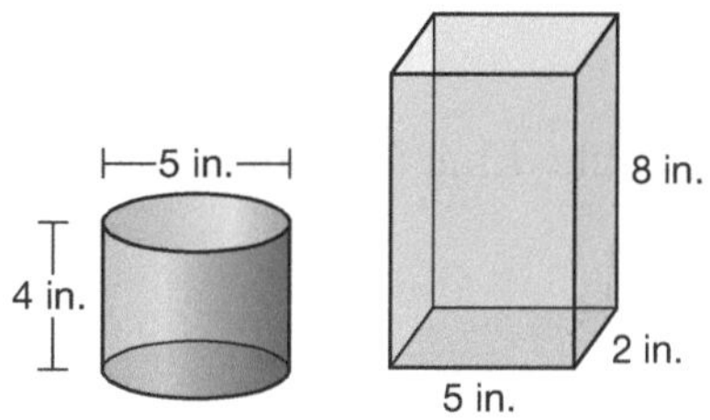

9. (67) **Analyze** How many reflections across the same line must be performed on a figure to restore it to its original state? How many rotations by 90° (in the same direction) must be performed to do the same?

10. If $\overline{AB}$ is tangent to circle C at A, what is m$\angle K$?
(58)

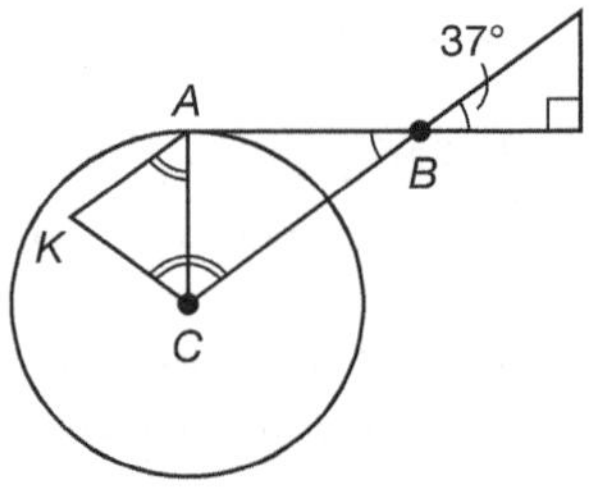

11. **Multiple Choice** What is the approximate length of a 288°-arc in a circle with a diameter of 12 centimeters?
(35)

A 30.16 cm **B** 15.08 cm
C 90.48 cm **D** 361.91 cm

12. **Tiling** A floor tile is in the shape of a regular hexagon with sides that are each 12 inches long. How many tiles would be needed to cover a 25-by-32-feet floor?
(66)

13. A day is chosen at random from a yearly calendar. Are the probabilities for each day of the week being chosen the same? Explain.
(Inv 6)

***14.** Find the lengths of the sides of kite *RSTU*. Round to the nearest tenth.
(69)

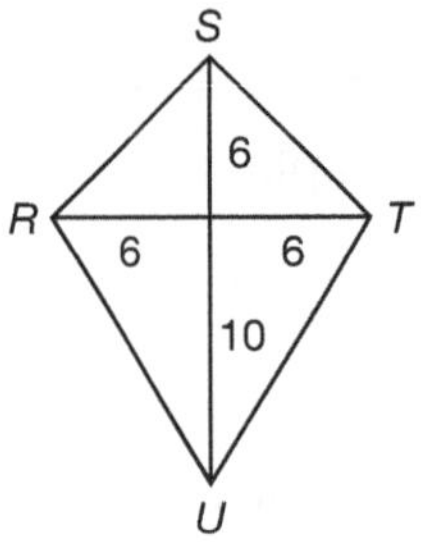

15. **Error Analysis** Jermaine found the perimeter of this irregular polygon to be 30. Explain what error he made and find the correct exact perimeter.
(57)

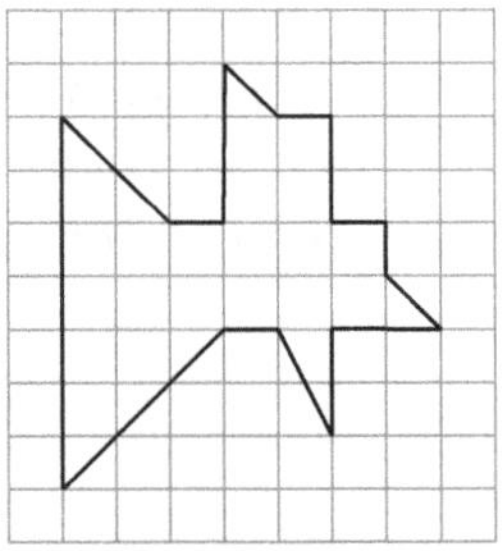

16. How many vertices does a polyhedron with 6 faces and 12 edges have?
(49)

17. Find the value of x in this circle. Line ℓ is tangent to the circle.
(64)

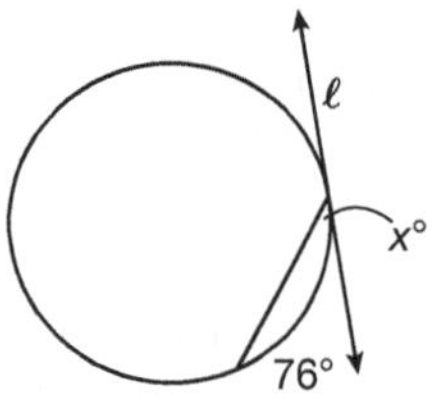

18. **Multi-Step** Classify the polygon with vertices $S(7, 2)$, $T(1, 2)$, $U(3, -3)$ and $V(5, -3)$. Find the area.
(57)

*19. In isosceles trapezoid $TUVW$, find UW if $TX = 23$ inches and $VX = 28.7$ inches.
(69)

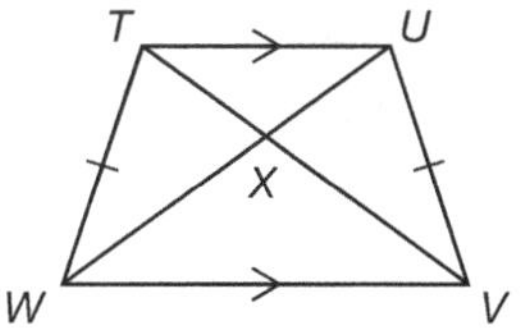

20. **Estimate** Estimate the measure of each angle in the triangle with vertices $(-4, 2)$, $(10, 10)$, and $(2, -7)$. Classify the triangle by its angles.
(13)

21. Find AD in the triangle at right.
(60)

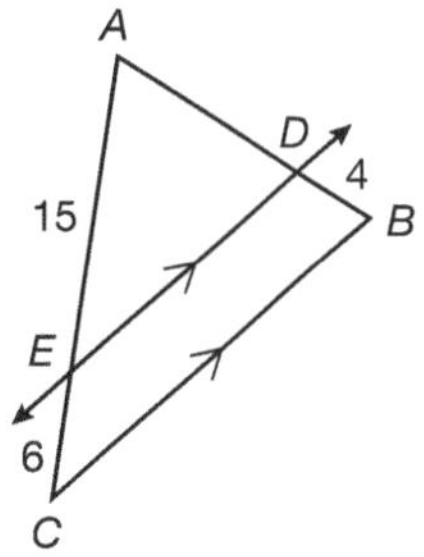

22. **Kitchen Skills** Howard is making frozen orange juice from concentrate. The mix comes in a cylindrical can that is 6 inches tall with a diameter of 3 inches. If the proper ratio of concentrate to water is 1:8, how much water does Howard need, to the nearest ten cubic inches?
(62)

23. Using the diagram at right, find PZ in terms of y if $TP = 7$ and $PM = y$. Point P is the circumcenter of the triangle.
(38)

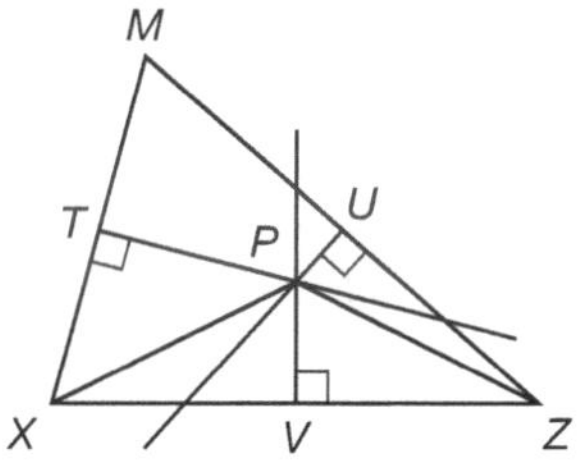

24. **Algebra** In $\triangle JLK$, $JK = 5$ and $m\angle JKL = 60°$. In $\triangle DEF$, $DE = (2x - 3y)$ and $m\angle DEF = (x + y)°$. If $KL = EF$, what are the values of x and y that make $\triangle JLK \cong \triangle DEF$ true?
(28)

*25. Find the measures of $\angle A$, $\angle B$, and $\angle D$ in trapezoid $ABCD$.
(69)

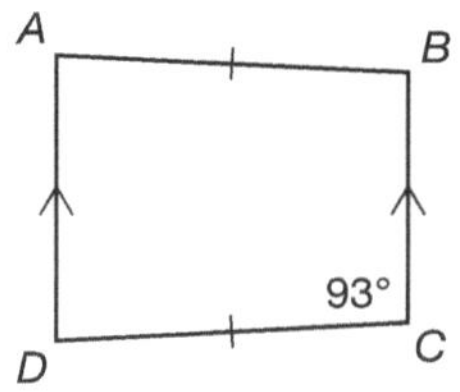

*26. Find $\sin b$, $\cos b$, and $\tan b$ in the triangle.
(68)

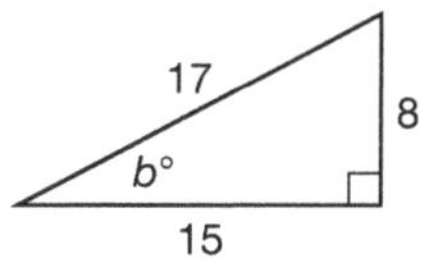

27. An altitude of a triangle is the ____________ line segment from a vertex to the line containing the opposite side of the triangle.
(32)

28. (68) **Generalize** Do you need to know the side lengths of a 30°-60°-90° triangle to find the sine or cosine of its angles? Explain.

29. (64) Find the value of x in the figure.

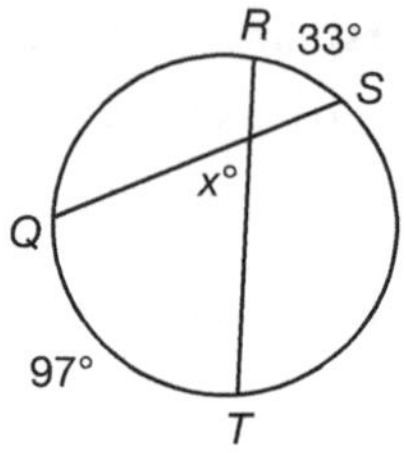

30. (67) **Multiple Choice** Which of the following, when performed on an equilateral triangle, might result in a nonequilateral triangle?

A rotation **B** reflection
C dilation **D** none of these

Name ______________________________ Date __________ Class __________

Finding Surface Areas and Volumes of Pyramids

LESSON 70

1. (69) Find m∠*P* and m∠*R* in kite *PQRS*.

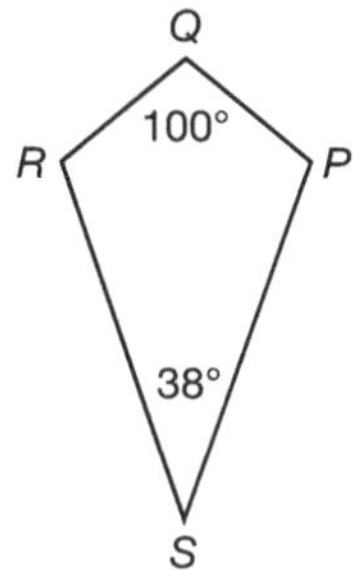

*** 2.** (70) What is the volume of a regular hexagonal pyramid with a height of 10 feet and base side lengths of 7 feet? Round your answer to the nearest cubic foot.

3. (40) **Multi-Step** Determine the perimeter of this figure.

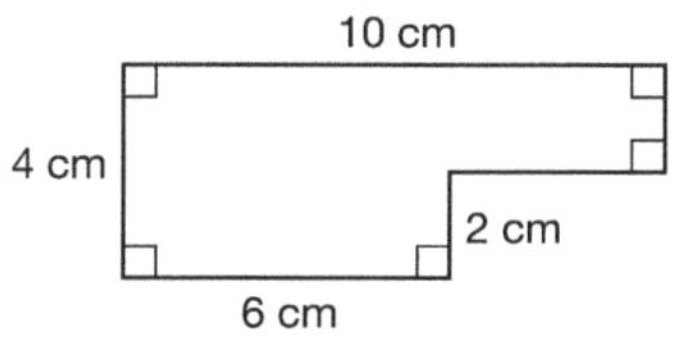

4. (65) Find the measures of the numbered angles that make the figure shown a rectangle.

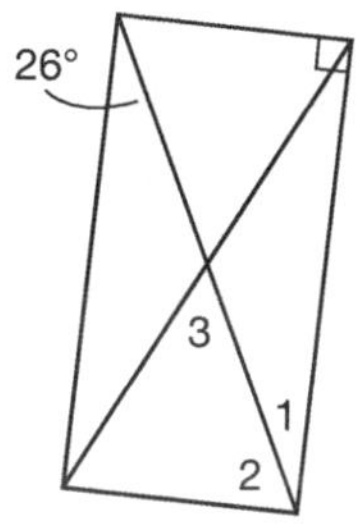

5. (55) **Bermuda Triangle** The Bermuda Triangle is a region in the Atlantic Ocean near the southeastern coast of the United States. The vertices of the triangle are Miami, Florida; San Juan, Puerto Rico; and Bermuda. In the figure, the dashed segments are midsegments. Find the perimeter of the midsegment triangle within the Bermuda Triangle. How does it compare to the perimeter of the Bermuda Triangle?

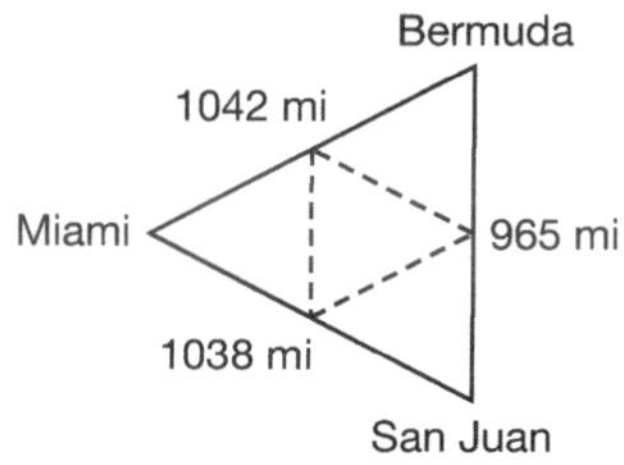

6. (66) **Sign Art** A sign maker is welding a sun-shaped design by dividing a regular hexagon into six equal triangles and arranging them along their base vertices to form rays of the sun. If the side length of the hexagon is 8 inches, what is the total area of one triangle?

7. (59) **Density** A certain crystal has a density of 34 grams per cubic centimeter. Find the mass, to the nearest hundredth of a gram, of the sample shown at right if the triangular face is an equilateral triangle.

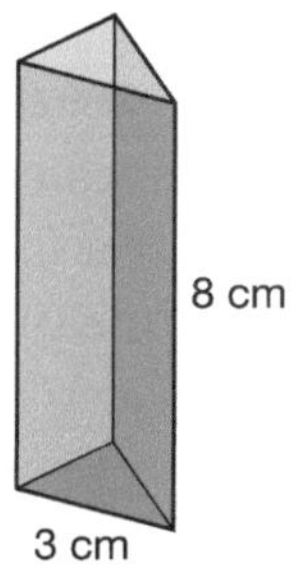

8. (68) Complete the following statement. In a 45°-45°-90° triangle, the ______ and ______ are equal. (***sine, cosine, tangent, hypotenuse***)

9. (56) **Write** How are 30°-60°-90° triangles and 45°-45°-90° triangles alike? How are they different?

10. (50) Find the value of x.

***11.** (70) What is the lateral area of a regular octagonal pyramid with base side lengths of 4 inches and a slant height of 10 inches?

12. (20) **Multiple Choice** The disjunction of p and q is true when
A p and q are both true, but not when either is false.
B either p is true, or q is true, or both.
C p and q are both false.
D either p is true, or q is true, but not both.

13. (37) **Multiple Choice** Which of the following is *not* parallel to $x = 2$?
A $0 = x$ **B** $x = 3y$
C $2x = 3$ **D** $x + 7 = 0$

14. (27) **Analyze** Write a two-column proof of the Converse of the Alternate Exterior Angles Theorem, "If two lines are cut by a transversal and alternate exterior angles are congruent, then the lines are parallel."
Given: $\angle 1 \cong \angle 2$
Prove: $j \parallel k$

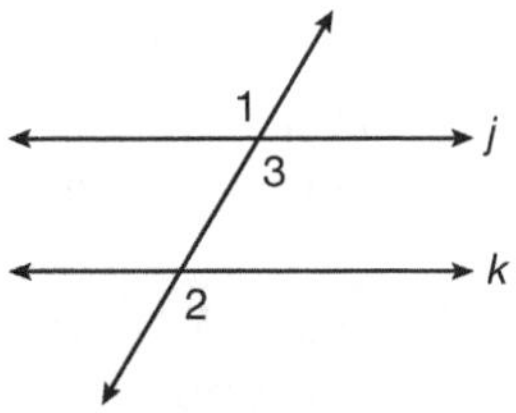

15. (69) **Algebra** Trapezoid $MNOP$ has a midsegment $\overline{QR}$. The parallel sides are $\overline{MN}$ and $\overline{OP}$. If $QR = 3x$, $MN = x + 3$, and $OP = 2x + 6$, find x and the length of each segment.

16. (Inv 6) **Games** A particular dart game is played using darts that can suction to a flat surface. A group of students is throwing these darts onto the tiled surface shown. If a dart lands on exactly one tile, what is the probability that it might land on one of the blue tiles?

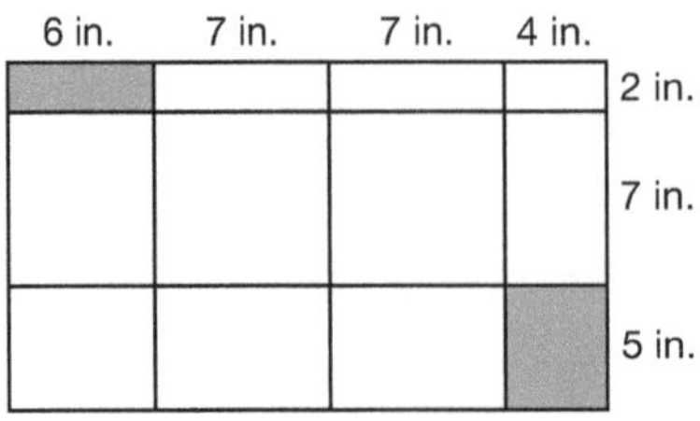

17. (66) **Multi-Step** An equilateral triangle has an apothem that is $7\sqrt{3}$ feet long. What is the area of the triangle?

18. (46) **Verify** Explain how you know these two triangles are similar, and then write the similarity statement.

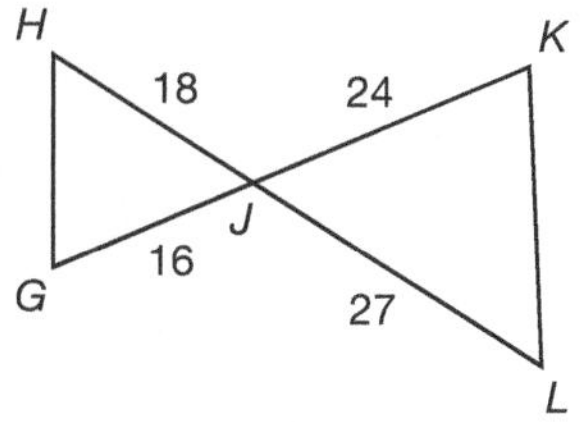

*19. (70) What is the surface area of a regular hexagonal pyramid with a slant height of 8 centimeters and a base side length of 2 centimeters? Round your answer to the nearest centimeter.

20. (67) **Error Analysis** Fernando said that $\triangle ABC$ was translated to form the image $\triangle A'B'C'$. Raquel said that it had to be rotated, not translated. Who is correct? Explain.

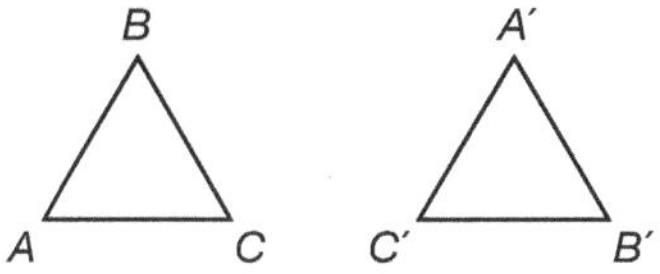

21. (56) **Coordinate Geometry** $\triangle RST$ is a 30°-60°-90° triangle with $S(-1, -4)$ and $T(9, -4)$, and $m\angle S = 90°$. What are possible coordinates of R?

22. (64) Find the measure of $\widehat{MNO}$ in the figure. Line ℓ is tangent to the circle.

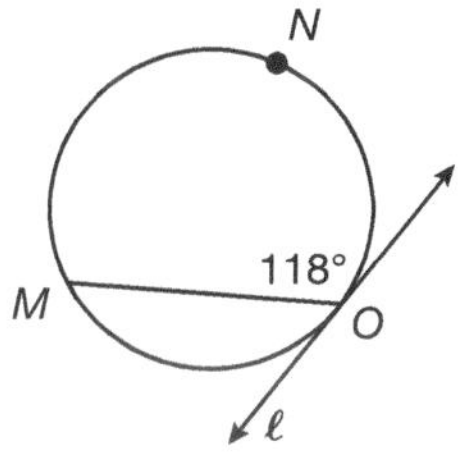

*23. (70) **Structures** When the Great Pyramid of Giza was first built, the side length of its square base was about 231 meters and the height of the pyramid was about 147 meters. What was its approximate lateral area? Round your answer to the nearest hundred square meters.

24. (69) Find the measures of $\angle F$, $\angle G$, and $\angle J$ in trapezoid $FGHJ$.

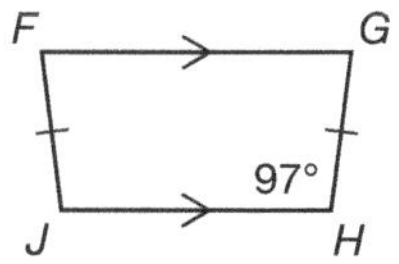

25. (50) **Verify** Show that the geometric mean of 12 and 300 is 60 by writing and solving a proportion.

26. (56) **Model** Draw a rectangle with a diagonal that is twice as long as its width. Write an equation to find the length of the rectangle.

27. (68) Use a calculator to find the length of MN. Round to the nearest hundredth.

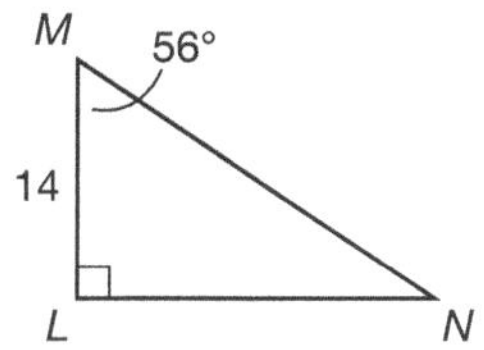

28. (34) **Algebra** The perimeter of parallelogram $ABCD$ is 84. Find the length of each side if $AB = 3BC$.

29. (31) **Formulate** Use the given two-column proof to write a flowchart proof.
Given: V is the midpoint of $\overline{SW}$, and W is the midpoint of $\overline{VT}$.
Prove: $\overline{SV} \cong \overline{WT}$

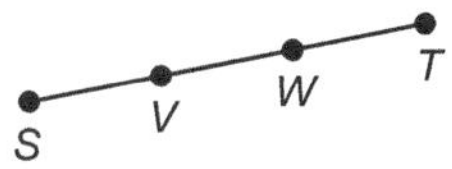

Statements	Reasons
1. V is the midpoint of $\overline{SW}$.	1. Given
2. W is the midpoint of $\overline{VT}$.	2. Given
3. $\overline{SV} \cong \overline{VW}$, $\overline{VW} \cong \overline{WT}$	3. Definition of midpoint
4. $\overline{SV} \cong \overline{WT}$	4. Transitive Property of Congruence

***30.** (70) **Construction** Steven is making two square pyramids. The first pyramid has a base length of 10 centimeters and its height is 20 centimeters. The second pyramid has twice the height of the first but only half the base length. What is the volume of the second pyramid? Round your answer to the nearest cubic centimeter.

Name ______________________ Date __________ Class __________

Translations

LESSON **71**

1. (61) **Analyze** Using the diagram, explain how you know that the bisectors of two consecutive angles of a parallelogram are perpendicular.

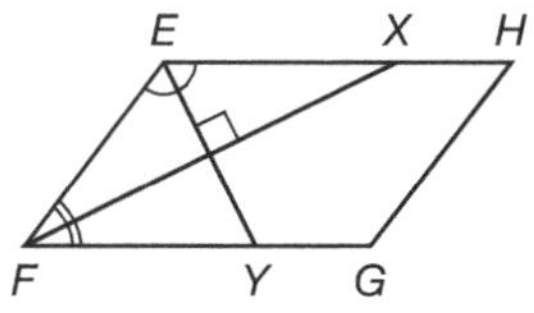

2. (70) A pyramid has a base area of 15 square centimeters and a height of 10 centimeters. What is the volume of the pyramid?

3. (33, 39) Determine whether these measurements (1.6, 1.8, 3.4) can be the side lengths of a triangle. If it is a triangle, determine whether it is an acute, obtuse, or a right triangle.

4. (62) **Bottled Water** A company wants to sell cylindrical bottles of water. If each bottle is to hold 0.5 liters, and will be 20 centimeters tall, what should the radius of each bottle be, to the nearest hundredth of a centimeter? *Hint:* $1\ cm^3 = 1\ mL$.

5. (71) To create a wallpaper pattern, this triangle will be translated as indicated by vector *u*. Apply the translation to the original triangle and then again to the image to create two triangle images for the pattern.

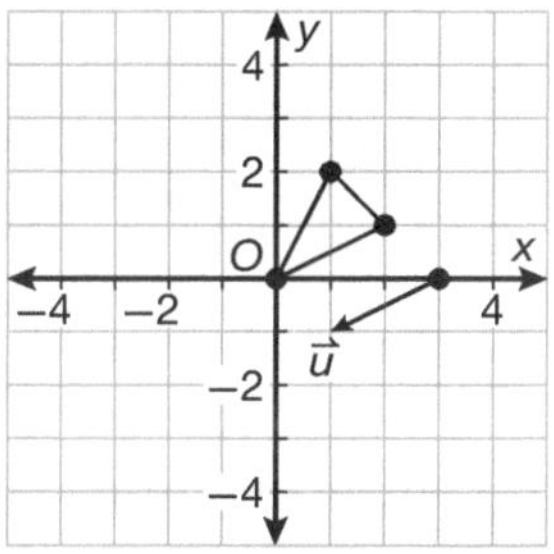

6. (71) **Algebra** The image of (5, *y*) after the transformation $v = \langle x, 11\rangle$ is (1, −6). Find the values of *x* and *y*.

7. (71) The points *P*(5, 5) and *Q*(−5, −5) are translated 4 units up and 3 units to the left. What are the coordinates of the images of the points?

8. (65) Is the parallelogram a rectangle, a rhombus, both, or neither?

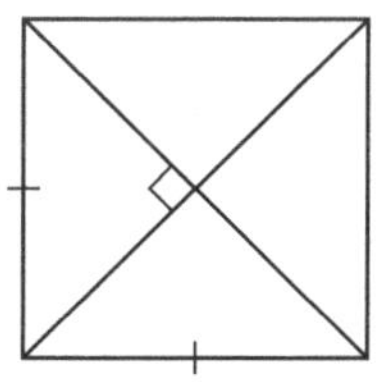

9. (69) A trapezoid has vertices at the points *E*(2, 3), *F*(3, 1), *G*(2, −2), and *H*(−1, 4). Use the distance formula to find the length of the midsegment of the trapezoid.

10. (70) What is the surface area of a regular pyramid with a lateral area of 10 square feet and a base area of 5 square feet?

11. (41) If trapezoids *RSTU* and *GHIJ* are similar, what is *GH*?

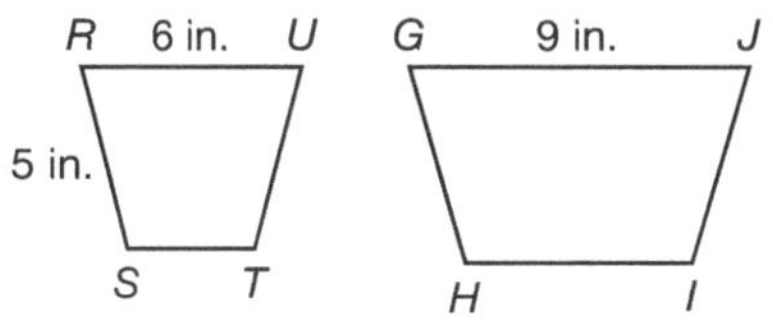

12. (37) Find the equation of the line perpendicular to $\frac{1}{2}y + 3x = 4$ that passes through the point (6, 5). Write in slope-intercept form.

13. (17) **Write** Write the inverse of the following statement.

If a triangle is equilateral, then the sides are congruent.

14. (67) **Design** The figure at right forms one quadrant of a logo. The completed logo is also shown. Identify the transformations performed on the original figure to form the completed logo.

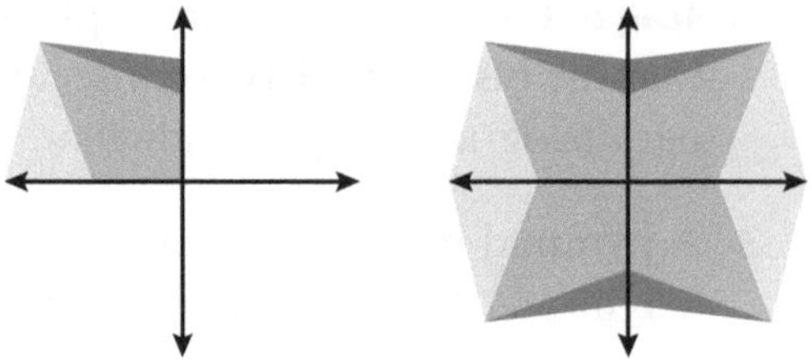

15. (70) **Structures** In Paris, there is a glass square-based pyramid in front of the Louvre Museum. The pyramid is about 70 feet tall and the side lengths of the base are about 115 feet. What is the approximate volume of the pyramid? Round your answer to the nearest cubic foot.

16. (71) **Multiple Choice** $\triangle DEF$ is translated so that the coordinates of E' are (0, 3). What are the coordinates of F' after the same translation?

A (1, −1) **B** (4, −2)
C (−2, −2) **D** (−2, 6)

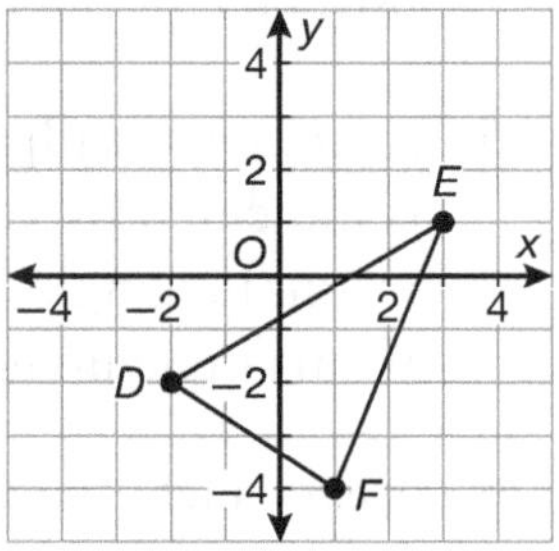

17. (Inv 7) **Model** Draw a 30°-60°-90° triangle with the longer leg measuring 1. Include all angle measures and side lengths.

18. (68) **Generalize** For what angle measures is the tangent ratio less than 1? greater than 1?

19. (Inv 7) Determine the missing side lengths in $\triangle STU$. Give exact answers. Approximate any values involving radicals.

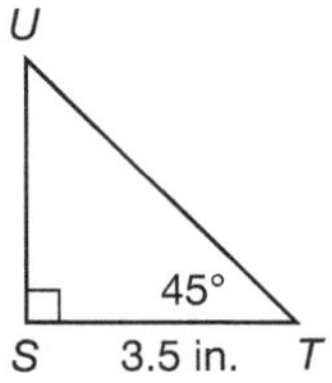

20. (66) **Interior Design** The part of a kitchen containing the sink, countertop, and refrigerator is in the shape of an equilateral triangle with 12-foot side lengths. What is the area of this triangle?

21. (39) **Justify** Which of the side lengths of $\triangle ABC$ is greatest? Explain how you know.

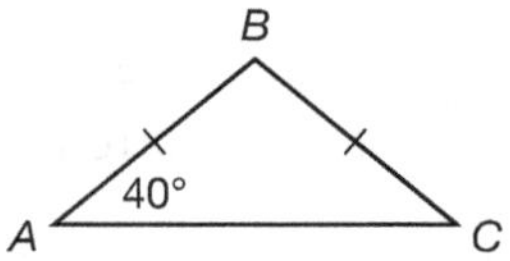

22. (48) **Multiple Choice** Which statement would contradict the claim that $\angle C$ and $\angle D$ are alternate exterior angles?

A Angles C and D are on the same side of the transversal.
B $m\angle C < 180°$
C $m\angle C = m\angle D$
D Angles C and D are on opposite sides of the transversal.

23. *(69)* Segment $\overline{VY}$ is the midsegment of trapezoid $UWXZ$. Find the length of $\overline{WX}$.

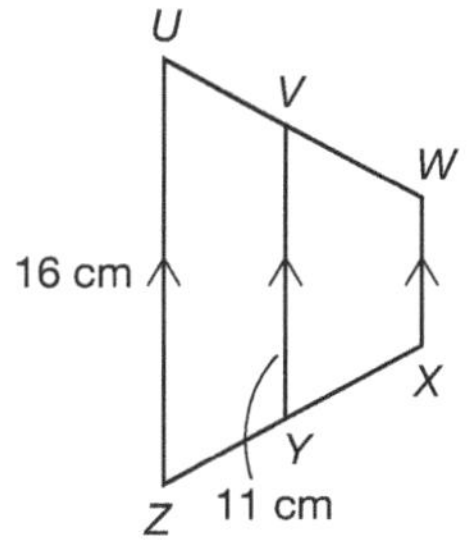

24. *(67)* **Analyze** A transformation takes $\triangle PQR$ to $\triangle P'Q'R'$. The vertices of the triangle are P, Q, and R are in clockwise order and the vertices P', Q', and R' are also in clockwise order. Which type of transformation could this *not* be?

A rotation　　**B** translation
C reflection　　**D** could be any of these

25. *(63)* What is the resultant vector of c and d, in component form?

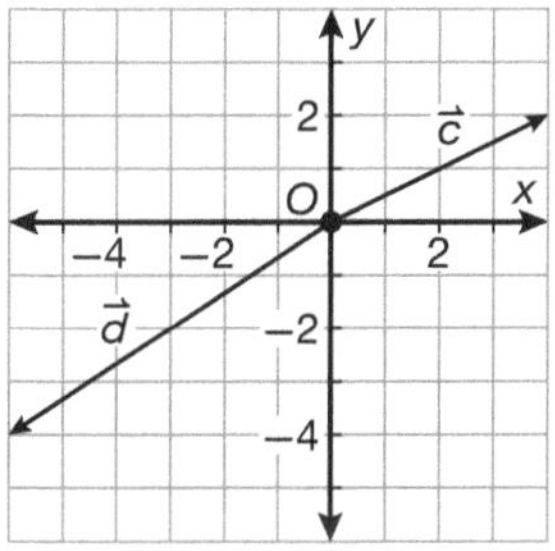

26. *(Inv 7)* In $\triangle DEF$, F is a right angle, $m\angle D = 45°$, and $DE = 3$ centimeters.

a. Draw a diagram of $\triangle DEF$.
b. Determine exact and approximate values for DF.

27. *(57)* **Surveying** A pond is overlaid with a coordinate grid with each square representing 5 square meters. Estimate the area of the pond.

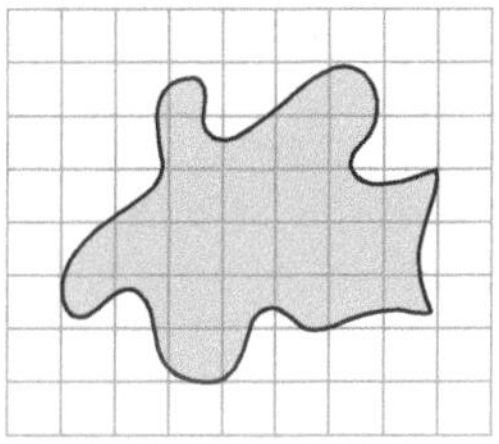

28. *(52)* **Multi-Step** Quadrilateral $KLMN$ has vertices at $K(3, 3)$, $L(7, 0)$, $M(3, -3)$, and $N(-1, 0)$. Classify the quadrilateral.

29. *(Inv 4)* Using the given triangles, list the sides x, y, and z in order from least to greatest.

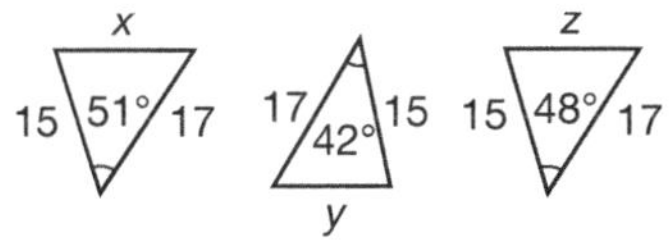

30. *(Inv 6)* Use the spinner at right to answer **a.** and **b.**

a. What is the probability of the pointer landing on gray? Express your answer as a fraction.
b. What is the probability of the pointer landing on white? Express your answer as a decimal.

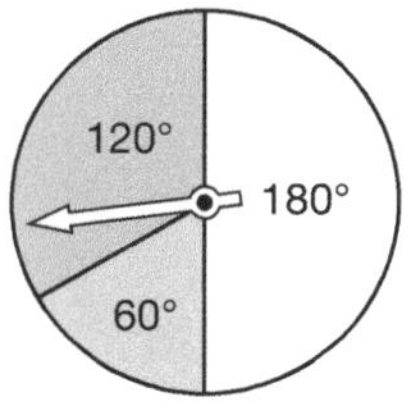

Name ______________________ Date ____________ Class ____________

Tangents and Circles, Part 2

LESSON 72

1. (40) **Painting** An artist will paint a detailed mural on the wall in the diagram at right, but cannot paint on the 1-by-8-foot window. If it takes him half an hour to paint one square foot, how long will it take him to paint the whole mural?

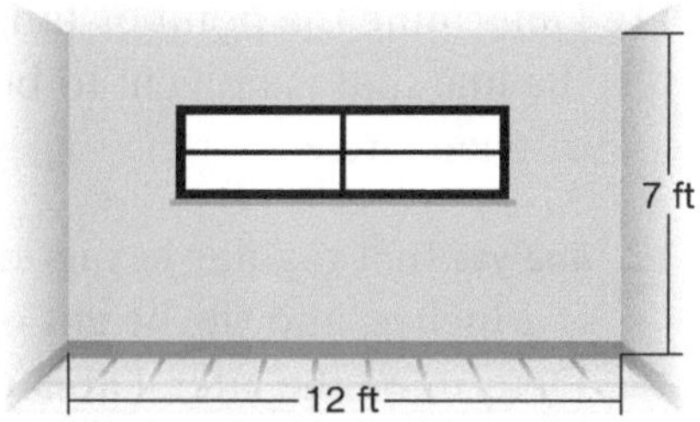

2. (58) **Multi-Step** Noncollinear segments $\overline{PQ}$ and $\overline{PR}$ are tangent to $\odot C$, which has a radius of 1 foot, 6 inches. If $CQ = 2PQ$, determine the perimeter of quadrilateral $CQPR$ in feet and inches.

3. (67) **Error Analysis** The quadrilateral shown was transformed, and Heather thinks the transformation was a translation. Explain why Heather is wrong.

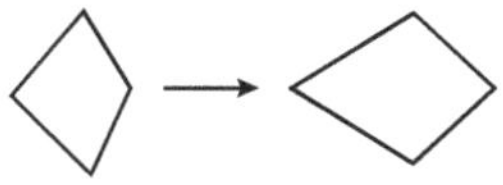

4. (17) Write the negation of the hypothesis and the conclusion in the statement.

   If a polygon has six sides, then it is a hexagon.

5. (72) Assume the segments that appear to be tangent are tangent. Find BE, CE, and DE.

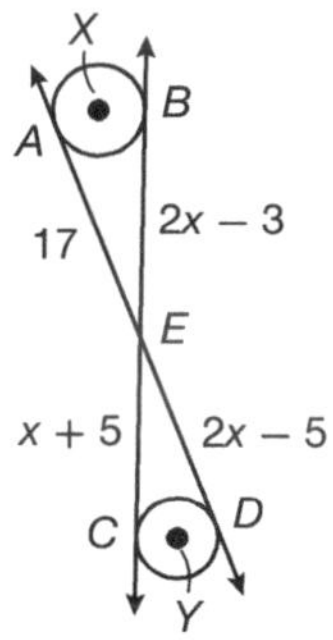

6. (Inv 7) **Model** Draw a diagram of a 30°-60°-90° triangle with a hypotenuse that is 6 inches long. Label the exact lengths.

7. (71) The translation $T{:}(x, y) \rightarrow (x - 2, y - 1)$ is applied to a circle with a center at (5, 4). What are the coordinates of the image of the center?

8. (62) Find the surface area of the cylinder to the nearest whole square meter.

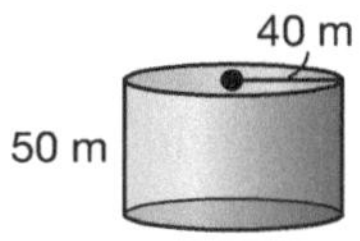

9. (36) **Multiple Choice** Which congruence theorem applies to these triangles?

   A HL Congruence Theorem **B** LL Congruence Theorem
   C HA Congruence Theorem **D** LA Congruence Theorem

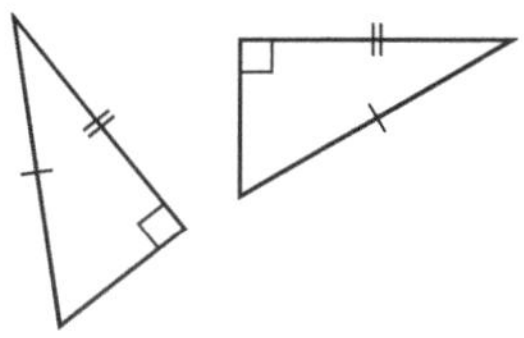

10. (37) **Algebra** Line a passes through the points (3, 2) and (5, 2). Line b passes through points (–2, 1) and (–8, 1). Are the lines parallel, perpendicular, or neither?

Tangents and Circles, Part 2

LESSON 72

11. (72) Determine the point of tangency and the equation of the line that is tangent to both circles. Find the radius of each circle.

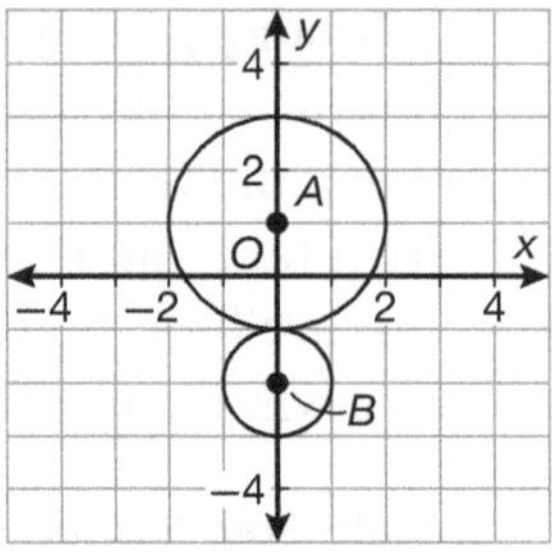

12. (70) **Analyze** In a regular hexagonal pyramid, the slant height is 2 inches, and the height of the pyramid is 1 inch. Determine the lateral area of the pyramid.

13. (55) **Riding Trails** The diagram at right represents horseback riding trails. Point B is the halfway point along $\overline{AC}$. Point D is the halfway point along $\overline{CE}$. The paths along $\overline{BD}$ and $\overline{AE}$ are parallel. If riders travel from A to B to D to E, and then back to A, how far do they travel?

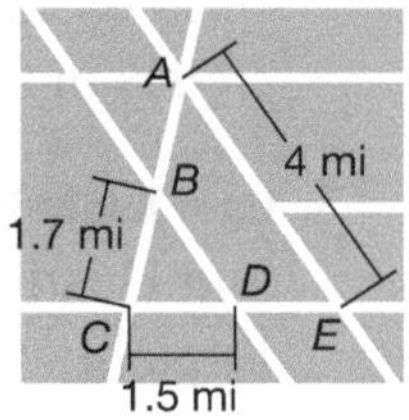

14. (71) Point $K(4, 11)$ is translated 5 units to the left. What are the coordinates of the image?

15. (38) Find the circumcenter of a triangle with vertices at (0, 0), (10, 0), and (5, 4).

16. (72) Determine the point of tangency and the equation of the tangent line. Find the radius of each circle.

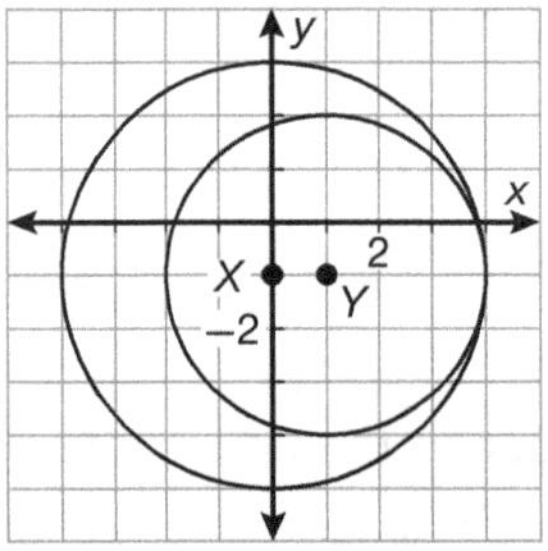

17. (71) What translation, in mapping notation, would move the point $H(3, -5)$ to $H'(0, -2)$?

18. (64) Find the value of x in the figure. Line ℓ is tangent to the circle.

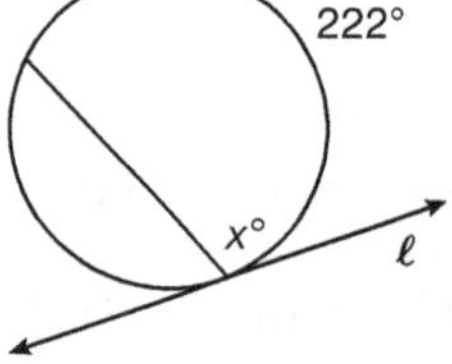

19. (66) **Write** What is the relationship between the apothem length of a square and the side length of the square?

20. $\overline{EF}$ is the midsegment of trapezoid *ABCD*. Find *EF*.
(69)

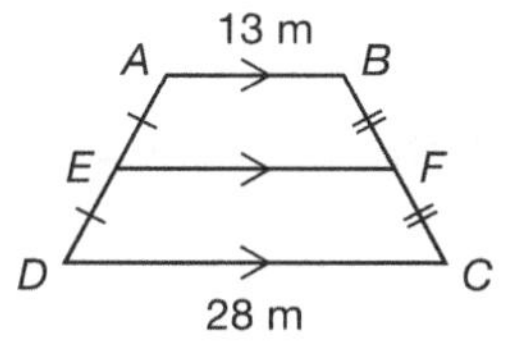

21. Any closed three-dimensional figure formed by four or more polygons that intersect only at their edges is called a ____________.
(49)

22. Given the point (1, 4), find the distance to the line $y = \frac{-3}{2}x - 1$.
(42)

23. Write a paragraph proof of the following.
(31)
Given: *N* is the midpoint of *MP*; *Q* is the midpoint of *RP*; $\overline{PQ} \cong \overline{NM}$
Prove: $\overline{PN} \cong \overline{QR}$

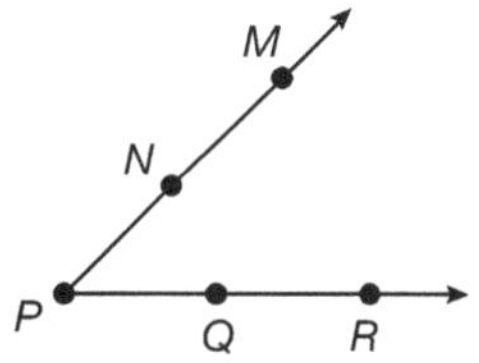

24. **Design** Martha wants to make a regular triangular pyramid out of construction paper. The base is an equilateral triangle. If the equilateral triangle has 10-inch side lengths, and she wants the slant height to be 5 inches, how much material does she need? Round your answer to the nearest square inch.
(70)

25. Is the parallelogram shown a rectangle, a rhombus, both, or is there not enough information to know?
(65)

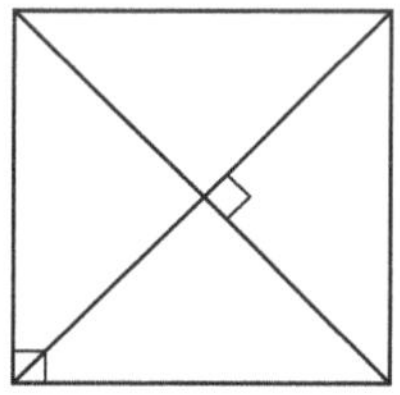

26. The ratio of the length of a rectangle to its width is 7:3. If the width of the rectangle is 42 centimeters, what is the length?
(41)

27. **Algebra** In $\triangle PQR$, $\angle SQR \cong \angle SRQ$, $PQ > PR$, $m\angle PSR = (4y + 9)°$ and $m\angle QSP = (6y - 24)°$. Find the range of values for *y*.
(Inv 4)

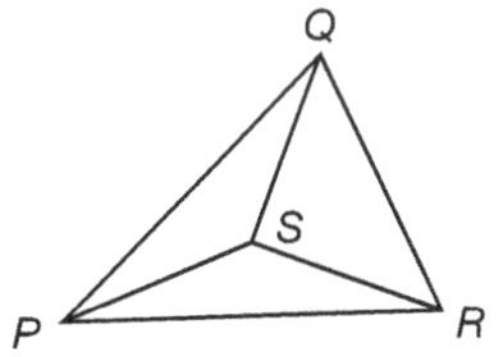

28. **Construction** A square section of a building frame is braced by two diagonal beams. If the section is 7 feet, 8 inches high, what is the length of each beam in feet and inches?
(Inv 7)

29. (59) **Railroad Cars** If the price of gravel is $25 per cubic yard, what is the approximate value of the gravel filling this railroad car?

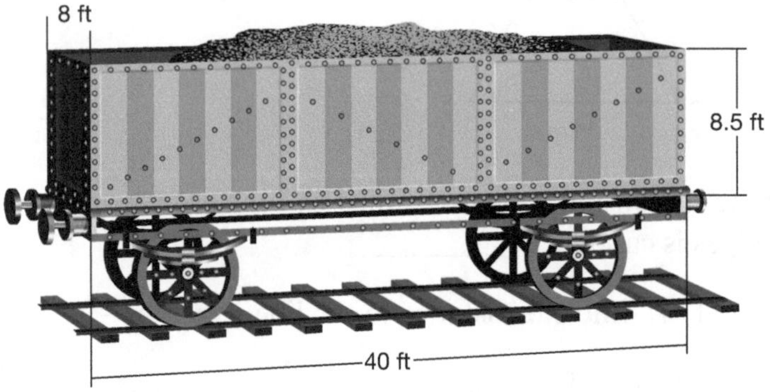

30. (72) **Model** Draw two circles with two common exterior tangents.

Applying Trigonometry: Angles of Elevation and Depression

LESSON 73

*1. **Algebra** A kite is flying at a 45° angle of elevation above the ground. Find the length of string if $x = 20$.
(73)

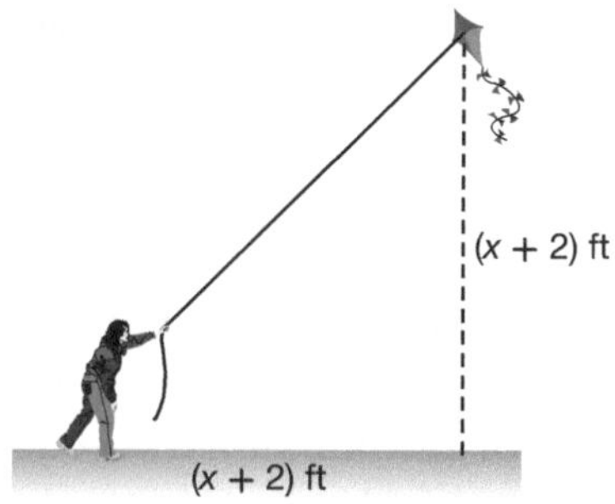

2. **Multiple Choice** Choose the best answer that compares $m\angle Y$ and $m\angle M$.
(Inv 4)

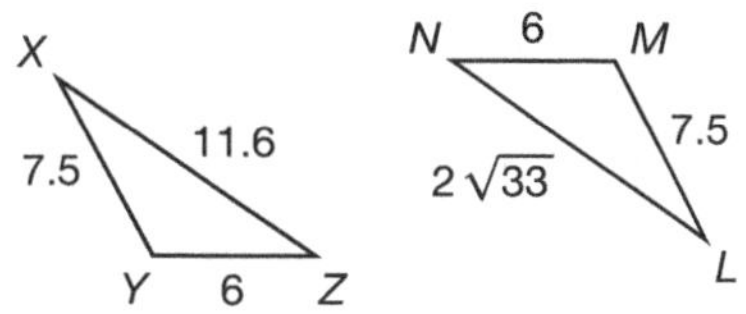

A $m\angle Y = m\angle M$ **B** $m\angle Y > m\angle M$
C $m\angle Y < m\angle M$ **D** Not enough information is given.

* 3. **Model** Draw three circles that share two common tangents.
(72)

4. **Insecticides** A company has developed a new type of insecticide for outdoor patios, which is based on attracting mosquitoes to the figure shown. Which sectors have the greatest probability of attracting mosquitoes?
(Inv 6)

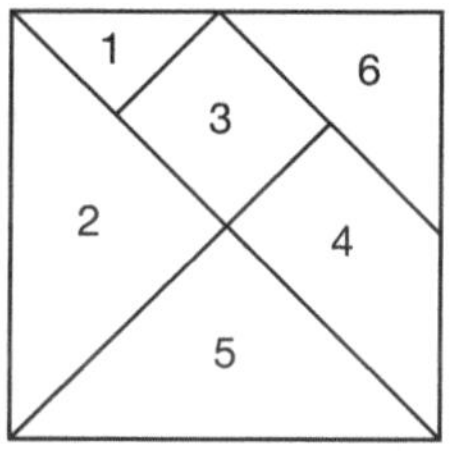

5. **Design** Jameson is making a set of regular pyramids as props for a school play. He makes the bases of all the pyramids with a 1-meter side length and a slant height of 2 meters. Determine a formula for the lateral area of the regular pyramid with n-sided base.
(70)

6. **Justify** Determine whether $\triangle DEF$ is a right triangle, if $\overline{AB} \parallel \overline{DE}$. Explain how you know.
(60)

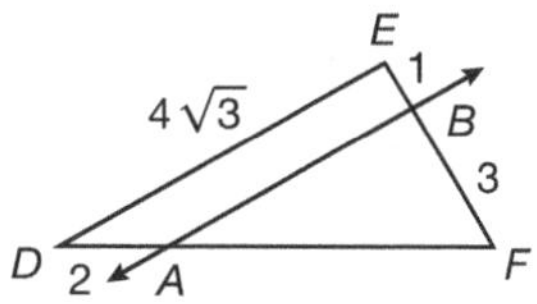

* 7. Assume the segments that appear to be tangent are tangent. Find x.
(72)

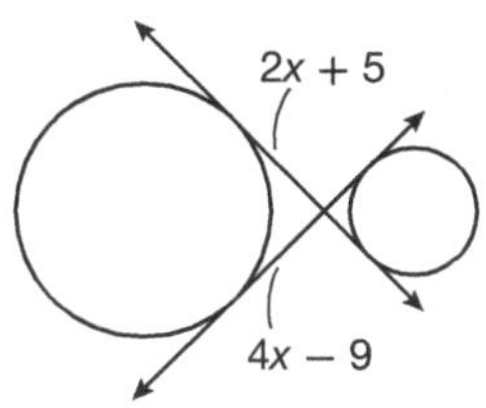

8. Find the length of the radius of a circle given an 8-centimeter chord that is 4 centimeters from the center of the circle.
(43)

9. What arc measure does the needle on a compass create as it goes from north to northeast?
(26)

10. *(40)* **Landscaping** A shop owner wants to build a brick patio, as shown at right. If each brick covers an area of 18 square inches, how many bricks will the shop need to cover the entire patio in brick?

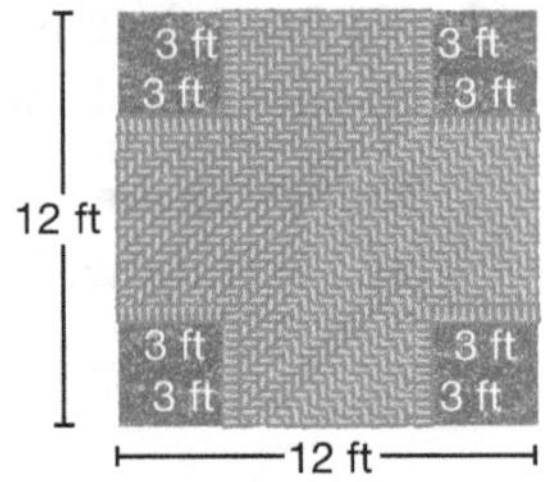

***11.** *(73)* A building's shadow is 136 meters long, and the sun is at an angle of elevation of 60° above the horizon. Find the height of the building. Leave your answer in radical form.

12. *(64)* Find the value of x in the figure.

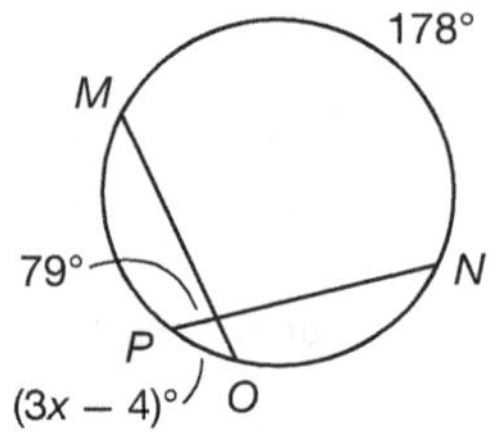

13. *(68)* **Verify** Find the cosines of 8°, 10°, 25°, 30°, 60°, 70° and 90°. Why is cosine never greater than 1?

14. *(Inv 7)* In $\triangle ABC$, A is a right angle, $m\angle B = 60°$, and $BC = 5$ inches.

a. Draw a diagram of $\triangle ABC$.
b. Determine AB.
c. Determine exact and approximate values for AC.

15. *(35)* Find the length of $\overset{\frown}{MD}$. Round to the nearest hundredth of an inch.

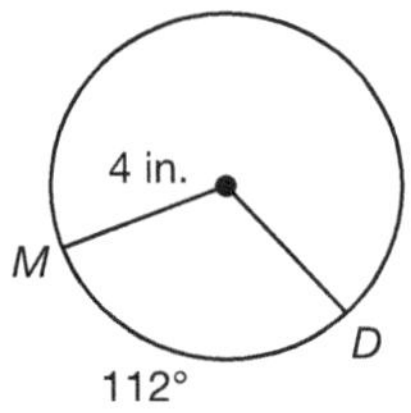

16. *(71)* **Verify** Quinton was asked to apply the vector translations $u = \langle 3, 8\rangle$ and $v = \langle -3, -8\rangle$ to a series of points. He reasoned that the two vectors would cause the points to move away from and then back to their original locations. Is he correct? Explain.

***17.** *(73)* **Multiple Choice** A pilot in a plane sees a lake at an angle of depression of 31°. The plane is cruising at 20,000 feet. How far away is the lake from the plane?

A 17,143 ft **B** 10,301 ft
C 23,333 ft **D** 38,832 ft

18. *(69)* Find the measures of $\angle B$, $\angle C$, and $\angle D$ in trapezoid $ABCD$ at right.

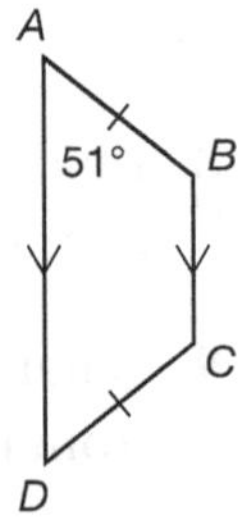

19. *(63)* **Flying** A pilot of a small airplane wants to travel at 225 kilometers per hour over the ground. She knows that she is flying directly into a wind that is blowing at 38 kilometers per hour. What should the speedometer of her airplane read, in order to maintain a ground speed of 225 km/hr?

20. *(71)* **Multi-Step** The translation vectors $u_1 = \langle 3, -2\rangle$ and $u_2 = \langle -1, -3\rangle$ are applied successively to each of the points $A(-2, 5)$, $B(-1, 3)$, and $C(1, 5)$. Find the coordinates of the image of each point after the translations.

21. List the side lengths of $\triangle JKL$ in order from least to greatest.
(39)

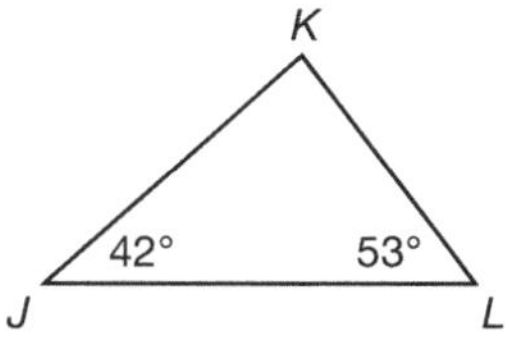

22. **Model** On a coordinate plane, show how to locate the midpoint of the hypotenuse $\overline{AB}$ of a right triangle, using the midpoints of its legs.
(11)

***23.** **Surveying** A surveyor measures a 65° angle of elevation to the top of an 800-foot building. How far is the surveyor from the base of the building, to the nearest foot?
(73)

Use the diagram to determine each length.

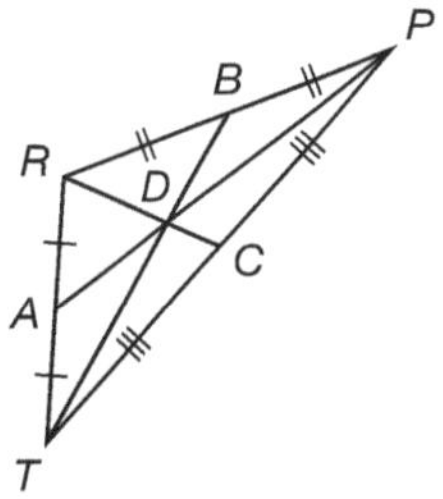

24. Given that $AP = 123$, determine DP.
(32)

25. Given that $BD = 63$, determine BT.
(32)

26. **Error Analysis** Giselle states that since the tile on the right is divided into three sections, there is a one-in-three chance of a fly randomly landing on any section. Is she correct? Explain.
(Inv 6)

27. **Algebra** What are the coordinates of the midpoint of $\overline{DE}$ with endpoints $D(5x - 3, 2 - 6y)$ and $E(2x + 3, 2y + 1)$?
(11)

28. **Justify** Is the quadrilateral shown a parallelogram? How do you know?
(61)

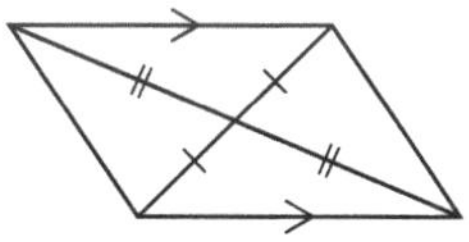

***29.** Assume the segments that appear to be tangent are tangent. Find CD, CE, and BC.
(72)

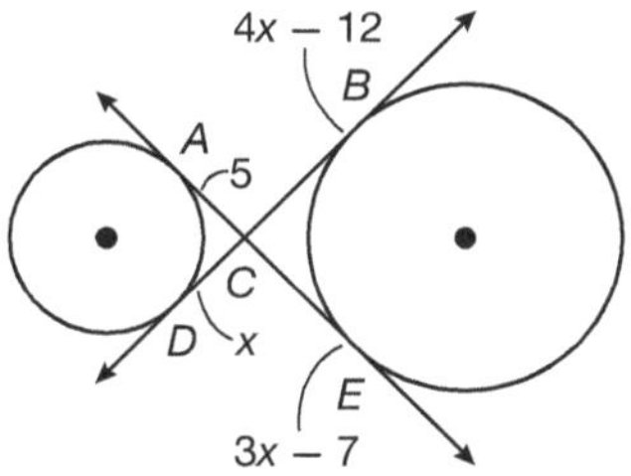

30. Identify each line or segment that intersects the circle.
(43)

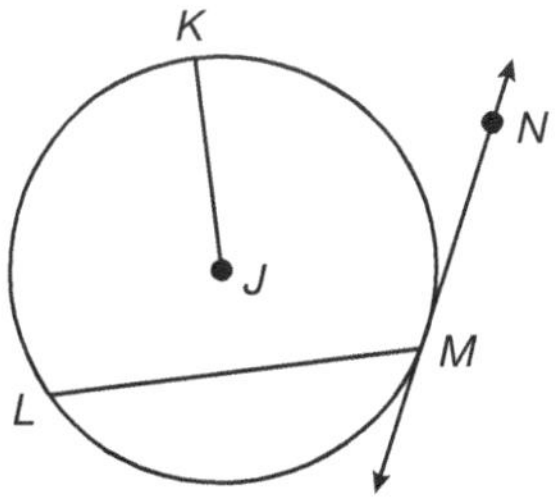

Reflections

LESSON 74

1. Find the measure of $\widehat{JKL}$ in the figure. Line ℓ is tangent to the circle.
(64)

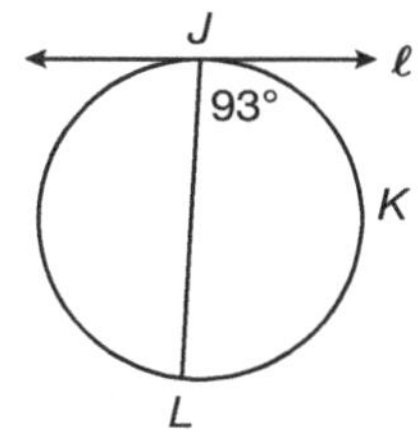

2. **Formulate** Write a transformation mapping for a reflection T across the line $y = -x$.
(74)

3. Find the distance between points (4, 0) and (5, 6).
(9)

4. Find DE. Round to the nearest hundredth.
(68)

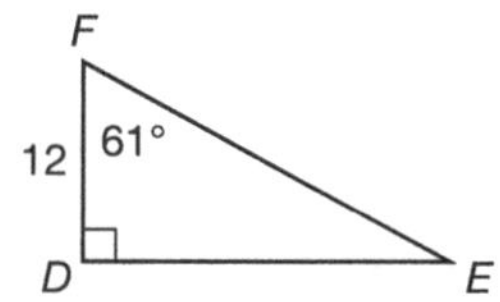

5. **Multiple Choice** Which of the following sets of numbers could be the side lengths of a right triangle?
(33)

A 6, 7, 8 **B** 5, $3\sqrt{3}$, $2\sqrt{13}$
C 7, $6\sqrt{89}$ **D** 5, 5, 9

6. **Algebra** In $\triangle PQR$, $\angle P$ is a right angle, $PQ = x$, and $QR = 2x$. In $\triangle STU$, $\angle S$ is a right angle, $ST = 10 - 3x$, and $TU = y + 2$. For certain values of x and y, you can use the HL Congruence Theorem to prove that $\triangle PQR \cong \triangle STU$. Determine these values of x and y.
(36)

7. If $\triangle JKL \sim \triangle PQR$, what is the value of a?
(41)

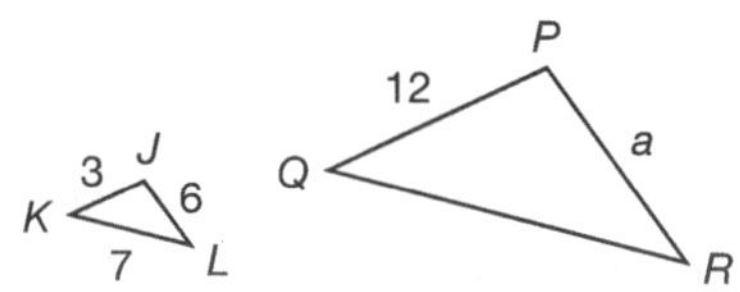

8. $\triangle ABC \sim \triangle WXY$, and the ratio of their corresponding sides is 4:1. If $BA = 12$, what is XW?
(44)

9. **Average Rainfall** Sanjay buys a rain barrel to store rainwater for his garden. If the average rainy day leaves 3 cubic feet of water in his barrel, and the barrel is 4 feet tall with a 1.5-foot radius, how many rainy days, on average, would it take to completely fill the rain barrel?
(62)

10. **Error Analysis** This circle has center A and radius $\overline{AB}$. Ava has calculated that $\angle A$ in $\triangle ABD$ is 65°. Is Ava correct? How do you know?
(58)

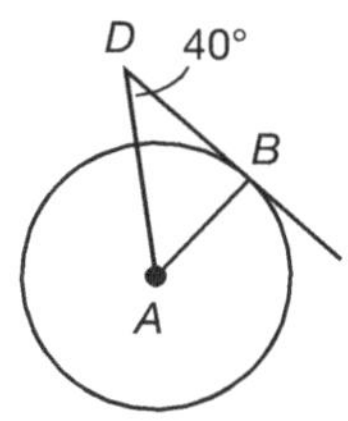

11. **Computer Generated Images** A computer-generated triangular prism is made by constructing a triangle with vertices (0, 0), (2, 5), (4, 0), translating it using T: $(x, y) \rightarrow (x + 4, y + 6)$ and connecting the vertices of the preimage to the corresponding vertices of the image. Sketch the triangular prism.
(71)

12. **Analyze** An equilateral triangle is reflected across a line containing one of its sides. What figure is formed by the image and preimage?
(51, 74)

13. What trigonometric ratio can a hiker use to determine the vertical distance to the lake, x.
(73)

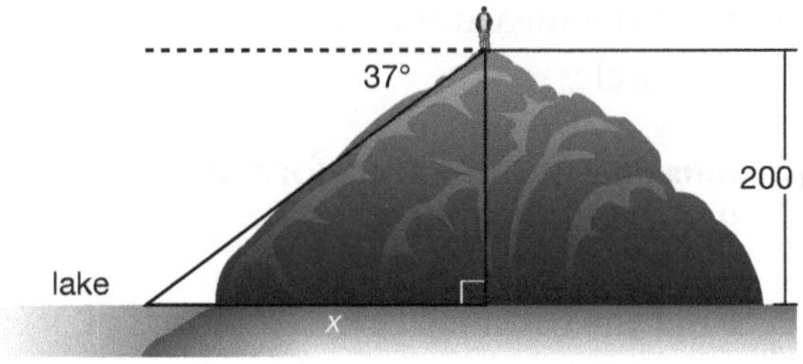

14. Triangle DEF has vertices $D(3, 4)$, $E(7, 2)$, and $F(6, 6)$. Graph the reflection of $\triangle DEF$ across the line $x = 2.5$.
(74)

15. Find the distance from the line $y = 3x - 1$ to $(5, 4)$.
(42)

16. Determine the missing side lengths in $\triangle PQR$. Give approximate answers to the nearest hundredth of a unit.
(Inv 7)

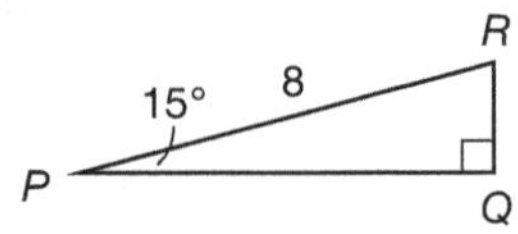

17. **Multi-Step** A triangle has sides that are 15 feet and 21 feet long, respectively. What range of values could be the perimeter?
(39)

18. **Justify** The measures of the angles of a triangle are $x°$, $(2x + 5)°$, and $(8x + 10)°$. Find the value of x. Provide a justification for each step.
(24)

19. Reflect $PQRS$ across the line $y = x$.
(74)

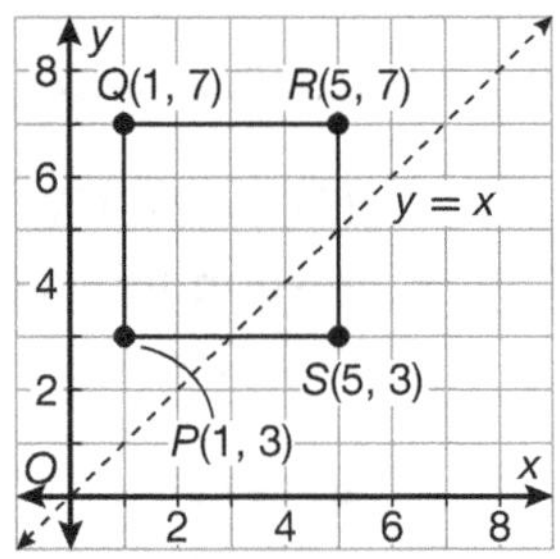

20. **Graphing Calculator** Use a graphing calculator to verify that the sine function varies between 0 and 1 by finding the sine of 7°, 14°, 23°, 56°, 78°, and 90°. Explain why sine cannot be greater than 1.
(68)

21. **Multi-Step** Classify the polygon with vertices $C(-2, -1)$, $D(4, 1)$, $E(5, -2)$, and $F(-1, -4)$. Find its area.
(57)

22. **Track Meet** The track at the high school is shown at right. What is the perimeter, to the nearest yard, of the track?
(40)

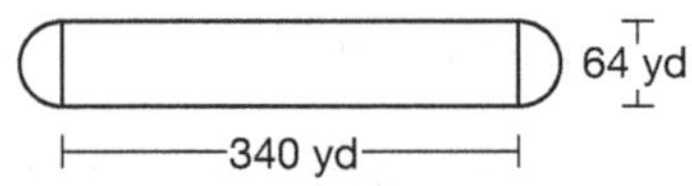

23. **Algebra** Line g passes through points $(3, -2)$ and $(4, 7)$. Line h passes through points $(1, 5)$ and $(-x, 4)$. What value of x makes these lines perpendicular?
(37)

24. Write the equation of the image of the line $y = 3x + 2$ after a reflection across the lines in parts **a** and **b**.
(74)

a. Across the line $y = x$.

b. Across the line $x + y = 0$.

25. **Write** In the figure shown, $\overline{AC}$ is tangent to both circles. $\overline{AD}$ and $\overline{AB}$ are also tangents. (72) Explain why $\overline{AB} \cong \overline{AD}$ even when the circles vary greatly in size.

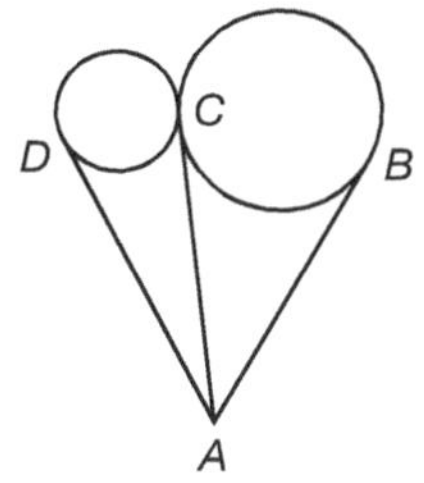

26. If quadrilateral $MNPR$ has three sides of equal length MN, NP, and PR—must the (34) quadrilateral be a parallelogram?

27. A building is 40 feet tall. If a person stands 40 feet from the bottom of the building (73) and sees the top, what is the angle of elevation from the person to the top of the building?

28. **Parasailing** A parasail is attached by a 40-foot rope to the boat that is towing it. If (73) the angle of elevation from the boat to the parasail is 34°, about how far above the water is the parasailer?

29. Determine the point of tangency and the equation of the (72) tangent line. Find the radius of each circle.

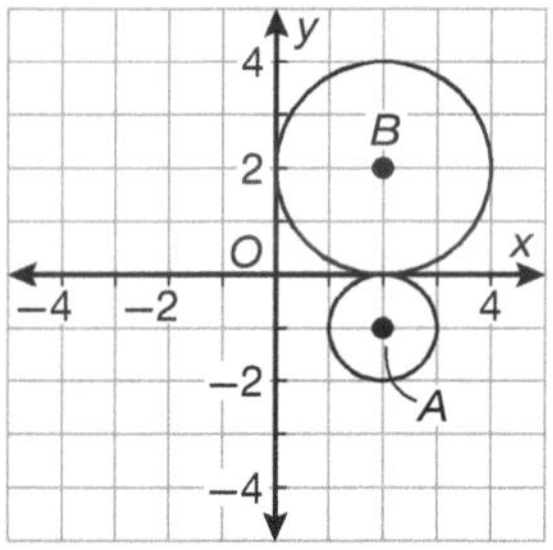

30. **Archaeology** The front of an ancient Greek temple includes (Inv 7) an isosceles triangle with base angles that each measure 30°. The legs of the triangle are each 13 yards long. Determine the height and the base length of the triangle, to the nearest tenth of a yard.

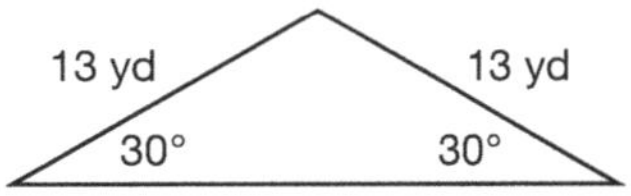

Name ______________________ Date ________ Class ________

Writing the Equation of a Circle

LESSON 75

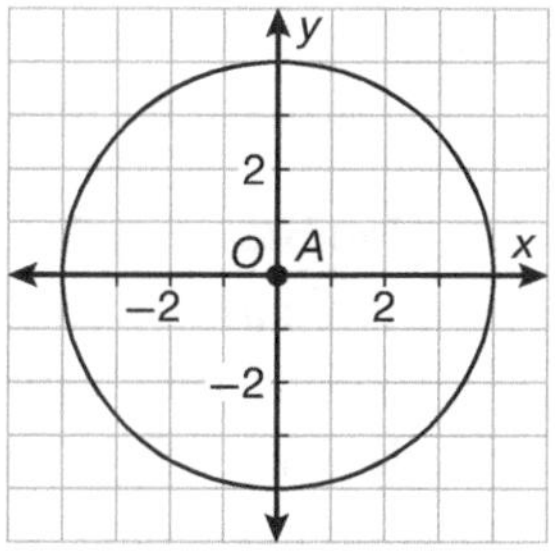

* **1.** Write the equation for $\odot A$.
(75)

2. **Navigation** A sailor on a ship sees the top of a distant hill at an 8° angle of elevation. The hill is 450 meters tall. How far is the sailor from the hill, to the nearest meter?
(73)

3. **Multiple Choice** Which is the most correct choice, given the two triangles?
(Inv 4)

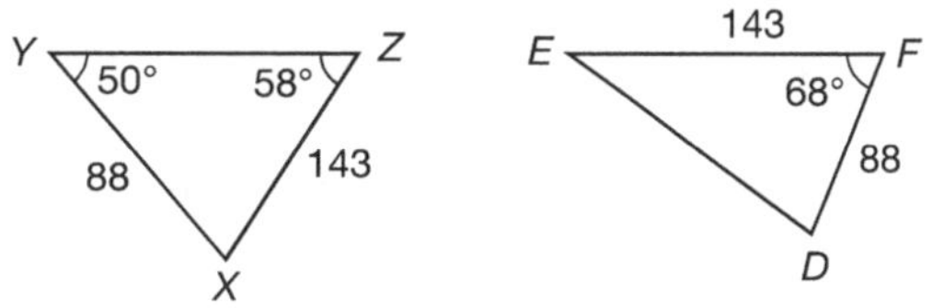

A $YZ > ED$ **B** $m\angle X > m\angle F$
C both **A** and **B** are correct **D** neither **A** nor **B** are correct

4. Find the geometric mean of 7 and 5.
(50)

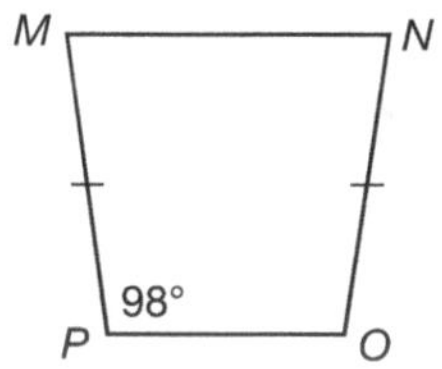

5. **Error Analysis** Minh-li claimed that $m\angle N = 98°$, because base angles of an isosceles trapezoid are congruent. Determine her error and find the correct value of $m\angle N$.
(69)

6. **Computer-Generated Images** A computer-generated, square prism is made by constructing a square with vertices (0, 0), (0, 2), (2, 2), and (2, 0), and then translating it using T: $(x, y) \rightarrow (x + 3, y + 4)$, and connecting the vertices of the preimage to the corresponding vertices of the image. Find the volume of the prism.
(71)

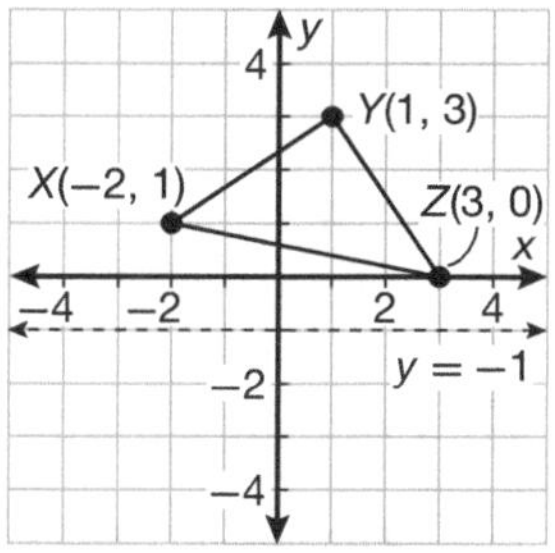

* **7.** Reflect $\triangle XYZ$ across the line $y = -1$.
(74)

8. **Construction** Yoshi wants to build a square-based pyramid. He wants to make the slant height of the pyramid twice as long as the height of the pyramid. If the side lengths of the base are 1 unit each and the magnitude of the lateral area is 11 units greater than the volume, how tall should Yoshi make his pyramid?
(70)

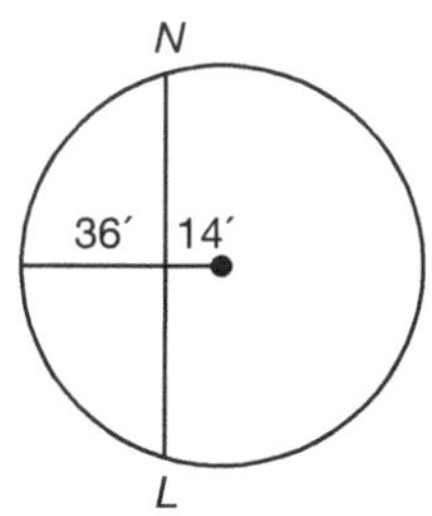

9. Find the length of chord $\overline{LN}$ in the circle at right.
(43)

10. **Graphing Calculator** Use a calculator to complete a table of values for sin x, cos x, and tan x, as x varies from 0° to 90° in increments of 10°.
(Inv 7)

a. Complete this sentence: sin x ________ from __ to __ as x increases from 0° to 90°.

b. Write similar sentences for cos x and tan x.

Writing the Equation of a Circle

LESSON 75

11. If a circle has an area of 144 square meters and a sector of that circle has an area of 12 square meters, what is the angle measure of the sector?
(35)

12. **Landscaping** A hexagonal area in a park has been cleared for a picnic area and a gazebo to be installed. The park director wants to construct a path from the gazebo in the center to the edge of the clearing. If the length of the path is 20 meters, how many square meters of park have been cleared?
(66)

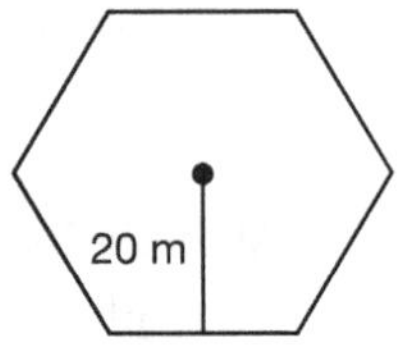

***13.** Write the equation for $\odot Q$ with a radius of 3, centered at $Q(2, 4)$.
(75)

14. If a circle has a radius of 7.5 inches, and a chord that is 7 inches long, what is the distance from the chord to the center of the circle?
(43)

15. Find the measure of $\angle D$.
(47)

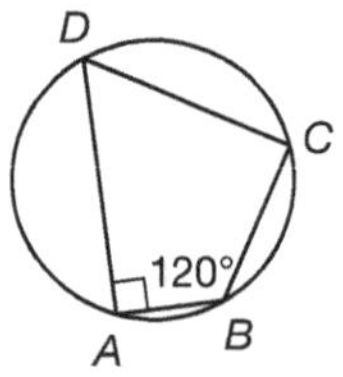

16. Find the magnitude of $\langle -3, 5 \rangle$ to the nearest tenth.
(63)

17. **Analyze** Determine the number of common tangents for the circles shown at right, then draw the tangents.
(72)

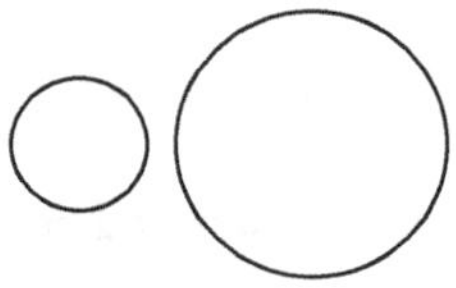

***18.** The equation of $\odot B$ is $x^2 + y^2 = 9$. Graph $\odot B$.
(75)

19. Find the slope of line f and then find the slopes of the lines that are parallel and perpendicular to f.
(37)

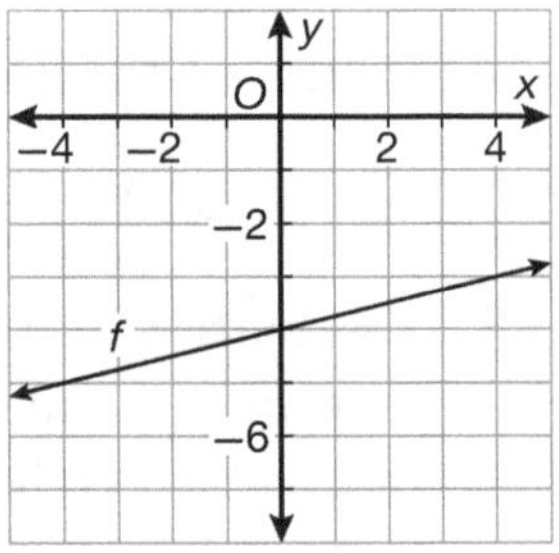

***20.** **Multiple Choice** A reflection across the line $y = 3$ maps (4, 0) onto:
(74)

A (4, 6) **B** (–2, 0)
C (7, 0) **D** (0, 4)

21. Find the length of $\overline{XY}$. Round to the nearest hundredth.
(68)

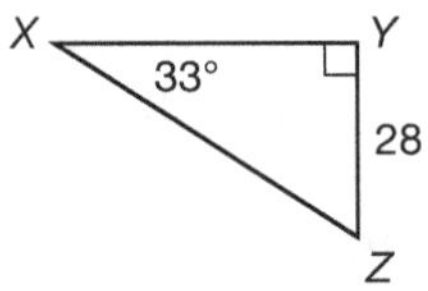

22. **Aviation** A plane is flying at an elevation of 10,000 meters and a speed of 300 kilometers per hour. The pilot sees a lake at an angle of depression of 60°. In how much time, to the nearest minute, will the plane be directly over the lake?
(73)

23. **Algebra** Rectangle $DEFG$ has vertices $D(x_1, 3)$, $E(0, 0)$, $F(3, 0)$, and $G(x_2, y_2)$. Find the values of x_1, x_2, and y_2.
(45)

24. Is this parallelogram a rectangle, a rhombus, both, or neither?
(65)

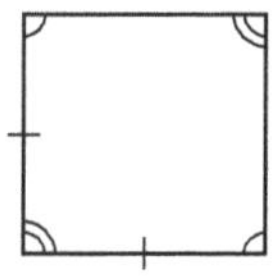

***25.** The unit circle and $\odot C$ with a radius of r are concentric. Circle D with a radius of s is centered at (8, 0). If circles C and D touch at one point, write all possible relations between r and s.
(75)

26. Analyze Write a paragraph proof of the following:
(31)
Given: Ray FD bisects $\angle EFC$, ray FC bisects $\angle DFB$
Prove: $\angle EFD \cong \angle CFB$

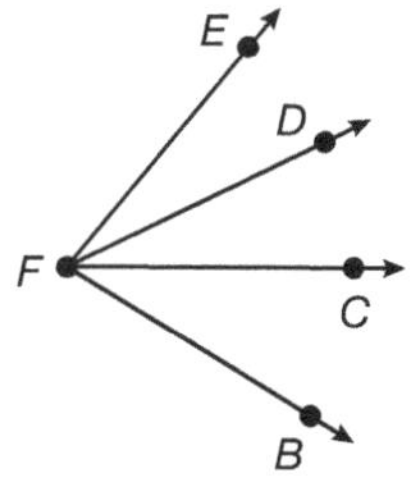

27. Multi-Step The perimeter of $\triangle ABC$ is 54 inches, and its side lengths are x, $x + 1$, and $x + 2$. If $\triangle ABC \sim \triangle PQR$, and the ratio of their corresponding sides is 1:2, what are the lengths of the sides of $\triangle PQR$?
(44)

28. Algebra Find the distance from the line $y = \frac{5}{3}x + 2$ to $(-5, 5)$.
(42)

***29.** Square $ABCD$ with vertices $A(3, 5)$, $B(1, 7)$, $C(-1, 5)$, and $D(1, 3)$ is reflected across the line $x = 3$. Verify that the reflection image has vertices $A'(3, 5)$, $B'(5, 7)$, $C'(7, 5)$, and $D'(5, 3)$.
(74)

30. Write Can a triangle have sides with lengths of 0.5 centimeters, 0.7 centimeters, and 0.3 centimeters? Explain why or why not.
(39)

Name ______________________ Date ____________ Class ____________

Symmetry

LESSON 76

1. (Inv 6) **Fountains** A woman turns her back to a circular fountain with a radius of 3 meters and randomly tosses a penny over her shoulder into the fountain. What is the probability that her penny lands on the triangular piece of art in the fountain?

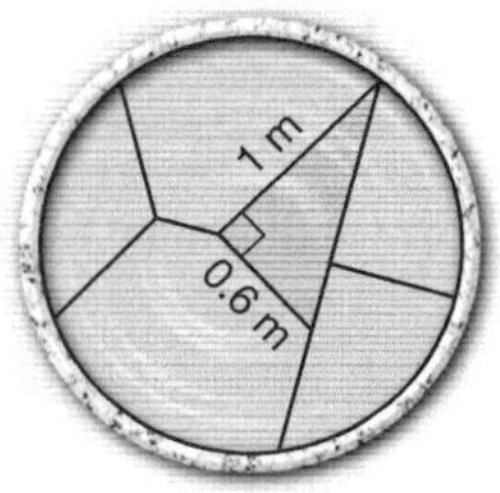

* 2. (76) Complete this chart. Can you make a conjecture about rotational symmetry based on the information you recorded?

Polygon	Triangle	Quadrilateral	Pentagon	Hexagon	Heptagon	Octagon	Nonagon	Decagon
Order of Rotational Symmetry	3							

3. (74) **Analyze** Genevive reflected $\triangle JKL$ with $J(-2, 3)$, $K(-2, 5)$, and $L(-4, 4)$ across the line $y = x$. Then she reflected $\triangle J'K'L'$ across the same line. What are the coordinates of $\triangle J''K''L''$?

4. (37) **Multiple Choice** Which of the following is *not* perpendicular to $12y = 4x - 6$?
A $y = -3x + 4$ **B** $-y + 3x = 12$
C $2y + 6x = 4$ **D** $-9x = 3y - 7$

* 5. (75) Graph the equation $x^2 + y^2 = 36$.

6. (69) In isosceles trapezoid $QRST$, find QS if $TU = 7.8$ feet and $RU = 3.5$ feet.

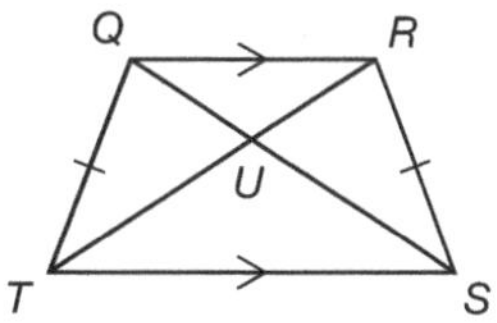

7. (25) **Generalize** On which diagonal can you cut a kite and have two congruent triangles?

8. (48) **Multi-Step** Complete this indirect proof by writing the indirect proof for the second case.

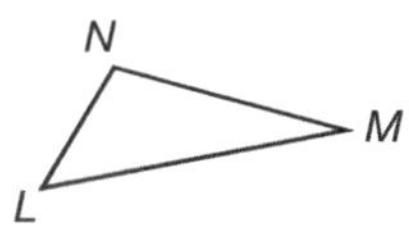

Given: $m\angle N > m\angle M$
Prove: $LM > LN$
Indirect Proof: First, assume LM is not greater than LN.
So, $LM < LN$ or $LM = LN$.
Case 1: ($LM < LN$): If $LM < LN$, then $m\angle N < m\angle M$ because the longer side would be opposite the larger angle (Theorem 39-1). The inequality $m\angle N < m\angle M$ contradicts the given information, so LM is not less than LN.
Case 2: ($LM = LN$): ______________________________
The assumption LM is not greater than LN is false, so $LM > LN$.

* **9.** (76) **Error Analysis** Akeelah identified this symbol as having 180° rotational symmetry. Explain her error.

10. (63) **Ballooning** A hot air balloon is rising at a rate of 6 feet per second. There is an updraft of 2 feet per second. If there were no updraft, how fast would the balloon be rising?

11. (70) What is the lateral area of a square pyramid where the length of one side of the square is 5 centimeters and the slant height is 10 centimeters?

12. (40) **Verify** Use what you know about areas of composite figures to verify that you can use the formula $A = 3(as)$ to find the area of the regular polygon in the figure.

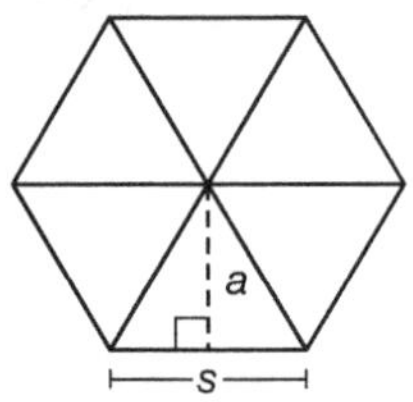

13. (46) If two triangles have two pairs of corresponding congruent angles and the included sides are proportional, what similarity theorem or postulate applies?

***14.** (76) **Algebra** Does the function $y = x^2 + 7$ have a line of symmetry? If so, name the line of symmetry.

15. (55) Segment QR is a midsegment of $\triangle MNP$. Find the values of x and y.

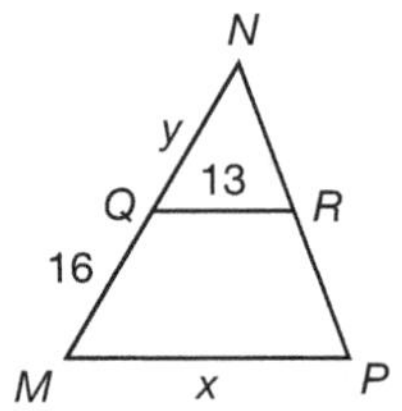

16. (12) **Multiple Choice** In this figure, $\angle 5$ and which other angle can prove the lines parallel using the Converse of the Corresponding Angles Theorem?

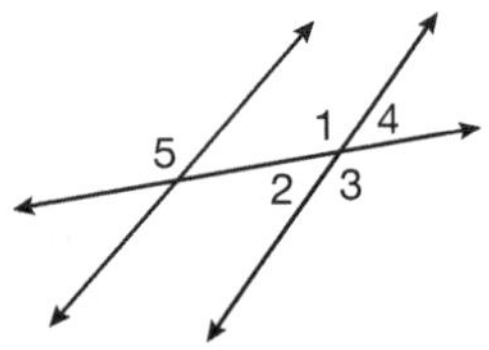

A 1 **B** 2
C 3 **D** 4

***17.** (75) **Verify** Check by calculation that the points $P(6, 1)$ and $Q(4, 5)$ lie on $\odot C$ with center $(1, 1)$ and radius 5.

18. (Inv 7) **Algebra** Use this triangle to determine the value of z.

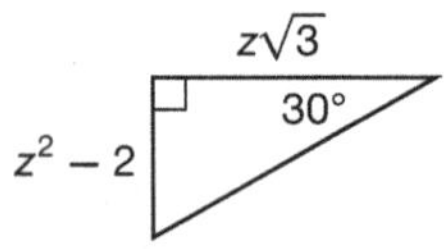

19. (66) Find the area of a regular decagon with 14-centimeter side lengths and an apothem that is 21.5 centimeters long.

20. (73) **Hiking** A hiker looks down from the top of a hill to a lake. The hill is 400 meters tall, and the angle of depression to the lake is 50°. How far away is the lake, to the nearest meter?

*21. (76) **Flags** Tell whether each flag has rotational symmetry. If yes, determine the angle of rotation and the order.

22. (45) Rectangle $ABCD$ has vertices $A(0, 4)$, $B(6, 4)$, $C(6, 0)$, and $D(0, 0)$. If E is the midpoint of DC, find the coordinates of E.

23. (34) The diagonals of parallelogram $DEFG$ intersect at P. Find GE, GF, $m\angle DFG$, and $m\angle GDE$ if $DE = 15$, $EP = 8$, and $m\angle EFG = 130°$.

*24. (75) **Multiple Choice** Which is the equation of a circle with center $(-3, 4)$ and a radius of 6?

A $(x + 3)^2 + (y - 4)^2 = 16$ **B** $(x + 3)^2 + (y - 4)^2 = 36$

C $(x - 3)^2 + (y + 4)^2 = 36$ **D** $(x - 3)^2 + (y - 4)^2 = 36$

25. (Inv 7) **Analyze** Explain why the tangent of 90° is undefined. Name one other degree measure for which the tangent is undefined.

26. (41) In the proportion $\frac{15}{6} = \frac{8}{y}$, what is the value of y?

27. (60) **Streets** On the map, 5th Ave., 6th Ave., and 7th Ave. are parallel. What is the length of Main St. between 5th and 6th Avenue?

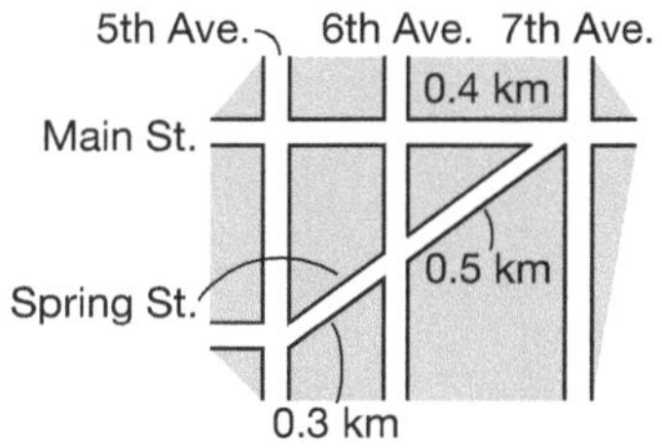

28. (42) **Algebra** Find the point on the line $y = -x - 4$ that is closest to $(4, 4)$.

29. (63) **Write** Could opposite vectors also be defined as vectors with the same direction but opposite magnitude? Why or why not?

30. (74) Reflect square *KMRW* across the line $y = x + 2$.

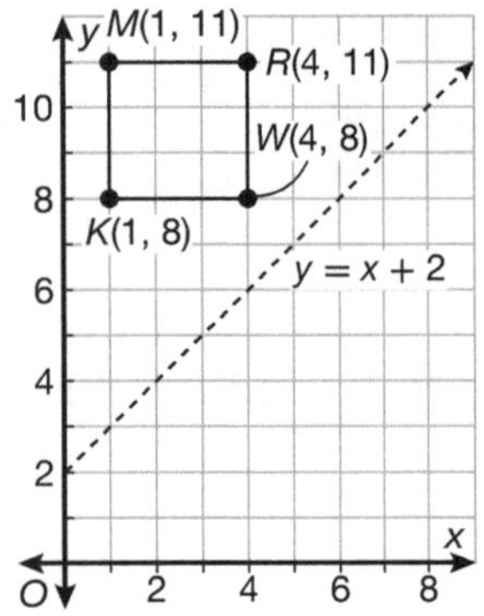

Name ______________________ Date __________ Class __________

Finding Surface Areas and Volumes of Cones

LESSON 77

* **1.** Calculate the lateral surface area of a cone with a radius of 3 centimeters and a slant height of 5 centimeters.
(77)

* **2.** **Multiple Choice** Which inequality gives the range of the cosine function?
(Inv 7)

A $0 < y < 1$ **B** $y > 0$

C $0 \leq y \leq 1$ **D** $y \leq 1$

3. **Rockets** A model rocket's fuel tank is in the shape of a cylinder with a radius of 1 foot and a height of 3 feet. To the nearest hundredth, how much fuel can the rocket hold if one cubic foot holds 7.5 gallons of fuel?
(62)

4. Find the range of possible lengths of the third side of a triangle if the other two side lengths are 115 feet and 266 feet.
(39)

5. **Multiple Choice** If _______ are congruent, then lines p and q are parallel.
(12)

A $\angle 1$ and $\angle 2$ **B** $\angle 2$ and $\angle 4$

C $\angle 1$ and $\angle 8$ **D** $\angle 1$ and $\angle 7$

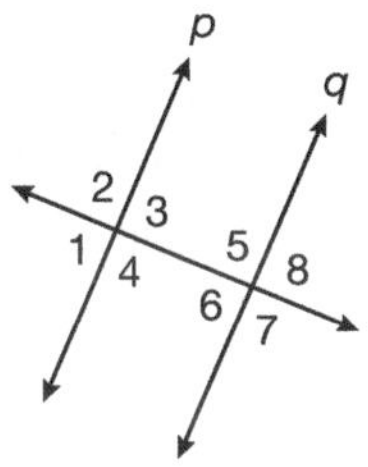

6. **Municipal Planning** On a grid of a city, the fire station is located at the origin, (0, 0). One square on the grid represents one square mile. The fire station's new siren can be heard in an area described on the grid as $x^2 + y^2 = 10$. Would a house located at (0, 5) be able to hear the new siren? What is the farthest distance, to the nearest hundredth mile, that a house could be from the fire station and still hear the siren?
(75)

7. **Model** Draw three internally tangent circles that are tangent to each other at exactly one point.
(72)

8. **Algebra** $\triangle PQR \sim \triangle KLM$. Given $PQ = x - 2$, $QR = y^2$, $RP = 6$, $KL = 9$, $LM = 12$, and $MK = 18$, find the values of x and y. Then, find the perimeter of $\triangle PQR$.
(44)

9. What is the radius of a circle if the area of a 60° arc is 6π?
(35)

10. Compare PS and PQ.
(Inv 4)

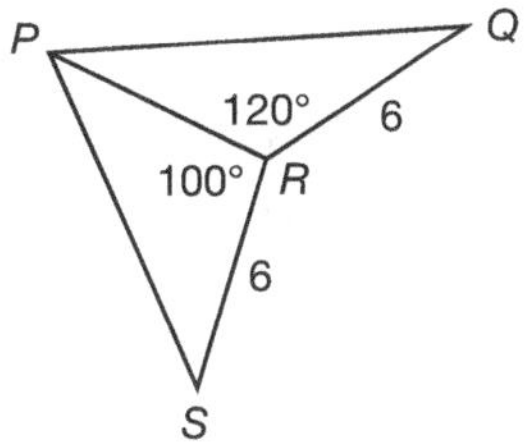

***11.** Calculate the surface area of a cone with a radius of 7 inches and a slant height of 10 inches. Round your answer to the nearest square inch.
(77)

12. Triangle PQR has vertices $P(-2, 1)$, $Q(2, 2)$, and $R(0, 5)$. What are the coordinates of $\triangle P'Q'R'$ after $\triangle PQR$ is reflected across the line $x = 1$?
(74)

*13. (76) **Multi-Step** Does quadrilateral *HJKL* with the given vertices have line symmetry or rotational symmetry? $H(3, 3)$, $J(2, -1)$, $K(0, -1)$, and $L(-1, 3)$.

14. (36) Which congruence theorem applies to these triangles?

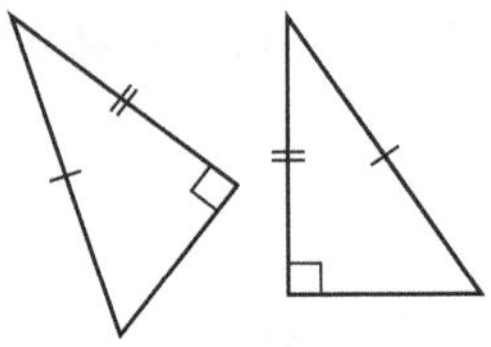

15. (73) **Surveying** A surveyor knows the height of a building is 70 meters. If the angle of elevation to the top of the building from where he stands measures 17°, how far is the surveyor from the building, to the nearest meter?

16. (53) **Estimate** A triangular loom is made from wooden pieces that form a 45°-45°-90° triangle. Pegs are placed every half-inch along the hypotenuse and every $\frac{1}{4}$ inch along each leg. If the loom has a 15-inch hypotenuse, estimate how many pegs are on the loom.

17. (69) **Design** Blake is making a kite. The frame is a quadrilateral with diagonals that are perpendicular. Does this guarantee that Blake is making a kite-shaped object? Explain.

*18. (77) **Cooking** A waffle cone has a diameter of 7 centimeters and a height of 14 centimeters. What area of waffle dough is needed to make the cone, to the nearest square centimeter?

19. (64) Find the measure of $\widehat{JKL}$ in the figure. Line ℓ is tangent to the circle.

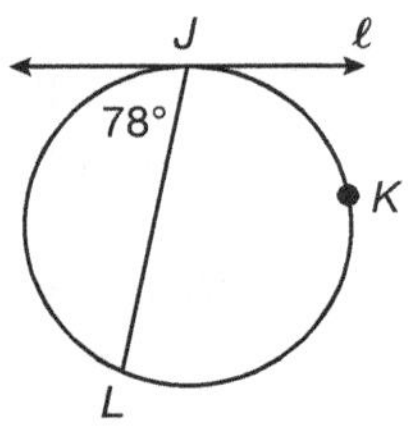

20. (75) Write the formula for $\odot Q$ with a radius of 2, centered at $Q(0, 3)$.

21. (41) The lengths of the sides of a pentagon are 6, 7, 8, 9, and 10 units. A similar pentagon has side lengths of 21, 24.5, 28, 31.5, and 35 units, respectively. By what factor are the side lengths of the smaller pentagon multiplied to get the side lengths of the larger pentagon?

*22. (76) **Write** Describe the lines of symmetry and the rotational symmetry of a parallelogram.

23. (65) **Justify** The vertices of parallelogram *LMNP* are $L(-4.5, -3.5)$, $M(-2, -1)$, $N(1.5, -1.5)$, and $P(-1, -4)$. Is it a rhombus or a rectangle? Explain.

24. (33) **Algebra** Write an inequality to show the possible values for x that make this triangle obtuse.

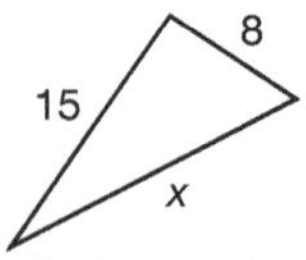

*25. (76) Name a type of triangle that has exactly one line of symmetry.

26. (46) **Write** Explain why the AA Postulate could also be called the AAA Postulate.

*27. Calculate the volume of a cone with a 1-meter radius and a height of 2 meters. Round your answer to the nearest tenth of a cubic meter.
(77)

28. What is the relationship between inscribed angles that intercept the same arc?
(47)

29. A circle has a diameter of 21 inches. A chord is 5 inches from the center. How long is the chord to the nearest tenth of an inch?
(43)

30. **Formulate** Write a paragraph proof.
(31)
Given: $\angle JKL$ is a right angle.
Prove: $\angle 1$ and $\angle 2$ are complementary angles.

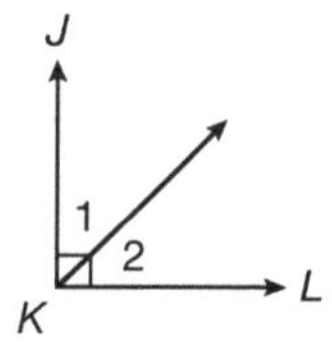

Name ______________________________ Date ____________ Class ____________

Rotations

LESSON 78

1. (75) Write an equation for $\odot A$.

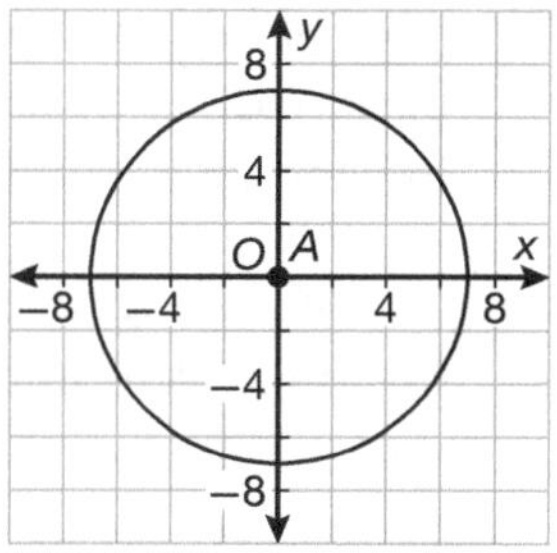

2. (44) **Multiple Choice** Brennan's house has a perimeter of 2500 feet. The perimeter of Shaniqua's house is 0.8 times as large. Which is the correct ratio of the perimeter of Brennan's house to the perimeter of Shaniqua's house?

A 4 to 5 **B** 1 to 8

C 5 to 4 **D** 25 to 0.8

3. (72) Assume the segments that appear to be tangent are tangent. Find x.

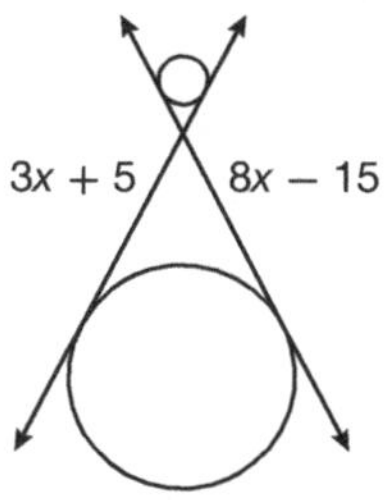

4. (66) **Error Analysis** Robin finds that a hexagon has an apothem length of $\frac{\sqrt{3}}{2}s$, where s is the side length, but Gustavo finds that it is $\sqrt{3}\,s$. Which student is correct? What error has the other made?

5. (Inv 5) **Multiple Choice** Which of these diagrams could not be the net of a triangular pyramid?

A

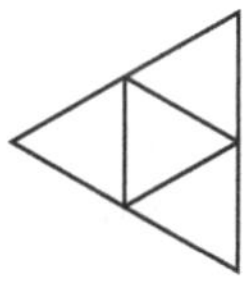

B

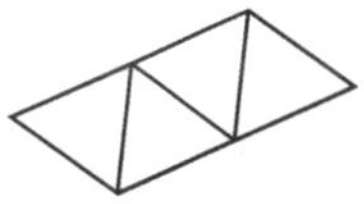

C

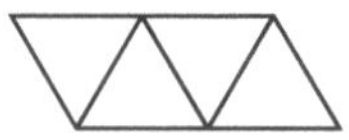

D

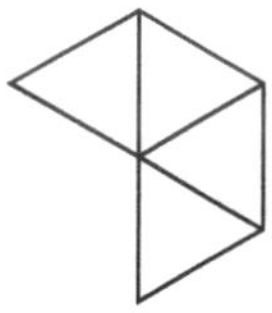

* **6.** (78) $\triangle FGH$ has vertices $F(4, 5)$, $G(1, 2)$, and $H(5, 1)$. Graph $\triangle FGH$ and its image after a rotation of 270° counterclockwise about the origin. List the coordinates of the vertices of $\triangle F'G'H'$.

7. (76) **Write** Describe the lines of symmetry and the rotational symmetry of a non-isosceles trapezoid.

8. (37) Find the line parallel to $y - 7 = 3(x + 4)$ that passes through the point (2, 3). Write the equation in slope-intercept form.

9. (45) **Coordinate Geometry** Use coordinate geometry to show that segments that join the midpoints of sides of a quadrilateral form a parallelogram.

10. (74) **Design** An ecology organization is having a new logo designed. The logo and its reflection across the line $x = 4$ are shown at right. Complete the logo.

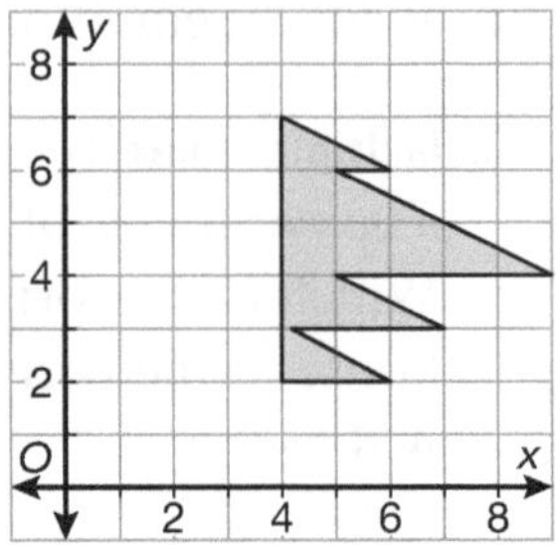

*11. (78) $\triangle ABC$ has vertices $A(-2, 4)$, $B(3, 6)$, and $C(1, 3)$. Graph $\triangle ABC$ and its image after a rotation of 90° counterclockwise about the origin. List the coordinates of the vertices of $\triangle A'B'C'$.

12. (34) Find the value of x, y, and z in the parallelogram.

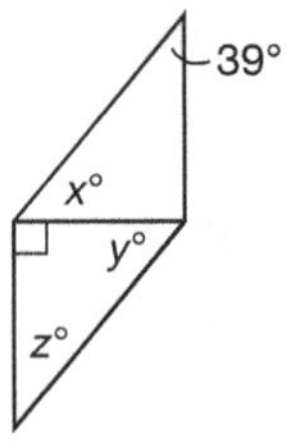

*13. (77) **Generalize** A special cone has the property that its radius is the same length as its height. Determine a formula for the volume of such a cone in terms of the radius, r.

14. (62) **Refreshments** A large cylindrical cooler is $2\frac{1}{2}$ feet high and has a diameter of $1\frac{1}{2}$ feet. It is $\frac{3}{4}$ full of water for athletes to use during their soccer game. Estimate the volume of water in the cooler, to the nearest gallon. *Hint: 1 gallon = 231 in³*

15. (70) **Multi-Step** The height of a regular square pyramid is equal to the side length of the base. The expression $3x - 17.5$ represents the height and $6y - 3$ represents the side length of the base. If $y = 7$, what is x? What is the volume of the pyramid? What is its surface area?

16. (32) **Model** For what type of triangle can the orthocenter be in the triangle's exterior: acute, right, or obtuse? Sketch an example.

17. (73) **Aviation** A pilot in a plane notices a lake at an angle of depression of 13°. The plane is flying at an altitude of 10,000 feet. How far is the pilot from the lake, to the nearest foot?

18. (Inv 4) Compare the measures of $\angle I$ and $\angle L$.

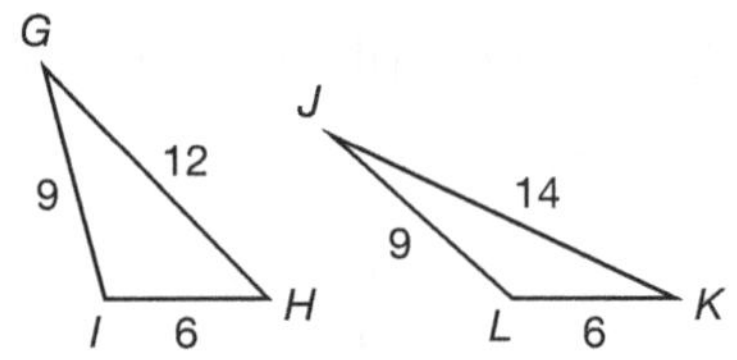

*19. (77) **Design** Rissa is making a cone, including the base, out of paper. She wants the height of the cone to be 12 centimeters and the radius of the cone to be 5 centimeters. How much paper will Rissa need?

20. (72) Assume the segments that appear to be tangent are tangent. Find AC, CD, CE, and BC.

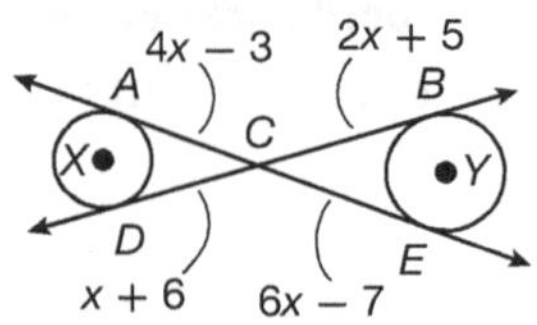

*21. (78) $\triangle RST$ has vertices $R(1, 4)$, $S(2, 1)$, and $T(4, 5)$. Graph $\triangle RST$ and its image after a rotation of 90° about the origin.

22. Find the distance from (5, 3) to the line $y = \frac{4}{3}x$.
(42)

23. **Analyze** Maribeth and Claudia are standing on opposite sides of a building. Maribeth is looking at the roof of the building with a 45° angle of elevation and Claudia is looking at the roof of the building with a 30° angle of elevation. If the building is 104 feet tall, how far away is Maribeth? How far away is Claudia? Round both answers to the nearest foot.
(73)

24. **(Masonry)** A mason is laying bricks for a fountain. The water is to pour out of a semicircular gap in the structure with a 3-foot diameter, and there will be a brick trapezoidal patio around the fountain, as shown in the diagram. If each brick covers 24 square inches, estimate the number of bricks needed to build the patio and fountain.
(40)

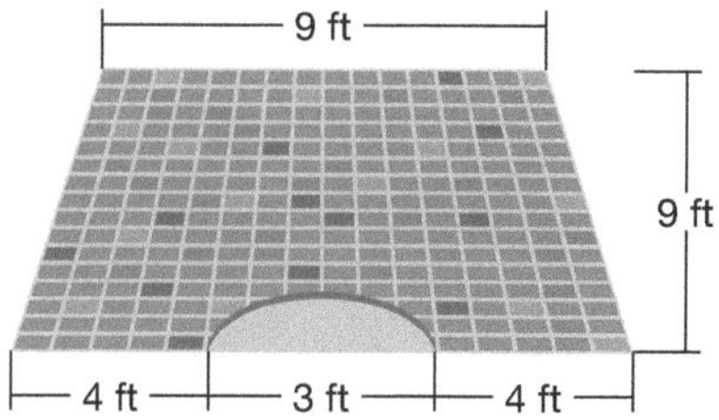

25. Write a valid conclusion from these statements using either the Law of Syllogism or the Law of Detachment, then state which law you used.
(21)

If it is Sunday or a holiday, then the mail will not be delivered today.It is Sunday or a holiday.

26. **Analyze** For what natural-number values of n does the equation $y = x^n$ have a line of symmetry?
(76)

27. **Algebra** If in $\triangle ABC$, $m\angle ABC = 62°$, $AB = 11$, and $m\angle BCA = (22x - 11)°$, and in $\triangle DEF$, $m\angle DEF = 62°$, $DE = 11$, and $m\angle EFD = (25x - 44)°$, what value of x will make $\triangle ABC \cong \triangle DEF$ by AAS Congruence?
(30)

28. Find the measure of $\angle FGI$.
(47)

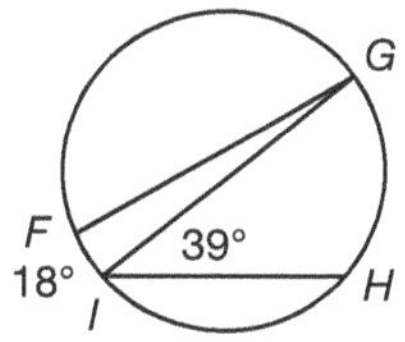

*29. $\triangle JKL$ has vertices $J(-5, -3)$, $K(-2, -5)$, and $L(-3, 1)$. Graph $\triangle JKL$ and its image after a rotation of 180° about the origin.
(78)

30. **Write** Explain why the slant height of a cone is always greater than the height of a cone.
(77)

Name ______________________ Date __________ Class __________

Angles Exterior to Circles

LESSON 79

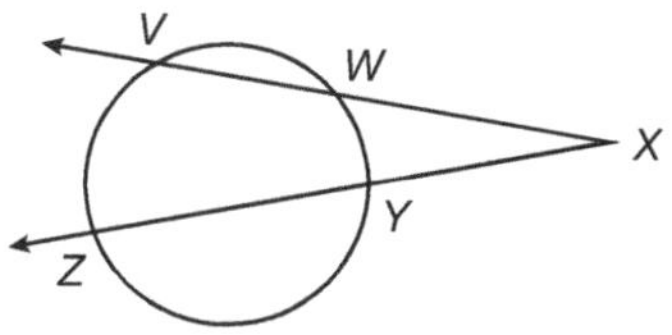

* **1.** (79) **Multiple Choice** Which of the following is true of $\angle X$?

A $m\angle X$ is greater than $m\widehat{VZ} - m\widehat{WY}$.
B $m\angle X$ is less than $m\widehat{WY}$.
C $m\angle X$ is less than $m\widehat{VZ}$.
D $m\angle X$ is greater than $m\widehat{VZ}$.

2. (63) **Flying** A pilot is flying his airplane in winds blowing south at 20 kilometers per hour. What is the vector the pilot needs to fly along in order to have a velocity of 80 kilometers per hour north?

* **3.** (78) Sketch the image of the figure after a rotation of 270° counterclockwise about the origin.

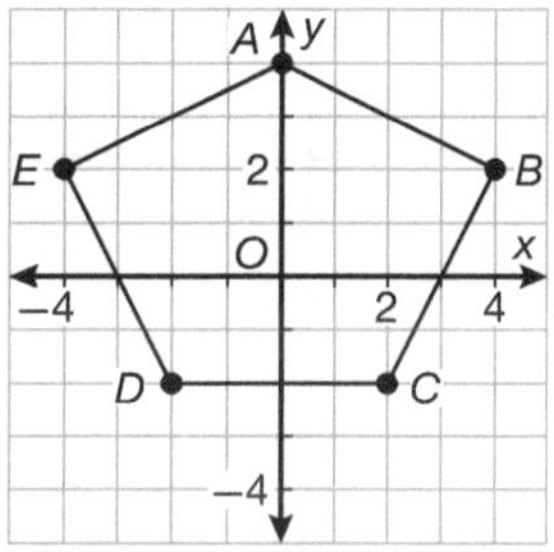

4. (14) **Multiple Choice** Which is a counterexample to the following conjecture?

If a triangle is scalene, then it is obtuse.

A triangle with side lengths of 3, 4, and 4.5 units
B triangle with side lengths of 3, 4, and 6 units
C triangle with angle measures of 20°, 40°, and 120°
D triangle with angle measures of 45°, 45°, and 90°

5. (75) Write the equation for the circle at right.

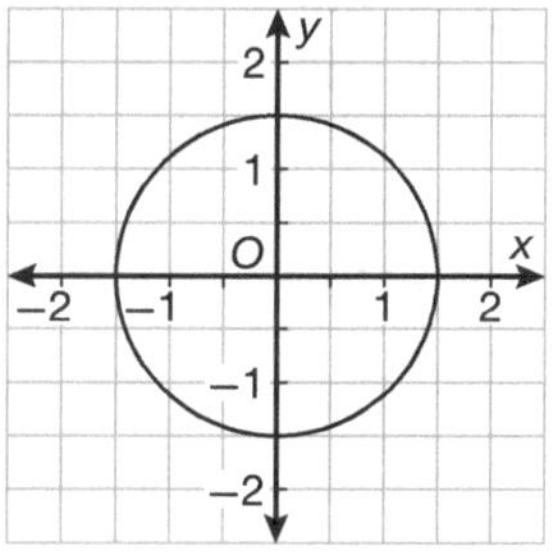

6. (39) **Error Analysis** Maddie measured the side lengths of a triangle and found them to be 2.4 centimeters, 3 centimeters, and 0.55 centimeters. How does she know that her measurements are incorrect without checking again?

7. (77) **Generalize** A property of a special cone is that its radius is the same as its height. Determine a formula for the total surface area of such a cone in terms of the radius, r.

* **8.** (79) **Verify** What is $m\angle BAC$?

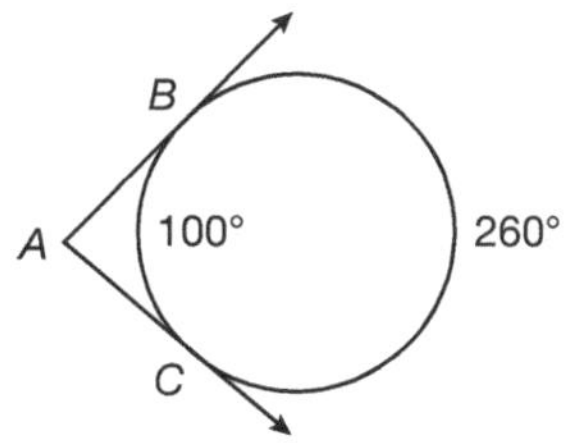

9. (45) Find the perimeter of a regular hexagon when the endpoints of one side are (2, 4) and (2, 2).

10. Algebra Find the range of values for x using the Hinge Theorem.
(Inv 4)

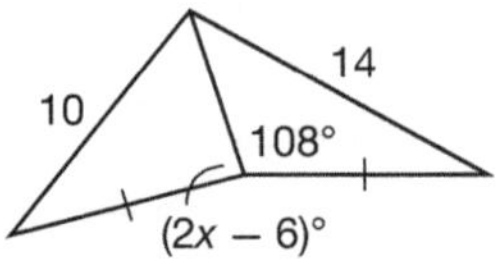

11. Write Describe the lines of symmetry and the rotational symmetry of a kite.
(76)

12. Multiple Choice Which could be the graph of cos x?
(Inv 7)

A

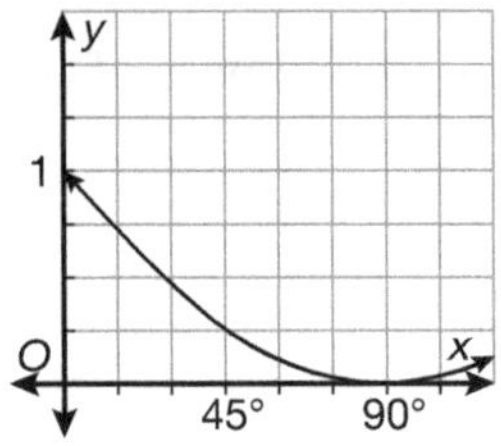

B

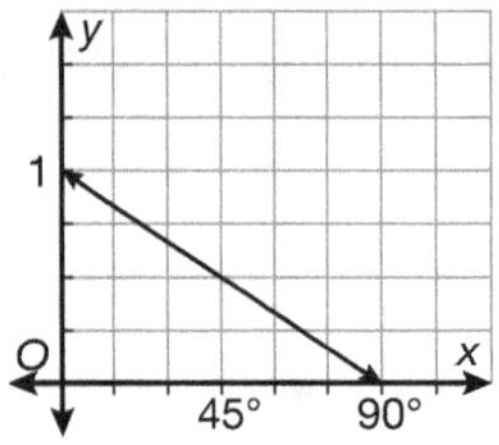

C

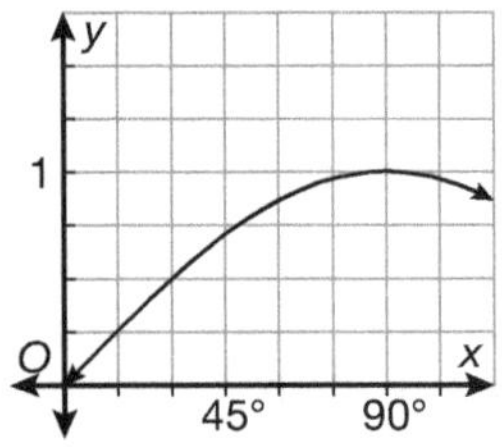

D

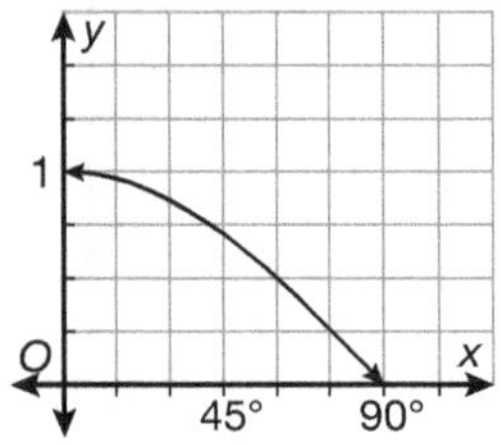

13. Chess A chessboard can be a model of a coordinate grid, where each space is 1 unit from its neighbors. In two moves, a chess piece starts at point X and moves to point Y. What vector represents this movement?
(71)

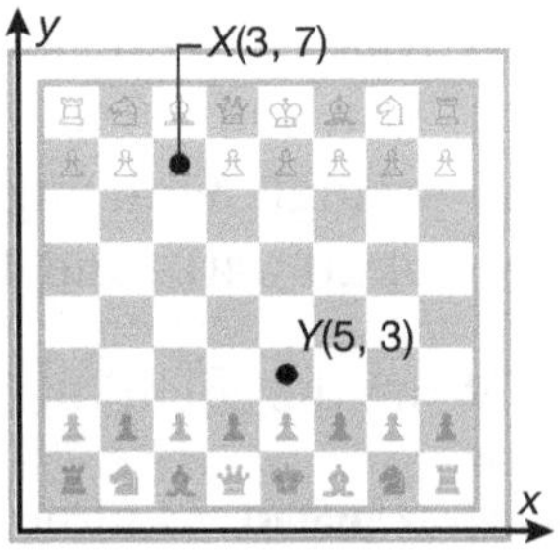

14. What is the volume of a cone with a radius of 8 millimeters and a slant height of 17 millimeters, to the nearest tenth of a millimeter?
(77)

15. Verify What are two similarities that show $\triangle ABC \sim \triangle ADE$?
(46)

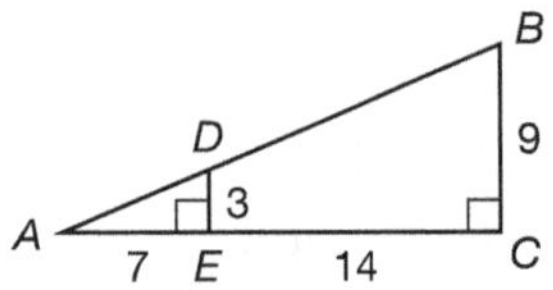

16. Find the distance between the line $y = x$ and the point (2, 8).
(42)

***17.** $\triangle DEF$ has vertices $D(3, -3)$, $E(0, -1)$, and $F(-2, -4)$. Graph $\triangle DEF$ and rotate it 180° counterclockwise about the origin. List the vertices of its image $\triangle D'E'F'$.
(78)

18. (69) **Painting** Kevin is painting a trapezoid in a mural. The height of the trapezoid is 3 feet and the length of the midsegment is 6 feet. If he can paint 9 square feet with one ounce of paint, how many ounces of paint does he need?

19. (72) Given that $C(-1, 2)$ is on circle A and $D(4, -1)$ is on circle B, determine the point of tangency of the two circles and the equation of the tangent line. Find the radius of each circle.

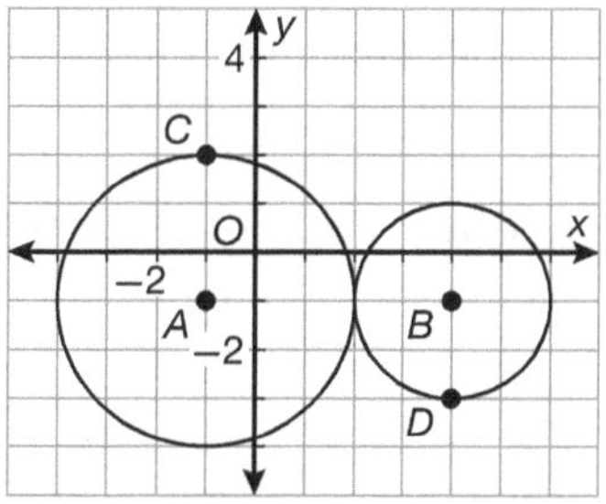

20. (58) **Logos** This logo consists of a circle tangent to the sides of a rhombus. The diagonal $\overline{AE}$ of the rhombus is 156 millimeters long, and the diameter $\overline{BF}$ of the circle is 60 millimeters long.
   a. Prove that $\triangle AOB$ is similar to $\triangle BOC$.
   b. What is the perimeter of the whole logo?

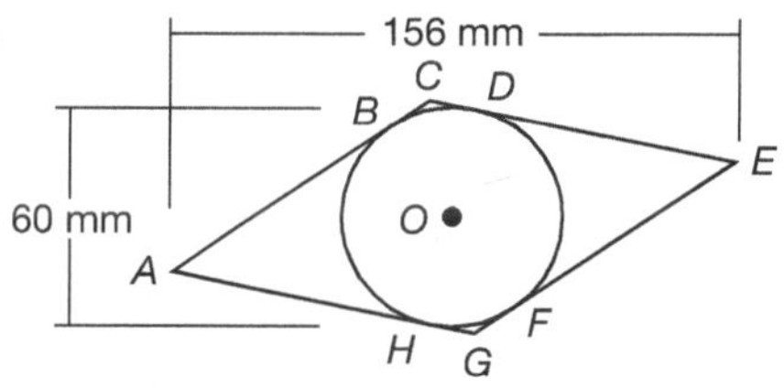

*21. (79) Find $m\angle Q$. $\overrightarrow{QR}$ is tangent at R.

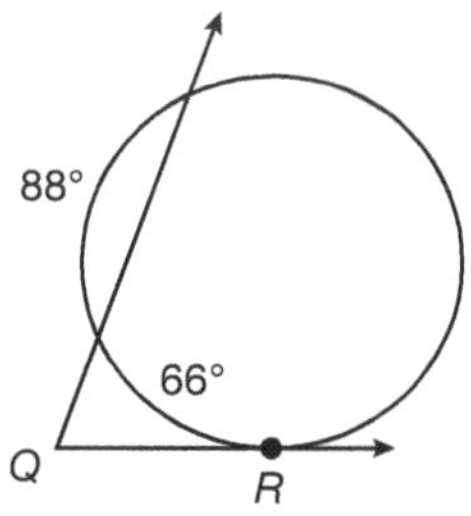

*22. (78) Line segment $\overline{AB}$ has endpoints $A(-4, -2)$ and $B(-1, 5)$. Graph the line segment, and then rotate it 180° counterclockwise about the origin. List the coordinates of the endpoints of its image, $\overline{A'B'}$.

23. (36) Use the Leg-Angle Congruence Theorem to show that $\triangle BCD \cong \triangle EFG$.

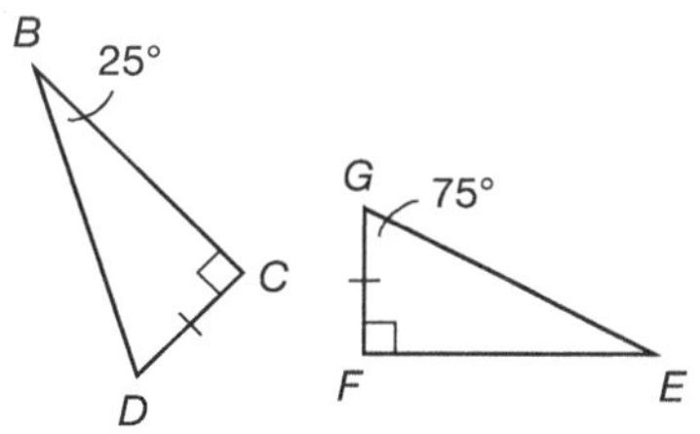

24. Write the equation of a circle with a center at (5.2, −3.4) and a diameter of 7.
(75)

*25. **Analyze** Write a paragraph proof of the third case of Theorem 79-1.
(31)
Given: secants $\overline{LJ}$ and $\overline{LN}$
Prove: $m\angle JLN = \frac{1}{2}(m\widehat{JN} - m\widehat{KM})$
Hint: Draw $\overline{JM}$.

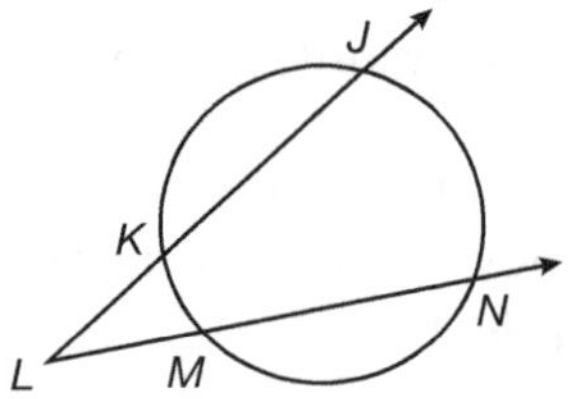

26. **Write** Explain how to find the other two side lengths of a 30°-60°-90° right triangle if you only know the length of the shorter leg.
(56)

*27. Find m∠1 in the figure below. Rays that appear to be tangent are tangent.
(79)

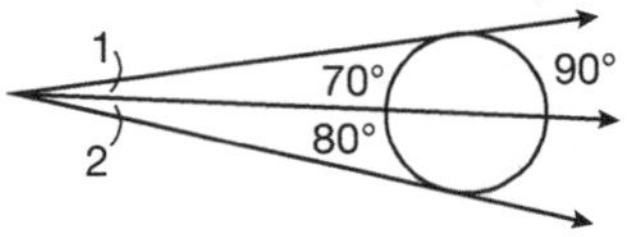

28. **Multi-Step** What is the lateral surface area of a right square pyramid if the area of its base is 64 square inches, and its height is 3 inches?
(70)

*29. **Gemstones** A piece of raw peridot is cut into a rectangular pyramid. Then, a triangular face is cut at each vertex. Find the number of sides, faces, and edges after all five vertices of the pyramid have been replaced by triangular faces. Verify your answers using Euler's Formula.
(49)

30. **Algebra** Find the value of x that makes the triangle a right triangle. Assume the side labeled $3x - 2$ is the largest side.
(33)

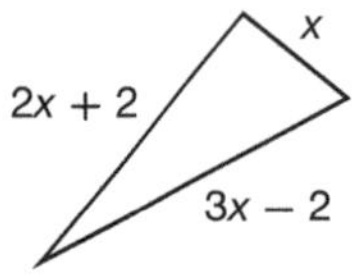

Name ______________________ Date __________ Class __________

Finding Surface Areas and Volumes of Spheres

LESSON 80

1. (50) Find the value of x.

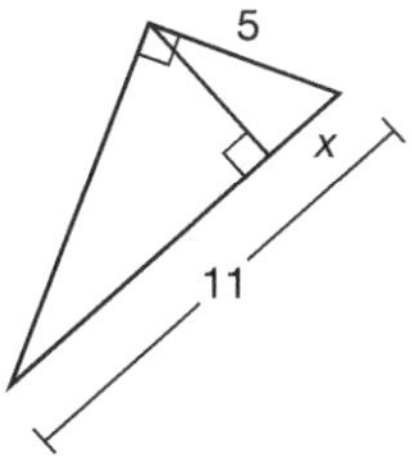

* **2.** (80) Find the surface area of a sphere with a radius of 25 inches, to the nearest tenth.

3. (64) Find the value of x and the measure of $\overset{\frown}{CD}$ in the figure. Line ℓ is tangent to the circle.

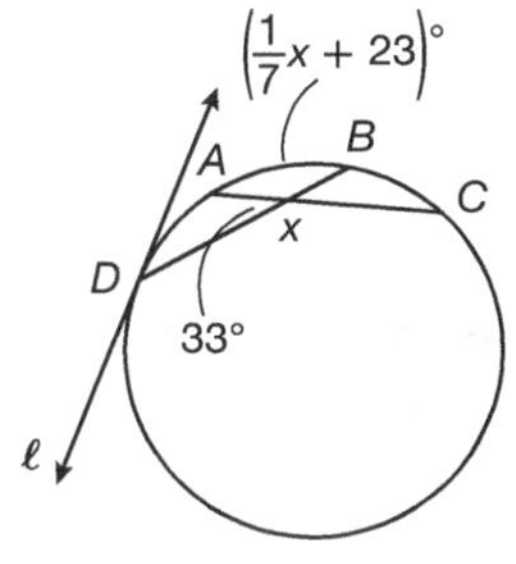

4. (37) Which pair of lines are parallel and which are perpendicular?

$y = 3x + 4$ $\quad$ $3y = x - 3$

$9y = -3x + 7$ $\quad$ $y = \frac{1}{3}x - 6$

5. (79) Find the measure of an angle formed by two tangents to a circle if they intercept an arc that measures 238°.

6. (73) **Write** Explain the relationship between the angle of elevation from point A to point B and the angle of depression from point B to point A.

7. (61) **Justify** Can it be concluded that this quadrilateral is a parallelogram? Explain.

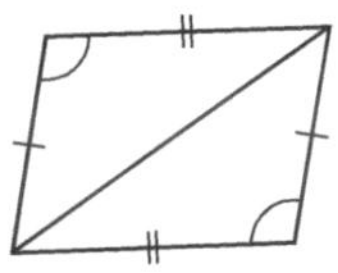

* **8.** (80) Find the approximate surface area and volume of a hemisphere with a diameter that is 23 yards long.

9. (40) **Vacuuming** Randy must vacuum his apartment, the floorplan of which is shown at right. If he vacuums one square foot per second, how long will it take him to vacuum his whole apartment, in minutes?

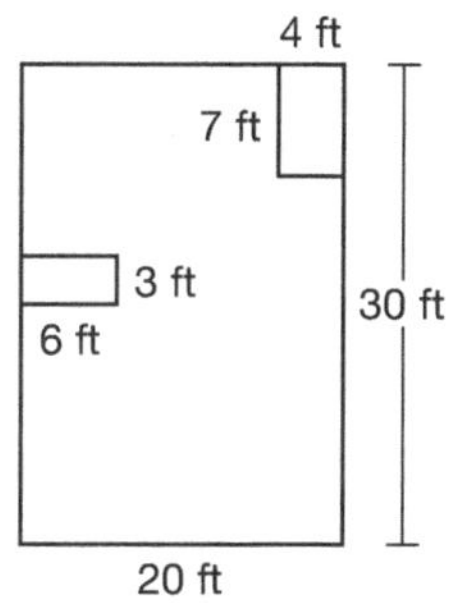

10. (78) Line segment $\overline{MN}$ has endpoints $M(-3, 3)$ and $N(4, -1)$. Graph the line segment, and then rotate it 270° counterclockwise about the origin. List the endpoints of its image, $\overline{M'N'}$.

11. (69) **Manufacturing** A factory manufactures kites that are each half blue and half red. Each kite has sides that are 8 inches and 1.5 feet long. The shortest diagonal of each kite is 10 inches long. What area of the kite is dyed red, to the nearest square inch?

12. **Algebra** Find the angle measures of quadrilateral *MNPQ* in the figure at right.
(47)

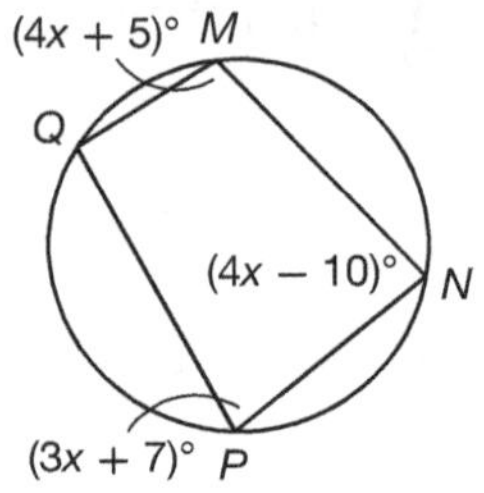

13. **Algebra** Write the inverse of the conditional statement. Is the inverse true?
(17)

If 3x + 2 = *11, then* x − 6 = −3

14. Find the magnitude of $\langle 6, -10 \rangle$ to the nearest tenth.
(63)

15. Find $m\angle TPR$ in the figure at right. $\overrightarrow{PR}$ is tangent to the circle at *R*.
(79)

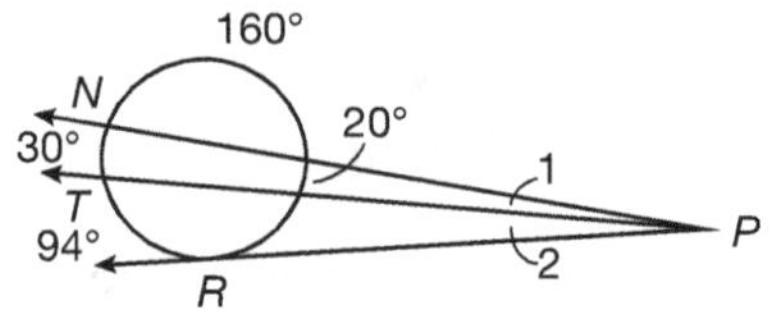

16. **Write** You are given two points on a circle. Is it possible to find an equation of the circle? Is it possible if you are given three non-collinear points? Explain.
(75)

***17.** **Globes** A globe has a circumference of 3 feet. Find the approximate volume of the globe.
(80)

18. **Write** What information would you need to know to conclude that the probability of a randomly chosen point on the figure shown here being blue is exactly 50%?
(Inv 6)

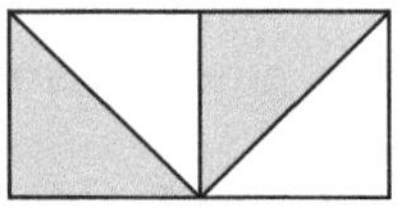

19. **Algebra** Square *DEFG* has vertices $D(x_1, 3)$, $E(6, 3)$, $F(6, 7)$, and $G(x_2, y_2)$. Find the values of x_1, x_2, and y_2.
(45)

20. **Algebra** Find the distance from the center of a circle with a 14-inch diameter to a chord that is 11 inches long.
(43)

21. Find $m\angle 1$ in the figure at right.
(79)

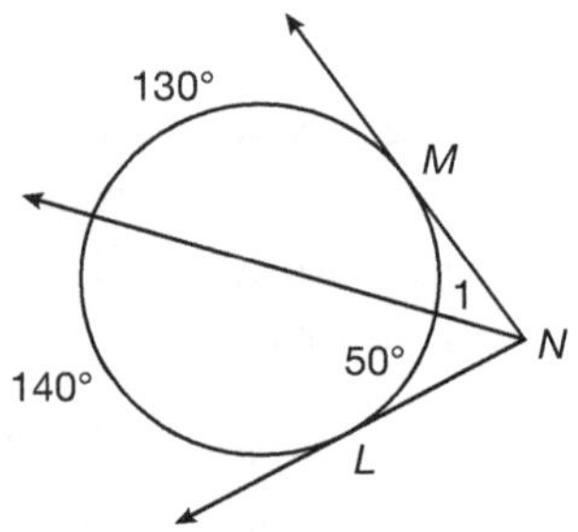

22. $\triangle BCD \sim \triangle QRS$. The ratio of their corresponding side lengths is 1:6. Given $BD = 2$, what is *QS*?
(44)

23. **Props** For a school play, Anita needs to build a regular, hexagonal pyramid. If the side lengths of the base are 3 inches and the slant height is 10 inches, what is the area of the piece of cardboard that Anita needs to use to make the pyramid, including the base?
(70)

24. **Multiple Choice** Which hypothesis below belongs to the converse of the following statement? *If two numbers are both odd or both even, then the sum of the numbers is even.*
(17)

A *Two numbers are odd and even*
B *The sum of two numbers is odd*
C *The sum of two numbers is even*
D *Two numbers are both odd or both even*

25. (77) **Food Preparation** What volume of ice cream will fit inside a cone that has a diameter of 2 inches and a lateral area of 15.7 square inches?

26. (41) Quadrilateral *LMNO* is similar to quadrilateral *BCDE*. If $m\angle B = 65°$, $m\angle C = 125°$, $m\angle D = 50°$, and $m\angle E = 120°$, what is the measure of each angle in quadrilateral *LMNO*?

***27.** (80) Find the approximate volume of the sphere at right.

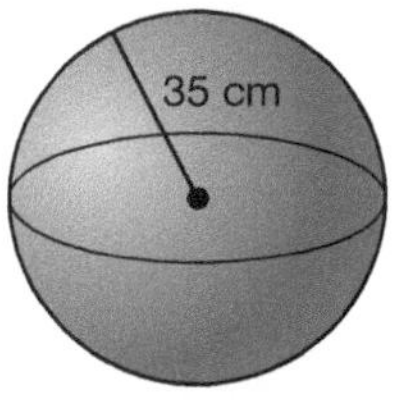

28. (35) Find the radius of the circle in which the area of a sector with a 45° interior angle is 2π.

29. (76) **Analyze** Make a conjecture for what natural values of n does the graph of the equation $y = x^n$ have rotational symmetry.

30. (78) Quadrilateral *JKLM* has vertices $J(1, 1)$, $K(2, 6)$, $L(5, 4)$, and $M(4, 0)$. Graph the quadrilateral, and then rotate it 180° counterclockwise about the origin. List the coordinates of the vertices of its image $J'K'L'M'$.

Name ______________________________ Date ____________ Class ____________

Graphing and Solving Linear Systems

LESSON 81

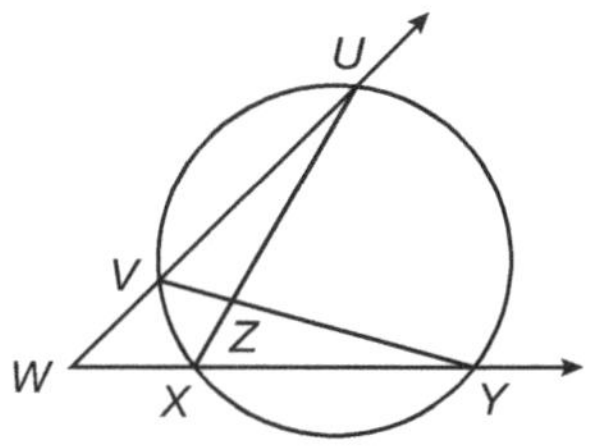

1. (79) **Justify** Two secants intersect in the exterior of the circle shown. Explain why it is true that for all cases, $m\angle UZY$ will be greater than $m\angle W$.

* **2.** (81) Solve the system of linear equations.

$y = 5x - 4$

$y = \frac{2}{3}x + 1$

3. (20) **Generalize** Suppose statement p is true, but statement q is not true.

a. Which is true: the statement "If p, then q," its converse, both, or neither? Use a truth table to answer.

b. If a biconditional is formed from the statement and its converse, is the biconditional true? Explain why or why not.

4. (55) Segment JK is a midsegment of $\triangle FGH$. Find the values of x and y.

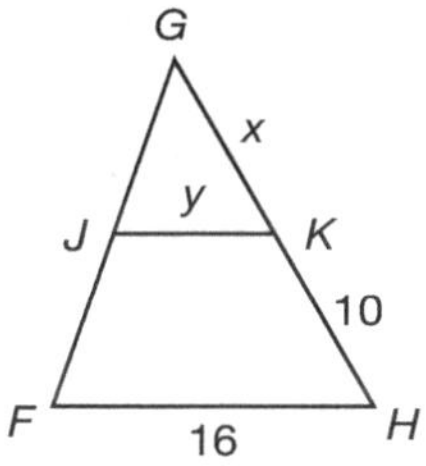

5. (Inv 7) **Multiple Choice** Which graph is the graph of tan x?
Hint: make a table of values.

A

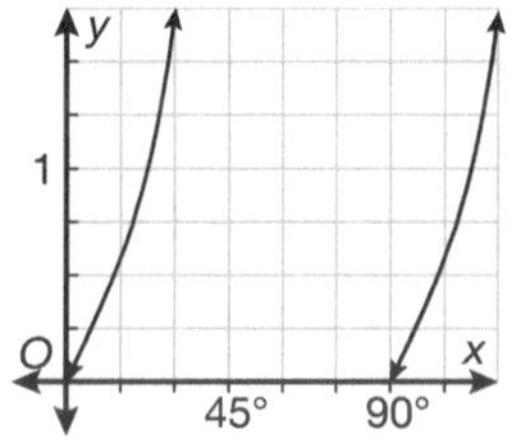

B

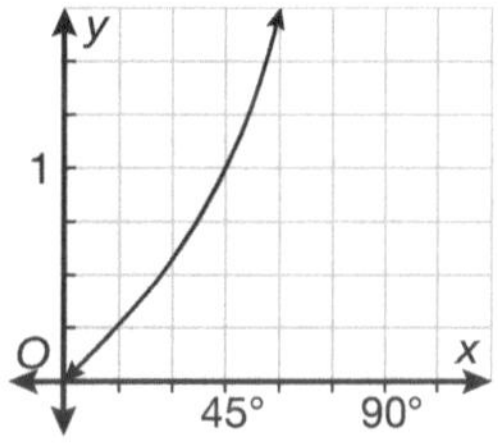

C

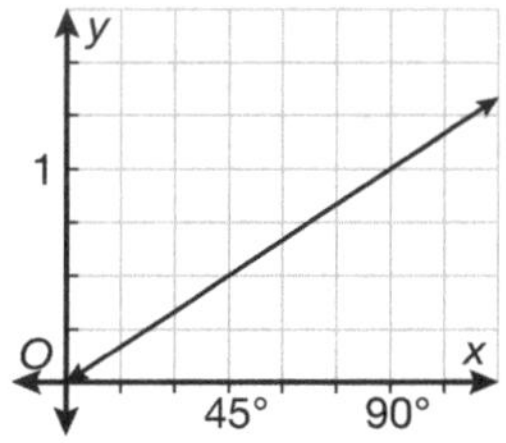

D

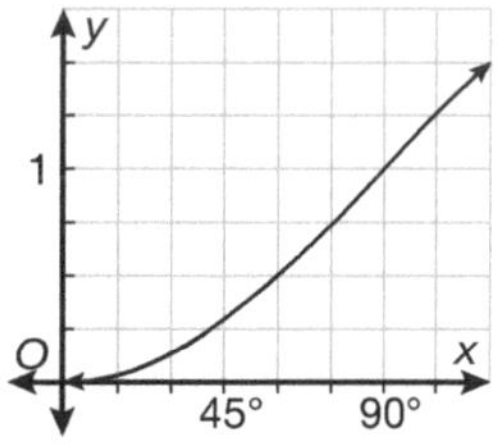

6. (77) **Manufacturing** A manufacturing company makes cone-shaped drinking cups. The height of the cone is 15 centimeters. What is the radius if the cone has a volume of 45π cubic centimeters?

* **7.** (Inv 8) **a.** Sketch this equilateral triangle and its rotation 60° clockwise about point F.

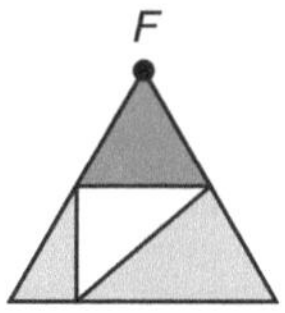

b. Repeat part **a** for clockwise rotations of 120°, 180°, 240°, and 300° about the apex of the original figure.

c. Describe the type and order of symmetry of your pattern from part **b**.

8. (69) **Generalize** Can the area of a trapezoid be calculated from its height, h, and the length of its midsegment, m? If so, determine a formula for the area in terms of h and m.

9. What is the volume of a cone with a base area of 6π square centimeters and a height of 7 centimeters? Leave your answer in terms of π.
(77)

*10. **Multi-Step** A circle with an area of 121π square inches is spun about its diameter to make a sphere. What is the volume of the sphere to the nearest cubic inch?
(80)

11. Determine the missing side lengths in $\triangle JKL$ to the nearest tenth of a centimeter.
(56)

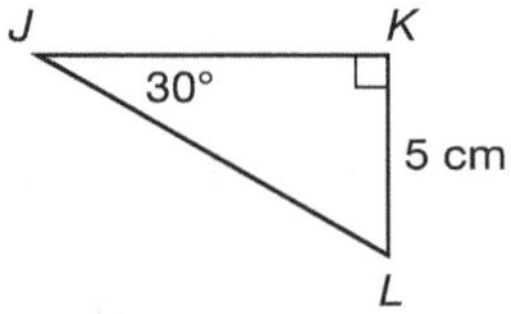

*12. **Pizza** One pizzeria sells a regular pizza for \$6 plus \$1.50 for each additional topping. Another pizzeria sells a regular pizza for \$8 plus \$0.50 for each additional topping. What number of toppings would make the regular pizzas from both places the same price? How much would a regular pizza cost with this number of toppings?
(81)

13. **Write** Is every equilateral triangle isosceles? Is every isosceles triangle equilateral? Explain.
(51)

14. **Theater** Elsie needs to make a paper hat shaped like a right cone. The hat must be 18 inches tall, and have a base radius of 4 inches. How much paper does she need, to the nearest square inch? *Hint: She does not need paper for the base of the cone.*
(77)

15. Find $m\angle C$ in the figure at right if $m\angle AFB = 100°$.
(79)

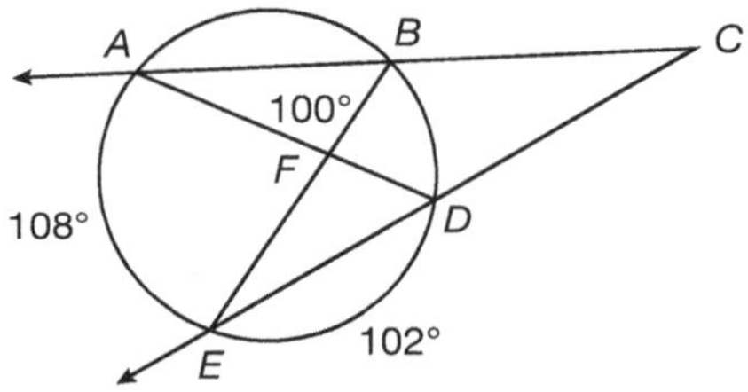

16. How many faces are there on a solid with 5 vertices and 8 edges?
(49)

17. Where is the orthocenter of a right triangle located?
(32)

18. **Multiple Choice** What is the hypothesis of the following conjecture?
(14)

If a pair of corresponding angles formed by a transversal ℓ are congruent, then lines m *and* n *are parallel.*

A *A pair of angles are corresponding angles*

B *A pair of angles are formed by a transversal*

C *Lines* m *and* n *are parallel*

D *A pair of corresponding angles formed by a transversal ℓ are congruent*

*19. **Algebra** The solution of a system of equations is $(-1, 1)$. One equation is $y = -x$ and the other equation is $y = \frac{2}{3}x + b$. What is the value of b?
(81)

20. Given that $\triangle JKL \sim \triangle PQR$, $JK = 21$, $PQ = 28$, and $QR = 48$, what is KL?
(46)

*21. **Write** Explain how the surface area and the volume of a sphere are different.
(80)

22. (Inv 4) **Algebra** Find the range of values of x that would cause $m\angle S$ to be larger than $m\angle P$.

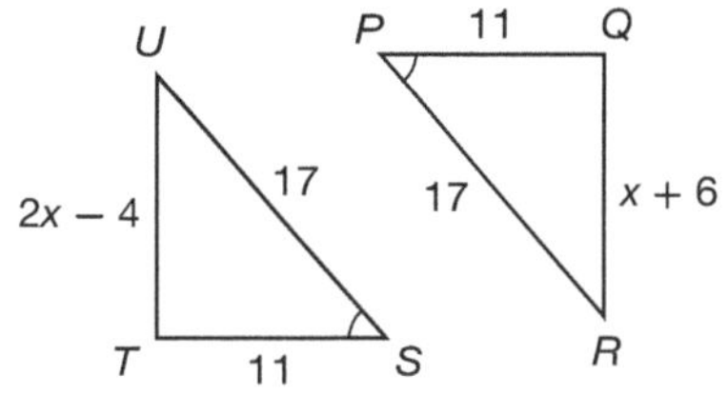

23. (Inv 5) **Model** Draw a net of a pentagonal pyramid.

24. (42) Find the distance to the nearest hundredth from the origin to the line $y = x + 6$.

*25. (81) **Error Analysis** Hector subtracted two equations, shown below. When he substituted into the original equations, he obtained two different answers. Where did he make his mistake? What is the correct answer?

$$y = \frac{5}{2}x + 1$$
$$\underline{-(y = -x - 3)}$$
$$0 = \frac{7}{2}x - 2$$
$$x = \frac{4}{7}$$

$$y = \frac{5}{2}\left(\frac{4}{7}\right) + 1$$
$$= \frac{17}{7}$$

$$y = -\left(\frac{4}{7}\right) - 3$$
$$= -\frac{25}{7}$$

26. (45) **Coordinate Geometry** A parallelogram has vertices $W(-6, -2)$, $X(-4, -2)$, $Y(x, y)$, and $Z(-4, -3)$. Find all possible values for x and y.

27. (36) In $\triangle ABC$ and $\triangle DEF$, $\angle B$ and $\angle E$ are right angles, $\overline{AC} \cong \overline{DF}$ and $\overline{BC} \cong \overline{EF}$. What theorem can be used to prove that $\triangle ABC \cong \triangle DEF$?

*28. (80) Find the volume of a sphere with a radius of 7 meters to the nearest square meter.

29. (78) **Propellers** The propeller of an airplane rotates counterclockwise. Find the angle of rotation required for propeller blade P to move to position P'. Explain.

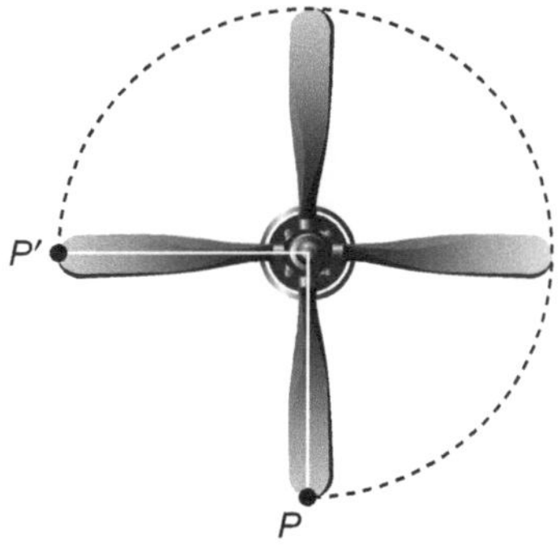

30. (39) Find the range of possible lengths for the third side of a triangle with two sides that are 22 centimeters and 14 centimeters long, respectively.

Name ______________________ Date __________ Class __________

More Applications of Trigonometry

LESSON 82

1. (82) Find θ_1 and θ_2 to the nearest degree.

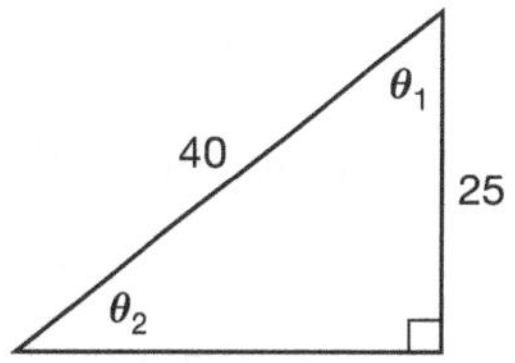

2. (69) **Multi-Step** A trapezoid has vertices at the points $P(1, 3)$, $Q(4, 6)$, $R(6, 6)$, and $S(0, 0)$. Determine which segments are the bases of the trapezoid. Explain.

3. (Inv 6) **Carnival Games** A carnival game involves dropping a ping-pong ball down a chute so that it randomly lands on a platform that is shown on the right. The player wins a prize if the ball lands in the square or an extra game token if the ball lands in the trapezoid. Both the square and the trapezoid are 5 centimeters tall. What is the probability of a player winning a prize? ...winning a token? ...winning nothing?

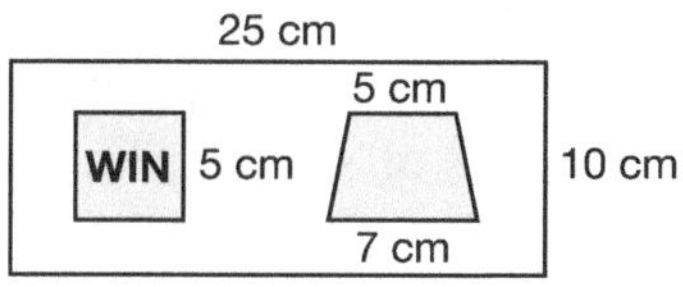

* **4.** (81) **Algebra** The solution to the linear system $x = -3$, $y = mx - \frac{7}{2}$ is $(-3, 1)$. What is the value of m?

5. (52) Quadrilateral $KLMN$ is a rhombus with its center point labeled P. If $m\angle PKL = 57°$, what is $m\angle PLK$?

6. (43, 68) **Write** Explain how to use trigonometry to find the length of the radius of a circle, given a 9-inch chord that is 2.2 inches from the center of the circle. What is the length of the radius?

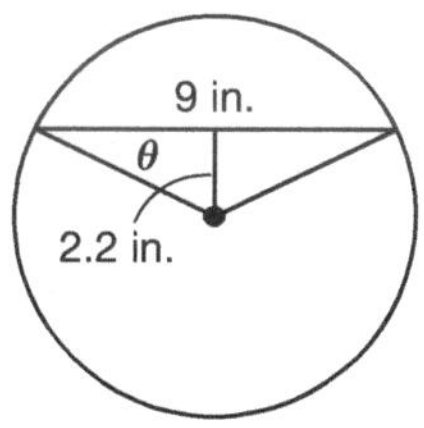

7. (80) Find the approximate surface area of a sphere whose great circle has an area of 85.2 square centimeters.

8. (47) Find $m\angle SRT$ in the figure at right.

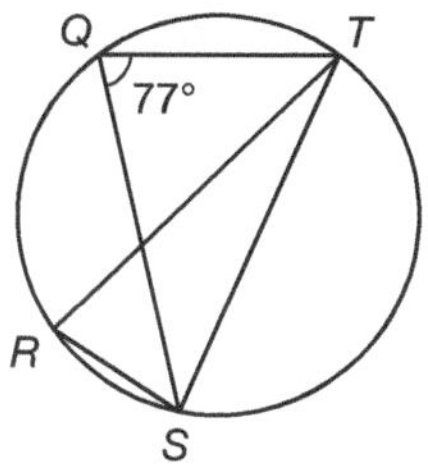

9. (71) The vertices of a triangle are $J(0, 1)$, $K(4, 2)$ and $L(3, -1)$. The triangle is translated according to the vector $\langle -4, 2 \rangle$. Find the coordinates of the vertices of the image.

***10.** (82) **Multiple Choice** Which statement is *not* true about the right triangle shown?

A $\tan^{-1}\frac{b}{a} = \tan^{-1}\frac{a}{b}$ **B** $\tan^{-1}\frac{b}{a} = \sin^{-1}\frac{b}{c}$

C $\cos^{-1}\frac{a}{c} = \sin^{-1}\frac{b}{c}$ **D** $\tan^{-1}\frac{a}{b} = \cos^{-1}\frac{b}{c}$

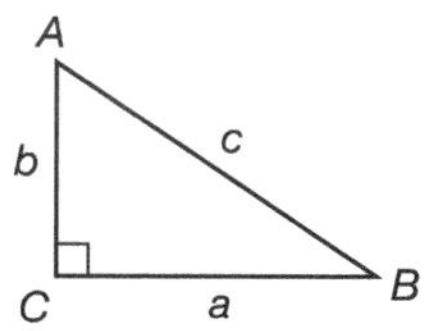

11. (76) How many lines of symmetry does a regular pentagon have?

12. (60) **Justify** Determine whether lines $\overline{NO}$ and $\overline{PQ}$ are parallel. How do you know?

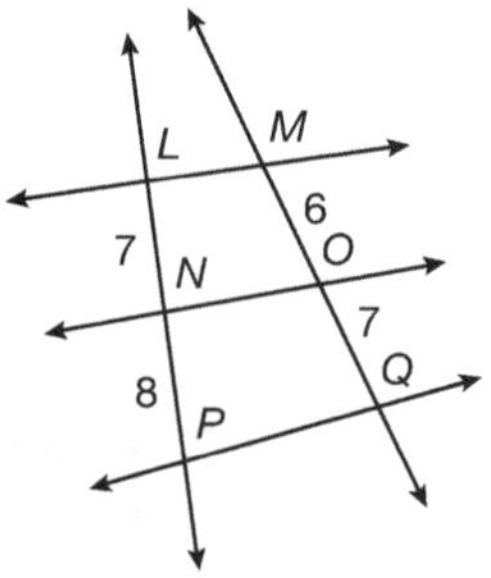

13. (34) **Multiple Choice** Which quadrilateral has diagonals of equal lengths?

A parallelogram　　**B** kite
C rhombus　　**D** rectangle

14. (Inv 8) **Retail Displays** Cans of soup are stacked in a triangular shape as a display in a supermarket. If there are 8 rows of soup cans, how many cans of soup are in the display?

***15.** (82) **Surveying** A surveyor needs to calculate the angle of the sun using the shadow cast by the building. Use the diagram to find θ to the nearest degree.

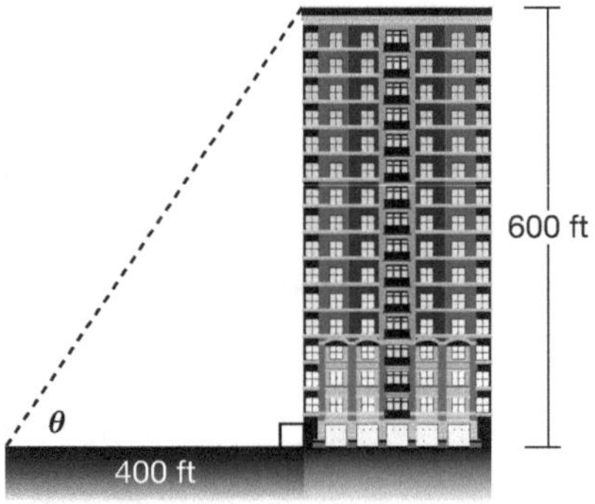

16. (74) **Error Analysis** Reuben calculates that a reflection of $\triangle TLV$ across the line $x + y = 0$ maps the three points as follows:

$T(3, 1) \rightarrow T'(-3, -1)$
$L(4, 2) \rightarrow L'(-4, -2)$
$V(-2, 4) \rightarrow V'(2, -4)$

a. Plot Reuben's reflection. What error has he made?
b. Plot the correct reflection image $\triangle A'B'C'$ and $\triangle ABC$ on the same graph.

17. (51) **Justify** In $\triangle LMN$, $m\angle L = 140°$ and $m\angle M = 20°$.

a. Determine $m\angle N$, and classify $\triangle LMN$ by its sides and angles.
b. Which angle is the vertex angle, and why?

***18.** (72) **Landscaping** A garden is constructed with two paths that are tangent to each of the circular flower beds. Are there other possibilities for common tangent paths in the garden? If so, sketch the possibilities.

***19.** (81) Find the solution for the following system of equations.
$y = -2x - 5, y = x + 1$

20. (79) Find $m\angle 2$ in the figure at right.

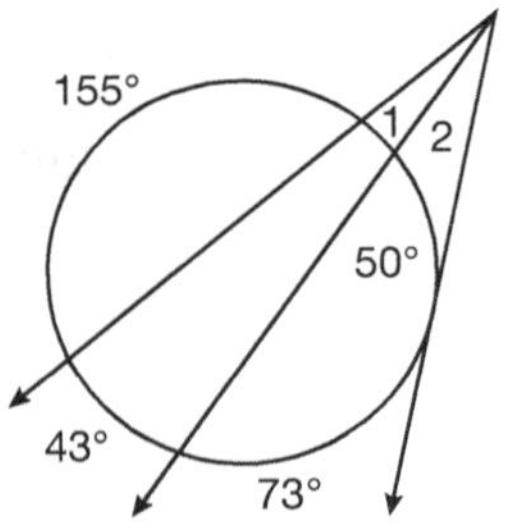

21. (16) **Generalize** Substitute (x, y) for (x_2, y_2) into the slope formula, and transform it into a linear equation. Describe this form of the equation of a line. How can the slope-intercept form be found from it?

*22. Find the solution for the system of equations. $y = \frac{3}{2}x + 4$, $y = -\frac{1}{3}x - \frac{10}{3}$
(81)

23. **Art** Javier is tracing a circular pattern for an art project. He places the two endpoints of a diameter at (3, 4) and (9, 12). What is the equation of the circle Javier traces out?
(75)

24. Find the value of x and y in the figure shown.
(50)

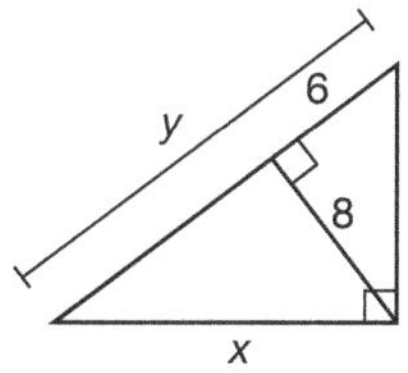

25. Find the approximate surface area and volume of a hemisphere with a radius of 20 inches.
(80)

26. **Algebra** Find the value of x that makes $\triangle RST$ a right triangle.
(33)

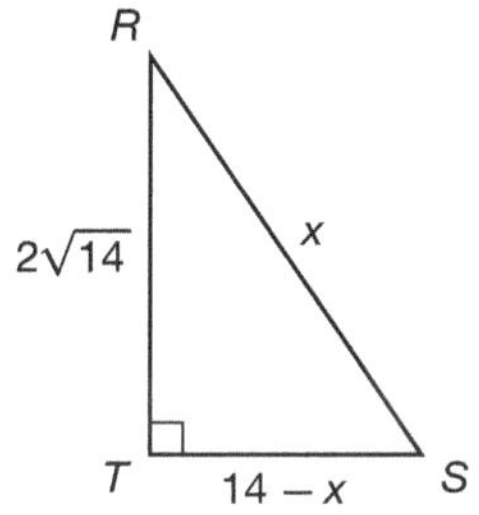

27. **Justify** Fill in the missing justifications in this proof of the Converse of the Same-Side Interior Angles Theorem.
(27)
Given: $\angle 1$ is supplementary to $\angle 2$.
Prove: $p \parallel r$

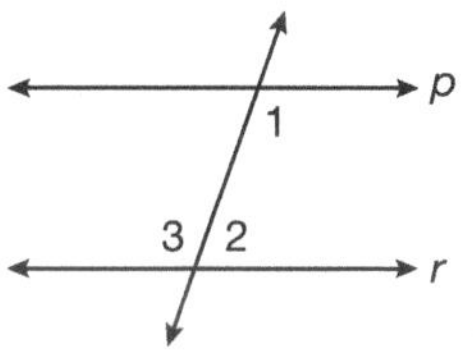

Statements	Reasons
1. $\angle 1$ is supplementary to $\angle 2$	1.
2. $m\angle 1 + m\angle 2 = 180°$	2.
3. $m\angle 2 + m\angle 3 = 180°$	3.
4. $m\angle 1 + m\angle 2 = m\angle 2 + m\angle 3$	4. Transitive Property of Equality
5. $m\angle 1 = m\angle 3$	5.
6. $p \parallel r$	6. Converse of the Corresponding Angles Postulate

*28. **Algebra** The perimeter of a right triangle is 12 inches and the legs are $x + 2$ and $x + 1$. The hypotenuse is $x + 3$. What are the measures of the two acute angles, to the nearest degree?
(82)

29. Determine the perimeter of this figure.
(40)

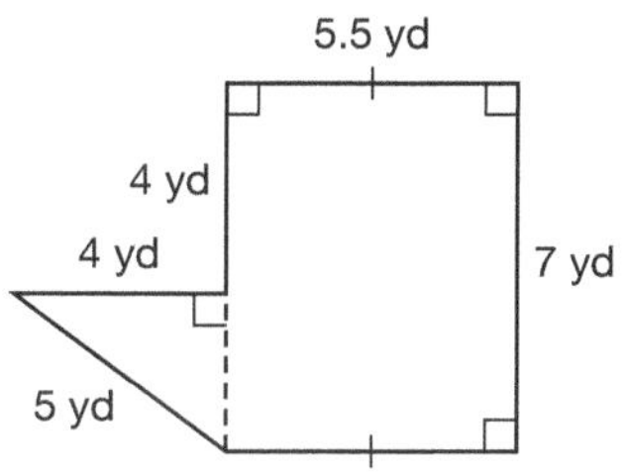

30. The perimeter of equilateral $\triangle WXY$ is 24 inches. If $\triangle WXY \sim \triangle RST$, and the ratio of their corresponding sides is 4:1, what are the lengths of the sides of $\triangle RST$?
(44)

Name ______________________ Date ____________ Class ____________

Vector Addition

LESSON 83

1. Given $\tan X = \frac{5}{4}$, which angle in $\triangle RST$ is $\angle X$, θ_1 or θ_2?
(82)

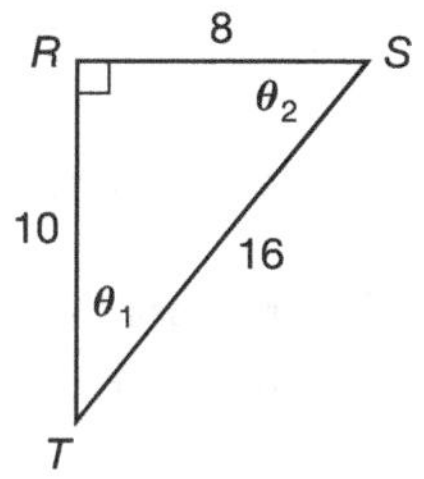

2. What is the perimeter of a regular hexagon with an apothem length of $28\sqrt{3}$ meters?
(66)

3. **Analyze** How many lines of symmetry does a semicircle have? How many lines of symmetry does a circle have?
(76)

4. In $\triangle PQR$ and $\triangle STU$, $PQ = UT$, $PR = TS$, and $m\angle RPQ = m\angle UTS$. Which triangles are congruent?
(28)

5. Compare $m\angle ADB$ and $m\angle DBC$ in the figure shown.
(Inv 4)

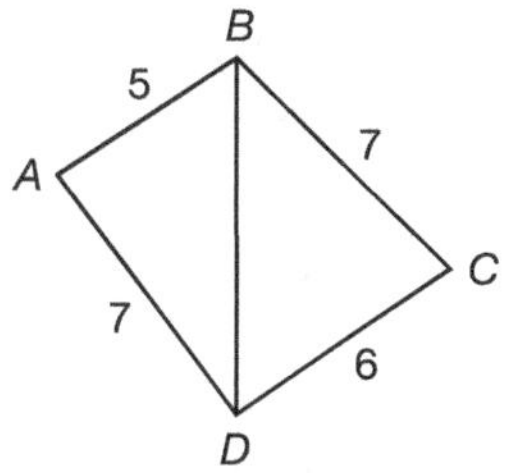

***6.** Find the magnitude of the sum of the vectors $\langle 4, 5\rangle$ and $\langle -2, 2\rangle$. Round your answer to the nearest hundredth.
(83)

7. Find the exact length of the hypotenuse of a 45°-45°-90° right triangle with a side length of 5 inches.
(53)

8. **Candles** Kyle bought a candle in the shape of a right cone. The candle has a height of 7 inches and a base radius of 1 inch. What is the volume of the candle to the nearest hundredth?
(77)

***9.** Classify this prism.
(49, Inv 5)

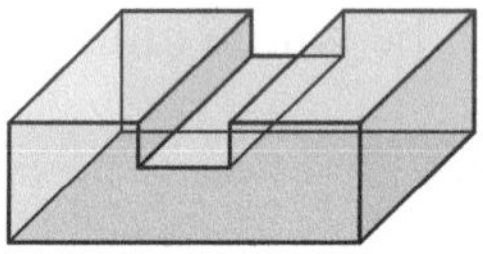

***10.** **Running** A runner runs diagonally across a field. She runs 80 meters north and 50 meters east. How far did she run and what angle did her path make with the horizontal, to the nearest degree?
(83)

11. A reflection across the line $x = 4$ maps $\odot C$ to $\odot C'$. Find the coordinates of the center and the radius of $\odot C'$.
(74)

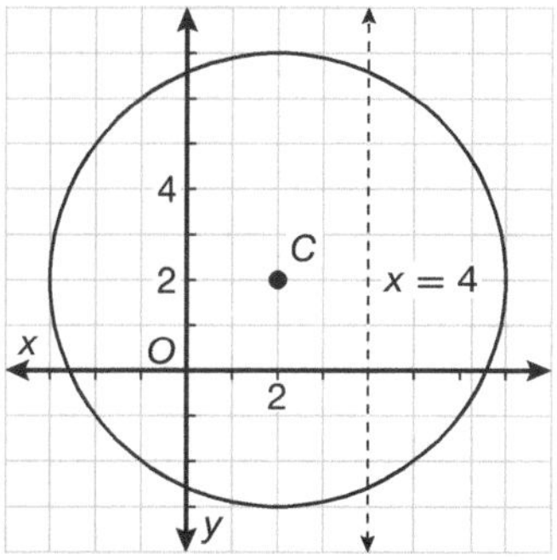

12. **Estimate** Estimate the volume of a cylindrical fuel drum with a height of 68 centimeters and a radius of 33 centimeters.
(62)

***13.** **Multiple Choice** The direction of each vector is given in degrees counterclockwise from the positive x-axis. Which of the following is incorrect?
(83)

A $\langle 3, 4\rangle$, 53° **B** $\langle 7, 2\rangle$, 16°
C $\langle 4, 7\rangle$, 30° **D** $\langle 2, 5\rangle$, 68°

14. (Inv 2) **Justify** Cyndie knows that r and s are parallel, so she writes "$\angle 4 \cong \angle 8$". What postulate or theorem justifies her statement?

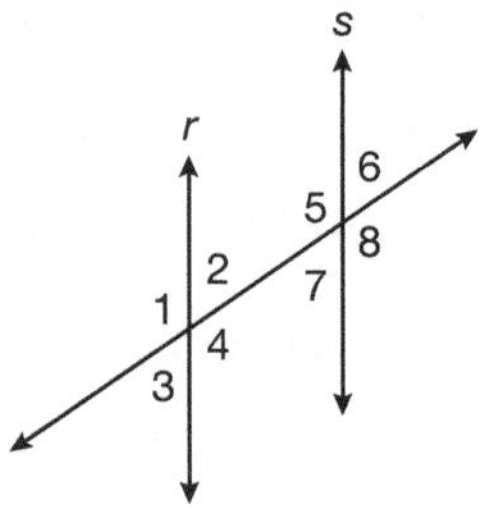

15. (81) **Algebra** A system of equations has no solution. One equation is $y = 6x + 4$ and the other equation is $y = \frac{a}{2}x - 1$. Find the value of a.

16. (40) **Crafts** Students at Franklin School are cutting out and decorating cardboard letters for a display. If they remove two squares from a rectangular piece of cardboard to form the letter E, what is the area of the letter they must decorate?

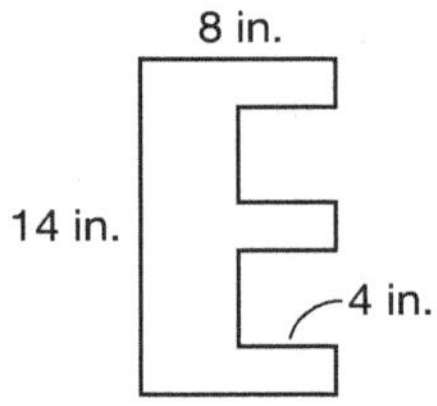

***17.** (83) **Algebra** Find the resultant vector sum of $\vec{a}$, $\vec{b}$, and $\vec{c}$ if $\vec{a} = \langle 2, 3 \rangle$,
$\vec{b} = 2\vec{a}$, and $\vec{c} = -\vec{a}$.

18. (45) **Coordinate Geometry** A square is placed on the coordinate plane so that two vertices are located at (0, 0) and (0, b). Give possible locations for the other two vertices.

19. (73) **Bird Watching** Vic sees a bird resting on a telephone pole. He is standing 40 meters from the base of the pole and he sees the bird at an angle of elevation of 17°. How far is Vic from the bird, to the nearest meter?

20. (80) **Write** Why can the radius and volume of a sphere never both be whole numbers?

21. (Inv 5) **Multiple Choice** Which of these figures is not the net of a cube?

A
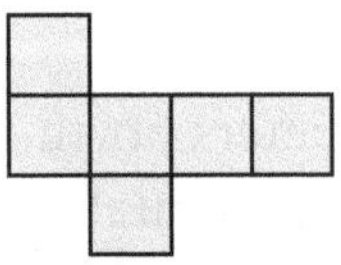

B
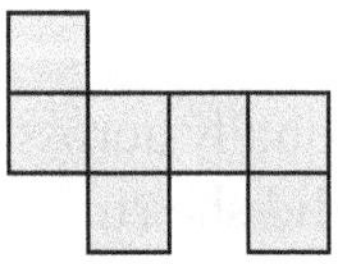

C
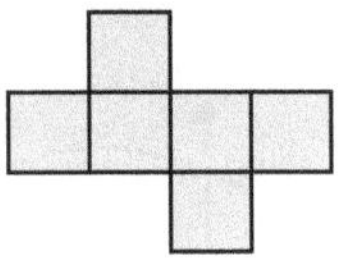

D
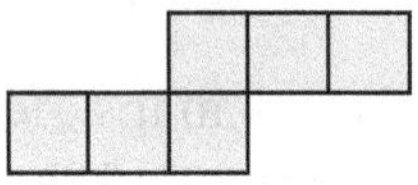

22. (82) Simplify the expression $\tan^{-1}[\tan(15°)]$.

23. (42) What is the distance from $(-1, -4)$ to the line $y = 0$?

24. (73) **Hiking** A hill makes an angle of elevation of 34°. If a hiker climbs to an altitude of 40 meters, what distance has he walked? Round your answer to the nearest meter.

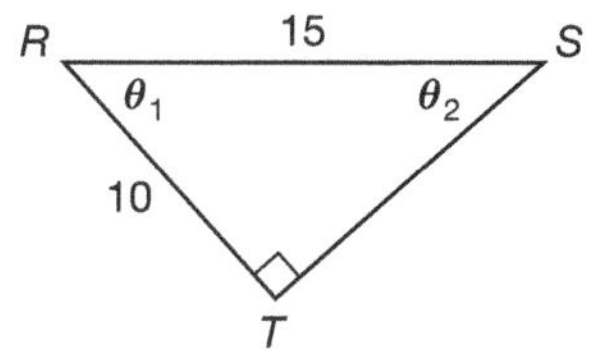

25. Find the measures of the acute angles in the right triangle. Round your answer to the nearest degree.
(82)

26. **Analyze** How many solutions will the system of equations $y = 2$ and $y = 4$ have? Why?
(81)

27. **Algebra** Two lines are perpendicular. One line has an equation of $rx + 3y = 4$ and the other line has an equation of $\frac{2}{s}x + y = 6$. Find a linear equation to describe the relationship between r and s.
(37)

28. **Multi-Step** Use the head-to-tail method to find the resultant vector of the sum of $\vec{a} = \langle 6, 5\rangle$, $\vec{b} = \langle 3, -2\rangle$, and $\vec{c} = \langle 7, -1\rangle$. Then find its magnitude to the nearest hundredth.
(83)

29. Find the volume, surface area, and lateral surface area of a cube with edge lengths of $4\sqrt{3}$ inches.
(59)

30. **Error Analysis** A student was asked to find $m\angle C$.
(79)

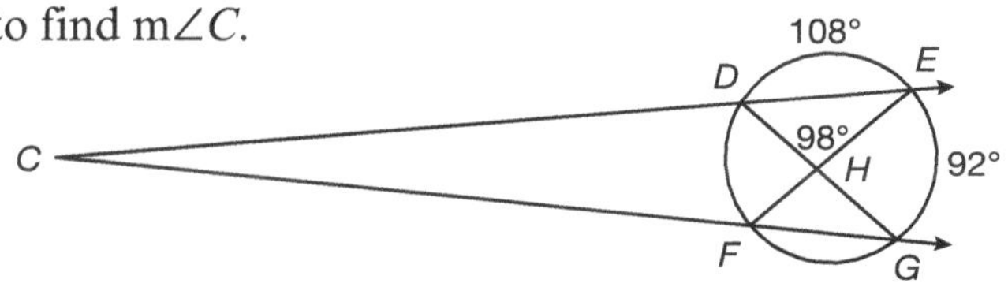

$$m\angle DHE = \frac{1}{2}(m\widehat{DE} - m\widehat{FG})$$
$$98° = \frac{1}{2}(108° - m\widehat{FG})$$
$$44° = -\frac{1}{2}m\widehat{FG}$$
$$-88° = m\widehat{FG}$$

The student didn't know how to finish. Explain the student's error and calculate $m\angle C$.

Name ________________________________ Date ____________ Class ____________

Dilations

LESSON 84

* **1.** Apply a dilation to $\triangle ABC$ using a scale factor of 2 and center D.
(84)

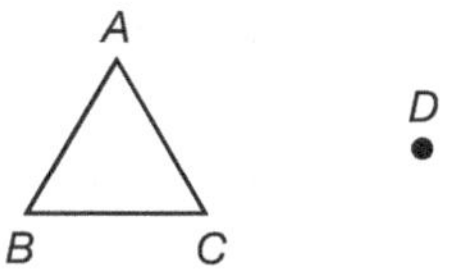

2. Find the solution for the system of equations. $y = 2x + 6$, $y = 2$
(81)

3. **Cooking** One cup is equivalent to 14.44 cubic inches. If a one-cup cylindrical measuring cup has a radius of 1.75 inches, what is its height to the nearest tenth?
(62)

4. **Predict** If $\odot B$ is enlarged, but continues to pass through point A, will it remain tangent to $\odot C$? If not, when will it *not* be tangent to $\odot C$?
(72)

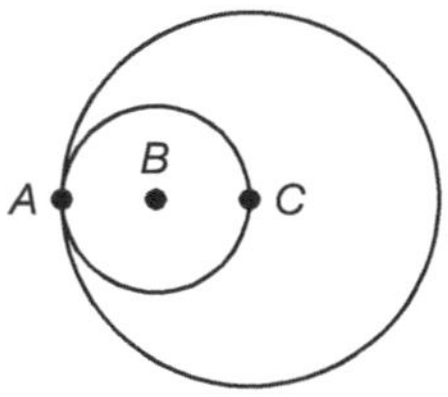

5. **Snow Sculpture** Lee is making a figure out of snow. If he makes his figure out of three spheres of snow with radii that are 1 foot, 2 feet, and 3 feet, respectively, what total volume of snow does he use, to the nearest cubic foot?
(80)

6. **Algebra** If two vectors have the sum of $\langle 3, a \rangle$ and one vector is $\langle 6, a \rangle$, what is the value of the other vector?
(83)

7. **Multiple Choice** The paths in a park are shown. Which of these routes represents the longest walk?
(39)

A A to B to D **B** A to D to B

C C to B to D **D** C to D to B

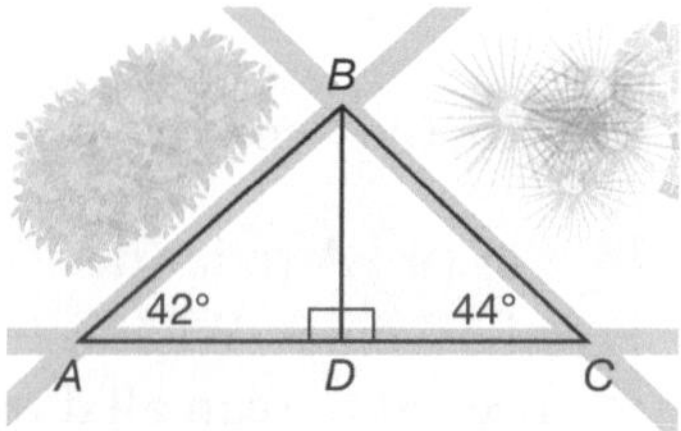

8. **Write** Explain how to determine whether a parallelogram is a rectangle.
(52)

9. Rectangle $MNPQ$ has vertices $M(6, 6)$, $N(6, 3)$, $P(-3, 3)$, and $Q(-3, 6)$. Graph its image after a dilation with the center at the origin and a scale factor of $\frac{1}{3}$.
(84)

10. Given $\cos X = \frac{3}{5}$, what is the measure of $\angle X$, θ_1 or θ_2?
(82)

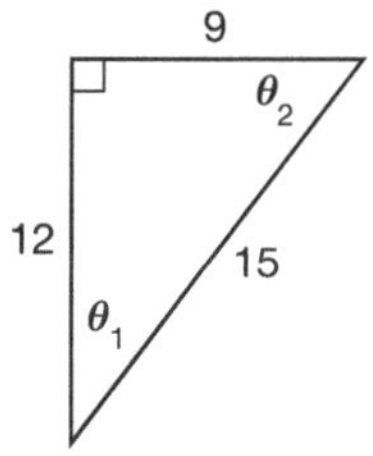

11. **Verify** Show, using an indirect proof, that it is impossible for the area of the base of a regular pyramid to equal the lateral surface area of the pyramid.
(70)

12. Use Euler's Formula to determine how many faces a polyhedron with 15 edges and 10 vertices has.
(49)

13. (58) **Astronomy** The Moon's orbit is not exactly circular, but the average distance from its surface to Earth's surface is 384,000 kilometers. The diameter of the Moon is 3476 kilometers. Find the distance to the nearest kilometer from the surface of Earth to the visible edge of the Moon, if the Moon is directly above the observer. *(Note: the figure is not drawn to scale.)*

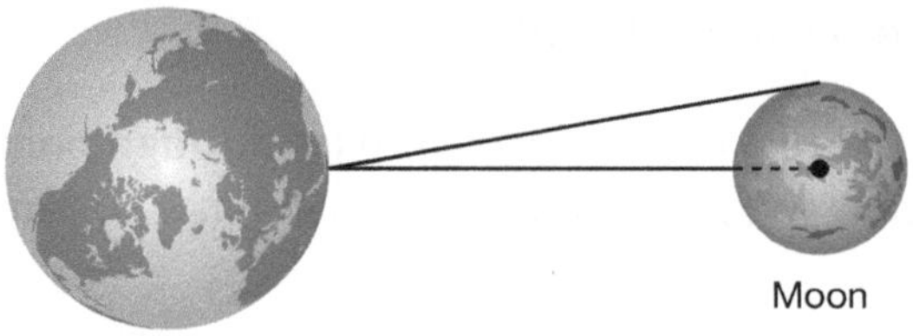

14. (78) $\triangle MNP$ has vertices $M(6, 1)$, $N(2, 1)$, and $P(1, 4)$. Graph $\triangle MNP$ and rotate it 270° counterclockwise about the origin. List the coordinates of the vertices of $\triangle M'N'P'$.

15. (45) Rhombus $STUV$ has vertices $S(3, -1)$, $T(6, 3)$, $U(x, y)$, and $V(7, -4)$. Find x and y.

*16. (83) **Multi-Step** Find the angle the resultant vector makes with the horizontal if $\vec{a} = \langle 4, 3 \rangle$ and $\vec{b} = \langle -2, 3 \rangle$. Round your answer to the nearest degree.

17. (10) Use the Venn diagram to write a conditional statement.

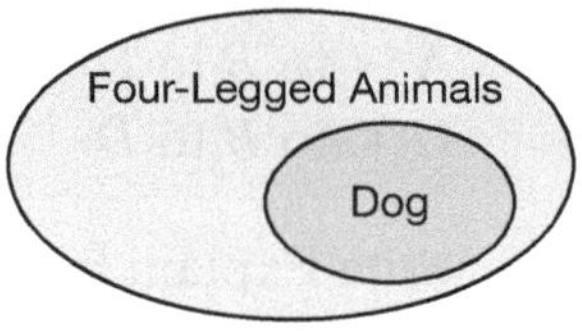

18. (35) **Radar** A radar device scans an arc of 80° out to a distance of 10 miles. What is the minimum number of such devices needed to scan all directions around an area? What would the area of the overlap be? Express your answer in terms of π.

*19. (84) **Photocopiers** A rectangular design with sides that are 12 centimeters long and a width of 8 centimeters is enlarged on a photocopier by 175%. What are the dimensions of the enlarged design? How do the areas of the original design and the copy compare?

20. (47) **Algebra** Find the value of a if $\overline{JL}$ is a diameter.

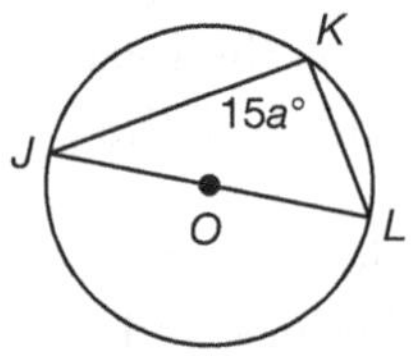

21. (65) **Write** How do you know that one half of a diagonal is congruent to one half of the other diagonal in a rectangle?

22. (75) What is the equation of a circle centered at $(-1, 5)$, with a diameter of 16?

23. (82) Find the measures of the acute angles in the right triangle. Round your answers to the nearest degree.

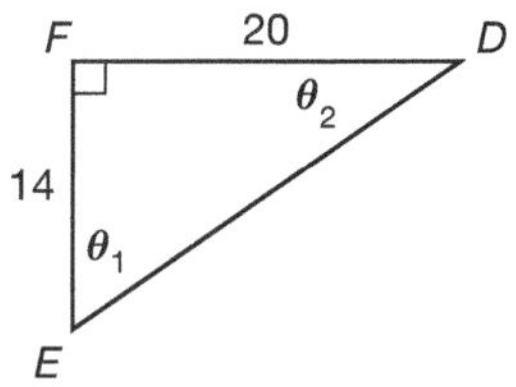

24. (50) If 3.2 is the geometric mean between two values, what is the product of the two values?

25. (41) For every 13 pennies in a bag of coins, there are 3 dimes and 1 quarter. If there are 325 pennies in the bag, how many dimes and quarters are there?

26. (83) Use the head-to-tail method to find the resultant vector of the sum of $\vec{d}\langle -2, -1\rangle$, $\vec{e}\langle 5, 4\rangle$, and $\vec{f}\langle -5, -1\rangle$.

27. (12) **a.** Identify two pairs of same-side interior angles in this figure.
b. Given that ∠3 and ∠8 are supplementary, prove that lines *a* and *b* are parallel.

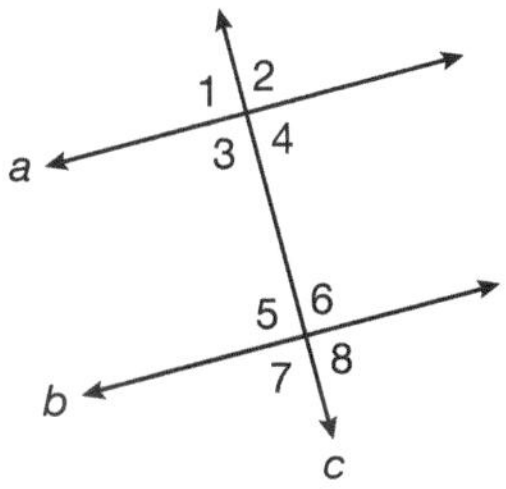

28. (Inv 8) **Formulate** Monostrips are formed by placing black or white square tiles in a row, from left to right. The order of tiles matters: for example, ■■□ and □■■ count as different monostrips.

a. How many different 5-tile monostrips can you form?

b. How many of these monostrips have exactly 2 black tiles?
Hint: Count like this:

■■□□□ □■■□□ ...
■□■□□ □■□■□ ...
■□□■□ ...
■□□□■

c. How many different *n*-tile monostrips can you form? How many of these have 2 black tiles?

29. (43) **Algebra** A circle has a diameter of 15 inches, and a chord that is 7 inches long. What is the distance from the chord to the center of the circle? Express your answer in simplified radical form.

***30.** (84) Draw the image of $\triangle XYZ$ under a dilation with scale factor $\frac{1}{2}$ and center *C*.

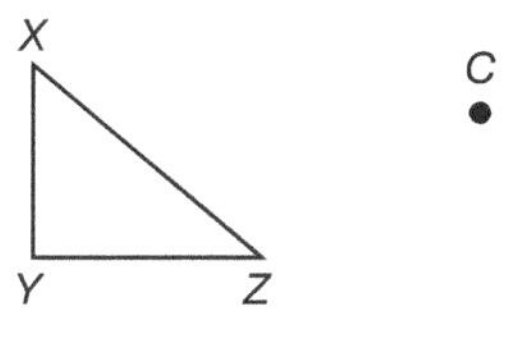

Name ______________________ Date __________ Class __________

Cross Sections of Solids

LESSON 85

1. (82) **Architecture** This decorative gate uses right triangles as supports. Find θ to the nearest degree.

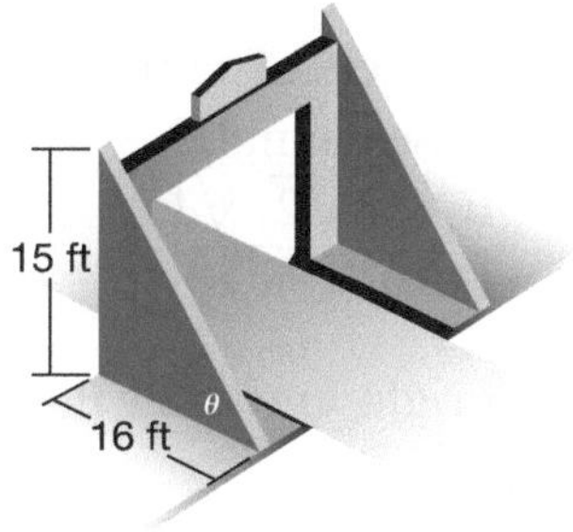

* **2.** (85) **Multiple Choice** Which of the following solids could not give a triangular cross section?

A cube **B** triangular prism
C square pyramid **D** cylinder

3. (71) What vector translates $\triangle ABC$ onto $\triangle A'B'C'$?

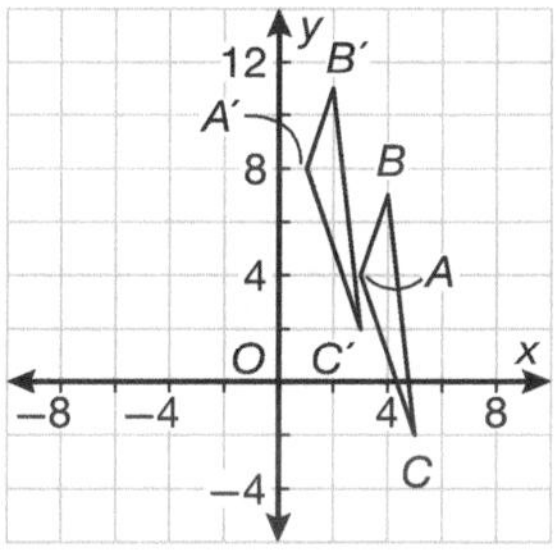

4. (44) **Algebra** If $\triangle GHJ \sim \triangle LMN$, $GH = x^2 + 2$, $HJ = y - 4$, $JG = 6$, $LM = 36$, $MN = 2$, and $NL = 12$. Find the values of x and y. Then, find the ratio of the two triangles' perimeters.

* **5.** (84) Apply a dilation to $\triangle QRS$ using a scale factor of $\frac{1}{3}$ and center C.

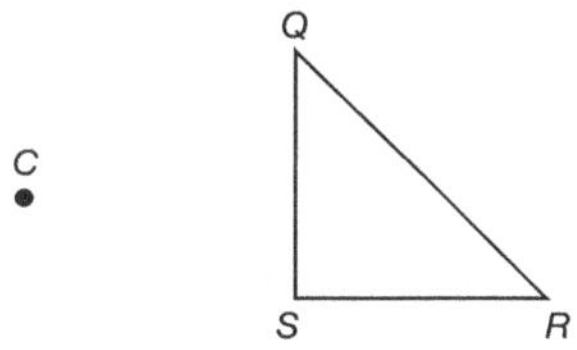

6. (77) **Hobbies** Victor has an hourglass made of two 4-inch-tall right circular cones connected at their vertices. After the sand has run for a time, there is only 0.883 in^3 of sand in the top half, making a cone 1.5 inches tall from the vertex. What is the radius at the top of the cone of remaining sand?

7. (51) **a.** Isosceles $\triangle JKL$ has a vertex angle at K. Its perimeter is 26 inches, and $JK = 7.5$ inches. Determine JL.

b. The bisector of $\angle K$ intersects $\overline{JL}$ at M. Determine JM.

8. **Verify** Segment DE is a midsegment of $\triangle ABC$. Find the coordinates of D and E.
(55)

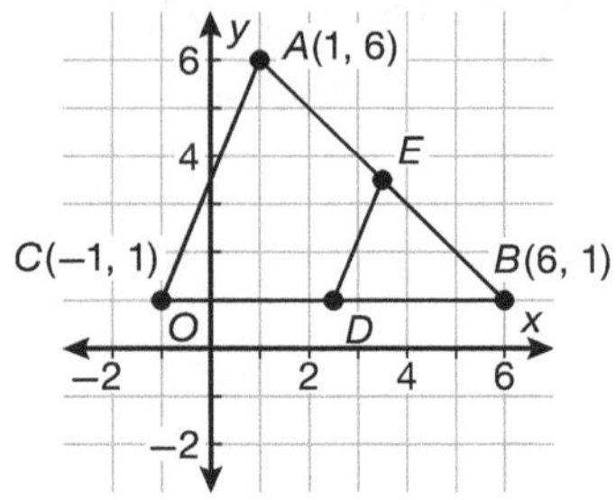

9. **Multiple Choice** Which of the following sets of numbers could be the side lengths of an obtuse triangle?
(33)

A $7, 3\sqrt{5}, 2$ **B** $4, 3\sqrt{2}, \sqrt{17}$
C $11, 19, 17$ **D** $16, 4\sqrt{5}, 8$

*10. **Model** Describe the cross section at right and draw it.
(85)

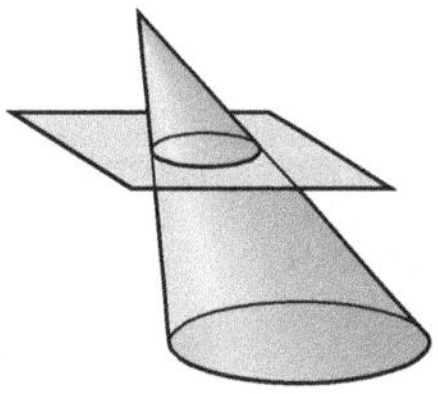

11. **Analyze** Are all right triangles with side lengths that are Pythagorean triples similar to each other? If so, explain why. If not, are any of them similar?
(46)

12. Compare ZY and WZ in the figure at right.
(Inv 4)

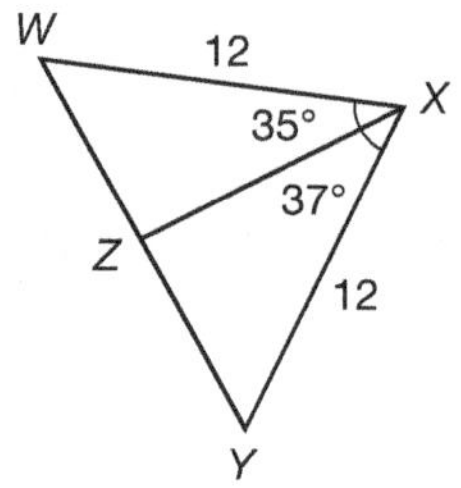

*13. $\triangle ABC$ has vertices $A(-3, 2)$, $B(1, 4)$, and $C(-1, -3)$. Apply a dilation with the center at the origin of the coordinate plane and sketch the graph. Use a scale factor of 2.
(84)

14. **Generalize** How many edges does a triangular prism have? … a rectangular prism? … a pentagonal prism? Based on these answers, write a formula for the number of edges in a prism with an n-sided base.
(49)

15. **Multi-Step** Use the head-to-tail method to find the resultant vector of $\vec{c} = \langle -2, 4 \rangle$, $\vec{d} = \langle -6, 1 \rangle$, and $\vec{e} = \langle 7, 4 \rangle$. Then, find its magnitude to the nearest hundredth.
(83)

16. **a.** This parallelogram contains two equilateral triangles. Sketch the figure and translate it right by the distance of one side length.
(Inv 8)

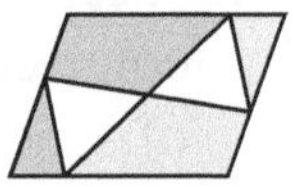

b. Repeat part **a** for three more translations. What type of pattern have you created? What type of symmetry does it have?

17. **Error Analysis** On Todd's last math assignment, he was given a 37° angle formed by a tangent and a chord of a circle, and he was asked to find the measure of the arc that subtends it. Recalling a theorem from class, he wrote down the answer as 18.5°, but his teacher marked the question incorrect. What was his mistake?
(64)

18. Use the Hypotenuse-Leg Congruence Theorem to show that $\triangle ABC \cong \triangle DEF$.
(36)

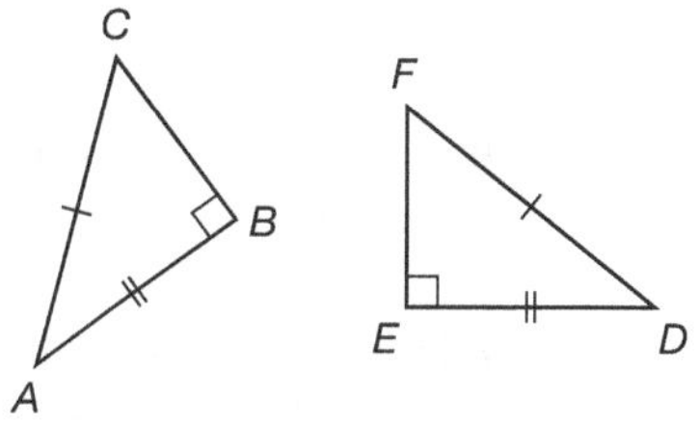

19. Rectangle *GHJK* has vertices *G*(2, 4), *H*(4.5, 4), *J*(4.5, −1), and *K*(2, −1). Reflect *GHJK* across $y = 2x$ and graph the image.
(74)

*20. **Algebra** Find the perimeter of a cross section of the square pyramid shown. The cross section of the pyramid makes a square and it is taken halfway between the vertex of the pyramid and the bottom of the pyramid. The original height of the pyramid is 8 inches and the base side lengths are 4 inches. Round your answer to the nearest whole inch.
(85)

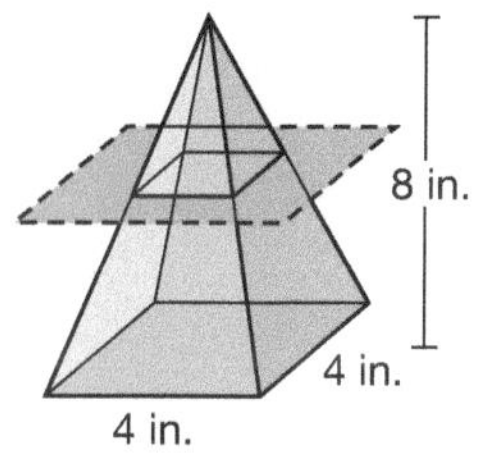

21. **Food Packaging** A cylindrical soup tin has a diameter of 7 centimeters and a height of 13 centimeters. Ignoring the thickness of the tin's walls, how much soup is it able to hold?
(62)

22. Quadrilateral *WXYZ* is a rectangle. Find *XY* and *WY*.
(52)

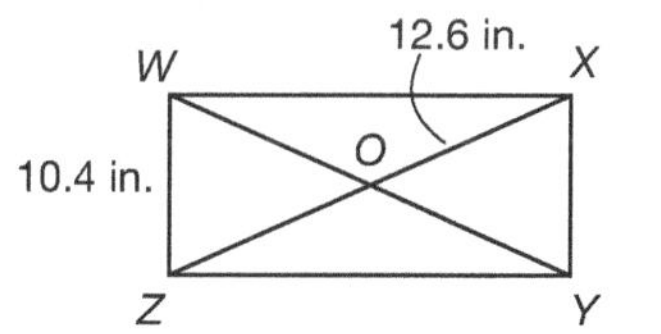

23. Explain why $\triangle PQR \cong \triangle STR$.
(30)

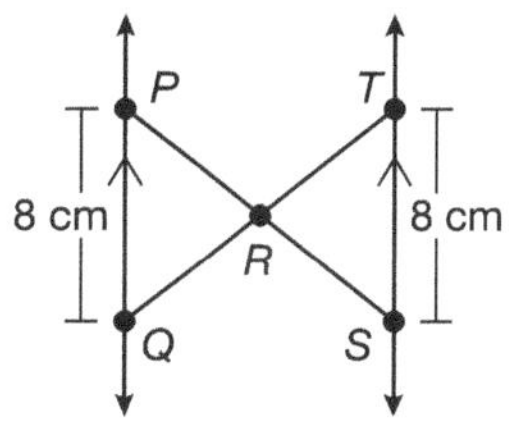

24. **Sailing** A sailboat is traveling directly across a lagoon at a velocity of 15 meters per second. If the water is flowing perpendicular to the sailboat at a velocity of 8 meters per second, what is the actual direction of the sailboat to the nearest degree?
(83)

Cross Sections of Solids

LESSON 85

25. Find m$\angle A$.
(79)

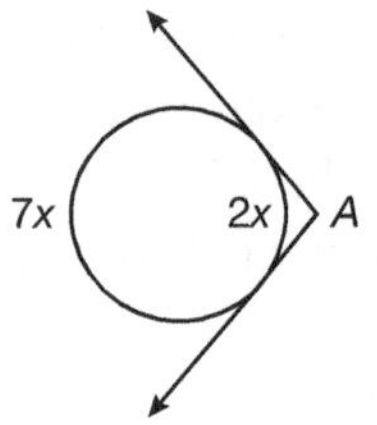

26. **Analyze** What is the order of rotation of a circle? How many lines of symmetry does a circle have?
(76)

***27.** **Breakfast** A chef is slicing a bagel into two halves along its side as shown. Describe the cross section.
(85)

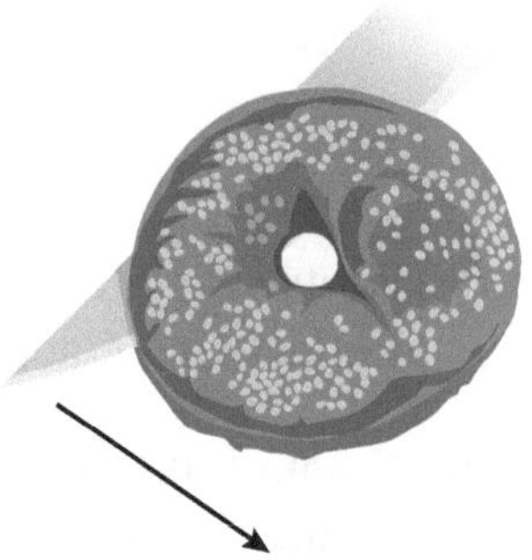

28. In the diagram, $ABCD \sim EFGH$. Find the measure of $\angle A$ and $\angle C$.
(41)

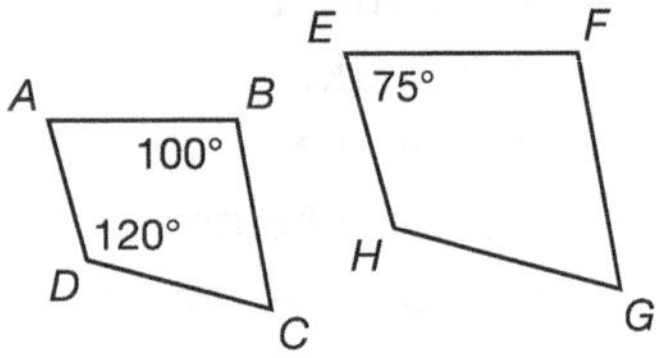

***29.** $\triangle M'N'P'$ is the image of $\triangle MNP$ after a dilation centered at the origin. Identify the type of dilation and find the scale factor.
(84)

30. Triangle ABC is rotated 120° in a counterclockwise direction and then rotated 190° in a clockwise direction about the origin. What clockwise rotation is equivalent to this set of rotations?
(78)

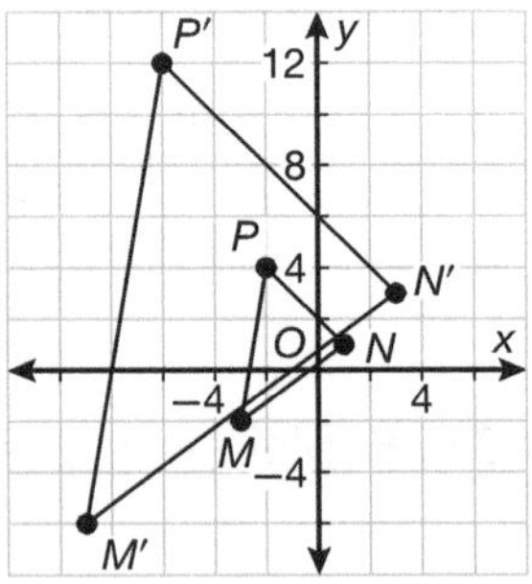

Name ______________________ Date __________ Class __________

Determining Chord Length

LESSON 86

* **1.** In ⊙C, what is VZ?
(86)

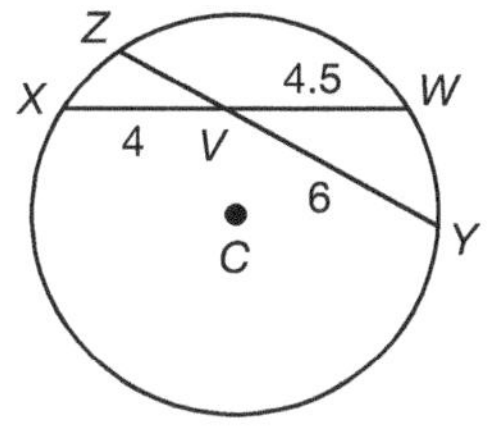

2. (**Map Reading**) When Erin drew a circle around the intersection of two straight trails on a map, she found the trails intersected an arc of 85° on one side of the intersection and 103° on the opposite side. What is the measure of the angle between the two trails?
(64)

3. **Generalize** A cone has one-third the volume of a cylinder with the same height and radius. Does such a cone also have less surface area than the circular cylinder? Explain.
(77)

4. Find the distance from (5, 3) to the line $x = -2$.
(42)

5. **Generalize** Describe how to determine the probability of a pointer on a spinner *not* landing on a given sector.
(Inv 6)

6. Apply a dilation to $\overline{ST}$ using a scale factor of 4 and center C.
(84)

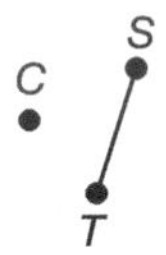

7. $DEFG$ is a parallelogram. If $\angle D$ is one-eighth the size of $\angle G$, what is the measure of each angle?
(34)

8. Find θ_1 and θ_2 to the nearest degree.
(82)

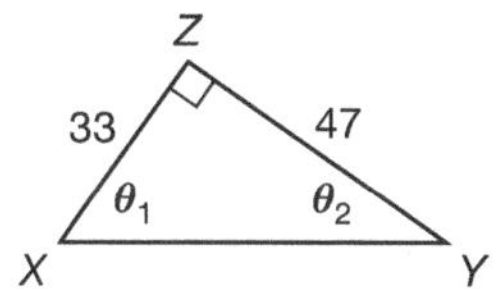

9. Add the vectors $\langle 1, 5\rangle$ and $\langle -1, -5\rangle$. What kind of vectors are these?
(63)

10. **Verify** Verify that $A(4, -1)$, $B(1, 0.5)$, and $C(-2, 2)$ are collinear.
(45)

***11.** The plane shown intersects a diameter of the cylinder. Find the perimeter of the cross section. The radius of the cylinder is 5 centimeters and the height is 18 centimeters.
(85)

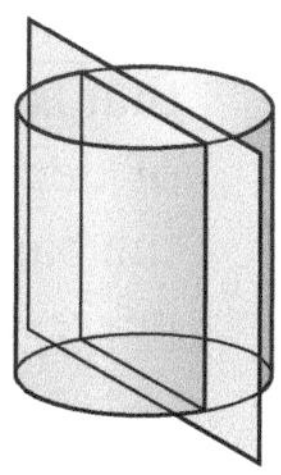

12. (**Gardening**) Gordon's outdoor fountain is in the shape of the lower half of a sphere. If the diameter of the hemisphere is 12 inches, what volume of water does the fountain hold to the nearest cubic inch?
(80)

Determining Chord Length

13. (66) Find the perimeter of the regular polygon shown, to the nearest foot.

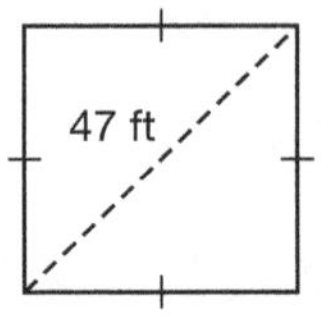

***14.** (86) **Analyze** $\overline{AB}$ and $\overline{CD}$ are chords in the same circle, and they intersect at point E. If $AE = CE$, What is the relationship between the two intersecting chords?

15. (18) **Multiple Choice** What is the best description for $\angle S$ in $\triangle STU$?

A right angle **B** remote interior angle
C complementary angle **D** exterior angle

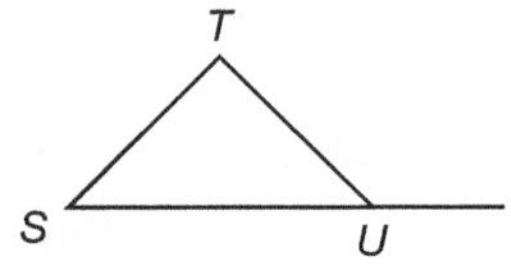

***16.** (86) **Algebra** Two chords of a circle, $\overline{FG}$ and $\overline{CD}$, intersect at E. $FE = 2$, $GE = 3 + 2x$, $CE = 6$, and $DE = x$. Write and solve an equation for x.

17. (83) **Multi-Step** Find the angle that the resultant vector of the vectors $\langle -3, 5\rangle$ and $\langle 6, 4\rangle$ makes with the horizontal. Round your answer to the nearest degree.

18. (79) **Algebra** Find the measure of each angle in the triangle shown.

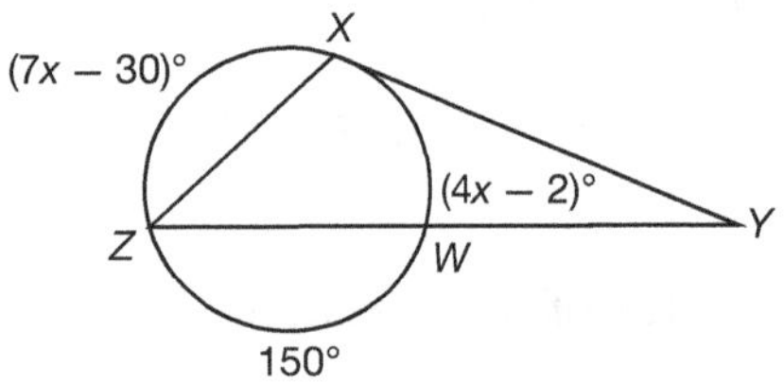

19. (84) Pentagon $ABCDE$ has vertices $A(0, 4)$, $B(4, 0)$, $C(2, -4)$, $D(-2, -4)$, and $E(-4, 0)$. Apply a dilation with the center at the origin of the coordinate plane. Use a scale factor of $\frac{1}{4}$.

20. (56) Find the values of x and y. Express your answers in simplified radical form.

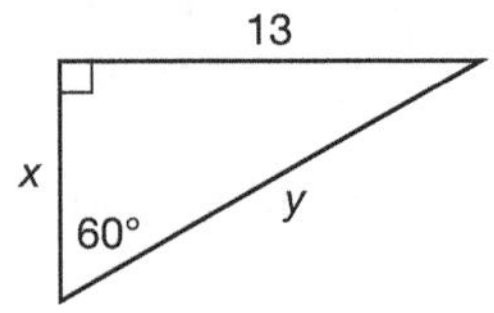

21. (31) **Write** In the diagram, $\angle A \cong \angle B$. Use a paragraph proof to show that $m\widehat{FE} = m\widehat{HG}$.

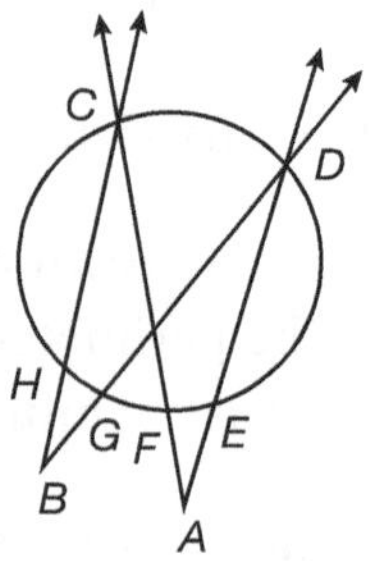

22. (73) **Fire Protection** A forest ranger stands in a tower that is 40 meters tall. If he sees a fire at an angle of depression of 6°, how far away is the fire from the base of the tower? Round your answer to the nearest tenth of a meter.

*23. (85) Find the perimeter of the cross section of the equilateral triangular prism shown. The sides of the triangle are 8 centimeters long.

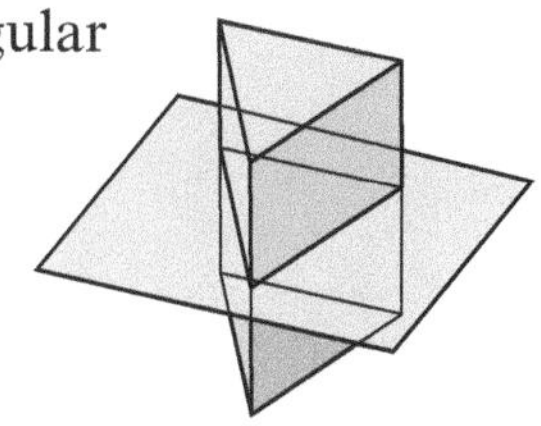

24. (70) Pet Supplies Charlie's fish tank is shaped like a regular pentagonal pyramid. If the area of the base is 200 cm^2 and the height of the fish tank is 18 centimeters, what volume of water is needed to fill the fish tank?

25. (21) Use the Law of Detachment to write a conclusion based on the following statements.

On Sundays, sandwiches are 25% off.
Today is a Sunday.

*26. (86) **Algebra** Two chords of a circle, $\overline{FG}$ and $\overline{HJ}$, intersect at K. $FK = 5$, $GK = 3 - 2y$, $HK = y - 4$, and $JK = 4$. Write and solve an equation for y.

27. (40) Railways A train station's rail tunnel has a semicircular opening large enough for a train to pass through, as shown. What is the area of the rail tunnel's opening, to the nearest square meter?

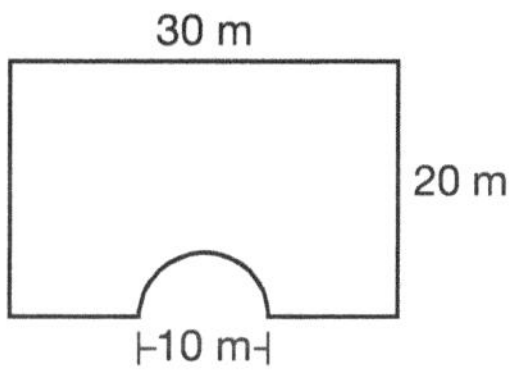

28. (Inv 5) **Error Analysis** Jean-Paul drew the net shown for a pentagonal prism. What is wrong with his net? How could he fix it?

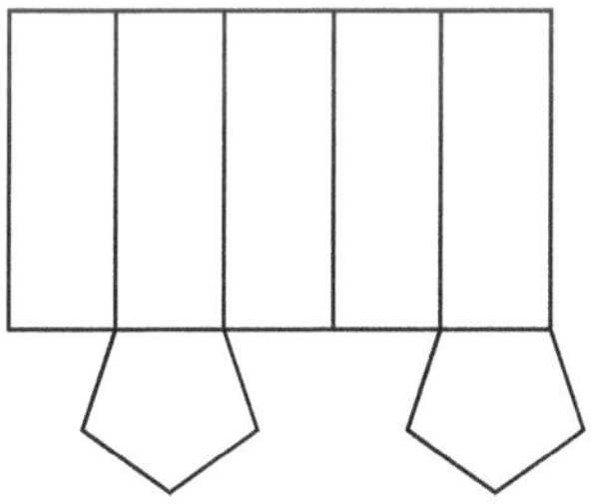

29. (53) Find the length of the hypotenuse of a 45°-45°-90° right triangle with a leg that is $13\sqrt{2}$ centimeters long.

*30. (85) **Multiple Choice** Which of the following could *not* have a square cross section?

A square pyramid
B sphere
C cube
D triangular prism

Name ______________________________ Date __________ Class __________

Area Ratios of Similar Figures

LESSON 87

* **1.** (87) **Archeology** A dig crew is asked to start excavating a site that is 4 meters by 5 meters. After this site is studied and some artifacts are uncovered, the crew is then asked to expand the site by a factor of 7 in each direction. What will be the total area of the site after this expansion?

2. (77) **Estimate** Estimate the surface area of a right circular cone with a slant height of 13.78 centimeters and a radius of 5.21 centimeters.

3. (55) In the figure at right, $\triangle ABC$ has midsegment $\overline{DE}$. Find the coordinates of D and E.

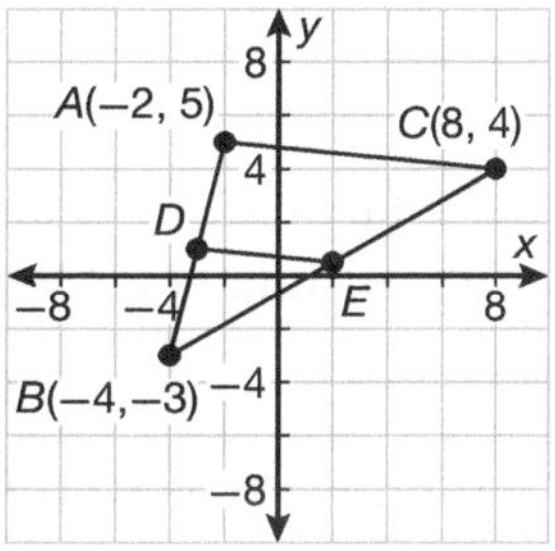

4. (84) Rectangle $JKLM$ has vertices $J(-4, 2)$, $K(-4, -6)$, $L(4, -6)$, and $M(4, 2)$. Apply a dilation with the center at the origin of the coordinate plane. Use a scale factor of $\frac{1}{2}$.

5. (39) Write three inequalities that follow from the Triangle Inequality Theorem for a triangle with side lengths of a, b, and c.

* **6.** (86) Two chords of a circle, $\overline{AB}$ and $\overline{CD}$, intersect at E. If AE and $BE = 6$ and $CE = 8$, determine DE.

7. (70) What is the volume of the regular pyramid shown below?

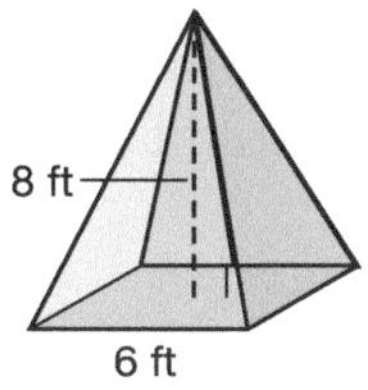

8. (81) **Cost Comparison** Two cafes are having a sale on coffee. The first one charges \$2.50 for a regular, plain coffee and \$0.75 for each additional flavoring. The second one charges \$3.25 for a regular, plain coffee and \$0.50 for each additional flavoring. If Brynna buys one regular coffee, how many additional flavorings would make her drink from each location cost the same? What is that price?

9. (52) **Error Analysis** Jerrod and Anthony are defining a rectangle. Whose definition is correct? Explain.
Jerrod: *"A rectangle has a pair of sides that are parallel and it has a right angle."*
Anthony: *"A rectangle is a parallelogram with one right angle."*

*10. (87) Two squares are related by a scale factor of 5. If the smaller square has a perimeter of 32 inches, what is the perimeter of the larger square?

*11. (47) **Algebra** Find the measure of $\angle H$.

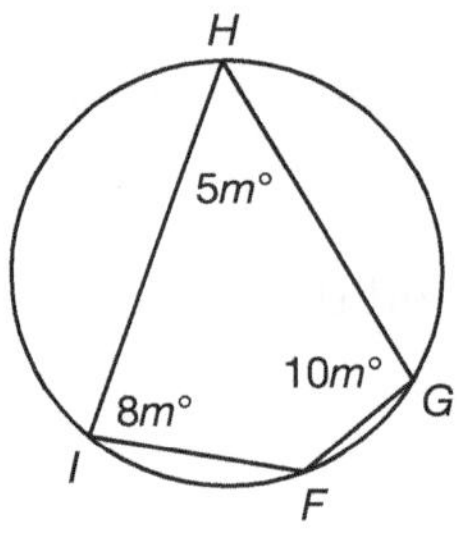

12. (80) **Baseball** A baseball is a spherical ball. The hide of a baseball covers the outside of the ball. If the ball has a radius of 4 centimeters, what area of material is needed for the hide to the nearest tenth?

13. (85) **Write** Explain how you could get a triangular cross section from a cube.

14. (56) If the hypotenuse of a 30°-60°-90° triangle is 4, what are the lengths of the other two legs?

*15. (87) **Multiple Choice** Kite $RSTU \sim HIJK$. If $HJ = 2RT$ and $KI = 2SU$, what is the area of kite $HIJK$, compared to the area of $RSTU$?

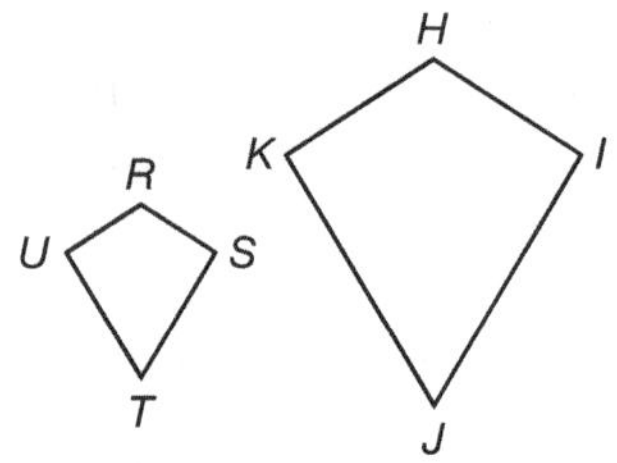

A The area is twice as large.
B The area is three times as large.
C The area is four times as large.
D The area is eight times as large.

16. (53) **Parks** Oakdale Park takes up one square block that is 300 feet on each side. Two diagonal sidewalks join the opposite corners. To the nearest foot, how long is each diagonal sidewalk?

17. (16) Graph the line with equation $x + 2y = 8$.

*18. (86) In the circle, what is QT?

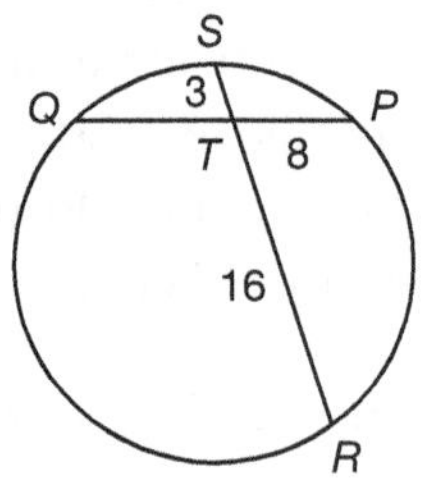

19. (32) If the length of a median of a triangle equals 16.5, what is the distance from the centroid to the opposite side?

20. (83) **Multi-Step** Use the head-to-tail method to find the resultant vector of $\vec{a} = \langle 2, 2 \rangle$, $\vec{b} = \langle -3, -2 \rangle$, and $\vec{c} = \langle 4, -3 \rangle$. Then find its magnitude to the nearest hundredth.

21. (37) **Algebra** Line x passes through points $(1, -3)$ and $(3, k)$. Line y passes through points $(2, 4)$ and $(4, 7)$. What value of k makes these lines parallel?

22. (85) Find the area of the cross section of the triangular prism to the nearest hundredth. Each side of the base is 8 centimeters long.

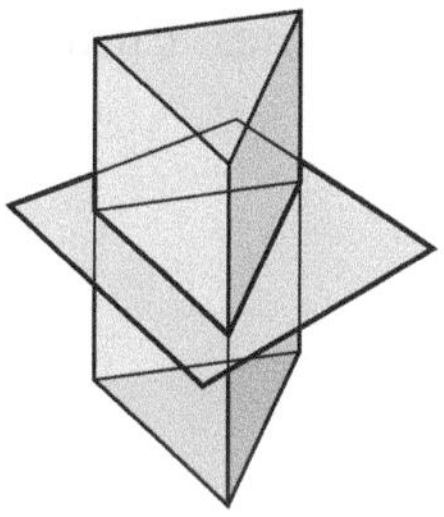

23. (69) **Analyze** Does the midsegment of an isosceles trapezoid divide the trapezoid into two similar trapezoids? Explain.

***24.** (87) A regular hexagon has a perimeter of 36 centimeters and an area of 93.5 square centimeters. A similar hexagon is constructed with a similarity ratio of 3:7. Find the perimeter and area of the larger hexagon.

25. (Inv 5) **Write** How are a solid's net and its surface area related?

26. (72) **Compact Discs** Do the interior circle and exterior circle of a compact disc have any common tangents? Are they tangent circles?

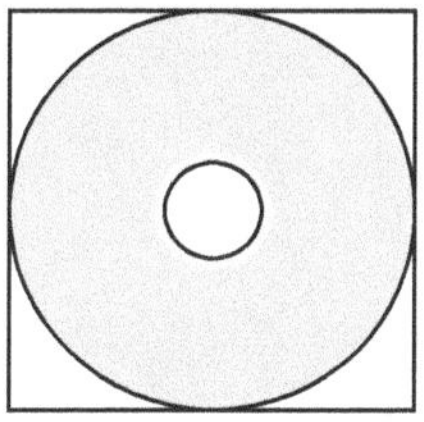

27. (57) **Write** Explain how to find the perimeter of the polygon with vertices at $(-2, 3)$, $(3, 1)$, $(-2, -1)$, and $(-3, 1)$.

28. (Inv 7) Use *sine*, *cosine*, or *tangent* to fill in each blank in this statement: The ____ function increases from 0 to 1 as angle measures increase from 0° to 90°, while the ______ function decreases from 1 to 0.

*29. **Multiple Choice** What is the missing segment length in this figure?
(86)

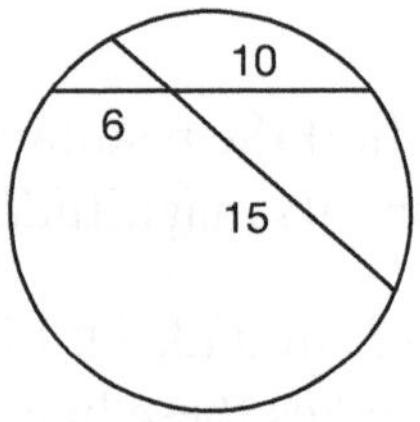

A $2\sqrt{15}$ B 15
C 4 D 25

30. A cube has a surface area of 54 square inches. Find its volume.
(59)

Name ______________________ Date ____________ Class ____________

Graphing and Solving Linear Inequalities

LESSON 88

* **1.** (87) Determine the area of the smaller parallelogram in the diagram if the similarity ratio is 3:11.

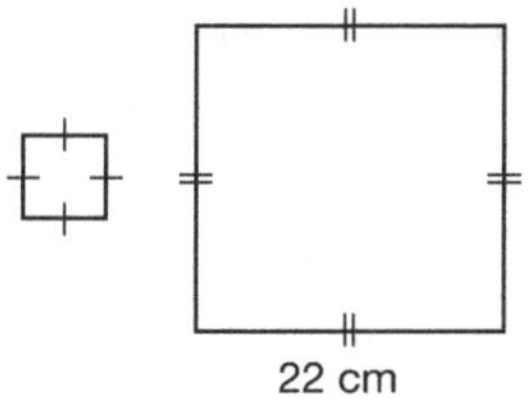

2. (77) **Biology** The Eastern Auger is a type of snail that has a cone-shaped shell, which is about 2.25 inches long and has a 0.5-inch radius. Approximately what is the surface area of the Eastern Auger's shell? Assume that the base is flat.

* **3.** (88) Solve the linear inequality $6x + 3y > 9$ for y.

4. (85) **Analyze** A square pyramid has a cross section that passes through the vertex and intersects two opposite corners of the base. What is the area of the cross section if the height of the pyramid is 70 centimeters and the base is 50 centimeters wide? Round your answer to the nearest hundredth of a square centimeter.

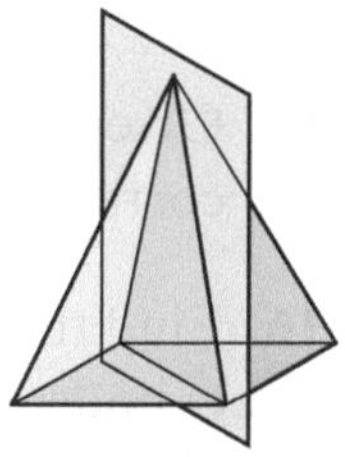

5. (17) Write the converse of the following statement about positive numbers x and y. Which is true—the statement, its converse, both, or neither?

If $\frac{x}{y} > 1$, *then* $x > y$.

6. (82) **Justify** Is this expression true for all x? $\sin^{-1}x = \frac{1}{\sin x}$. If so, prove it. If it is not true, find a counterexample.

7. (86) **Algebra** Use this figure to write and solve an equation for a.

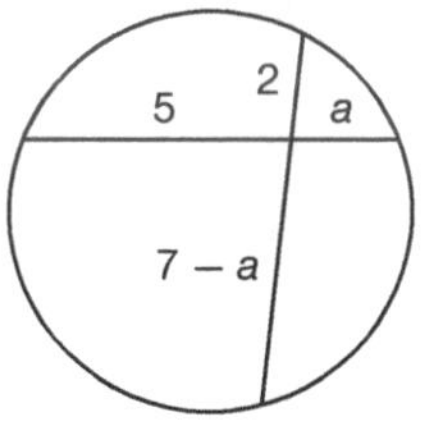

8. (37) Write the equation of a line perpendicular to $y = \frac{2}{5}x + 7$.

9. (66) **Multiple Choice** Which of the following values represents the area of an equilateral triangle with 30-centimeter side lengths?

A $450\sqrt{3}$ cm^2 **B** $225\sqrt{3}$ cm^2

C $\frac{450}{\sqrt{3}}$ cm^2 **D** $\frac{225}{\sqrt{3}}$ cm^2

10. (34) Find the values of x, y, and z in the parallelogram.

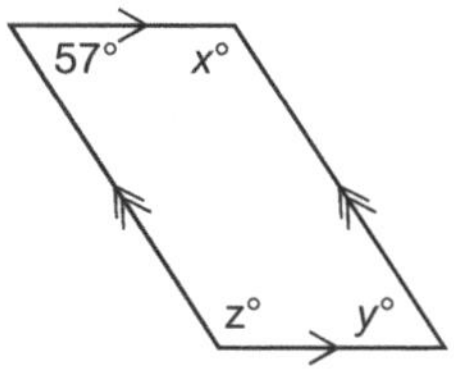

11. (81) **Economics** The supply of Brand A is represented by $y = 2x + 15$, where y represents the price in dollars and x represents the number of units. The demand for Brand A is represented by $y = \frac{1}{3}x + 75$. What are the optimum number of units and the price for Brand A?

***12.** (88) Graph $4 + 2y > 8x - 4$.

*13. (87) **Scale Models** The scale model of a barn is shown at right. It has four sides that are congruent rectangles. It is modeled after a rectangular barn with a length of 24 feet and a height of 12 feet. If the scale factor used is 1:16, what is the total exterior area of the model?

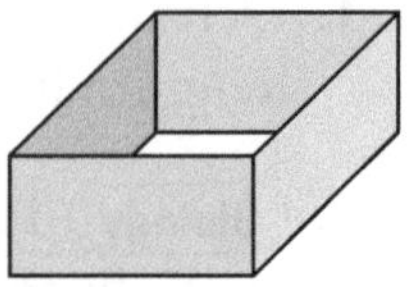

14. (78) $\triangle ABC$ has vertices $A(-4, -3)$, $B(-3, 1)$, and $C(1, -2)$. Graph $\triangle ABC$, and then rotate it 90° counterclockwise about the origin. List the coordinates of the vertices of $\triangle A'B'C'$.

15. (87) Given $\triangle FGH \sim \triangle XYZ$, find the ratio of the perimeters if the ratio of their corresponding sides is 1:8.

16. (85) Find the area of the cross section of the cylinder at right, through the cylinder's diameter. The radius is 5 centimeters and the height is 18 centimeters.

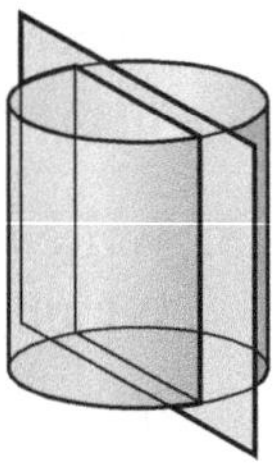

17. (57) **Multi-Step** Classify the polygon with vertices $R(1, 2)$, $S(-2, 5)$, and $T(9, 4)$. Find the perimeter. Round your answer to the nearest hundredth.

18. (53) Find the area of a 45°-45°-90° right triangle that has a 14-meter hypotenuse.

*19. (73) **Analyze** Jin is measuring the distance between himself and the city monument shown below from various heights in the 8-story building where he works. He knows that the monument is 50 feet from the base of the building and that each floor is 15 feet higher than the last. As Jin climbs up the stories of the building, will the angle of depression increase at a steady rate? Will his distance from the monument increase at a steady rate? Explain why or why not.

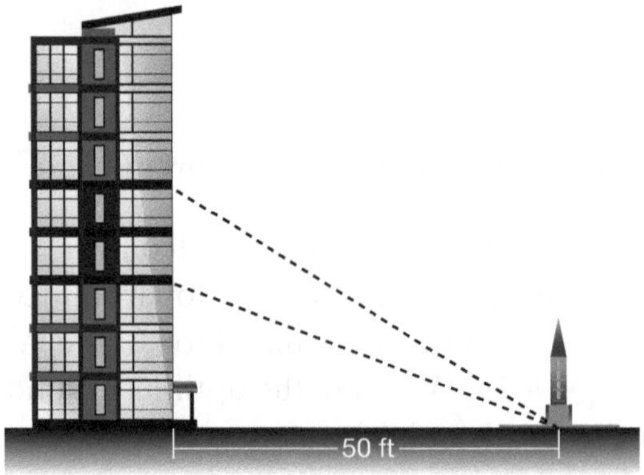

*20. (88) Graph $-3y \geq 2x - 6$.

21. (41) What is the value of x in the proportion $\frac{6}{x+2} = \frac{3}{5}$?

22. (28) **Algebra** A pair of corresponding angles in two congruent triangles measure $(3x + 80)°$ and $(4x + 70)°$. What is the value of x?

23. (86) **Architecture** In this circular stained-glass window, what is the length of the horizontal crosspiece?

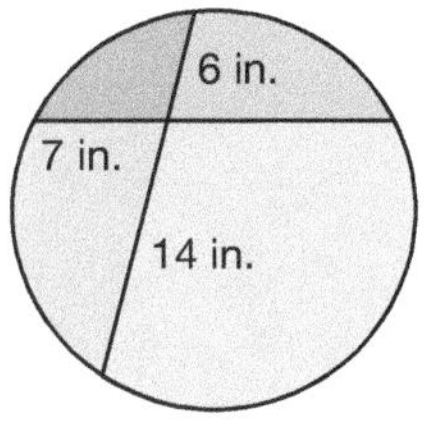

*24. (87) **Error Analysis** Raquel states that since the ratio of the areas of two similar polygons is 4:9, the ratio of their perimeters must be 4:9. Is she correct? Explain why or why not.

25. (75) **Analyze** The equation $(x - h)^2 + (y - k)^2 = r^2$ is one way of representing a circle with radius r and center (h, k). Expand the equation. Then, determine the radius and center of the circle $x^2 + y^2 + 2x - 6y + 1 + 9 - 25 = 0$.

26. (50) Find the values of x and y to the nearest hundredth in the triangle shown.

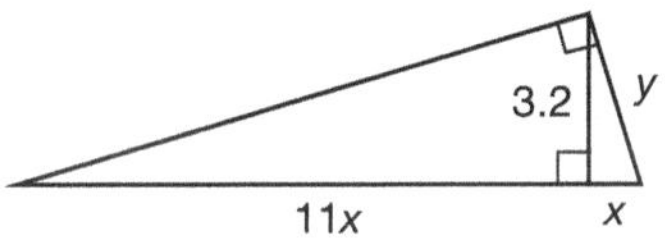

27. (39) If a triangle were constructed with the largest third side possible, which angle would measure the least, if the two given sides were 8 meters and 5 meters long, respectively?

*28. (88) **Landscaping** Veruka is building a rectangular fence in her backyard. However, she only has 20 meters of fencing. If x represents the length and y represents the width of the rectangle in meters, graph the set of possible values for x and y. Use your graph to determine whether Veruka can build a fence with a length of 10 meters and a width of 2 meters.

*29. (79) **Algebra** Find the measure of each angle in the triangle.

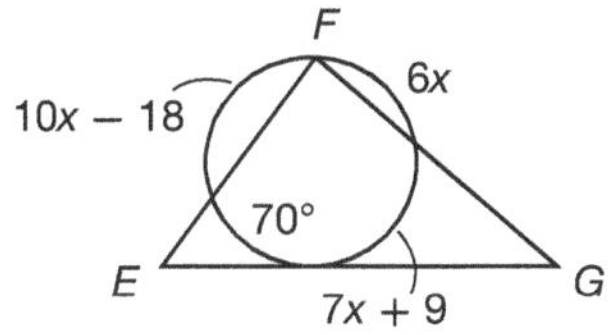

30. (11) Determine the midpoint M of the points $P(-5, 4)$ and $Q(10, 0)$.

Name ______________________________ Date __________ Class __________

Vector Decomposition

LESSON 89

1. *(58)* Points A and B are on $\odot C$, with $\angle AOB$ acute. OB is 4 inches and BD is 3 inches. $\overline{OA}$ is extended to D with $\overline{BD}$ tangent to $\odot C$.
   a. Determine OD.
   b. Determine AD.

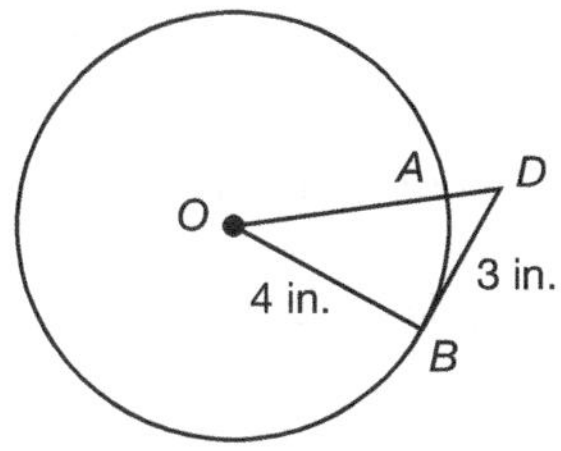

* 2. *(89)* Find the component form of a vector with a magnitude of 4 and a direction of 35°.

3. *(86)* **Analyze** Use Theorem 86-1 to prove that if $\overline{AB}$ and $\overline{CD}$ are chords of a circle and $\overline{CD}$ bisects $\overline{AB}$, then $(CE)(DE) = \frac{1}{4}(AB)^2$.

4. *(71)* **Multiple Choice** $\triangle ABC$ is translated so that the coordinates of B' are (1, 5). What are the coordinates of C' after the same translation?
   A (4, 1) **B** (4, −1)
   C (1, 4) **D** (−1, 1)

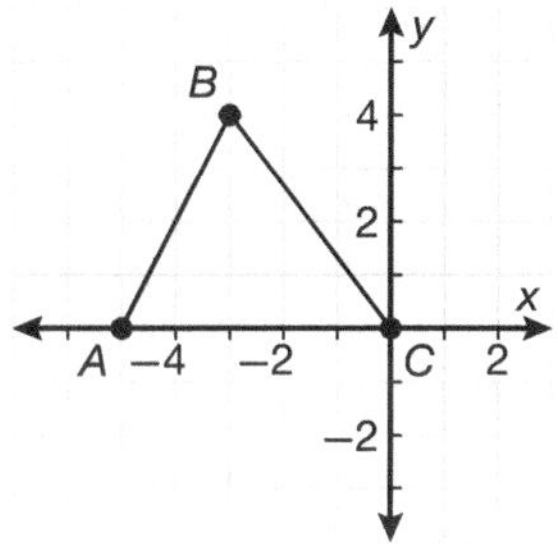

5. *(83)* **Kayaking** A kayaker is traveling across a river at a velocity of 5 kilometers per hour. If the current is traveling at a rate of 2 kilometers per hour in a direction perpendicular to the kayaker's movement, what is the actual speed of the kayaker to the nearest hundredth?

6. *(9)* If the coordinates of one endpoint of a segment are (4, 5) and the segment extends vertically downward 4 units, what would be the coordinates of the other endpoint?

7. *(41)* Given $\triangle BCD \sim \triangle JKL$, find KL.

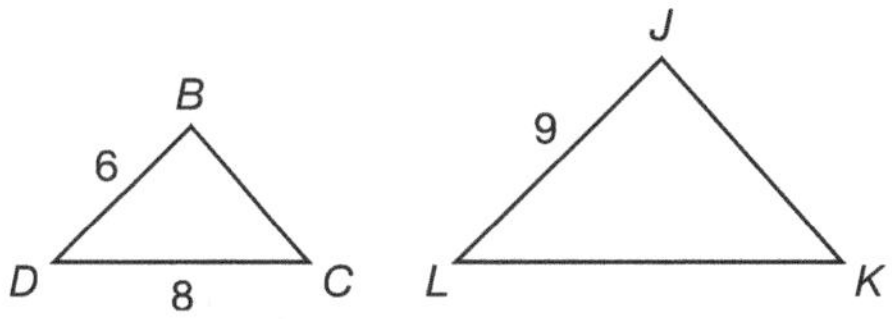

8. *(76)* **Analyze** If a regular polygon has an angle of rotational symmetry of 6°, how many sides does the polygon have?

* 9. *(88)* Sketch the graph of $y \geq -2x - 3$.

10. *(59)* **Construction** A builder drills a hole with a 1-inch radius through a cube of concrete, as shown in the diagram. This cube will be an outlet for a water tap on the side of a house.
   a. Find an expression involving π that gives the surface area of the cube. *Hint: Do not include the hole.*
   b. Find the lateral area of the cylinder to the nearest tenth of a square inch.

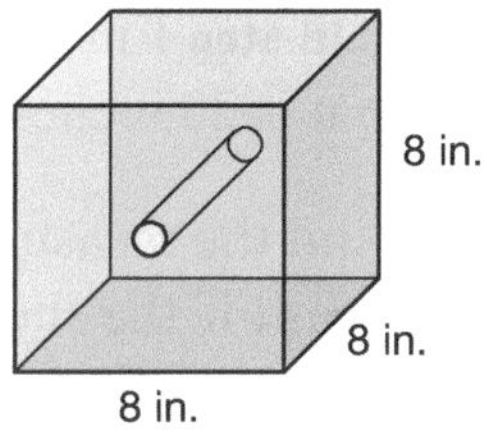

11. (85) **Baking** Warren must cut a carrot cake in half that is in the shape of a wide cylinder, for a catered event. If the cake is 5 inches tall with a diameter of 12 inches, and he cuts along its diameter, what is the perimeter of the cross section?

12. (87) **Multiple Choice** The side length of a regular hexagon is 3 times as long as the side length of a similar hexagon. Which is a true statement about these two hexagons?

A The smaller hexagon's perimeter is $\frac{1}{9}$ and its area is $\frac{1}{3}$ the size of the larger.

B The smaller hexagon's perimeter is $\frac{1}{3}$ and its area is $\frac{1}{9}$ the size of the larger.

C The smaller hexagon's perimeter and its area are each $\frac{1}{3}$ the size of the larger.

D The smaller hexagon's perimeter and its area are each $\frac{1}{9}$ the size of the larger.

13. (50) Find the value of x in the triangle at right to the nearest tenth.

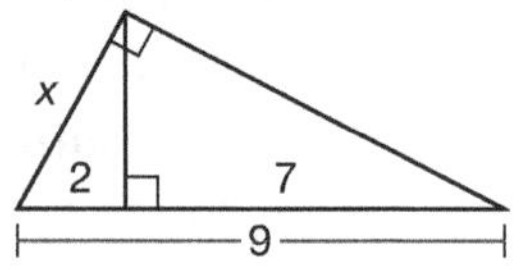

14. (38) Find the circumcenter of a triangle with vertices at (6, −2), (−2, −8), and (−6, −2) in a coordinate plane.

***15.** (89) **Algebra** Vector $\vec{v}$ has a magnitude of x and a direction of θ. Find the magnitude and angle of a vector that is 3 times longer than $\vec{v}$ and that points in the opposite direction.

16. (83) **Model** On a coordinate plane, draw a parallelogram using the vectors $\langle 3, 5\rangle$ and $\langle 1, 6\rangle$ and find the sum of the two vectors.

***17.** (Inv 8) What is the 15th triangular number? What is the 20th triangular number?

***18.** (88) **Transport** The density of rice is 782 kilograms per cubic meter and the density of wheat flour is 528 kilograms per cubic meter. A small cargo ship can carry 120,000 kilograms. Write an inequality for the total volume of rice (x), and flour (y), that the ship can carry.

***19.** (89) The hour hand on a clock points to 7. If the vector represented by the hour hand has a magnitude of 5 inches, what is the magnitude of its horizontal component?

20. (53) **Multi-Step** Find the perimeter and area of a 45°-45°-90° triangle with a hypotenuse that is 20 inches long to the nearest hundredth.

21. (79) Find the measure of the angle exterior to a circle made by one tangent and one secant if the shorter arc measure between the tangent and secant is 54° and the longer one is 112°.

22. (35) Find the circumference based on the arc given assuming, that $\overline{AB}$ is a diameter.

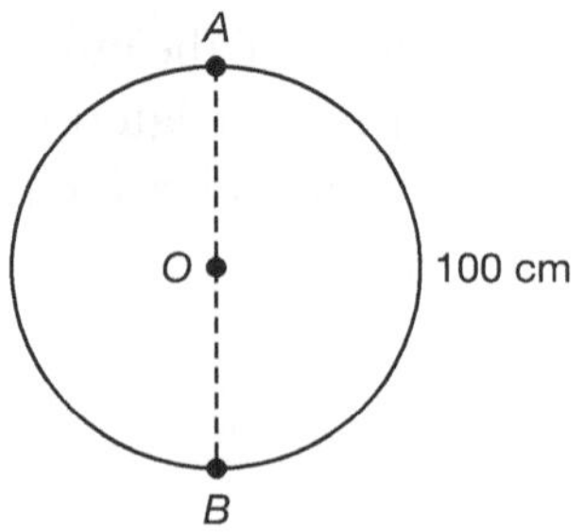

23. (87) Two similar triangles have areas of 76 square centimeters and 931 square centimeters. Determine the ratio of their perimeters.

24. (52) **Justify** The endpoints of the diagonals of a quadrilateral are (−4, −3), (−5, 8), and (6, 9), (7, −2). Determine whether the quadrilateral is a rectangle. Explain how you know.

25. (84) The center of the dilation at right is the origin of the coordinate plane. The preimage is rectangle *JKLM*, and the image is rectangle *J′K′L′M′*. Identify the type of dilation and find the scale factor.

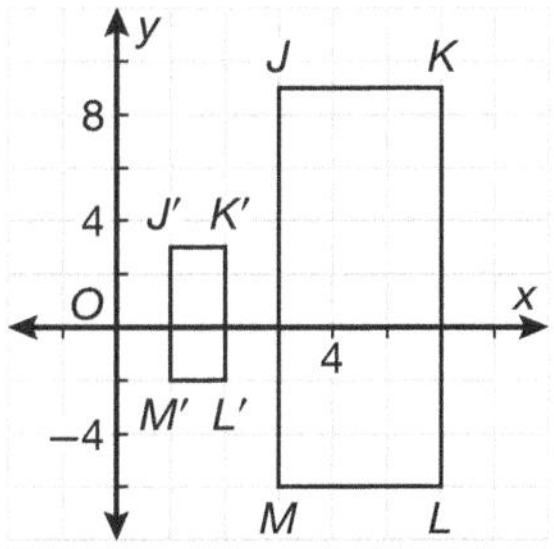

26. (82) **Construction** For maximum accessibility, a ramp should have a slope between $\frac{1}{12}$ and $\frac{1}{16}$. What is the range of the measure of the angle between the horizontal and the ramp, rounded to the nearest degree?

*27. (89) **Error Analysis** A student found the components of a vector with an angle θ and a magnitude of a. The student's answer was $\langle a\sin\theta, a\cos\theta\rangle$. Explain the error.

28. (56) If the hypotenuse of a 30°-60°-90° triangle is 125, what are the lengths of the two legs?

29. (Inv 4) In the given triangles, order the angles *x*, *y*, and *z* from smallest to largest.

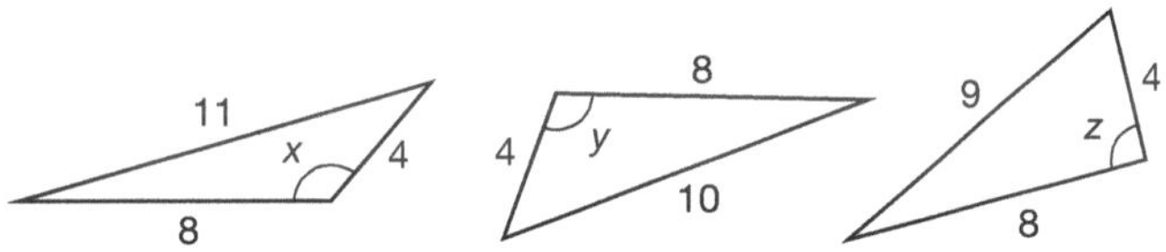

30. (88) Graph $4x + 3 < 2y - 5$.

Name ______________________ Date ____________ Class ____________

Composite Transformations

LESSON 90

1. (36) **Multiple Choice** Which corresponding parts of these triangles are shown to be congruent?

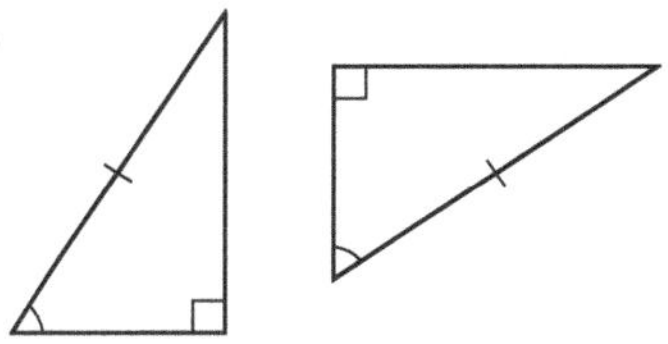

A hypotenuses, pair of acute angles, pair of right angles
B pair of legs and pair of right angles
C pair of legs and pair of acute angles
D hypotenuses and pair of legs

* **2.** (90) Reflect $\triangle DEF$ across line q, and then translate the image along u.

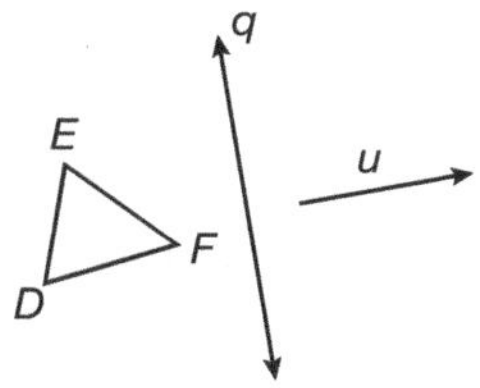

3. (88) Solve the strict linear inequality $27x - 3y < 9$ for y.

4. (77) **Manufacturing** A toy manufacturer is pouring melted plastic into a right cone-shaped mold to make a part of a toy. The mold has a slant height of 13 centimeters and a base radius of 5 centimeters. What is the approximate volume of the conical mold?

5. (57) **Landscaping** A graph showing the top of a circular fountain has its center at (4, 6). The circle representing the fountain passes through (2, 1). What is the exact area of the space covered by the fountain?

6. (69) In isosceles trapezoid $MNOP$, find the length of $\overline{MQ}$ if $NP = 51.7$ centimeters and $PQ = 24.8$ centimeters.

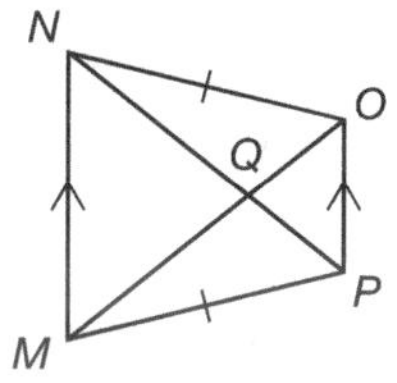

7. (73) A bird is flying 120 feet away from two bird watchers who are standing together. They estimate that the bird is 60 feet above them. What is the angle of elevation at which they see the bird?

8. (40) Determine the area of this composite figure.

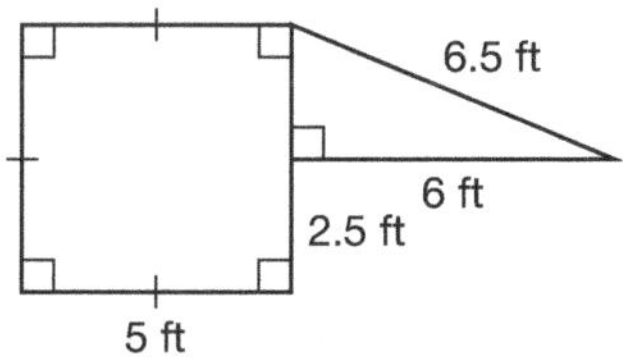

9. (7) Suresh claims, "the expression $4n - 1$ will always result in a prime number." Find a value of n that disproves his conjecture.

10. (83) **Sailing** The wind moving a sailboat is blowing 60° north of east at a velocity of 60 feet per second. The current is moving west at a velocity of 22 feet per second. What is the magnitude and angle of the sailboat's speed and course?

11. (86) Determine the exact value of AC in this circle.

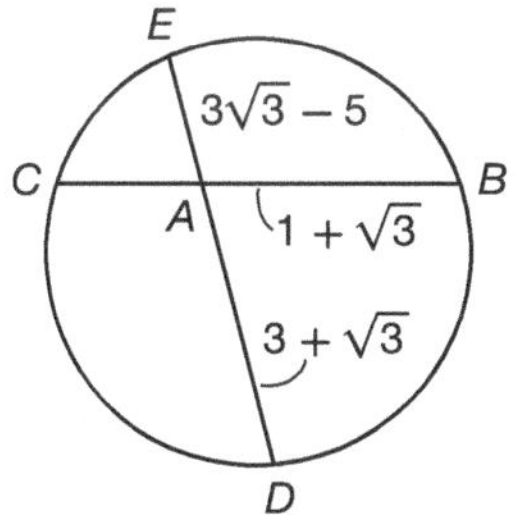

12. (80) **Generalize** Construct a formula for the volume of a sphere in terms of its diameter, d.

13. Given that $\triangle ABC \sim \triangle DEF$, $AB = 15$, $DE = 20$, and $EF = 16$, what is the length of BC?
(46)

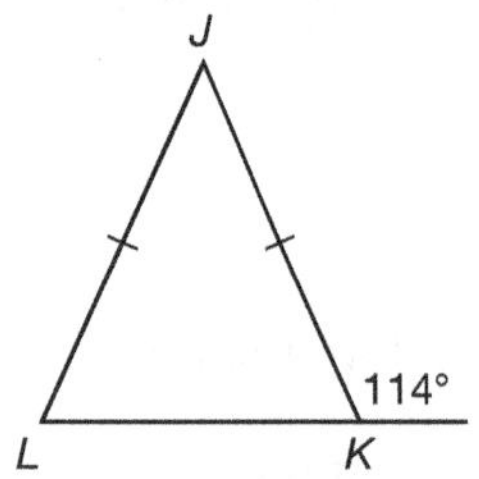

14. Show that the measure of the exterior angle at vertex K is greater than the measure of either remote interior angles.
(39)

15. Algebra The points M, N, and P are midpoints of $\triangle FGH$, $GH = 4x - 6$, and $MP = 15$. Find x and GH.
(55)

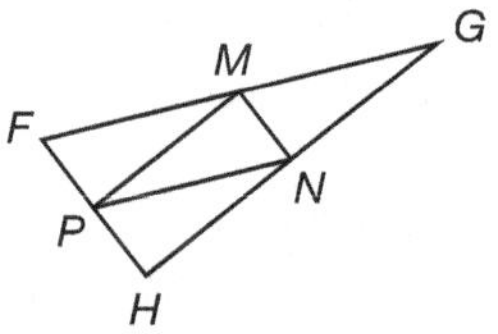

16. Multi-Step Two similar equilateral triangles have a scale factor of 2:5. Find the perimeter and area of the larger triangle if the smaller triangle has a side length of 8 inches.
(87)

***17. Error Analysis** Quan reflected a triangle across line x, followed by a reflection across line y, as shown. Did Quan perform the reflections correctly? Explain.
(90)

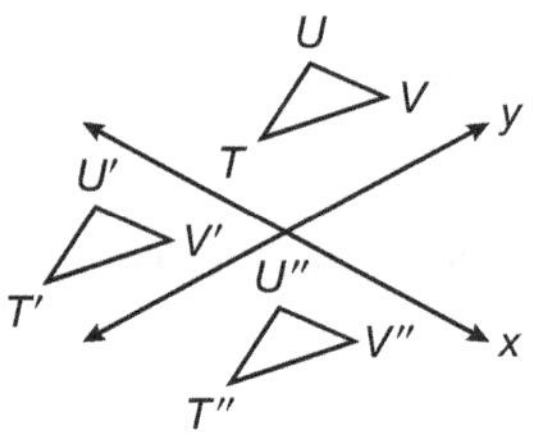

18. Algebra A reflection R across the line $x = a$ maps $(2, 4) \rightarrow (7, 4)$. Write and solve an equation for a.
(74)

19. Apply a dilation to $\triangle ABC$, at right, using a scale factor of 2 and P as the center.
(84)

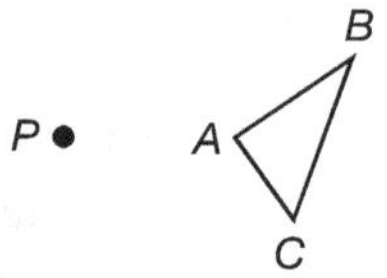

20. Analyze A vector has a magnitude x, where $x > 0$, and an angle θ such that $90° < \theta < 180°$. Find an expression for the component form of the vector in terms of θ.
(89)

***21. Logos** A skateboarding company is designing a logo for its new line of skateboards. The company's designers transformed its logo, SK8 as shown. Which two transformations did the company use?
(90)

22. Find the geometric mean between 5 and 8 in simplified radical form.
(50)

23. a. State the converse of the following statement.
(20)

If the time is 9 p.m., then it is evening.

b. Determine whether the statement is true and whether its converse is true.

24. Quadrilateral *WXYZ* is a rectangle. Find *WK*.
(52)

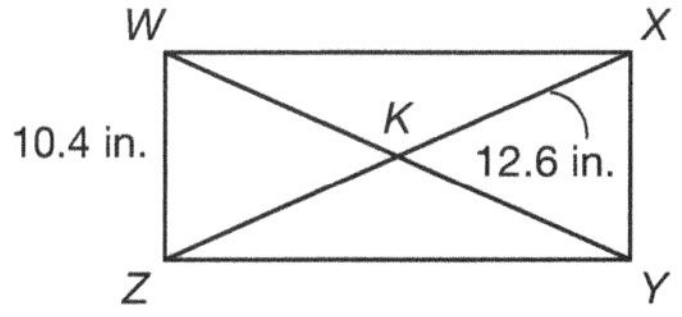

25. **Generalize** Two circles intersect at exactly two points. How many common tangents do they share?
(72)

26. Find the measure of angle x.
(64)

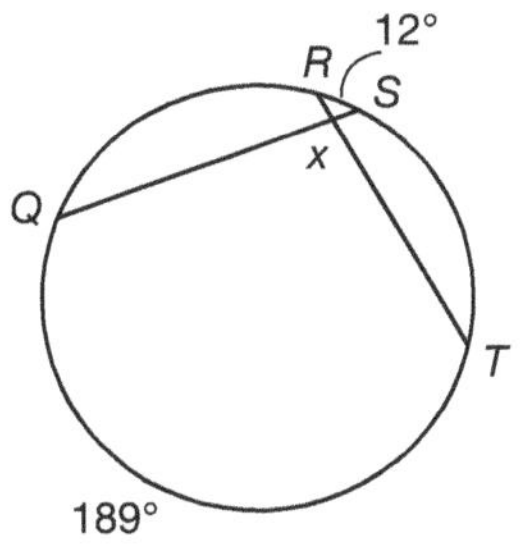

27. **Justify** A vector has vertical and horizontal components of −3 and 4, but it is not known which is the x-component and which is the y-component. Name the angle measures this vector could possibly have. Explain your answer.
(89)

28. **Justify** Determine whether lines $\overleftrightarrow{KL}$ and $\overleftrightarrow{MN}$ are parallel. How do you know?
(60)

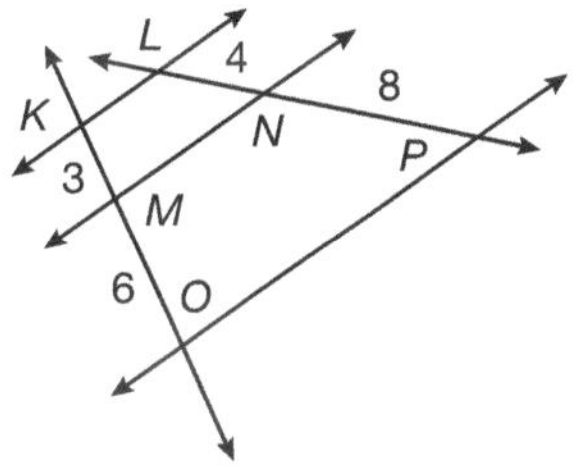

29. **Fund Raising** Justin is running a bake sale to raise money for a class trip to the local science center. He is selling bran muffins for \$1.00 and blueberry muffins for \$1.50 and needs to have total sales of at least \$650. Graph the inequality of the number of bran muffins (x), and blueberry muffins (y), he needs to sell.
(88)

***30.** Rotate $\triangle XYZ$ 90° counterclockwise about point P, and then translate the image along v.
(90)

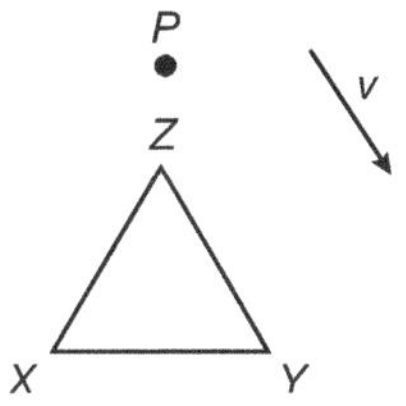

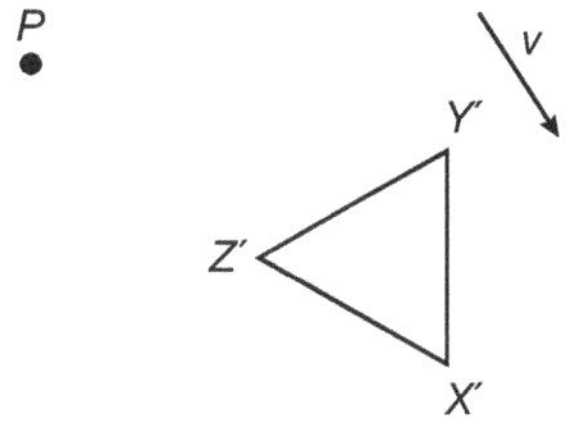

Name ____________________ Date __________ Class __________

Introduction to Trigonometric Identities

LESSON 91

* **1.** Sketch a tessellation using congruent images of this kite.
(Inv 9)

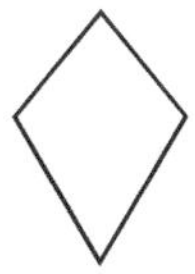

* **2.** **Write** How would you go about finding a value of θ where $\sin \theta = \tan \theta$? What is that value?
(91)

3. Sketch the graph of $f(x) < x + 2$.
(88)

4. **Multi-Step** A dragonfly is flying parallel to the ground up a hill that has a slope of 27°. If the dragonfly is flying at a speed of 16 feet per second, and the wind is blowing up the hill at a speed of 4 feet per second, what are the horizontal and vertical components of the dragonfly's speed over the ground?
(89)

* **5.** Draw two lines of reflection that will transform rectangle $STUV$ to rectangle $S'T'U'V'$ as shown.
(90)

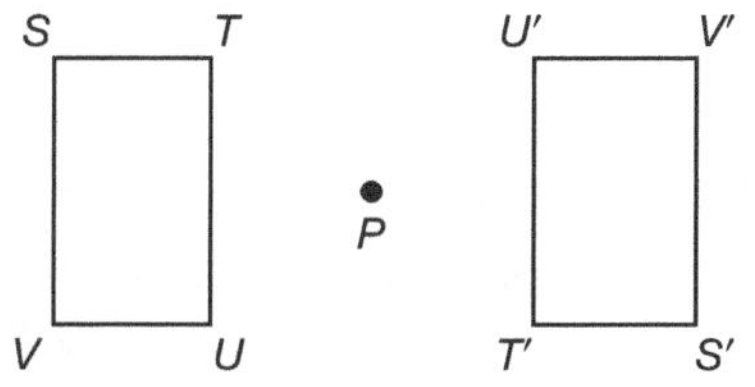

6. **Analyze** If a regular polygon has an angle of rotational symmetry of 15°, how many sides does it have?
(76)

7. What is the surface area of a sphere with a radius of $\frac{4}{\sqrt{\pi}}$ centimeters?
(80)

8. **Coordinate Geometry** A triangle has vertices at (2, 6), (4, −5), and (−3, 0). Classify the triangle by its sides.
(45)

9. A circle's radius is $4b$. Find the area of a 60° sector of this circle in terms of π and b.
(35)

10. If the length of the shorter leg of a 30°-60°-90° triangle is 68, what are the lengths of the other leg and hypotenuse?
(56)

***11.** Perform a glide reflection by reflecting $\angle ABC$ across line w and along $\vec{u}$.
(90)

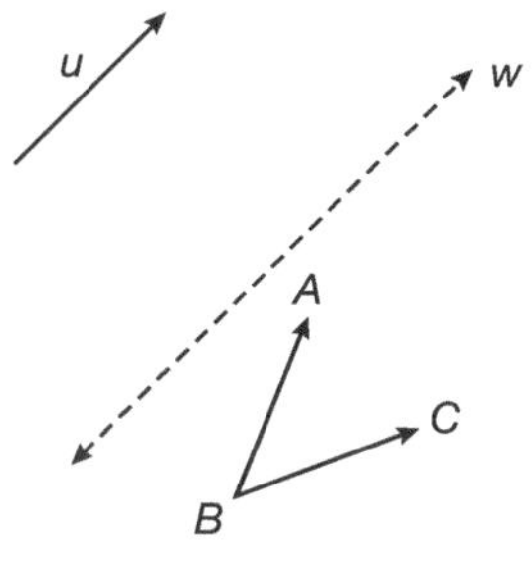

12. **Verify** A student says that a vector with a magnitude of x and an angle of 196° will have components that are negative. If $x > 0$, is the student correct? Explain.
(89)

13. **Analyze** All solids can have a cross section of a point. Explain how this is possible with a sphere, a cube, and a cylinder.
(85)

14. **Algebra** Use this figure to write and solve an equation for x.
(86)

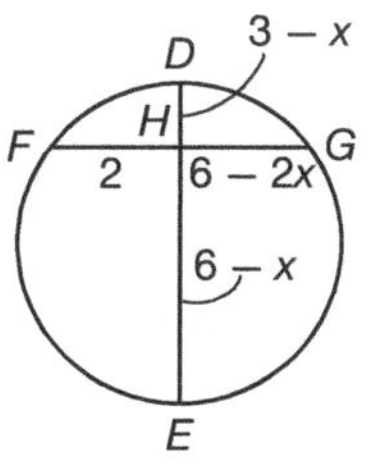

15. (47) What is the ratio of the measure of an arc to the measure of its inscribed angle?

16. (80) **Tennis** A tennis ball is made of two equally sized patches of material. If the diameter of the tennis ball is 3 inches, what is the area of each patch to the nearest hundredth?

17. (Inv 4) Compare *QR* and *SR*.

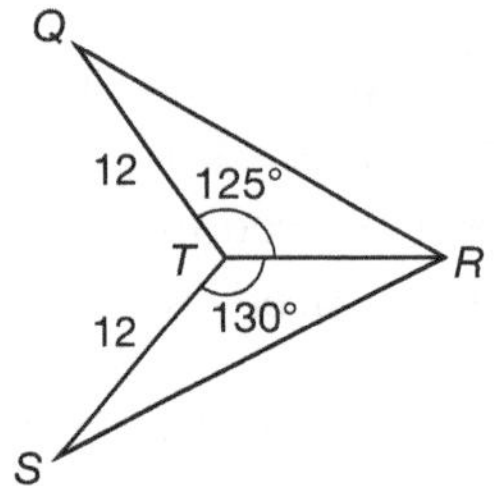

18. (70) **Architecture** Jan is designing a square-based pyramid that will be in front of a building. If the sides of the square are to be 6 feet long and the height of the pyramid is to be 4 feet, how much material does Jan need to construct the pyramid, including the base?

***19.** (90) In the diagram, $\triangle ABC$ undergoes a glide reflection. Copy the diagram and draw in the reflection line and the translation that occurred.

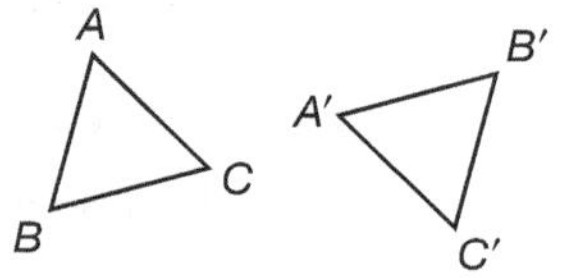

20. (61) **Multiple Choice** Which statement is not true about all parallelograms?
A Opposite angles are congruent.
B Consecutive angles are supplementary.
C Diagonals perpendicularly bisect each other.
D Opposite sides are congruent.

21. (62) **Containers** A cylindrical juice container has the dimensions show. To the nearest cubic inch, how much juice does the container hold?

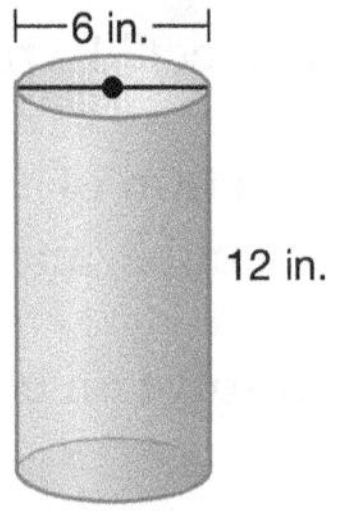

22. (85) **Analyze** If the height of a cylinder is 31.4 centimeters, and the area of the cross section parallel to a circular face has the same area as the cross section perpendicular to the circular faces through a diameter of each face, what is the radius of the cylinder?

23. (24) A rectangular table has a length of $3x - 2$, a width of $2x + 1$, and an area of $2x + 28$. Solve for x and provide a justification for each step.

***24.** (91) Write $\tan^2\theta$ in terms of $\cos\theta$.

25. (53) **Sawmills** To make the best use of the wood from each tree, sawmill operators must trim each log on four sides to make the largest square beam possible. If a log has a 20-inch diameter, find the width of the square beam that can be made from that log.

26. (42) Find the distance from $(-5, 12)$ to the line $x = 6$.

***27.** (91) **Algebra** For what value of θ does $\cos^2\theta = 3\sin^2\theta$?

28. (44) Roderick wants to know how tall the flagpole in his schoolyard is, but he cannot measure it directly. He knows that his shadow and the shadow of the flagpole form similar triangles. The length of his shadow is 2.25 feet and he is 6 feet tall. If the flagpole's shadow is 20.25 feet, how tall is the flagpole?

29. (83) **Bridges** A cable is suspended diagonally to hold the supports of a bridge. If there is a 200-pound vertical load and a 500-pound horizontal load, what is the total tension load of the cable? What is the angle the cable makes with the horizontal? Round your answers to the nearest tenth.

***30.** (91) **Error Analysis** Desi tried to prove that $\tan\theta = \frac{\sin\theta}{\sqrt{1 - \sin^2\theta}}$. His work is shown below. Where did he make his error?

$$\tan\theta = \frac{\sin\theta}{\sqrt{1 - \sin^2\theta}}$$

$$\frac{a}{b} = \frac{a}{c} \cdot \frac{1}{\sqrt{1 - \left(\frac{a}{c}\right)^2}}$$

$$\frac{a}{b} = \frac{a}{c} \cdot \frac{1}{\sqrt{c^2 - a^2}}$$

$$\frac{a}{b} = \frac{a}{c} \cdot \frac{1}{\sqrt{b^2}}$$

$$\frac{a}{b} = \frac{a}{c} \cdot \frac{1}{b}$$

$$\frac{a}{b} = \frac{a}{b} \cdot c$$

Name ________________________________ Date __________ Class __________

Quadrilaterals on the Coordinate Plane

LESSON 92

1. (71) **Multiple Choice** $\triangle DEF$ is translated so that the coordinates of E' are $(-2, 2)$. What are the coordinates of F'?

A $(0, -1)$ **B** $(-1, 0)$
C $(1, 0)$ **D** $(1, 1)$

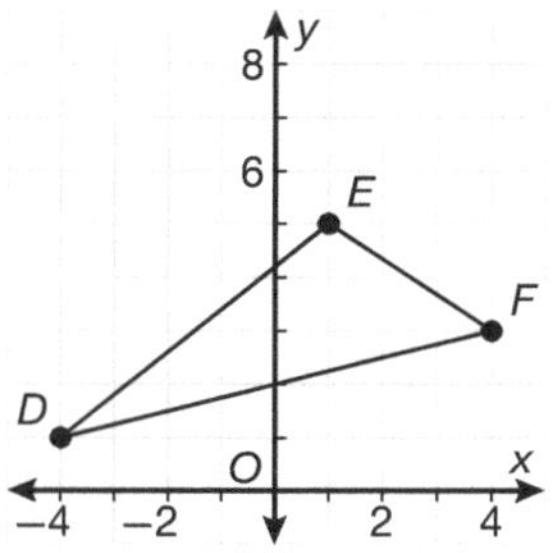

2. (89) Find the horizontal and vertical components of a vector with a magnitude of 80 and an angle of 12°.

***3.** (92) Quadrilateral $ABCD$ has vertices $A(3, 1)$, $B(5, 3)$, $C(2, 3)$, and $D(1, 2)$. Quadrilateral $EFGH$ has vertices $E(-1, 3)$, $F(-3, 5)$, $G(-3, 2)$, and $H(-2, 1)$. Prove that $ABCD \cong EFGH$ by determining corresponding side lengths and slopes.

4. (39) What is the longest side in the figure shown?

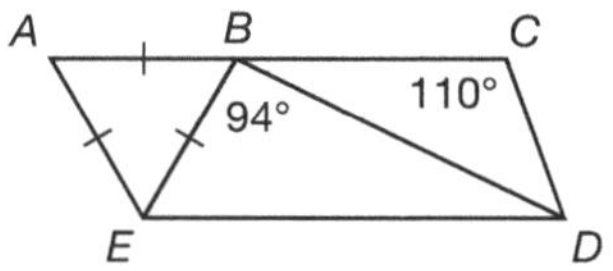

5. (37) Write the equation for a line that is perpendicular to and a line that is parallel to the line $y = 0.2x - 4$.

***6.** (Inv 8) **Generalize** Into how many segments do n points on a line divide that line? *Hint: Try putting 1, 2, and 3 points on a line and look for a pattern.*

7. (79) **Multi-Step** Find $m\widehat{BF}$ on the larger circle and $m\widehat{CE}$ on the smaller circle.

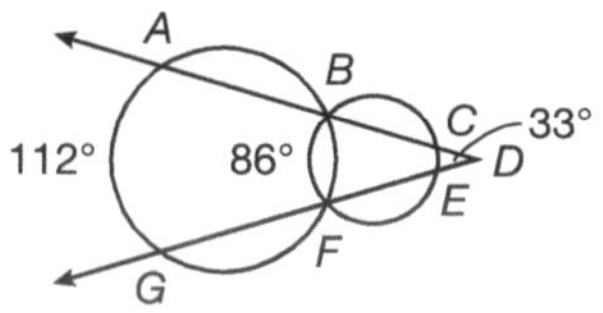

***8.** (92) The vertices of quadrilateral $WXYZ$ are $W(0, 3)$, $X(3, 2)$, $Y(-2, -3)$, and $Z(-5, -2)$. Prove that $WXYZ$ is a parallelogram by determining the slope of each side.

9. (58) **Analyze** Use Theorem 58-2 (if a line in the plane of a circle is perpendicular to a radius at its endpoint on the circle, then the line is tangent to the circle) to show *indirectly* that, if line ℓ intersects $\odot C$ at P but is *not* perpendicular to $\overline{CP}$, then line ℓ intersects $\odot C$ at one other point Q, and $\angle CPQ$ and $\angle CQP$ are congruent acute angles.

***10.** (92) Prove that quadrilateral $PQRS$ is a trapezoid.

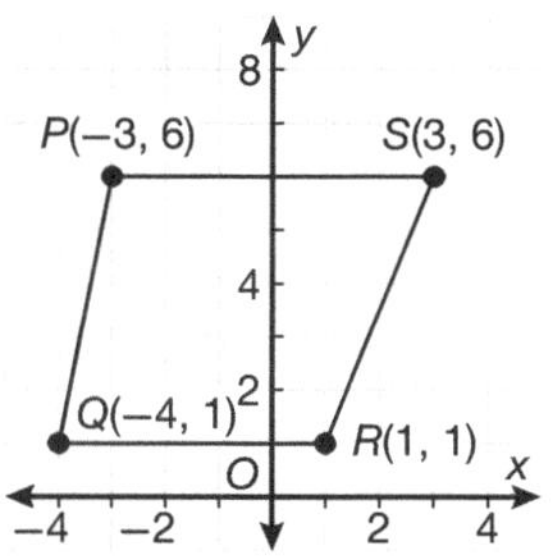

11. (63) **Boating** A boat sails along the vector $\langle 3, 4 \rangle$, then sails along the vector $\langle 1, 5 \rangle$. What vector can it use to go directly back to where it started?

12. (Inv 5) Draw the net of a pentagonal pyramid.

***13.** (91) **Verify** Use a right triangle to prove that $\cos\theta = \frac{1}{\sqrt{1 + \tan^2\theta}}$.

14. If $AG = 10$ and $DB = 16$, find GF and BG to the nearest tenth.
(32)

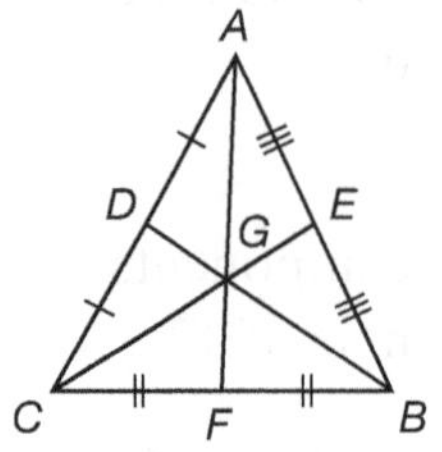

15. **Dartboards** A dartboard has a diameter of 20 inches, with a center circle that has a 5 inch diameter.
(Inv 6)

a. If you assume that throwing a dart is a random event, what is the probability of hitting the center circle?

b. In reality, is the probability of hitting the center circle different from what you calculated in part **a**?

16. Apply a dilation to $\overline{FG}$ using a scale factor of $\frac{1}{2}$ and center C.
(84)

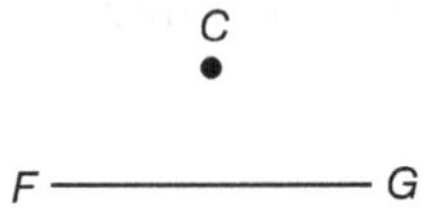

17. **Aviation** A plane takes off and flies at an angle of 30° from the ground. After a certain amount of time, the plane has reached an altitude of 3000 meters. Use trigonometry to find the horizontal distance of the plane from its starting point to the nearest hundredth.
(73)

18. **Analyze** A log that is 5 meters long is rolling down a hill. The lateral surface area of the log is 31.4 square meters. How many times will the log revolve if the hill is 62.8π meters long?
(62)

19. Find the circumference of circle O based on the arc given.
(35)

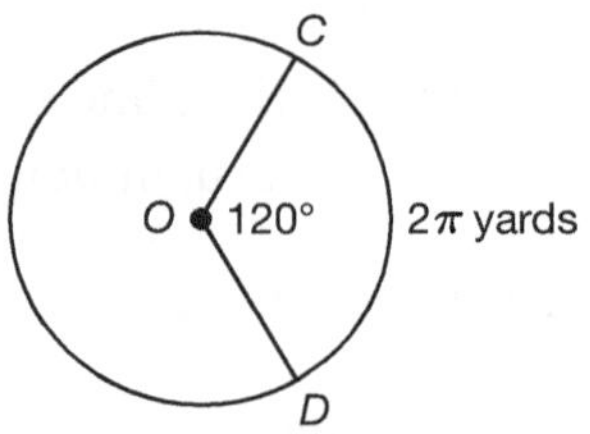

***20.** Prove that quadrilateral $JKLM$ with vertices $J(1, 1)$, $K(4, 1)$, $L(5, 4)$, and $M(2, 5)$ is congruent to quadrilateral $NOPQ$ with vertices $N(5, 7)$, $O(8, 7)$, $P(9, 4)$, and $Q(6, 3)$.
(92)

***21.** A boat is at coordinates (2, 0). The boat is towing a parasail. The coordinates for the parasail rider are (4, 6). If the angle of elevation is x, what is the tangent of x?
(73)

22. Reflect the figure across ℓ_1, and then reflect the image across ℓ_2.
(90)

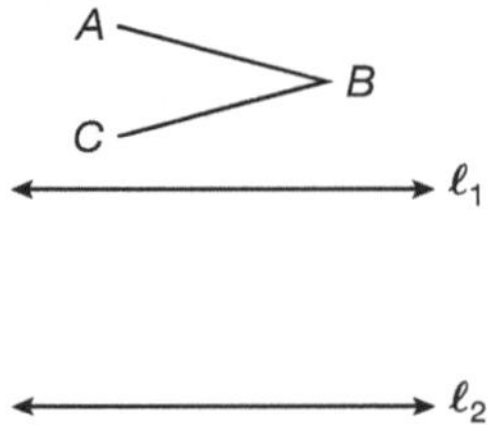

23. Solve for $\cos\theta \cdot \tan\theta$ in terms of $\sin\theta$.
(91)

24. (43) The chord of a circle is 28.3 inches long, and is 11.2 inches from the center of the circle. What is the length of the radius of the circle to the nearest inch?

25. (70) **Timekeeping** An hourglass is a device used to measure time. A particular hourglass is made of two congruent, regular, square-based pyramids attached at the two vertices of the pyramids. One of the two pyramids is filled with sand. What volume of sand is needed if the height of each pyramid is 5 inches and the side lengths of each square is 3 inches?

26. (21) Do the statements below show use of the Law of Syllogism or the Law of Detachment?

If William wakes up before 5 a.m., then he goes running that day. Today, William woke up before 5 a.m. Therefore, he will go running today.

27. (90) **Write** Ray drew equilateral triangle $\triangle EFG$. He then drew two lines, l_1, and l_2, that made a 60° angle through the center of the triangle. Ray reflected the triangle across l_1, and then across l_2. Describe the similarities and differences between the final image and the original triangle.

***28.** (Inv 9) Continue the tessellation of this pentagon that begins with

a. the given translation; **b.** the given rotation.

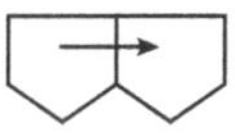

***29.** (82) **Playgrounds** A slide for a preschool's playground should have a slope between $\frac{1}{4}$ and $\frac{1}{6}$. What is the range of the measure of the angle between the slide and the ground rounded to the nearest degree?

30. (91) **Algebra** If $\frac{\cos\theta}{\sin\theta} = 12$, what is the value of $\tan\theta$? Then find θ to the nearest degree.

Name ______________________ Date __________ Class __________

Representing Solids: Orthographic Views

LESSON 93

***1.** (93) **Model** This orthographic drawing shows the front, top, and side views of a solid. Sketch the solid.

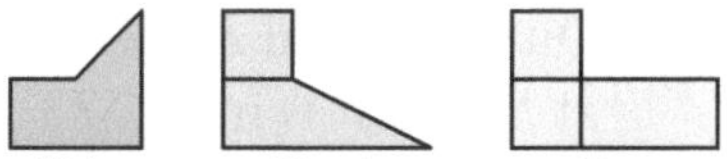

Side Front Top

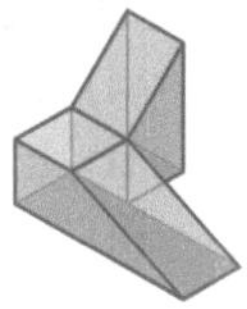

2. (88) Graph the region described by the inequalities $2x - y > -1$, $x + y < 1$, and $x - y < 1$.

3. (91) **Algebra** If $\tan^2\theta = 3.2$, what does $\cos\theta$ equal?

4. (62) **Compact discs** Compact discs have the dimensions shown. Each disc is 1 millimeter thick. Find the volume in cubic centimeters of a stack of 25 discs. Round to the nearest tenth of a centimeter.

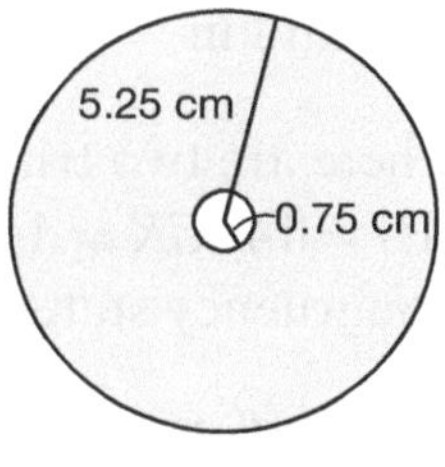

5. (80) **Pottery** Brandon crafted a clay bowl on a pottery wheel in the shape of a hemisphere. After the clay hardens, Brandon will paint only the outside of the bowl. If the radius of the bowl is 6 inches, what surface area will he paint to the nearest square inch?

6. (90) **Multiple Choice** Which of these best describes the composite transformation in the diagram?

A glide reflection **B** glide rotation
C reflection then translation **D** translation then reflection

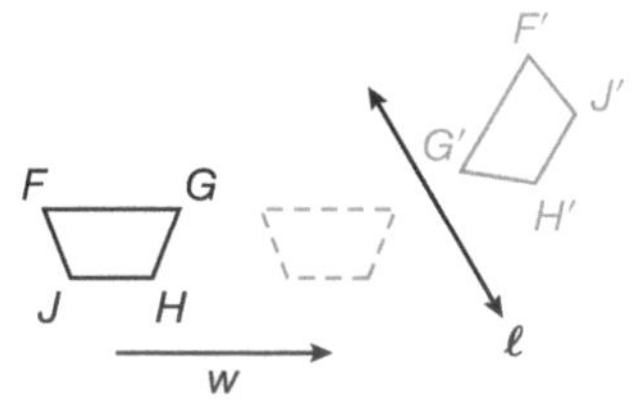

7. (87) Two similar triangles have areas of 76 square centimeters and 931 square centimeters, respectively. Determine the ratio of their perimeters.

8. (61) **Write** Quadrilateral $ABCD$ has vertices $A(-3, 3)$, $B(4, 1)$, $C(-1, -2)$, and $D(-5, -1)$. Could you make the quadrilateral a parallelogram by moving any point? Explain why or why not.

***9.** (93) **Multiple Choice** This orthographic drawing shows the front, top, and right-side views of a solid. Which of these sketches represents the solid?

Front Side Top

A

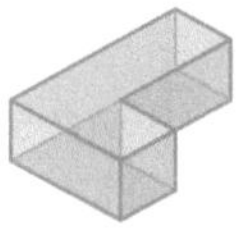

B

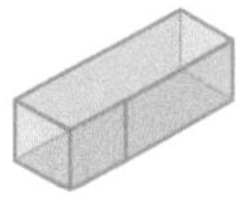

C

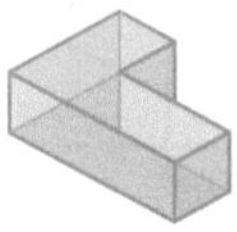

D

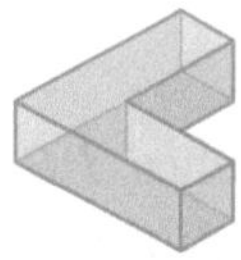

10. (82) **Multi-Step** For the right triangle with vertices $K(-2, -2)$, $L(1, -3)$, and $M(3, 3)$, find the side lengths to the nearest tenth of a unit and the angle measures to the nearest degree. $KL = 3.2$, $LM = 6.3$, $KM = 7.1$; $\angle K = 63°$, $\angle M = 27°$, $\angle L = 90°$

11. (52) Quadrilateral *KLMN* is a rhombus with diagonals that intersect at *S*. What is m$\angle KSL$?

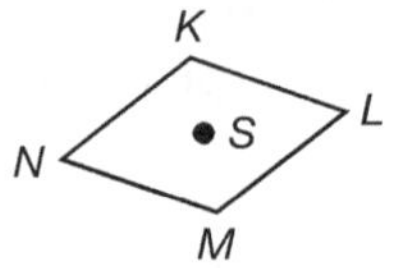

12. (37) **Multiple Choice** Which of the following are perpendicular lines?
i) $x + y = 1$,
ii) $x - y = 3$, and
iii) $y - x = 5$

A i and ii
B i and iii
C ii and iii
D i and ii and i and iii

13. (25) There are two triangles, $\triangle AGK$ and $\triangle JOV$, with side lengths as follows: $AG = 14$, $GK = 15$, $KA = 13$, $OJ = 14$, $JV = 15$, and $VO = 13$. Write a congruency statement for the triangles.

14. (40) **Error Analysis** Sarita is standing at *P* and wants to travel to *C*. She reasons that since the area of quadrilateral *ABCD* is greater than the area of polygon *APQRCD*, she will be taking a shortcut if she travels along $\overline{PQ}$ and then $\overline{QR}$, rather than by traveling along $\overline{PB}$, then $\overline{BR}$. Explain why she is wrong.

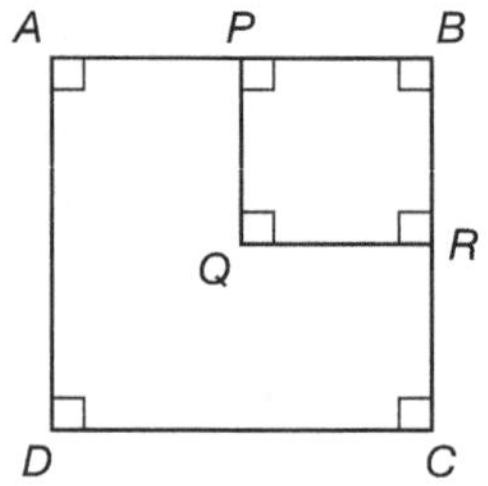

15. (42) **Algebra** Given the equation $y = 3x - 4$ and the point $C(0, 6)$, find the point on the line that is closest to *C*.

16. (57) **Civil Planning** The diagram represents train tracks surrounding a children's zoo. Find the area enclosed by the tracks. The side lengths of each square represents 1 meter.

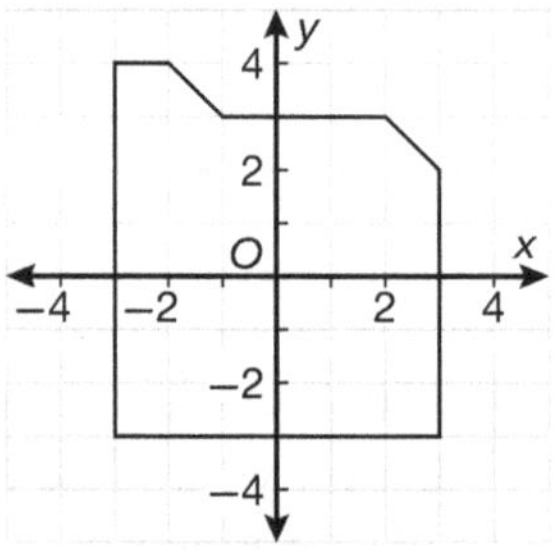

17. (80) What is the surface area of a sphere with a radius of 5.5 meters?

18. (85) **Woodworking** Mark has a cube-shaped block of wood he wants to cut. He wants to make a cut through the plane of the midpoints of the three edges adjacent to one of the vertices. What shape is this cross section?

***19.** (92) Prove that *UVWX* is a parallelogram by determining its side lengths and slopes.

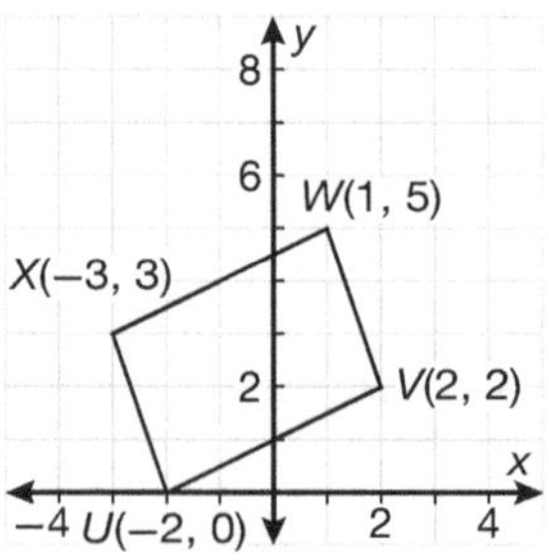

20. (81) **Algebra** The solution to a linear system is (3, 2). One equation is $y = 3x + b$ and the other equation is $y = 2$. What is the value of *b*?

21. (25) If $\triangle QPR \cong \triangle DEF$, and $QP = 5$ inches, $PR = 7$ inches, and $DF = 8$ inches, what are the lengths of the other sides?

***22.** (93) **Model** Construct an accurate orthographic drawing of a square pyramid with slant height and side lengths of 2. Include horizontal and vertical dimensions.

*23. (63) **Physics** Newton's Second Law says the force on an object is the net acceleration, which is a vector, multiplied by the mass. A block on a ramp is under the force of gravity at about 10 m/s^2 down and a friction force of 4 m/s^2 up and 8 m/s^2 to the left. What is the net acceleration on the block?

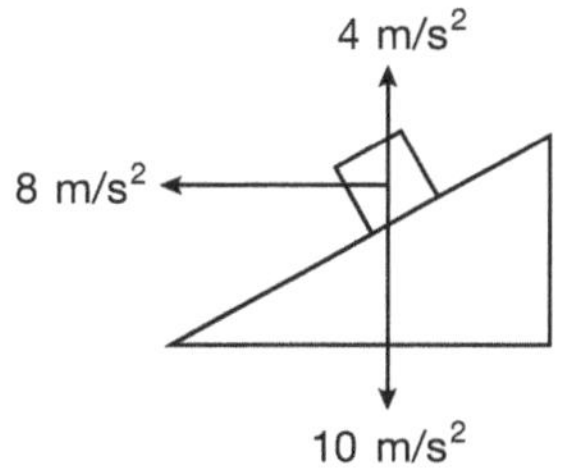

24. (86) **Algebra** Two chords of a circle, $\overline{DE}$ and $\overline{FG}$, intersect at C with segment lengths $CD = 3$, $CE = x + 2$, $CF = 6 - x$, and $CG = 5$. Write and solve an equation for x.

25. (55) Segment UV is a midsegment of $\triangle RST$. Find RT.

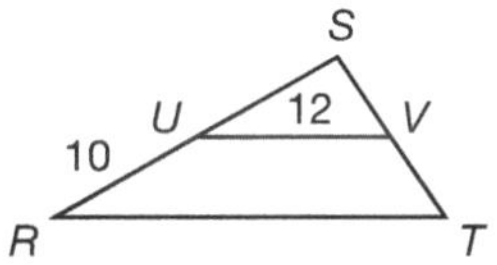

*26. (92) **Verify** The vertices of quadrilateral $MNOP$ are $M(2, 2)$, $N(3, 0)$, $O(6, 4)$, and $P(5, 6)$. Prove that $MNOP$ is a parallelogram by determining its side lengths.

27. (91) Find an expression for $\cos\theta$ in terms of $\tan\theta$.

*28. (93) **Model** Draw the front, top, and side orthographic views of this solid.

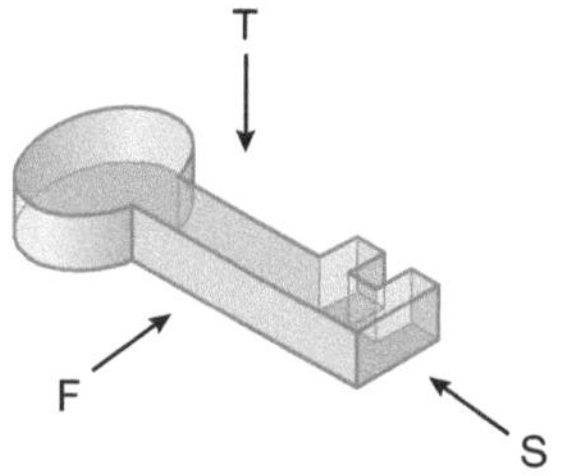

29. (89) Find the horizontal and vertical components of a vector with a magnitude of 44 and an angle of 275°.

30. (46) Find the value of x in the diagram.

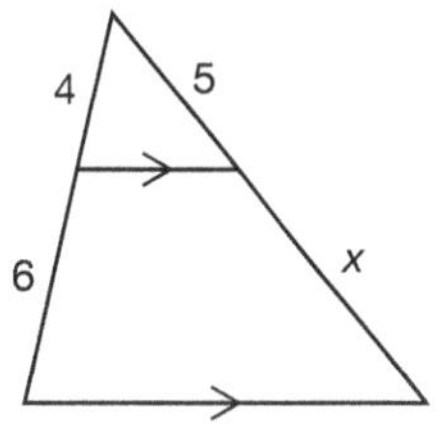

Name ______________________ Date __________ Class __________

Law of Sines

LESSON 94

1. (41) What is the similarity ratio between these two similar trapezoids?

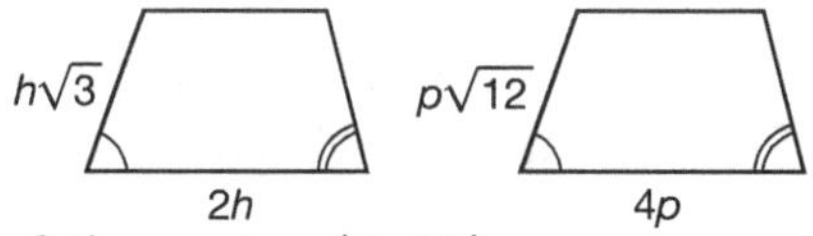

* **2.** (63) **Error Analysis** Humberto sees a bird fly the length of the vector $\langle 4, 10\rangle$ and then fly the length of the vector $\langle 14, 14\rangle$, where 1 unit is 1 kilometer. Humberto said that since the bird flew for a total of an hour, the bird's velocity for the trip was 30 km/h. What mistake did Humberto make?

3. (64) **Wheels** A wheel has a square built in for support. When the wheel is rolling on a flat road, what will be the measure of the angle between the road and a chord from one of the sides of the square when the cord meets the road?

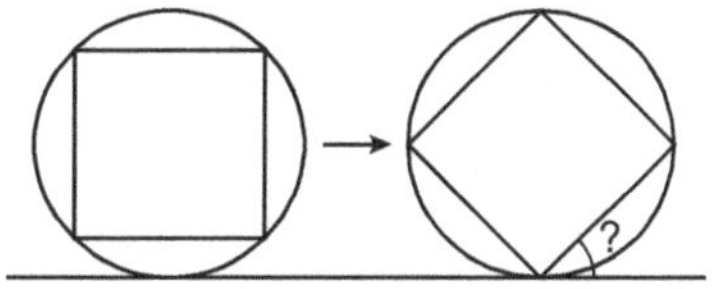

4. (53) **Softball** A softball diamond is a square that is 90 feet long on each side. To the nearest tenth, what is the distance from home plate to second base, at the opposite corner?

5. (92) The vertices of quadrilateral *ABCD* are *A*(3, 7), *B*(8, 8), *C*(7, 3), and *D*(2, 2). Prove that *ABCD* is a parallelogram by determining the slope of each side.

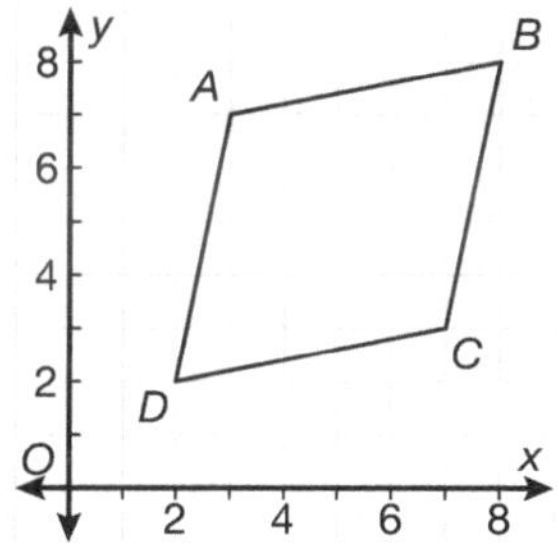

6. (70) **Multi-Step** What is the volume of a pyramid with an equilateral triangle for a base and a height equal to the base side length? Express your answer in terms of *s*, the length of a side of the base.

* **7.** (94) **Aircraft** An observer sees a helicopter at an angle of elevation of 30° and an airplane at an angle of elevation of 65°. The pilot of the airplane sees the helicopter at an angle of depression of 79.87°. The observer uses a laser to find that the helicopter is 300 meters away. How far is the helicopter from the airplane, to the nearest meter?

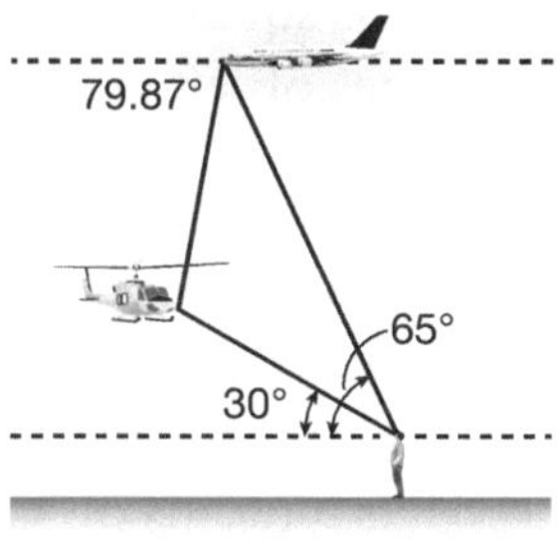

8. (Inv 4) **Algebra** Find the range of values for *x*.

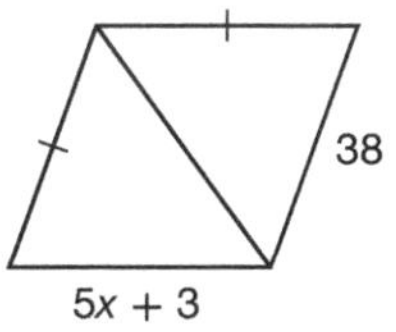

9. (84) Pentagon $QRSTU$ has vertices $Q(1, 1)$, $R(2, 0)$, $S(1, -1)$, $T(-1, -\frac{1}{2})$, and $U(-1, \frac{1}{2})$. Sketch a dilation of $QRSTU$ with the center at the origin. Use a scale factor of 6.

***10.** (94) Use the Law of Sines to find PR to the nearest whole number.

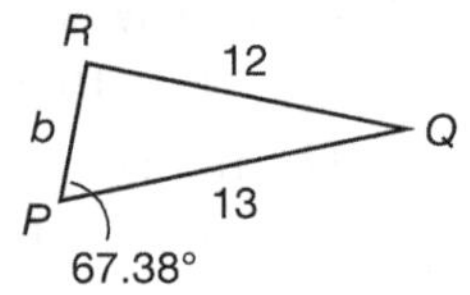

11. (91) Find an expression for $\tan^2\theta$ in terms of $\sin\theta$.

***12.** (93) **Model** Draw the front, top, and side orthographic views of this solid.

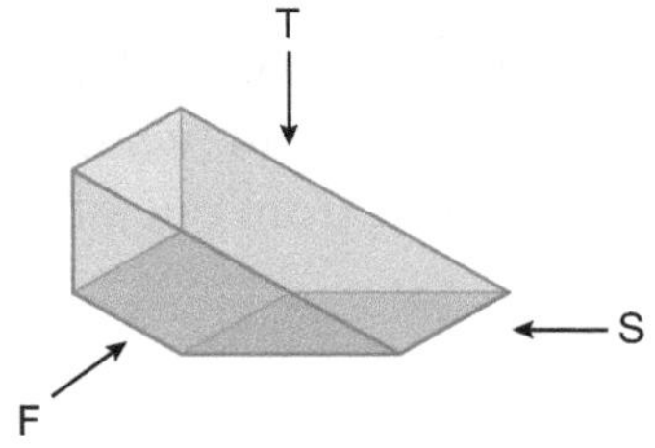

13. (92) **Multiple Choice** Which could be the slopes of the sides of a trapezoid, in clockwise order?

A 0, 2, 0, 3 **B** $3, -\frac{1}{2}, \frac{1}{2}, 5$

C 1, 4, 2, 3 **D** $1, 5, -1, -\frac{1}{5}$

14. (47) **Algebra** Find the measure of x in the figure.

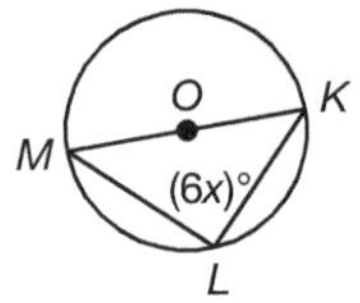

15. (77) The volume of a cone is 96π cubic centimeters. If the radius of the cone is 6 centimeters, what is the surface area of the cone to the nearest tenth?

16. (66) A regular pentagon has 45-inch side lengths and an apothem that is 31 inches long. Find the perimeter and area of the pentagon.

***17.** (94) **Algebra** Express the Law of Sines in terms of only the cosine function.

18. (Inv 9) This square tile has rotational symmetry of order 4 about its center but no lines of symmetry. Construct a tessellation that has rotational symmetry about the center of each square and about the vertex of each square.

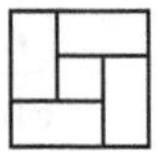

19. (75) **Painting** Gregory is painting a mural design on his wall. He has already painted a grid pattern where 1 unit is 1 foot. He wants to paint concentric circles that will be centered at point $(1, -1)$ on his grid. If the first circle has a radius of 1 foot, what is the equation of this circle?

***20.** (94) **Analyze** Nadim is given a Side-Side-Angle relationship in which the angle between sides a and b can either be obtuse or acute. Can the student find two answers for the length of side c that might both be correct? Explain.

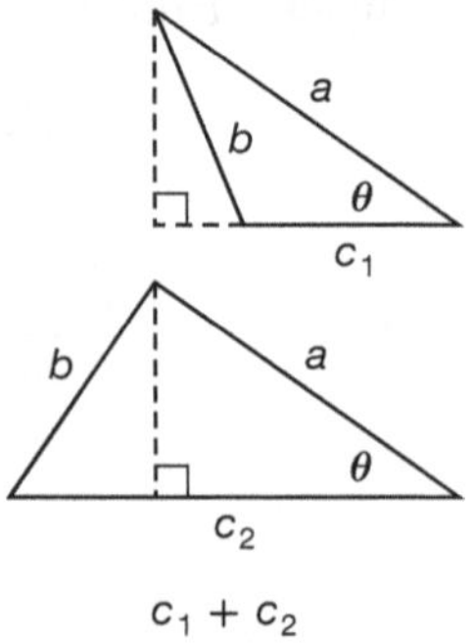

21. (80) **Verify** Show that the volume and the surface area of a sphere have the same value only if the radius is 3 units.

22. (72) Determine how many common tangents the circles have and draw the tangents.

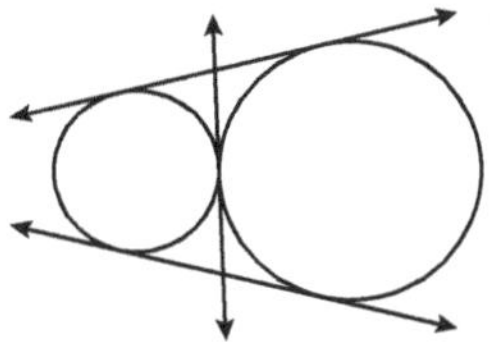

23. (28) If $\triangle ABC \cong \triangle DEF$, $AB = DE$, $BC = EF$, $m\angle ABC = (7x - 36)°$, and $m\angle DEF = (3x + 16)°$, then what is x?

24. (Inv 6) **Model** Design a spinner with 4 sectors so that the probability of the pointer landing on one sector is 3 times greater than any of the others.

25. (36) Which congruence theorem applies to these triangles?

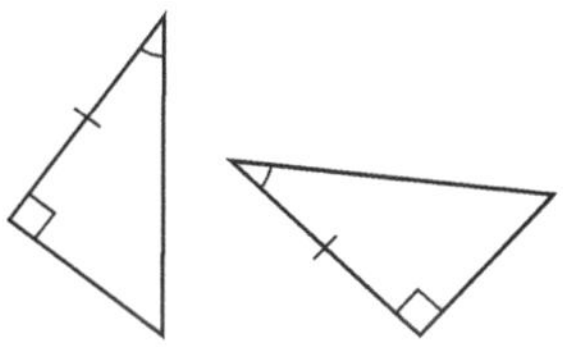

26. (33) **Multiple Choice** Which of the following sets of numbers does not form a right triangle?

A 3, 4, 5 **B** $2\sqrt{2}, 2\sqrt{2}, \sqrt{8}$
C $2\sqrt{2}, 2, 2$ **D** $7, 6\sqrt{2}, 11$

27. (57) **Rock Garden** The illustration depicts a rock garden, with the side of each square representing 1 foot. If there should be one basalt rock for every 2 square feet of rock garden, find an estimate for how many basalt rocks should be used.

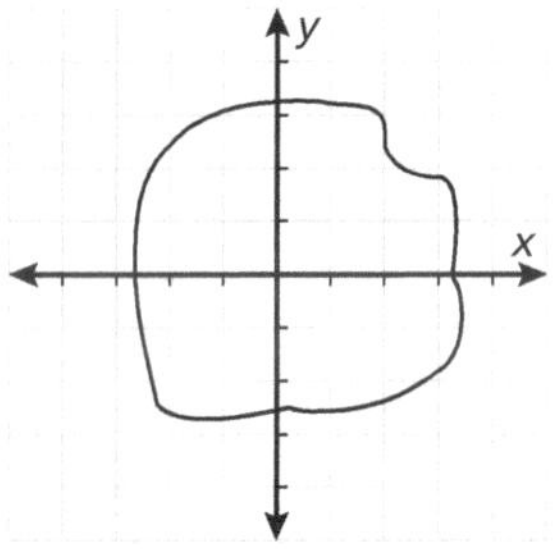

28. (86) **Algebra** Two chords of a circle, $\overline{RS}$ and $\overline{TU}$, intersect at V. $RV = 13 - c$, $SV = 5$, $TV = 7$, and $UV = c - 1$. Write and solve an equation for c.

29. (88) Graph $y > -2x + 3$.

***30.** (93) **Model** This orthographic drawing shows the front, top, and left-side views of a solid. Sketch the solid.

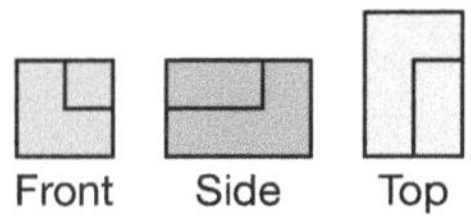

Name ______________________ Date __________ Class __________

Equations of Circles: Translating and Dilating

LESSON 95

1. (93) **Furniture** This orthographic drawing shows front, top, and left-side views of a child's chair. Sketch the chair.

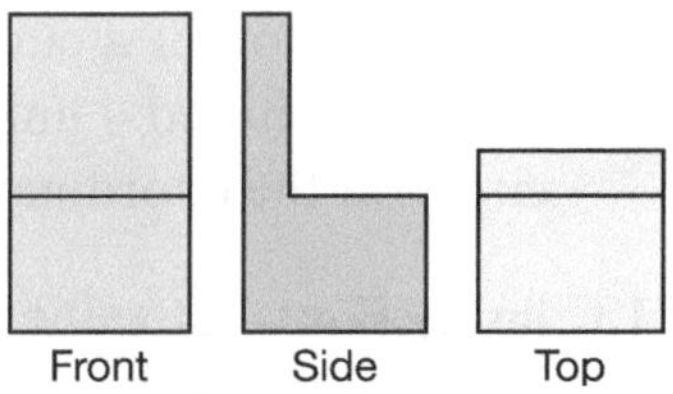

2. (79) Find the measure of the angle exterior to a circle made by two secants to the circle if the shorter arc is 60° and the longer one is 150°.

3. (89) **Football** A quarterback throws a football at a velocity of 50 miles per hour, at a 30° angle above the horizontal. What is the horizontal speed of the football, to the nearest tenth?

4. (33) **Algebra** Write an inequality to show the least value of x that would make the triangle acute.

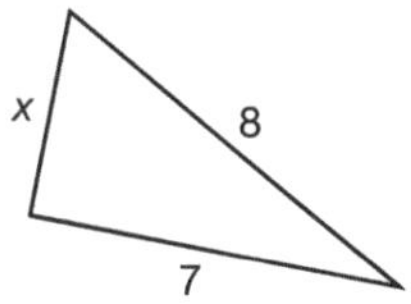

*** 5.** (95) The equation of a circle is $x^2 + y^2 = 9$. Write the equation of this circle after it is shifted 8 units to the right. Draw the original circle and the shifted circle on the coordinate plane.

6. (50) **Verify** Show that the geometric mean of $\frac{1}{2}$ and $\frac{1}{32}$ is $\frac{1}{8}$.

7. (90) Reflect the triangle across the horizontal line that goes through point C. Then reflect the image across line t.

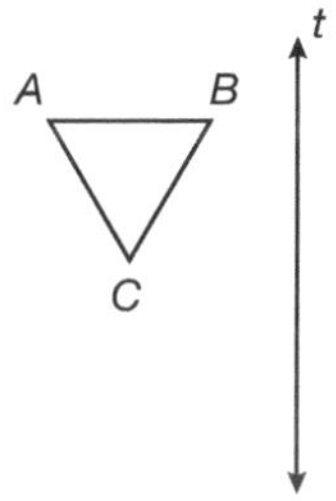

*** 8.** (95) **Multi-Step** The equation of a circle is $x^2 + y^2 = 144$. Find the equation of the circle after it is dilated by a factor of ¼, then is shifted 1 unit to the right and 4 units down.

*** 9.** (94) Find AC. Round your answer to the nearest hundredth.

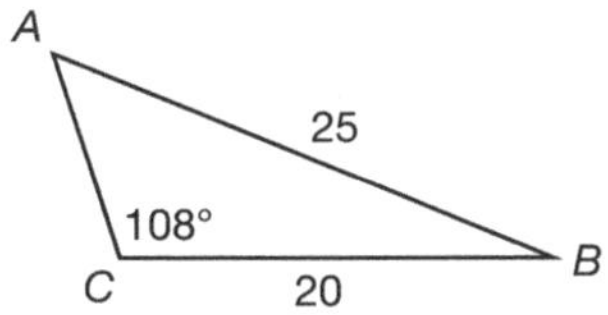

10. (83) **Skiing** A skier skis downhill at a velocity of 14 meters per second (m/s). If there is a wind coming towards him up the hill at a velocity of 2 m/s, what is his actual magnitude? What would his velocity be if the wind were traveling *with* him down the mountain at the same velocity?

11. (46) Find the value of x in the diagram.

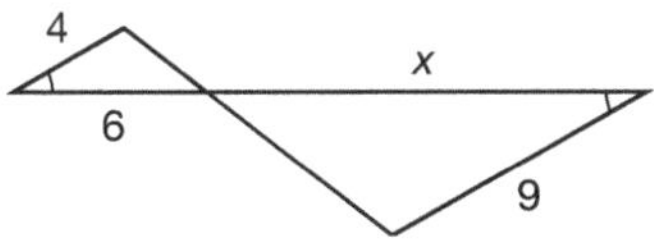

*12. (95) The equation of a circle is $x^2 + y^2 = 36$. Write the equation of this circle after it is shifted 4 units upward. Draw the original circle and the shifted circle on the coordinate plane.

13. (12) **Justify** For what value of y are line m and n parallel? State a theorem to justify your answer.

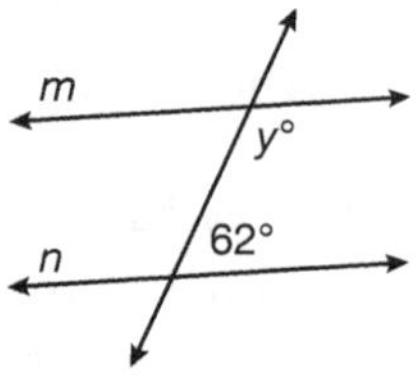

14. (91) **Analyze** At what value between 0° and 180° is the tangent function undefined? Explain why it is undefined at this value.

15. (94) Find the length of $\overline{LM}$. Round your answer to the nearest hundredth.

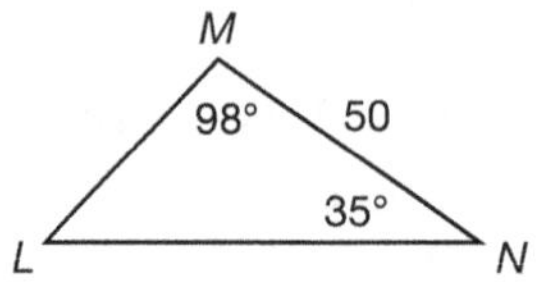

16. (37) **Multiple Choice** Which of the following are parallel lines?

i) $y = 2x + 7$ **ii)** $y = 2(x - 4)$ **iii)** $y - x = 7$

A i and ii **B** i and iii

C ii and iii **D** i, ii, and iii

17. (92) **Error Analysis** Noemi says that quadrilateral *CDEF* is a trapezoid. Explain why she is mistaken.

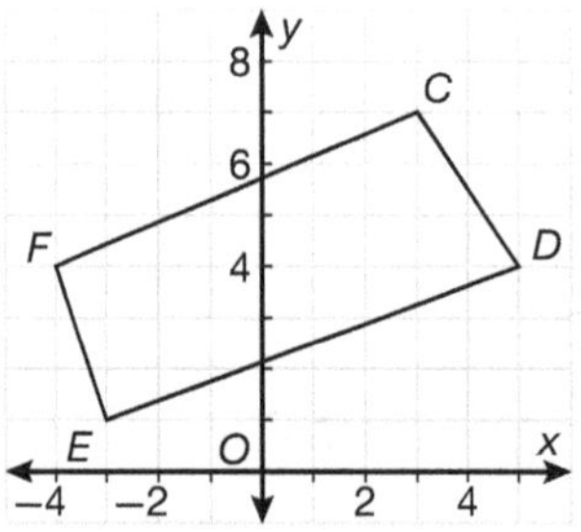

18. (53) Find the exact length of a leg of a 45°-45°-90° right triangle with a hypotenuse of 31 centimeters.

*19. (94) **Formulate** Express the Law of Sines using only the tangent function.

20. (65) If $x = 3$, is this parallelogram a rhombus, a rectangle, both, or neither?

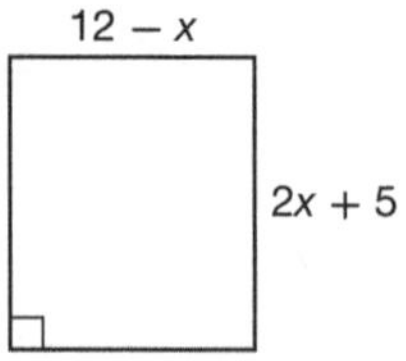

21. (Inv 1) If two parallel lines are cut by a transversal, and the alternate interior angles formed measure $(3x - 10)°$ and $(-x + 60)°$, find the value of x.

22. (85) **Carpentry** A carpenter is cutting a cylindrical piece of wood. If he makes a cut that is parallel to the base, what is the shape of the cross section?

23. (Inv 8) **Design** A wallpaper pattern consists of nested squares, as shown in the diagram. Does this pattern have rotational symmetry? If so, what is the order of rotational symmetry?

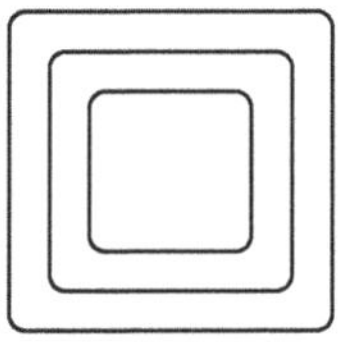

*24. (95) The equation of a circle is $x^2 + y^2 = 16$. Find the equation of the circle after it is dilated by a factor of 3. Draw the original circle and the dilated circle on the coordinate plane.

25. (58) How far apart are the centers of these two circles?

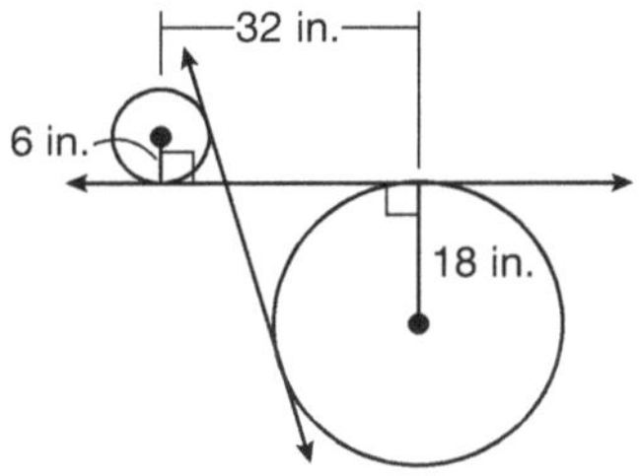

26. (78) Quadrilateral $QRST$ has vertices $Q(5, -6)$, $R(6, -4)$, $S(3, -1)$, and $T(1, -3)$. Graph the quadrilateral, and then rotate it 90° counterclockwise about the origin. List the coordinates of the vertices of quadrilateral $Q'R'S'T'$.

27. (43) A chord of a circle is 15 inches long, and 12 inches from the center of the circle. What is the length of the radius of the circle?

28. (93) **Model** Draw the front, top, and side orthographic views of this solid.

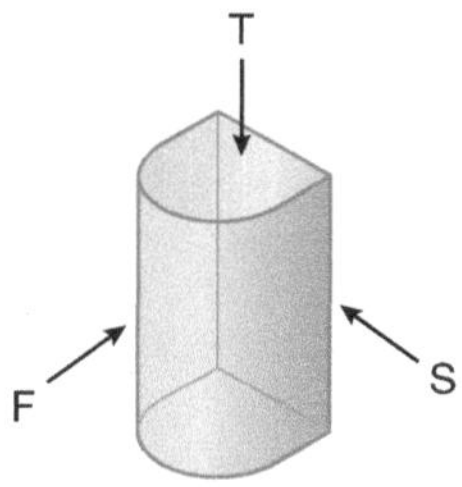

29. (61) Is this statement sometimes, always, or never true?
A rhombus is a parallelogram.

30. (27) Write a two-column proof showing that $m\angle 1 = m\angle 3$.

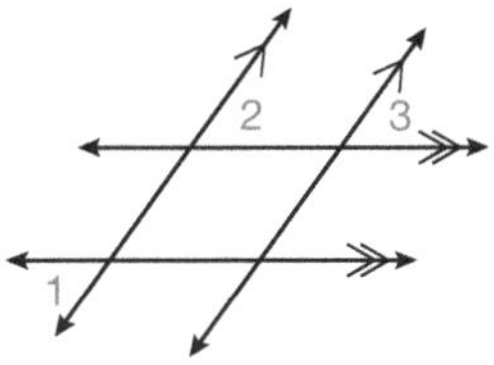

Name ______________________ Date ____________ Class ____________

Effects of Changing Dimensions on Perimeter and Area

LESSON 96

1. (94) Find the length of $\overline{DE}$. Round your answer to the nearest hundredth.

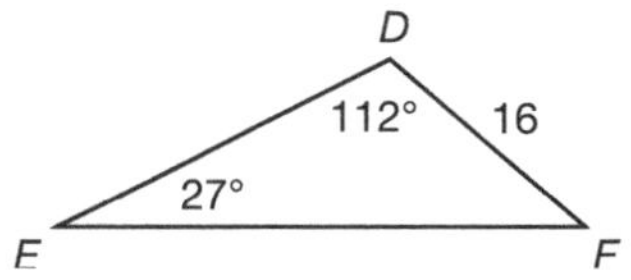

2. (86) Two chords of a circle, $\overline{JK}$ and $\overline{LM}$, intersect at N. $JN = KN$, $LN = 3$, and $MN = 12$.

a. Sketch the circle and the two chords, showing the given information.

b. Determine JN.

3. (37) **Algebra** Line m passes through points $(5, -3)$ and $(2, -6)$. Line n passes through points $(4, y)$ and $(-2, 3)$. What value of y makes these lines perpendicular?

* **4.** (95) The equation of a circle is $x^2 + y^2 = 100$. Write the equation of this circle after it is shifted 3 units upward. Draw the original circle and the shifted circle on the coordinate plane.

* **5.** (96) **Multi-Step** The perimeter of a square is 16 centimeters. If the area is doubled, what is the new side length?

6. (Inv 5) Is the net at right the net of a cube? Explain.

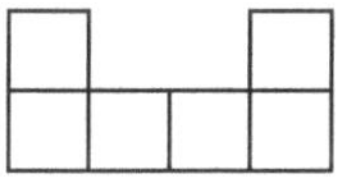

* **7.** (62) **Milk** After fresh milk was stored in a 452-cubic-inch cylindrical jar for half a day, it separated into a 2-inch band of cream and a 14-inch band of low-fat milk. What is the radius of the can?

8. (40) **Miniature Golf** A hole on a miniature golf course is in the shape given in the diagram, with dimensions in feet. What is the exact amount of artificial turf needed to resurface this hole? What is the amount rounded to the nearest tenth? The regions that appear to be semicircles are semicircles.

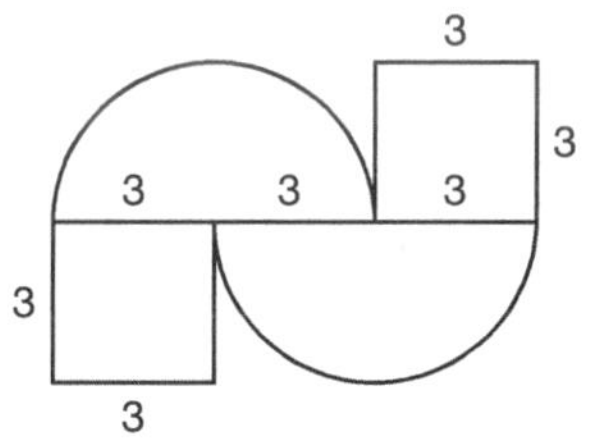

9. (78) Triangle ABC has been rotated counterclockwise about the origin. The original vertices were located at $A(-5, -8)$, $B(-3, 2)$, and $C(-1, -8)$. After the rotation, the vertices were located at $A'(-8, 5)$, $B'(2, 3)$, and $C'(-8, 1)$. What was the angle of rotation?

10. (94) **Write** Can you use the Law of Sines to find the other measures of $\triangle EKG$? Explain.

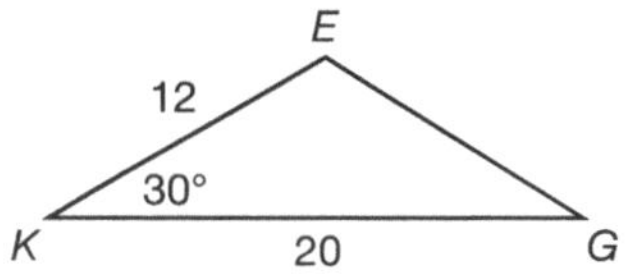

***11.** (96) **Algebra** The circumference of a circle is πx. If the radius is increased by a factor of 2, what is the area of the circle, in terms of π?

Effects of Changing Dimensions on Perimeter and Area

12. (44) Find the value of k in these similar polygons.

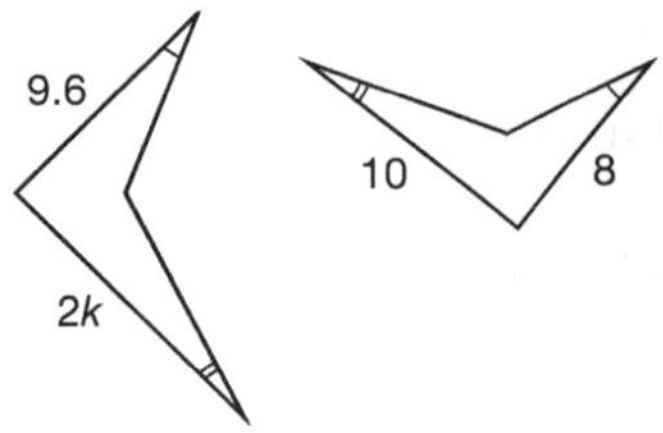

***13.** (95) The equation of a circle is $x^2 + y^2 = 64$. Write the equation of this circle after it is shifted 1 unit to the right. Draw the original circle and the shifted circle on the coordinate plane.

14. (90) **Error Analysis** What has Leif done incorrectly in the glide reflection from $ABCD$ to $A''B''C''D''$?

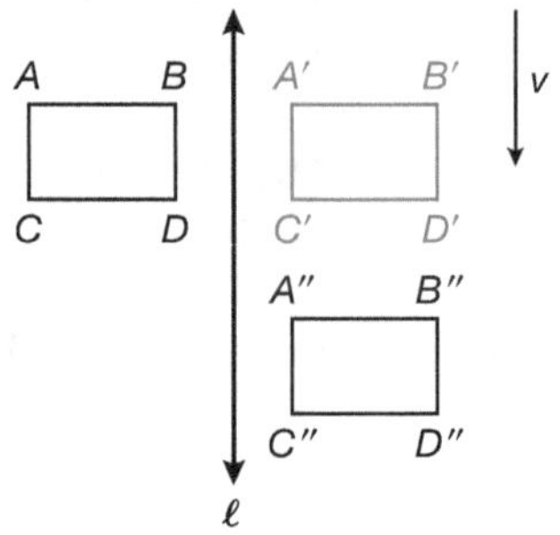

15. (66) **Multiple Choice** Which is the area of a pentagon with side lengths of 44 feet and a 50.5-foot apothem?

A 3703.3 ft^2 **B** 11,110 ft^2
C 555.5 ft^2 **D** 5555 ft^2

16. (60) **Shadows** A streetlight is mounted at the top of a 15-foot pole. A 6-foot-tall man walks away from the pole along a straight path. If it is dark and the streetlight provides the only light, how long is the man's shadow when he is 40 feet from the pole, to the nearest tenth of a foot?

17. (93) **Model** This orthographic drawing shows the front, top, and left-side views of a solid. Sketch the solid. Classify the solid.

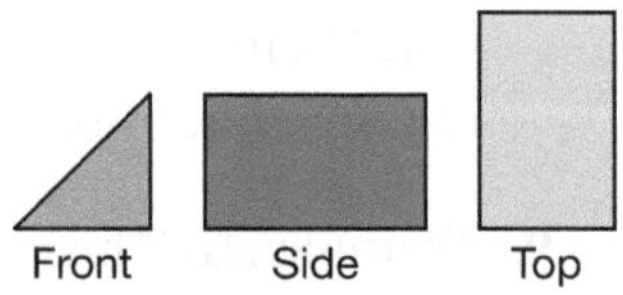

18. (85) **Write** Two cross sections of a cylinder are being compared. One is parallel to the base and the other is slanted through the base. Which will have the larger area? What shape will the cross sections have? Explain.

19. (30) In the diagram given, what piece of information is needed to conclude that $\triangle ABC \cong \triangle DEF$?

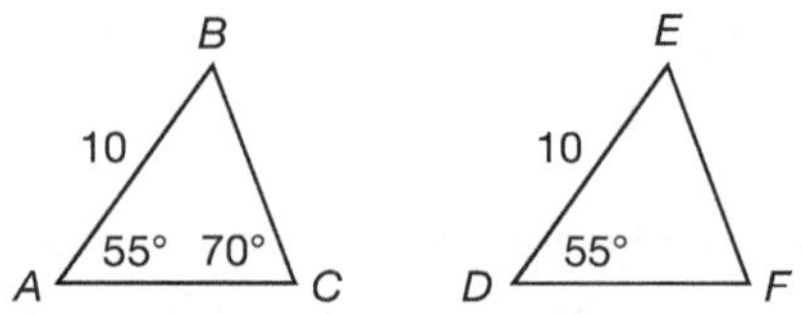

***20.** (96) **Converting Units** If a playground covers 10 square yards, how many square feet does it cover? Explain how you can use dilations to answer this question.

21. (56) **Multi-Step** Find the value of x in the figure shown.

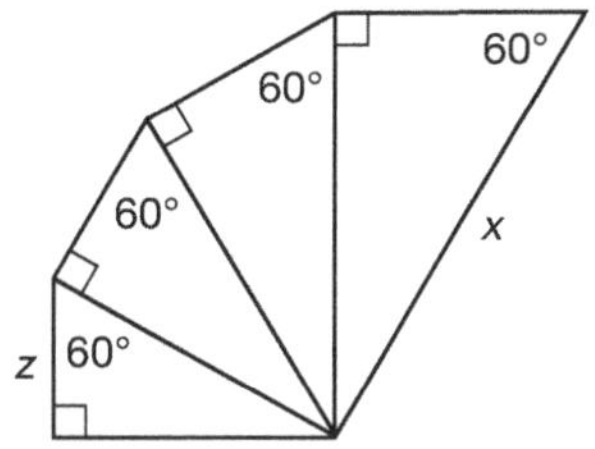

22. (87) **Architecture** A model of a pyramid for an art gallery has glass triangular lateral faces, each with a base of 3 feet and a height of 4 feet. The scale of the model is 2:41. How many square feet of glass will be needed for each triangular glass pane?

23. (49) Classify the solid. How many vertices, edges, and bases does it have?

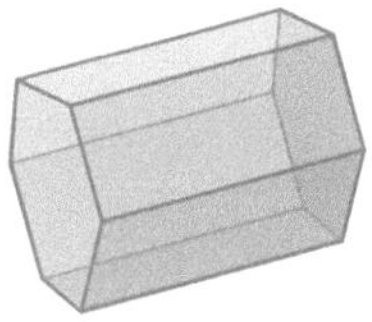

24. (80) Find the surface area of a sphere with a 12-inch radius to the nearest square inch.

25. (35) Find the circumference of this circle based on the arc given.

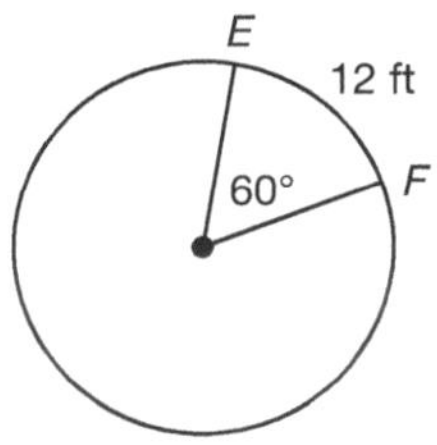

26. (71) **Verify** Show that the area of a right triangle with vertices $A(0, 0)$, $B(0, 5)$, and $C(4, 0)$ under the translation T: $(x, y) \rightarrow (x - 2, y + 1)$ remains constant.

***27.** (95) A circle whose equation is $x^2 + y^2 = 25$ is shifted 1 unit down and 2 units to the left. What is the equation for the shifted circle? Graph the shifted circle.

28. (Inv 3) Each exterior angle of a regular polygon is 10°. How many sides does the polygon have?

29. (91) **Verify** Use the diagram to show that $\frac{\tan \theta}{\sin \theta}$ is equivalent to $\frac{1}{\cos \theta}$.

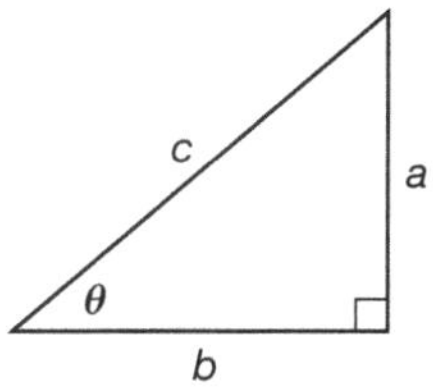

***30.** (96) **Architecture** An architect makes a replica of a clock tower. If the replica has dimensions that are ten times smaller than the clock, what is the ratio between the replica's circumference and the actual circumference?

Name ______________________ Date __________ Class __________

Concentric Circles

LESSON 97

1. **Error Analysis** Julius found the sine of $\angle F$ to be $\frac{13}{5}$. Identify and correct his mistake.
(Inv 7)

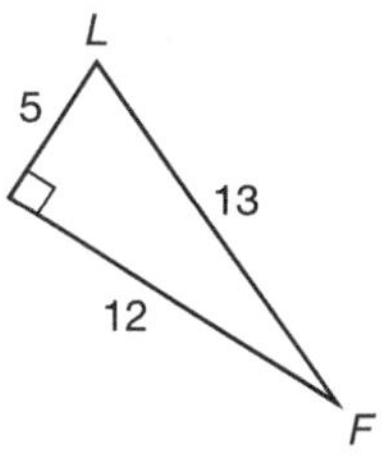

2. Polygon *ABCDE* has vertices $A(0, 1)$, $B(0, 5)$, $C(-2, 2)$, $D(-4, 5)$, and $E(-4, 1)$. Sketch the reflection of *ABCDE* across the line $y = x$.
(74)

* 3. Find the exact area of the annulus between two concentric circles, one with a 15-inch radius and the other with a 2-inch radius.
(97)

4. Write the equation of a circle centered at $(-4, 3)$ with a radius of 1000.
(95)

5. **Physics** A camper uses a pole to hold up an awning. The pole is at a 60° angle and has 30 pounds of force on it. What is the horizontal component of the force in pounds?
(89)

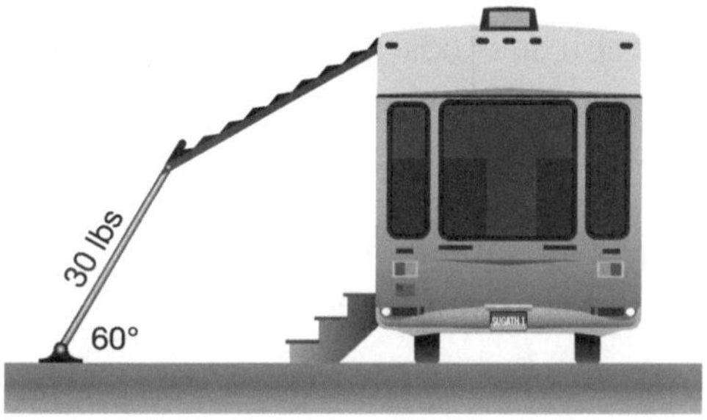

6. **Ballooning** The passengers on a hot-air balloon see a playground at an angle of depression of 16°. Later, they see the playground at a 36° angle of depression. At both times they were 150 meters above the ground. Have they moved closer or farther from the playground, and by how many meters? Round your answer to the nearest meter.
(73)

* 7. **Probability** This figure is made up of concentric circles on a flat surface, with dimensions as shown. If a coin is randomly dropped onto the figure, what is the probability it will land on the shaded region?
(97)

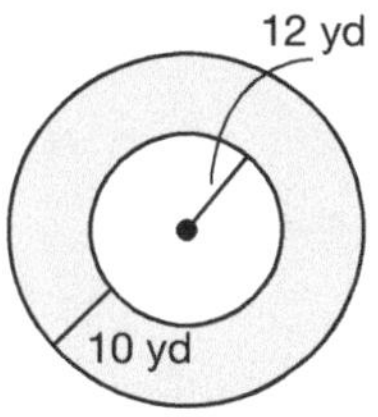

8. $\triangle MNP$ has vertices $M(3, 3)$, $N(5, 1)$, and $P(1, 1)$. Apply a dilation centered at $(1, 2)$ with a scale factor of 2 to $\triangle MNP$. Find the coordinates of the vertices of the image.
(84)

9. **Multiple Choice** This trapezoid is made up of congruent equiangular triangles. What is its perimeter?
(51)

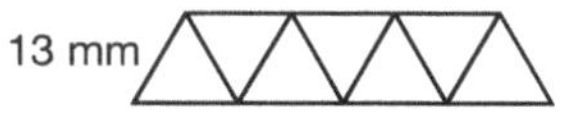

A 104 mm **B** 117 mm
C 273 mm **D** 130 mm

10. Graph the inequality $y \leq \frac{3}{2}x - 3$.
(88)

11. (62) **Metalworking** A sheet of metal that is 8 feet long and 6 feet wide is to be cut into cylindrical cans like the one shown. How many lateral surfaces for the cans can be cut from the metal sheet with as little waste as possible?

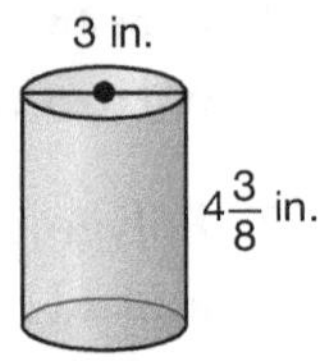

12. (45) **Write** Describe four coplanar points that do not form a quadrilateral.

*13. (96) Find the perimeter of the new image if each dimension of the triangle shown is dilated by a factor of 3.

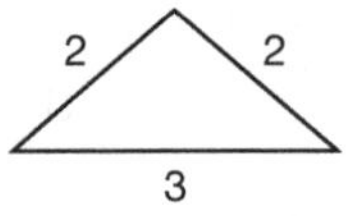

*14. (96) **Write** How could you change one dimension of a trapezoid to triple its area?

*15. (97) Find the area, in terms of π, of the annulus between these concentric circles.

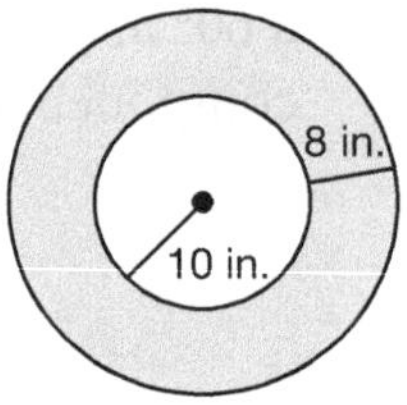

16. (82) **Write** Simplify the expression $\cos\left[\cos^{-1}\left(\frac{4}{5}\right)\right]$. Explain why your answer is correct.

17. (94) What are the possible measures for θ_1 and θ_2? Round your answers to the nearest degree.

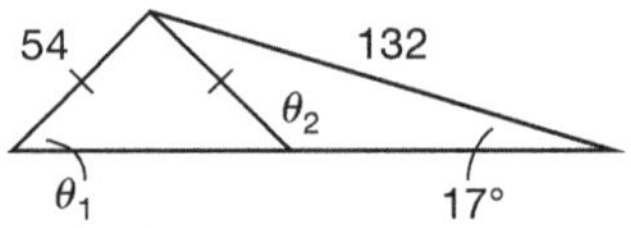

18. (92) **Analyze** Determine coordinate-based criteria for a quadrilateral to be each of the following: a rhombus, a rectangle, and a trapezium.

19. (67) **Sports** This simplified plan shows part of an Olympic complex. The boundary of the complex will be completed by rotations of the segments $\overline{AB}$ and $\overline{BC}$ through 120° clockwise and 120° counterclockwise about the central fountain F. Determine the perimeter of the whole complex.

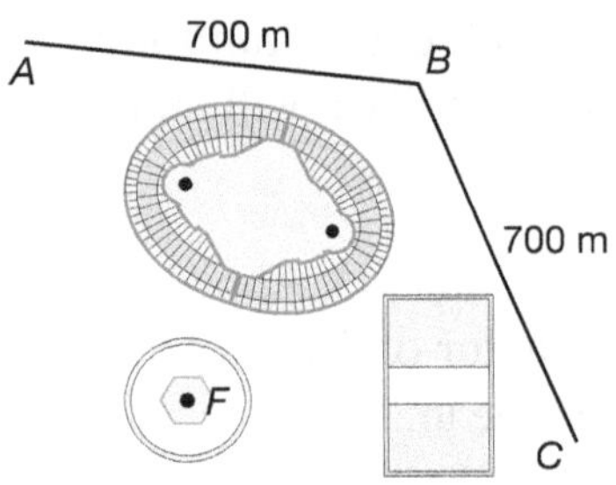

20. (22) **Multi-Step** Find the area of a rectangle with a diagonal of 13 and a side length of 5.

21. (Inv 9) **Write** Consider this tessellation of a parallelogram.

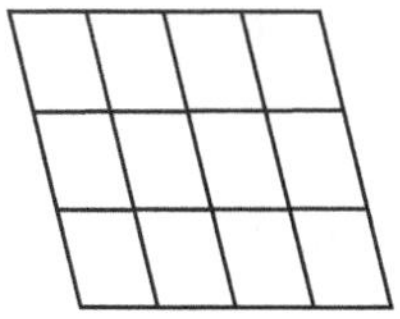

a. The tessellation has translation symmetries that are based on combinations of two vectors. Explain how these vectors are related to the sides of the original parallelogram.

b. The tessellation also has rotational symmetry. What angle must the rotation be? Where could its center be?

c. Explain why the tessellation has no reflection symmetry.

***22.** (96) **Mapping** A map has a scale of 1:250. If a map represents a community center by a square with an area of 100 square centimeters, what is the actual area of the community center, in square meters?

23. (57) **Multi-Step** Classify the polygon with vertices $P(2, 1)$, $Q(7, -1)$, $R(2, -3)$, and $S(-3, -1)$, and find its perimeter. Give your answer in simplified radical form.

***24.** (97) **Write** Write the equations for the concentric circles shown with center $(5, -4)$. How are the equations alike? How are they different?

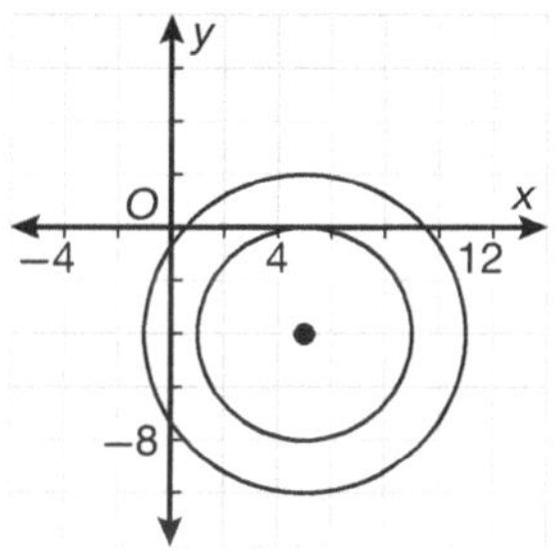

25. (95) The equation of a circle is $x^2 + y^2 = 169$. Write the equation of this circle after it is shifted 6 units down. Draw the original circle and the shifted circle on the coordinate plane.

26. (52) Quadrilateral $KLMN$ is a rhombus with its center point labeled S. What is $m\angle NSM$?

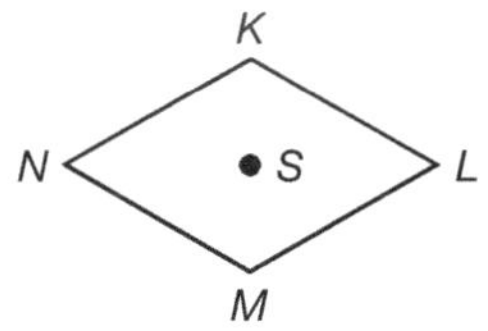

27. (17) Assume the following conditional statement is true. State its converse. Is the converse true?

If Noel does not clean her room, she will not be able to find her shoes.

28. (41) These triangles are similar. Find w.

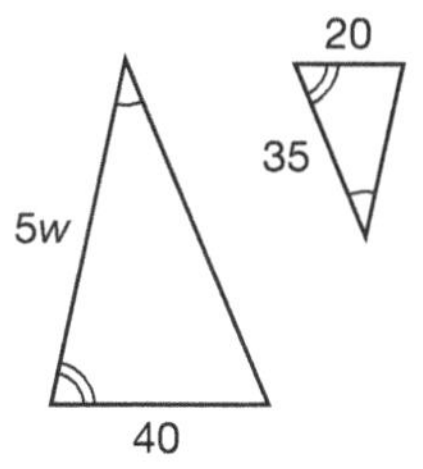

29. (47) **Algebra** If an arc measures 96°, and the measure of its inscribed angle is $(2x + 3)°$, what is the value of x?

30. (10) Use the Venn diagram to write a conditional statement.

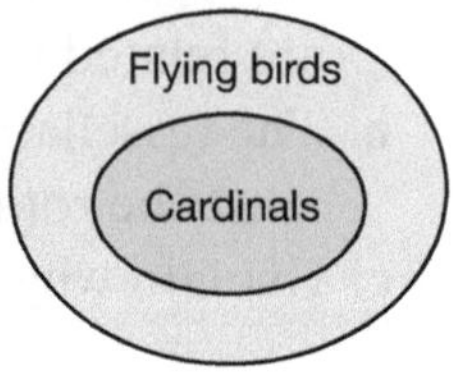

Name ______________________ Date __________ Class __________

Law of Cosines

LESSON 98

* **1.** *(98)* **Algebra** Find θ. Round your answer to the nearest degree.

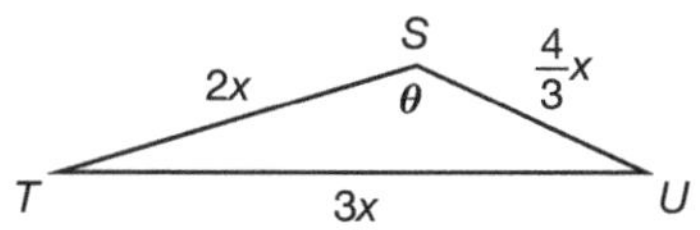

2. *(95)* **Write** A circle whose equation is $x^2 + y^2 = 4$ is dilated about its center by a factor of 3 and shifted 3 units to the left and 2 units down. Franklin performs the dilation first, then the translation, while Benjamin performs the translation first, and then the dilation. Will the two students' images be the same? Justify your reasoning. What is the equation of the new circle?

* **3.** *(97)* **Track and Field** A circular track, shown at right, needs to be repaved. What is the area of the track's surface to the nearest square meter?

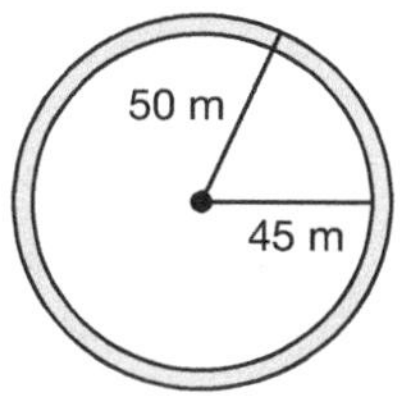

4. *(43)* If two chords are congruent, and one is 3 inches from the center of the circle, then what is the distance from the center to the other chord?

5. *(63)* Find the magnitude of vector $\langle 3, -4 \rangle$.

6. *(55)* Segment TU is a midsegment of $\triangle QRS$. Find the values of x and y.

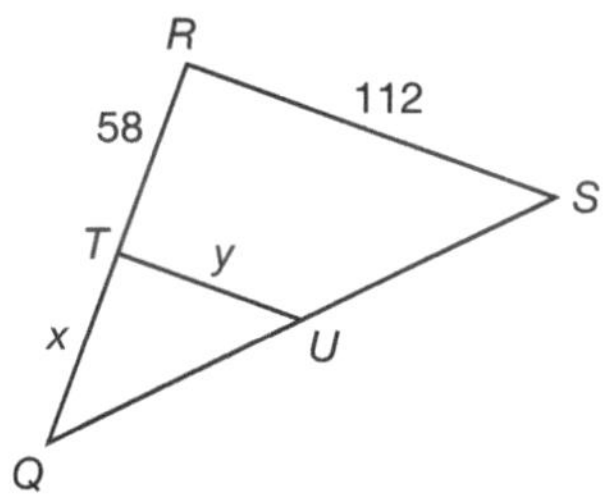

7. *(91)* **Algebra** If $\frac{\sin \theta}{\tan \theta} = 0.6$, find the value of $\cos \theta$. Then find θ to the nearest degree.

8. *(31)* Write a paragraph proof showing that $m\angle 1 = m\angle 2$.

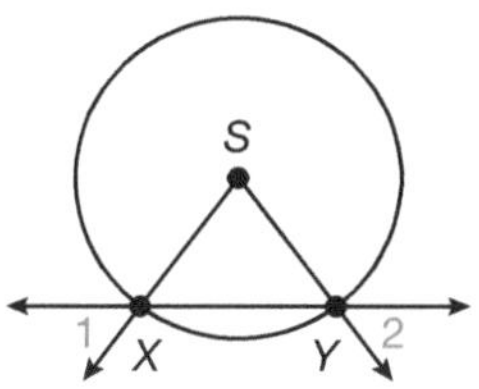

9. *(85)* **Architecture** In a regular square pyramid that has a height of 100 feet and a base with 200-foot-long sides, there is a second floor located halfway up the pyramid. What is the area of this floor?

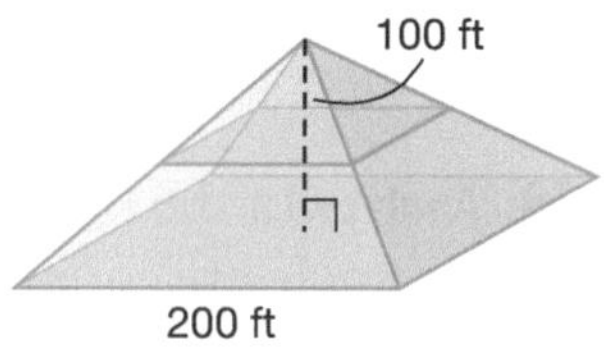

10. *(89)* **Analyze** Vector u has a magnitude of 3 and an angle of 30° from the positive x-axis. How many unique vectors in the same plane with the same initial point as u have a magnitude of 2 and are perpendicular to u? List them.

*11. Find θ. Round your answer to the nearest degree.
(98)

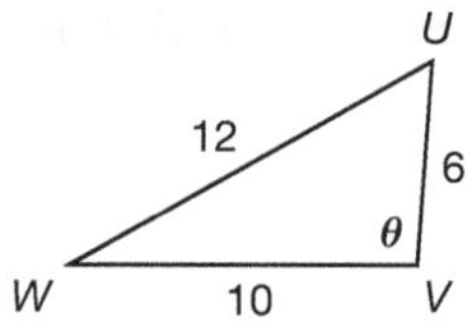

12. Prove that $\triangle JKL \cong \triangle PQR$.
(36)

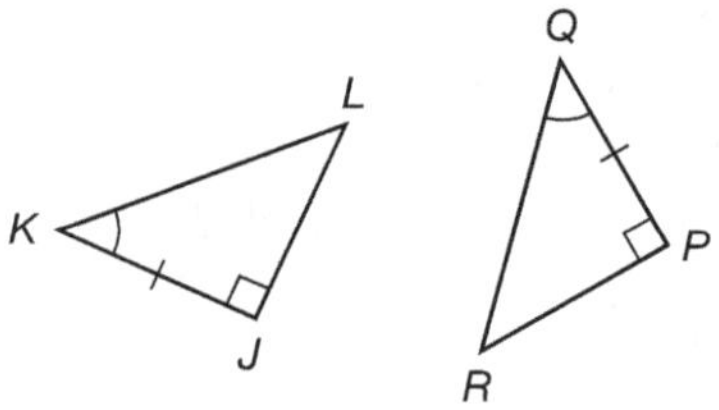

13. Find the perimeter of this square if the length but not the height is shrunk by a factor of $\frac{1}{6}$. Write an expression for the perimeter of the new rectangle based on the original perimeter, P.
(96)

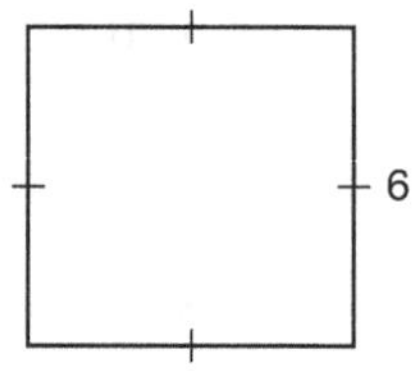

14. If the coordinates of one endpoint of a segment are $(-1, -3)$ and the segment extends from this point to the left by 7 units, what is the coordinate of the other endpoint?
(9)

15. **Carpentry** A wooden frame is built in the shape of a parallelogram. The carpenter knows that $\overline{AB} \cong \overline{CD}$ and $\overline{AC} \cong \overline{BD}$. Using a tape measure, she determines that $BC = AD$. Is the frame a rectangle, rhombus, both, or neither?
(65)

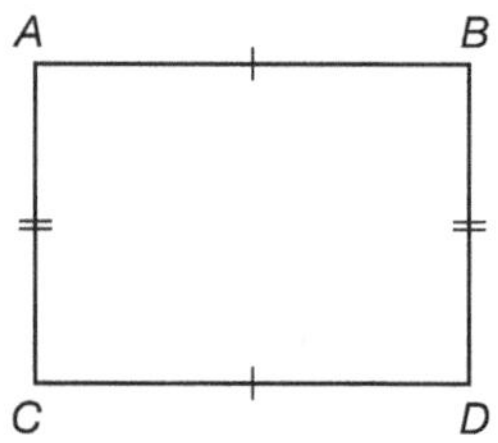

16. What value of x completes the equation $\sin 60° = \cos x$?
(68)

*17. Write the equations for these concentric circles, centered at $(-1, 0)$. Explain how the equations are similar and how they are different.
(97)

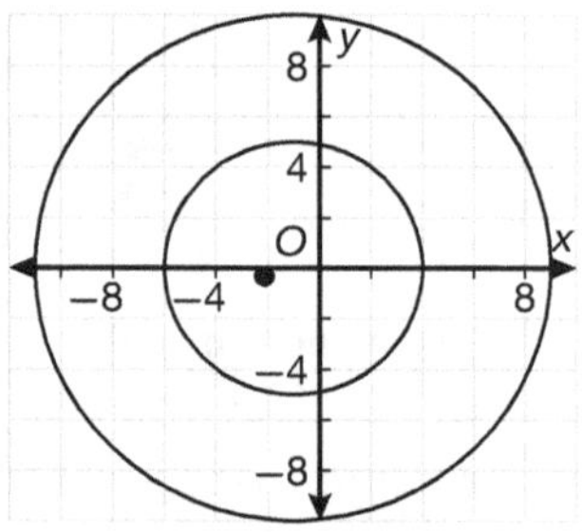

*18. **Write** Explain why the Law of Cosines is identical to the Pythagorean Theorem when it is used in a right triangle.
(98)

19. **Analyze** In the figures below, it is given that two sides and an angle are congruent between the two triangles. Explain why it cannot be concluded that the triangles are congruent.
(94)

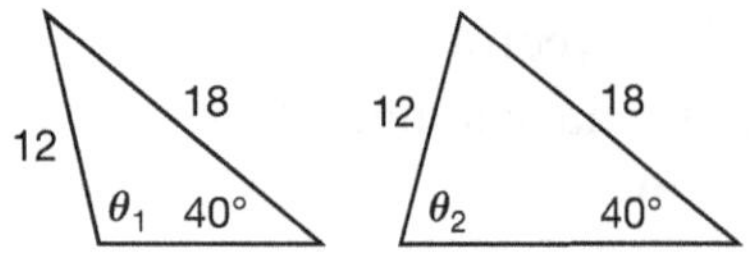

20. In a two-column proof, prove that $KL > HL$, given
(Inv 4) that $\overline{JK} \parallel \overline{HL}$, $\overline{JK} \cong \overline{HL}$, and $m\angle KML > m\angle HML$.

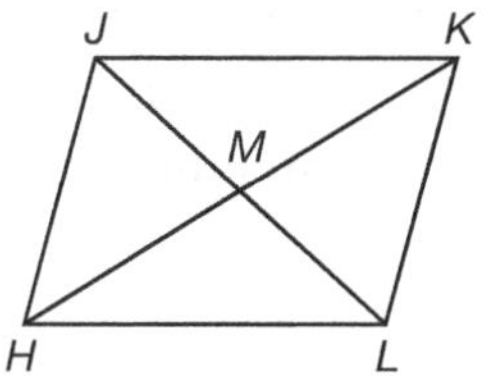

21. Find the exact length of the leg of a isosceles right
(53) triangle with a hypotenuse of 75 inches.

*22. **Kites** Shannon is flying a kite. She has released
(98) 55 feet of string. Adrian sees the kite from 35 feet away. How far is Shannon from Adrian if the kite makes a 95° angle between them? Round your answer to the nearest foot.

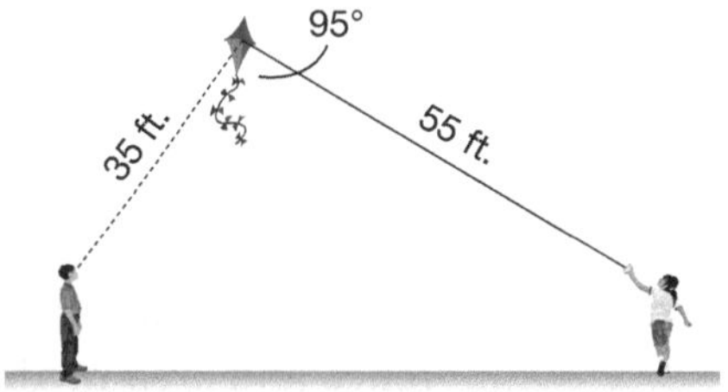

23. **Error Analysis** Kaelie believes she has found a
(91) new trigonometric identity below based on $\sin^2\theta + \cos^2\theta = 1$. Identify any errors she made and explain why she is wrong.

$$\sin^2\theta + \cos^2\theta = 1$$
$$\sqrt{\sin^2\theta + \cos^2\theta} = \sqrt{1}$$
$$\sin\theta + \cos\theta = \pm 1$$

24. Find the value of x in the figure.
(64)

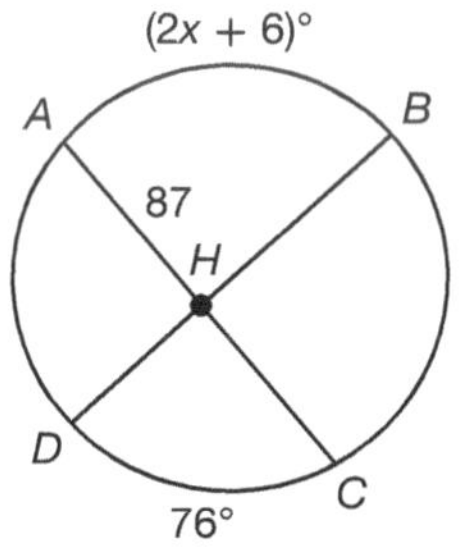

25. **Multiple Choice** The set of probabilities for a spinner experiment are 41% red, 34% blue,
(Inv 6) and 25% green. The measures of the central angles for the sectors of the spinner are:

A red: 120°; blue: 120°; green: 120°
B red: 145°; blue: 125°; green: 90°
C red: 120°; blue: 105°; green: 75°
D red: 160°; blue: 60°; green: 140°

26. **Packaging** Two identical round vases are packed into a box.
(72) There is reinforcement cardboard to keep the vases from smashing into each other. How many tangents and common tangents are there?

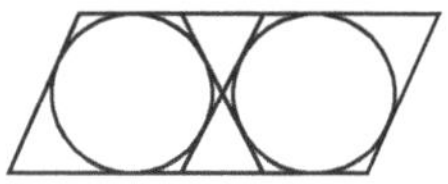

27. **Multi-Step** A square has coordinates $D(1, 2)$, $E(-1, 2)$, $F(-1, 4)$, and $G(1, 4)$.
(96) If a pair of parallel sides of the square is dilated by a factor of 3, what shape does the image take? What are the perimeter and area of the image?

*28. **Probability** The figure below is made up of concentric circles with dimensions as (97) shown. If a coin is randomly dropped onto the figure, what is the probability it will land on one of the shaded regions, assuming it lands in only one region?

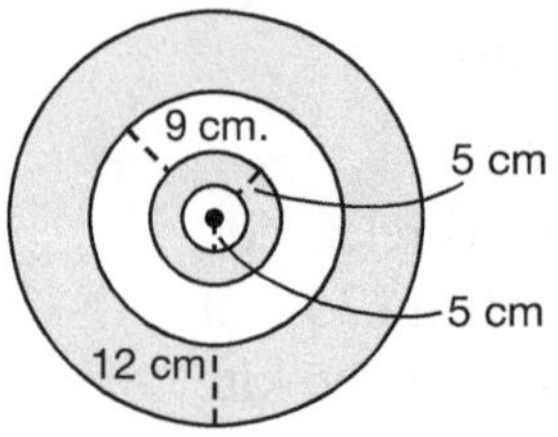

29. **Analyze** Two circles' radii have a ratio of 4:7. How do the measures of the (87) circumference and area of the larger circle compare to the circumference and area of the smaller circle?

30. Reflect the triangle across line t, and then reflect the image across line m. (90)

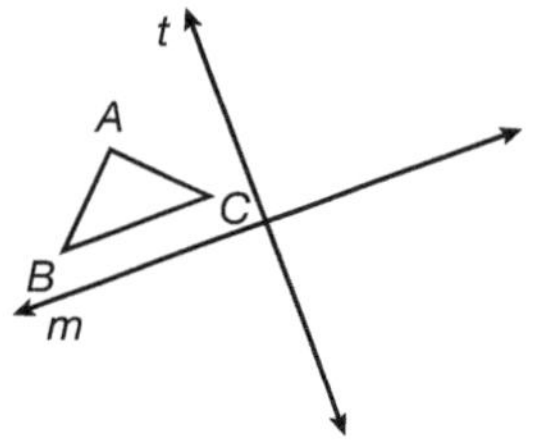

Name ______________________ Date __________ Class __________

Volume Ratios of Similar Solids

LESSON 99

* **1.** (98) Find x. Round your answer to the nearest tenth.

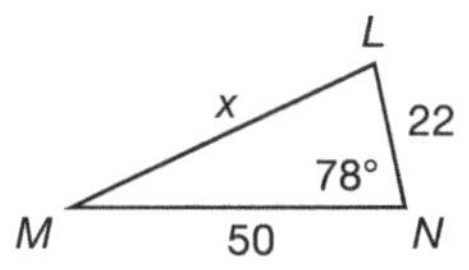

2. (56) **Multi-Step** Find the perimeter of a 30°-60°-90° triangle where the longer leg is 630 millimeters. Give your answer in simplified radical form.

3. (93) **Plumbing** A pipe junction consists of three cylindrical pipe sections positioned at right angles to one another. Using the three orthographic views, sketch the pipe junction.

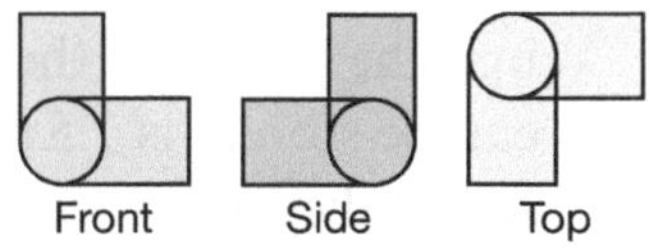

* **4.** (99) Two similar right rectangular prisms R and S have a scale factor of 3:4. The base of R is 3 centimeters by 4.5 centimeters and its height is 9 centimeters. Determine the area of each face of S.

* **5.** (99) Two similar rectangular pyramids P and Q have a scale factor of 4:5. The base of P is 6 inches long and 4 inches wide. Each sloping edge of P is 10 inches long. Determine the perimeter and side lengths of Q.

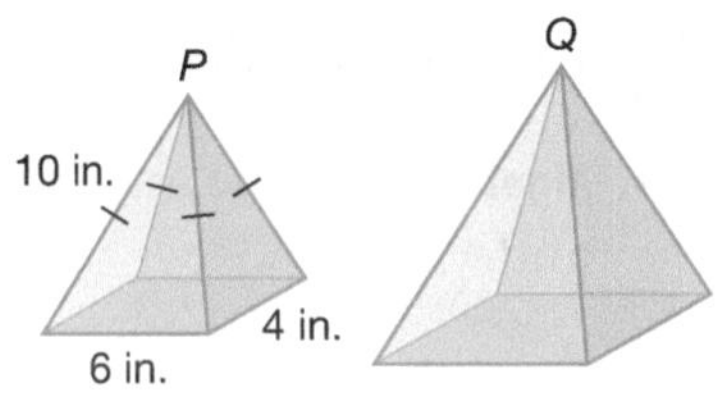

6. (16) **Predict** A family of lines have equations of the form $x - ay + a^2 = 1$.

a. Describe the line corresponding to $a = 0$.

b. What happens as a increases?

7. (94) Find θ. Round your answer to the nearest degree.

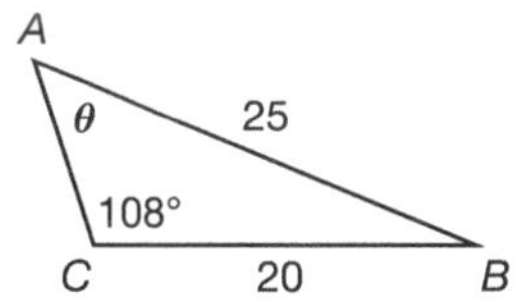

8. (96) The ratio of the lengths of a trapezoid's bases is 2:1. The trapezoid's height is equal to the length of its long base. If the height of the trapezoid is doubled, what is the ratio of the new trapezoid's area to the original trapezoid's area?

* **9.** (98) **Mapping** The map shows the distance between three landmarks. Find all three angles. Round each measure to the nearest tenth.

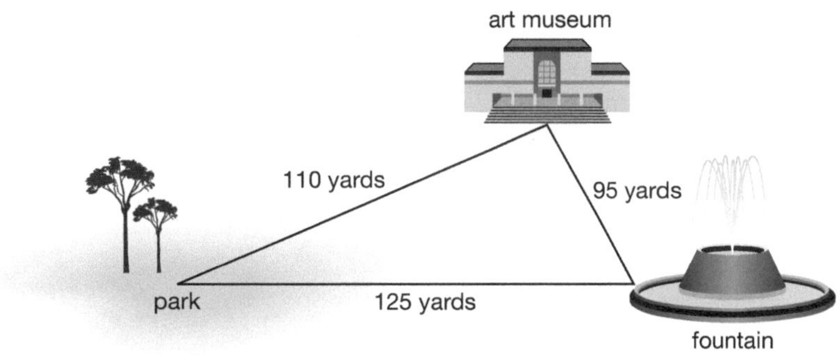

10. The sides of two similar polygons have a similarity ratio of 8:13. What is the ratio (87) of the perimeter of the smaller polygon to the perimeter of the larger polygon? What is the ratio of the area of the smaller polygon to that of the larger polygon?

*11. (97) **Compact Discs** The length of a song on a compact disc is proportional to the area of the disc it takes up. The radius of the central hole, where no music can be stored, is 7.5 millimeters. If a ten-minute song takes up the shaded region in the diagram at right, how many minutes of music can the entire disc hold, to the nearest minute?

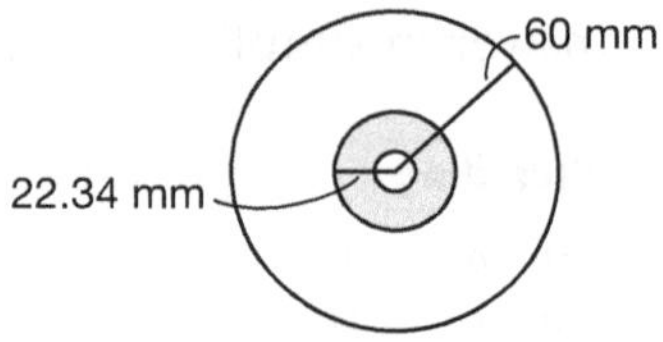

12. (62) **Canning** A particular can of tuna has a height of 1 inch and a diameter of 3 inches. The label on the can covers the entire lateral side. What is the area of the label?

13. (69) Find the lengths of the sides of kite *ABCD*. Round to the nearest tenth.

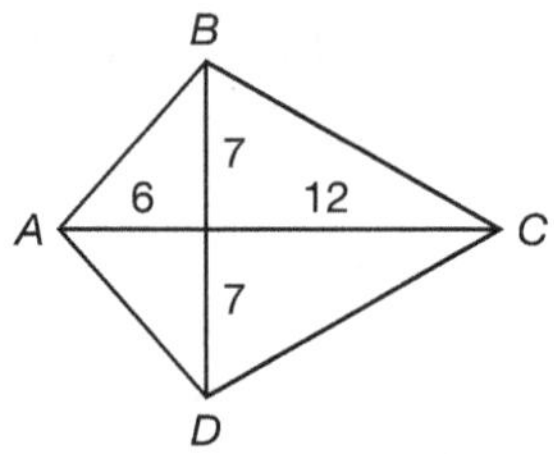

*14. (98) **Algebra** Find the angles of a triangle if the sides are x, $2x$, and $\frac{3}{2}x$.

15. (50) Find the geometric mean of 12.1 and 5.6.

16. (40) **a.** Determine this figure's perimeter.
b. Determine its area.

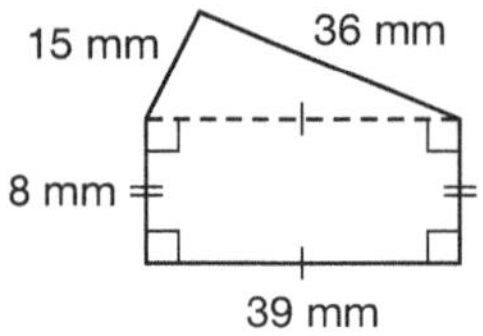

17. (91) **Formulate** Write an identity for tangent in terms of only cosine.

*18. (99) **Analyze** Prove that if two regular triangular pyramids have a scale factor of $a:b$, then the ratio of the areas of their corresponding faces is $a^2:b^2$.

19. (39) List the side lengths of the triangle from smallest to largest.

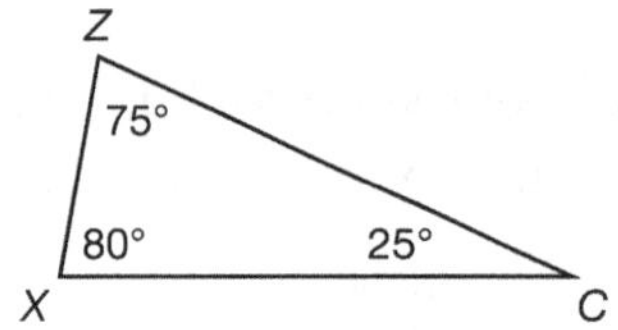

20. (97) **Baking** A bagel with a diameter of 12 inches has a hole with a radius of 1 inch. What is the area of one face the bagel, to the nearest tenth of a square inch?

21. (34) **Algebra** Find an expression for the height of parallelogram *PTRW* in terms of x.

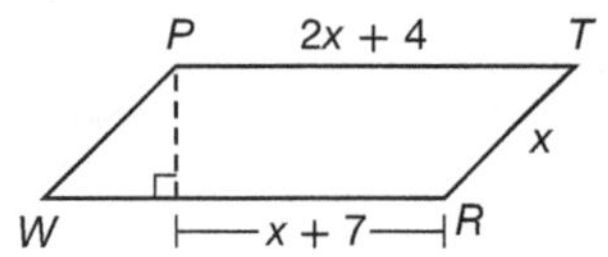

22. *(61)* The measures of three interior angles of a parallelogram are 33°, 57°, and 33°. What is the measure of the fourth interior angle?

23. *(45)* **Error Analysis** Luka wrote the following as she was trying to prove that $\triangle RTF$ is equilateral. Find and correct any errors she made.

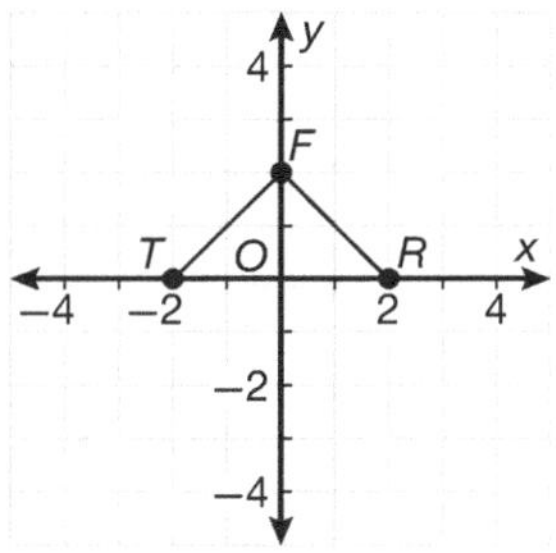

$TF = \sqrt{2^2 + 2^2} = \sqrt{4 + 4} = \sqrt{16} = 4$

$FR = \sqrt{2^2 + 2^2} = \sqrt{4 + 4} = \sqrt{16} = 4$

$TR = 4$

24. *(88)* **Model** The price of eggs is at least a dollar less than three times the price of milk. Write a linear inequality that models this relationship and sketch the graph of it.

***25.** *(99)* These two similar triangular pyramids have a scale factor 2:5. Determine their respective surface areas.

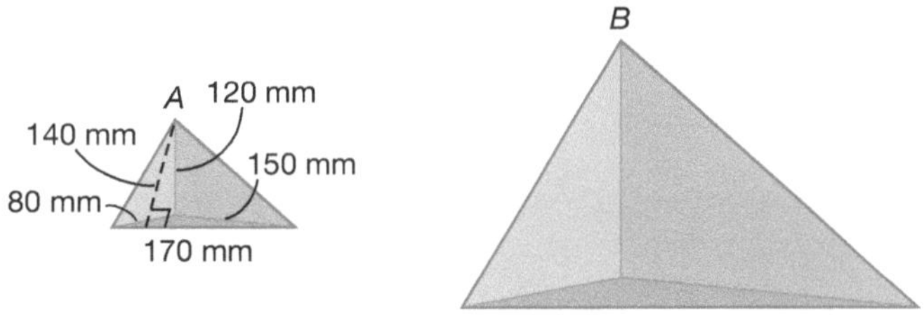

26. *(58)* **Multiple Choice** R is an exterior point of $\odot C$, and $\overline{RP}$ and $\overline{RQ}$ are tangent to $\odot C$ at P and Q. Given that $\angle PCQ$ is a right angle, what type of quadrilateral is $PCQR$?

A kite **B** parallelogram

C square **D** none of these

27. *(95)* The equation of a circle is $x^2 + y^2 = 121$. Write the equation of this circle after it is translated 6 units to the left. Draw the original circle and the translated circle on the coordinate plane.

28. *(94)* **Multiple Choice** Which is closest to the length of $\overline{RS}$?

A 24 **B** 14

C 12 **D** 17

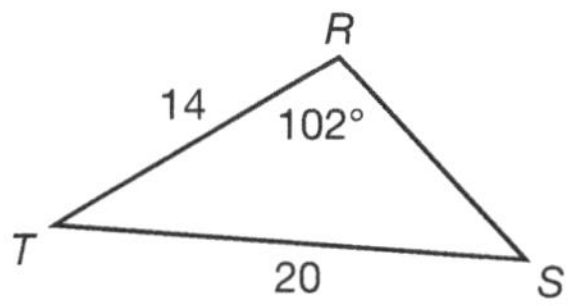

29. *(66)* **Algebra** If a regular hexagon with 40-inch side lengths were divided into six congruent equilateral triangles with vertices connecting at the center, what would be the length of their corresponding congruent sides?

30. Prove that this quadrilateral is a trapezoid.
(92)

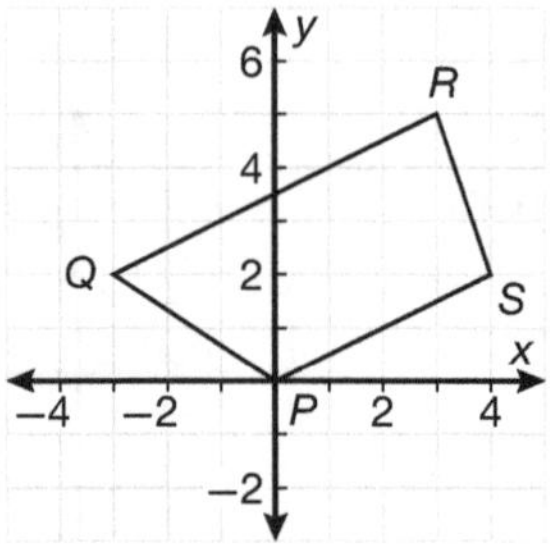

Name ______________________ Date __________ Class __________

Transformation Matrices

LESSON 100

* **1.** In the concentric circles shown, find the area of the annulus in terms of π.
(97)

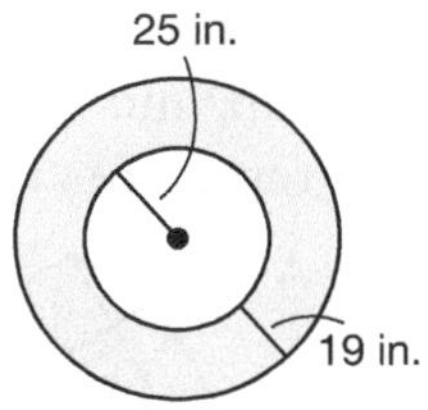

2. **Meteorology** Meteorology equipment at a research station measures the velocity of the wind on a particular day, given by the vector $\langle 60, 5 \rangle$. Find the magnitude of the wind.
(83)

3. Identify the type of transformation shown at right.
(67)

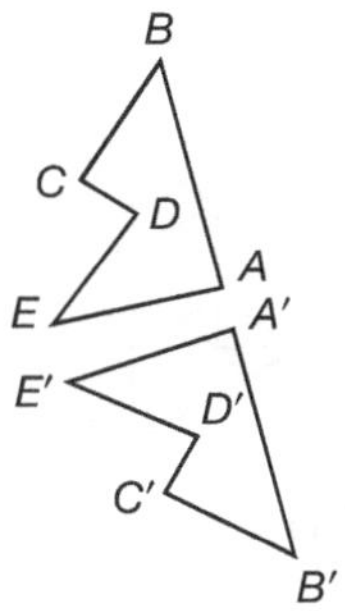

4. **Multiple Choice** A pair of similar solids A and B have a scale factor of 3:5. Identify the correct equation for the surface area of B in terms of the surface area of A.
(99)

A $S_B = \frac{3}{5}S_A$ **B** $S_B = \frac{25}{9}S_A$

C $S_B = \frac{9}{25}S_A$ **D** $S_B = \frac{125}{27}S_A$

* **5.** Find the translation matrix for $\triangle LMN$.
(100)

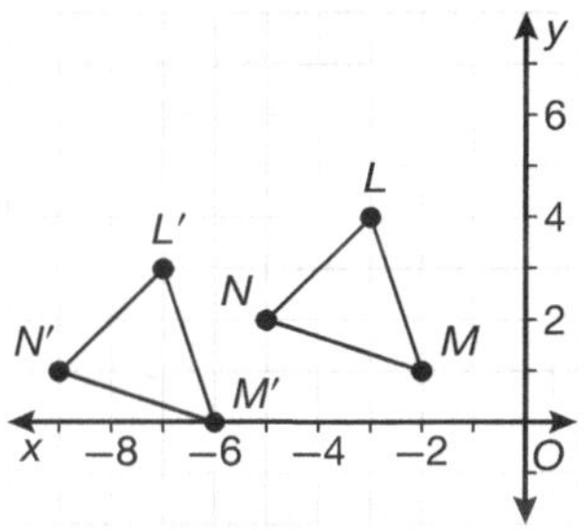

6. **Algebra** If $\cos^2\theta$ equals 0.4, what does $\sin\theta$ equal?
(91)

7. **Algebra** What is the arc measure of $\widehat{JK}$ if $v = 3.2$?
(47)

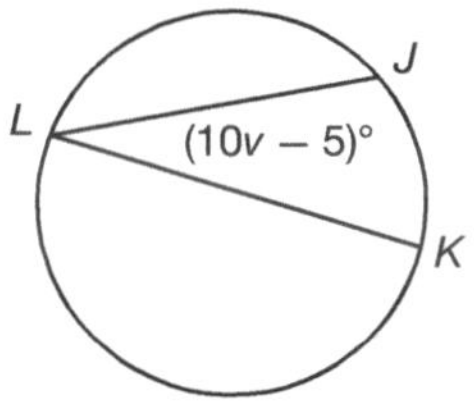

8. Two segments are divided proportionally. The first segment is divided into parts that are 12, 18, and x units long. The second segment is divided into parts that are y, 9, and 13 units long. What are the values of x and y?
(60)

9. Where is the orthocenter of a right triangle located?
(32)

* **10.** **Dancing** A certain type of dance uses the step pattern of three steps forward and three steps to the right. If everyone is dancing in the same direction, what 2×1 matrix could be used to define this step?
(100)

11. (93) **Multiple Choice** This orthographic drawing shows the front, top, and side views of a solid. Which of the sketches below represents the solid?

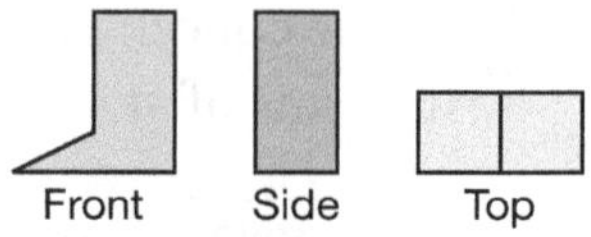

A

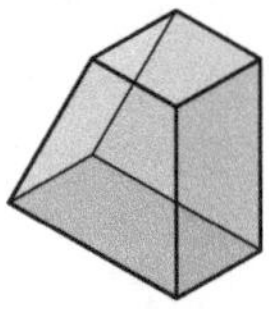

B

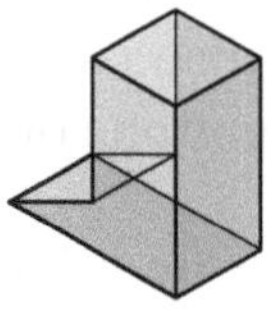

C

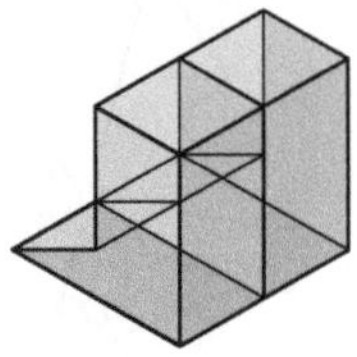

D

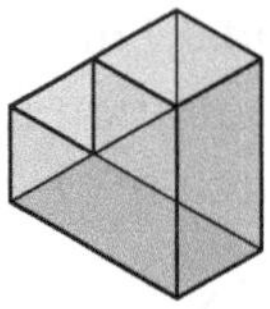

12. (75) Write an equation for $\odot C$ with a 2.5 radius, centered at the origin.

***13.** (99) These two similar cylinders have a scale factor of 3:2. Determine the base radius and height of cylinder D.

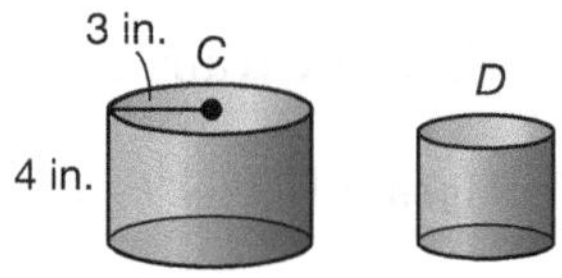

14. (89) Find the horizontal and vertical components of a vector with a magnitude of 15 and an angle of 37°.

15. (Inv 5) Sketch the net of a pentagonal pyramid.

***16.** (98) **Multi-Step** Find all angle measures in the triangle. Round each answer to the nearest degree.

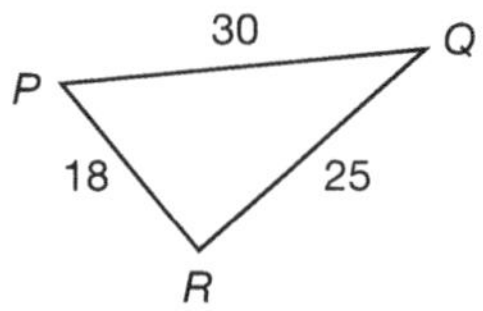

17. (52) A quadrilateral has diagonals that are perpendicular, but are not the same length. Classify the quadrilateral.

***18.** (99) **Visual Arts** A sculpture consists of two similar square pyramids with a scale factor of 3:8. The smaller pyramid has a base that is 30 millimeters long and each of its triangular faces has a 36-millimeter height. Determine the area of each face of the larger pyramid.

19. (72) Determine how many common tangents the internally tangent circles have and draw the tangent(s).

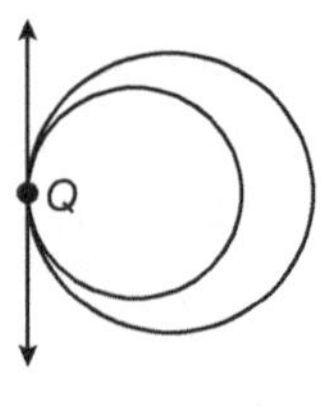

***20.** (98) **Write** Which law can be used to find the side lengths of a triangle, given the three angle measures—the Law of Sines, the Law of Cosines, both, or neither? Explain.

21. (59) **Cheese** This equilateral triangular prism represents a wedge of cheese that is to be coated with wax to prevent it from drying out. What is the exact surface area that needs to be coated with wax?

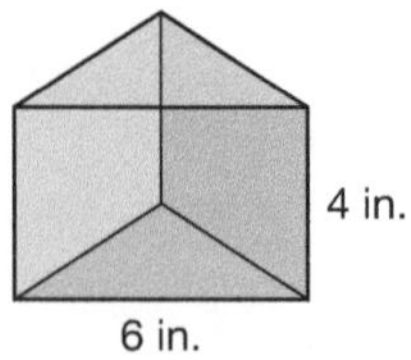

22. **Formulate** Determine a formula for the total surface area of a square pyramid with a side length of s and a slant height of l.
(70)

*23. **Error Analysis** Donna wrote the matrix $\begin{bmatrix} -3 & 1 \\ -3 & 1 \end{bmatrix}$ for the translation three units left and one unit up. Explain Donna's error and correct the matrix.
(100)

24. How can the equation $y^2 + 1 = x$ be altered to make it symmetrical along the x-axis?
(76)

25. If parallelogram $QRST$ is similar to parallelogram $JKLM$, $JK = 12$, $QR = 45$, and $LM = 15$, find ST.
(44)

*26. **Formulate** A circle is given by the equation $(x + 3)^2 + (y - 2)^2 = 9$. Another circle is a dilation of the first circle by a factor of 3. What is the equation of the second circle?
(95)

xy^2 *27. **Algebra** A translation moves a line segment up by $2x$ units and then down by $x - 1$ units. Write the matrix for this translation.
(100)

28. **Multi-Step** Find the surface area of a sphere with a circumference of 28 inches, to the nearest square inch.
(80)

29. What is the value of y in the proportion $\frac{15}{45} = \frac{33}{y}$?
(41)

30. In the given diagram, if P is the center of the circle and $\overline{BC}$ and $\overline{AD}$ are diameters, prove that $\triangle PAB \cong \triangle PCD$, using a two-column proof.
(27)

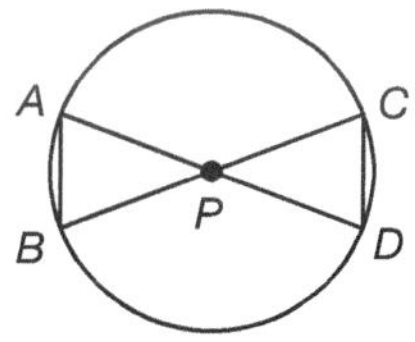

Name ______________________ Date __________ Class __________

Determining Lengths of Segments Intersecting Circles

LESSON 101

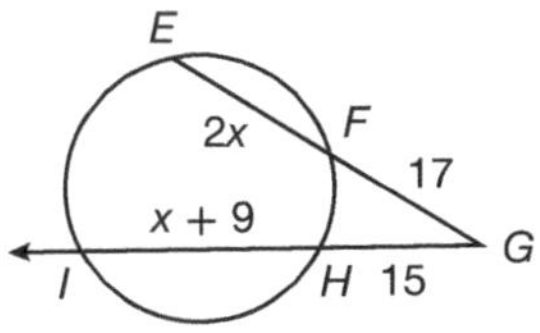

* **1.** (101) Find the length of $\overline{EG}$ to the nearest tenth of a unit.

* **2.** (88) What shape is made by the graph of the solution to $|x| + |y| \leq 2$?

3. (63) A boat travels to $\langle 3, 4 \rangle$ using its own power. However, the wind pushes it by $\langle 1, -1 \rangle$. What is the final position of the airplane?

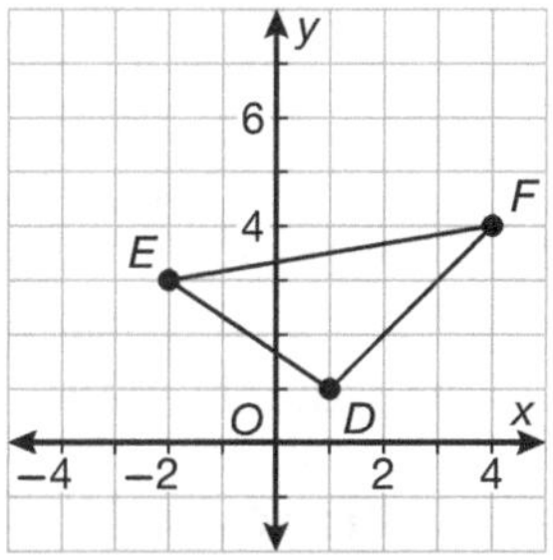

* **4.** (100) **Multi-Step** Find the matrix representation of the triangle shown. Then, write a matrix to translate the triangle 3 units to the right. Finally, write the matrix for the translated triangle.

5. (78) A quadrilateral is rotated 99° in a clockwise direction, and then rotated 231° in a counterclockwise direction about the origin. What single rotation is equivalent to these rotations?

6. (37) **Algebra** Two lines are parallel. One line has an equation of $y = \frac{2}{k}x + 7$ and the other line has an equation of $2y = \frac{h}{6}x + 4$. Find possible values for k and h.

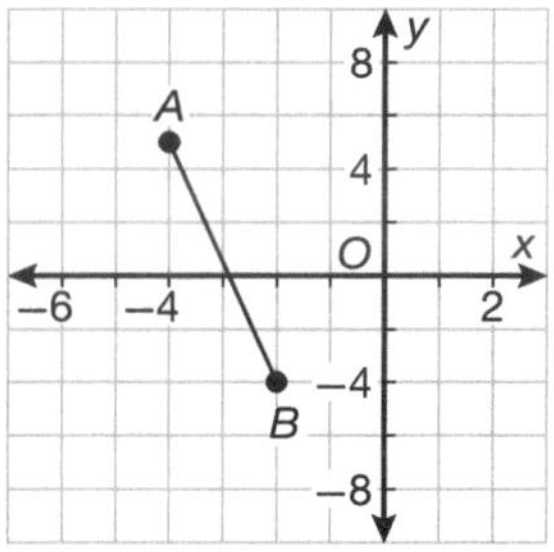

7. (11) Determine the midpoint M of $\overline{AB}$.

8. (91) Solve for $\tan \theta$ in terms of $\sin \theta$.

* **9.** (99) **Packaging** A flour package in the shape of a right triangular prism comes in two sizes. The smaller size has right triangular bases with leg lengths of $\frac{3}{4}$-inch and 1-inch, and is 4.5 inches long. The larger package has a similar shape to the smaller one, but is twice the size. Find the face areas of the larger package.

* **10.** (101) Find the exact value of x in the diagram if p is tangent to the circle.

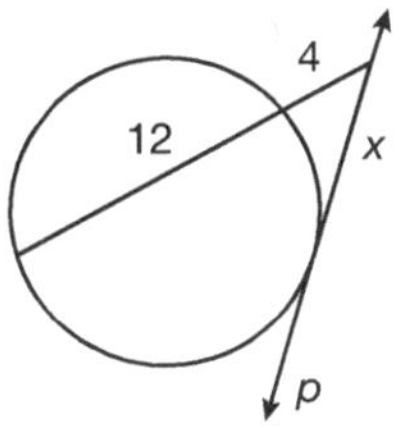

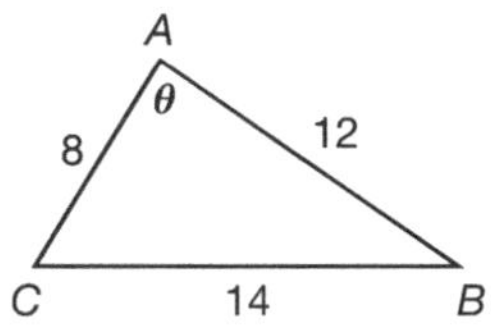

11. (Inv 7) Draw a 45°-45°-90° triangle with 1-unit long legs. Include all angle measures and side lengths.

* **12.** (98) Find θ in the triangle shown. Round your answer to the nearest degree.

13. Find the matrix that represents the translation of a line segment five units left and three units up.
(100)

***14.** In the concentric circles, find the area of the annulus in terms of π.
(97)

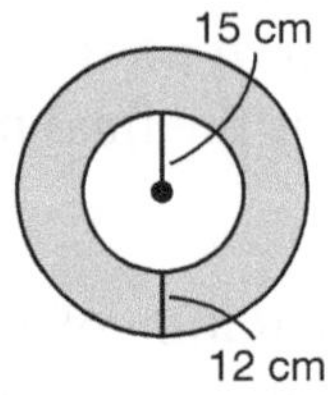

15. **Analyze** A system of equations with one solution is $y = ax - 1$, $y = bx + 1$, where $a > b > 0$. Describe where the intersection of these two lines will be on the coordinate plane.
(81)

***16.** **Multiple Choice** Which is the length of $\overline{AB}$?
(101)

A $4\sqrt{2}$ centimeters **B** 32 centimeters
C 24 centimeters **D** $24\sqrt{2}$ centimeters

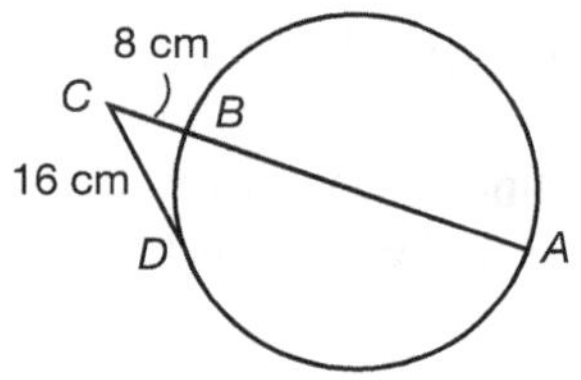

17. In $\triangle PQR$, $PQ > QR$. Can $\triangle PQR$ be equiangular? Explain.
(51)

***18.** **Algebra** If a line is translated $3x$ units right and $2x$ units down, what is the matrix for the translation?
(100)

19. Find the length of $\overline{EF}$. Round your answer to the nearest hundredth unit.
(94)

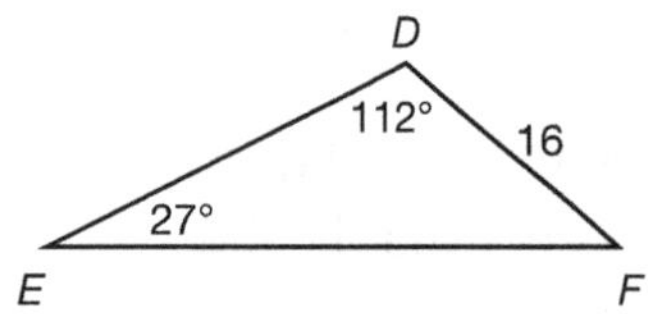

20. Four of the interior angles of a convex pentagon measure 100°. What is the measure of the fifth angle?
(Inv 3)

***21.** Find the length of $\overline{HJ}$ in the figure.
(101)

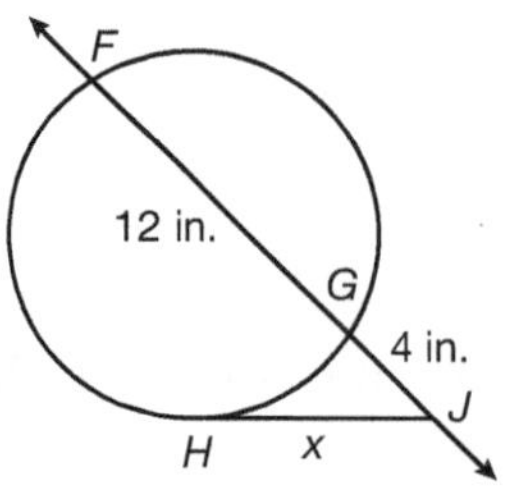

22. (53) **Multi-Step** Determine the difference in the perimeters of two 45°-45°-90° triangles if one has a hypotenuse of 20 feet and the second has a hypotenuse of 10 feet. Round your answer to the nearest foot.

23. (99) These two similar right rectangular prisms have a scale factor of 4:9. Determine the area of each face of S.

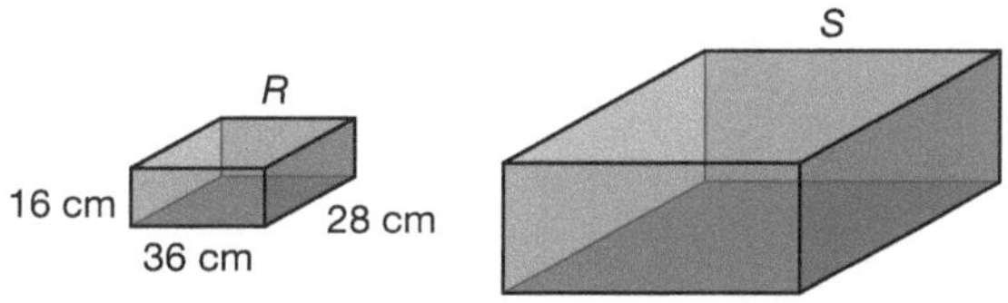

24. (42) Find the distance from $(-6, -2)$ to the line $y = -5$.

25. (57) **Multiple Choice** Triangle LMN has an area of 13 square units. Given the coordinates of $L(-1, 2)$ and $M(1, -1)$, which of the following is *not* a possible location for N?

A (7, 3) **B** (5, 6)
C (−5, 5) **D** (−6, −2)

26. (71) The points $H(3, -5)$ and $I(-5, -8)$ are translated 11 units down. Determine the coordinates of each translation point.

27. (85) **Algebra** Find the area of the circular cross section of a cone that is parallel to the cone's base and is two-thirds of the way from the vertex to the base of the cone. The height of the cone is 3 centimeters. The radius of the base is 3 centimeters. Round your answer to the nearest hundredth square centimeter.

*28. (96) **Predict** Describe the effect on the area of a square if its diagonals were dilated by $\frac{1}{4}$.

29. (11) **Multiple Choice** Which point is the midpoint of the line segment joining M and N?

A R **B** S
C T **D** U

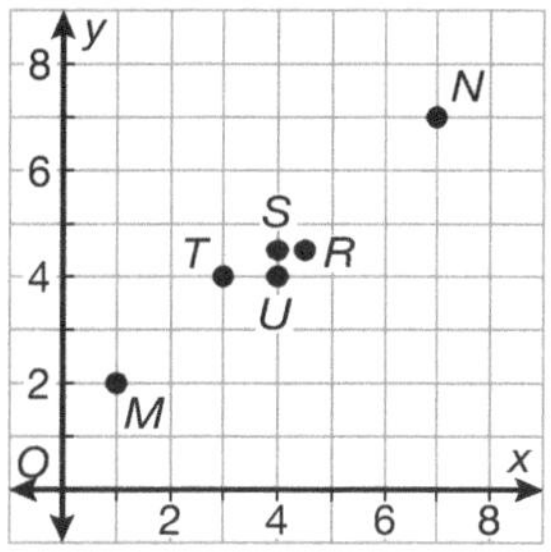

30. (65) **Carpentry** Find the length of metal needed to make the pair of braces in the shelving unit shown if one diagonal brace is 6 feet long.

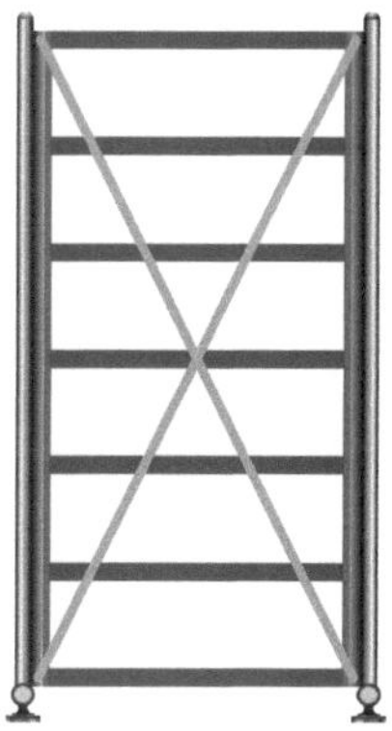

Name ______________________________ Date __________ Class __________

Dilations in the Coordinate Plane

LESSON 102

* **1.** (97) **Probability** A target is made up of concentric circles with dimensions as shown. Assuming it is lying face-up on a flat surface, what is the probability that a coin dropped onto it will land on the shaded region?

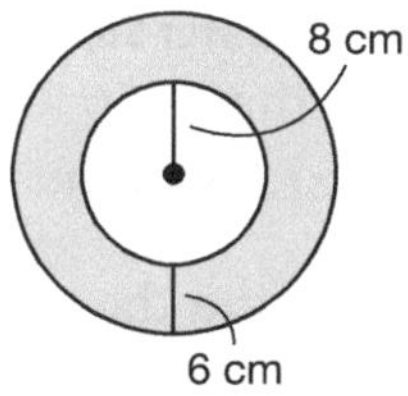

* **2.** (102) Find the image of the point $(-4, 5)$ under a dilation with a scale factor of 7, centered at the origin.

3. (66) **Algebra** A regular hexagon has an apothem that is $13\sqrt{3}$ feet long. What is the area of the hexagon?

4. (101) What is the value of y in the diagram?

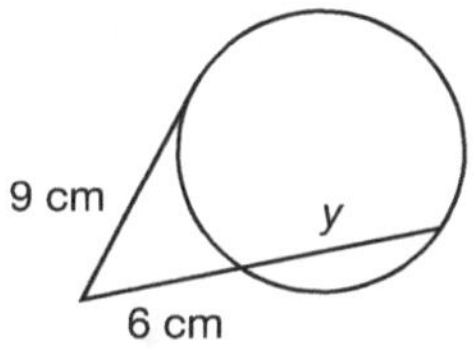

5. (83) **Hiking** A hiker travels along a trail with vertical distance of 6 meters and a horizontal distance of 50 meters, then climbs up a cliff that rises 75 meters over a horizontal distance of 12 meters. Write a vector to describe the displacement of this hike.

* **6.** (98) Find the value of x. Round your answer to the nearest hundredth unit.

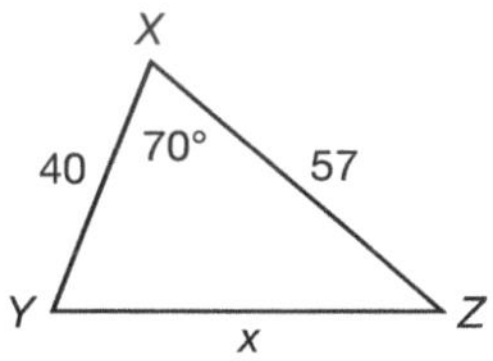

7. (39) **Maps** At right is a partial map of three Texas cities. List the distances between cities in order from greatest to least.

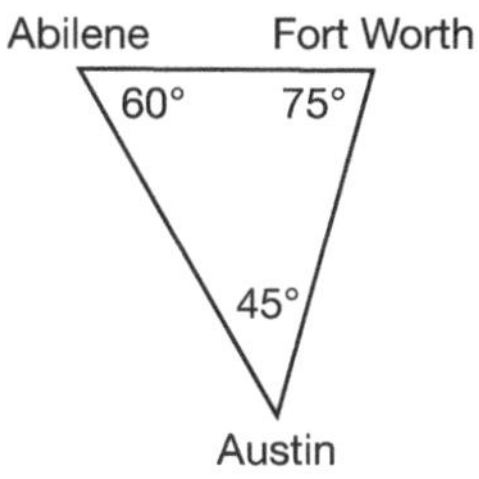

8. (59) **Analyze** A right rectangular prism has a width that is equal to the length and a height that is twice the length. The volume of the prism is 432 cubic feet. Find the surface area.

* **9.** (102) Find the vertices of the given triangle after the dilation $D_{O,\,0.75}\,(x, y)$ is applied.

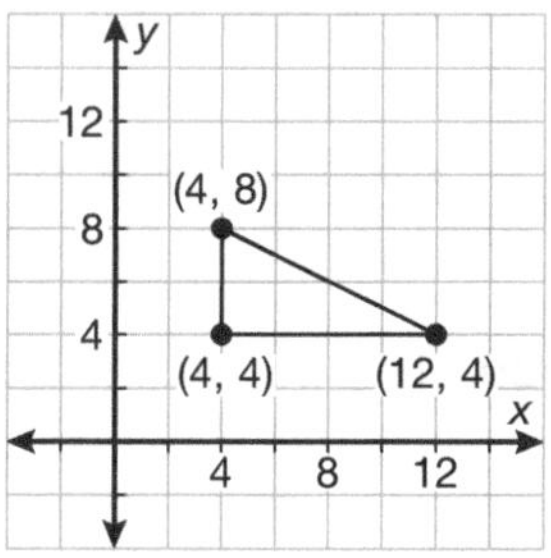

10. (96) **Analyze** A rectangle is dilated by a factor of 12. If the area of the image 576 square units, what was the original area?

11. **Water Supply** A large water tank servicing a rural district is in the shape of a cylinder
(62) that is 56 feet tall and has a diameter of 40 feet. If one cubic foot is equal to about 7.5 gallons, find the volume of the tank to the nearest thousand gallons.

*12. Find the value of x in the diagram.
(101)

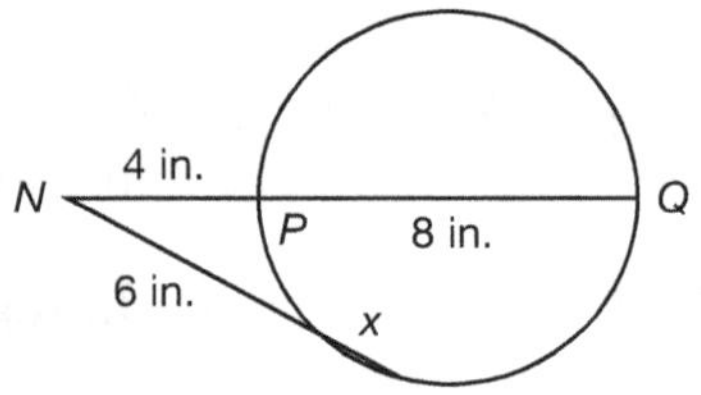

*13. **Space Exploration** A 1:16 scale model of a spacecraft
(99) is a truncated right cone with a base radius of 6.2 inches, a top radius of 2.1 inches, and a height of 5.0 inches. The height of the cone before it was truncated was 7.4 inches. Determine the surface area and volume of the model and the surface area and volume of the actual spacecraft to the nearest square or cubic foot, respectively.

*14. **Multiple Choice** If the triangle shown is dilated with a scale
(102) factor centered at the origin so that T' has the coordinates $(9, -6)$, what are the coordinates of S'?

A $(12, 3)$ B $(12, -3)$

C $(-12, 3)$ D $(3, 12)$

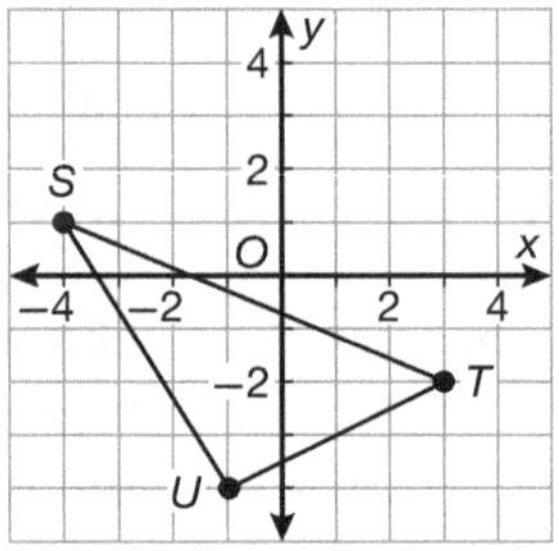

15. **Generalize** A three-dimensional object is made by adjoining
(77) two congruent cones along their circular faces. If the length from vertex to vertex of the new shape is h, and the radii of the initial cones is r, determine an expression for the surface area of this object.

16. **Verify** In $\triangle ABC$ at right, show that $\overline{BC} \parallel \overline{DE}$, if D and E are
(55) the midpoints of their respective sides. *Hint: Find the slope of each segment.*

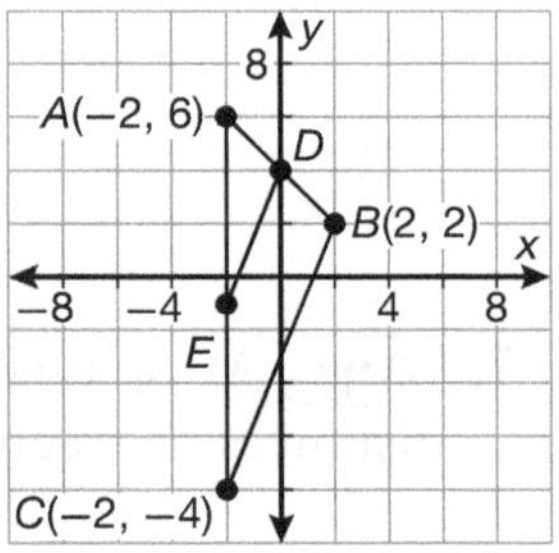

17. If a horizontal vector has a magnitude of x and a vertical
(89) vector has a magnitude of x, what is the angle measure of the resultant vector when they are summed? What is its magnitude?

18. Find the matrix that represents the translation of a triangle
(100) 3 units down and 4 units right.

*19. **Multi-Step** Find the matrix representation of the line segment.
(100) Then, write a matrix to translate the line segment 2 units down. Finally, write the matrix for the translated line segment.

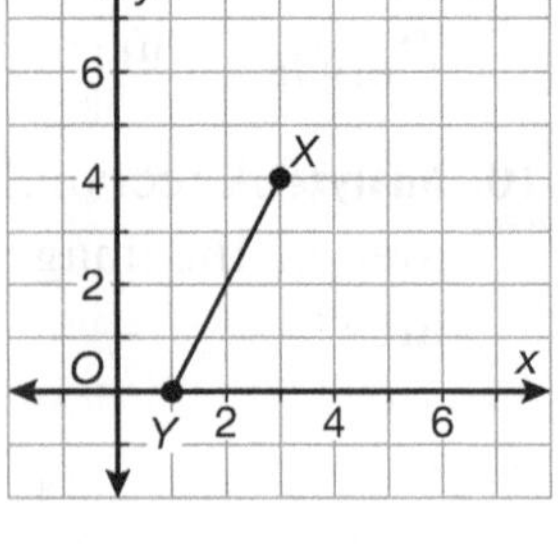

20. Two chords of a circle, $\overline{ST}$ and $\overline{XY}$, intersect at point V. Find
(86) VT if $SV = 5.4$, $XV = 3.9$, and $VY = 1.8$.

21. (31) **Error Analysis** Dantrell wrote a paragraph proof that included the statement, "By the Vertical Angles Theorem, ∠1 and ∠3 are supplementary." How can his statement be reworded to make it a true statement?

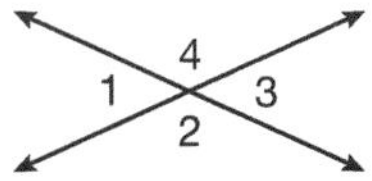

22. (72) Assume the segments that appear to be tangent are tangent. Find *AC*, *CD*, *CE*, and *BC*.

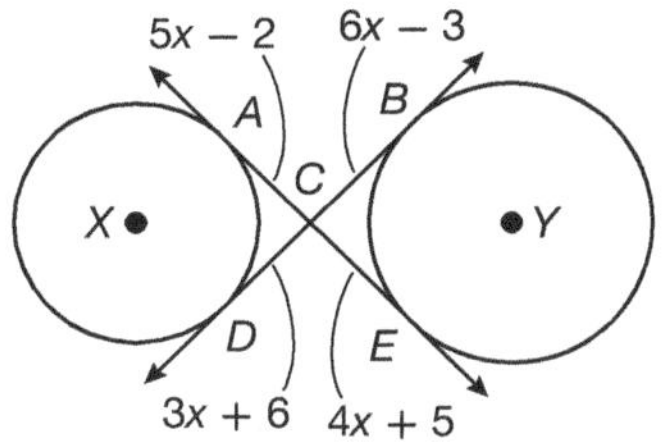

23. (46) Draw two triangles that are similar by Angle-Angle Similarity.

24. (Inv 6) **Graphics** Digital images are comprised of thousands of pixels, which are small points of light that combine to make the larger picture. A screen that is 8 inches tall by 13 inches wide displays a photograph of the Earth on a black background. The radius of the image of the Earth is 3 inches. If a pixel is chosen at random, what is the probability that it will be a part of the black background?

25. (82) **Multi-Step** For the triangle with vertices $X(0, 0)$, $Y(0, 4)$, and $Z(-2, 0)$, find the side lengths to the nearest tenth of a unit and the angle measures to the nearest degree.

***26.** (102) **Algebra** Show the point matrix multiplication with a scale factor of 3 for the given image.

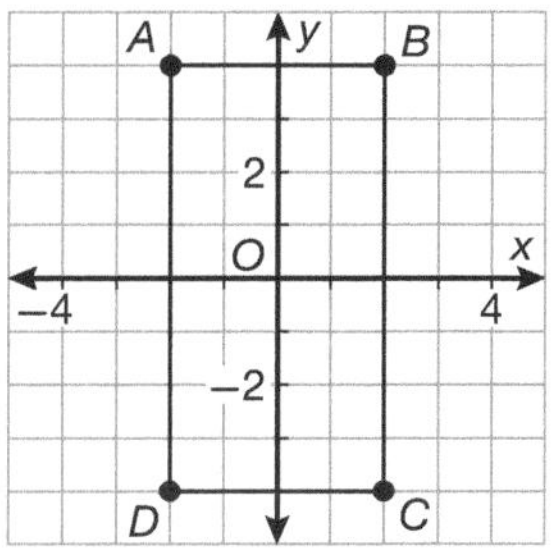

27. (18) **Algebra** The angles of a triangle measure $(x^2 - 2x)°$, $(6x + 3)°$, and 12°. Write and solve an equation for x. Which solution determines the angle measures?

28. (50) Find the geometric mean of 35 and 57 to the nearest tenth.

***29.** (101) **Write** Explain how the Tangent-Secant Product Theorem is a special case of the Secant Product Theorem.

30. (36) Which congruence theorem applies to these triangles?

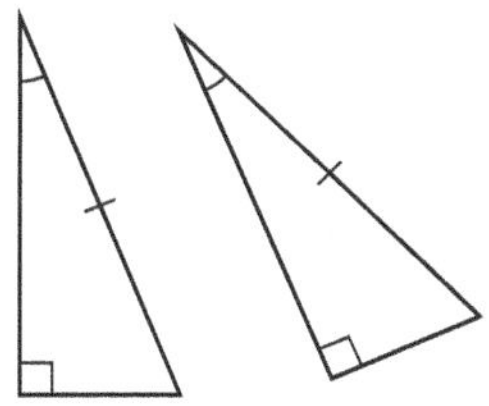

Name ______________________ Date __________ Class __________

Frustums of Cones and Pyramids

LESSON 103

* **1.** (102) Find the point matrix for the given rhombus and apply a scale factor of 1.5 to find the vertices after dilation.

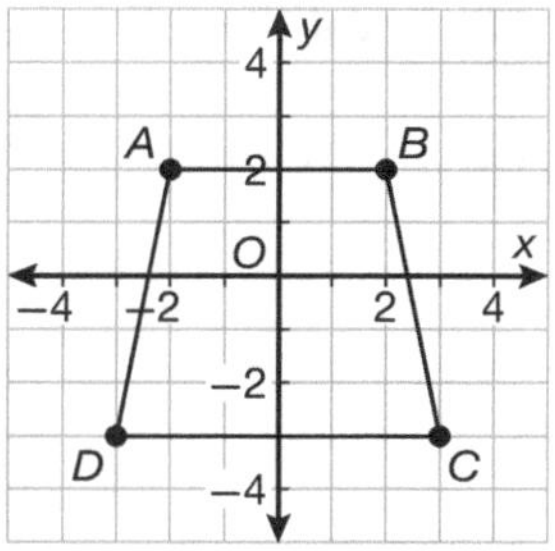

2. (79) Find the measure of the longer arc between two secants if the shorter arc is 50° and the exterior angle is 33°.

3. (94) **Error Analysis** Farnaz and Samantha each solved for x. Which student is correct? Explain the error the other one made.

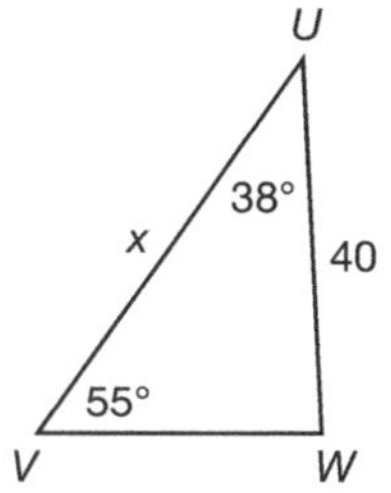

Farnaz:

$$\frac{x}{\sin 38°} = \frac{40}{\sin 55°}$$

$$x = \frac{40(\sin 38°)}{\sin 55°}$$

$$x \approx 30$$

Samantha:

$$\frac{x}{\sin 87°} = \frac{40}{\sin 55°}$$

$$x = \frac{40(\sin 87°)}{\sin 55°}$$

$$x \approx 49$$

* **4.** (103) **Algebra** The area of the base of a square pyramid is x^2 and the height is y. If the frustum is $\frac{5}{8}$ the height of the pyramid, and the smaller base of the frustum has an area of 16 square units, what is an expression for the volume of the frustum?

5. (Inv 7) Use $\triangle XYZ$ to determine the exact sine, cosine, and tangent of 35°.

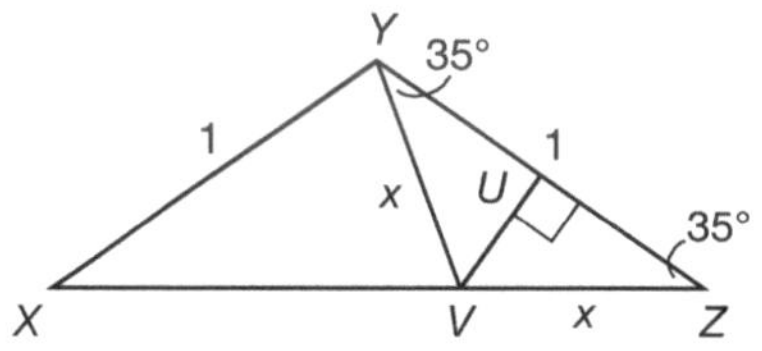

6. (61) If the acute corners of a right triangle are folded to align with the right angle, will the result always be a parallelogram? … a rectangle?

7. (Inv 4) Compare FH and AB.

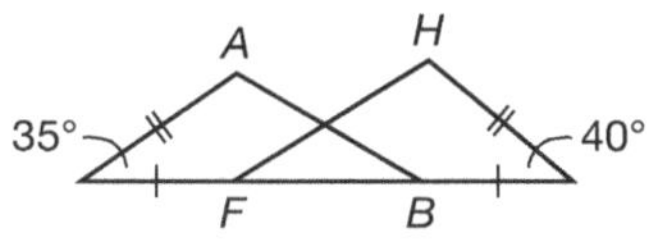

* **8.** (102) **Write** What is the meaning of the subscript O in the dilation notation $D_{o,k}(x, y) \rightarrow (kx, ky)$?

9. (47) **Algebra** Find the measure of each angle in quadrilateral $JKLM$.

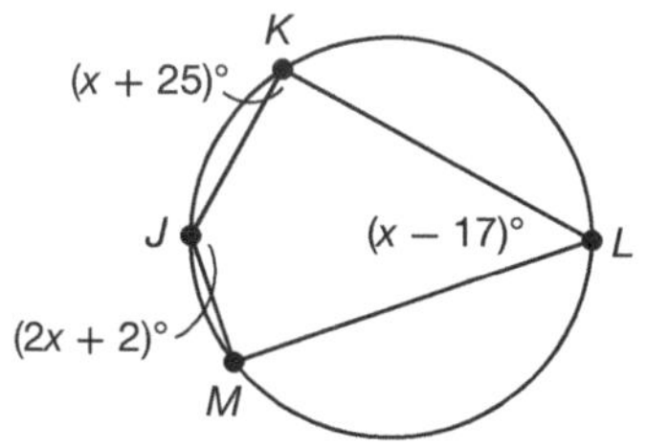

10. (21) **Robotics** Leah programs an industrial robot with the following logical rules:

If there is a green item in the tray, paint it blue.

If there is a blue item in the tray, attach a widget to it.

What can Leah conclude will happen if she puts a green item in the robot's tray?

11. (Inv 9) **Model** Sketch a figure which *cannot* be tessellated.

12. (73) In the diagram, which angles are not angles of elevation or depression?

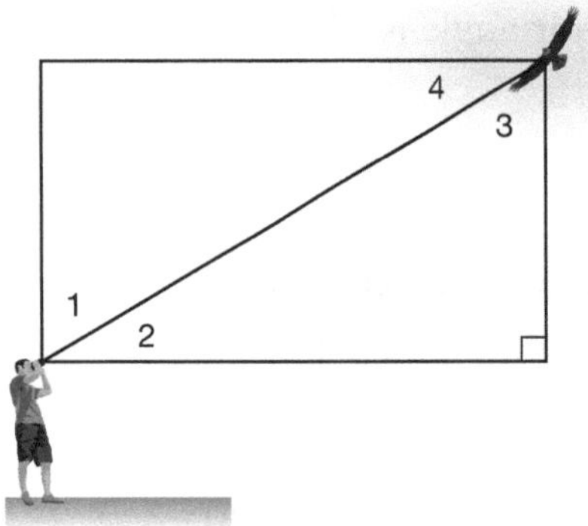

13. (58) **Algebra** R is an exterior point of $\odot C$, and $\overline{RP}$ and $\overline{RQ}$ are tangent to $\odot C$ at P and Q. Given that $m\angle CPR = (x^2 - x)°$ and $m\angle PRQ = (9x)°$, prove that $CPRQ$ is a square.

***14.** (101) **Mountaineering** In the diagram shown, a mountain climber stands at the top of a mountain that is 2640 feet above sea level. The diameter of the earth is approximately 7920 miles. Assuming the earth to be spherical, how far away can the mountain climber see, to the nearest mile?

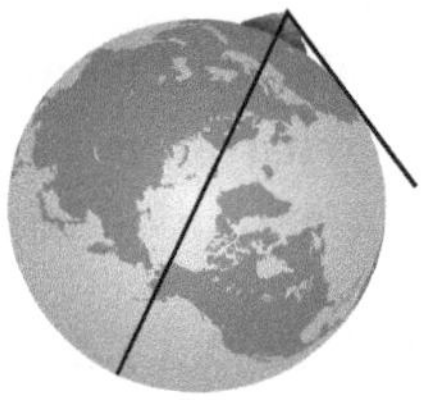

***15.** (98) Find θ. Round your answer to the nearest degree.

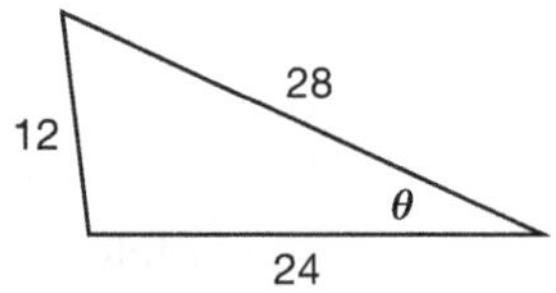

16. (69) A trapezoid has vertices at the points $W(-3, 2)$, $X(1, 0)$, $Y(-1, -2)$, and $Z(-3, -1)$. Use the distance formula to find the length of the midsegment of the trapezoid.

17. (43) If a circle has a radius of 4.5 inches, and a chord through the circle is 5 inches long, what is the distance from the chord to the center of the circle?

***18.** (103) Find an expression for the volume of the frustum of a cone that is $\frac{1}{6}$ the height of the cone.

19. (84) A dilation with a scale factor of 3 is applied to the rectangular prism at right. Find the surface area and the volume of the image that results.

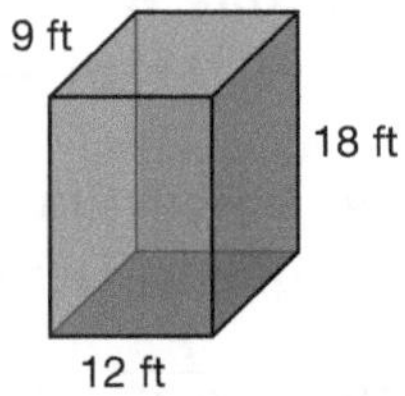

20. (Inv 10) **Write** Explain what it means for a fractal to be self-similar.

***21.** (102) Find the result of the dilation $D_{0,3.5}(x, y)$ on the points (4, 6) and (−2, −4).

22. (88) Are the points (1, 2), (2, 9), and (−2, 3) part of the solution set of $y > 2x + 3$?

23. *(80)* Find the surface area of a sphere whose great circle has a 52-meter circumference, to the nearest tenth.

*24. *(100)* **Multi-Step** $\overline{BC}$ has endpoints (−6, −3) and (−2, −1). If the line segment is translated 3 units up and 2 units left, what is the point matrix of the translated line segment?

*25. *(103)* **Cooking** A decorative teapot makes a cone shape. If the teapot stands 1 foot tall with a base diameter of 8 inches, what is the volume of half a pot of tea? Round your answer to the nearest tenth of a cubic inch.

26. *(64)* **Write** If two chords intersect at right angles, what can you say about the measures of the two opposite arcs? Explain how you know.

27. *(32)* **Mobiles** Hugh is making a triangular shape for a mobile to hang above his baby's crib, which should remain level. He measures the medians of the triangle to be 2.4, 3.2, and 3.75 inches. From which point should he suspend the triangle? How far is this point from each vertex, to the nearest tenth of an inch?

*28. *(103)* **Multiple Choice** Which of these could *not* be a formula for finding the volume of a frustum?

A $V = \frac{1}{3}h(B_1 + \sqrt{B_1B_2} + B_2)$ **B** $V = \frac{1}{3}(h_1B_1 - h_2B_2),\ h_2 > h_1$

C $V = \frac{1}{3}\pi h({r_1}^2 + r_1r_2 + {r_2}^2)$ **D** none of the above

29. *(68)* Use a special right triangle to find the value of tan 60°.

30. *(101)* **Architecture** An architect designs the circular window shown in the diagram. If the diameter of the window is 18 inches, and the architect wants exactly half of the shorter crosspieces to pass in front of the window, what should the total length of the shorter crosspieces be, to the nearest half-inch?

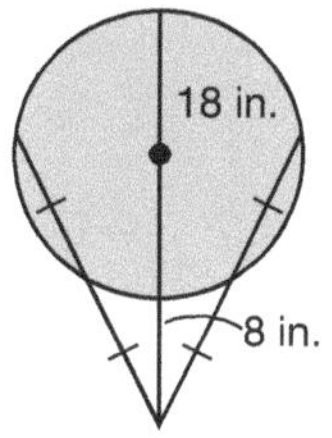

Name ______________________ Date ____________ Class ____________

Relating Arc Lengths and Chords

LESSON 104

* **1.** Use the figure shown and the given, $\overline{AD} \cong \overline{BC}$, to find $m\widehat{AD}$.
(104)

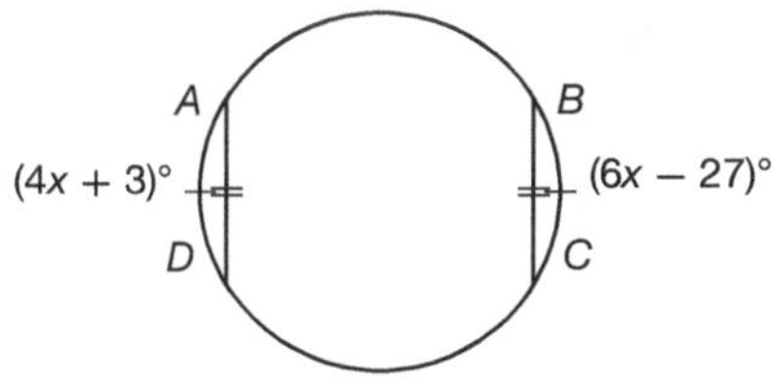

2. **Public Transportation** A bus route runs close to three large apartment complexes located at (0, 0), (6, 0), and (0, 2). The transportation agency wants to add a bus stop that is the same distance from each complex. Where should the stop be located?
(38)

* **3.** **Multi-Step** Two similar cylinders, C and D have a scale factor of 9:4. Cylinder C has a base radius of 3 feet, 6 inches and a height of 5 feet, 9 inches. Determine the surface area of cylinder D in square meters, to the nearest hundredth. Use the conversion factor 1 inch = 2.54 centimeters.
(99)

4. Reflect rectangle $JKLM$ across the line $x + y = 0$.
(74)

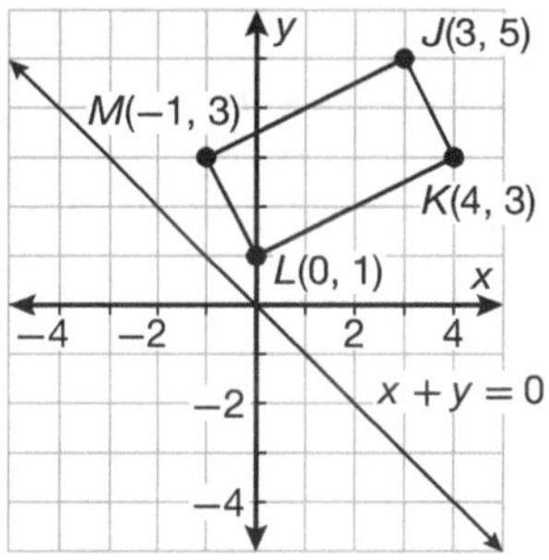

5. Show the point matrix multiplication for a dilation with a scale factor of 2 if the vertices of a triangle are (3, −1), (4, 0), and (0, 9).
(102)

6. Perform a reflection of quadrilateral $ABCD$ across line l_1, followed by a reflection across line l_2.
(90)

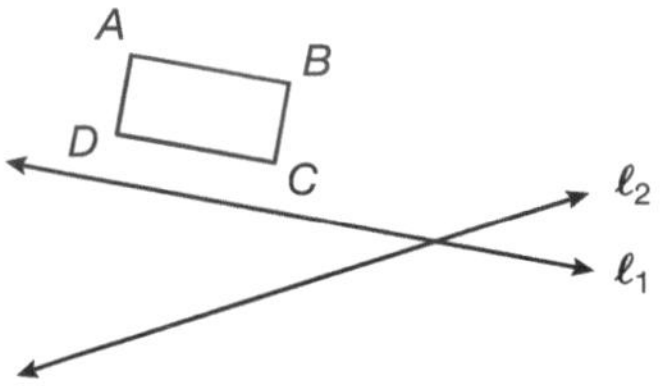

7. **Multiple Choice** Which of the following statements is true of a rectangle but not true of a square?
(52)

A All sides are congruent.
B The diagonals are perpendicular.
C The interior triangles created by the diagonals are two obtuse and two acute triangles.
D The diagonals bisect opposite angles.

8. Three of the vertices of a parallelogram are located at (1, 0), (4, 3), and (5, −2). Give all possible answers for the coordinates of the fourth vertex.
(34)

* **9.** Find the value of x in the diagram.
(101)

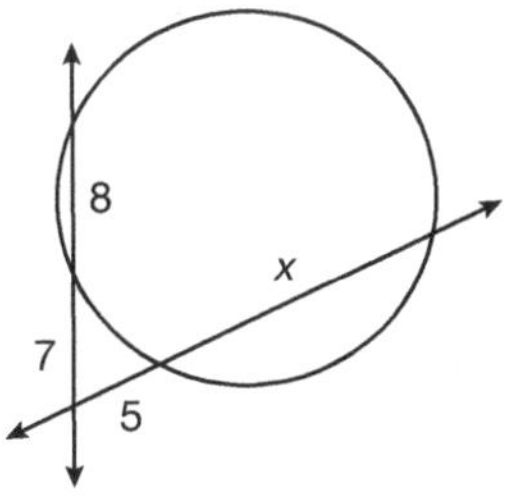

10. (81) **Multiple Choice** Which linear system has no solution?

A $y = -x, -y = x - 1$ **B** $y = 2x + 4, \frac{1}{4}y = x - 3$

C $4y = x, 2y = 2x$ **D** $x + y = 6, y = x - 4$

***11.** (104) Find the value of x if $m\overparen{RT} = 96°$ and $m\overparen{SU} = (x^2 + 4x)°$.

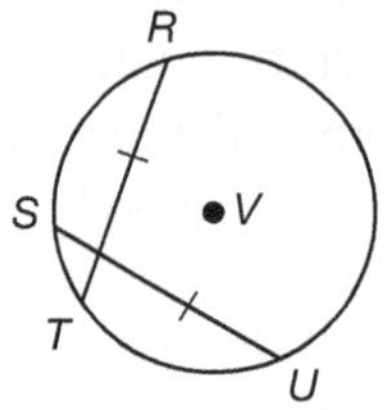

12. (45) A regular hexagon has six congruent sides and six congruent 120° angles. The figure shows a hexagon with a side length of L in a coordinate plane with one side on the x-axis and one vertex on the y-axis. Determine the coordinates of each vertex in terms of L.

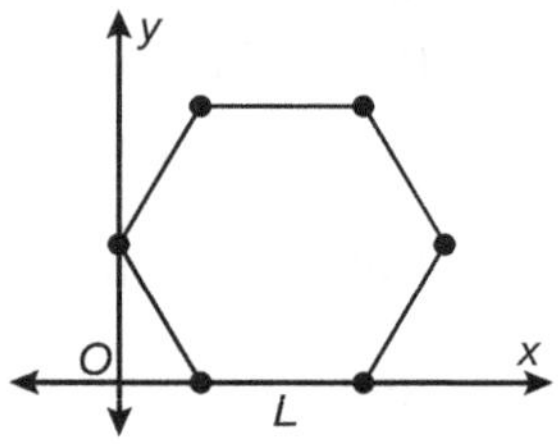

***13.** (103) Find the volume of the frustum shown. Round your answer to the nearest tenth.

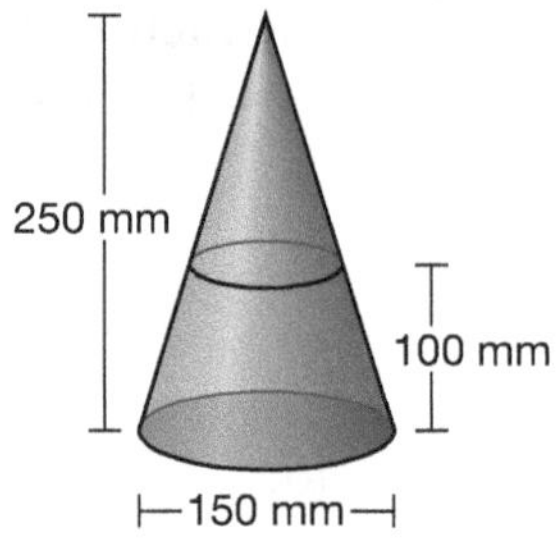

14. (96) A circle is dilated by a factor of 4. If the radius of the dilated circle is 12, what is the exact circumference of the original circle?

***15.** (104) Use the figure shown at the right and the given information to find $m\overparen{MN}$.

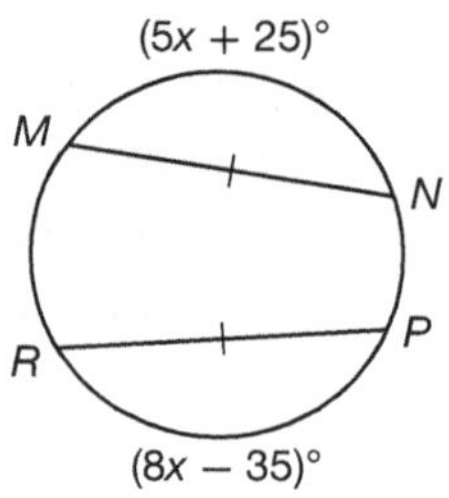

16. (96) **Write** Each side of a square is doubled. Describe how the area of the resulting square compares with the area of the original square.

17. (Inv 8) How many line segments can you draw between 9 noncollinear points?

***18.** (102) Find the vertices of the resulting triangle, if the given triangle is dilated by a factor of 3, centered at the origin.

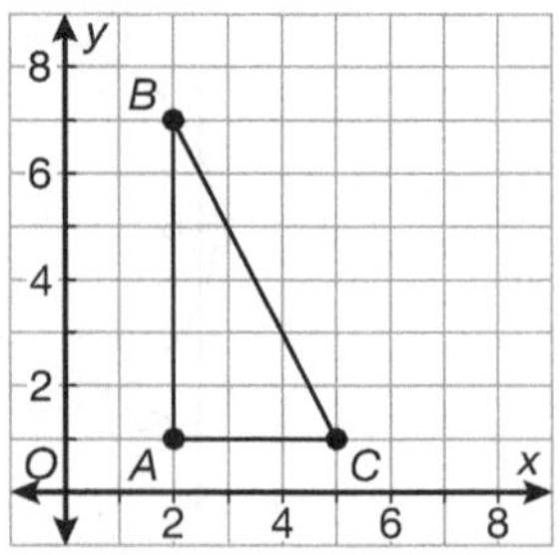

19. (60) Two segments are divided proportionally. The first segment is divided into parts that are 36, 42, and x units long, respectively. The second segment is divided into parts that are 24, y, and 30 units long, respectively. What are the values of x and y?

*20. Describe the translation of the graph $y = x^2$, and then write a 2×1 matrix to represent the translation.
(100)

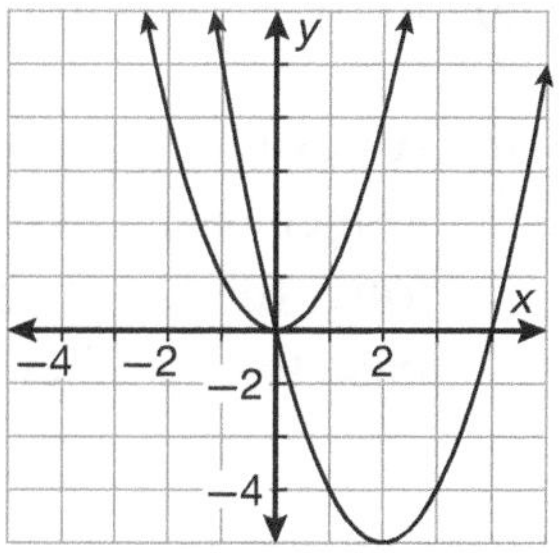

21. **Algebra** If $\frac{1}{\tan^2\theta} = 0.6$, what does $\sin\theta$ equal?
(91)

*22. **Multi-Step** Find the volume of the frustum at right. Round your answer to the nearest whole number.
(103)

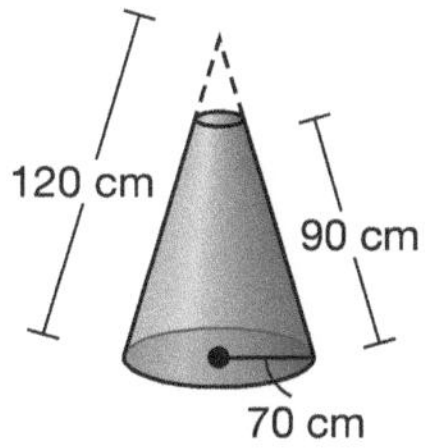

23. What shapes, and how many of each, make up the net of a hexagonal prism?
(Inv 5)

*24. **Write** Circle E is divided as shown in the figure. Describe the parts that are congruent and explain why they are congruent. Find the measures of $\angle CED$, $\widehat{AB}$, $\angle AED$, and $\widehat{BC}$, given that $m\angle BEA$ is 130°.
(104)

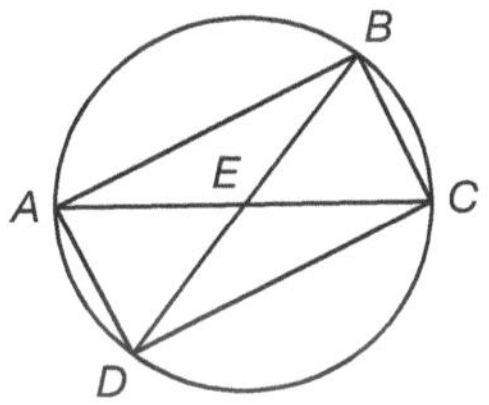

25. The vertices of quadrilateral $EFGH$ are $E(-3, -3)$, $F(1, -1)$, $G(3, 5)$, and $H(-3, 2)$. Prove that $EFGH$ is a trapezoid.
(92)

26. **Algebra** Use the Law of Cosines to find the value of x in $\triangle PQR$.
(98)

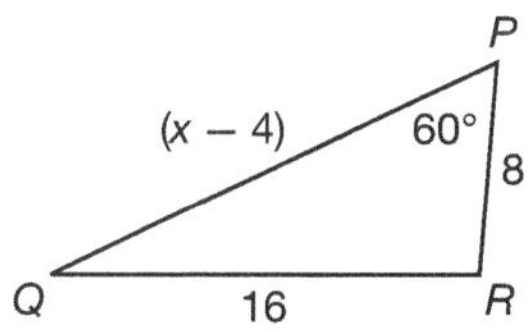

27. **Multi-Step** Find the perimeter of a 30°-60°-90° triangle with a 12-centimeter hypotenuse. Give your answer in simplified radical form.
(56)

28. Find the volume of the frustum shown. Round your answer to the nearest whole number.
(103)

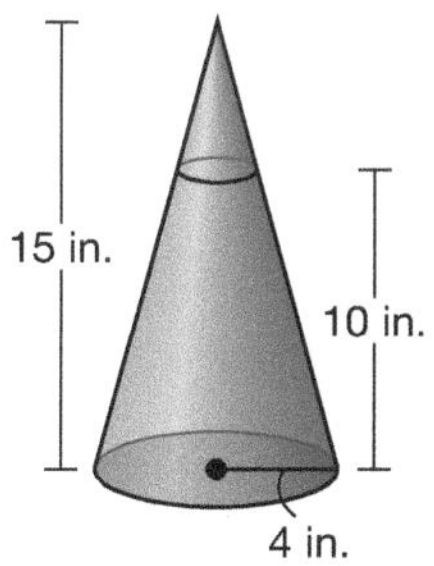

29. Find the distance from (5, 3) to the line $y = 2$.
(42)

30. A hexagonal figure is formed by two congruent isosceles trapezoids joined at their longer bases. What is the area of the figure if the shorter bases are 10 centimeters long, the longer bases are 25 centimeters long, and the distance from one shorter base to the other is 13 centimeters?
(40)

Name ______________________ Date __________ Class __________

Rotations and Reflections in the Coordinate Plane

LESSON 105

* **1.** Simplify $\begin{bmatrix} 6 & -1 \\ 3 & 2 \end{bmatrix}\begin{bmatrix} 5 & 2 \\ -8 & 4 \end{bmatrix}$.
(105)

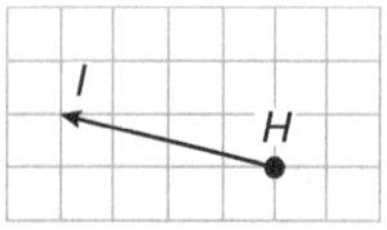

2. Write vector $\overrightarrow{HI}$ in component form.
(63)

3. **Multi-Step** A triangle has vertices $A(3, 2)$, $B(6, 1)$, and $C(2, -4)$. Find all the lengths and measures in the triangle. Round angle measures to the nearest degree and side lengths to the nearest tenth.
(98)

4. Figures *LMNO* and *PQRS* are similar. The ratio of their corresponding sides is 4:7. If the perimeter of *PQRS* is 87.5 centimeters, what is the perimeter of figure *LMNO*?
(44)

5. **Advertising** The figure at right shows the background for a company's logo. In order for the design to be symmetrical, what must be true about $\widehat{AB}$, $\widehat{AC}$, $\overline{AB}$, and $\overline{AC}$? Explain your reasoning.
(104)

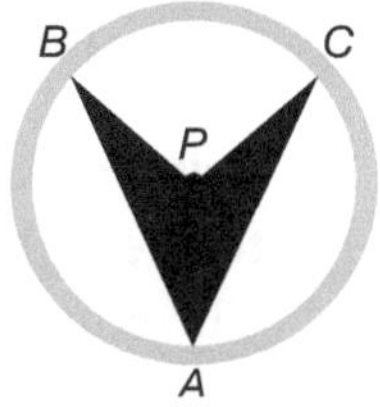

6. The equation for $\odot A$ is $(x + 2)^2 + (y - 3)^2 = 2.25$. Circle *B* has the same center as $\odot A$ and has a radius of 5. Write the equation of $\odot B$.
(75)

7. Find the volume of this frustum. Round your answer to the nearest whole number.
(103)

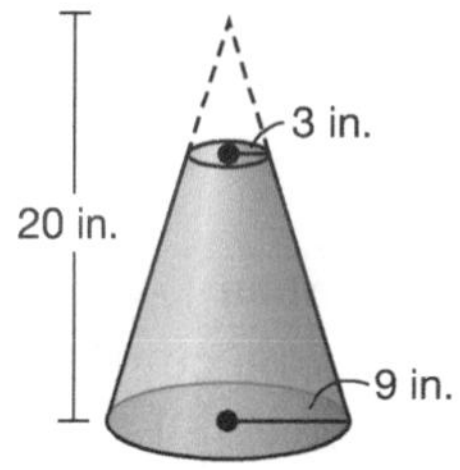

8. **Multiple Choice** This orthographic drawing shows the front, top, and right-side views of a solid. Which of these sketches represents the solid?
(93)

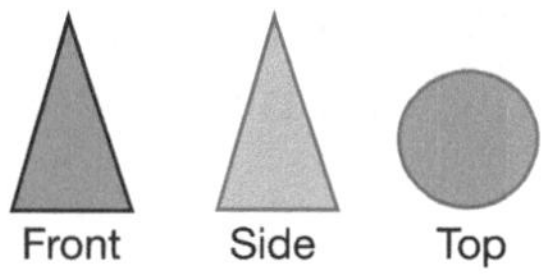

A

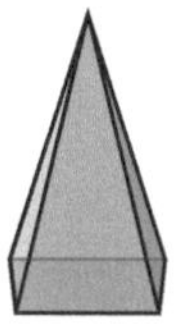

B

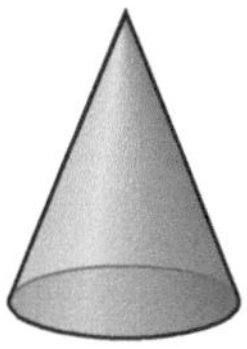

C

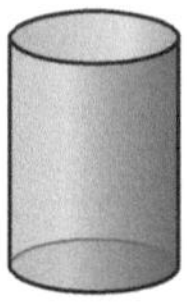

D

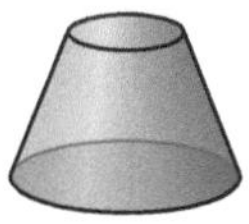

9. Solve this system of equations.
(81)

$y = \frac{3}{2}x - 3, x = 2$

Rotations and Reflections in the Coordinate Plane

LESSON 105

10. (70) **Formulate** Determine a formula for the volume of a tetrahedron with side length equal to $2m$.

***11.** (105) The vertices of $\triangle JKL$ are $J(-6, 2)$, $K(-6, -3)$, and $L(1, -3)$. Use matrix multiplication to reflect the image across the x-axis. Draw the preimage and the image in a coordinate plane.

12. (99) Two similar pentagonal prisms have a scale factor of 4:9. If the volume of the smaller prism is 100 cubic meters, find the volume of the larger prism to the nearest cubic meter.

13. (78) Copy the figure at right. Then, draw the rotation of the figure 180° about the point shown.

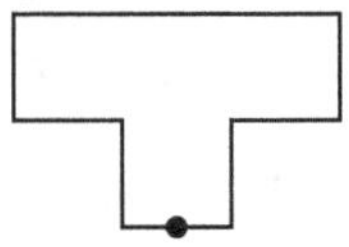

14. (95) **Multiple Choice** A circle given by $x^2 + y^2 = 49$ is shifted 5 units to the right and 6 units downward. It is also dilated by a factor of 2. The equation of the shifted and dilated circle is:

A $(x - 5)^2 + (y + 6)^2 = 196$ **B** $(x - 5)^2 + (y + 6)^2 = 14$

C $(x + 5)^2 + (y - 6)^2 = 196$ **D** $(x + 5)^2 + (y - 6)^2 = 14$

15. (95) **Analyze** The equation of a circle is $(x - 3)^2 + (y + 4)^2 = 16$. The circle is dilated by a scale factor of 0.5. What translation of the original figure would have translated the center of the circle to the same coordinates as the center of the new image after dilation?

16. (49) **Food Preparation** A deli worker has a large block of cheese in the shape of a cube. She makes one cut through the block parallel to one of the faces. What is the shape of the remaining block?

17. (102) **Write** For which values of k is a dilation a reduction? For which values of k is a dilation an enlargement?

***18.** (105) Triangle XYZ has vertices $X(-5, -1)$, $Y(-4, 3)$, and $Z(-1, 1)$. Determine the point matrix of the image for a 180° rotation about the origin of $\triangle XYZ$. Graph $\triangle XYZ$ and its image in a coordinate plane.

19. (101) Find the value of z in the diagram.

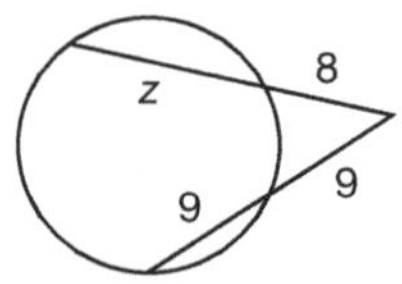

20. (20) In the city of Logica, there are two types of buses. Downtown buses are blue and suburban buses are green. State the disjunction of "A bus is a downtown bus," and "A bus is green." Is the disjunction true or false?

21. (104) Use the figure shown at right and the fact that $\overline{AB} \cong \overline{CD}$ to find the measure of $\widehat{AB}$.

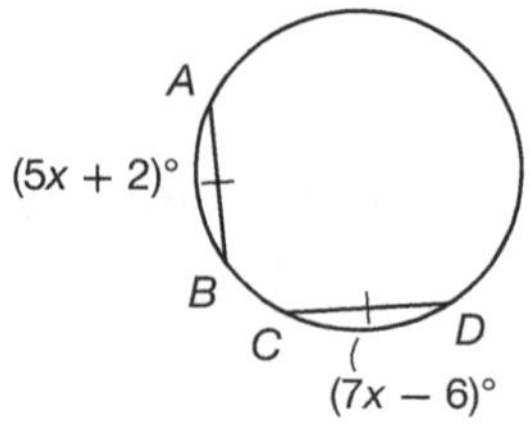

22. (Inv 3) What is the sum of the interior angles of a convex decagon?

23. (51) **Algebra** In an isosceles triangle, the vertex angle measures $3(x + 5)°$ and the base angles measure $(2x - 47)°$. Determine the angle measures.

***24.** (105) Trapezoid $TUVW$ has vertices at $T(-2, 2)$, $U(-1, 2)$, $V(0, 1)$, and $W(-3, 1)$. Determine the image matrix for a 90° rotation about the origin of trapezoid $TUVW$. Graph trapezoid $TUVW$ and its image in a coordinate plane.

25. (53) What is the ratio of the areas of two 45°-45°-90° right triangles if one has a hypotenuse of 14 yards and the other a hypotenuse of 7 yards?

26. (39) **Multiple Choice** Which group of line segment lengths can be used to form a triangle?

A 3, 5, 8 **B** 5, 9, 18
C 4, 7, 9 **D** 6, 8, 16

27. (83) **Coordinate Geometry** One vector is parallel to the y-axis and is perpendicular to a second vector. These two vectors are added and the resultant vector makes a 45° angle with the horizontal and has a magnitude of $5\sqrt{2}$. What is the magnitude of each of the two original vectors?

28. (72) **Model** Draw four circles, each pair of which share two common tangents.

29. (103) **Multi-Step** Find the volume of the frustum of the cone shown with a slant height of 25 centimeters and a radius of 10 centimeters. The frustum is $\frac{2}{3}$ the height of the cone. Round your answer to the nearest whole cubic centimeter.

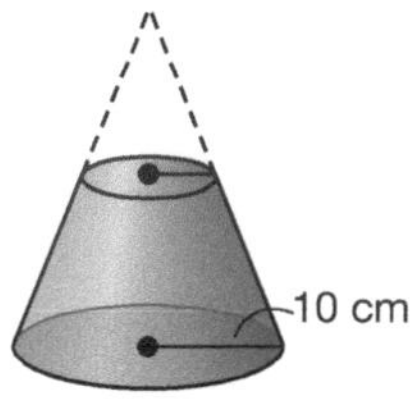

30. (65) The sides of a rhombus are 5 inches long. One diagonal is 6 inches long. What is the length of the other diagonal?

Name ______________________________ Date ____________ Class ____________

Circumscribed and Inscribed Figures

LESSON 106

* **1.** (106) **Multi-Step** Find the circumferences of the inscribed and circumscribed circles if the equilateral triangle has a side length of 12 centimeters.

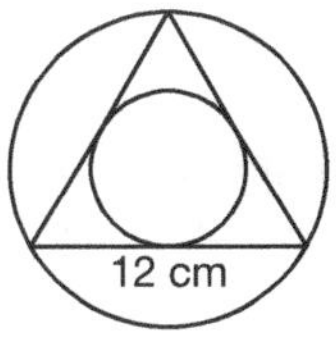

2. (100) **Multiple Choice** Which of the following transformation matrices represents a translation?

A $\begin{bmatrix} 1 & 0 \\ 0 & 1 \end{bmatrix}$ **B** $\begin{bmatrix} 0 & 0 \\ 2 & -2 \end{bmatrix}$ **C** $\begin{bmatrix} -1 & -1 \\ 0 & 0 \end{bmatrix}$ **D** $\begin{bmatrix} 1 & 2 \\ 1 & 2 \end{bmatrix}$

3. (71) Point M has coordinates $(-6, 5)$. What is the vector that translates $\triangle MNP$ to $\triangle M'N'P'$?

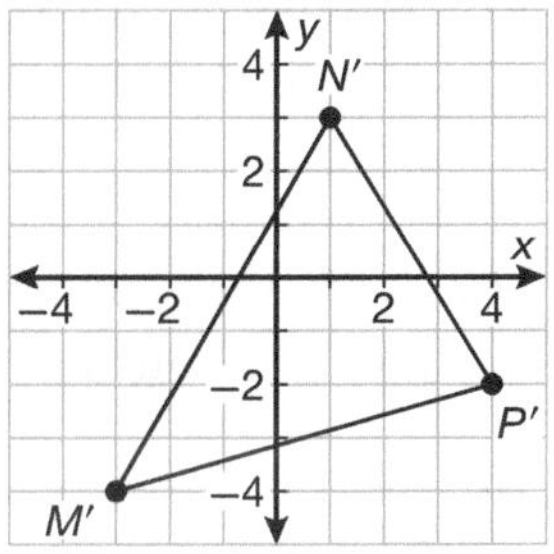

4. (50) What is the geometric mean of 4 and 9?

5. (62) **Algebra** A cylinder has a height that is twice the length of the diameter of its base. The volume of the cylinder is 100.48 cubic centimeters. Find the surface area to the nearest square centimeter.

* **6.** (105) Triangle ABC has vertices $A(3, 4)$, $B(7, 2)$, and $C(4, -3)$. Determine the image matrix for a 270° counterclockwise rotation of $\triangle ABC$ about the origin. Graph $\triangle ABC$ and its image in a coordinate plane.

7. (82) **Multi-Step** For the right triangle with vertices $D(-2, 0)$, $E(4, 3)$, and $F(4, 0)$, find the side lengths to the nearest tenth of a unit and the angle measures to the nearest degree.

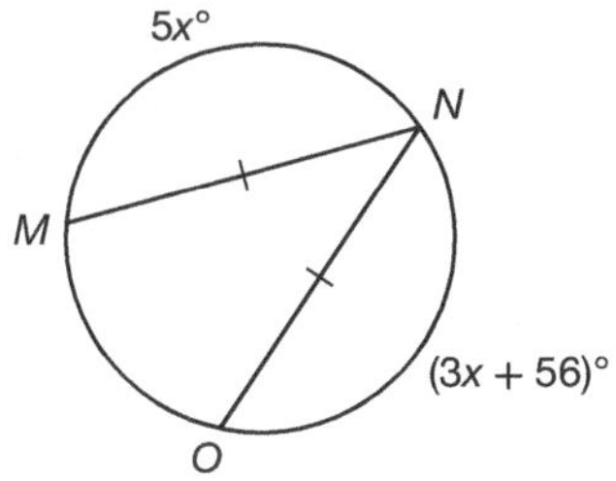

8. (104) Use the figure to find $m\widehat{MN}$.

9. (88) Sketch the graph of $y > \frac{1}{2}x - 1$.

10. (17) Write the contrapositive of the statement "If a quadrilateral has exactly one pair of parallel sides, then it is a trapezoid." Is the contrapositive true?

11. (103) Find the volume of the frustum of the square pyramid shown. Round your answer to the nearest hundredth of a cubic meter.

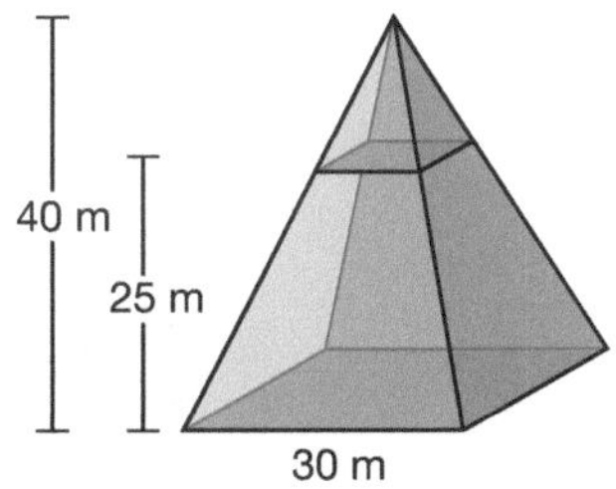

12. (92) **Analyze** A parallelogram has coordinates $A(-1, 1)$, $B(-3, -3)$, $C(3, -2)$, and $D(p, q)$. How many possible coordinates exist for D? Find them.

13. (59) A right rectangular prism has a length, width, and height that are all equal. The volume of the prism is 343 cubic meters. Find the surface area.

14. (76) How could you make the equation $y = x^2$ symmetrical along the x-axis?

15. (86) **Algebra** Two chords of a circle, $\overline{AB}$ and $\overline{CD}$, intersect at E. This figure's dimensions are: $AE = 5$, $BE = z$, $CE = 3$, and $DE = 7z - 4$. Write and solve an equation for z.

***16.** (106) **Carpentry** Sawmills use inscribed squares to cut the most economical beams of wood from logs. Using the illustration at right, find the ratio between the length of the side of a beam and the radius of the log.

17. (35) **Records** If the record player has a radius of 17 centimeters, what is the arc length traced by its needle moving half of a rotation?

18. (97) **Justify** Determine if the circles shown are concentric. Explain your reasoning.

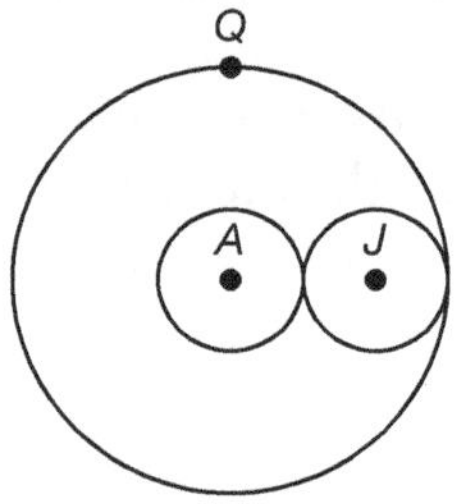

19. (66) Find the area of a regular hexagon with sides that are 22 inches long.

***20.** (105) Simplify $\begin{bmatrix} -5 & 0 \\ 2 & -7 \end{bmatrix}\begin{bmatrix} 3 & 1 & -1 \\ -2 & 6 & -3 \end{bmatrix}$.

21. (104) Use the figure shown to find $m\widehat{CD}$ if $\odot P \cong \odot T$.

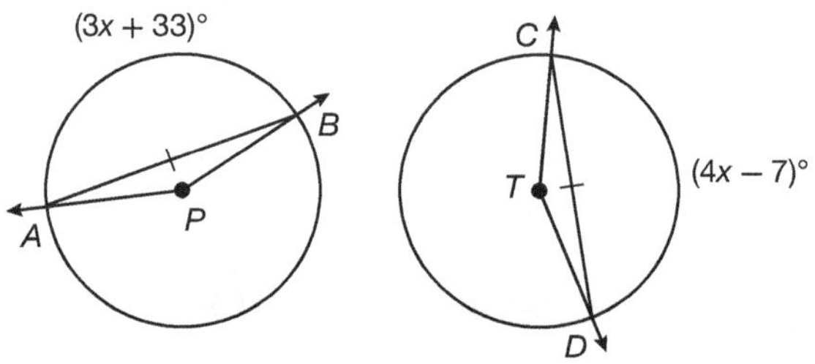

22. (39) In $\triangle JKL$, $JL = 4$, $LK = 2.7$, and $KJ = 2.9$. List angles J, K, and L from greatest to least measure.

23. (57) **Algebra** Find the area of the polygon bounded by the equalities $y = x$, $x = 6$, $y = 4$, and $x = 0$.

24. (93) **Error Analysis** Melanie drew an orthographic view of this solid. Determine if any of these views are incorrect, and if so, draw the correct view.

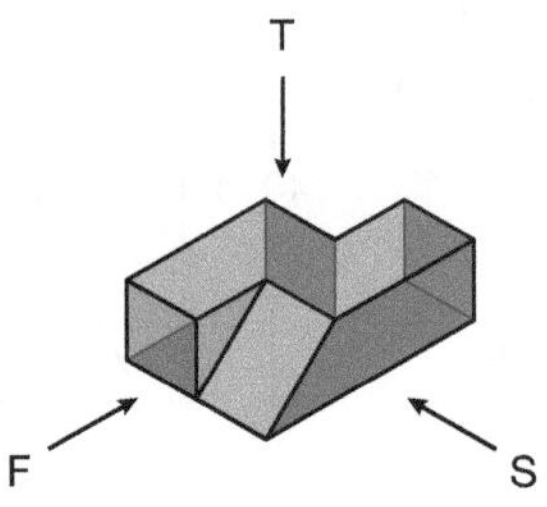

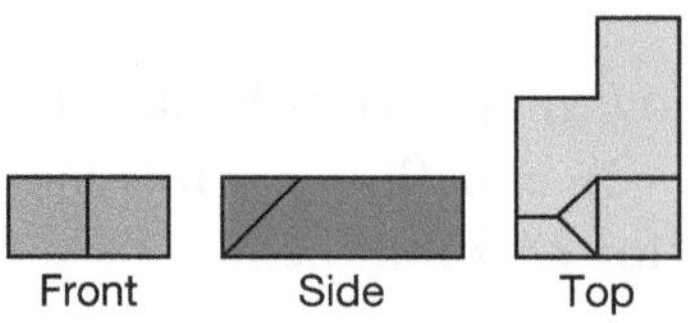

*25. Find the perimeter of a regular decagon inscribed in a circle having a radius of 10. Round your answer to the nearest tenth.
(106)

*26. The vertices of $\triangle XYZ$ are $X(3, -1)$, $Y(5, -5)$, and $Z(7, -1)$. Use matrix multiplication to reflect the image across the y-axis. Draw the preimage and the image in a coordinate plane.
(105)

27. Segment JK is a midsegment of $\triangle FGH$. Find the value of x and the lengths of $\overline{JK}$ and $\overline{FH}$.
(55)

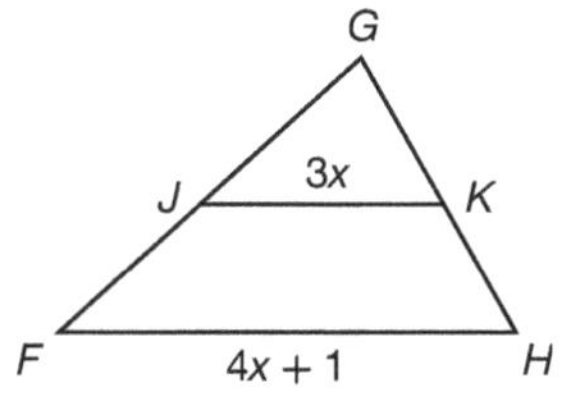

28. Find the vertices of the image of $D_{O, \frac{3}{2}}(x, y)$ for a triangle with vertices $(-3, 0)$, $(5, 2)$, and $(2\ -4)$.
(102)

29. **Model** Draw two triangles that are similar by SSS.
(46)

*30. **Algebra** A regular polygon is inscribed in a circle. If the circle has a radius of r and the polygon has a side length of r, what type of polygon is it?
(106)

Name ______________________ Date __________ Class __________

Maximizing Area

LESSON **107**

1. (104) Use this figure to find $m\widehat{AD}$.

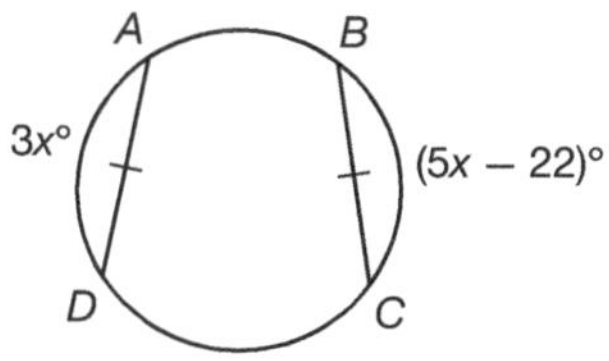

2. (99) **Packaging** A package of rice in the shape of a right triangular prism comes in two sizes. The smaller size is 4.5 inches tall and has right triangular bases with legs that are 0.75 and 1 inch long, respectively. The larger size is similar to the smaller but with double the dimensions. Find the surface area of the larger package.

*** 3.** (107) Triangle A is a right triangle with side lengths of 3, 4, and 5 inches. Triangle B is an equilateral triangle with side lengths of 4 inches each. Find the perimeters of each of these triangles and predict which will have the greater area. Verify your answer.

4. (49) What is the name of a right solid whose bases are five-sided polygons and whose lateral faces are rectangles?

5. (64) Find the value of x in the figure.

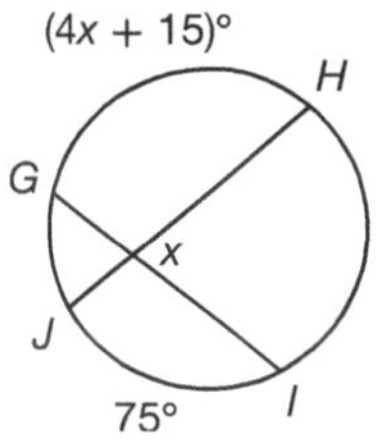

6. (14) Find a counterexample to the following conjecture.

If the product of two numbers is positive, then both numbers are positive.

7. (105) Triangle DEF has vertices $D(-4, -5)$, $E(-1, 5)$, and $F(2, -5)$. Determine the image matrix for a 360° rotation of $\triangle DEF$ about the origin. Graph $\triangle DEF$ and its image in a coordinate plane.

*** 8.** (107) Determine the largest possible area for a hexagon with a perimeter of 12 centimeters. Round the area to the nearest tenth.

9. (41) Triangles DEF and XYZ are similar. If $DE = 3(XY)$, what is the ratio of the perimeters of the triangles?

10. (Inv 6) A square has side lengths of 5 centimeters. A second square is drawn inside the first by connecting the midpoints of each side. Find the probability that a point chosen at random within the larger square will fall inside the smaller square.

***11.** (106) Describe the diagram in two ways.

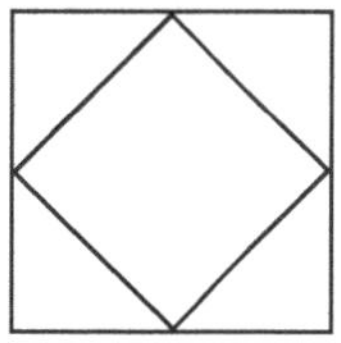

12. (68) What is $\sin M$?

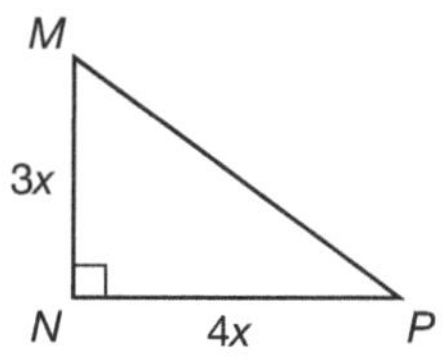

13. (102) **Multiple Choice** What are the coordinates of the preimage point in the dilation $D_{O,4}(x, y) \rightarrow (20, -4)$?

A (80, −16) **B** (5, −1)

C (−1, 5) **D** (−16, 80)

14. (68) What angle has a tangent equal to 1?

15. (101) **Error Analysis** Jeremy suggests that the value of x in the figure shown must be 5 inches. Is he correct? If not, give the correct answer.

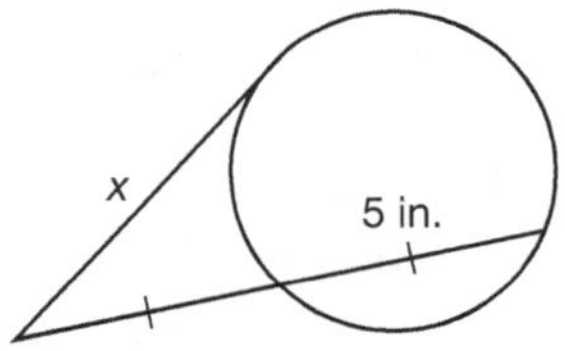

***16.** (107) What is the minimum perimeter that will enclose a triangular area of 100 square feet? Round your answer to the nearest tenth of a foot.

17. (86) Find b in the figure at right.

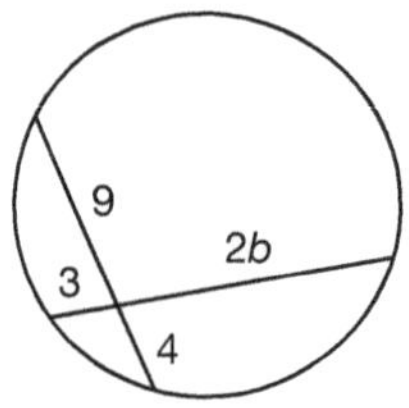

***18.** (106) A regular hexagon has a perimeter of 60 inches. What is the area of a circle inscribed in the hexagon?

19. (58) **Algebra** $\overleftrightarrow{AB}$ is tangent to $\odot Z$ at B, $m\angle ZAB = (3x + 72)°$, and $m\angle AZB = (13 - 2x)°$. Determine the value of x.

20. (103) **Formulate** Write a formula for finding the volume of a frustum of a cone that is half the height of that cone.

21. (90) Translate the triangle along v, and then reflect it across line t.

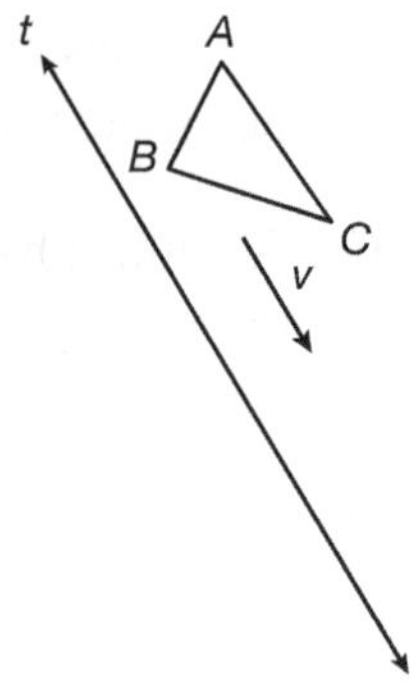

22. (105) Simplify $\begin{bmatrix} 4 & 2 & -7 \\ -1 & -3 & 5 \end{bmatrix}\begin{bmatrix} 9 & 6 \\ 3 & 5 \\ 1 & -2 \end{bmatrix}$.

23. (36) **Write** The congruence theorems for right triangles are derived directly from the general Triangle Congruence Theorems and Postulates SAS, SSS, AAS and ASA. Which of these is HA Right Triangle Congruence derived from? Explain.

24. (Inv 7) **Algebra** Let $s = \sin x$, $c = \cos x$, and $t = \tan x$. Determine an equation for t in terms of c and an equation for t in terms of s.

25. (106) A regular pentagon is inscribed in a circle with a radius of 7. Find the perimeter of the pentagon. Round your answer to the nearest tenth.

26. Is the following statement always, sometimes, or never true?
(52)

The diagonals of a square, a rhombus, and a rectangle are congruent.

27. **Targets** A target sits on a grid. It has a center circle whose equation is $(x + 3)^2 + (y - 2)^2 = 9$. An outer circle of the target is a dilation of the center circle by a factor of 3. What is the equation of the outer circle?
(95)

***28.** **Corrals** A farmer wants to build a rectangular corral for his horse. The farmer has 64 feet of fencing. What is the maximum area that the farmer can surround with his fencing?
(107)

29. **Generalize** A three-dimensional figure is formed by adjoining two congruent cones along their circular faces. If the length from vertex to vertex of the new shape is h, and the radius of the initial cones is r, determine a formula for the volume of this figure.
(77)

30. **Analyze** Which point of concurrency in a triangle is the center of a circle that contains all three vertices? How is it found?
(32, 38)

Name ______________________________ Date __________ Class __________

Introduction to Coordinate Space

LESSON 108

*** 1.** *(108)* State the coordinates of the points on the graph.

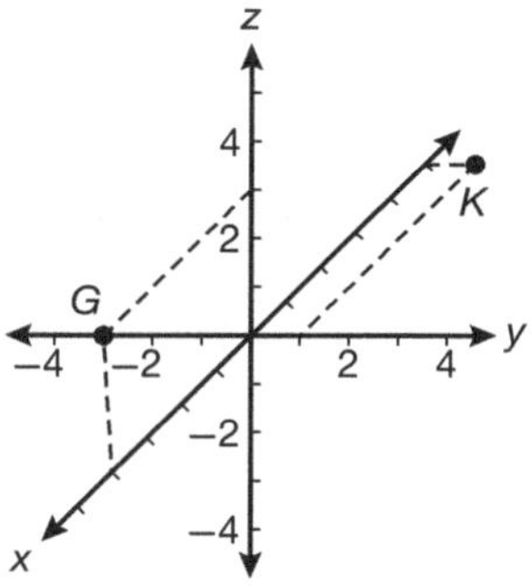

2. *(86)* Two chords of a circle, $\overline{AB}$ and $\overline{CD}$, intersect at P. $AP = 8$, $BP = x$, $CP = 2$, and $DP = 2x + 3$. Write and solve an equation for x.

3. *(105)* **Justify** If a triangle is represented by the matrix $\begin{bmatrix} -1 & -3 & 3 \\ -3 & 3 & 1 \end{bmatrix}$ and its image matrix after a transformation is $\begin{bmatrix} -3 & 3 & 1 \\ 1 & 3 & -3 \end{bmatrix}$, was the triangle rotated about the origin, or was it reflected? If it was reflected, was it across the x-axis or the y-axis? If it was rotated about the origin, was it by 90°, 180°, 270°, or 360°? Explain your reasoning.

4. *(69)* **Farming** A water trough for horses is in the shape of a trapezoidal prism. The lengths of the parallel sides of the trapezoid faces are 15 inches and 21 inches. If the water level is such that it just touches the midpoints of each leg of the trapezoid faces, what is the length of the water level across the face?

5. *(106)* Find the perimeter of the rectangle that is inscribed in a circle. The radius of the circle is 14 centimeters and $\theta = 130°$. Round your answer to the nearest tenth of a centimeter.

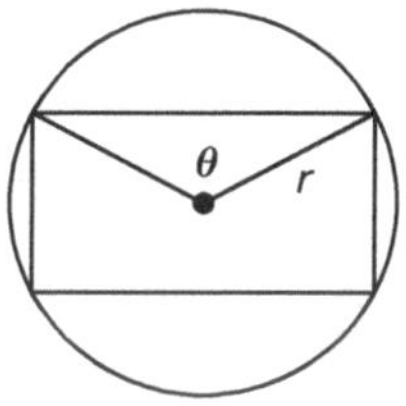

6. *(45)* Prove that the line containing the points $(3, -1)$ and $(7, 1)$ is perpendicular to the line containing the points $(-2, 4)$ and $(0, 0)$.

7. *(101)* **Write** Describe how to use the Secant-Tangent Product Theorem to solve for the length of the tangent segment in the given diagram.

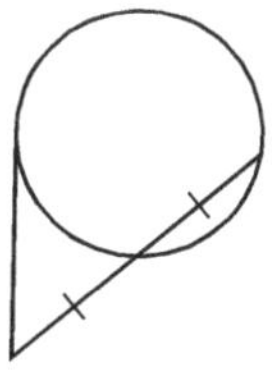

8. *(97)* **Write** Given the equations of two circles, how can you tell whether the circles are concentric or not?

9. *(88)* **Error Analysis** Oliver drew this graph as the solution to the inequality $x + y > 1$. Find and correct Oliver's mistake.

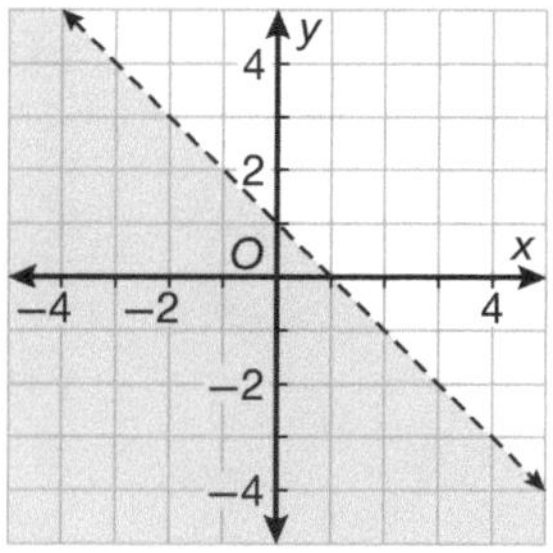

10. *(50)* Find the geometric mean of $\sqrt{3}$ and $\sqrt{13}$.

***11.** *(108)* **Algebra** Does the point $(5, -2, 6)$ lie on the line defined by the equation $(x, y, z) = (1, 0, -3) + t(2, -1, 5)$?

12. *(75)* The equation of $\odot C$ is $(x - 2)^2 + y^2 = 25$. Graph $\odot C$.

***13.** *(107)* What is the least possible area of the square that contains a circle with a radius of 10 inches?

14. *(104)* **Art** Dante is painting two arcs of equal length on a circle. If the length of the chord associated with one arc is 5 centimeters, how long should he make the chord that corresponds to the other arc? Explain how you know.

15. (86) Two chords of a circle, $\overline{AB}$ and $\overline{CD}$, intersect at P. $AP = x - 1$, $BP = 9$, $CP = 6$, and $DP = x + 1$. Write and solve an equation for x.

16. (52) **Algebra** Find the value of x in this rhombus.

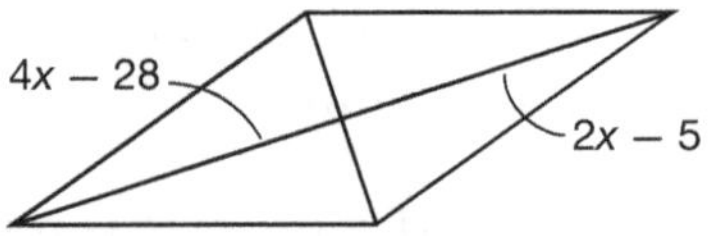

***17.** (108) Plot the points $K(4, -3, -3)$ and $L(3, -4, -4)$.

18. (80) **Sports** A soccer ball needs to be filled with air. What is the volume of air needed if the ball is to be a perfect sphere with a radius of 4 inches?

***19.** (107) Determine the largest possible area that can be contained by an octagon with a perimeter of 16 inches. Round your answer to the nearest tenth.

20. (94) **Multi-Step** Find the perimeter of $\triangle PQR$. Round your answer to the nearest whole number.

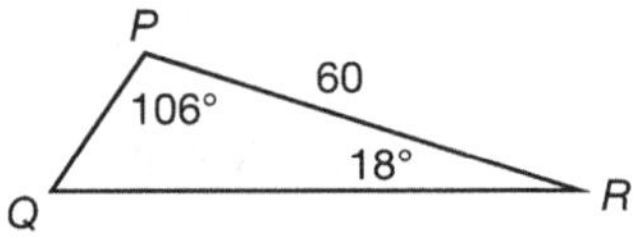

21. (61) **Write** Describe what information is needed to prove that a quadrilateral is a parallelogram.

22. (40) **Lunch** Alyssa has taken a roughly-semicircular bite out of her sandwich, as shown. If each bite she takes is about the same size as her first bite, how many bites in all will it take for Alyssa to eat her entire sandwich?

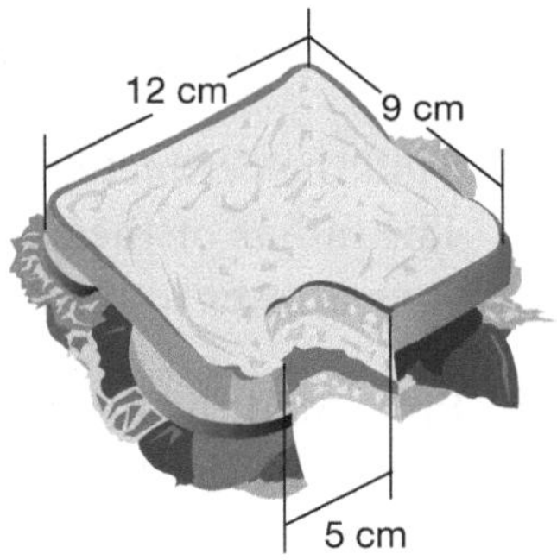

23. (106) A regular pentagon circumscribes a circle with a radius of 8. Find the perimeter of the pentagon to the nearest tenth.

24. (73) **Diving** A scuba diver is in the water, as shown, and he sees a coral at an angle of depression of 18°. He knows that he is 100 feet from the boat and sees it at a 30° angle of elevation. If the scuba diver is 12 feet above the coral, how far is the boat from the coral, to the nearest foot?

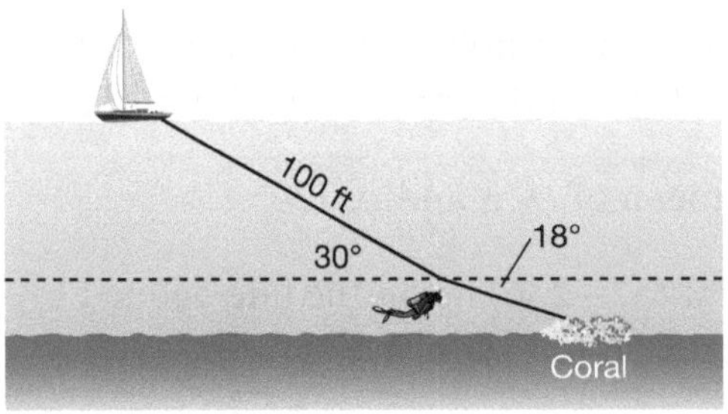

***25.** (108) **Multiple Choice** Which point is collinear with the points $(-1, 4, 4)$ and $(-10, 1, -8)$?

A $(5, 6, 10)$ **B** $(2, 2, 8)$
C $(-7, 2, -4)$ **D** $(10, 8, 20)$

26. (78) The endpoints of $\overline{AB}$ are $A(1, 3)$ and $B(2, 5)$. Graph $\overline{A'B'}$ after $\overline{AB}$ has been rotated 90° counterclockwise about the origin. Then, graph $\overline{A''B''}$ after $\overline{A'B'}$ has been rotated 180° counterclockwise about the point $C(-3, -1)$.

***27.** (107) What is the minimum length of wire needed to secure an area of 34 square centimeters? Round your answer to the nearest tenth.

28. (81) **Algebra** A system of equations has no solution. One equation is $y = -\frac{1}{3}x - 4$ and the other equation is $x = by + 1$. What is the value of b?

29. (100) **Analyze** Describe the translation of the graph $y = x^3$, and then write a 2×1 matrix to represent the translation.

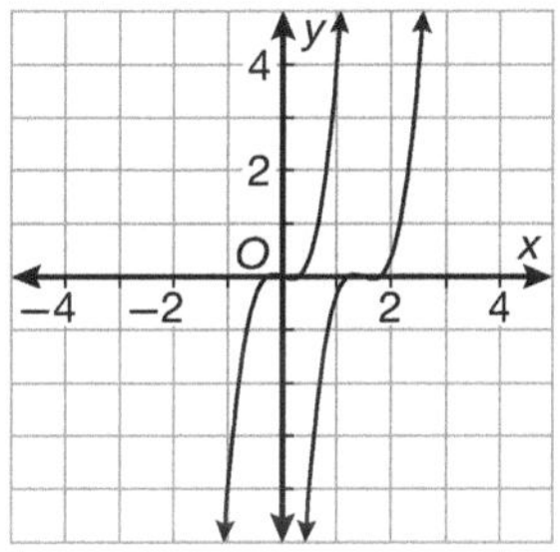

30. (24) Solve for θ. Show your steps.

$\sin \theta + \sin^2\theta = 1.25 - \cos^2\theta$

Name ________________________________ Date __________ Class __________

Non-Euclidean Geometry

LESSON 109

1. (104) **Wheels** Some wheels have support spokes equally spaced along the circumference to keep the wheel from breaking. How can you confirm that the arc length between the first and third spokes is equal to the arc length between the second and fourth spokes?

*** 2.** (109) Triangle JKL is on a sphere with radius 10 centimeters. Its angles measure 90°, 80°, and 45°. What is the area of $\triangle JKL$ to the nearest tenth of a square centimeter?

3. (20) **Multiple Choice** Sonja always has a salad for lunch on Tuesdays. Which statement is true?

A If Sonja has a salad for lunch, then it is a Tuesday.
B Sonja has a salad for lunch if and only if it is a Tuesday.
C If it is a Tuesday, then Sonja has a salad for lunch.
D All of these are true.

4. (84) A dilation with a scale factor of $\frac{1}{4}$ is applied to this rectangular prism. Find the surface area and the volume of the image that results.

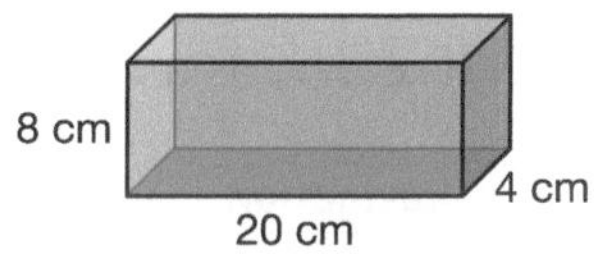

5. (105) The vertices of $\triangle QRS$ are $Q(1, 1)$, $R(5, 3)$, and $S(2, -3)$. Use matrix multiplication to first rotate the triangle 90° about the origin, and then reflect the image across the x-axis. What is the image matrix?

6. (38) **Write** Do you need to construct all three perpendicular bisectors of a triangle to locate its circumcenter? Explain.

7. (74) What point does a reflection across the line $y = x$ map (x, y) onto?

8. (103) **Analyze** The frustum of a cone is 10 inches tall. The base radius is 3 inches and the upper radius is 2 inches. The frustum of a square pyramid is also 10 inches tall. It has a base square with side lengths of 3 inches and an upper square with side lengths of 2 inches. Which frustum has the greater volume?

*** 9.** (108) Determine the coordinates of two points that lie on the line $(x, y, z) = (4, 0, 0) + t(1, 0, 1)$.

10. (66) A regular hexagon can be divided into six equilateral triangles. The height of each triangle is 6 centimeters. What is the perimeter of the hexagon? What is the area?

***11.** (60) **Justify** Determine whether $\overline{BC}$ and $\overline{EF}$ are parallel. How do you know?

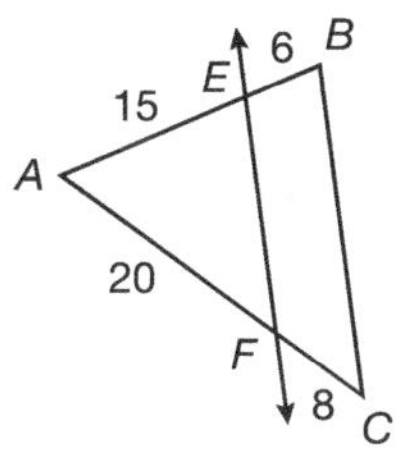

12. (87) The sides of two equilateral triangles are in the ratio 1:4. The area of the larger triangle is 64 square feet. What is the area of the smaller triangle?

*13. (109) In spherical geometry, the shortest distance between two points is the minor arc of a __________.

14. (96) **Write** Marina has a photograph that is 5 inches by 7 inches. She wants to enlarge the photo so that the length and width are each tripled. Describe how the area of the photo will change.

15. (104) Use the figure shown at the right to find m$\widehat{QS}$.

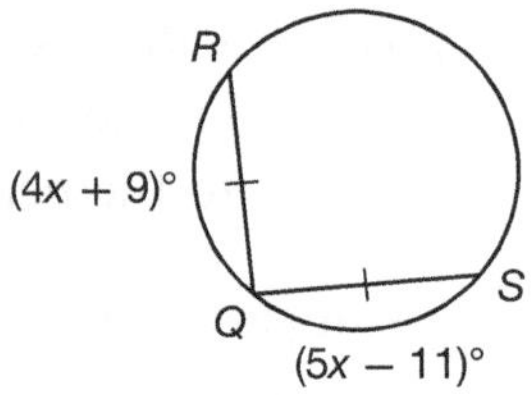

16. (107) Emma wants to use 100 centimeters of wire to enclose either a triangular area or a rectangular area. What is the largest possible area that she can enclose?

17. (63) **Multiple Choice** What is the magnitude of the vector ⟨5, 7⟩, to the nearest whole unit?

A 6 units **B** 7 units
C 8 units **D** 9 units

18. (79) If $\angle AEC$ is a right angle and $\overrightarrow{EB}$ bisects $\angle AEC$, find m$\widehat{AB}$.

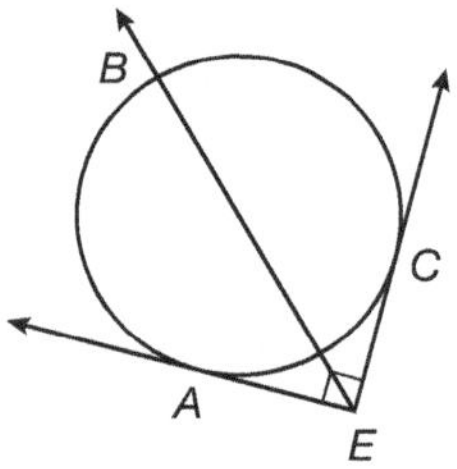

*19. (109) **Navigation** A boat sailing on the Atlantic Ocean traveled along a triangular path with vertices at 77°, 56°, and 90°. If Earth has a radius of 3960 miles, what is the area of the triangle that the boat traveled around?

20. (91) **Algebra** If $\sin^2\theta = 0.12$, what does $\cos\theta$ equal?

*21. (108) **Verify** Show that the point (1, −8, −4) lies on the line through the points (4, −5, −1) and (3, −6, −2).

*22. (106) **Error Analysis** Eddie was asked to find the perimeter of the largest square that can be inscribed in a circle with a 7-inch radius. His answer was 56 inches. What is the correct answer and what was Eddie's mistake?

23. (56) **Closets** A storage closet is built underneath a staircase. Find the height of the closet to the nearest tenth.

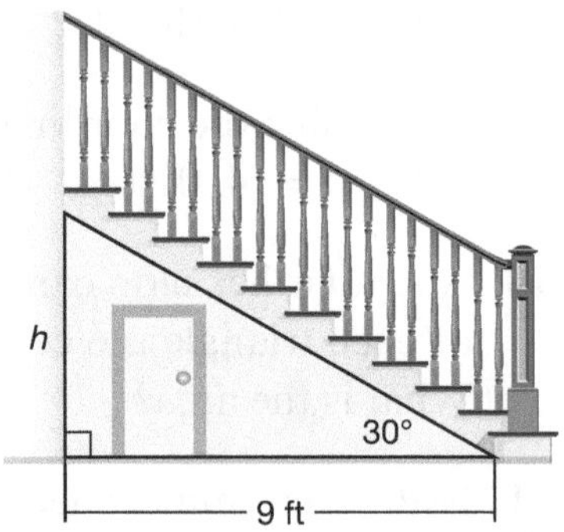

24. (85) **Art** Tracy wants to make a circle in her art class using a cone that has a radius of 4 centimeters and a height of 20 centimeters. If she cuts the cone parallel to the circular face 5 centimeters from the vertex, what is the area of the circle that is formed? Round your answer to the nearest hundredth.

25. (108) **Multiple Choice** Which of these points is collinear with the points (1, −4, 6) and (2, 5, 8)?

A (4, 23, 12) **B** (0, 5, 4)
C (3, 22, 10) **D** (−1, −14, 2)

26. (20) Consider the statements, "A quadrilateral has four right angles," and "A quadrilateral is not a rectangle." Which is true: their conjunction, their disjunction, both, or neither?

27. (89) **Ornithology** An ornithologist, someone that studies birds, put radio tags on two birds and released them at the same time from the same place to study their migration. After two days, one bird was 27 miles away at 210 degrees southwest and the other was 22 miles away at 120 degrees southeast. How far apart were the birds from each other, to the nearest tenth of a mile?

28. (107) What is the maximum area of an octagon with a perimeter of 24 centimeters, to the nearest tenth?

29. (67) Triangle *PQR* has been reflected to form $\triangle P'Q'R'$. Is the slope of the line of reflection positive, negative, zero, or undefined?

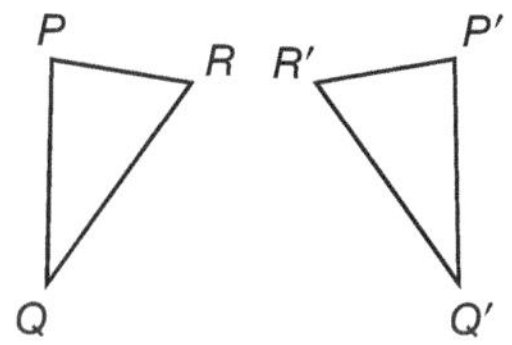

30. (43) What is the diameter of a circle in which a 9.2-centimeter chord is 4.3 centimeters from the center of a circle?

Name ____________________ Date __________ Class __________

Scale Drawings and Maps

LESSON 110

1. (65) **Error Analysis** Based on the information that $\overline{AB} \parallel \overline{CD}$, $\overline{AD} \parallel \overline{BC}$, and that $AC \neq BD$, Suzanne concludes that the figure on the right must be a rhombus. Yvonne argues that there is not enough information to know that for sure. Who is correct? Why?

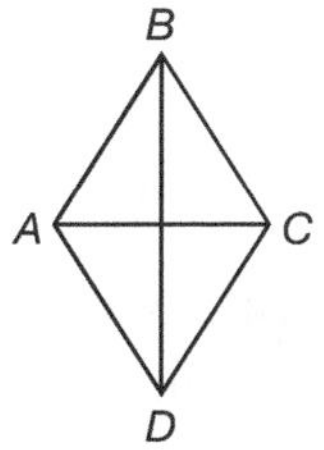

2. (51) **Multiple Choice** The perimeter of an equiangular triangle with side lengths s, t, and u is:

A $3s$ **B** $3t$

C $3u$ **D** All of the above

3. (35) What is the total arc length highlighted in blue? Write your answer in terms of π.

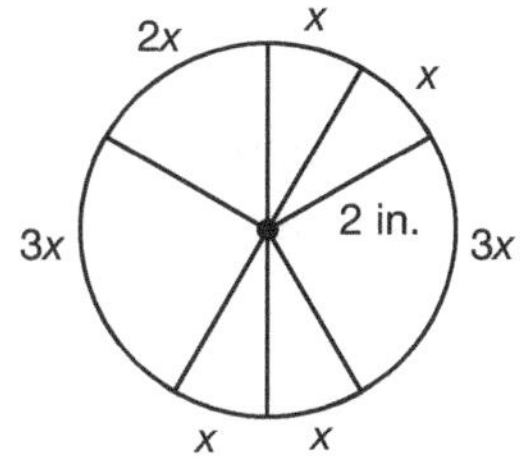

4. (108) **Write** Explain why the line passing through the points $(-2, 3, 1)$ and $(5, 1, 1)$ can either be written as $(x, y, z) = (-2, 3, 1) + t(7, -2, 0)$ or $(x, y, z) = (5, 1, 1) + t(7, -2, 0)$.

5. (53) **Automotive Repair** A mechanic raises a car hood to inspect the engine. To keep the hood from falling, the mechanic positions the prop rod from the base to the hood. If the base of the prop rod is 67 centimeters from where the hood connects to the car, how long is the rod?

6. (105) Simplify $\begin{bmatrix} 10 & -2 \\ 5 & 1 \end{bmatrix}\begin{bmatrix} -1 & -3 \\ -4 & 0 \end{bmatrix}$.

***7.** (109) Find the area of a triangle that is on a sphere with a radius of 8 centimeters and whose angle measures have a sum of 215°. Round your answer to the nearest tenth of a square centimeter.

8. (108) **Algebra** Determine the equation of the line that passes through the points $G(3, 1, -2)$ and $H(6, 9, 3)$.

9. (47) If an arc is 148°, and the measure of its inscribed angle is $(3x - 4)°$, what is the value of x?

10. (102) **Write** Describe two successive dilations that would cause the preimage to coincide with the image.

11. (98) **Multi-Step** Find the perimeter of the triangle. Round your answer to the nearest tenth.

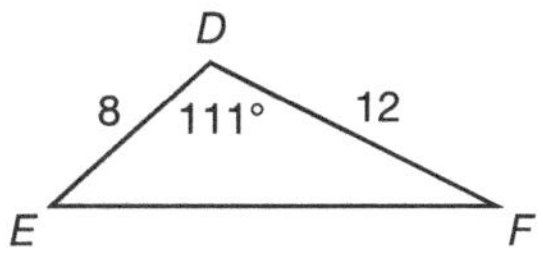

12. (76) **Algebra** Does the function $y = x^3$ have a line of symmetry? Does it have rotational symmetry? If so, what is the order of rotational symmetry?

13. Find the perimeter of the rectangle that is inscribed in the circle.
(106) The radius of the circle is 8 inches and $\theta = 55°$. Round your answer to the nearest tenth.

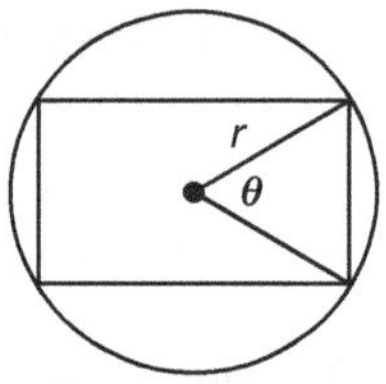

14. **Multiple Choice** For a given perimeter, which of the following shapes
(107) has the greatest area?

A an equilateral triangle **B** a square
C a pentagon **D** a regular dodecahedron

15. Determine the point of tangency and the equation of the
(72) tangent line which is tangent to both circles. Find the radius of each circle.

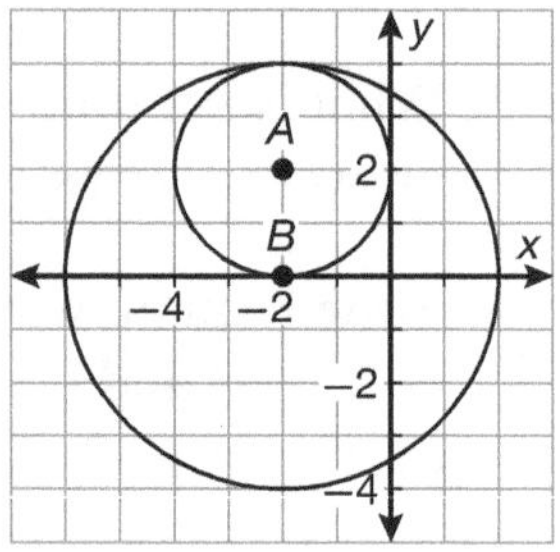

16. (**Maps**) Philadelphia is 12.1 centimeters away from
(110) Washington, D.C. on a map. If their actual distance is 139 miles, what is the scale of the map? Round your answer to the nearest hundredth.

17. A cylinder has a height that is three times the length of the diameter.
(62) The volume of the cylinder is 509 cubic meters. Find the approximate surface area.

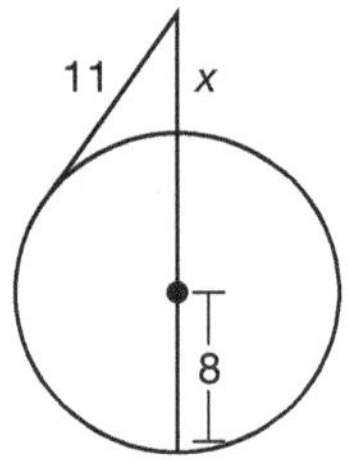

18. **Algebra** Find x to the nearest tenth of a unit.
(101)

19. (**Navigation**) A ship sets out on a course traveling 6 miles per hour at
(83) 60° north of east. If the current is traveling at an equal speed at 30° north of east, what is the actual speed and direction of the ship to the nearest tenth?

***20.** (**Astronomy**) In a model of the solar system, Mercury is 4 feet from the sun. Its actual
(110) distance from the sun is 36.0 million miles. If Jupiter is 483.4 million miles from the sun, how far would it be from the sun in the same model? Round your answer to the nearest foot.

***21.** Find the area of $\triangle LMN$ if the radius of the sphere is
(109) 4 centimeters.

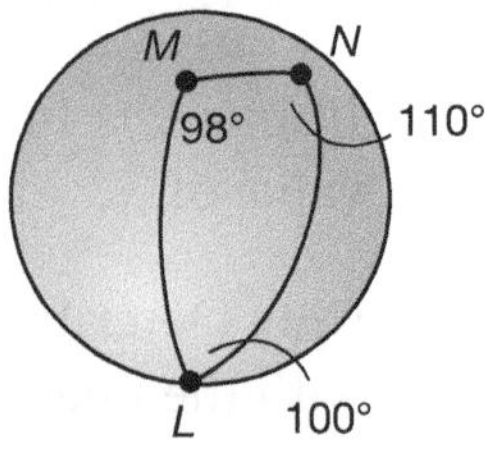

***22.** **Model** Draw a scale drawing of your classroom. Include the
(110) desks, the chalkboard, and other objects in the classroom. You can either measure the distances or estimate them.

23. (**Fashion**) Helga has 31.5 inches of material that she will use to make two square
(44) designs on a shirt. The similarity ratio for the squares is 2:5. How long will each side of each square be?

24. **Write** Two different circles have arcs of equal length. Does this mean that the chords
(104) created by connecting the endpoints of each arc are equal in length? Explain.

25. **Algebra** Find the side length of a square if it is inscribed in a circle with a radius, r. What is the side length of a square circumscribing the circle?
(106)

26. **Multiple Choice** This orthographic drawing shows the front, top, and left-side views of a solid. Which of these sketches represents the solid?
(93)

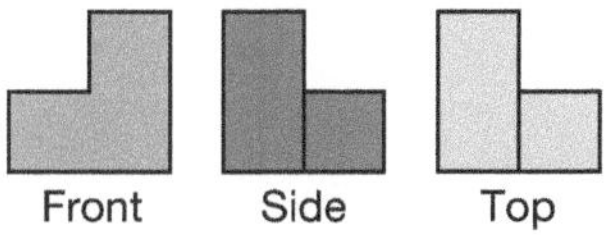

A

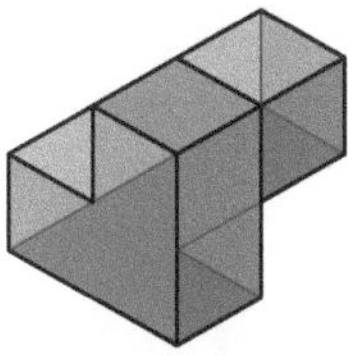

B

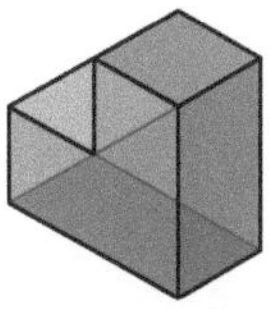

C

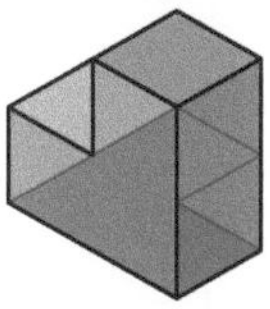

D

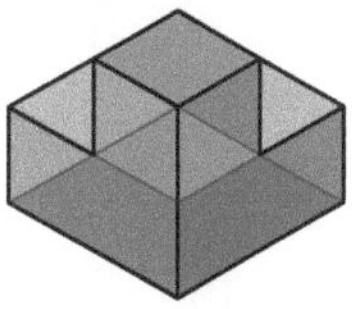

27. **Multi-Step** Classify the polygon with vertices $W(-3, -1)$, $X(1, 1)$, $Y(0, 3)$, and $Z(-2, 2)$. Find the area. Give your answer in simplified radical form.
(57)

*28. Classify the triangle on the sphere as equilateral, isosceles, or scalene.
(109)

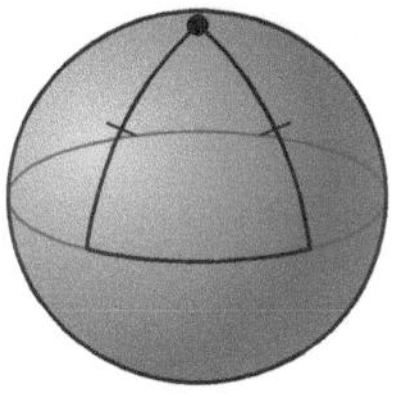

29. **Generalize** Determine a formula for the surface area of a sphere in terms of its diameter, d.
(80)

30. If two parallel lines are cut by a transversal, and the alternate interior angles formed measure $(-2x + 40)°$ and $(3x - 15)°$, find the measure of each angle.
(Inv 1)

Name ______________________ Date __________ Class __________

Finding Distance and Midpoint in Three Dimensions

LESSON 111

1. (95) A circle whose equation is $x^2 + y^2 = 36$ is shifted 5 units up and 2 units to the left. What is the equation for the shifted circle? Graph the shifted circle.

2. (74) Onto what point does a reflection across the line $y = x$ map the point $(-2x, 3y)$?

3. (78) Quadrilateral *JKLM* was rotated counterclockwise about the origin. The original vertices were located at $J(4, -2)$, $K(6, 1)$, $L(-1, -3)$, and $M(0, 2)$. After the rotation, the vertices were located at $J'(2, 4)$, $K'(-1, 6)$, $L'(3, -1)$, and $M'(-2, 0)$. What was the angle of rotation?

4. (111) Find the midpoint of $D(-10, 2, 13)$ and $E(-4, -2, 5)$.

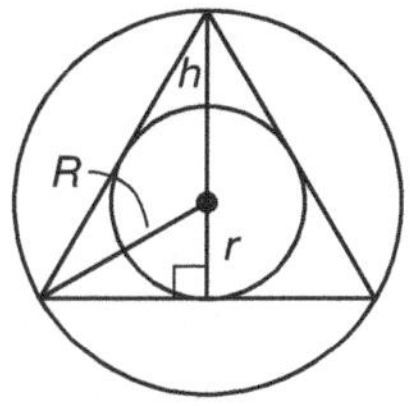

5. (106) **Multi-Step** Find expressions for R and r if the height of the equilateral triangle is h.

6. (65) A rhombus has diagonals that are 10 and 24 units long, respectively. Find the perimeter of the rhombus.

7. (108) **Error Analysis** Donald states that the point (13, 18, 16) must lie on the line defined by the equation $(x, y, z) = (4, 3, 5) + t(3, 5, 4)$. Is he correct? Explain why or why not.

8. (59) **Landscaping** Ingrid is planning to build a plastic greenhouse for her plants. Which of these frames will require more plastic?

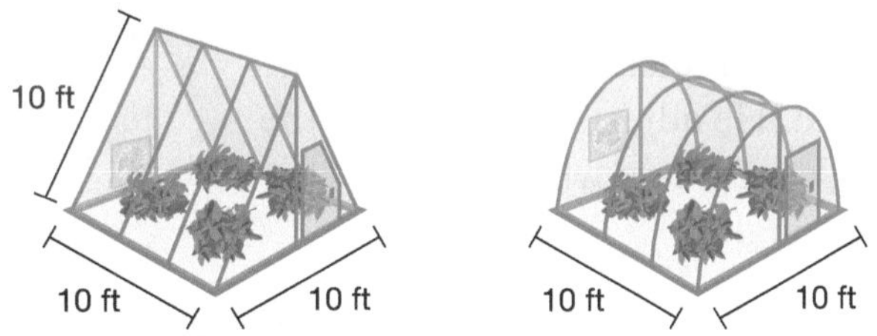

9. (81) **Algebra** A system of three equations has no solution. One equation is $y = 2x + 7$, another equation is $2y = mx + 8$, and the third equation is $y = 3nx + p$. What are the values of m, n, and p?

***10.** (111) **Space Exploration** Two astronauts are repairing a satellite telescope as shown in the figure. The first astronaut is 6 feet in front of the satellite, and the second astronaut is 3 feet behind the satellite. How far apart are the astronauts from each other? Round your answer to the nearest tenth of a foot.

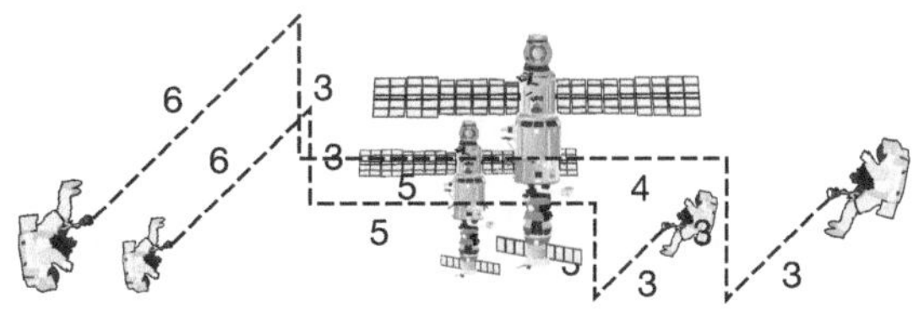

***11.** (111) Find the midpoint M and distance d between $V(3, 7, -6)$ and $W(-4, -8, 7)$.

12. (55) **Algebra** Points J, K, and L are midpoints of $\triangle FGH$, shown at right. If $FG = 4x + 18$ and $KL = 5x - 12$, what is the length of $\overline{FG}$?

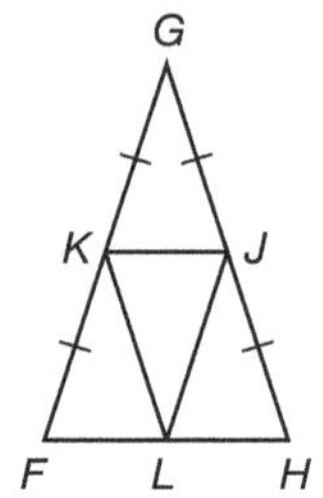

13. (100) Find the matrix that would represent the translation of a quadrilateral $\frac{1}{2}$ unit up and 4 units left.

14. (46) Draw two triangles that are similar by SAS. Explain how you made your sketches.

***15.** (110) **Chemistry** An iron atom has an atomic radius of 140 picometers (pm). If a model of the atom has a diameter of 4 centimeters, what is the scale factor?

16. (12) **Justify** Write and solve an equation for the value of x that allows you to apply the Converse of the Same-Side Interior Angles Theorem. Explain your answer.

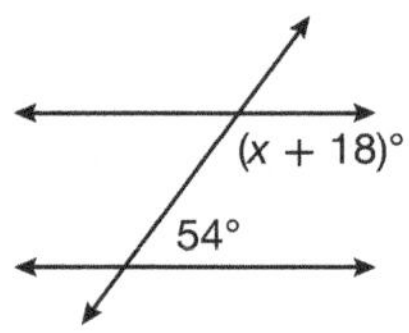

***17.** (Inv 11) Find two numbers that are in the golden ratio to 15. Round your answers to the nearest hundredth.

18. (99) **Milk Cartons** These two milk cartons are similar in shape. If the smaller carton holds 32 ounces, what volume does the larger hold?

19. (69) **Justify** Rogelio has a set of sticks arranged to form an isosceles trapezoid. He adjusts them so that the figure has right angles. Explain why the new figure must be a rectangle.

20. (109) **Formulate** If the sum of the angles of a spherical triangle are 181°, does that mean that the triangle is large or small, relative to the size of the sphere? Explain. Use the formula for the area of spherical triangles to justify your answer.

21. (33) **Algebra** Determine the value of x in the figure at right. Write your answer in simplified radical form.

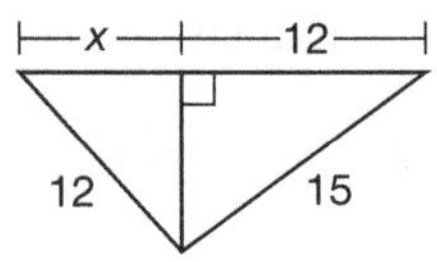

22. (103) **Gift Wrapping** Harris wrapped a present for a friend in the shape of a frustum of a square pyramid. If the present was 21 centimeters tall and the two square faces had side lengths of 15 centimeters and 25 centimeters, what was the volume of his present?

23. (109) Name a line, a segment, and a triangle on the sphere.

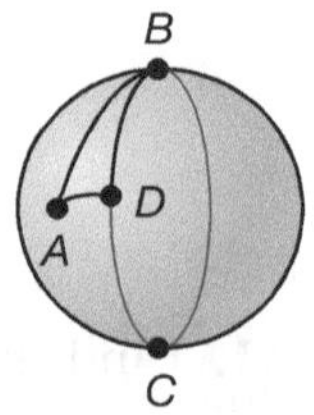

***24.** (111) Find the distance between $A(-1, 2, -3)$ and $B(-6, -5, 4)$.

*25. (110) **Multiple Choice** The scale model of the base of a building is 6 centimeters by 8 centimeters. What would be a reasonable scale factor for the building?

A 1 cm : 1 ft **B** 1 cm : 2 m
C 1 cm : 100,000 cm **D** 1 cm : 6 in.

26. (66) **Algebra** Write an expression for the side length s of a regular n-sided polygon with area A and apothem length a.

27. (70) What is the lateral area of a regular pentagonal pyramid with a side length of 6.2 inches and a slant height of 4 inches?

28. (107) **Generalize** Derive a formula to find the minimum perimeter, P, required to enclose a rectangular area, A.

29. (50) Write three similarity statements for these triangles.

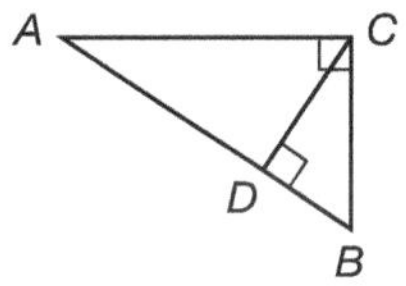

30. (Inv 9) **Write** An abstract mosaic design has two types of tile. One tile is octagonal.

a. Given that the design is a semiregular tessellation, sketch a section of it.
b. Describe the symmetries of the design.

Name ______________________ Date __________ Class __________

Finding Areas of Circle Segments

LESSON 112

* **1.** (112) Determine the area of the shaded circle segment. Round your answer to the nearest square centimeter.

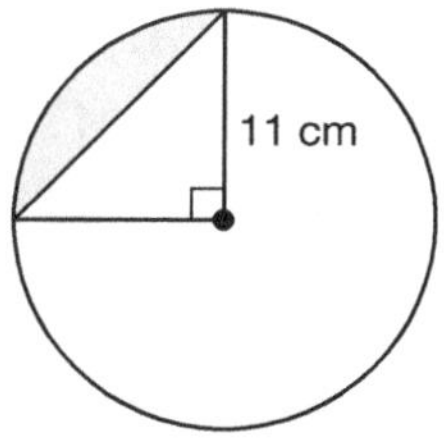

2. (69) **Design** Andres is designing a logo for the math club. He wants the symbol to include a trapezoid with one base length being 4 centimeters and the midsegment being 10 centimeters. What length should he make the other base?

* **3.** (111) Find the exact distance between $P(-1, 7, -5)$ and $Q(12, 11, 10)$.

4. (107) **Error Analysis** A student determines that the maximum area that can be contained by a triangle with a perimeter of 30 centimeters is 30 square centimeters, since a right triangle with side lengths 5, 12, and 13 centimeters can be drawn. Is the student correct?

5. (93) **Multiple Choice** This orthographic drawing shows the front, top, and right-side views of a solid. Which of these sketches represents the solid?

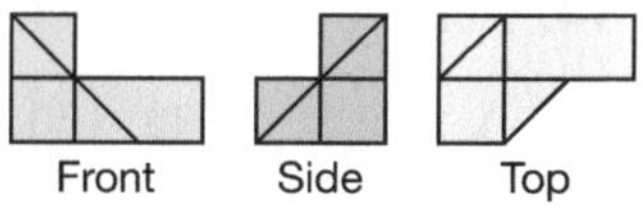

A

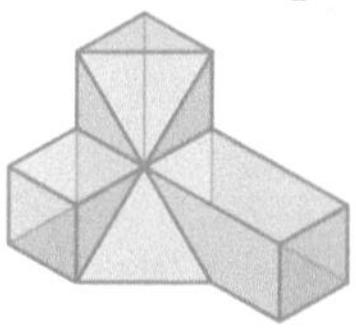

B

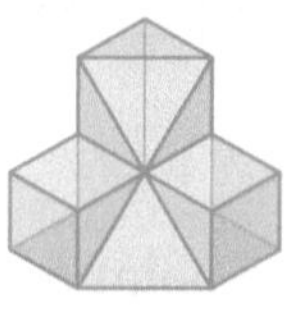

C

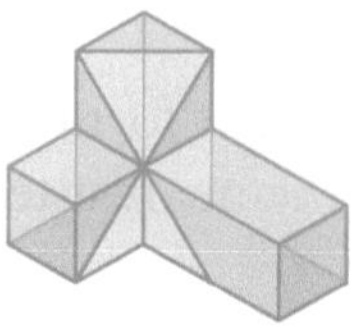

D

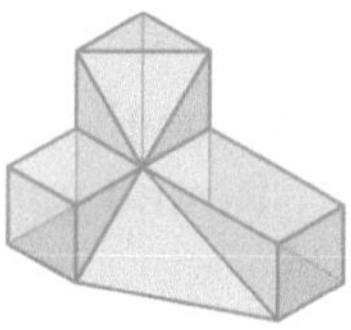

6. (34) **Model** If three of a parallelogram's vertices are located at $(-4, 2)$, $(-1, 3)$, and $(-1, 6)$, what are all the possible coordinates of the fourth vertex?

7. (105) Use the figure at right to answer the following questions.
a. Write the matrix representing the vertices of the polygon.
b. Find the image matrix for a 90° rotation about the origin.
c. Graph the image.

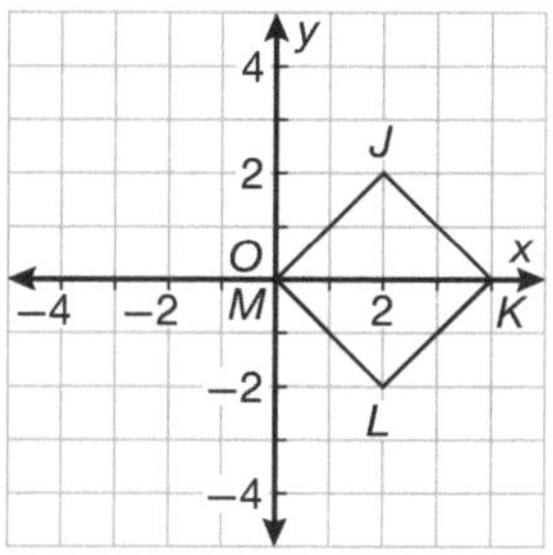

8. (96) A square has an area of 36 square centimeters. If each side of this square is multiplied by x, the resulting square has an area of 900 square centimeters. Find the value of x.

9. (110) **Astronomy** A scale model of the sun has a diameter of 8 feet. If the sun's actual diameter is 865,000 miles, what is the scale factor? Express your answer in scientific notation with two significant digits.

10. **Justify** $\overline{AP}$ is parallel to $\overline{BQ}$ and perpendicular to $\overleftrightarrow{PQ}$.
(58)

a. Circle A's radius is $\overline{AP}$. Is $\overleftrightarrow{PQ}$ tangent to $\odot A$? Why or why not?

b. A second circle, $\odot D$, has $\overleftrightarrow{PQ}$ as a tangent at point Q. On which line does the center of $\odot D$ lie?

*11. **Multi-Step** Determine the area of the shaded circle segment in this kite, to the nearest tenth of a square inch.
(112)

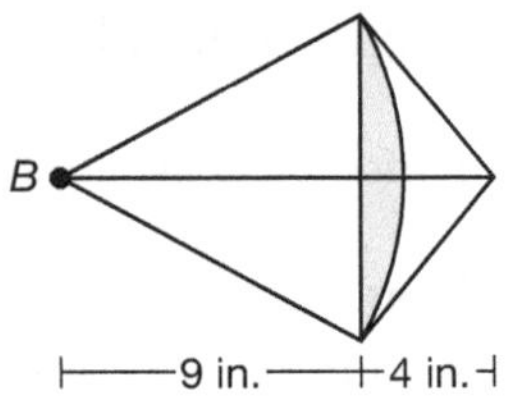

12. In spherical geometry, which postulate does not hold true?
(109)

13. **Write** Two different circles have chords of equal length. Does this mean that the arcs that correspond to each of the chords are equal in length? Explain.
(104)

14. **Multiple Choice** Which statement is *not* true?
(82)

A $\tan\left(\frac{15}{10}\right) = \tan\left(\frac{3}{2}\right)$ B $\tan\left(\frac{14}{16}\right) = 90° - \tan\left(\frac{16}{14}\right)$

C $180° - \tan\left(\frac{4}{2}\right) = \tan\left(\frac{1}{2}\right)$ D $\tan\left(\frac{20}{15}\right) = 90° - \tan\left(\frac{3}{4}\right)$

15. Describe the diagram in two ways.
(106)

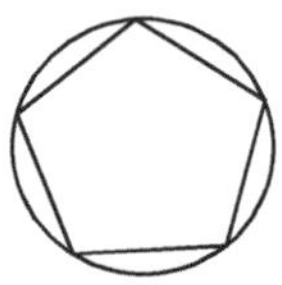

xy² 16. **Algebra** Given the point $D(1, -1)$, find the point on the line $y = -\frac{3}{2}x - 6$ that is closest to D.
(42)

*17. A circle has a radius of 5 inches. Determine the area of the segment formed by a chord with a central angle of 36°. Round your answer to the nearest tenth of a square inch.
(112)

*18. A line segment has an endpoint at $(-7, 3, 8)$. If the segment's midpoint is at $(2, -4, 9)$, what are the coordinates of the other endpoint?
(111)

19. **Farming** A farmer wants to fill a conical silo to half its capacity. Would he fill more than half the height or less than a quarter of the height? Explain.
(103)

20. If $\triangle ABC \cong \triangle LMN$, and $AB = 9.3$ centimeters, $BC = 3.2$ centimeters, and $LN = 4.6$ centimeters, what are the lengths of the other sides?
(25)

21. **Verify** Show that the origin lies on the line defined by the equation $(x, y, z) = t(4, 1, 3)$.
(108)

22. Rotate the figure 90° clockwise about point P, and then translate the image along v.
(90)

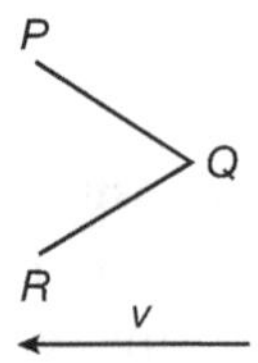

23. **Packaging** A tin can is designed to have a radius of 2 inches and a height of 3 inches. To the nearest hundredth of a square inch, how much paper is needed to wrap a label around the can?
(62)

24. (71) **Programming** A programmer is making a video game. He wants to program a button with a command that moves a player's character along the vector $\langle -4, 2 \rangle$. If a player's character starts at the point (8, 3) and the button is pressed three times, what should the character's final position be?

A (−8, 3) **B** (−7, −2)
C (−4, 9) **D** (9, 2)

***25.** (112) Determine the area of the shaded part of this figure, to the nearest tenth of a square foot.

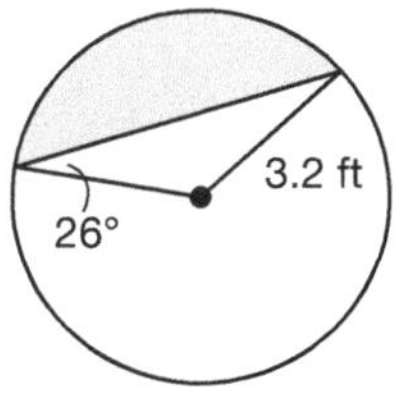

26. (102) **Formulate** Anushka performs a dilation on a figure such that all the points of the figure remain the same. Write the dilation map for her transformation.

27. (39) Explain whether it is possible or not to construct a triangle with side lengths of $x + 7$ inches, $x - 11$ inches, and $2x + 1$ inches.

28. (65) **Multiple Choice** Which statement is *not* true of all rhombuses?

A Both pairs of opposite angles are equal.
B The diagonals bisect the opposite angles.
C All consecutive sides are equal.
D All consecutive angles are perpendicular.

***29.** (111) Find the midpoint of (12, 3, 3) and (−4, 7, −9).

30. (Inv 3) **Algebra** In a regular polygon, the sum of half of the angles is 1260°. How many sides does this polygon have?

Name ______________________ Date ___________ Class ___________

Symmetry of Solids and Polyhedra

LESSON 113

* **1.** (113) Determine whether the solid has plane symmetry. If it does, show the symmetry in a drawing.

2. (87) **Algebra** Two rectangles are in the similarity ratio of 4:3. The smaller rectangle has a length of 9 feet and a width of 3 feet. What is the perimeter of the larger rectangle?

3. (111) Find the length of the diameter of a sphere whose radius has endpoints $C(3, 4, -2)$ and $D(6, -3, 8)$, where C is the center of the sphere.

4. (40) **Furniture Restoring** Yuan is restoring the top of his desk, shown at right. He has cut a circular hole in the top, which has a 2-inch radius for computer wires to pass through. What area will he need to paint, to the nearest inch?

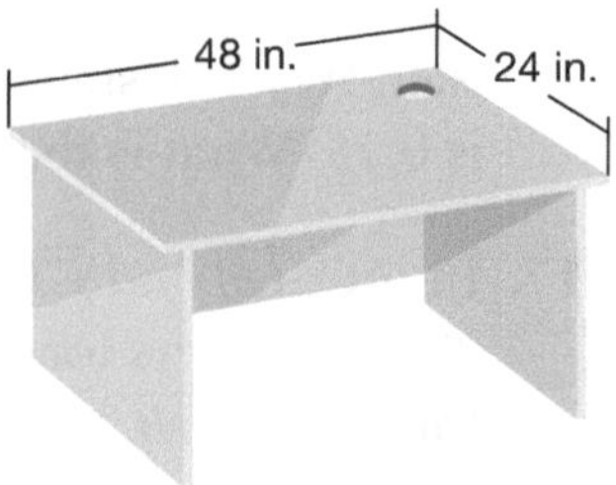

5. (68) Find the perimeter of right $\triangle ABC$ if $m\angle A = 42°$ and the hypotenuse is 12 centimeters. Round to the nearest hundredth of a centimeter.

6. (Inv 6) **Multiple Choice** Which does *not* represent the geometric probability associated with a single region of this tangram?

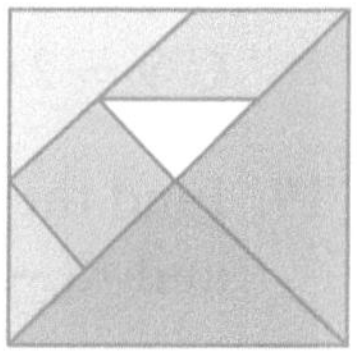

A $\frac{1}{2}$ **B** $\frac{1}{4}$

C $\frac{1}{16}$ **D** $\frac{1}{8}$

7. (105) The vertices of $\triangle JKL$ are $J(2, 1)$, $K(6, 1)$, and $L(4, 5)$. Use matrix multiplication to reflect the image across the y-axis and then rotate the triangle 180° about the origin. What is the image matrix?

* **8.** (112) Determine the area of the shaded circle segment, to the nearest hundredth of a square inch.

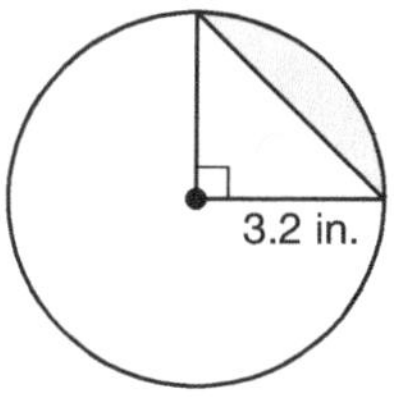

9. (Inv 11) Determine the sums of the first seven Fibonacci numbers, the first eight Fibonacci numbers, and the first nine Fibonacci numbers.

***10.** (92) **Formulate** A parallelogram has coordinates $W(3, -1)$, $X(a, b)$, $Y(7, 6)$, and $Z(c, d)$. Write equations for c and d in terms of a and b.

11. (56) **Home Improvement** Michaela is attaching a shelf to a wall and will use a metal bar for support, as shown. What length of metal does she need to use?

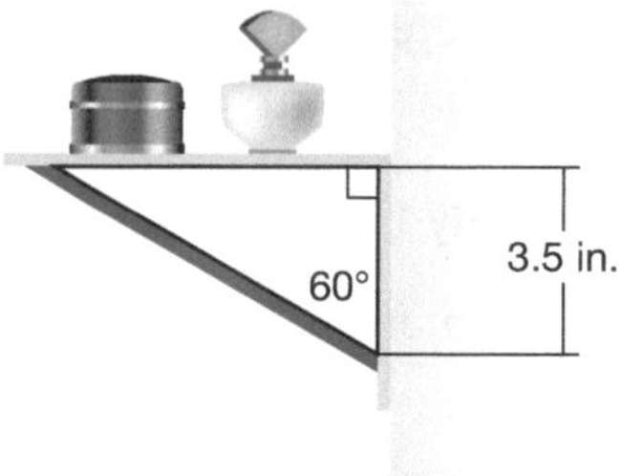

12. (Inv 8) What is the 90th triangular number?

*13. Determine whether the solid has rotational symmetry. If it does, give the angle of rotational symmetry and the order of symmetry.
(113)

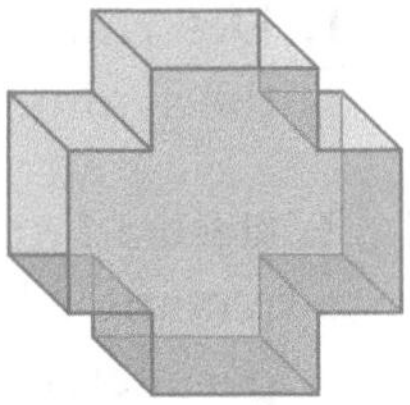

14. (Chemistry) An iron atom has an atomic radius of 140 picometers (pm). If a model of the atom is a sphere with a volume of 30 cubic inches, what is the scale factor between the model and an actual iron atom? Round your answer to the nearest hundredth.
(110)

15. **Error Analysis** Ella attempted to graph the inequality $y < 1.5x + 2$. Identify any errors she has made.
(88)

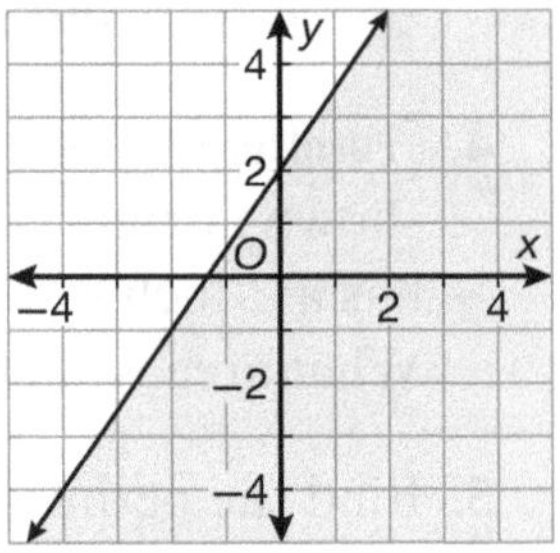

16. **Multi-Step** The sine of one acute angle in a right triangle is 0.75. What is the sine of the other acute angle?
(Inv 7)

*17. In $\odot C$, $\overline{CA}$ and $\overline{CB}$ are perpendicular radii that are each 28 centimeters long. Determine the area of the circle segment formed by $\overline{AB}$, to the nearest square centimeter.
(112)

18. **Multiple Choice** The equation of the line at right is:
(16)

A $y = 2x - 1$ **B** $y = -2x + 1$
C $y = 2x + 1$ **D** $y = -2x - 1$

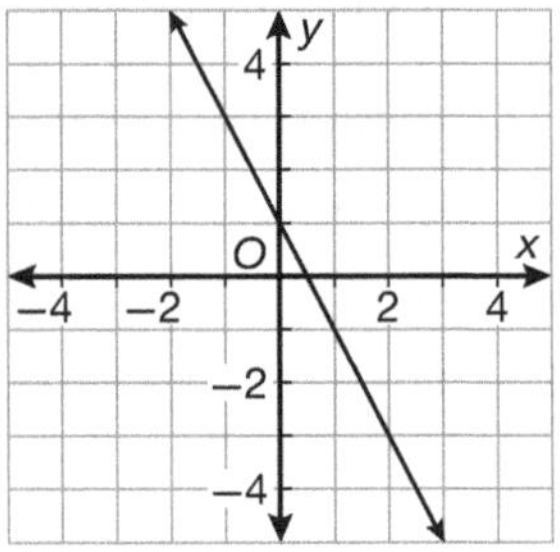

19. Find the midpoint of $J(4.5, 3.25, 8.6)$ and $K(-2.5, 6.75, -2.6)$.
(111)

*20. Determine whether this solid has plane symmetry, symmetry about an axis, or neither.
(113)

21. The perimeter of $\triangle EFG$ is 35.7 inches, and $\angle E \cong \angle G$. If $EF = 12.2$ inches, determine EG.
(51)

22. A tangent and a secant are drawn from an external point P to a circle. The tangent is 8 meters long and the part of the secant inside the circle is 12 meters long. How long is the secant?
(101)

23. **Verify** Use the relationship $A_{\text{segment}} = A_{\text{sector}} - A_{\triangle}$ to verify that the area of this segment is given by $\left(\frac{1}{4}\pi - \frac{1}{2}\right)r^2$.
(112)

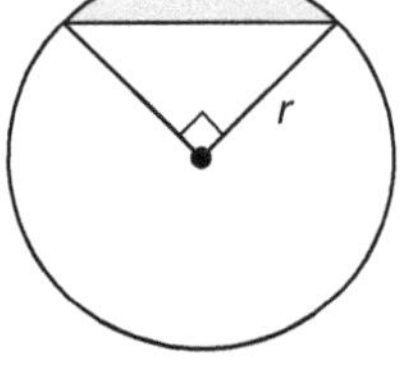

24. *(16)* Determine the slope of the line passing through (−4, 0) and (2, 4).

25. *(83)* **Force** A beam supports a structure that leans against it. The beam carries a 15-pound vertical load and a 25-pound horizontal load. What is the total load that the beam is carrying?

26. *(77)* **Generalize** Two cones are similar, but one has twice the surface area. How are the volumes related?

27. *(107)* **Art** Bruce wants to build a rectangular picture frame out of clay. He can stretch the clay to a maximum length of 32 centimeters. What is the greatest area the picture frame can enclose?

***28.** *(113)* Tell whether this solid has plane symmetry, symmetry about the given axis, or neither.

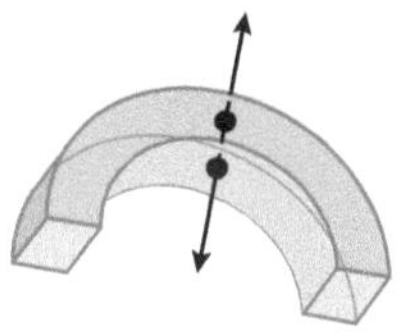

29. *(49)* How many vertices does a polyhedron with 22 edges and 10 faces have?

30. *(108)* **Analyze** Will the line connecting the points $A(-2, 4, 6)$ and $B(3, 5, 6)$ ever intersect the line connecting the points $C(8, -3, -4)$ and $D(13, -2, -4)$? Explain.

Name ______________________ Date __________ Class __________

Solving and Graphing Systems of Inequalities

LESSON 114

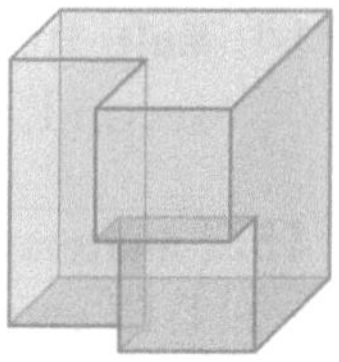

*1. Determine if the solid has plane symmetry. (113)

2. The length of the hypotenuse of a right triangle is 17 centimeters. Name one pair of possible leg lengths. (9)

3. Find θ_1 and θ_2 to the nearest degree. (82)

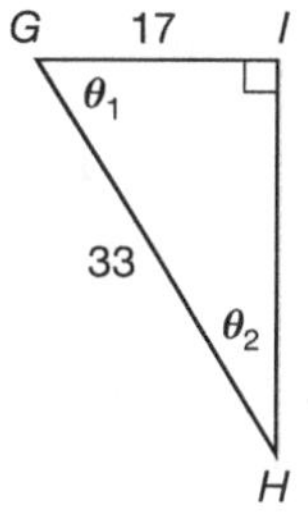

4. **Multi-Step** Show that (4, −4, 5) is the point of intersection of the line $(x, y, z) = (-2, 0, 1) + t(3, -2, 2)$ and the line through the points (3, 5, 11) and (5, −13, −1). (108)

5. Determine the area of the shaded circle segment, to the nearest tenth of a square centimeter. (112)

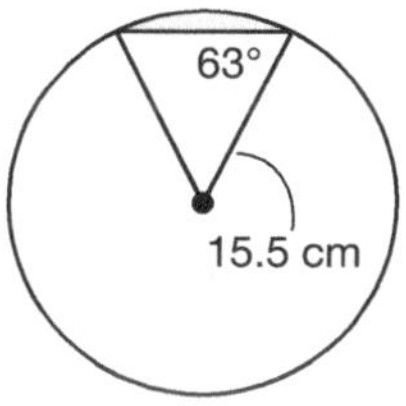

*6. Graph the region described by the inequalities $y \geq x$ and $y \leq x - 3$. (114)

7. **Weather** A particular spherical weather balloon has a radius of 10 meters at a certain altitude. What is the volume of air in the balloon? (80)

8. The first iteration of a fractal is shown. Sketch the second iteration of the fractal. (Inv 10)

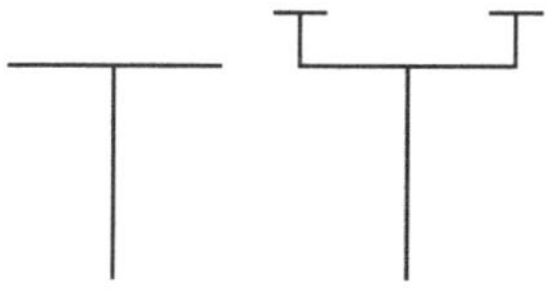

9. A cube with sides that are 6 units long has one vertex at the origin. Determine the distance between the origin and the vertex that is diagonally opposite it through the cube. (111)

*10. The drawing shows a part of a solid and its center of rotation. Draw the complete solid with an order of rotational symmetry of 4. (113)

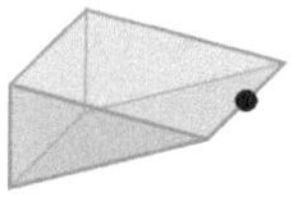

order: 4

11. **Write** What is the direction of a zero-magnitude vector? (89)

*12. **Lighthouses** Two lighthouses are placed along a shoreline. The first one can light the region below the line $y = 2x + 5$ on a map and the other can light the region above the line $y = -x + 1$ on the same map. Graph the region that at least one lighthouse can light. (114)

13. Find LN in the triangle. Round your answer to the nearest hundredth. (94)

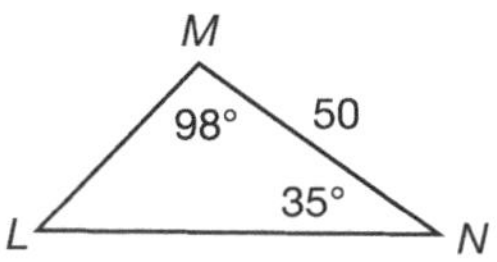

14. (53) **Multi-Step** The hypotenuse of one 45°-45°-90° right triangle is 53 feet while a leg of a second, similar triangle is 37.5 feet. Which triangle has the greater area?

15. (Inv 11) **Anatomy** In the diagram, A is 1.9 centimeters, B is 1.17 centimeters, C is 0.42 centimeters, E is 0.68 centimeters, G is 1.89 centimeters, and H is 3.06 centimeters. Which ratios of these lengths are approximately equal to the golden ratio?

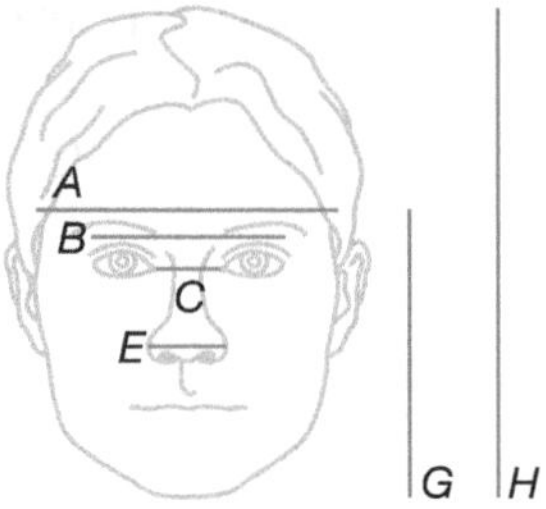

16. (84) Triangle ABC has vertices $A(-3, 2)$, $B(-4, -2)$, and $C(2, 1)$. Apply a dilation centered at $(3, -3)$. Use a scale factor of 3. *Hint: First, translate the preimage, △ABC, so the center is at the origin. Then, apply the dilation. Finally, translate the figures so the preimage returns to its original location, and identify the coordinates of* A′, B′, *and* C′.

17. (52) **Algebra** Find the value of x in this rhombus.

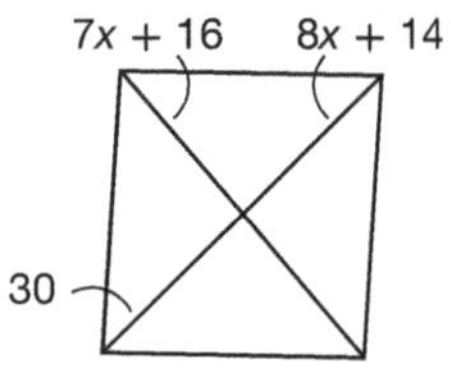

***18.** (114) Graph the region described by the inequalities $y > 3x + 2$ or $y > 2x$.

***19.** (97) **Formulate** What is an expression for the area of a shape composed of a circle with a radius g that has had a circle of radius r cut out of it?

20. (112) **Error Analysis** Patrice wrote this expression for the area of the segment shown: $\frac{2}{3}\pi(9)^2 - \frac{1}{2}(9)\left(\frac{9\sqrt{3}}{2}\right)$. Correct Patrice's error.

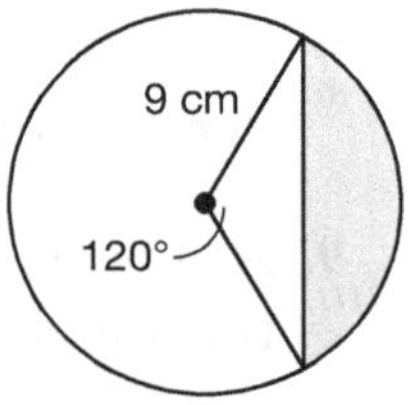

21. (75) **Multiple Choice** Circle C has the equation, $(x - 5)^2 + (y - 2)^2 = 16$. If ⊙$C$ is translated right 2 units, what is the equation of its image, ⊙C'?

A $(x - 3)^2 + (y - 2)^2 = 16$ **B** $(x - 5)^2 + (y - 4)^2 = 16$
C $(x - 7)^2 + (y - 2)^2 = 16$ **D** $(x - 5)^2 + (y - 2)^2 = 36$

22. (60) Find the length of $\overline{IF}$ in the triangle at right.

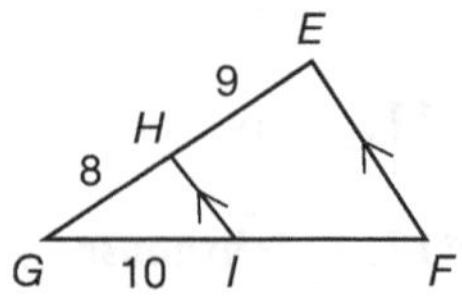

23. (91) If $\cos^2\theta = 0.45$, what is the value of $\sin\theta$ to the nearest hundredth?

24. Determine whether the solid has plane symmetry, symmetry about an axis, or neither.
(113)

25. **Generalize** If a polygon circumscribes a circle, is the polygon regular? What if the circle circumscribes the polygon?
(106)

26. **Photography** A photographer takes a photo of the ridge above him from the bottom of a gorge. If he knows the gorge is 110 meters deep and his angle of elevation is 78°, how far should he focus the lens to obtain the clearest photo of the ridge of the gorge? Round your answer to the nearest meter.
(73)

27. **Buildings** The front of the building shown is to be surfaced with bricks. The building has two 3-by-7-foot doors and ten 2.5-by-2.5-foot windows that will not be covered with brick. If each brick covers 0.5 square feet, how many bricks will be needed?
(40)

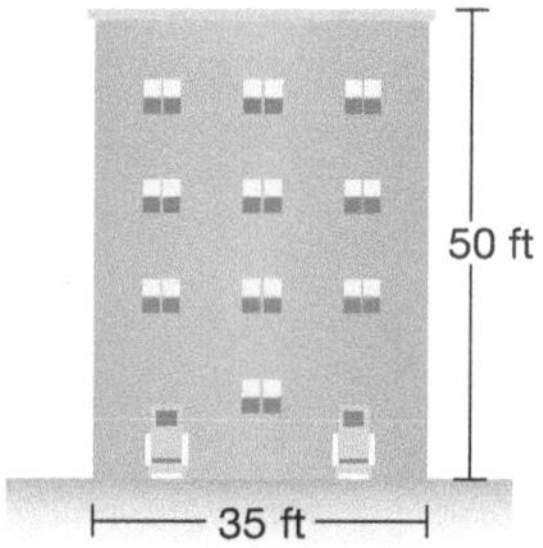

*28. Graph the region described by the inequalities $y \geq 2x$, $y \geq -2x$, and $y \leq x + 2$.
(114)

29. **Verify** Stacy says that a triangle with side lengths of 8.7, 10.1, and 13.6 is a right triangle. Is she correct?
(33)

30. **Analyze** The coordinates for the image of point $P(x, y)$ under a transformation are $P'(\frac{4}{5}y - \frac{3}{5}x, \frac{4}{5}x + \frac{3}{5}y)$. Identify the transformation as a rotation, translation, or reflection, and specify the center of rotation, line of reflection, or translation vector.
(67)

Name ______________________ Date __________ Class __________

Finding Surface Areas and Volumes of Composite Solids

LESSON 115

1. Find the surface area of the solid. Assume that the prism and pyramid are right.
(115)

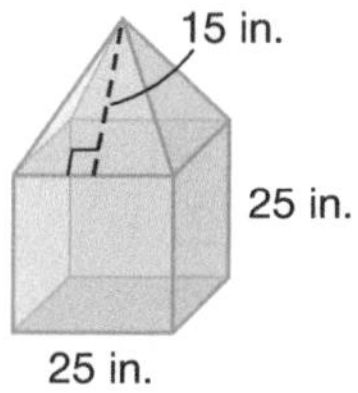

2. Find the matrix that would represent the translation of a triangle 4 units left and 8 units down.
(100)

3. **Analyze** What are two possible shapes for a cross section of a cube?
(85)

4. Determine whether the solid has plane symmetry, symmetry about an axis, or neither.
(113)

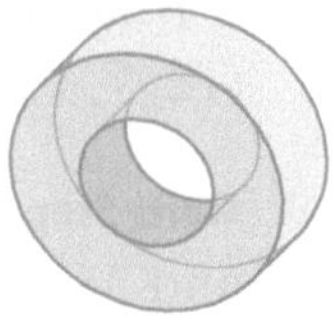

5. Find the measure of the smaller arc between two secants if the larger arc measure is 114° and the exterior angle is 29°.
(79)

6. In the figure, $\overline{MO} \cong \overline{NP}$. Find m$\widehat{NP}$.
(104)

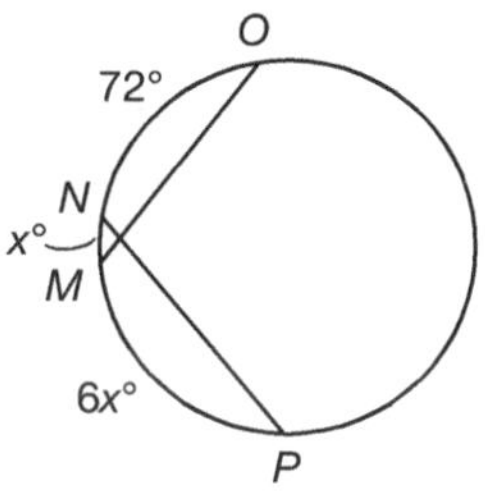

7. **Astronomy** Four moons are in the same circular orbit around a planet. The arc measure between moons A and B is 55°, and the arc measure between moons C and D is 33°. If $\overline{AC}$ and $\overline{BD}$ intersect at E on the planet, what is m$\angle AEB$?
(64)

* 8. **Analyze** Can points A, L, and F on the sphere at right be considered a triangle? Explain why or why not.
(109)

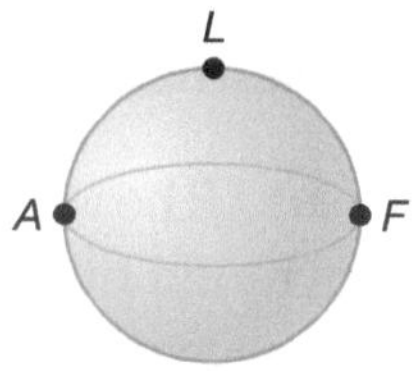

*9. Graph the solution to $y - x > 4$ or $3y + x < 6$ and label the point (3, −4). Is (3, −4) in the solution set?
(114)

10. A circle has a radius of 5.2 meters. Determine the area of the segment formed by a chord with a central angle of 120°. Round your answer to the nearest hundredth.
(112)

11. Find the volume of the solid to the nearest tenth. Assume that the cylinder is a right cylinder.
(115)

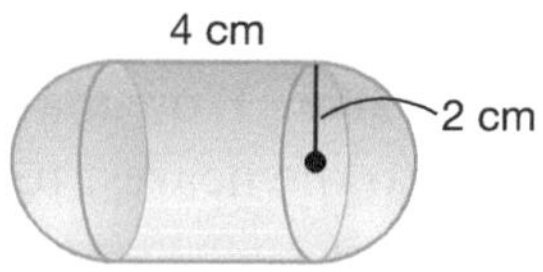

12. In an isosceles triangle, the vertex angle measures $2(x + 7)°$ and the base angles measure $(3x - 37)°$. Determine the angle measures.
(51)

13. **Multiple Choice** The coordinates of three vertices of a parallelogram are (1, 2), (2, −3), and (−3, −1). Which cannot be the coordinates of the fourth vertex?
(61)
A (0, 6) **B** (−2, −7)
C (−2, 8) **D** (−4, 3)

14. Describe the diagram in two ways.
(106)

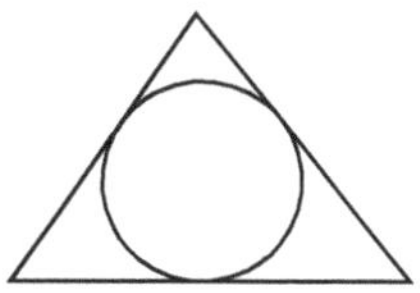

15. **Write** Write three statements that form a syllogism.
(21)

*16. Is $(-1, -4)$ a solution to the disjunction of $y > 3x - 2$ and $2x - y > 1$? Is $(2, 3)$?
(114)

17. Find the volume of this solid. The prisms are right prisms.
(115)

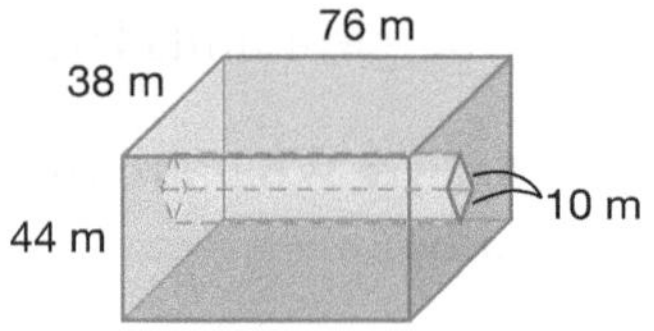

18. $\overline{XY}$ has a midpoint of $(4, -3, 6)$. Point X has coordinates $(12, 7, 1)$. What are the coordinates of point Y?
(111)

19. **Multi-Step** Draw quadrilateral $JKLM$ with vertices $J(2, 4)$, $K(2, -3)$, $L(-3, -3)$, and $M(-3, 4)$. In the same coordinate plane, draw the image under the dilation $D_{O, \frac{1}{2}}(x, y)$. What is the relationship between the areas of the two quadrilaterals?
(102)

20. **Error Analysis** The two triangles are similar. Daphne found the value of x to be 8. What was her error?
(41)

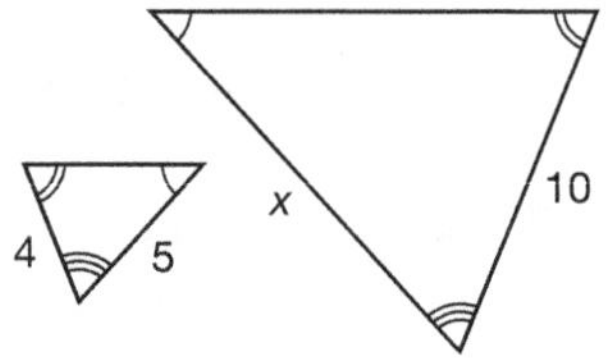

21. **Verify** Show that quadrilaterals $ABCD$ and $EFGH$ are congruent, and identify the type of quadrilateral(s) they are.
(92)

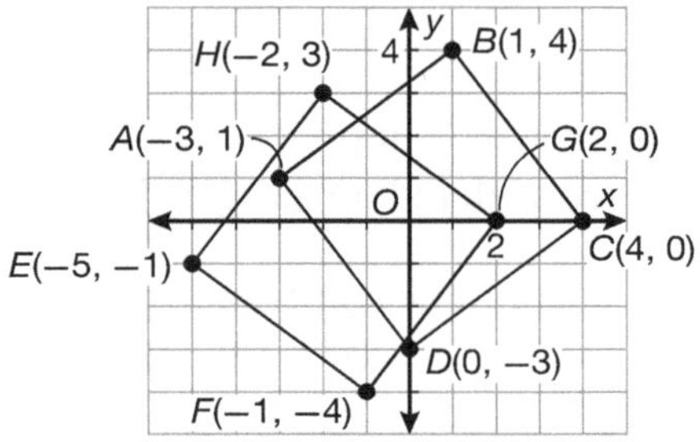

22. **Art** Rhea is making a regular heptagon-based pyramid out of paper maché. To cover the lateral surface of the pyramid, she needs 70 square inches of paper maché. If the slant height of the pyramid is 2 inches, what are the side lengths of the heptagon?
(70)

*23. **Silos** How many cubic feet of grain can the silo hold to the nearest tenth?
(115)

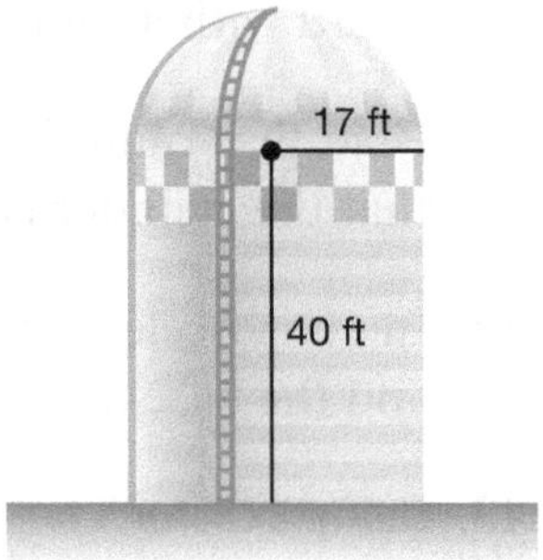

24. **Analyze** Does the function $y = x^4$ have a line of symmetry? Does it have rotational symmetry?
(76)

25. (98) **Surveying** A surveyor uses trigonometry to find the height of a building by measuring the distance from the top of one to the top of the other. Find θ. Round your answer to the nearest degree.

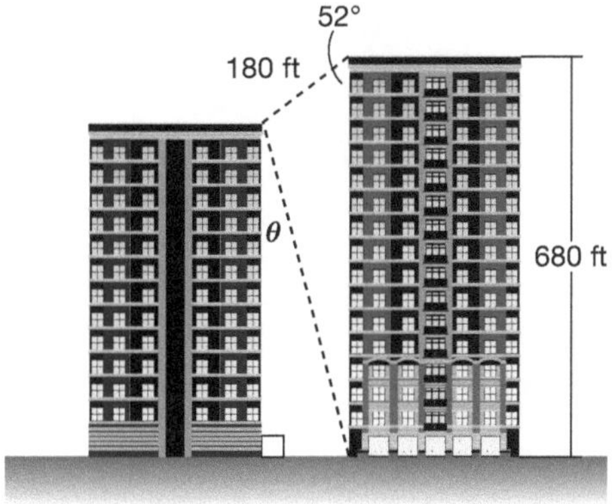

26. (36) Which congruence theorem applies to these triangles?

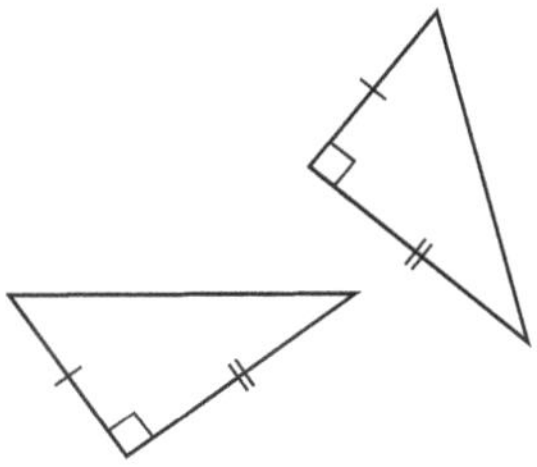

27. (113) A regular polygon has 120 sides. What angle of rotational symmetry does the polygon have?

28. (55) **Algebra** The points D, E, and F are midpoints of $\triangle ABC$. If $DF = 2x + 1$ and $BC = 14$, find x and DF.

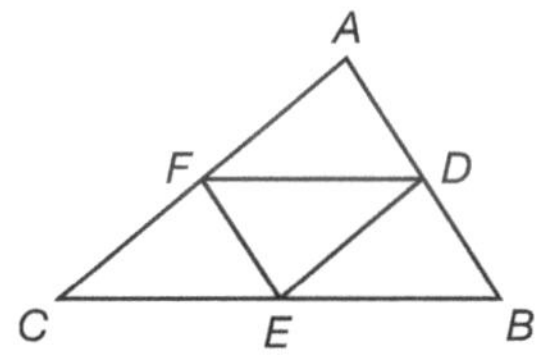

*29. (114) **Baseball** In baseball, the term *foul ball* refers to a ball that is hit and its trajectory goes outside of two rays, one formed by home base and first base and the other formed by home base and third base. For a diagram of a baseball diamond with home base at (3, 2) and first base at (5, 4), write a disjunction of simplified inequalities whose solution is the area where a foul ball would go.

30. (34) Two congruent parallelograms make the following shape. Describe $m\angle JKL$ in terms of x.

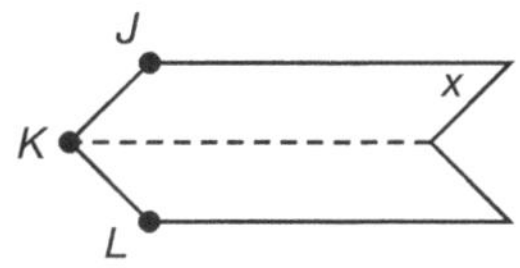

Name ______________________ Date ___________ Class ___________

Secant, Cosecant, and Cotangent

LESSON 116

1. (96) **Elasticity** A certain elastic band will break if stretched so that its total length is more than 22 inches. The plastic band is placed around a spherical balloon with a radius of 1.7 inches. If the balloon is inflated so that its radius doubles, will the elastic band break? Explain.

2. (112) **Architecture** Determine the combined areas of the four circular segments of glass used in this stained-glass window. Round your answer to the nearest square inch.

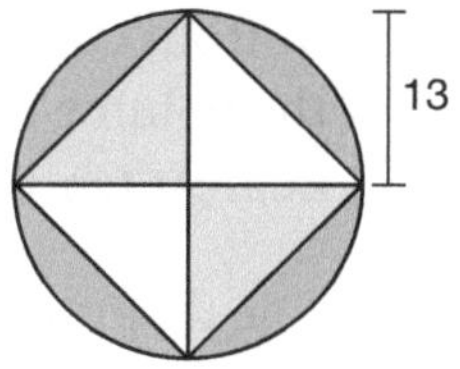

* 3. (116) **Multiple Choice** Which of the following is not a possible value for sec θ?

A 1.46 **B** 8.99
C -0.89 **D** -19.02

* 4. (115) **Algebra** The surface area of this composite solid made of two cones is $(3\sqrt{13} + 15)\pi$. Find the radius, r.

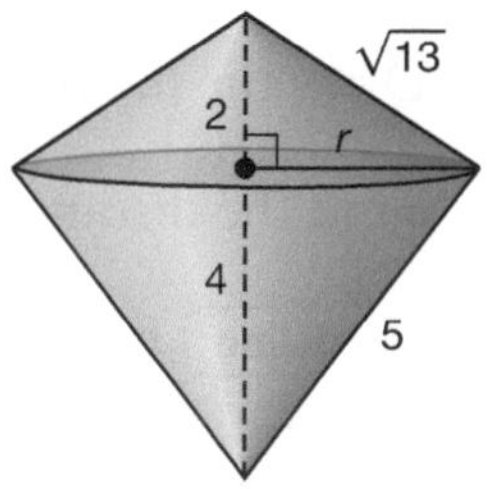

5. (63) **Exercise** Doug is walking on a treadmill. If the conveyor belt is moving at 3.6 miles per hour backward, how fast and in what direction must Doug walk in order to stay on the treadmill?

* 6. (81) **Write** List all the possible reasons why a system of two linear equations could have no solution and explain why there is no solution in each case.

7. (114) A region is bound by the vertices (1, 2), (3, 5), and (4, 0). Find the coordinates of a point inside the region and a point outside the region.

8. (31) **Analyze** In the diagram, $\angle 1$ and $\angle 2$ are complementary. Write a paragraph proof to show that $\angle 2$ and $\angle 3$ are complementary.

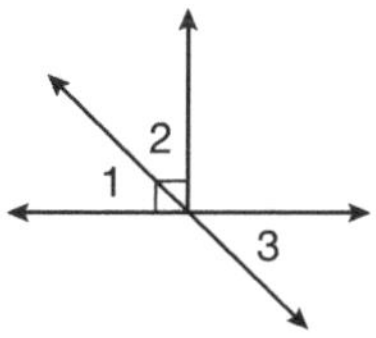

9. (108) **Error Analysis** Joanna is trying to place a segment with vertices (3, 2) and (4, 5) in a three-dimensional coordinate system. She decides the new coordinates are (0, 3, 2) and (0, 4, 5). Explain her error and correct it.

*10. (115) Find the volume of the composite solid. Assume that the pyramid is right. Give your answer to the nearest tenth of a cubic inch.

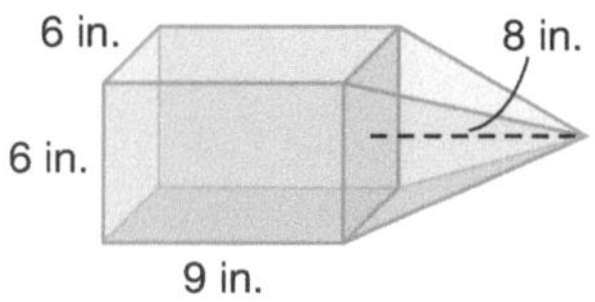

11. (57) **Multi-Step** Classify the polygon with vertices $L(1, -1)$, $M(-3, -3)$, and $N(-3, 2)$. Find the perimeter. Give your answer in simplified radical form.

12. (114) **Write** How is it that a conjunction of linear inequalities might have no solution, but a disjunction of the same inequalities would always have a solution?

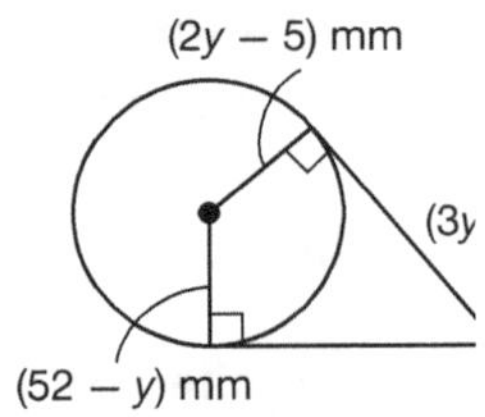

13. *(58)* **Algebra** Determine the perimeter of this quadrilateral.

14. *(103)* **Storage** A rubber stopper for a bottle is in the shape of a frustum of a cone with a height of 5 centimeters. If the top circle has a radius of 1 centimeter and the bottom circle has a radius of 3 centimeters, what is the volume of the stopper? Round your answer to the nearest tenth of a cubic centimeter.

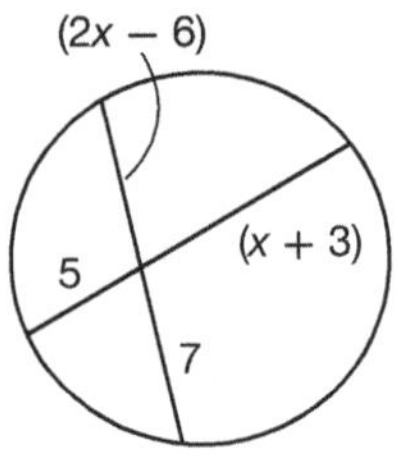

15. *(86)* The diagram shows intersecting chords in a circle. Find the value of x to the nearest hundredth.

***16.** *(116)* **Analyze** The sine and cosine functions always give a value between 1 and –1. Is the same true for secant and cosecant? Explain.

17. *(Inv 5)* Draw the net of a pentagonal pyramid.

18. *(111)* Find the distance between $Y(5, 5, 5)$ and $Z(-5, -5, -5)$.

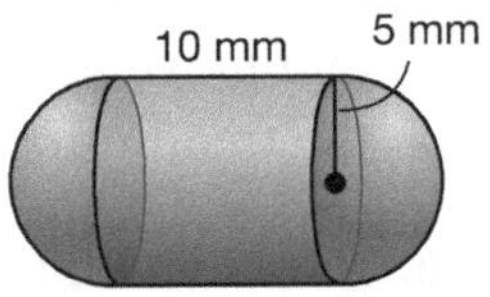

***19.** *(115)* **Medicine** Find the surface area of this medicine capsule to the nearest tenth. Assume that the cylinder is right and each of the ends are hemispheres.

20. *(78)* The endpoints of line segment $\overline{XY}$ are $X(-3, -2)$ and $Y(-1, 1)$. Graph $\overline{X'Y'}$ after $\overline{XY}$ has been rotated 180° about the origin.

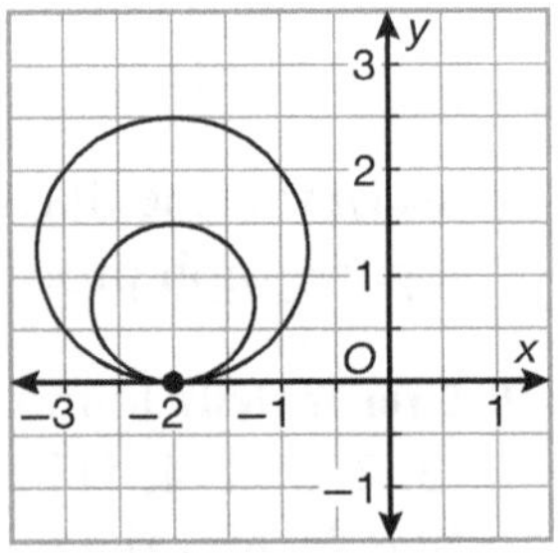

21. *(72)* Determine the point of tangency and the equation of the tangent line in the diagram at right.

***22.** *(116)* **Algebra** If the hypotenuse of a right triangle is 4 and $\tan \theta = \frac{a}{b}$, find $\csc \theta$, $\sec \theta$, and $\cot \theta$.

23. *(98)* Find the value of x to the nearest hundredth if $\overline{AC}$ bisects $\angle A$.

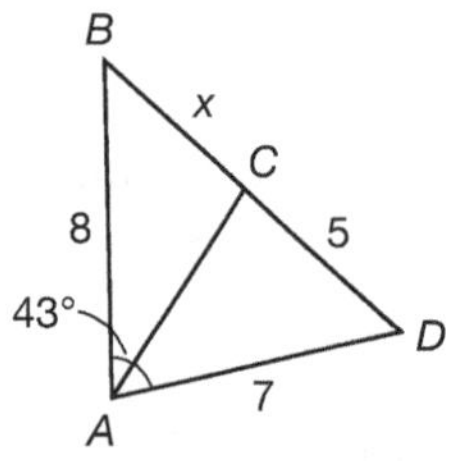

24. *(91)* **Multi-Step** If $\cos \theta \cdot \tan \theta = 0.8$, find the value of $\cos \theta$. Then, find θ to the nearest degree.

25. *(7)* Use inductive reasoning to write the next three steps of this series:
3, 5, 7, 11, 13, 17, …

26. Given a fixed perimeter, which shape has the greatest area?
(107)

27. Determine whether this wheel has rotational symmetry. If it does, give the angle of rotational symmetry and the order of symmetry.
(113)

***28.** **Formulate** Write an expression for $\sin \theta$ in terms of $\sec \theta$.
(116)

29. A circle whose equation is $(x + 2)^2 + (y - 7)^2 = 81$ is shifted 4 units upward and 8 units to the left. What is the equation for the shifted circle? Graph the shifted circle.
(95)

30. Using the diagram, prove $\triangle BAM \cong \triangle CAM$.
(30)

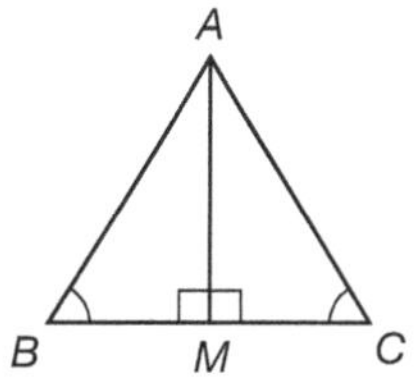

Name ______________________________ Date ____________ Class ____________

Determining Line of Best Fit

LESSON 117

1. *(115)* **Error Analysis** Describe and correct the error in finding the volume of the composite solid. Give your answer to the nearest tenth of a cubic unit.

$V = \frac{1}{3}\pi(4^2)(5) + \frac{1}{3}\pi(4^2)(5)$

$V = 26\frac{2}{3}\pi + 26\frac{2}{3}\pi$

$V = 53\frac{1}{3}\pi$

$V = 167.5$

The volume is approximately 167.5 cubic units.

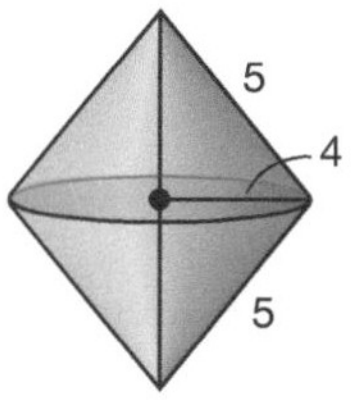

2. *(52)* Is the following statement always, sometimes, or never true?

A square is both a rhombus and a rectangle.

3. *(115)* **Barn Construction** The exterior of the barn shown will be entirely covered with metal sheeting. To the nearest square foot, how much metal sheeting is needed to cover the building?

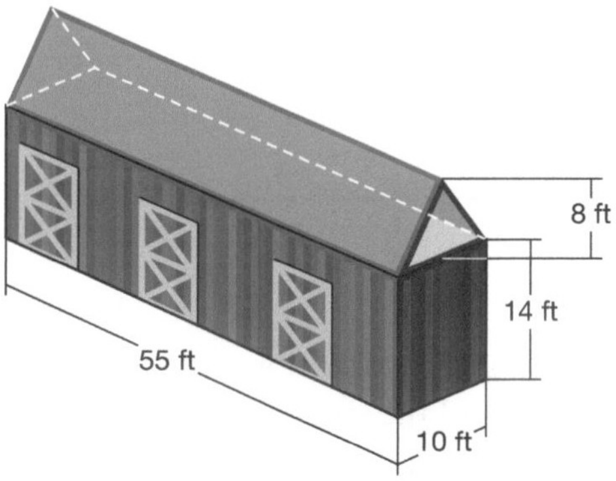

4. *(18)* **Algebra** An exterior angle of a triangle measures $(45 - y)°$. The two remote interior angles measure $(2y + 12)°$ and $(31 - y)°$. Determine the value of y.

5. *(98)* **Multi-Step** Find all the missing angle measures and lengths in the triangle shown. Round each answer to the nearest whole number.

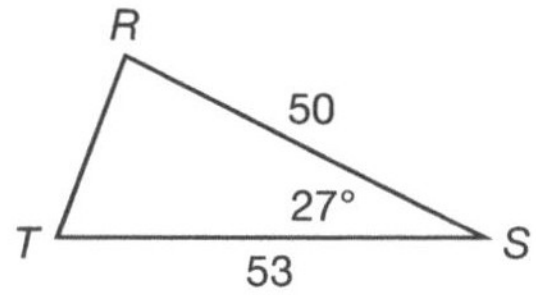

6. *(87)* A triangle has a base of 1.5 meters and a height of 6 meters. A second, similar triangle has three times the base and height of the original triangle. What is the area of the second triangle?

7. *(90)* **Model** Draw two lines of reflection that will transform rectangle $STUV$ to rectangle $S'T'U'V'$.

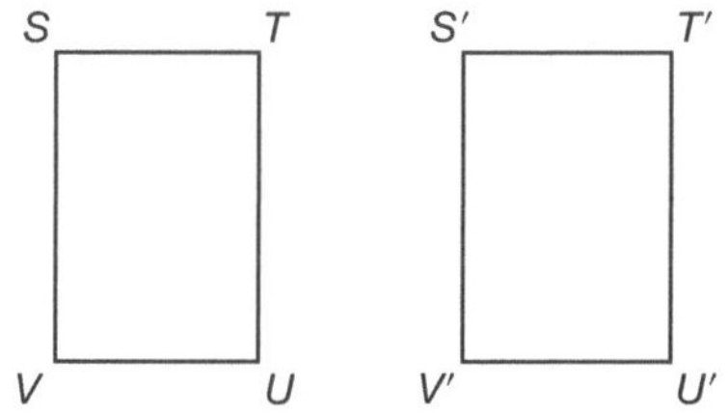

8. *(114)* What are the vertices of the region that is the solution of $y \leq -x + 1$, $y \leq 3x + 5$, and $y \geq \frac{1}{3}(x - 1)$? Give a point in the region that is not on the boundary.

9. Find LJ in the triangle at right.
(60)

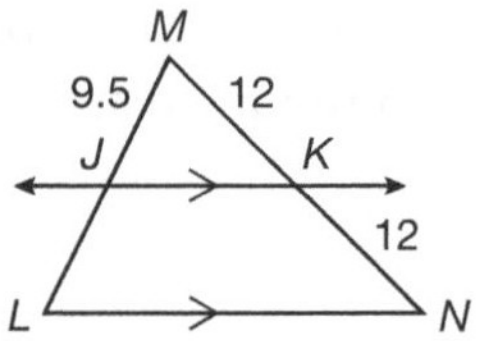

*10. $\triangle JKL$ has vertices $J(1, 3)$, $K(0, 5)$, and $L(-2, -2)$. Apply a dilation centered at $(-3, 4)$. Use a scale factor of $\frac{1}{2}$. Find the coordinates of the vertices of the image. *Hint: Draw axes at $(-3, 4)$ and find the coordinates of* J, K, *and* L *as if this was the origin. Apply the dilation, then find the coordinates of each image point with respect to the actual origin.*
(84)

*11. **Estimate** Draw the line of best fit in the scatterplot. Then, describe the correlation.
(117)

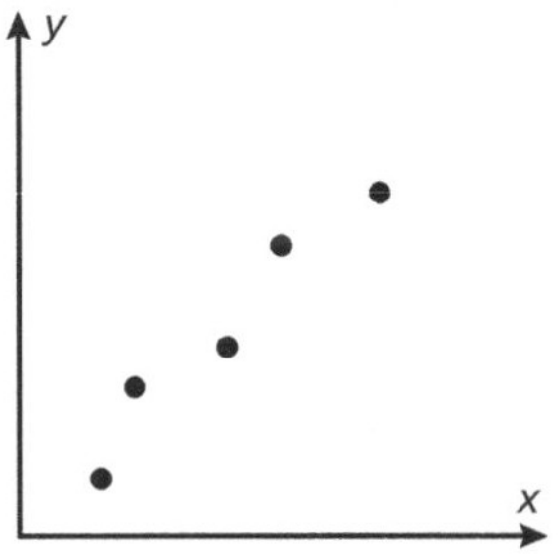

*12. Solve $\tan\theta$ in terms of $\csc\theta$.
(116)

13. **Algebra** As part of their training for a triathlon, Tila and Jamaal must run to and then swim across a circular pond. Find the length of Tila's total route to the nearest meter.
(101)

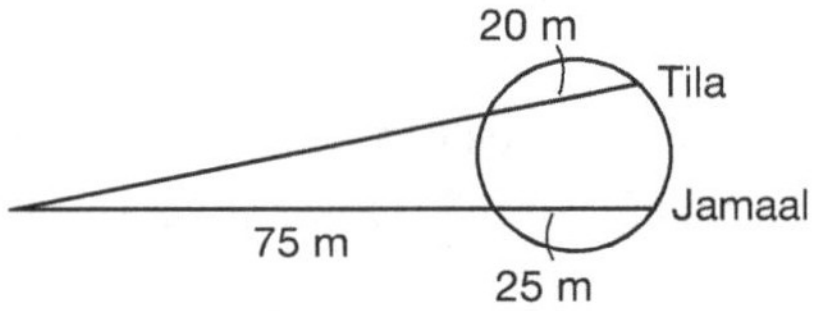

*14. **Write** Would you expect the data relating the number of days a student is absent and the student's grades to show a positive or a negative correlation? Explain.
(117)

15. Find the radius of this circle to the nearest hundredth of a meter.
(35)

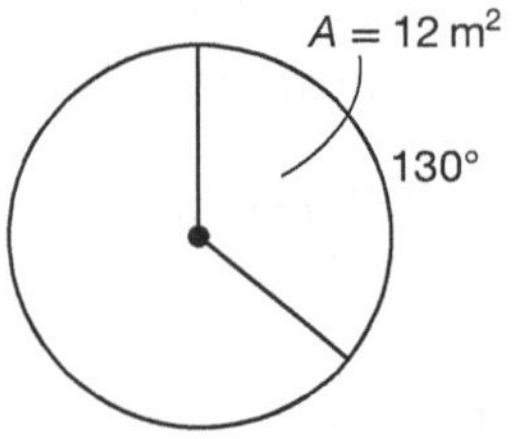

16. (44) **Architecture** A building has a base that is twice as long as it is wide, and the area is 50 square meters. If a contractor wants to make a scale drawing on an $8\frac{1}{2} \times 11$ inch piece of paper, what is the largest scale he could use that would be a whole number?

*17. (117) According to the scatterplot, approximately what is the average number of hours of daylight per day one could expect for the month of June?

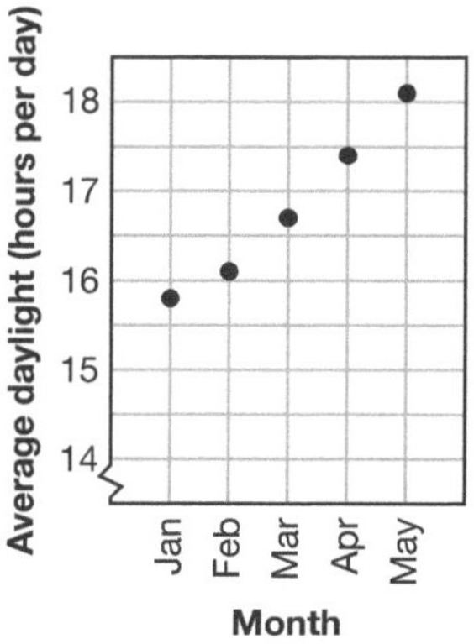

*18. (75) **Write** Using the equation of a circle and a line, explain why a circle and a line can intersect in at most two points. *Hint: Solve the general equation of a line for one variable and substitute into the general equation of a circle.*

19. (76) How many lines of symmetry does the figure below have? What order is the rotational symmetry?

*20. (116) **Multiple Choice** Which of the following is *not* a possible value for csc θ?
A 1.12 **B** 14.24
C −8.76 **D** −0.12

21. (104) Use the figure shown at right to find WY.

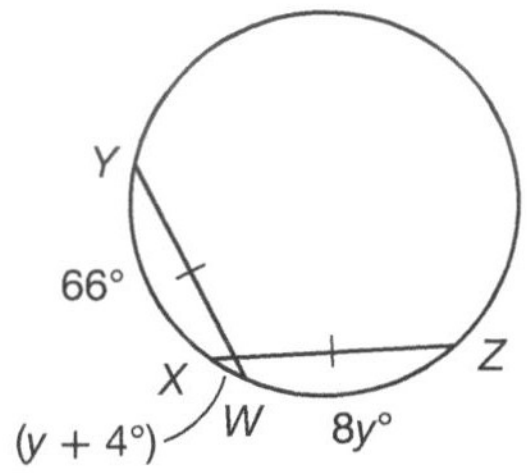

22. (105) **Justify** $\triangle ABC$ was either reflected across an axis or rotated about the origin. If the triangle is represented by the matrix $\begin{bmatrix} 2 & -3 & -2 \\ 2 & 6 & -6 \end{bmatrix}$ and the image matrix is $\begin{bmatrix} -2 & 3 & 2 \\ 2 & 6 & -6 \end{bmatrix}$, was the triangle reflected or rotated about the origin? If it was reflected, was it across the x-axis or the y-axis? If it was rotated about the origin, was it by 90°, 180°, 270°, or 360°? Explain your reasoning. Name the line of reflection or angle of rotation in your explanation.

23. (113) How many plane symmetries does a regular square pyramid have? Describe them.

24. (48) Write an indirect proof showing that a right triangle cannot have an obtuse angle.

25. (70) What is the lateral area of a regular pyramid with a base perimeter of 10 inches and a slant height of 10 inches?

26. If the volume of the smaller of these two similar solids is 17.2 cubic meter, what is the volume of the larger?
(99)

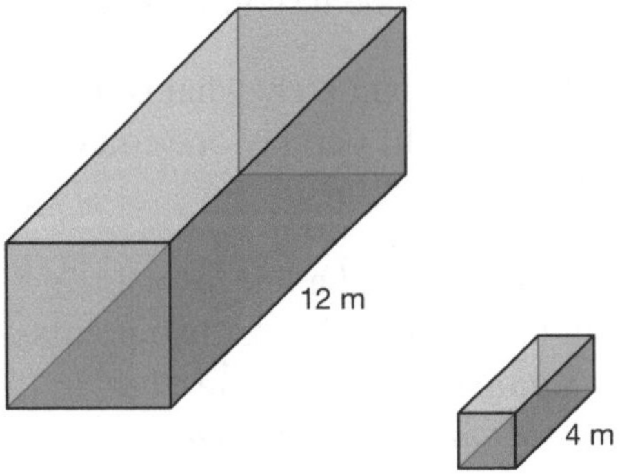

*27. **Verify** Use trigonometric identities to verify $\tan \theta = \frac{\sin \theta}{\sqrt{1 - \sin^2\theta}}$.
(91)

28. **Flight** The diagram shows a plane taking off. If the acceleration due to lift is 11.14 m/sec^2 at 63.9° to the horizontal, and gravity pulls straight down at 9.8 m/sec^2, what is the resultant acceleration vector felt by the passengers?
(83)

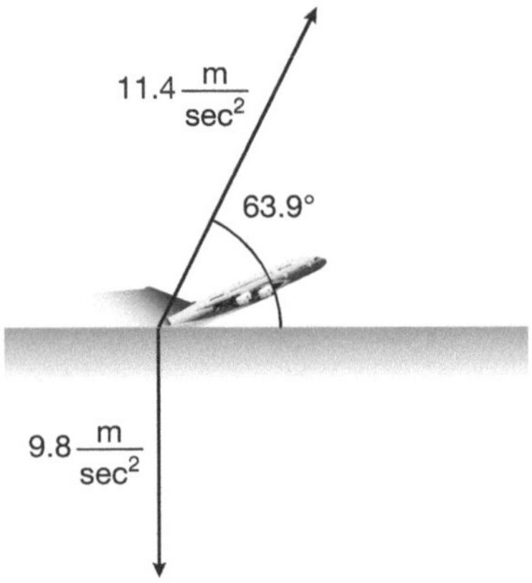

29. **Horticulture** Sunflower seeds grow in a special pattern: each spiral of seeds has the same number of seeds as the previous two spirals combined. If the first two spirals have 3 and 4 seeds, respectively,
(Inv 11)

a. how many seeds are in the tenth spiral?

b. how many seeds are there in the first ten spirals altogether?

*30. **Multiple Choice** Which scatterplot shows a correct line of best fit?
(117)

A 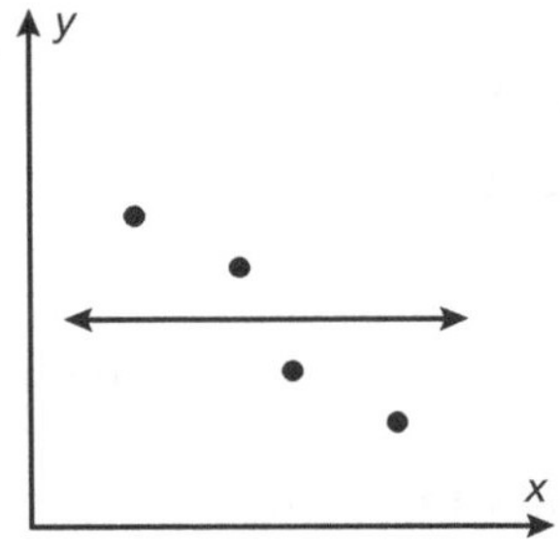

B 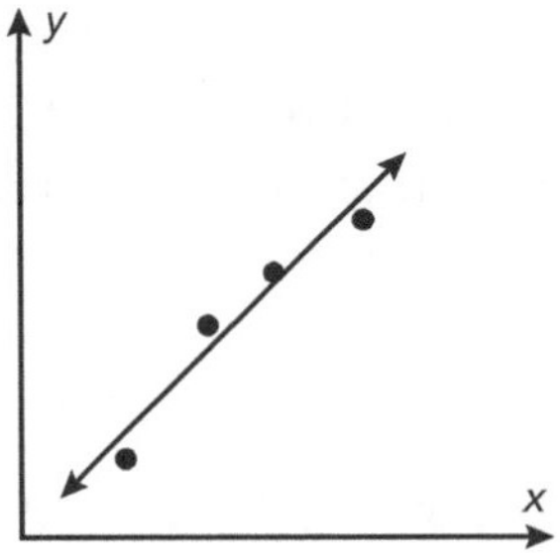

C 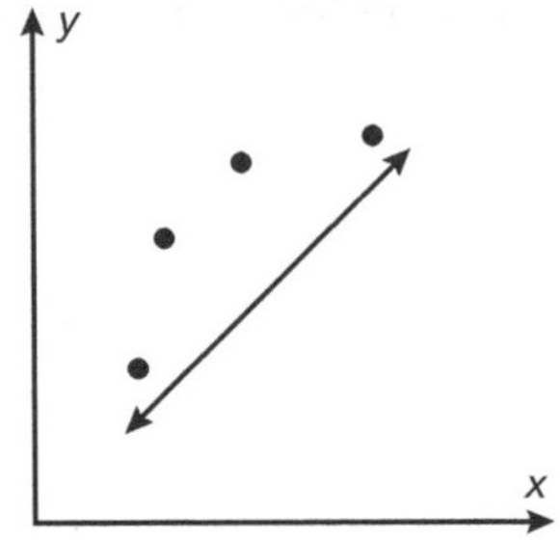

D 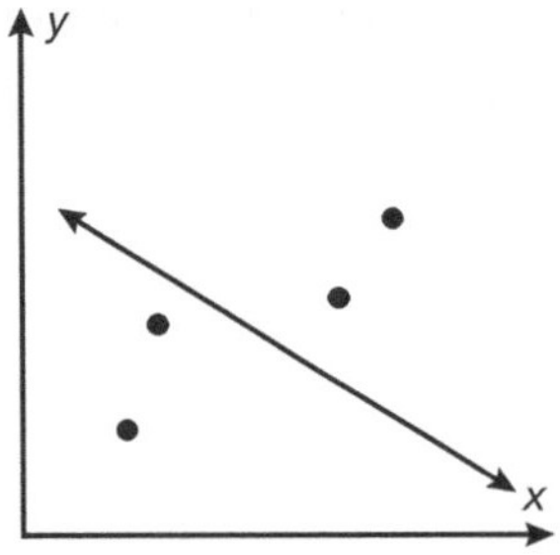

Name ______________________ Date __________ Class __________

Finding Areas of Polygons Using Matrices

LESSON 118

* **1.** (118) **Flooring** Bart wants to paint a design on his tiled floor. He determines the vertices of the polygon he is going to paint are located at $(-5, 7)$, $(-1, 15)$, $(5, 2)$, $(0, -8)$, and $(-10, -3)$. What is the area Bart wants to paint?

* **2.** (117) Describe the correlation in the scatterplot.

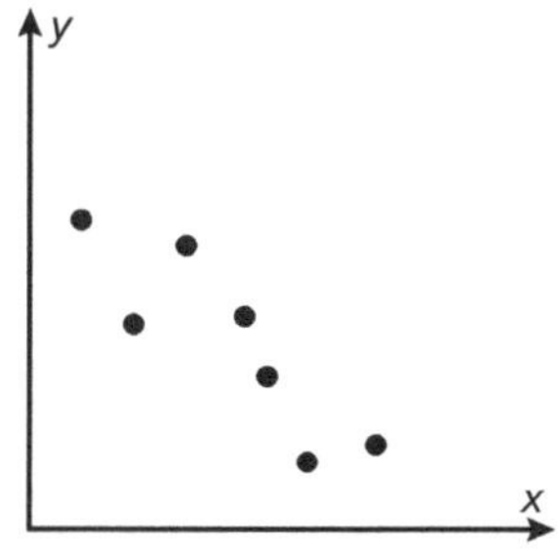

* **3.** (118) **Architecture** On a grid of the floor plan of a building, the corners of the building are located at the points $(5, 7)$, $(7, 0)$, $(1, -5)$, and $(-6, 2)$. If one unit represents one yard, what is the area of the actual floor?

4. (116) **Analyze** Explain what happens to the graph of cosecant and secant when $\sin\theta = 0$ and when $\cos\theta = 0$.

5. (42) What is the distance between the point $(-9, 4)$ and the line $y = 3$?

6. (64) **Write** Using Theorem 64-1, explain why, if a tangent to a circle has a point of tangency, T, and $\overline{TA}$ is a diameter of the circle, then $\overline{TA}$ is perpendicular to the tangent.

7. (115) Find the volume of this right cylinder from which a smaller right cylinder has been removed. Give your answer to the nearest tenth of a cubic centimeter.

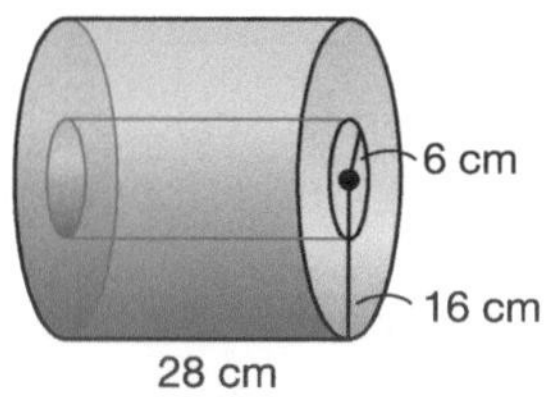

* **8.** (118) Calculate the determinant of $\begin{bmatrix} 5 & 4 \\ 4 & 5 \\ 2 & 1 \end{bmatrix}$.

9. (112) Determine the area of the shaded part of the circle by determining the area of the segment and subtracting that from the area of the circle. Write your answer in terms of π.

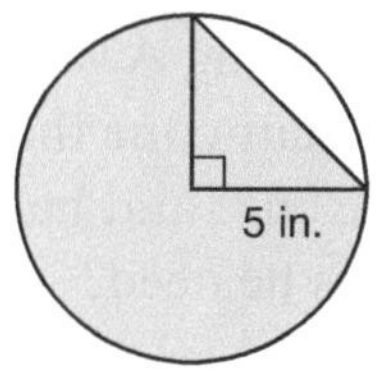

10. (114) **Analyze** A region is defined by the disjunction of the inequalities $y > -x + 2$ and $y < x + 2$. Graph the region, then add $y > -2x + 3$. If $y > -2x + 3$ were included in the disjunction, would the region be larger?

11. (93) Draw front, top, and side views of the solid at right.

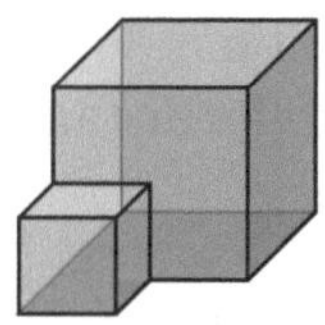

12. (76) **Algebra** Find the equation of the line of symmetry of the function $y = |x - 3|$.

*13. **Multi-Step** Find the circumferences and areas of the inscribed and circumscribed circles if the regular hexagon has a side length of 10 inches.
(106)

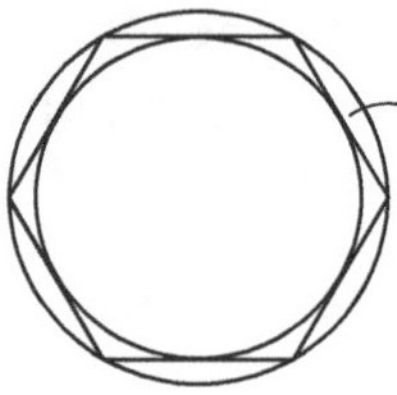

14. **Multiple Choice** The conjecture, "The bisector of an angle divides the angle into two congruent acute angles," has
(14)
A no counterexamples. B many counterexamples.
C exactly one counterexample. D exactly two counterexamples.

15. Find the line perpendicular to $y = 12x - 4$ that passes through the point (4, 1).
(37)

*16. Calculate the determinant of $\begin{bmatrix} 1 & 2 \\ 0 & 0 \end{bmatrix}$.
(118)

*17. **Formulate** If the height and radius of a cone are H and R, respectively, what is a formula for the area of the circular cross section that is h units from the vertex of the cone?
(85)

*18. **Write** Is the line in the scatterplot a good choice for line of best fit? Explain why or why not.
(117)

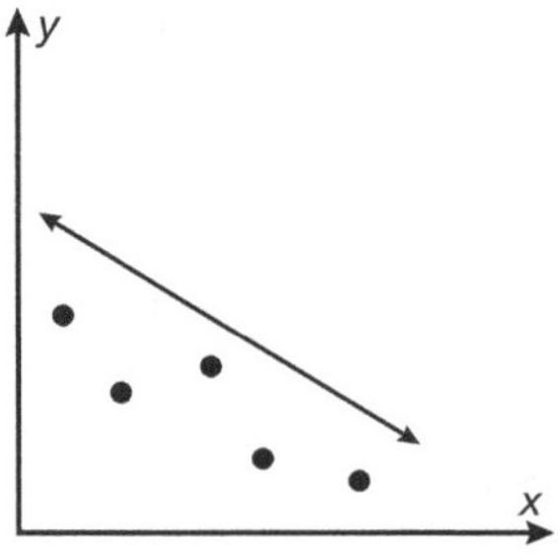

19. An isosceles right triangle has a hypotenuse of 16 feet. What is the perimeter, to the nearest tenth of a foot?
(53)

20. What is the equation of a circle with a radius of 5 and a center point located at (6, −2)?
(75)

21. **(Megaphones)** Matteo is making a homemade megaphone out of newspaper for Recycling Awareness Week at his school. He plans to have the megaphone be a right circular cone that is 2 feet long, with an opening that is 8 inches across at one end, and be as thick as three sheets of newspaper. How much newspaper does he need?
(77)

22. In this figure, $\overline{VU}$ is a diameter. What is the measure of $\angle VTU$?
(47)

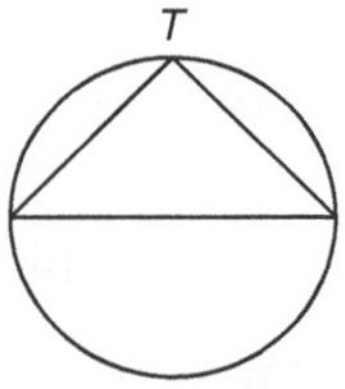

23. **(Flight)** An airplane is flying at an elevation of 1 mile. Its location is 35 miles east and 140 miles south of the airport. Another airplane is flying at an elevation 2.25 miles, and its location is 300 miles west and 95 miles north of the airport. Find the distance to the nearest tenth of a mile between the planes.
(111)

24. $\triangle ABC$ and $\triangle DEF$ are similar and have sides related by the ratio 3:4. If the area of $\triangle ABC$ is 15.3 square units, what is the area of $\triangle DEF$?
(87)

25. **Multiple Choice** Which of the following values of θ is not in the domain of $\cot \theta$?
(116)
A 90° B 0°
C 45° D 270°

26. (115) **Construction** A construction company is having cinder blocks specially made for the walls of a building. For structural support, each block must contain approximately 3000 cubic inches of concrete. How tall should each block be to meet the specifications? Give your answer to the nearest whole inch.

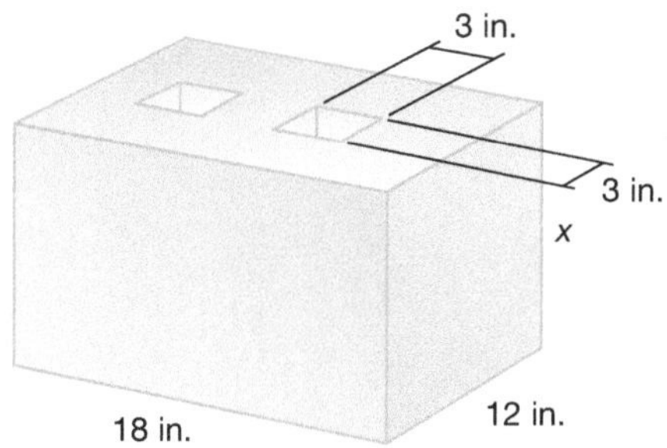

27. (73) Looking down from her balcony, Celeste sees her car at a 25° angle of depression. The balcony is 16 feet above the ground, and Celeste is about 5 feet tall. How far away is she from her car, to the nearest foot?

*28. (117) **Error Analysis** Oscar and Reena drew different lines of best fit in a scatterplot. Which line of best fit is more suitable for the data in the scatterplot? Explain.

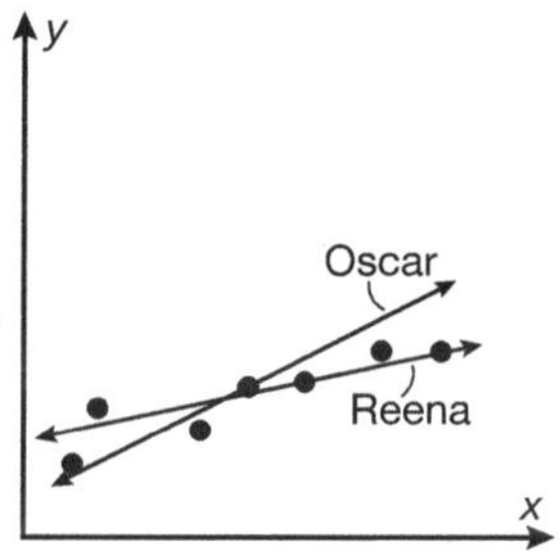

*29. (118) Calculate the area of the pentagon with vertices (0, 2), (−3, 1), (−2, −1), (1, −1), and (3, 1).

30. (88) Solve the system of inequalities $y > 5x + 1$ and $y \leq 5x - 11$.

Platonic Solids

LESSON 119

1. (116) **Error Analysis** Brittney solves sin θ in terms of csc θ like this: $\sin\theta = \frac{\sqrt{\csc^2\theta - 1}}{\csc\theta}$. Write the correct answer and explain Brittney's error.

2. (49) Using Euler's formula, determine how many edges a polyhedron with 10 vertices and 7 faces has.

*3. (119) Which of the Platonic solids can be classified as a pyramid?

*4. (119) **Multiple Choice** Which of the following is *not* a net for a tetrahedron?

A

B

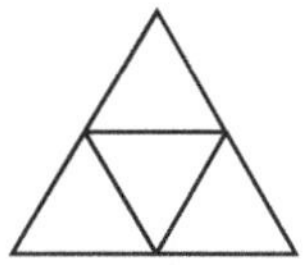

C

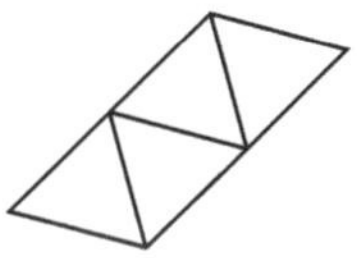

D

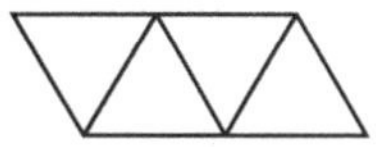

5. (113) **Write** A rectangular prism has lengths of 7 units, 3 units, and 5 units. What are the dimensions of the prism after a rotation of 270°? Explain your answer.

6. (98) **Multi-Step** Find the perimeter of this triangle. Round your answer to the nearest tenth.

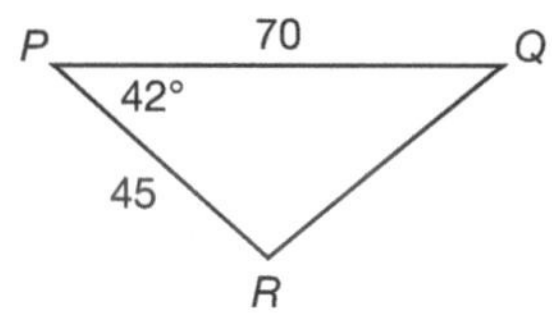

7. (82) The function $y = 8x + 1$ makes an angle with the positive x-axis. What is the angle measure to the nearest degree?

*8. (118) **Write** The area of a triangle with vertices (0, 0), (a, b), and (c, d) is equal to $\frac{1}{2}$ times the determinant of $\begin{bmatrix} a & b \\ c & d \end{bmatrix}$. Use this to explain the formula for the area of a convex polygon about the origin given in Lesson 118.

9. (40) **Sewing** A tailor is cutting out the pattern shown to make a dress. Find the area of the tailor's pattern to the nearest tenth of a square inch.

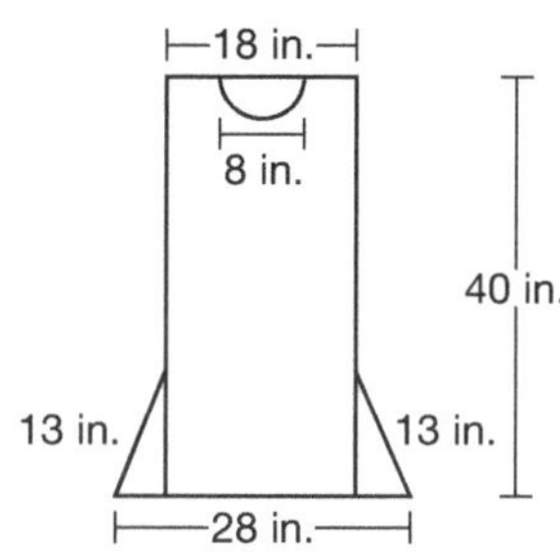

*10. (118) **Write** Use the determinant area formula to explain why the area is dilated by a^2 when the side lengths of a convex polygon are dilated by a.

11. (68) Use a trigonometric ratio to find the value of x in the diagram to the nearest hundredth.

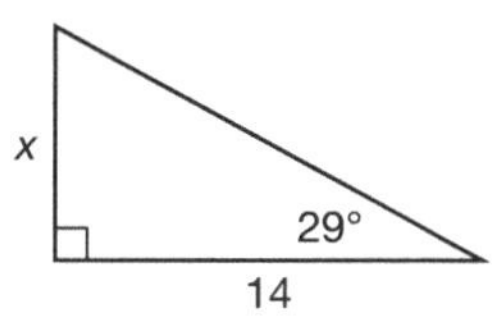

*12. (Space Walks) Two astronauts are moving in space on unassisted space walks.
(108) The first astronaut begins at (3, −1, 4) and moves to (9, 2, 11). The second begins at (−49, −15, −2) and moves to (−38, −11, 4). Show that the astronauts will meet at the point (39, 17, 46) if they stay on the same linear paths.

13. **Multiple Choice** In which scatterplot is there a strong positive correlation?
(117)

A

B
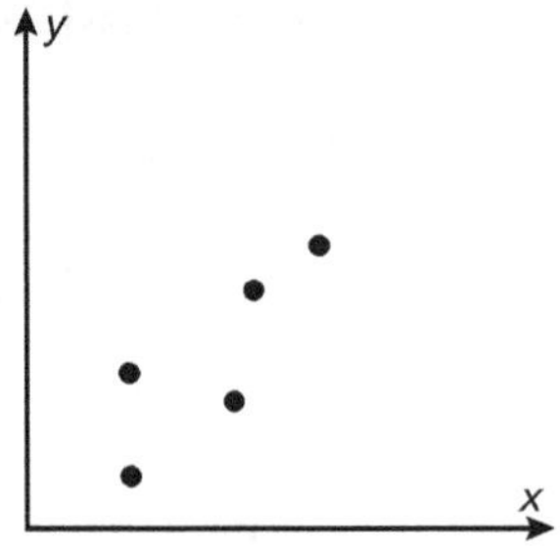

C
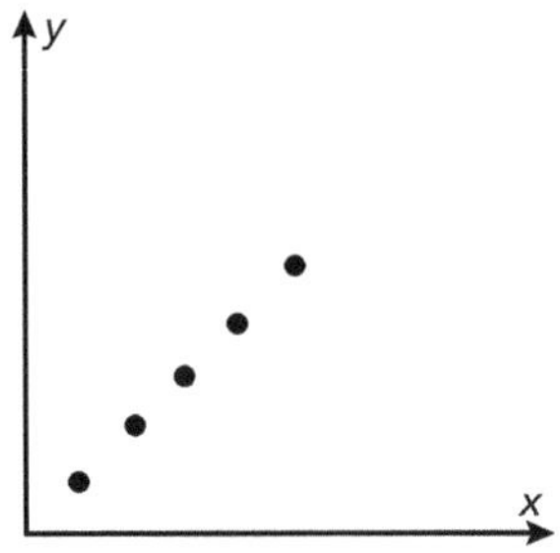

D
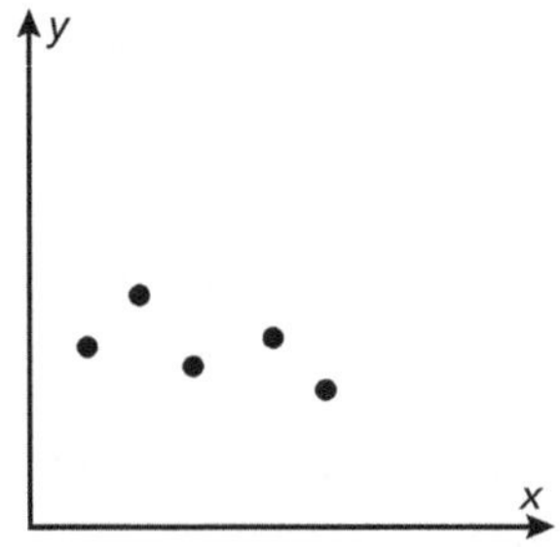

*14. How many axes of rotation does a tetrahedron have?
(119)

15. In the circle shown, chords $\overline{AB}$ and $\overline{CD}$ intersect at E. Find the value of x.
(86)

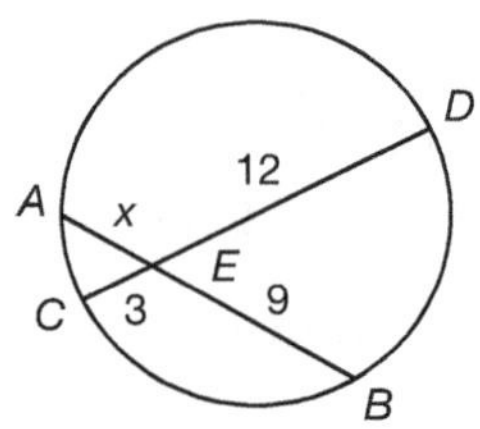

*16. **Analyze** Calculate the area of the triangle with vertices (2, 3), (4, 5), and (1, 6).
(118)

17. (Storage) Alastair's attic is in the shape of a rectangular pyramid. If the floor's dimensions are 10 feet by 20 feet, and the height of the attic is 6 feet, what volume can theoretically be stored in Alastair's attic?
(70)

18. **Analyze** What geometric figure will result from dilating a circle centered about the origin with a 5-unit radius by a scale factor of 0?
(84)

19. Graph the solution of the conjunction of $2x + 3y > 1$ and the disjunction of $x - 3y \geq 1$ and $5y - 4x \geq 10$.
(114)

20. (29) Find the value of x. Give your answer in simplified radical form.

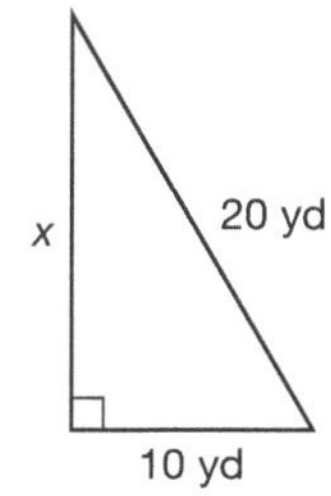

21. (112) **Design** The logo for a communications corporation is a regular pentagon inscribed in a circle with a radius of 3 inches. Determine the combined area of the five circle segments in square inches, to the nearest tenth.

22. (71) **Algebra** The point $(x, -3)$ is translated 3 units right. The image has coordinates $(3, -3)$. Find the value of x.

23. (89) **Running** Beth runs 150 meters at 43° north of west. Which is larger, her northward displacement or her westward displacement, and by how much? Round your answer to the nearest tenth.

24. (52) Is the following statement always, sometimes, or never true?

A square is a rhombus.

25. (115) **Products** A jar of peanut butter with a 3.5-inch diameter has had a 1-inch-radius hemispherical scoop taken out of it. What volume of peanut butter remains in the jar, to the nearest tenth?

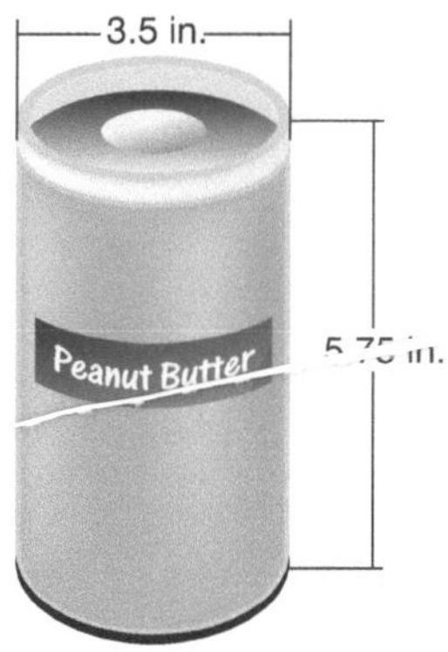

26. (106) **Algebra** Find the side length of an equilateral triangle in terms of r, if it is inscribed in a circle with a radius, r. What is the side length if the triangle circumscribes the circle instead?

27. (116) Use trigonometric identities to find the tangent of an angle when the secant of that angle is $\frac{3}{2}$. Express your answer in simplified radical form.

28. (94) **Multi-Step** Find the perimeter of the triangle. Round your answer to the nearest whole number.

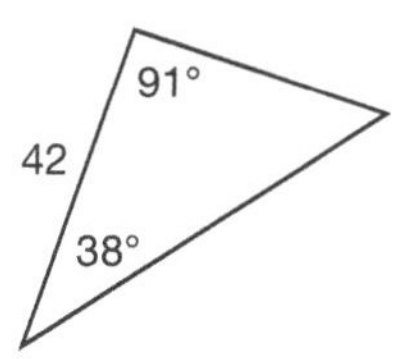

*29. **Analyze** Which Platonic solids can produce a cross section that is a pentagon?
(119)

30. Find the value of a in this scalene triangle.
(94)

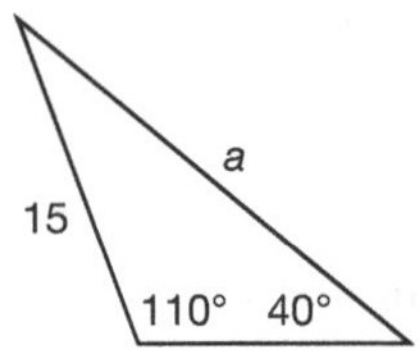

Name ______________________ Date __________ Class __________

Topology

LESSON 120

1. (100) The triangle ABC is translated 4 units right and 3 units down. Write a point matrix for $\triangle ABC$ and find the matrix that transforms $\triangle ABC$ to $\triangle A'B'C'$.

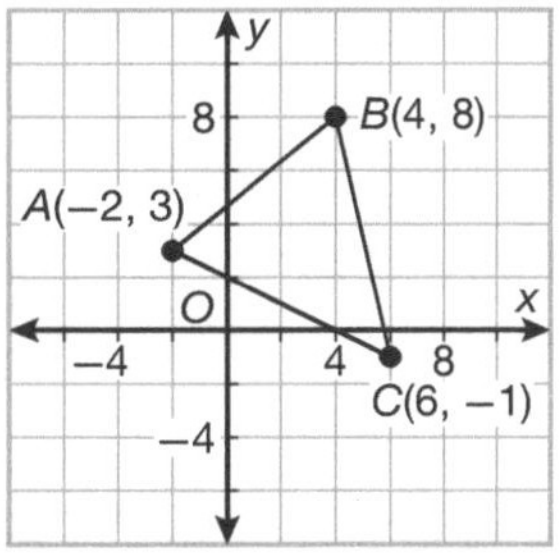

2. (107) Given a fixed area, which shape will have the least perimeter?

3. (88) **Multiple Choice** Which region represents the conjunction of $y \geq 3x + 1$ and $y \leq -x$?

A A **B** B

C C **D** D

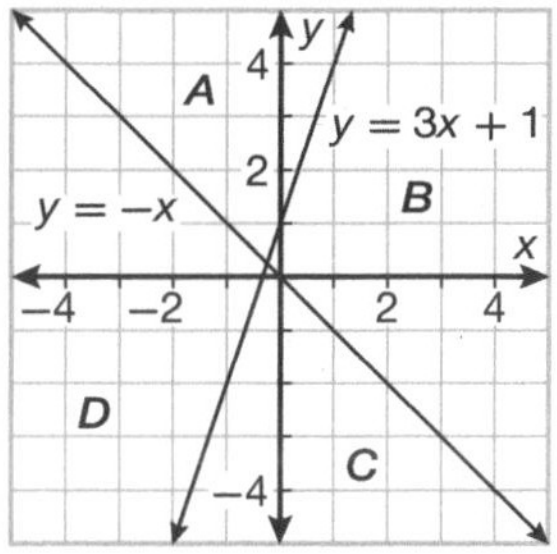

4. (118) **Verify** Use the determinant area formula to verify that the area of a square with a side length of s has an area of s^2.

5. (104) Find x and $m\widehat{KJ}$, if $\overline{JL} \cong \overline{JM}$, $\overline{JM} \cong \overline{KN}$, and m = 120°.

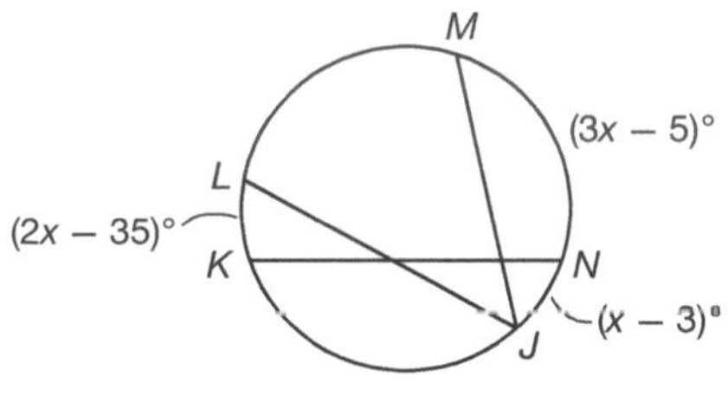

6. (90) A composite transformation reflects a figure over the x-axis, rotates it 120°, and then flips it across the y-axis. Will the resulting image be the same, regardless of which order these transformations are performed? Explain.

7. (79) What is the measure of $\angle A$?

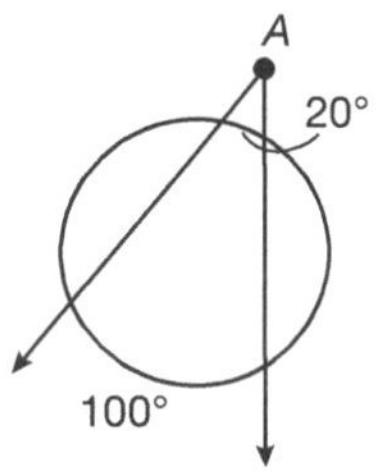

8. (116) **Multi-Step** Is $\sin\theta = \dfrac{\sqrt{1 + \cot^2\theta}}{\cot\theta}$ true? Use trigonometric identities to prove it or use a counterexample to disprove it.

9. Find *FD*.
(50)

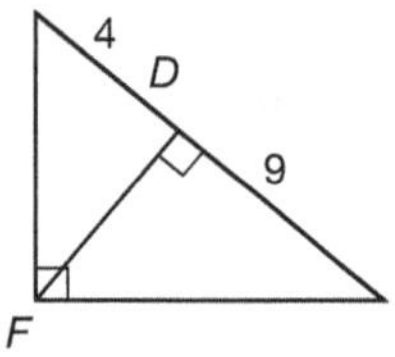

10. **Games** During a board game, Bhavna has pieces at points (2, 5), (−3, 1), and (1, −6) on the game board. Imagine the pieces are the vertices of a polygon. What is the area of the polygon?
(118)

11. **Lighthouses** A lighthouse flashes its light to warn ships that are closer than 1500 meters away. If the lighthouse keeper knows his lighthouse is 50 meters tall, at what angle of depression should he begin flashing the light at the ship? Round your answer to the nearest hundredth.
(73)

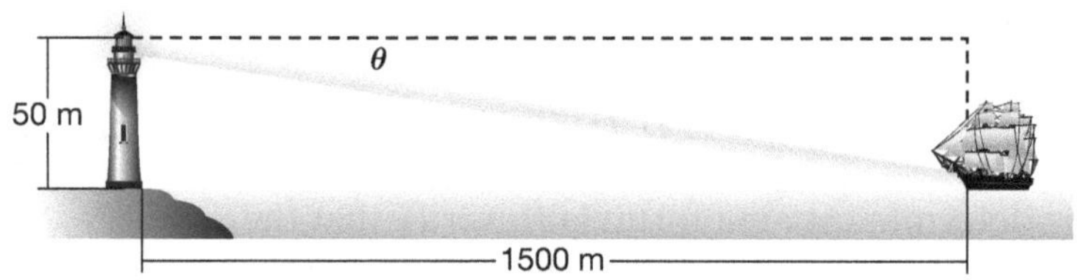

(Not to scale)

***12.** A square pyramid has vertices $R(1, 1, 2)$, $S(3, 1, 2)$, $T(3, -1, 2)$, and $U(1, -1, 2)$. If the vertex of the pyramid is $V(2, 0, 6)$ what is the height of the pyramid?
(111)

***13.** **Write** The faces of a soccer ball are regular polygons. Why is a soccer ball not an example of a Platonic solid?
(119)

***14.** **Multiple Choice** Which letters are topologically the same whether they are uppercase or lowercase?
(120)

A a and P | **B** b and D
C e and D | **D** J and k

15. **Algebra** Find x if $AB = x + 6$.
(55)

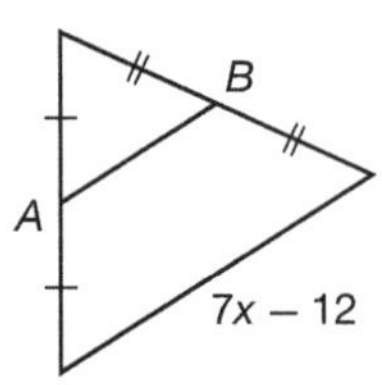

***16.** Draw a net for an octahedron.
(119)

17. To the nearest whole square centimeter, find the surface area of a sphere with a 15-centimeter radius.
(80)

18. (112) **Civil Engineering** Determine the area of the circle segment of this bridge, to the nearest square yard.

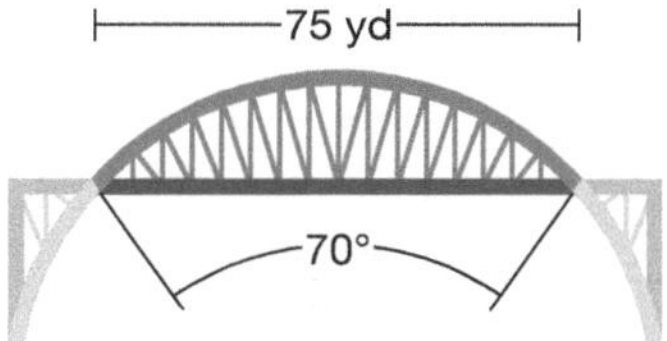

19. (98) **Multi-Step** A triangle has vertices $X(-2, 3)$, $Y(1, 1)$, and $Z(-1, -3)$. Find all the measures in the triangle. Round angles to the nearest degree and sides to the nearest tenth.

***20.** (89) **Physics** When an object rests on a surface, a force vector called the *normal force* holds the object up. This vector is always perpendicular to the surface. Find the horizontal and vertical components F_V and F_H of the normal force, vector F_N in the diagram, if the normal force is 12 pounds. Round your answers to the nearest hundredth of a pound.

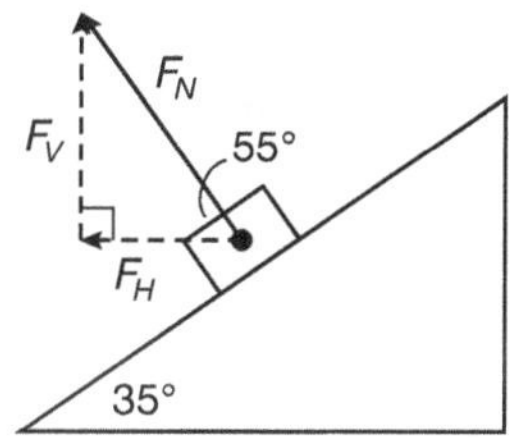

21. (11) **Formulate** The point x is the midpoint of a and b on the number line. The point y is the midpoint of c and d on the number line. Determine an expression for the midpoint of x and y. Interpret your result.

***22.** (120) **Analyze** Is a knotted loop of string topologically equivalent to an unknotted loop of string? Explain.

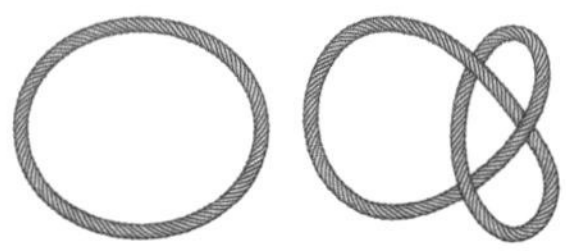

23. (112) **Formulate** Determine a formula for the area of a segment with a central angle measure of $0° < x° < 180°$, in a circle with a radius, r.

24. (27) Write a two-column proof to show that if two parallelograms both have an area of A and a base of b, corresponding to heights h_1 and h_2 respectively, then $h_1 = h_2$.

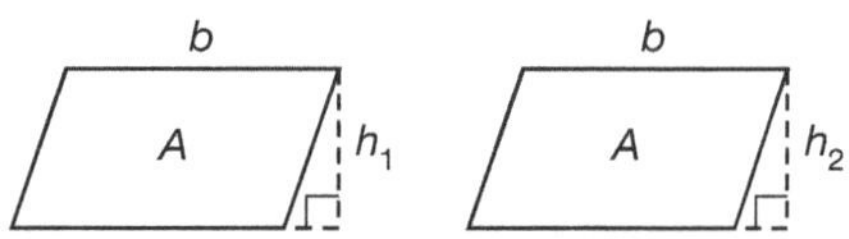

***25.** (120) **Error Analysis** Joseph conjectures, "A closed soup can is topologically distinct from an open soup can." Identify and correct his error.

26. (111) Find the distance between $P(2, 5, 6)$ and $H(-2, 7, 1)$.

27. (117) Describe the correlation shown in the scatterplot as negative or positive, and strong or weak.

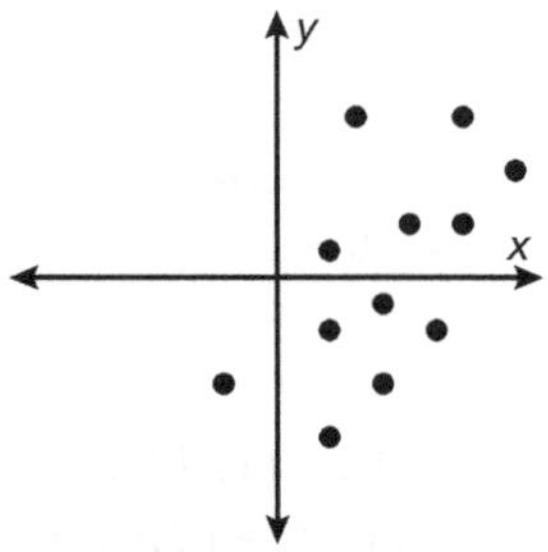

***28.** (120) **Write** Could a fork and a spoon be considered topologically equivalent? Explain.

29. (51) **Basketball** Shirley is playing basketball and wants to pass the ball, but is not sure to which teammate to throw the ball. She decides to pass the ball to whomever is closest. To whom should she pass the ball, and why?

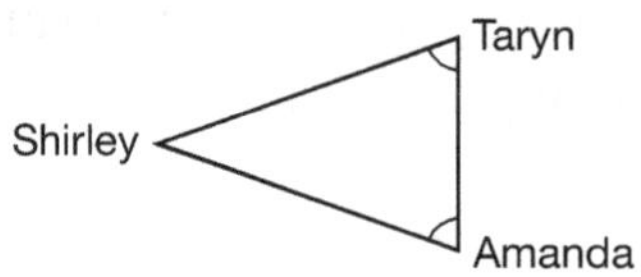

30. (113) The drawing shows a part of a solid and its center of rotation. Draw the complete solid with order of rotation 3.

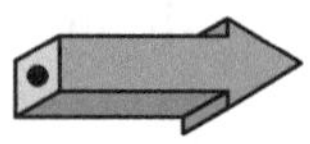

4500939736
August 21, 2026
Printed in the U.S.A